W9-CID-583

Western Linguistics: An Historical Introduction

To my family

Western Linguistics

An Historical Introduction

Pieter A.M. Seuren

BLACKWELL
Publishers

Copyright © Pieter Seuren 1998

The right of Pieter Seuren to be identified as author of this work has been asserted in accordance with the Copyright, Designs and Patents Act 1988.

First published 1998

2 4 6 8 10 9 7 5 3 1

Blackwell Publishers Ltd
108 Cowley Road
Oxford OX4 1JF, UK

Blackwell Publishers Inc.
350 Main Street
Malden, Massachusettes 02148, USA

All rights reserved. Except for the quotation of short passages for the purposes of criticism and review, no part of this publication may be reproduced, stored in a retrieval system, or transmitted, in any form or by any means, electronic, mechanical, photocopying, recording or otherwise, without the prior permission of the publisher.

Except in the United States of America, this book is sold subject to the condition that it shall not, by way of trade or otherwise, be lent, resold, hired out, or otherwise circulated without the publisher's prior consent in any form of binding or cover other than that in which it is published and without a similar condition including this condition being imposed on the subsequent purchaser.

British Library Cataloguing in Publication Data

A CIP catalogue record for this book is available from the British Library.

Library of Congress Cataloging-in-Publication Data

Seuren, Pieter A.M.
    Western Linguistics. An Historical Introduction / Pieter A.M. Seuren
        p.   cm.
    Includes bibliographical references and index.
    ISBN 0-631-20890-9 (alk. paper). — ISBN 0-631-20891-7 (pbk. : alk. paper)
        1. Linguistics--History.   I. Title.
    P61.S48   1998
    410'..9—dc21   97-42247
                                                                        CIP

Camera-ready copy supplied by the author
Printed in Great Britain

This book is printed on acid-free paper.

Contents

Preface

Modern linguistics has, regrettably, grown accustomed to living without its history. This is unfortunate not only because it makes for a limited horizon and deprives one of the pleasure of being conversant with the past (we all have a deep-seated wish to know about the past: man is a historical animal), but also because it creates the risk of continuously re-inventing the wheel. There are, of course, already quite a number of books available detailing the history of linguistics, but they are often not directly relevant to the concerns and issues that are at play in modern theoretical linguistics, as their principal aim is to achieve a systematic reconstruction of the past. While this is the historian's noble and indispensable task, the linguist is more interested in the historical backgrounds of his actual professional interests. I have, therefore, written this book as a linguist, which I am, not as an historian, which I am not.

The present book thus looks at the history of the subject from the angle of what occupies the minds of present-day theoretical linguists. And since methodology is among the primary concerns nowadays, a great deal of attention has been devoted to issues of methodology and of philosophy of science. The reader will thus find, at often unexpected points in the text, discussions of and references to modern issues in linguistic theory. This has been done with the purpose of making explicit the continuity of the questions at hand. This strategy also made it possible to show more clearly if, when and how progress was made, and how sometimes important issues were lost sight of in modern linguistics, much to its disadvantage.

Given this purpose, it proved necessary to go into the actual issues to a much greater extent than is customary in current textbooks on the history of linguistics. And it requires the 'long view', the identification of those currents of history, both large and small, that have led to the present state of affairs. The book is, therefore, meant as a synthesis of history and theory, so that the student can follow the coming about of the key notions of his subject through the course of time, and thus gain an extra dimension of understanding.

The main guiding principle of this book is given by the question 'If linguistics is justified in claiming the status of a real science (which is doubtful), when and how did the application of scientific methodology come about, and what mistakes have been made in this respect?' It is from this overarching point of view that the book tries to paint the notions, discoveries, principles, techniques that have, through the ages, contributed to the modern state of affairs in general linguistic theory, including its weaknesses, gaps and unevenly distributed interests.

Organizing the book around this question implied a certain selectivity. Unlike current studies on the history of linguistics, this book does not aim at completeness in the sense that everything needs to be mentioned. On the contrary, I have tried to avoid overburdening the reader with details, names and dates, and to concentrate on a handful of large issues that have dominated the history of linguistics throughout. This gives more unity to the book, and it will, hopefully, make for pleasanter reading.

In taking this perspective I have restricted myself to the western or Graeco-Roman tradition, thus neglecting the Chinese, the Indian, the Mesopotamian (cp. Black 1989), the Judaeic, and the Arabic traditions, despite their sometimes monumental achievements. This decision is not simply due to considerations of size and of expertise, but to other reasons as well.

First, there is the fact, not often recognized in the literature, that all non-western traditions of linguistic inquiry, with the possible exception of China, have been strongly dominated by religion in one form or another. Very often, thought about language was mainly focussed on the interpretation and preservation of ancient sacred texts of divine or semi-divine origin, such as the Bible, the Koran, or the Vedic hymns. In this respect the Graeco-Roman tradition is essentially different. This tradition has been characterized from the very beginning by a sharp rejection of religious thought and is therefore basically secular and non-religious. Neither Homer, whose Iliad and Odyssey came closest to the status of a canonical text in the Greek world, nor the Christian Bible played a significant part in the coming about of linguistics in the western world. Graeco-Roman linguistics has its origins first in the philosophical question, central to Greek philosophy, of truth as correspondence between what is said and what is the case, and secondly, in the Hellenistic period, in the practical necessity of having to teach Greek to Egyptian and other non-Greek children. Not that the religious element has always been completely absent. On the contrary, there have been episodes, especially in the work of St. Augustin and during the Middle Ages, when attempts were made to turn linguistics into applied theology, but these attempts clearly lost out against the strong secular strand inherited from the Greeks.

Most of the other traditions, on the contrary, show a much stronger influence of, and sometimes even domination by, religious forces. Here too, of course, there are degrees. The Indian tradition, for example, with Pāṇini's work as the most outstanding achievement, seems to have been significantly less religious and more secular than the Judaeic or the Arabic traditions, though there, too, occasional secular elements are found. In this respect, the Indian tradition comes closest to what we consider scientific linguistics (cp. Staal 1972). In fact, modern scholarship has recognized many features in ancient Indian grammatical analysis that have been rediscovered in present-day linguistics.

A further reason for excluding the non-western traditions is the fact that they are often also strongly directed at practical, usually political or commercial, aims, such as the development of a writing system, or the furthering of an ideology with the help of a metaphorical interpretation of an ancient canonized text. Basic scientific research, with the primary aim of *understanding*, was hardly ever germane to those traditions. True, as has been said, the Graeco-Roman tradition is rooted at least in part in the necessity to teach Greek as a foreign language and thus had a clear practical purpose as well, but, as is shown in section 1.2, this exercise was, right from the start, permeated by existing philosophically motivated methods of linguistic analysis, and parallelled by purely philosophical investigations of language in the post-

Aristotelian schools of philosophy. Eventually, the practical and the philosophical currents merged to give rise to what is known, in the western world, as traditional grammar.

The decisive reason, however, for not taking other linguistic traditions into account has been the consideration that there is no evidence of any influence from non-western on western linguistics, despite the fact that the interest of western scholars in the other traditions dates back to the first half of the eighteenth century. There may have been some influence the other way round, from western on non-western linguistics, but that can only have been relatively recent, in the general context of the expansion of western power and culture.

This book differs from existing genres also in that I have felt free to express value judgements wherever I considered that to be appropriate, but always with a holy respect for the historical facts and a proper historical perspective. I have presented these value judgements in the hope that the reader will take them to be an invitation to think about the issues and to apply and test his or her own standards and thus form a personal opinion.

Besides bringing history and theory together, the book also aims at a synthesis of grammar and meaning. One thing this book makes clear is that while these two were united in one coherent tradition from Antiquity till the 19th century, modern developments separated them to the point where they became two, even three, distinct streams. For many years, linguists, psychologists and semanticists have formed largely separate groups, each with their own ways of thinking, standards and perspectives. We should, therefore, not be surprised to find that now that they are meeting up again they are finding it difficult to understand each other's viewpoints and methodologies. One purpose of the book is to help bring about a better understanding of the situation, and thus perhaps also a better integration of the academic populations concerned.

The book consists of two parts. Part 1 contains the chapters 1 to 4 and deals with the history of what is normally considered to be linguistics proper, concentrating on the study of grammar. Chapter 1 deals with Antiquity, the Middle Ages and the subsequent period till the end of the 17th century. Chapter 2 takes us into the 18th and 19th centuries. During this period the study of language form and the study of meaning began to be separated, the latter being extremely tentative and lost between an incipient psychology and a mind-oriented logic. In the early 20th century logic takes off and goes its own course, leaving grammar and psychology to battle with each other. The chapters 3 and 4 describe the rise of 20th century theoretical linguistics in Europe and in America, respectively, first as structuralist linguistics then as formal grammar, with generative grammar at centre stage in chapter 4. They show, among other things, how, after logic, psychology was also shed by the linguists during the 1930s.

Part 2 is about the study of meaning. Modern semantics has been dominated for some time by logical model-theory. Although, as is shown in chapter 6, model-theoretic semantics is not adequate for natural language, a good knowledge of logic is indispensable for a linguist who wants to understand meaning. Chapter 5, therefore, explains the basic notions of logic and describes the main lines of its history, against the background of model-theory. It leads up to chapter 6, which first explains the basic notions of model-theoretic semantics, showing its fundamental weaknesses, and then explains some principles of a more suitable semantics, which has to be discourse-oriented. Anaphora and presupposition play a prominent role there. Chapter 7 discusses the question of how meaning links up with grammar. Two strategies are distinguished, a Platonic tradition according to which sentence meaning is reflected in a separate 'deep' or semantic structure, distinct from surface structure, and an Aristotelian tradition which rejects the notion of a separate semantic structure and wants to see meaning reflected directly in surface structure. The latter is followed mostly by logically oriented, the former by generative linguists. The book ends with a description of the rise and fall of the Generative Semantics movement that came about during the 1960s.

This book is meant for all those who, for professional or other reasons, want to hear about the main issues that have arisen during the two thousand odd years of the history of theoretical linguistics. The professionals will, I hope, find it useful and entertaining to read about historical developments while at the same time being challenged as to the main parameters of their discipline. If this book makes them subject the philosophical and methodological foundations of their work to renewed scrutiny it will have fulfilled its purpose.

It took a lifetime of teaching, reading and thinking to find and mould the insights and to summon the courage required for writing this book. While I was working on it I read, of course, a pile of new literature. But I also reread most of the stuff I went through as a beginning linguist and saw the notes and glosses I had scribbled in the margins of the old books, or found again the chits of scrap paper with my comments on them, and was surprised to find, on the one hand, how intensive my reading had been in those days, but, on the other hand also, how narrow my grasp of the issues. This gave me hope because, apparently, I had not deluded myself in thinking that over the past forty years my understanding of the issues and their history had gained in depth and breadth. It also made me feel that writing this book was a worthwhile exercise.

It was also an extremely pleasant exercise, not least because of the wholehearted support and practical help from my colleagues at the Nijmegen Arts Faculty, especially Ad Foolen, Haike Jacobs, Wus Kloeke, Henk Schotel and Leon Stassen, and also from Camiel Hamans and Jan Noordegraaf, all of whom lent me their books or their knowledge, read parts of the manuscript and made me correct and add enough details for me to realize that my, and perhaps anyone's, knowledge only goes skindeep.

Nijmegen, May 1997   P.A.M.S.

Acknowledgements

The author and publisher gratefully acknowledge the following for permission to reproduce copyright material:

Academic Press, Inc. for extracts from F. Newmeyer, *Linguistic Theory in America. The First Quarter-Century of Transformational Generative Grammar*, 1980.

Addison Wesley Longman Ltd for extracts from G. Bursill Hall, *Grammatica Speculativa of Thomas of Erfurt*, 1972. Reprinted by permission of Addison Wesley Longman Ltd.

Cambridge University Press for extracts from W. von Humboldt, *On Language. The Diversity of Human Language-Structure and its Influence on the Mental Development of Mankind* (trans. Peter Heath), 1988.

Harvard University Press for extracts from W.V.O. Quine, *From a Logical Point of View*, copyright © 1953, 1961, 1980 by the President and Fellows of Harvard College. Reprinted by permission of Harvard University Press.

Henry Holt & Co., Inc. for extracts from L. Bloomfield, *Language*, 1933.

Kluwer Academic Publishers for extracts from D. Dowty, *Introduction to Montague Semantics*, 1981; Z.S. Harris, *Papers on Syntax*, 1981.

Macmillan Publishing Co., Inc. for extracts from Ch. Hockett, *A Course in Modern Linguistics*, 1958.

MIT Press for extracts from N. Chomsky, *Aspects of the Theory of Syntax*, 1965 and *The Minimalist Program*, 1995; R. Jackendoff, *Semantics and Cognition*, 1983.

Mouton de Gruyter for extracts from N. Chomsky, *Syntactic Structures*, 1957 and *Current Issues in Linguistic Theory*, 1964; W.J.M. Levelt, *Formal Grammars in Linguistics and Psycholinguistics*, Vols I and II, 1974.

Oxford University Press for extracts from A. Gardiner, *The Theory of Speech and Language*, 1932; R. Harris, *The Linguistics Wars*, 1993; W. and M. Kneale, *The Development of Logic*, 1962.

Plenum Press for extracts from N. Chomsky, *The Logical Structure of Linguistic Theory*, 1975.

Prentice Hall for extracts from P.S. Peters, *Goals of Linguistic Theory*, 1972.

Random House UK Ltd for extracts from R. Monk, *Ludwig Wittgenstein. The Duty of Genius*, 1990.

Routledge for extracts from J. Andresen, *Linguistics in America 1769-1924*, 1990; G. Huck and J. Goldsmith, *Ideology and Linguistic Theory*, 1995; B. Russell, *Portraits from Memory*, 1956; Also figure 11 of Ogden and Richards, *The Meaning of Meaning*, 1923.

The University of Chicago Press for extracts from Z.S. Harris, *Methods in Structural Linguistics*, 1951.

The University of Michigan Press for figure 5 from E. Nida, *Morphology*, 1949, p.87.

The University of Wisconsin Press for extracts from L. Hjelmslev, *Prolegomena to a Theory of Language* (trans. F. Whitfield), revised English edition, copyright 1961, 1989. Reprinted by permission of the University of Wisconsin Press.

The publishers apologize for any errors or omissions in the above list and would be grateful to be notified of any corrections that should be incorporated in the next edition or reprint of this book.

PART 1

CHAPTER 1

Linguistics from Antiquity till the seventeenth century

1.0 Preamble

This chapter is the first leg of our trip through the history of linguistics. It covers the long road from the earliest Greek linguistic conceptualizations in the fifth and fourth centuries BC to the end of the seventeenth century, when grammatical description became a profession. Obviously, it is not possible to cover such a long period completely in barely 45 pages. The mere thought seems frivolous, especially since many of the main lines of thought and some fundamental approaches or 'philosophies' have their roots in Antiquity. But then, there are quite a number of excellent works which, taken together, provide a well-nigh complete survey of existing scholarship regarding this period. We may mention, for example, Allen (1948), Arens (1955), Barwick (1957), Borst (1957-1963), Coseriu (1975), Householder (1994a, 1994b), Hovdhaugen (1982), Pinborg (1967, 1975), Robins (1967), Steinthal (1890-1891), Taylor (1994), and many other valuable studies.

The point of this chapter is thus not to provide a complete survey. It is selective in a number of ways. First, we will select and emphasize those notions and techniques which are of special relevance to modern linguistics. Too often one finds that students and professionals alike are not or hardly aware of the earliest origins of the concepts and analytical means they consider central to linguistics, and it is hoped that this chapter will make them realize that many of those concepts and analytical tools do, in fact, go back to the very beginnings of linguistics.

In this context special attention is devoted to the tension between word linguistics and sentence linguistics. We shall see that in the beginning grammatical theory was heavily concentrated on the word as the unit of description and analysis. Only much later did the sentence come up as the primary structural unit, which is the point of view almost universally accepted nowadays. Although the earliest proposals for a sentence linguistics date back to the Stoics (who were unable, unfortunately, to do much about it), and were later elaborated by the 6th century Latin grammarian Priscian and taken up again in the Middle Ages, word linguistics persisted till way into the 20th century: de Saussure and Gardiner, for example, as we shall see in chapter 3, still thought that the sentence was a free, 'creative' product of language use, not a unit of the language system.

We shall likewise emphasize the distinction between underlying semantic form and surface structure, which goes back, essentially, to Plato and even to his great predecessor Heraclitus of Ephesus. This issue is not elaborated but just touched upon from time to time. A much fuller treatment is provided in chapter 7, especially in section 7.1.

The Platonic tradition, with its assumption of an underlying 'semantic' form, contrasts with the Aristotelian tradition, where no such underlying form is postulated. Both traditions have been immensely influential. The enormous influence of Aristotle through his logic and through his categories will become apparent in this and almost all following chapters.

We shall also highlight the importance of the opposition between eco-logism and formalism, which finds its counterpart in the ancient controversy between anomalism and analogism, the former a part of the Platonic, the latter of the Aristotelian tradition.

Finally, we stress the historical importance of the eternal triangle of language, thought and world. This triangular relation, brilliantly schematiz-ed in Ogden & Richards famous semiotic triangle (1923:11), dominates vir-tually all thinking about language from the very beginning (the only notable exception being the American structuralist notion of a linguistic theory without meaning – see chapter 4).

A further aim of this chapter is to show what motivated the originators of linguistics. Why did they shape the ideas that form the basis of linguistics? In what context? For what purpose? Here we touch on wider issues of historical and cultural context, including some very practical circumstances, such as the demand for the teaching of Greek as a foreign language (see 1.2.2).

Then we shall, with big strides, enter the Middle Ages and try to find our way through the tangled web of theories and developments of those centuries. This is not an easy task, mainly because ever since they came to an end, the Middle Ages, quite generally, have been subjected to a form of malign neglect so thorough and so vicious that its effects are still felt today, despite the many excellent studies produced by medievalists. There are two related dif-ficulties here. First, we want to make a proper selection of those aspects that are relevant to present-day linguistics, and, secondly, we must impose the correct interpretation, one that is not biased by the modern point of view (we are all prone to giving in to the coquettish wish to see ourselves prefigured in history). This danger is, of course, present everywhere, but especially so in matters concerning the Middle Ages, with their often abstruse and overdiffer-entiated terminologies. For the purpose of this chapter it seemed best to con-centrate on the generally enigmatic theory of Speculative Grammar, which, though despised by later grammarians and philosophers, was kept alive in one form or another in ecclesiastical circles. It thus led some kind of under-ground, para-academic existence, but its influence remained strong, owing to the power and status of the scholarly institutes run by the Church and its religious orders.

The Renaissance period is, again, treated selectively. We only select three main figures, Linacre, Scaliger, and Sanctius, leaving the many others who worked and wrote on language undiscussed. The most important figure of the three is no doubt Sanctius, who is given pride of place on account of his almost prophetic vision of deep semantic structure (in the Platonic tradition), and his adumbrations of a transformational relationship between deep and surface sentence structure.

Finally we get to the seventeenth century. Here our view is directed mostly to France and the powerful Port Royal tradition, which incorporated some of the ideas proposed by Sanctius, though not at all wholeheartedly, as will be shown. The towering figure of Leibniz, though largely belonging to the seventeenth century, is discussed in the next chapter, since his ideas were way ahead of his time.

At this point we make a break. The following chapter dovetails into the 18th century, when linguistics became an established intellectual profession. It was then that the period of small, general theoretical treatises on grammar came to an end and big descriptive grammars began to be made.

1.1 The tradition of Plato and the Stoa

- *Plato's dialogue Cratylus*

The earliest document, in Western civilisation, of linguistic analysis is the dialogue *Cratylus*, written by the Greek philosopher Plato (428-348 BC) in his middle period. Before we discuss the actual dialogue, some background information is called for. The *Cratylus* is called after the 5th century BC philosopher of that name, a follower of Heraclitus. This is important because Plato was, through Cratylus, heavily influenced by Heraclitus.

- *Heraclitus*

Heraclitus of the city of Ephesus in Asia Minor (now Turkey) lived approximately 535-480 BC. He was one of the Presocratic philosophers of nature, who tried to establish the unity of matter despite its manifest variety. According to Heraclitus, the world is characterized by constant change: nothing is ever the same, everything is in constant flux. It is, for example, impossible to step into the same river twice, because the second time it is no longer, in a very material sense, the same river. His most famous phrase is, of course: *pánta rheî*, 'everything flows'. He took it that the original form of matter is fire, the most changeable and volatile of all. The constant change consists, in principle, in a downward process of densification and then again an upward process of rarification: from fire into air into water into earth, and back into water, air and fire. From these four 'elements', fire, air, water and earth, all other varieties of matter are derived.

But this was not all. Heraclitus understood, apparently, that this was not good enough as a theory of nature. Although he surmised that the circular process of change from fire to earth and back to fire was fundamental or axiomatic in some as yet unclear sense, the actual system according to which this and other processes in nature takes place is hidden from direct observation and must be reconstructed by careful theory-building. This system, the *lógos* (Latin: *ratio*) or 'harmony', is immanent in the world, a part of its very nature. In fact, he considered the immanent lógos to be God. Two famous sayings of Heraclitus are 'Nature likes to hide herself' and 'Invisible harmony is stronger than visible harmony'. We may infer that Heraclitus realized fully that he was still very far from unravelling the mysteries of nature, though he may not have realized that it would take some twenty centuries before a serious start would be made with the physical sciences.

- *Cratylus and the problem of identity*

Clearly, this philosophy of nature had to lead to a crisis around the notion of identity: how is it possible to identify objects over time if they are never identical? One of Heraclitus' followers, the Athenian philosopher Cratylus, drew the ultimate conclusion and said that, since a thing cannot remain itself over time it is impossible to refer to the same thing twice. One cannot refer to things other than by pointing. Any form of language use is deceit. He spent the last years of his life in silence. Apparently, Cratylus saw that the use of language to refer to things requires a certain permanence, an identity over time, of the things referred to. But as he did not succeed in defining criteria of identity or permanence he saw no other way out than to live by his ideas and give up speaking.

- *Plato taught by Cratylus*

The same Cratylus had taught the young Plato in Athens (presumably while he still spoke) the principles of Heraclitean philosophy, and it is generally believed that this lies at the bottom of Plato's philosophy of an eternal world of 'ideas', which would account for the fixity of things despite the constant changes in the material world. It certainly is the basis of Plato's notions of language, set forth in his dialogue *Cratylus*, where it is assumed that each word has an underlying form expressing the meaning of that word in a regular and transparent way. The reconstruction of the 'original' underlying word form and its meaning was called *etymología*, our 'etymology', from the Greek *étymos*, 'true', and the suffix *-logía*, 'knowledge'.

- *The dialogue* Cratylus

The dialogue is a conversation between Socrates, one Hermogenes, an otherwise unknown Athenian, and Cratylus on the nature of truth and, in particular, on the question of the truth inherent in words. Hermogenes and Cratylus disagree about the nature of words, and Socrates tries to adjudicate between them. In the end, Socrates, most probably voicing Plato's own point of view, takes a middle position between the two, though with a clear preference for Cratylus.

Cratylus defends the view that language is inherently 'true to life', since words are given by nature, and not by convention. They essentially depict what they stand for, though to see that one has to dig a little below the surface. To illustrate this, Socrates and he go through a long list of words and names, providing what have since then been called *etymologies* ('true word forms'). For example, the name of Poseidon, the god of the seas, seems justified because he is restrained by the sea as he walks: the sea is a 'bond' ('desmós') to his 'feet' ('podôn'), though it may also be because 'he knows much': 'pollà eidôs', with substitution of -*s*- for -*ll*-. And 'thought' is called 'phrónēsis' because of all that 'moves and flows' ('phorâs roû') it is the 'thinking' ('nóēsis'). (The implicit reference to Heraclitus' theory of *pánta rheî* is obvious.) The ultimate (nowadays one would say 'axiomatic') elements, the words that cannot be analysed as compounds made up of other words, are sound-symbolic, motivated by their sounds. The sound *r*, for example, symbolizes rapid repetitive movement; on the other hand, the sound *l* is appropriate for everything that is smooth and soft, while the high front vowel *i* lends itself naturally to the expression of whatever is delicate and subtle. Different languages use the symbolic value of the sounds in different ways, just like a tool can be realized in different materials. Strictly speaking, this theory entails that the word *horse* should be seen as a natural property of the animals thus called, as much as their typical size, shape and constitution. Word forms are seen primarily as *ideophones*, symbolizing and depicting the reality of things.

Hermogenes defends the opposite view, later taken up forcefully by Aristotle. For him word forms are arbitrary and conventional. There is no inherent justification for word forms, which are no more than a product of social convention. Socrates then expresses the view that word forms should, as far as possible, be seen as non-arbitrary and motivated by the things they denote, though a certain amount of convention and arbitrariness should be allowed for as well.

- *Truth considered a property not only of sentences but also of words*

It is important to realize that this whole discussion is about truth. For us, truth is a property of (propositions in) sentences, not of words. To say that a word is true, is, for us, a category mistake. But in Plato's days this was not at all obvious. When Plato wrote the *Cratylus* he apparently still held the view that truth could be predicated of sentences (propositions) as well as of words. Early on in the dialogue, almost at the beginning, we read (385C):[1]

Socr.:	But now tell me, do you distinguish between speaking the truth and speaking falsehoods?
Herm.:	I do.
Socr.:	So there are true and false sentences?
Herm.:	Absolutely.
Socr.:	And a sentence that says the things the way they are is true, while one that says the things the way they are not is false?
Herm.:	Yes.
Socr.:	So it is possible to use a sentence for truth as well as for falsity?
Herm.:	Most certainly.
Socr.:	Now, if a sentence is true, is it true only as a whole and are its parts not true?
Herm.:	No no, the parts are true as well.
Socr.:	Does this apply only to the large parts and not to the small parts, or to all parts?
Herm.:	To all parts, I think.
Socr.:	Is there a smaller part of a sentence than a word?

[1] In this and later chapters, translations are mine unless otherwise indicated.

Herm.:   No, that is the smallest part.
Socr.:   And the word is called a part of the true sentence?
Herm.:   Yes.
Socr.:   A true part, is that what you mean?
Herm.:   Yes.
Socr.:   And are not the parts of a falsehood also false?
Herm.:   That is what I mean.
Socr.:   So one may call a word true or false, just like a sentence?
Herm.:   Yes, why not?

The whole remainder of the dialogue then deals with the question of 'truth in words'. Since this question is meaningless to the modern reader the dialogue has suffered from a great deal of misunderstanding and puzzlement. In the proper historical perspective, however, of the early search for the notion of truth in connection with questions about the nature and origin of language, the Cratylus dialogue makes perfect sense, and so does the etymologizing.

- *'Etymologies' are arbitrary but reveal notion of semantic form*
One further factor has contributed to the modern lack of appreciation with respect to the *Cratylus*. To the modern eye, the Cratylean 'etymologies' are, on the whole, fanciful and speculative, deserving Cratylus, and by implication Socrates and Plato, the qualification of a 'glib and unscientific etymologist' (Cary et al. 1953, s.v. *Cratylus*). The idea that we can learn about the world by looking at the words that denote the things in it is, of course, absurd. We accept the essential 'arbitrariness of the linguistic sign', as de Saussure put it, in his *Cours de linguistique générale* (1916). This lack of empirical backing has, in modern times, caused the dialogue to come into some disrepute.

Some recent authors, however, feel that a re-appraisal is in order. Hovdhaugen (1982) defends the dialogue:

> *Cratylus* is a magnificent work. Again and again it has attracted scholars of different professions, stimulating them, irritating them, and frequently leaving them bewildered. Is Plato really serious in Cratylus — what does he believe and where does he stand? It is vain to look for satisfactory answers to these questions. Plato has presented the problems in all their complexity, raising many questions and answering very few.   Hovdhaugen (1982:31)

Although Hovdhaugen is no doubt right in saying that Plato reviewed the central questions and considered possible answers, there is a further dimension to the ancient notion of etymology, which is not mentioned in the existing literature although it is immediately relevant to present-day theory of grammar. The point is that Plato saw a hidden, semantically 'pure' form behind the surface forms of language. Unfortunately, however, lacking the modern notion of syntactic structure, he projected this idea on word forms, where it applies much less than in sentential structures.

In Antiquity, the activity of more or less speculative etymologizing was not frowned upon at all. Many ancient treatises have been preserved on 'the propriety of words', in which the authors base their prescriptions as to the proper use of language on what they take to be the true origin of the words discussed. This kind of prescriptive etymologizing remained popular till the early Middle Ages, especially with those philosophers and students of language who had Platonic or Stoic leanings (Luhtala 1994:1463-4). The underlying thought goes back to Heraclitus, according to whom the world, and language with it, is transient and ever-changing, and conceals its real nature. The system which must be there in the apparent chaos is not open to direct inspection but must be unearthed by painstaking observation and theory building. Through Plato and other philosophers this thought was handed down and further developed by the philosophers of the Stoa.

Interestingly, some of the etymologies current in ancient times were not very far off the mark and some were even correct. For example, it was commonly accepted, during the first centuries AD, that the Latin word *virtus* ('moral strength', 'virtue') was derived from *vir* ('man'), so that *virtus* would originally have meant 'manliness'. We now know this to be historically correct, even if it shows a cultural prejudice with regard to the virtues of women. Some etymologies were based on contraries, the so-called etymologies 'a contrario'. Thus, Latin *lucus* ('forest') was derived from 'a non lucendo', i.e. 'because there is no light there'. This, again, is correct in principle. *Lucus* is a cognate of *lux* ('light') and meant at one time 'open space in a forest'. By metonymy it then came to mean 'forest' (not unlike the English word *town*, originally 'fence', later in particular 'town walls', and then, by metonymy, 'town').

- *Naturalness sought in words, not in sentences*

Etymologizing was practised mainly by those philosophers who felt that language is a product of nature, and not, or only in a minor sense, of convention. Here modern linguistics agrees: language is basically a natural phenomenon; if it has certain conventional aspects these are peripheral and largely limited to the lexicon. Yet modern linguistics rejects the ancient practice of etymologizing. This gives rise to the question of why we reject ancient practice while we accept the ancient view. In part, the answer is, of course, that ancient etymologizing suffered from a severe lack of empirical and other methodological criteria. But the main answer is that the Ancients sought naturalness and 'truth' where it is not to be found, in words. They should have looked for it in sentences. Words are largely conventional, or 'arbitrary' as modern terminology goes. Sentences, on the other hand, have a structure which is not at all arbitrary but heavily, though not fully, determined by natural constraints imposed by the structure of thoughts and by the natural, autonomous machinery of syntax as a species-specific means of expressing thoughts. This is, of course, an extremely interesting aspect.

When philosophizing about language the early ancient philosophers were not so different from ordinary people nowadays, who think that language is just a collection of words. There is no clear focus on grammatical rules and structures. Words is what people commonly see and have in mind when they speak about language. This explains why, in Antiquity, the important Heraclitean assumption of an underlying system was applied more to words than to sentences. Though both the word-centered and the sentence-centered view lived side by side, when it came to actually formulating transformational relationships between the presumed underlying ideophonic expressions on the one hand and surface expressions on the other, it was word transformations, not sentence transformations, that were produced. The ancient etymologies are thus the deficient expression of the otherwise profound insight that linguistic surface form conceals the 'deeper' reality of meaning.

In due course, the notion of (assertive) sentence did come to the foreground, but without a proper notion of structure. In his late dialogue *Sophist* Plato defined a sentence as a combination of a nominal and a verbal expression, later called 'subject' and 'predicate', respectively, taking this as a tentative basis for a definition of truth: if the predicate applies to the subject the sentence is true, otherwise false. Aristotle took this up and turned it into a more systematic theory of sentence structure and of truth and falsity. The main contribution, however, to the 'philosophy of the sentence' was made by the Stoics.

- *The Stoic notion of sentence as expression of thought*

The Stoic philosophers saw a sentence (or utterance: the distinction was not yet made) as an expression of a mental representation of a state of affairs. A sentence (utterance) was seen as meaningful physical sound reflecting a non-physical thought which, if true, in turn reflects a state of affairs involving physical objects (referents). We see here the making of a *theory of signs*: the sentence (utterance) is a sign of a thought which, if true, reflects a state of affairs in the physical world. We also see a notion of truth as primarily a property of thoughts. If truth (or falsity) are predicated of a sentence it is a property derived from the underlying thought. We shall see in the following section that Aristotle, like Plato, wavers, in his definition of truth: on the one hand he proposes an analysis of the linguistic sign along lines that are identical with what is reported about the Stoics, defining truth as primarily a property of *thoughts*, but on the other hand he defines truth as a correspondence between what is *said* and actual states of affairs, without any reference to underlying thought processes.

- *The Stoic notion of semantic form*

The Stoics, in any case, made a clear distinction between a sentence as a linguistic structure and the underlying thought as a mental or cognitive structure. The proper conception of thoughts was seen as subject to a permanent rational system guiding and producing proper ideas and true thoughts. It is here that we find the origins of the modern concept of *semantic analysis* or, in the terminology of some, *logical form*, as an abstract mental structure underlying the surface form of a sentence. What the Stoics did not have, however, was a clear concept of 'structure'. Our modern notion of structure is a great deal clearer and much better defined, but this degree of clarity and explicitness was not achieved until very recently, a few decades ago, in the tradition of European and American structuralism. (The 19th century German linguistic tradition, for example, of 'innere' (inner or semantic) and 'äussere' (outer or surface) form, also still lacked a clear notion of structure, with the result that no significant progress was made.)

- *Both sentences and semantic structures representable as tree diagrams*

Nowadays, a linguistic structure is represented as a specific kind of graph, normally called a 'tree structure' which specifies the hierarchically ordered constituents of the structure. More is said about this in section 4.4.5. Here it suffices to see that both the underlying semantic representation or 'logical form' and the surface structure of a sentence are representable as tree structures. Once this is clear the question can be asked how these two classes of tree structures are related to each other, what rule system maps a semantic structure onto a surface structure or vice versa. We now know that such a rule system is by definition transformational, as it transforms tree structures of one level into tree structures of another level. But the Stoics were unable to attain this insight as their notion of structure was still severely underdeveloped.

- *The ancient notion of transformation: word transformation*

Instead, what is found in the ancient literature is a notion of 'transformation' applied not to sentence structures but to word forms. This notion 'word transformation' is found in Plato's *Cratylus* (394B), where he makes Socrates say:

> In like manner a person who knows about words looks at their meaning and is not put out if a letter or two is added or moved or taken away, or indeed if the meaning of the word lies in altogether different letters.

Interestingly, Plato, or rather Socrates in the dialogue, immediately runs into the trap of unconstrained transformations, well-known to modern grammarians. The notion of transformation described in this passage, and used throughout Antiquity, is unconstrained and allows one to transform anything into anything. This is precisely what Socrates now sets out to do. He continues:

> Thus the two names *Astyanax* ['king of the city'] and *Hector* ['holder'], which we use for the same person, have only the letter *t* in common. And what letter has the word *Archépolis* ['ruler of the city'] in common with the latter two? Yet it means the same, and many other words mean just that: 'king'.

Aristotle follows suit, more or less, in *De Poetica* (1457b-1458a), but only in the context of deriving poetic nouns from 'ordinary' ones, never as a method of etymologizing (translation by Ingram Bywater (Aristotle 1946)):

> Whatever its structure, a Noun must always be either (1) the ordinary word for the thing, or (2) a strange word, or (3) a metaphor, or (4) an ornamental word, or (5) a coined word, or (6) a word lengthened out, or (7) curtailed, or (8) altered in form. ... A word is said to be lengthened out when it has a short vowel made long, or an extra syllable inserted; e.g. *pólēos* for *póleōs*, *Pēlēiádeō* for *Pēleídou*. It is said to be curtailed, when it has lost a part. ... It is an altered word when part is left as it was and part is of the poet's making; e.g. *dexíteron* for *déxion*.

Here he mentions the transformations of addition ('lengthening out'), deletion ('curtailing'), and of substitution and transposition ('alteration'), as part of a series of poetic devices. We may assume that Aristotle took his notion of word transformation from Plato but used it for a different, more marginal, purpose.

- *Varro and word transformations*

The Platonic concept of word transformation by juggling sounds ('letters') is found also, for example, in *De Lingua Latina* by the Latin author *Marcus Terentius Varro* (116-27 BC). Varro, whose inspiration came at least in part from Plato and the Stoa, derives words from their presumed semantic base via etymologies, just like Cratylus, and in hardly less fanciful ways. The relation between the alleged underlying semantic word forms and their surface counterparts is defined 'by the deletion or addition of letters, and through their permutation and modification' ('litterarum enim fit demptione aut additione, et propter earum traiectionem aut commutationem' (bk 5, ch.6)). Here we have a mathematically precise definition of the notion 'elementary transformation' as used in modern transformational grammar, but applied to word forms, not to sentences. The latter step was not taken until much later (see 1.5.2 on Sanctius).

- *Modern notion of semantic form goes back to Heraclitus, Plato, Stoa*

While the practice of etymologizing with the aim of establishing motivated word forms died down towards the end of Antiquity, the idea that each *sentence* corresponds to an underlying semantic form somehow lived on, mostly in the Stoic tradition, albeit without any precise notion of 'structure'. This idea found its way into the Middle Ages and thus into the traditional lore of modern thinking. Until the advent of behaviourism and its corresponding school of linguistics, American structuralism, it was commonplace to see sentences as the more or less incidental 'clothing' of the more essential real stuff, the underlying thoughts, both being structured according to their own specific rules and principles. We now see that this part of our traditional thinking has its roots in the ideas of Heraclitean, Platonic and Stoic philosophers from the 5th century BC onwards about invisible systems governing the visible phenomena of the world.

1.2   The Aristotelian tradition

A different tradition from the one established by Plato and continued in the Stoa became prominent shortly after Plato's death, with the Macedonian philosopher Aristotle, likewise in Athens. We shall discuss two aspects of Aristotle's influence on linguistics, first his influence, via the notion of truth, upon modern model-theoretic formal semantics, and then the way he influenced theories of grammar in Antiquity.

1.2.1 Aristotle's theory of truth: where things went wrong

- *Verbal and cognitive notions of truth*

In one respect, Aristotle's theory of truth has had a profound influence on the development of modern model-theoretic formal semantics in the tradition of Russell, Tarski and Montague. Aristotle defended two distinct notions of truth, both within the general frame of truth as correspondence. In some passages he presents truth as a property of *thought*, just like the Stoics did later, but in other passages truth is defined as a property of what is *said*, without any reference to underlying thoughts. The former we call the *cognitive* notion, the latter the *verbal* notion of truth. In both cases the property in question is that of correspondence between the bearer of the property, i.e. thought or sentence, on the one hand and an actual state of affairs on the other.

- *The formalism of logic based on verbal notion of truth*

Aristotle also elaborated the first logical system in history, logic being a formal calculus for the preservation of truth given a set of sentences. All existing forms of logic take *sentence* structures, not *thought* structures, as the formal 'abacus' to do the computation with, clearly because sentence structures are more accessible than thought structures. For Aristotle it was important that an elementary structural analysis at sentence level, in terms of subject and predicate, was available. Aristotle's logical principles, quite apart from his actual logical system, have been enormously influential throughout the history of logic, so much so that present-day logic maintains the Aristotelian *principles*, even if the actual *machinery* of his predicate calculus and syllogisms has been replaced. As a result, modern logic is still entirely a calculus on sentential structures, not on thought structures, and model-theoretic formal semantics, a direct offspring of modern logic, has become a semantic theory that establishes correspondence relations between what is *said* and what is the case, and not between what is *thought* and what is the case.

This is an essential point, and also a point of criticism with regard to present-day formal semantics, since this dominant modern paradigm of linguistic semantics fails to take into account the cognitive structures and processes occurring in the minds of the humans who transfer meanings by using language. Curiously, the ones most aware of the strangeness of this situation are the computational linguists, who face the hard reality of making programs that do what humans do. David Israel, a leading computational linguist, writes, in his review of Cresswell (1985):

> It is quite likely that an adequate semantics of natural languages – in particular, an adequate semantics of propositional attitude reports – cannot be formulated in complete isolation from accounts of the creatures who use these languages and, in turn, are both the producers and the [primary] subjects of those reports.
>
> Israel (1987:363)

Let us look at the details. In *De Interpretatione* (*Perì Hermēneías*) Aristotle presents a Stoic notion of the linguistic sign. In the first paragraph he says:

> The sounds are symbols of impressions of the soul, and written characters are again symbols of the sounds. And just as writing is not the same for all men, neither are the sounds. But the mental impressions of which the sounds are signs ARE the same for all mankind, and so are the actual things of which the impressions are images.

(Aristotle adds writing as a fourth element, besides the sounds (symbols), the mental impressions and the actual world, but this is only a minor point.) The impressions can only be images of actual things if there is a regular correspondence between the two, i.e. if they are true. And a sentence can only be true, in a derived sense, if the thought it expresses is true. This was mentioned above in connection with the Stoic notion of sign, but it originates with Plato. In Plato's *Sophist* (260B) we see the Eleatic Stranger converse with Theaetetus (translation De Rijk 1986:190-191, with a minor adjustment):

> ES: We saw that 'what is not' is one kind among the rest, spread out over the whole domain of things that are.
> Th.: Yes.
> ES: Therefore the next question is, whether it mixes up with thought and speech.
> Th.: Why that?
> ES: If it does not mix up with them, everything must be true; but if it does, there will be false thought and false speech. For thinking or saying 'things that are not', *that* is, it would seem, falsity occurring in thinking and speech.

For Plato, therefore, truth and falsity can be predicated, first of thinking, then of saying.

In accordance with this, Aristotle (*Metaphysics* 1027^{b}25) speaks of truth and falsity as properties primarily of thoughts:

> For falsity and truth are not properties of actual things in the world (so that, for example, good things could be called true and bad things false), but properties of thought.

And again (*Metaphysics* 1051^{b}1-16) we see that Aristotle treats truth and falsity primarily as properties of 'opinions', i.e. thought, and only secondarily of spoken sentences (translation by Warrington (Aristotle 1956:243), with some adjustments):

> Now truth and falsity depend, in the case of objects, upon their being united or divided; he who thinks of what is divided that it is divided, or of what is united that it is united, is right; but he whose thought is contrary to the real condition of the objects is in error. This being so, *when* do 'truth' and 'falsity' exist or not exist? We must be clear about the meaning of these terms. You are not white *because* we truly think you are, but it is because you are white that we speak the truth when we say you are.

The Stoics agree. Sextus Empiricus (2nd cent. AD) informs us, in his book *Against the Mathematicians* VIII,11:

> [The Stoics] say that the signifier, the signified, and the referent are all three connected. The signifier is the vocal sound, as in *Dion*. The signified is the thought content expressed by the vocal sound, such as we understand it when it actually presents itself to our thought, while those who do not speak our language do not understand it even if they hear the sound. As to the referent, that is the corresponding outside object, Dion himself. Of these three elements two are physical, the sound and the referent, but the third is non-physical, the thought content signified or the expressible. It is the expressible that is true or false, but not just any expressible, because there are complete and incomplete expressibles. Only the assertion is a complete expressible, and the general definition of the assertion is precisely: 'That which is true or false is an assertion'.

On this point, therefore, Aristotle, Plato and the Stoics are of one mind.

However, when it comes to actually *defining* truth and falsity Aristotle moves away from the mental dimension and concentrates more on the relation between what is *said* and what is the case. In *Metaphysics*, at 1011^{b}26, truth is defined as a correspondence relation between a sentence and the world, and falsity as the absence of correspondence, without any mention of the thought underlying the sentence (translation by Warrington (Aristotle 1956:142)):

> We begin by defining truth and falsehood. Falsehood consists in saying of that which is that it is not, or of that which is not that it is. Truth consists in saying of that which is that it is, or of that which is not that it is not.

Here, too, Plato precedes Aristotle. In the *Sophist* (262D-263B), just after the passage quoted above, Plato first makes the Eleatic Stranger define a sentence (*lógos*) as a synthesis of noun and verb (or, perhaps better, a nominal and a verbal expression, i.e. subject and predicate). He then makes him propose a true and a false sentence about his interlocutor Theaetetus, 'Theaetetus is sitting' and 'Theaetetus is flying'. Then we read:

> ES: And the true sentence says the things about you the way they are.
> Th.: What else?
> ES: And the false one says things that differ from the way they are.
> Th.: Yes.
> ES: That is, it says things that are not as if they were.
> Th.: More or less, yes.

Clearly, in this passage, truth and falsity are predicated of sentences, not of thoughts, a legitimate but secondary use of these predicates.

Both Plato and Aristotle waver between thoughts ('opinions') and sentences as bearers of the truth values. The tradition has never considered this to be serious. Yet it would seem that we have reason now to say that the tradition has underestimated the importance of this point, which is considerable. In the context of modern studies of language the point at issue is quite serious, for two related and important reasons.

- *Empirical reason: truth is co-determined by cognition*

The first reason is that it is *empirically incorrect* to say that a sentence, or, if one wishes, utterance, is the bearer of a truth value, while the underlying thought is nothing but the mental counterpart of the sentence (utterance). Sometimes, there are elements in the thought which are neither expressed in the utterance nor recoverable from it, yet are constitutive of the meaning and the truth-conditions. In Antiquity, the Sophists had their set examples, like *There is a pleasant breeze*, which, if true, is true not by simple correspondence between the utterance and the weather, since it is impossible to formulate the conditions that must be fulfilled by the wind for it to be called 'pleasant' without taking into account language-independent factors of personal preference on the part of some person who is presented by the speaker as the 'viewpoint holder', 'protagonist', or, as we shall say, 'viewer', usually the speaker himself.

Much clearer examples of this nature have been actively studied in psycho-linguistics over the past twenty years,[2] but totally neglected in philosophy and linguistic semantics (see 6.1.5.2 and 6.1.5.4 for a more extensive discussion). A sentence like *The ball is to the right of the man* is true for the situations a, b and d, and false for c, in fig. 1. But for b it is true only if the man embodies the viewpoint from which the predicate 'to the right of' is evaluated, as in, for example, *The man knows where the ball is; it is to his right*. For a and d it is the viewer (usually the speaker) whose viewpoint guides the evaluation, as in *The viewer sees where the ball is; it is to the right of the man*.

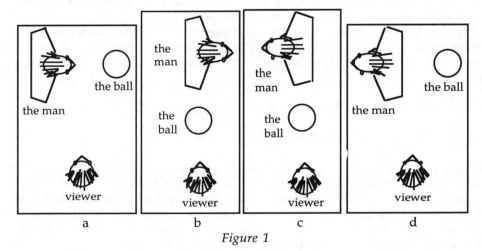

Figure 1

Another example showing that truth values may depend on extraneous cognitive factors is mentioned in Seuren (1985:21) (see also 6.1.5.2 below):

(a)   Each of the 25 rooms in the hotel has a shower.
(b)   Each of the 25 students in the class has a supervisor.

The first of these is false if the rooms share a shower, even if that shower is explicitly assigned to these rooms. But the second sentence is true if the students share an assigned supervisor. That is, for (a) to be true there must be a one-to-one mapping between rooms and showers, whereas an analogous mapping is not required for the truth of (b). This raises questions regarding the meaning, and the satisfaction conditions, of the verb *have*. We are forced to incorporate into the meaning description of this verb an element that refers the language user to commonly available knowledge about the way things are done in hotels, or in faculties, or wherever. Without such knowledge it is impossible to establish the truth value of such sentences.

The truth conditions of such sentences are therefore co-determined by non-linguistic, encyclopedic knowledge about the world, i.e. by a cognitive faculty.

---

[2] E.g. Miller & Johnson-Laird (1976:381-414); Levelt (1989:48-54); Carlson-Radvansky & Irwin (1993); Levinson (1996).

This is a very serious threat to the idea that truth is a correspondence between *utterances* on the one hand and states of affairs on the other, and supports the notion of truth as correspondence between *thoughts* and states of affairs. This does not mean that, from now on, we should never again speak of true or false utterances. Such a decision would go against natural usage and be counterintuitive. But we must realize that when we say of an uttered sentence that it is true or that it is false it is taken for granted that such a truth value assignment is conditional upon any extraneous cognitive information that may have a bearing on the utterance's meaning.

An immediate important consequence of this is that the calculus of truth values of sentences in a model can no longer be regarded as compositional, i.e. computable from the component parts and their position in the structure.

- *Consequences for model theory*

The second reason why it is important to distinguish between the verbal and the cognitive concept of truth lies in the consequences for model theory as a theory of linguistic meaning. Modern formal semantics is entirely Aristotelian in spirit. It concentrates entirely on the relation between sentential structures and classes of states of affairs ('possible worlds'), without taking into account at all the fact that it is human beings, endowed with cognitive faculties, that produce true or false statements in the shape of sentential structures. This is an essential flaw in the general set-up of present-day formal semantics, which is, in fact, quite unable to account for examples of the kinds illustrated above. We see now that this error goes back to the days of Plato and Aristotle, and that it would certainly be worth our while to try and develop a semantic theory more along Stoic than along Aristotelian lines.

- *Cognitive notion of truth has never been formalized*

The Stoic notion of truth and falsity as properties of thoughts has, however, never led to a logical machinery, the reason being that there can be no logic without some structural analysis and no clear notions existed, or indeed exist, about the structure of thoughts and their connections with available cognitive content. The only structural analysis that has so far become available applies to sentences, not to thoughts. It was, therefore, the sentence-based or *verbal* notion of truth that became dominant, as opposed to the thought-based or *cognitive* notion. The enormous prestige acquired by logic over the centuries further enhanced the dominance of the verbal notion of truth. When we now speak of the 'Aristotelian notion of truth' we mean the verbal notion according to which the sentence, not the thought, is the bearer of the truth value. The point is taken up again in section 2.6.4.

- *Ogden & Richards' semiotic triangle*

It is interesting to note, in this connection, that Ogden & Richards' (1923) notion of the linguistic sign, expressed in their famous 'semiotic triangle', leans towards the Stoic point of view but retains the Aristotelian notion of truth, though only as an 'imputed relation', as shown in fig. 2.

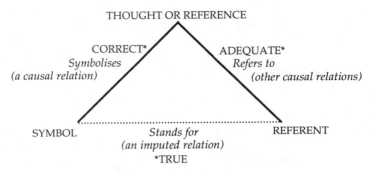

THOUGHT OR REFERENCE

CORRECT* ADEQUATE*
Symbolises *Refers to*
(a causal relation) *(other causal relations)*

SYMBOL   *Stands for*   REFERENT
(an imputed relation)
*TRUE

Figure 2   Ogden & Richards' semiotic triangle

Ogden and Richards pointedly fail to show the primary truth relation, which holds between the thought and its 'referent', i.e. the actual state of affairs in the world. What they call the relation of 'adequacy' is in fact the primary truth relation.

Nowadays we are in a position to develop a somewhat more precise idea of how thoughts are structured, which means that the time has come to be more consistent and start defining truth as a relation between a thought on the one hand and an actual state of affairs on the other, and not as an 'imputed relation' between an uttered assertive sentence and a state of affairs. The construction of a logic and a semantics along these lines, with thought structures as the abacus for the logical computations, should be an exciting and challenging exercise.

1.2.2 The Alexandrine philologists

For a discussion of Aristotle's role in the early development of grammatical theory it is necessary that something be said first about his biography, and that of his pupil Alexander, since the first beginnings of linguistics as a sustained scientific activity distinct from philosophy were, at least in part, a result of Alexander's exploits.

● *Aristotle and Alexander the Great*
Aristotle (384-322 BC) was the son of a Macedonian physician, the court physician of the Macedonian king Amyntas II, father of Philippus II and grandfather of Alexander the Great. Macedonia was not reckoned to be part of Greece, in those days. Macedonian was not a Greek language or dialect, but a totally different language (about which virtually nothing is known). And the Macedonians were, strictly speaking, considered barbarians, i.e. non-Greeks, even though the Greek language was widely used and Greek culture was rapidly penetrating. Young Aristotle studied philosophy with Plato for about twenty years, until Plato's death in 348-347. Not being too enthusiastic about Plato's successor in the Academy, he left Athens and spent a few years in Asia Minor (the present Turkey) and on the island of Lesbos, until he was called by Philippus II, in 343-342, to assume the task of educating the crown prince

Alexander, later called 'the Great' (356-323 BC). This he did till about 340, when Alexander's education became more directed at military matters.

Under Philippus' reign the cities of mainland Greece were brought on and off under Macedonian authority, often against fierce resistance. Athens, in particular, whipped up by the powerful public orator Demosthenes, remained an obstinate enemy of Macedonian domination. When Philippus was assassinated, in 336, Alexander, barely eighteen years old, assumed power and re-established order in Greece, including Athens, leaving no doubt about his authority (he exterminated the city of Thebes, to set an example). The following year, in 335, Aristotle returned to Athens to set up a new college of philosophical and other studies, called the Lyceum (Lýkeion, after a nearby shrine of Apollo Lýkeios).

Meanwhile, Alexander started on the greatest military expedition in ancient history, his conquest of all the land between the Indus and the Nile, including Egypt and the Persian Empire. Within less than ten years he became master of the Eastern world and rose to mythical proportions. He died, however, in 323, thirty-three years old, from the effects of an injury incurred during his many battles, before he could realize his dream of conquering Arabia and even Italy. After his death there was a great deal of strife about his succession. In the end, the great empire was split up among some of his generals. Ptolemy, probably Alexander's elder bastard half-brother, took Egypt and became the founder of the dynasty that ended, almost three centuries later, with Cleopatra.

- *Relevance of Alexander's campaign for linguistics*

The relevance of Alexander's campaign in the present context lies in what happened to the Greek language as a result of it. Before the campaign, Greek was one of the many languages spoken, in more or less garbled versions, in market places throughout the Near and Middle East. But Alexander's campaign brought about an enormous change in this respect. Wherever he went he left behind Greek, or anyway Greek speaking, officials to rule according to his directives. This means that in those places where the new form of government was firmly established Greek became the language of government, and hence the language of status. Whoever was to climb the social ladder had to know proper Greek. A sudden and massive demand thus developed for the teaching of Greek as a foreign language, especially in Egypt, which was the most powerful and the best organized among the new Hellenistic kingdoms.[3]

- *Foundation of the Museum, the first university*

Around the year 280 BC a university, the *Museum* ('abode of the Muses'), was established in the capital Alexandria (founded by Alexander a few decades earlier) by the aged Ptolemy and/or his son Ptolemy II for the advancement of

---

[3] Cp. Robins (1994:4645): 'The Macedonian rulers systematically imposed the Greek language and Greek literature on their subject peoples for anyone aspiring to a general standard of education. ... Greek as a foreign language was now a major educational activity.'

the sciences as they had been started by Aristotle, to counteract the intellectual influence of Athens. Professors were appointed in different subjects, some of them linguists or 'philologists'. We know from documentary evidence that the Alexandrine philologists were concerned with critical editions of ancient literary texts, in particular Homer, always with the aim of establishing what they thought of as the original, pure forms of Greek words and sentences. Given the pronounced normative character of their philological work we may surmise that they had also been assigned the practical task of developing teaching material for the new schools. This explains their activity in formal grammar, in conjunction with their text-critical work.

• *Early Alexandrine grammar*
The early Alexandrine linguists found themselves in a predicament, since they needed linguistic, in particular grammatical, analysis for the purpose of formal grammar teaching. Authoritative literary texts were, of course, of great help in teaching the foreign learners, but formal grammar was needed as well. A certain amount of grammatical analysis was available, developed in the philosophical tradition of the preceding two centuries, in particular the works of Aristotle, who was, understandably, favourite among the Alexandrines as he was the most illustrious exponent of Macedonian culture and glory. However, what was provided by the philosophical tradition was too little to suffice for the Alexandrines' purpose.[4] Many more notions and a great deal of new terminology had to be developed from scratch.[5] Moreover, a

---

[4] According to ancient sources, the philosopher Democritus, who held that language is a product of convention and not of nature, had made the distinction between verbs and nouns, though confusing this with that between subject and predicate. He also discovered the process of morphological derivation ('from *thought* we say *think*, but from *justice* we can say nothing'; Diels & Kranz 1951, 68B26). According to Aristotle (*Rhet.* 1407[b]7; *Poet.* 1456[b]15), the Sophist Protagoras had distinguished various nominal genders and verbal moods. Plato uses the distinction between subjects (nouns) and predicates (verbs) to define truth (*Sophist* 263B-D). The term *case* is the English version of the Latin word *casus*, literally 'fall', esp. 'fortuitous fall'. Latin *casus* is again a loan translation of the Greek word *ptōsis*, which occurs for the first time in Plato (*Rep.* 604C) in the context of the vicissitudes of life, which are like the ways dice may come down in a poker game. Aristotle uses the term for morphological variations of word stems, whether nominal or verbal. In Stoic writings it gets restricted more and more to nominal flection, as in the normal modern use of the term. The details of this development are unknown, though it is known that some confusion existed already in Antiquity. Aristotle knew, in addition, about homonyms, synonyms and paronyms ('words that differ by their "case", such as *grammar* and *grammarian*, or *courage* and *courageous*'; *Categ.* 1[a]12-15), simple and compound nouns, indefinites, declension and conjugation, sentences, negation, imperatives, questions, wishes, assertions, subject and predicate, and perhaps a few more things. A considerable amount of linguistic analysis was, therefore, available. Yet much more remained to be developed.

[5] Unfortunately, much is unknown about these early developments in scientific grammar, not least because the writings of the greatest of the Alexandrinians, Aristarchus, have been lost in their entirety. What we know about them is little and indirect. Consequently, there is some controversy in the scholarly literature about questions of development and attribution. One point about which there is particular controversy is the origin of the

model had to be chosen for what was to be considered 'proper Greek', to be described or approximated by the rules of grammar to be developed.

A lively research activity thus came about directed, on the one hand, at establishing what could be taken as the 'purest' form of Greek, and, on the other, at the normative grammatical description of that variety. The variety of Greek settled upon was the dialect of Attica as used in Athens during the late 5th century BC. This Attic Greek continued to serve as the normative model for 'pure' or 'classical' Greek throughout Antiquity and after.

- *Origin of the term 'grammar'*

The grammatical analyses and descriptions that were produced were used and interpreted as prescriptions for the proper use of the language: Alexandrine linguistics was strictly prescriptive and normative. The term *grammar* has its origin in these developments. Its Latin equivalent is *grammatica*, which is short for *ars grammatica*, a loan translation from the Greek *téchnē grammatikḗ*, i.e. 'the art of writing'. Plato had used this term in his dialogues *Cratylus* (431E) and *Sophist* (253A), but in the original sense of 'art of writing', i.e. the use and concatenation of written characters to represent words and sentences. In the centuries after Aristotle, however, the term began to be used for what we now call 'grammar', though always with strictly normative connotations: 'the art of writing correct Greek or Latin'.

- *Grammars in the classroom: teaching Greek as a foreign language*

Unfortunately, the documentary evidence on the period between 300 and 50 BC is extremely scarce, which makes it difficult to put together an adequate account of the course of events. Householder informs us (1994b:931-2) that

---

names of the Greek cases: nominative, genitive, dative, accusative and vocative. The most plausible theory seems to be that these names were introduced by the Alexandrinians. They smack of school practice. The *nominative* case (Greek: onomastikè ptōsis) is the form you use to give your name. It was also called, in Latin, *casus rectus* (Greek: orthè ptōsis), i.e. the word form that has not begun yet to 'fall' into the 'oblique' cases. The *genitive* is the form you present your family or clan (Greek: génos) name in. The *dative* (Greek: dotikè ptōsis) is the form to refer to the one you give something to. The accusative (Greek: aitiatikè ptōsis) is, probably, the form to refer to the person you take to court (from *aitía* 'accusation'), though others say that this term has a philosophical origin, from the other meaning of the homonymous word *aitía*, 'cause'. According to them the Latin loan translation is incorrect, and should be *causativus*. The *vocative* case (Greek: klētikè ptōsis) is used to refer to the person called at (Latin *vocare* 'call'). All these names refer to what were, for the Hellenistic speakers of Greek, prototypical uses of the cases in question. De Mauro (1971:239-332) argues extensively in favour of a philosophical, and against a philological, origin of the case names, trying to supply them all with philosophical meaning. His argument is based on statistics: datives, for example, do not, in fact, very frequently occur in construction with a verb of giving in the texts that are available. Other uses are far more frequent. However, what counts is not the frequency but the prototypicality of the use in question. And here the 'give' notion of the dative clearly wins out: ask anyone to provide a sentence with a dative, and the answer will in most cases be a sentence with a verb of giving. The philosophical meanings assigned to the cases are, moreover, for the most part far-fetched and weakly supported.

between ca. 250 and 50 BC grammatical sketches (*téchnai*) were being written, as aids for teachers, in the Alexandrine tradition. According to him :

> If ... an ordinary man wishes to decline a strange [i.e. as yet unknown, PS] noun correctly or form the correct aorist of a new verb that he has met in reading, and there is no complete Greek grammar or dictionary available, how does he do it? He might ask a *grammatikos*, but how did he, in turn, find out? The normal answers given to this question were two: (a) analogy, and (b) usage. Analogy means (to the grammarian) finding the rules for saying that two or more words are inflected alike, when one is well-known but not the other. Usage means finding out how Demosthenes or Thucydides inflected the word, or else how one's college-educated neighbor did so. By and large, *grammatikoi* began to set themselves up as experts on both analogy (knowledge of the correct inflection) and usage (knowledge of the dialect of Demosthenes, etc.).

Thus, in actual practice, the teaching of Greek as a foreign language consisted of the teaching of inflectional paradigms and other possible grammatical regularities, together with the teaching of texts written by classical authors with the aim of developing usage, a good 'ear' for the language.

● *Linguistics started as applied linguistics*
The work done by the Alexandrines marked the beginning of what we now call 'linguistics'. And if we are right in linking this with a widespread demand for the teaching of Greek it began, strictly speaking, as applied linguistics, the teaching of Greek as a foreign language. It is clear that from then on the study and analysis of language was no longer the exclusive province of philosophers. Professional linguists began to be heard as well.

● *Dionysius Thrax*
One particular document from that period must be mentioned specifically, the *Téchnē Grammatikē* traditionally attributed to Dionysius Thrax, who lived ca. 100 BC and had been trained by the Alexandrines.[6] It is a very short treatise of barely 30 small pages, and is the first document in western history that aims at providing a grammatical description of a language, in this case Greek. It starts with a discussion of what grammar amounts to ('Grammar is the expert knowledge of the language forms mostly used by the poets and the prose writers'), the proper reading technique (i.e. aloud, with the right accents and pauses, and in the correct literary style), the accents, punctuation, rhapsody (four lines), the letters of the alphabet, syllables, pronunciation, nominal expressions ('names'; three pages), verbs (one page), verb conjugation, participles, articles, pronouns, prepositions, adverbs, conjunctions. It ends with an appendix on verse metres. It thus set the pattern for all subsequent grammars of European languages till well into the 18th century, which all consist, entirely or largely, of a discussion of 'letters' (speech sounds), syllables, words

---

[6] There is considerable uncertainty as to its authenticity and its period. According to Householder (1994:932) the most probable theory is that it consists of earlier and later parts, some even from the third century AD. We shall stay away from this controversy and consider the work from the point of view of its influence and status in Antiquity and later.

and word classes and their morphology if any. This little work has been enormously influential in the western grammatical tradition, introducing, among other things, a number of grammatical terms that have since become standard. It ushers in a period of almost two millennia during which much of the effort of linguists went into the establishment and delineation of word classes and their function in sentence structures. During that whole period, linguistics will be largely concerned with questions of taxonomy, but the need for explanatory theories will be felt and there will be a great deal of speculation, especially as regards the relations between language, thinking and reality. But any approximation of empirical theory construction will have to wait till the 20th century.

1.3 Anomalism and Analogism, or Ecologism and Formalism

• *Two traditions: analogism and anomalism*
We thus see the outlines of two different traditions emerging in Antiquity. On the one hand, there is the tradition that developed along Heraclitean, Platonic and Stoic lines. On the other, there is the tradition of Aristotle and the Alexandrine philologists. It is generally believed (on the basis of evidence from Varro and Sextus Empiricus) that for a few centuries, from roughly 300 till 50 BC, these two traditions were at odds with each other, though there is a conspicuous scarcity of direct documentary evidence on this. We follow the commonly held view that such a controversy did indeed exist during that period, adherents of the former being called *anomalists*, or 'lovers of exceptions', from the Greek word *anōmalía* 'exception', and of the latter *analogists*, or 'lovers of regularity', from the Greek word *analogía* 'regularity', used in particular for the regularities expressed in morphological paradigms (see for example 'Analogy and Anomaly' in Cary et al. (1953)). There were, in any case, the two traditions, one carried by the Stoa and the other by the Alexandrines. So why not call them by the traditional names of anomalism and analogism, respectively. (In discussing these two schools we shall concentrate on the opposition between ecologism and formalism as methodological alternatives in the study of language.)

The differences between the two schools were profound. The anomalists were philosophers, mostly belonging to the Stoa, not practising linguists like the analogists. The absence of practical demands enabled them to engage in purely theoretical arguments about the nature of language, the relation between language and thought, or between language and logic, the notion of 'sign' and how language can be considered to be a system of signs, the origin of language as part of human nature, and similar abstract topics. Language, for them, was a product of nature and therefore likely to show all the quirks and capriciousness one finds in nature, yet be governed by an underlying system that would explain all. To the extent that they developed actual grammatical notions and terminology it was always against the background of the general idea that language, as given by nature, is but the expression of thought. In their eyes, the semantic function of language was primordial and paramount. Behind the surface structure of each sentence lurks a semantic structure reflecting the thought expressed by the sentence in question.

The Alexandrine philologists were in a very different situation. Driven by practical demands they had no time for deep philosophies. Their sympathy lay with Aristotle, who defended a conventionalist view of language. For them, human languages are purely conventional systems, which can, to a certain extent, be changed and improved upon by competent specialists. They had no time for the niceties of the language, their primary concern being the establishment of what they saw as the regular declinational and conjugational paradigms of Greek. Whatever appeared to be odd, or against the rules, was reasoned away as an impurity that had, unfortunately, crept into the language but should ideally be expurgated from it. The kind of contemporary Hellenistic Greek spoken in Egypt was considered inferior, to be brought back to the purer form of 5th century Attic Greek and possibly even further. That the language had changed was the unhappy consequence of the moral decay of mankind since the old days of heroism and virtue.

The important point is that, for the Alexandrines, language is a system of conventional word forms, which are not 'true' or given by nature, as was maintained by the anomalists. They stressed the arbitrary nature of the 'etymologies' proposed by their opponents. On this score, as we have seen, the Alexandrines were clearly right. On the other hand, they failed to see beyond words into sentence grammar. The anomalist philosophers were somewhat stronger on this point, and their contention that language is given by nature makes best sense from the point of view of sentence grammar, even if they themselves may have had only dim intuitions in this respect. Both parties thus had their reasonable and their less reasonable points of view.

• *The two schools merge in first century BC*
By the first century BC the controversy apparently died down. A synthesis was achieved both in the actual practice of grammar writing and in the more theoretical treatises. Authors like Varro, mentioned above, show influences from both sides, with perhaps a preference for one over the other. It is the combination of the two schools that produced what we now know as 'traditional grammar'. The actual debate between anomalists and analogists shifted from the description and analysis of language to stylistics. The anomalists became 'asianists', with a preference for novel and unexpected stylistic turns and word uses. The analogists became 'atticists' and favoured a sober use of language and style, avoiding unusual forms of expression.[7] We shall leave the controversy there, but for one important point, which keeps recurring in the history of linguistics and is illustrated clearly in the ancient debate between the anomalists and the analogists.

---

[7] For this aspect of the controversy see Norden (1898).

- *Difference of method: formalism and ecologism*

The point is one of method. It concerns the way in which linguistic theorists deal with the facts of language. Two main approaches can be distinguished in this respect, which we shall dub *ecologism* and *formalism*. It will soon be clear that the ancient analogists belong in the formalists' camp, whereas the ancient anomalists represent ecologism.

For the formalists, language is a formal system describable in terms of rules for the acoustic or visual expression of meanings, and whatever appears to go against the system tends to be regarded as a nuisance, attributable to deplorable interference from outside sources. Formalists tend to play down the fact that language occurs as a natural faculty of the human race and is therefore an empirical object to be approached by hypotheses that aim at empirical adequacy. They prefer to approach the task of analysing language with a formal system that has been developed elsewhere, usually in logic or mathematics, and tend to impose their a priori, preconceived system on what they perceive as the facts of language. Keen observation of facts is not their strongest point. Instead, they usually underestimate the difficulties posed by natural languages. And when these are pointed out to them they are prepared to take them into account only to the extent that their system is not messed up too badly. Facts that might show the unviability of their approach are usually ruled out of order and attributed to the weakness (or dumbness) of the humans who use language. For them, language is a product of ingenuity, 'something which we could have cooked up ourselves ... had this not, in effect, already been done (perhaps none too well)' (Travis 1981:1).[8]

In the ecologistic approach, on the other hand, language is primarily seen as a product of nature, and hence as an object for empirical research. The expectation is that language, like nature, will manifest itself in all kinds of unexpected variations on and deviations from an as yet largely unknown rule or norm system. Regularities are wonderful, but, as in the rest of nature, they are not always readily detectable and they tend to leave room for idiosyncrasies or, as they are commonly called, exceptions. For an ecologist, language is an object of wonder, a 'storehouse of unimaginable complexities and surprises, to be discerned by looking very closely' (Travis 1981:1), and, we may add, by exerting patience and mulling over the facts in our minds until a bright idea springs up and shows them in their true light.

- *Both approaches have their merits and their drawbacks*

Both approaches have their merits. Formalism gives the linguist a better awareness of the properties, mathematical and other, of the descriptive and analytical system he is using. It makes explicit all kinds of implicit precon-

---

[8] The following statement by the extreme formalist Bertrand Russell is highly illustrative in this respect (Russell 1956:197): 'I am allowed to use plain English because everybody knows that I could use mathematical logic if I chose. Take the statement: "Some people marry their deceased wives' sisters". I can express this in language which only becomes intelligible after years of study, and this gives me freedom.' (See also note 13 in chapter 5)

ceptions about the formal properties of the analyses and descriptions deliver- ed. The importance of this was made manifest, in this century, in the early development of transformational grammar, when it was shown that Bloom- field's concept of grammar was in fact that of a system of context-sensitive re- write rules, while the concept of grammar used in information technology around the middle of the century was that of a probabilistic Markov system (see section 4.7.1 for a detailed discussion of these notions). Once these precon- ceptions were made explicit they could be questioned, and found inadequate. It took a few intelligent formalistic minds to achieve this important step for- ward in our knowledge of grammar systems.

The ecologists, on the other hand, have the experience, the familiarity with the data, and the general knowledge of the terrain required for a judi- cious selection of a hypothesis that may have a reasonable chance of success. Ecologists live with the data, they know their way around the jungle of language and understand a great deal even if much of it is, for the moment, at a pretheoretic or preformalized level.

The two approaches also have their drawbacks, especially when they are pushed to extremes. The formalist risks becoming blinkered by the mathema- tics of his system, losing sight of the reality the system should be about. The ecologist runs the risk of becoming an antitheorist, rejecting anything formal and concentrating entirely on data collecting, without any theoretical perspec- tive. Some ecologists have been seen to reject the very notion of an underlying system, on the pretext that the use of language is 'free' and 'creative', in some ill-defined sense. Both extremes occur, as anyone familiar with the field will know. And such extremes are, of course, to be avoided.

Ecologism is more complete than formalism. It encompasses the whole lengthy process from the first inklings of wonder about linguistic facts, via the gradual detection of regularities and conception of semi-formal theories, to the final stage of constructing advanced formal systems and even implement- ing them. Formalism, clearly, covers only the last few stages of this drawn out process, and thus risks missing out on the rich ecological basis of language.

Ideally, the two approaches should be in complementary harmony. Both the formalists and the ecologists should be able to search for the best theory – the theory with the most extensive generalizations over the facts of any language under description, and of language in general, minimizing the excep- tions. Thus united, the two approaches might find it not too difficult to agree on the status and causal explanation, if any, of the exceptions, the drags of the rule system agreed upon. Reality, however, has shown itself to be quite dif- ferent. What one sees most of the time is two different mentalities and a well- nigh unbridgeable gap.

• *Modern repetition of old opposition*

Nowadays we see a repetition of the ancient clash. Modern model-theoretic semantics, established by the American philosopher and logician Richard Montague (1931-1971), represents formalism. The formal semanticists are the latter-day analogists. Their analytical and descriptive tools are largely taken from logic and its special branch, model theory, and applied to the analysis and description of natural language sentences. For this school, natural languages are instances of 'formal' languages as developed in logical theory. (Likewise, it is commonly said in circles of computational linguists that natural languages are instances of computer languages.) To avoid the complexities of natural language formal semanticists usually limit themselves to what they call a 'fragment' of the language under description. Needless to say, the fragments selected are on the whole highly restricted and tend to coincide with what their rule systems can handle. Contrary facts brought up by critics are then said to be irrelevant as they do not belong to the 'fragment'. This would not be so bad if the fragments chosen could easily be extrapolated to the language as a whole. In fact, however, such an extrapolation invariably turns out to be problematic to the point of being unrealistic.

Ecologism is typically represented, nowadays, by theoretical linguistics, where empirical adequacy is of prime importance. (The ecologistic character of modern linguistics clearly goes back to its origins in 18th century Romanticism – see section 2.3.) For modern linguistics, natural language is an auto-nomous object of investigation, to be studied in its own right, as a phenomenon connected with human nature. Natural languages are not instances of formal logical languages (nor, for that matter, of computer languages).[9]

While in Antiquity the ecologist approach was represented by philosophers and philosophical logicians of Stoic persuasion, and formalism was in the hands of the professional grammarians of Alexandria, in modern times the roles are reversed. Now it is the professional linguists that carry out the ecologists' programme, whereas the logicians and computational linguists, and in general those who approach language from a mathematical angle, represent formalism.

1.4 Late Antiquity and the Middle Ages[10]

1.4.1 Apollonius Dyscolus, Donatus and Priscian

- *Apollonius Dyscolus*

What is known about linguistic theory in the Greek world during the first centuries of our era is largely based on the works of the Greek linguist

---

[9] The Chomsky-led school of linguistics is beginning to be an exception to the principle that modern linguistics is ecological. It is typical for this school to submit any programme of grammar writing for natural languages to stringent constraints that would show the essential uniformity of all languages. These unifying constraints are supported more by the desire to streamline the theory than by factual generalizations, and are thus evidence of a tendency towards formalism.

[10] It is impossible, in this context, to provide anything near a 'history of linguistics in late Antiquity and the Middle Ages'. All we can do is select a few highlights and place these in a historical context. For a thorough treatment of the history of linguistics in the Middle Ages, see Pinborg (1967).

Apollonius Dyscolus (ca. 110-175 AD), who lived and worked in Egyptian Alexandria. He must have been an enormously prolific writer, as 59 book titles are mentioned in various sources. Yet only four of these books have to some extent survived: *On the Pronoun, On Adverbs, On Conjunctions* and *On Syntax*. The last of these is of most interest with regard to the development of linguistic theory, as it is the first known work on sentence structure in history, though it leans heavily on Aristotle's syntactic notions expounded in his *Rhetoric*. (There is an excellent modern translation with commentary of Apollonius' work on syntax by Fred Householder (1981).)

Apollonius identifies and discusses what are now called 'government' and 'agreement', developing an early but already sophisticated theory of nominal cases. In his syntactic analysis of the sentence he distinguishes between the verb (predicate) and its argument terms, rather than between the predicate and just the subject, as Aristotle and the Stoics did.[11] He is puzzled by the fact that the subject is normally in the nominative case except when constructed with an infinitive, where it takes the accusative case. He also distinguishes impersonal, intransitive and transitive verbs, and identifies speech act verbs. In short, he introduced a number of central analytical notions into the study of language, some of which took many centuries to be developed further and become an integral part of grammatical and semantic analysis.

- *Donatus*

In the Roman world all we have is a limited number of grammar writers. The best known of them are Donatus and Priscian. *Donatus* (ca. 310–after 363 AD) wrote two grammar books, the *Ars Minor*, and an extended version, the *Ars Maior*. The latter is of the usual format: the 'letters', i.e. speech sounds and syllables, then the 'parts of speech' (partes orationis, word classes), of which he recognized eight (noun, pronoun, verb, participle, adverb, conjunction, preposition, interjection; adjectives were considered a subclass of nouns), and finally a number of literary style figures and mistakes against good language use. His purpose was pedagogical, for readers who already spoke Latin. He was the most influential grammarian in the early Middle Ages, up to the 11th century, when the teaching of Latin as a foreign language to inhabitants of lands with a Romance, Germanic or Celtic language was of prime importance.

- *Priscian*

Priscian (Latin: Priscianus, early 6th century) was quite a different figure, and more interesting from a historical point of view. His *Institutiones Grammaticae* consists of 18 books, 16 of which dealt with the conventional topics of 'letters' and word classes (always called 'partes orationis' or 'parts of speech'). These were brought in relation with the Aristotelian categories. The last two books deal with syntax and propose structural analyses meant to relate sentence structure to Aristotelian logic and metaphysics. The structure of sentences was seen as the result of an interaction between Aristotelian

---

[11] Cp. Householder (1981:3). For the history of the subject-predicate distinction see 2.6.3.

categories as expressed in word classes. In the abstract word order he proposed for Latin sentences, 'the noun precedes the verb because the substance expressed by the noun precedes the accidents expressed by the verb' (Luhtala 1994:1467).

- *The Aristotelian categories*

It is useful, in this context, to make a comment on the Aristotelian notion of category. In his *Categories*, and later also in his *Metaphysics*, Aristotle had proposed a system of ten categories: *substance, quantity, quality, relation, place, time, position, state, action* and *affection*. These ten Aristotelian categories are to be conceived of as the most primitive, axiomatic, non-composite predicates applicable to the (or any) world. They thus reflect Aristotle's ontology to the extent that any reality can be known and thought or spoken about. There is nothing incomprehensible in this, other than that Aristotle assigns 'substance' also to species like 'plant' or 'animal', which gave rise to interminable debates on universals and, for a long time, split the philosophical world into a realist and a nominalist camp. If 'substance' is withheld from species and assigned only to individuals there is not much difference with ontologial views current in modern analytical philosophy, where, if this degree of generality is achieved at all, (any) reality is laid out in terms of the parameters of *space* and *time*. In space are located (*position*) entities or individuals (*substance*), grouped in sets (*quantity*) and in *n*-tuples of sets (*relation*), according to their properties (*quality*). Each such structure is a *state*; time is a succession of states. Properties are causal in that they lead over time to effects exerted by active forces (*action*) upon entities affected (*affection*). The categories are thus meant to establish an isomorphism between the primitive categories (in the literal sense of 'predications') of thinking and speaking on the one hand, and the 'modes' of being on the other. (We have now become accustomed to the use of the term *category* in all three of these senses.) What Priscian attempted to achieve was, therefore, an implementation of this Aristotelian programme by recognizing the metaphysical categories in the formal categories of grammar. Modern model-theoretic formal semantics does essentially the same, in terms of set-theoretically defined models (see chapters 5 and 6 for further discussion).

- *Categories of being, thinking and speaking*

The importance of this can hardly be overestimated. It means that linguistic elements and linguistic structures are seen in the light of the categories of being and the categories of thinking. This provided a starting point for many centuries of speculative theorizing about the system underlying human language in general and specific languages in particular. The Greeks and Romans were not directly concerned with universal properties of human language, their linguistic horizon being extremely restricted. But during the Middle Ages and later, philosophers of language, whose linguistic environment was much more diverse, began asking questions about the unity of language as such, as opposed to the diversity of languages, and thus developed theories about universal grammar. Of course, those theories were, for a long time, very speculative and Aristotle, always a key figure, was not always of great help in this respect. But the questions began to be asked.

- Priscian's *Institutiones*

The *Institutiones* are more theory-oriented than other extant works of the late Roman period. According to the specialists (e.g. Pinborg 1967:22, Bursill-Hall 1972:14), Priscian's work was to a large extent a compilation, sometimes garbled (Covington 1982:22), of what had been done in the Greek world and much less an original contribution to the theory of language or the description of Latin. This may be true but it was largely through Priscian, who wrote in Latin and not in Greek, that these ideas penetrated into the Middle Ages and formed the basis of medieval and later theories about universal grammar.

Whereas Priscian tended to be forgotten during the early parts of the Middle Ages, probably on account of being too difficult and too scholarly for the mundane purpose of teaching Latin to youngsters, he was rediscovered as a result of the Carolingian Renaissance during the ninth century. After that he became the most popular source of grammatical and language-theoretical insights until the end of the Middle Ages (Kneepkens 1995). He almost became for grammar and linguistic theory what Aristotle was for philosophy and logic.

1.4.2 The Middle Ages: Speculative Grammar

- *The Carolingian Renaissance*

Until the ninth century no theoretical development of any kind took place. The Church became the paramount spiritual, cultural and worldly power, and curtailed education, emphasizing the teaching of Latin, this being the language of the Church. It was due to the worldly emperor Charlemagne (768-814) that proper education was reinstated. As part of his Carolingian Renaissance, the school curriculum called 'trivium' was restored from just school grammar to Grammatica, Rhetorica and Dialectica (i.e. logic), as it had been before. Both the arts and academic study were stimulated. Yet much of what Antiquity had contributed had been lost. Greek was no longer known, with the result that the enormous wealth of Greek literature, philosophy and other branches of learning had become inaccessible. Aristotle, for example, could not be read. Only Latin texts were read, and then only those that were considered ideologically 'correct'.[12] Reading the Latin grammarians was allowed, although the example sentences that were considered too pagan were often censured away. Understandably, therefore, the Carolingian Renaissance was severely hampered. Yet the way had been opened, in principle, to the highly sophisticated developments in philosophy, logic and the study of language witnessed by the 13th and 14th centuries, to which we turn now.

---

[12] The Latin poet Virgil, strangely enough, was among the 'correct' authors on account of his fourth Ecloga, which alludes to the coming of a saviour.

- *Opening up of medieval world through Arabic influence and urbanisation*

There can be no doubt that the period between 1250 and 1350 marks the heyday of linguistic theory in the Middle Ages. This was part of a general blossoming of culture and learning during that period, which was due to a variety of factors. One of the main factors was no doubt the presence of the Arabs and Moors in Southern Spain, and, to some extent, also in Sicily. They brought with them the richness of their culture, which included Aristotle, who was well-known and universally admired in the Arab world. His texts became available in Latin translations from the Arabic. (The Greek language remained practically unknown till after 1453, when Constantinople, the capital of the Greek speaking world, was conquered by the Turks and the Byzantine Greek scholars fled to Italy.) Another factor was the massive urbanisation that took place from the tenth century onward and led to a considerable improvement in the standard of living of the population at large and the formation of a powerful class of 'burghers' or town dwellers.[13]

- *Rediscovery of Priscian and birth of Speculative Grammar: the Modists*

Starting from the 12th century we see the influence of Priscian's ideas on theories regarding the relations between language, the world and thought:

> [T]he wind of change which was to alter the whole direction of the study of logic and philosophy had a similar effect on scholastic attitudes to grammar; this now came under the control of logic and metaphysics, the rules of grammar being derived and justified by recourse to logic and metaphysical theories of reality. Grammar therefore became a branch of speculative philosophy and although normative grammar continued to be taught, it was almost completely eclipsed until well into the fourteenth century.   Bursill-Hall (1972:16)

This led directly to what is known as the movement of *Speculative Grammar* ('Grammatica Speculativa').[14] The movement lasted from about 1250 till roughly 1320. As far as can be judged from the available evidence (modern knowledge of the period leaves much to be desired, due to the sorry state and the relative inaccessibility of the documentary sources), the doctrine of speculative grammar was dominant in the universities of mainland Europe and Britain during that period, after which it was superseded by British nominalist philosophy, which had no sympathy for the central tenets of Speculative Grammar. Covington, however, observes (1982:40-41) that although the Nominalists drove the Modists out of the philosophical court, they had no grammatical theory to put in its place.[15] As a result, Modistic grammar kept

---

[13] Significantly, no urbanisation took place within the papal state which cut through the middle of Italy. There, Rome remained the only urban centre of importance.

[14] Lyons (1968:15) points out that the term *speculative* should not be understood in the modern sense, but as derived from *speculum* ('mirror'), as reality was taken to be mirrored in language and thought. Covington (1982:47-48), however, rejects this as unsupported by evidence and holds that the term *speculative* just meant 'theoretical'.

[15] The Nominalists, like many modern philosophers, minimized their ontology to individuals and sets of individuals. Reference to abstract entities, therefore, had to be regarded as reification, a product of the mental machinery of abstraction and interpretation. They

being taught in the schools, in less philosophical and more practical versions, till as late as the 16th century.

What were its central tenets? Speculative Grammar is essentially an attempt at establishing a relation of regularity between the ontological and metaphysical categories thought to structure the real world, the mental categories of thought, and the grammatical categories of language. The term invariably used for these categories was 'modes' (modi): the 'modes of being' (modi essendi) were taken to be mirrored in both the 'modes of thought' (modi intelligendi) and the 'modes of signifying' (modi significandi), found in language. This school of philosophy of language is therefore normally called the *Modists* (Modistae). All formal categories in grammar were called 'modes': word classes, cases, genders, verb inflections, etc.

The modes of being were the standard and the point of departure for the modes of thinking and the modes of signifying. The modes of being were those of contemporary metaphysics, which was characterized by an extreme 'constructivism' in that enormously complex hierarchical metaphysical constructions were devised and applied to any object in sight. On the basis of the Aristotelian distinction between 'substance' and 'process', two main linguistic categories were distinguished: referential expressions (nouns and pronouns) and verbs (finite verbs, infinitives and participles), the former expressing stability, the latter change and variation. The differences between noun and pronoun, and between finite verb, infinitive and participle, were interpreted in terms of the metaphysical distinction of 'matter' (materia) and 'form' (forma), derived from Aristotle but put to heavy use in those days. Their ontology was rich, to say the least. Covington gives a clear account (1982:51-53):

> Each real-world object has not only an essence, which makes it what it is, but also a set of *modi essendi* 'modes of being', various properties that allow it to be conceived of in various ways. Thus, along with its conceptus of the thing itself, the intellect has access to *modi intelligendi*, various 'modes of understanding', that derive from the properties of the object that are 'co-understood' (*cointelliguntur*) along with the thing itself. The linguistic sign, in turn, signifies the concept (or rather signifies the thing via the concept) and consignifies the modes of understanding . . . ; the consignified properties are called *modi significandi*. . . .
>
> Since grammar is defined as the study of modes of signifying, it should follow that grammar is the study of the consignified properties, such as time, position, plurality, and the like — which is not the case. Grammar is actually the study, not of the properties themselves, but of the mechanisms or means by which the properties are encoded into language. Hence another distinction has to be introduced, the distinction between the properties of real world objects as consignified by words (e.g., time, consignified by the verb) and the properties of the word that make the consignification possible (e.g., verb tense); the proper concern of grammar is then the latter.

---

were thus forced to formulate a doctrine of *suppositio*, 'reference': how do abstract terms relate to ontological entities? Their attempts, however, remained unsuccessful, a fate shared by the formally and analytically much better equipped modern nominalists (see 6.1.2.3).

Later Modistae therefore distinguished between *modi significandi activi* 'modes of signifying', which are properties of the word, and *modi significandi passivi* 'modes of being signified', which are the properties of the real-world object that the word consignifies . . .

Given this distinction, grammar can be defined as the study of *modi significandi activi*, and all is well.

It was this all too luxuriant ontology that the later Nominalists objected to.

We have no hesitation in rejecting this approach to grammar, nor, as has been said, had the 14th century nominalist philosophers. Yet two things must be observed in defence of the Modists. First, this was the beginning of medieval theorising about universal grammar, and it strongly influenced later theories of universal grammar. Secondly, in the course of developing their conceptual constructions the Modists shaped a number of new analytical notions and succeeded in sharpening and refining the categories used in grammatical analysis. As their grammatical predecessors, they took immediate inspiration from Priscian, but they criticised him for his presumed lack of explanatory theory as well as for his deficient observations.

- *Thomas of Erfurt's* Grammatica Speculativa

The most famous *Grammatica Speculativa* is by Thomas of Erfurt, probably written between 1300 and 1310.[16] It deals specifically with the modes of signifying. The book is roughly 90 printed pages long. It consists of a *proœmium* (preamble), dealing with the notion 'modus significandi', a part called *etymologia*, which deals with the parts of speech, and a part called *diasynthetica*, standing for syntax. Just to have a taste of the kind of prose used, but also because of later responses to the questions discussed (see 1.5.1 on Scaliger), let us read some sections from the preamble:

The mode of signifying introduces equal factors which are called the active and passive modes of signifying. The active mode of signifying is the mode or property of the expression conferred on it by the intellect, by means of which the expression signifies the property of the referent. The passive mode of signifying is the mode or property of the referent as signified by the expression.

In addition it must be noted that, since the intellect uses the expression for signifying and consignifying, it attributes to it a double faculty, [a] the faculty of signifying, which can be called signification by means of which a sign or significant is effected, and so it is formally a word; and [b] the faculty of consignifying which is called the active mode of signifying by means of which the signifying expression creates the cosign or consignificant, and so it is formally a part of speech. Therefore, a part of speech is such accordingly by means of this faculty of consignifying or active mode of signifying according to an instance of the formal principle; however, it is a part of speech in relation to other parts of speech by virtue of this same active faculty of consignifying according to the intrinsic efficient principle.

---

[16] Its authorship has long been uncertain. It was thought to be the work of Duns Scotus, under whose name it was published as a separate work (Fernàndez 1902). Recently, the authorship of Thomas of Erfurt has been established (Pinborg 1967:132).

From this it is clear that the active faculties of consignifying or active modes of signifying in and of themselves refer primarily to grammar, inasmuch that they are principles relevant to grammar. But the passive faculties of consignifying or passive modes of signifying are not relevant, except accidentally, to grammar, because they are neither a formal nor an efficient principle of a part of speech, since they may be properties of referents; they may be relevant only insofar as their formal aspect is concerned, since in this way they do not differ greatly from the active modes of signifying, as we shall see. . . .

It should be noted immediately that since faculties of this kind or active modes of signifying are not fictions, it follows necessarily that every active mode of signifying must originate basically from some property of the referent. . . .

But to this it may be objected that ... negative properties ['privationes'] and fictions fall under no properties whatsoever since they are not entities, and yet the significative expressions of negative properties and fictions have active modes of signifying, e.g. blindness, chimaera, etc. We answer that it does not follow that the active mode of signifying of a word is always drawn from the property of the referent of that word of which it is a mode of signifying, but it can be derived from a property of the referent of another word and attributed to the referent of that word, and it suffices that these should not be incompatible. . . .

(transl. Bursill-Hall 1972:135-139, with adjustments)

- *Medieval Immediate Constituent Analysis*

An extremely interesting passage is found in chapter 89, where the principle of immediate constituent analysis is proposed, much in the way it was advanced by Wundt around the year 1900 and taken over by Bloomfield in his *Language* of 1933:

The principles of the construction. We shall, first of all, discuss these principles in general. There are four essential principles of constructing the sentence congruously and completely, i.e. material, formal, efficient, and final.

Constructibles are the *material* principle of constructing: what subject is to accident, constructibles are to construction. But the subject is the matter of the accident, for the accident cannot have matter from which but only in which it is realized. Therefore constructibles are the matter of the construction. And in any one construction there are not several but no more than two constructibles, because, as will become obvious, a construction comes about as the result of the dependency of one constructible on another; but one dependency can involve only two elements, dependent and determinant. Therefore, in any one construction there are only two principal constructibles, dependent and determinant.

This shows the error of those who say that the following is only one construction: *homo albus currit bene* ['the white man runs well']. For one has here several dependencies: one by which the Adjective determines the Substantive, the other by which the Verb determines the suppositum, the third by which the determinant determines the determinable. Therefore, we will not have one single construction here. Similarly, when we say: *Socrates percutit Platonem* ['Socrates beats up Plato']: because of several dependency relations of the Verb with respect to the suppositum preceding it and the oblique following it, this cannot be one single construction, as is obvious.   Bursill-Hall (1972:274)

Here we find the *grammatical* distinction between subject and predicate clearly present, though in a terminology that goes against already establish-ed practice (see 2.6.3): our subject, as a sentence constituent, is called *suppositum* by Thomas, while *subiectum* stands for that which bears a property or undergoes a process ('accidens'). And our *predicate* is Thomas's *Verb* (Verbum), though *Verbum* also stands for what we call *verb*, as opposed to its arguments.

Moreover, and even more importantly, we find a sophisticated notion of hierarchical constituent or tree structure, coupled with a first inkling of the modern idea that a tree structure may serve as a computational frame for a categorial calculus (we must anticipate here on 4.4.5 and 5.5).[17] We do, how-ever, need some terminological adjustments. Let us read *(immediate) constituent* for '(principal) constructible', *function* for 'determinant', *takes as argument* for 'determines' (the Latin has: 'dependet ad'), *term* for 'dependent' or 'determinable', *subject* for 'suppositum' (as already indicated), and *direct object* for 'oblique'. Moreover, Thomas is, apparently, at a loss when he has to denote the adverb *bene*, distinguishing it from the verb form *currit*: the former he calls simply the *determinant*, the latter is the *determinable*. If we intro-duce these terminological adjustments, we have a text that could almost serve in a modern textbook of linguistics:

> This shows the error of those who say that the following is only one construction: *homo albus currit bene* ['the white man runs well']. For one has here several dependencies: one by which the adjective takes as argument the substantive, the other by which the predicate takes as argument the subject, the third by which the adverb takes as argument the verb form. Therefore, we will not have one single construction here. Similarly, when we say: *Socrates percutit Platonem* ['Socrates beats up Plato']: because of several dependency relations — of the predicate with respect to the subject preceding it and the verb with respect to the direct object following it — this cannot be one single construction, as is obvious.

The Bloomfieldian notion of Immediate Constituent Analysis or hierarchi-cal tree structure (see 4.4.5) is clearly present. The example *Homo albus currit bene*, directly reminiscent of Bloomfield's *Poor John ran away*, has a tree structure as in (a), while *Socrates percutit Platonem* may be taken to corres-pond to the tree structure (b):[18]

---

[17] Hierarchical structure as a frame for dependencies is first found with Thomas's earlier contemporary, the Modist Martinus de Dacia. But Thomas refined the notions and gave the verb a central position (Pinborg 1967:127-130).

[18] Cp. the excellent essay by Robins (1980) on the exegesis of this passage in the *Grammatica Speculativa*. Covington (1982:61-62) disagrees: according to him the structure intended by Thomas is not to be interpreted as a Bloomfieldian consituency tree but rather as a dependency tree à la Tesnière. I believe that Covington is wrong here, as I fail to find a consistent interpretation of this passage in terms of Tesnière-type dependencies. This text does not contain the notion 'head of a construction', whether in Bloomfield's or in Tesnière's sense: neither *dependent* nor *determinant* is consistently interpretable as 'head', a fact acknowledged by Covington (1982:85). The only consistent explanation I can find is in terms of model-theoretic functions, an interpretation not considered by Covington. The question is, however, only of remote interest.

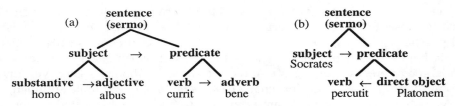

Figure 3   Tree diagrams reconstructed from Erfurt's
Grammatica Speculativa

- *Function-argument dependency*

Moreover, there is an implicit notion that the determinant of a binary branching is a function that takes the dependent (term) as input and passes on the associated value to the dominating node, thereby anticipating the categorial functional calculus of modern model theory (5.5.2). The arrows in (a) and (b) point from the argument to the function. Obviously, the Modists lacked any systematic notion of structure required for a consistent handling of tree structures, as well as the mathematical backing required for the categorial calculus. The former had to wait till the notion of algorithm found its way into generative grammar. The latter needed Frege and his notion of mathematical function. Moreover, we now know that the dichotomy between function and arguments does not imply binary branching as a function may take an *n*-tuple of arguments as input (see 5.5). But the Modists' insight remains amazing.

- *The notion of construction*

The final, syntactic part of Thomas's *Grammatica Speculativa* then goes on to discuss the notion of 'construction' (which is a product of the *mind*, the 'modi intelligendi', and no longer of reality, the 'modi essendi': only the grammatical forms were taken to reflect the modi essendi), the notion of 'congruity', split up in agreement ('similitudo') and government ('proportio'), and finally the ancient notion of 'completion' or predication ('perfectio sermonis').

- *The notion of 'complete sense'*

The ultimate aim of a construction is 'to generate a complete sense in the mind of the hearer resulting from the proper composition of constituents' (generare perfectum sensum in animo auditoris ex constructibilium debita unione). Therefore, the highest construction must always be between subject and predicate. Only the verb can be a predicate as it is the only word class capable of predication. An incipient notion of compositionality (see 5.5.1) is found in the following passage (where we read *subject* for 'suppositum' and *predicate* for 'appositum'; the difficult term *distantia* has been translated as 'predication'):[19]

---

[19] It is interesting to compare this passage with Frege (1906:302): '[Definitions] presuppose knowledge of certain primitive elements and their signs. The definition puts together a group of those signs according to certain principles, so that the meaning of this group is determined by the meanings of the signs used.'

The *proximate aim* <of the sentence> is the expression of a mental concept composed by way of predication (secundum distantiam). And I say "by way of predication" because a mental concept is sometimes composed without predication, as when I combine *homo* with *albus* without copula, as in *homo albus* ['white man']. But at other times a mental concept is composed by way of predication, as when I combine *homo* with *albus* with the help of a copula, as in *homo est albus* ['the man is white']. This kind of composition has the property of being true or false, as is said in *Peri Hermeneias* book I ch. 1. And since the intellect does not stop at the first composition, as it is incomplete, but proceeds from the first to the next, the final purpose of a construction is not the expression of the first composite concept but the expression of the last concept which is composed by way of predication. The *ultimate aim* of a construction, on the other hand, is to generate a complete sense in the mind of the hearer resulting from the proper composition of constructibles.

Secondly, it must be noted that just as a construction by itself comes about by the mere putting together of constructibles, and congruity arises from the proper composition of the constructibles, so completion comes about as a result of the proper composition of constructibles, but not of just any constructibles but only of the suppositum and the appositum, provided no dependency has been left unfinished keeping the sentence from its purpose, which is to express a composite mental concept and to generate a complete sense in the mind of the hearer.

This shows that three conditions must be fulfilled for the completion of a sentence. First, it must consist of a suppositum and an appositum. Since the final purpose of a complete construction is the expression of a mental concept that is composed by way of predication, it is proper that, just as there is predication in the composite mental concepts, there should be predication in the composition of the constructibles. And only the verb can be appositum, because is exists in the mode of predication. Then, conformity is required of all modes of signifying, just as it was required for congruity. And thirdly, it is required that no dependency be unfinished as that would keep the construction from its purpose, which is to generate a complete sense in the mind of the hearer.   Bursill-Hall (1972:312-314)

- *Speaker's 'complete sense' copied by hearer: communication*

One cannot fail to notice that each of the paragraphs quoted ends in an assertion of the thesis that the ultimate end of sentences consists in bringing about, in the hearer's mind, a copy of the thought conceived by the speaker. This conceptual rhyme is a certain indication of the importance attached by Thomas to the primary function of language, which is communicative.

1.5 The Renaissance and later

- *Causes of decline in the Middle Ages*

We will take leave of Speculative Grammar and the Modists here, as we can only touch on the highlights, and pass on to a discussion of the subsequent period where, as we shall see, much of what was achieved during the Middle Ages was lost and remained lost till our days. Only recently have medievalists succeeded in unlocking, if only up to a point, this arcane realm of learning. It is a great pity that the rediscovery of Medieval scholarship in recent times came too late for it to have had much influence on modern developments: what we could have learned from the Modists had, to a large extent, already been rediscovered, in a much more formal and mathematically oriented context, by the time their work was brought to our attention by dedicated medievalists.

What caused the decline, and ultimately the demise, of the Middle Ages during the 14th century is a complex question to answer. The ultimate cause is perhaps to be sought in a process of emancipation, all over Europe, from the all-powerful Church, as a result of improved education, increased urbanisation and higher standards of living, coupled with better communications by sea and by land. The invention of book printing will no doubt have contributed to the emancipation process. Moreover, the waves of Black Death, famine and terrible wars that devastated Europe during the 14th century will have forced people to rely more on their own devices than on prayers and divine intervention. In any case, if one thinks of emancipation one understands why those who closed down the Middle Ages and ushered in the new era of the Renaissance had such a strong feeling of passing from the dark into the light, from one world into another. The passage from the Middle Ages to the Renaissance was different from most other cultural transitions in history. Hardly ever does one find such a clear and definite change in cultural identity. When the Middle Ages were left behind there was a general feeling that a different, more enlightened world had been entered. The link with pagan Antiquity could be picked up again, and the intervening period was ignored as much as possible, the way one ignores and represses an embarrassing period in one's life. The very name 'Middle Ages' shows how that period was regarded as an interlude, rather than as a stage in the cultural advance of mankind. Whereas most other cultural transitions imply a sense of continued cultural identity besides the changes taking place, the transition from the Middle Ages to the Renaissance was a definite and conscious break, not a continuation.[20]

• *Inadequacies of medieval grammar; oblivion in later periods*
As regards the study of language, a more specific reason for the break with tradition was, in all likelihood, the fact that, in the end, the highly cultivated and specialized theories and analyses advanced by the last of the great medieval scholars, though both inspired and inspiring, came to nothing for lack of sufficient formal and technical expertise. An elaboration of the intuitions of, in particular, the Modists required the kind of formal mathe-

---

[20] Not that the Church lost all power. But the absolute dominion it held during the Middle Ages was considerably reduced. Spiritually the Church lost enormously by the many movements of religious Reformation that took hold of large sections of Europe, especially in the Northern parts. All these diverse movements had in common the rejection of the authority of the Pope or of any similar central holder of absolute spiritual power, which shows that much of the discontent that existed was generated by the position of power held by the Papacy. From the worldly point of view, the Church lost as well, as emperors, kings and local rulers gathered wealth and power at the expense of the Vatican. Yet a great deal of worldly power still remained invested in the Church. Bishoprics where the bishop was also the local holder or representative of state power existed till the end of the 18th century. And Catholic kings were often not averse from investing themselves with substitute spiritual power by forbidding any religion other than Catholicism, a measure that was invariably welcomed by the Church.

matical and logical knowledge that was not achieved until the 20th century. As a consequence, their successors did not quite know what to do with the filigree and arcane, but very creative theories worked out by the Modists. In the end, these theories were not elaborated any further. They were not entirely lost, not yet, though they were never really clarified and always remained enveloped in a haze of speculation and vagueness. The ideas kept cropping up in a diffuse and non-specific way in virtually all language-theoretic writings of subsequent ages, until they were really lost in the brazen cultural climate of the 20th century. When the same issues were addressed in the context of modern linguistics no distinct memory of them remained. The significance of the old medieval theories was recognized only post hoc.

We will now look a little more closely at the way the medieval scholars were treated in the Renaissance linguistic literature. We will see that Renaissance authors simply refuse to refer to their medieval predecessors, even if they must have known about them (as appears, inter alia, from the terminology used).[21] Instead, they refer lavishly to the ancient grammarians, not just Priscian but many others as well. The price of this reversal to Antiquity, however, was an immediate dramatic impoverishment of linguistic thought. The most striking feature of Renaissance linguistics is the loss of the rich and creative insights of the Medieval philosophers of language, which were replaced with the somewhat dried up notions culled from ancient authors.

1.5.1 Linacre and Scaliger

• *More actual descriptive grammars*
One feature of Renaissance linguistics is the proliferation of actual descriptive grammars, first only of Latin and Greek, later also of the new vernaculars that were becoming the languages of Europe. The Latin grammars were mostly written for pedagogical reasons, as the humanist scholars considered it important that classical Latin should be reinstated and medieval Latin abolished. Some, however, contained sections on the theory of language, in addition to the merely pedagogical parts. Purely theoretical treatises on language, such as the works of Scaliger and Sanctius discussed below, were much rarer.

• *Medieval grammarians ignored*
It is interesting to see how some of the earliest Renaissance grammarians are still implicitly in discussion with their medieval predecessors, in particular

---

[21] Curiously, this attitude is sometimes reflected in the modern scholars studying them. Schaars, for example, writes (1988:352-3): 'The Renaissance grammarians of Latin and Greek left the medieval ideas about syntax as developed by the Modists for what they were and reverted to, in particular, Priscian. ... During the Middle Ages Thomas of Erfurt was one of those who tried to apply logic to the study of grammar but, on the whole, the medieval systems of syntax remained stuck in arid collections of glosses. There was no fundamental change in the system of syntax.' This stands in contrast with Robins (1967:81): 'It was in syntax that the speculative grammarians made the greatest innovations and the most significant developments.'

the Modists, while the only authors they refer to by name are those of Greek and Latin Antiquity. No reference is ever made to medieval grammarians or philosophers of language. Let us look at two grammarians, Linacre and Scaliger, who published their works during the first half of the 16th century, the time when Erasmus was studying, teaching, travelling and, above all publishing and writing his letters. (Though our discussion might seem to imply some criticism with regard to the authors discussed this is not so. If there is a criticism it is one of the times they lived in, rather than of them individually. They simply acted according to the rules and values of their society.)

- *Linacre*

The English grammarian *Thomas Linacre* (1460-1524) wrote a pedagogical grammar of Latin, *De Emendata Structura Latini Sermonis*, published posthumously in 1524. No mention is found, in this work, of any medieval author, but classical and contemporary authors are mentioned liberally. Yet it is obvious from the text that Linacre owed a great deal to the Modists, especially in his syntactic notions. His syntax is more elaborate than in other contemporary and later works. He defines a construction as follows (Luhrman 1984:189):

> Thus a construction is the proper composition of parts of speech with respect to each other, as required by the correct rules of the grammar.

Both the conceptual content and the terminology used point to the Modists (cp. the passage from Thomas of Erfurt on constructions quoted above). Then, Linacre follows the English tradition, established by the early Modists Robert Kilwardby and Roger Bacon, of investigating and analysing the Priscianic notion 'persona' (Luhrman 1984:203-207). The problem, for them, was that 'person', on the one hand, characterizes the subject of a sentence, but on the other also the direct object of a transitive sentence, although in that position the 'person' is thought to have a different ontological status. For Priscian only subjects were 'person', but the medieval scholars had found that unsatisfactory as the same expressions occur as subject and as direct object and in other positions as well. We are not primarily interested here in the details of the question itself. What does occupy us here is the fact that, though Linacre clearly took part in a discussion that had been conducted in his country for a few centuries he does not refer to it. Apart from this, it may be observed that Linacre's treatment of the question at hand led to a much improved insight into the various semantic functions that can be fulfilled by noun phrases in the sentence and thus contributed to the distinction between word classes and functional sentence constituents, i.e. between the paradigmatic and the syntagmatic aspect of words and constituents (Luhrman 1984:202).

- *Scaliger*

The same negative attitude towards the Middle Ages is found with an otherwise very different author, the Italian *Julius Caesar Scaliger* (1484-1558), a younger contemporary of Linacre. His principal linguistic work is *De Causis Linguae Latinae*, published in 1540 and written for his adolescent son, not as a pedagogical grammar but as a theoretical sequel to one. His main allegiance was to Aristotle, of whom he says, at the end of the book (Luhrman 1984:226):

> But may it suffice to have laid down for you the foundations of science according to our first leader Aristotle, in the light of whose wisdom the darkness of the grammarians should be dispelled.

For Scaliger, grammar is principally about words, and words reflect the Aristotelian categories. This is not unlike the Modists' programme, but they are never mentioned, nor does Scaliger use the term 'modus', which a naïve observer might expect him to do. The book has the usual structure: after an introduction it discusses, in that order, sounds and letters, syllables, words (the central object of his study), nouns, verbs, pronouns, participles, prepositions, adverbs, interjections, conjunctions, syntax (9 pages out of 352), and, finally, on the last ten pages, general questions of methodology (analogy versus anomaly, etymology, use, normative principles and system). Syntax, for him, is ancillary, as it is thought to belong to speech ('usus') rather than to language (just like de Saussure's notion of syntax, almost 400 years later).

In the work he mentions by name, besides Aristotle, Galenus and Averroës, the ancient grammarians Priscian, Varro, Victorinus, Nigidius, Aulus Gellius, Diomedes and Quintillian and his older contemporary Linacre (Luhrman 1984:227). No medieval author is mentioned, although their influence is obvious. It is obvious, for example, that he harks back to Speculative Grammar in the following passage (Luhrman 1984:297), which is directly reminiscent of the first passage quoted above from Thomas of Erfurt's *Grammatica Speculativa*:

> One may have the following doubt: Are names that express figments real words? For they designate nothing. This can be solved thus. That which we call a being is sometimes a real being, like God, but sometimes also non-real, and this in two ways: a non-real being is either a negative property ['privatio'] or a figment — a negative property like "empty", a figment like "Phoenix". Such words do, therefore, not signify in the same way as normal words, like *Deus* signifies God. They signify a negative property thus: as the word *full* signifies the property of a space touched everywhere by physical matter, *empty* will signify its contrary. And although the contrary has no being, it is understood in virtue of that which is. Figments are understood more easily: they are like false expressions. For it is the same to say "Phoenix" and "a bird that causes its own return to life".

Of course, questions of non-being and reference to non-beings arise naturally from Aristotle's *Metaphysics* (and have kept philosophers busy till the present day, leading to abominations like Heidegger's 'das Nichts'). But the specific way and the terminology in which Scaliger deals with the issue point directly to Thomas of Erfurt, who is not mentioned.

1.5.2 Sanctius and the *Minerva*

• *Sanctius: life*

But let us look forward now, and consider the one high Renaissance grammarian who lifted both the description and the theory of language to a much higher level of sophistication, the Spaniard *Franciscus Sanctius* (Spanish: Sánchez; 1523-1600). His principal work on linguistic theory, *Minerva seu de Causis Linguae Latinae*, appeared in 1587. He was professor of rhetoric, Greek and Latin at the University of Salamanca, and was, for unclear reasons, badly harassed by the Inquisition until his very last days.[22] Sanctius was influenced, naturally for one born in Spain in those days, by Arabic scholarship, which continued the Greek, and in particular the Aristotelian, tradition, but also by Linacre and Scaliger, and by Petrus Ramus who is not discussed here.[23]

- The *Minerva*

The *Minerva*, however, is much more than just the product of its influences. It is, though clearly part of its tradition, marvellously innovative from both a descriptive and a theoretical point of view. Descriptively and observationally it is much richer than any earlier work. Theoretically it marks the beginning of a new period in which the Aristotelian categories are no longer taken to motivate categories in surface structures but in a semantic deep structure. A separate set of rules, the grammar, is then postulated to define the relation between the deep semantic structures and the surface structures. The *Minerva* has a format that deviates from the usual, and the contents is equally unconventional. Sanctius concentrates on syntax: 'Oratio sive syntax est finis grammaticae' ('The sentence, i.e. syntax, is the aim of grammar'), he says in chapter 2 of Book I, perhaps implicitly referring to Thomas of Erfurt, who insisted, as we have seen, that the purpose of the sentence is 'to express a composite mental concept and to generate a complete sense in the mind of the hearer'.[24] The *Minerva* consists of four books. Book I is called 'The Parts of Speech' and deals with the notion of grammar and with words (single stem words and compounds), word classes, nominal and verbal flection, and comparatives and superlatives. The syntax begins in Book II, which discusses noun phrases, including their function in the sentence with regard to the verb. It also includes an analysis of the Latin Ablative Absolute construction, and, again, a chapter on superlatives and comparatives. Book III discusses verbal syntax: intransitive versus transitive sentences, passives, impersonals, infinitives, passive participles, tenses, and also prepositions, adverbs and conjunctions. In Book IV we find a discussion of the relation between *surface structure* (oratio figurata) and *semantic structure* (oratio naturalis) (Breva-Claramonte 1983:235). It is

---

[22] Breva-Claramonte (1983:8-9) points out that Sanctius was a 'cristiano nuevo', i.e. a member of a Jewish or a Muslim family recently converted to Christianity. He suggests, not without reason, that this may have been the prime reason for the Inquisition's displeasure in his regard.

[23] See Breva-Claramonte (1983) for a thorough study of Sanctius.

[24] Jan Noordegraaf pointed out to me that *finis grammaticae* may also be read as 'the end of grammar', as it was customary to see rhetoric as the continuation of syntax, and to regard syntax as, so to speak, straddling the fence between grammar and rhetoric.

here that one finds Sanctius' startling ideas on two-level syntax and the relation of surface structures to meaning.[25]

- *Why the name 'Minerva'?*

For Sanctius, language is both systematic in itself and a product of human reason. He called the book *Minerva*, as the goddess Minerva ('Athena' in the Greek world) was considered to be the goddess of Reason (Breva-Claramonte 1983:97, 201). His aim was to lay bare the 'causes' of the Latin language (and with it, in principle, of all other languages). The word *causa* is understood in two ways which are distinct for us but not for Sanctius. On the one hand it stands for 'historical origin', and on the other for 'systematic causal factor'. He shared the belief, already common in Antiquity, that mankind was originally good, intelligent, logical and generally flawless, but for its inclination to decline. Therefore, the 'original language' must have been perfectly logical, a reliable mirror of reality and of thought about reality. To find the 'causes' of language in general and languages in particular one must, therefore, reconstruct the pristine form of language, which was perfectly logical and expressed the Aristotelian categories.

- *Emphasis on syntax; transformations on sentences*

And this is what Book IV is about. As appears from the summing up of its contents above, the *Minerva* concentrates almost entirely on syntax, which in itself makes it exceptional for its days. The syntax then proceeds without hesitation towards the final distinction between 'logical form', which is both historical and systematic ('synchronic'), on the one hand and surface form on the other. Here Sanctius falls back on the ancient quadripartite system of transformations which we encountered earlier, at the end of section 1.1, when we discussed Varro. The difference is, however, that this time the transformations from semantic to surface structure do not apply to word forms, as with Varro, but to sentence structures. True, this was not entirely Sanctius' own idea, as Priscian had already advanced suggestions in this direction when he introduced an abstract word order for Latin sentences in which the subject has to

---

[25] Chomsky (1966a) claims Cartesian ancestry for his notion of transformational syntax. Unfortunately, this claim ignores any history prior to the Port Royal grammar of 1660, as well as the philosophical background (Aarsleff 1970). For example, Chomsky (1966a:47) mistakenly attributes to Beauzée, who published a *Grammaire générale* in 1767, the theory that relative pronouns are short for full NPs, as in *the house of which I have acquired possession*, which is said to be short for 'the house, of which house I have acquired possession'. In fact, this goes back to Sanctius (Breva-Claramonte 1983:168; see Breva-Claramonte 1983:238-239 for further examples of this nature). Moreover, the notion of deep structure, and hence of transformation, as it arose in post-Bloomfieldian structuralist grammar (see section 4.5) is radically different from what is at issue here. Here we have transformation from a semantic structure to surface structure, the only transformational notion in linguistic history before 1950. In Chomskyan transformational grammar one has transformation from a semantically irrelevant, purely syntactic deep structure to surface structure — a notion that has no precedent in history (cp. note 25 of chapter 2). See also Breva-Claramonte 1983:240.

precede the predicate since the substance comes first and the accidents later (see the beginning of section 1.4). And, as we have seen, Priscian will have borrowed this idea from earlier Greek authors. But what Sanctius does is new in that he goes into the matter more systematically and in much greater detail. As a result, his ideas about deep and surface structure, and their interrelations, are much clearer than Priscian's, and, in addition, he hit upon an astonishing amount of facts and details of the Latin language.

First of all,[26] he discusses *deletion*, which he calls *ellipsis*. Each language has certain rules which permit the regular deletion of semantic elements, as in *I wish to drink*, which stands for 'I wish that I drink', and certain idiosyncratic cases where the deletion is recoverable on the basis of lexical knowledge, as in *I was at John's*, which is understood as 'I was at John's place', or the Shakespearean *I must away*, for 'I must go away' (I use English examples as long as these render exactly what Sanctius wished to express by means of his Latin examples). Then there is *addition*, which occurs, for example, when an adjective takes on the morphological markings for case, number and gender from the noun it is constructed with. Next there is *permutation* or *transposition*, as in Latin *mecum*, which means 'cum me', i.e. 'with me', or the relative *quibus de rebus*, which is derived from 'de quibus rebus' ('from which things'). Finally we have *substitution*, as in the biblical (Psalm 8) *lunam et stellas quae Tu fundasti* ('the moon and the stars that Thou hast fixed'), where the neuter plural *quae* needs a neuter plural head, like *negotia* ('things'), so that we can say that *quae* substitutes for *quae negotia*: 'which *things* you have fixed'.[27] Furthermore, there are transformations that are made up of combinations of the four elementary types mentioned, like Conjunction Reduction, or Subject Raising.[28]

- *Sanctius' general theory of language*

We thus have here a precursor of transformational grammar, based on the following considerations, all clearly represented in the *Minerva*, though in less modern terminology:

(a)   Given the relative success of humans in interpreting and manipulating the world by applying reason (thought), there must be a relation of cor-

---

[26] I rely on Breva-Claramonte (1983:218-219) for the following survey.

[27] Admittedly, this example is not very convincing, as it may also be described as a form of deletion. A better example is perhaps the substitution of the ablative case ending for a preposition, which is what, in Sanctius' view, the ablative case amounts to.

[28] Sanctius quotes here a sentence from the Latin comedy writer Terence (*Adelphi* 874), where the subject has been raised out of a finite clause (Breva-Claramonte 1983:217):

> Illum   ut   vivat   optant   ('they wish him to live')
> him-ACC that he-may-live they-wish

It should be noted that this form of Subject Raising, which was very common in colloquial Latin (Kühner & Stegmann 1955, vol. II:579-582), poses problems for present-day theories of syntax.

respondence between the categories and structures of reason (thought) on the one hand and those of the world on the other.

(b) Since language expresses reason (thought) in sentences, there must be a level at which the basic categories and structures of sentences mirror those of thought.

(c) Given the variety of languages and the semantic anomalies found within each language separately, that level cannot be the level of *surface structure*.

(d) Hence there must be a more abstract level at which sentences and reason (thought) meet, the level of *deep structure*.

(e) If that is so, each human must acquire a set of rules and principles that define the relationship between the deep and the surface structure of the sentences he utters in his language. Those rules and principles constitute the *grammar* of his language.

(f) Since (sets of) sentences are globally translatable from one language into another, and since all tribes and peoples on earth have a language, there must be a level, defined by *universal grammar*, at which all different languages are identical to the extent that translation is possible. As long as there is no evidence to the contrary, it is reasonable to assume that this universal level of representation is identical with the level of deep structure, so that all languages have largely identical deep structures.

(g) Since languages change in time, and language was originally created by man according to the faculty of Reason bestowed on him by God, there can only have been one pristine language, which reflected reason (thought) in a pure and unadulterated way. The sentences of this language were formed according to the rules of deep structure. The grammar of this 'ur'-language, therefore, was the grammar of thought.

The considerations (a) and (b) have an Aristotelian touch, but (c) and (d) have a more Platonic-Stoic flavour. The modern reader will note that the considerations (a)-(f) are normally subscribed to by those modern linguists and semanticists who see their discipline as a branch of cognitive psychology.[29] Only (g) is rejected, nowadays, as being speculative and romantic.

Sanctius did not provide a full formal specification of deep sentence structures, nor, therefore, of the mapping rules required to link them with surface structures. Yet he is surprisingly precise in formulating observations and problems. For example, he asks why it is that the subject always takes the nominative case with finite verbs but the accusative case with infinitives.[30] This is a far from trivial question, not only for Sanctius in his days but also for

[29] Those who see it as a branch of logic or of mathematics will not subscribe, but they are usually not very clear on the non-cognitivist foundations of their way of doing linguistics or semantics.

[30] This point was taken up later in Lancelot (1653), as noted in Lakoff (1969a:354). Cp. also note 28.

students of linguistics in our days. Both his theoretical acumen and his keen eye for observations and the theoretical problems raised by them make Sanctius a key figure in the history of linguistics.

1.5.3 Port Royal and after

The seven considerations given above became the foundations of linguistic thinking during the centuries that followed. Yet this did not happen imme- diately. The *Minerva* remained relatively obscure for some time, as one can understand considering the fact that it was published in central Spain, away from where most of the action was. It broke through around 1650 in France, when it was discovered by Claude Lancelot, a Port Royal grammarian.

- *The Port Royal group*

Port Royal (Wheeler 1994) was a 13th century convent near Paris, which at- tracted, around the middle of the 17th century, a group of Jansenist intellec- tuals who engaged in religious, philosophical and also linguistic studies. The best known among them are *Claude Lancelot*, an unassuming man dedicated to the service of God, the pursuit of knowledge and the teaching of the young (as education was the prime activity of the Jansenists), and *Antoine Arnauld*, an aristocrat, whose sister had been abbess of the Port Royal convent. Three works, published by Port Royal scholars, have played a decisive role in the further development of linguistic theory: Lancelot (1644), Lancelot & Arnauld (1660), and Arnauld & Nicole (1662).

- *How Sanctius did and did not influence the Port Royal grammarians*

The influence of Sanctius' *Minerva* is clearly traceable in these works, though less than one might expect, and with some surprising complications. In 1644 Lancelot brought out the first edition of his *Nouvelle méthode pour facilement et en peu de temps comprendre la langue latine*, a pedagogical grammar of Latin adopting principles, already widely in use in Northern Europe, includ- ing the North of France (Law 1996), that were meant to make learning easier (grammar rules in verse, better typography, etc.). This was 'a distinct success and was even used by young Louis XIV' (Wheeler 1994:3231), who was then just six years old but already King of France. The book soon reached a second print- ing. However, after the second printing Lancelot came across Sanctius' *Miner- va*, which made such an impression on him that he virtually rewrote the work, quadrupling its size. This became the third edition, of 1653. In the Pre- face to the third edition Lancelot writes (Lakoff 1969a:356):

> Having therefore been informed of the high reputation which Sanctius acquired in these latter times by a treatise on this subject [the Latin language], greatly esteemed by the learned, but rare and difficult to purchase, I contrived to get a copy of this treatise, which I perused with all possible attention, and at the same time with such satisfaction as I want words to express. ...
>
> Sanctius has dwelt particularly on the structure and connection of speech, by the Greeks called "syntax", which he explained in the clearest manner imaginable, reducing it to its first principles, and to reasons extremely simple and natural;

showing that expressions which seem contrary to rule, and founded on the caprice of language, are easily reduced to the general and ordinary laws of construction [i.e. of deep structure; PS], either by supplying some word understood, or by searching into the usage observed by writers of remote antiquity, of whom some vestiges are to be seen in those of later date; in short, by establishing a marvelous analogy and proportion through the whole language.

Robin Lakoff checked and found that Lancelot's discovery of Sanctius, which took place between the second and the third printing of *Nouvelle méthode*, did indeed have drastic consequences (Lakoff 1969a:356):

> The preface cited above is from the third edition, a work of some 900 pages. But there were two previous editions; and these, according to Lancelot, were written before he had access to Sanctius. It would be significant in our search for the origins of Lancelot's linguistic theories if there were noticeable differences between the first edition of the NML and the third. There is apparently no copy of any edition of the NML prior to the third in the United States; but I have been able to acquire a copy of the first edition from the Bibliothèque Nationale in Paris. This is a volume of some 200 (small) pages — about the size of the G[rammaire] G[énérale] R[aisonnée]. Looking at it, one would be hard put to find anything of interest at all, or even anything suggestive. It is a perfectly straightforward pedagogical grammar of Latin, and it contains none of the insights that the third edition of the NML was to contain. In short, Lancelot is telling the truth: it was his discovery of Sanctius, and his incorporation of the ideas of Sanctius into the third edition, that makes his book linguistically interesting.

It was through Lancelot that Sanctius' ideas penetrated the circle of Port Royal members. And indeed, some formulations in the *Grammaire générale et raisonnée* (Lancelot & Arnauld 1660), and *La logique* (Arnauld & Nicole 1662) allude to the theory of underlying syntactic-semantic form and the foundation in Reason of the underlying form, called 'simple form' by the Port-Royalists. There one immediately recognizes Sanctius, as when the *Grammaire* deals with adverbs in a way closely akin to similar analyses proposed by him (Breva-Claramonte 1983:179, 181):

> The wish people have to abbreviate the discourse is what has given birth to adverbs. For all that most of these particles do is signify in one word what one could mark by a preposition and a noun, like *sapienter*, 'wisely', for *cum sapientia*, 'with wisdom': *hodie* for *in hoc die*, 'today'.   Lancelot & Arnauld (1660:88)

Other than the few passages, however, where the notion of underlying form comes up in a vague and non-specific way, the *Grammaire* is a conventional work. Subject ('sujet') and predicate ('verbe' or 'attribut') are mentioned only as elements of 'ce qui se passe dans notre esprit' ('what happens in our mind'; p. 29), not as grammatical sentence constituents. The grammar proper consists of a discussion of spoken and written 'letters', of word classes and their flectional forms, of auxiliary verbs in the 'vulgar' languages (as distinct from Latin). The last, short, chapter is on syntax, and deals with rules of agreement and the semantic function of the nominal cases. The *Grammaire*, in other words, has the traditional structure of grammar books before Sanctius. In this way, and in the other ways mentioned, it is to be considered a retrograde development with respect to Sanctius, despite the enthusiasm with which Lancelot greeted

Sanctius' work in the third edition of 1654 of his *Nouvelle méthode*. (It is this work which is the main textual source for a detailed demonstration of Sanctius' influence, as has been shown in Lakoff (1969a).)

• *Possible causes of apparent reluctance to pay tribute to Sanctius*
In the light of Lancelot's ringing tribute to Sanctius quoted above, one wonders what may have caused the obvious reluctance of his colleagues in the Port Royal circle, and perhaps of himself, to show more of Sanctius' ideas in the *Grammaire* and *La Logique*. One should perhaps take into account that up till about 1660 their favoured position with the Court made the Port-Royalists not only a force to be reckoned with but also extremely vulnerable to the King's displeasure. This came when Louis XIV, who had meanwhile come of age and manifested himself as an absolute monarch if ever there was one ('l'état c'est moi', he declared in 1661), began to implement the ban which had been inflicted by the Church on the Jansenists in 1653 under Jesuit pressure. In 1709 he finally ordered the closure of Port Royal, which was destroyed in 1712. In this context it is understandable that the Port Royal members, being under a cloud themselves, should feel they had better be circumspect with an author who had once incurred the wrath of the Inquisition. It would be worth while to investigate the Port Royal attitude towards Sanctius in greater detail, against the background of the incredibly involved political situation in Paris during that period.

• *Influence of Port Royal grammar on later linguistic thought*
Be that as it may, the Port-Royalists gained high prominence in and outside France, and their works kept being reprinted and translated until well into the 19th century. And the fact that Sanctius was 'adopted' by Lancelot meant that his ideas would now spread all over Europe, but in the weakened and watered down form in which they were digested by the Port Royal scholars. The original Sanctius slid into oblivion.

• *The beginnings of Romanticism*
The late 17th century saw the beginnings of the great cultural movement called Romanticism. Among other things, Romanticism involved a reaction against the strictly rationalistic view, preached especially in France, according to which thought is independent of language and language is nothing but the rule-governed expression of pre-existing thought. This traditional view had been given new life by the Port Royal scholars, and has remained influential if not dominant till the present day. The 18th century, however, saw the emergence of an alternative, romanticist view, implying that language itself is one of the factors shaping the structure of thought. It is here that we find the origins of the ideas developed further by Humboldt and by the 20th century adherents of the Humboldt-Sapir-Whorf hypothesis about the relation between language and thought.

CHAPTER 2

The eighteenth and nineteenth centuries

2.0 Preamble

In the Preamble to the previous chapter we announced that we would leave the dovetailing of the 17th century into the modern period to this chapter. We are now well into what is known as 'the modern period', a period of fascinating developments, puzzles and confusions that are still as alive and relevant today as they were a couple of centuries ago.

During the 18th century Romanticism conquered Europe. Material well-being, an explosion of scientific knowledge and improved technologies had not only brought Europe to the beginning of the Industrial Revolution, it had also awakened a universal curiosity about the more distant past and the more remote regions of the world. Archaeology was born, satisfying the need to have physical contact with Antiquity. Captain Cook was voyaging around the world to chart unknown coasts and oceans. The financial backing for these explorations into the past and the geographical distance came from governments, aristocratic patrons and wealthy citizens, whose desire for direct evidence from and physical contact with those spheres of life that had hitherto belonged to myth and legend had now gained public acceptance and was officially recognized by states and other public funding authorities.

In this context the philosophical front changed dramatically, giving rise to 18th century Enlightenment, which emphasised the light of reason and the light of facts, against tradition and revelation, as sources of knowledge. A total revision of ethical principles ensued, resulting in new theories of state, law and social justice, based on natural principles rather than on divine authority. In epistemology, a balance was sought between reason and facts. Cartesian rationalism had cast doubts on facts, since the *cogito*-argument had shown the intrinsic impossibility of proving the reality of facts. All that remained was analytical, a priori deduction. This, however, proved too sterile and many philosophers felt that a rationally unproven faith in the reliability of the senses and of human experience in general was called for. This led to a weakening of Cartesian rationalism and a re-appraisal of, among other things, British empiricist philosophy, in particular Locke.

The first to express a romanticist anti-rationalism was the Neapolitan thinker and legal philosopher Giambattista Vico, who laid the foundations for a theory of the state and of the validity of law based on 'sensus communis', general communal feeling and good sense. The torch was taken over by the philosophers of the Enlightenment, and, later again, by the Hegelian and phenomenological traditions in German philosophy, including the much quoted Wilhelm von Humboldt. Yet the rationalist tradition never lost ground completely. During the 18th century, the rationalist and the romanticist ways of thinking lived side by side, contesting each other's right of existence and fighting over territory, much as their modern descendants still do in our day.

Abandoning the Cartesian view of the rational mind as the principle of thought, and of language as 'merely' the expression of thought, the new romanticist thinkers argued that thought is to a large extent shaped by language, thus giving rise to linguistic relativism and to what is now called the Humboldt-Sapir-Whorf hypothesis.

The 18th century also saw the beginning of institutionalized science. Chemistry, of course, saw the light of day in this period, but so did some other sciences, including phonetics. In linguistics proper, grammar became a separate and popular domain of scientific enquiry, especially in France. The French grammarians of the 18th century (now unjustly forgotten) contributed substantially to the grammatical know-how of modern linguistics. They also either revived or started discussions on general theoretical topics, such as the question of the normativity of grammar and with it the relation between facts of usage and linguistic descriptions, or the typology of speech acts. The 19th century discussions on general issues, such as the function and definition of subject and predicate, cannot be understood without the preparatory background of the 18th century French grammarians of the Enlightenment.

Next to this highly inspired and fruitful work on grammar and language theory, there was also the romanticist wish to find out about the origin of language, a topic that kept philosophers and men of letters busy throughout the 18th century. It was fashionable to think that the birth of language was triggered by the urge to produce poetry, especially vocal music which developed into singing and thus into language, but other scenarios were proposed as well, all equally speculative. The problem was that, unlike archaeology, linguistics had no empirical access to the history of language beyond the oldest written texts. This changed suddenly when, towards the end of the 18th century, it proved possible, by means of a systematic comparison of words in different languages, to replace speculation about the origin of language with empirically testable theories about the historical development of languages and their genetic relationships. At the same time it became possible to satisfy the desire to find out about hitherto unknown languages of far-away nations. It was thus that historical comparative linguistics came into being, together with anthropological linguistics, which studies exotic languages and cultures.

Romanticism did not mean a sudden interest in the psychological mechanics of language: that had to wait till the 20th century. This may seem surprising in the light of the scientific achievements of that period and the 17th century notion of man-as-machine. But the man-as-machine philosophy had remained little more than a philosophical position, which had not penetrated the world of those who studied language. It did inspire a few individuals, like Franz Joseph Gall (1758-1828) to develop mechanistic theories of the human mind (for which he was punished by the Church and had to leave Austria), but the times were not ripe yet for psychology as a theory of the workings of the mind. Up till about 1900 it was normal to equate the mind with a non-material 'soul' or 'willing self'. Linguists were thus not pushed to investigate the mechanics of language, as that would involve an investigation of the mechanics of non-material thought. The mental realm had to remain closed for yet another while.

In the 19th century, the most obvious and spectacular progress was made in historical linguistics. The results were so impressive and convincing that they have become part of general culture in the Western world: every individual with only a modicum of education knows about the Indo-European and other language families and has some notion of etymology based on sound laws and patterns of semantic change. As regards the systematicity of language and mental structures and processes, however, progress was slow and painstaking. It is a typical feature of the 19th century discussions in this area that disciplines were invoked, in particular psychology and sociology, that had themselves not yet grown to the point where they could be of use. Much of 19th century theorizing about language had, therefore, to remain speculative and intuitive rather than empirical and formal.

2.1   The running up: Romanticism

• *The European commercial and colonial expansion*
What happened to linguistics during the 18th and 19th centuries cannot be understood without a broader view of the historical situation around that time and of the developments that led up to it. As the 15th century drew to a close the maritime nations of Western Europe embarked on a programme of grand scale commercial and political expansion towards the Far East, motivated largely by the demand for oriental spices and luxury goods like silk, silver and gold. The spices were particularly important as they were needed for the preservation of food during the winter periods, which were steadfastly characterized by undernourishment and, consequently, by massive disease. (It was for very good reasons that the Catholic Church had fixed the period of Lent at the end of the winter, when there was hardly anything to eat anyway.) Overland trade routes did exist from India and China to Western Europe, but the expeditions were extremely costly and, above all, hazardous, with murderous brigands lurking around every corner. The only alternative, therefore, was the sea. But Africa had not yet been rounded, which meant that the goods had to be ferried partly over land, through the hands of Arab dominated peoples, who made a handsome profit out of this trade.[1] It was thus that the sea route around the Cape was explored in order to cut out the Muslim middlemen. The Portuguese and the Spanish were the first

---

[1] Typically, the French expression *cher comme poivre* ('dear as pepper') stands for 'inordinately expensive', as pepper was, though necessary for the preservation of food, hard to get by before the European colonial expansion. The English expression *for a peppercorn*, on the other hand, meaning 'at an insignificant price', clearly originates from the period after the expansion, when pepper had become cheap. In fact, the *Oxford English Dictionary* tells us that its first occurrence was in 1791.

to search for a direct sea route to the Far East. The Dutch, the English and the French soon followed suit. One of the earliest expeditions was led by Christopher Columbus, under the orders of the Spanish king. Thinking that he was on his way to India he landed in America in 1492, with the result that the western world was drawn into the expansion programme as well.

By the middle of the 17th century a gigantic maritime trade had come into being, extending from the Far East to America's east coasts and the Caribbean. Plantations had been set up on the western side, mainly in the Caribbean area. Slaves were captured, traded and put to work at great profit. The East and West Indies Companies of England, France and Holland were so strong that they exerted even political power over the territories that had been taken.

- *Romanticism: widening of geographical and historical horizons*

Meanwhile, a class of wealthy *grand bourgeois* arose in the colonizing countries of Western Europe. At first, these *nouveau riches* distinguished themselves more by their hard commercial sense and chauvinist biblical piety than by their cultural refinement or sophistication. Gradually, however, the young men and women born into the *grandes bourgeoisies* of the countries concerned began to feel that their status entitled them to enhanced knowledge and above all direct experience of the world at large, its cultures and their history. A general need was felt for a widening of horizons, both geographically and historically. It was the realization of that wish that characterizes the era of Romanticism, which started somewhere in the 18th century and lasts till the present day: the values that define Romanticism are still values of today.

- *Captain Cook's voyages and Charles Darwin*

The late 18th century thus saw the emergence of initiatives to set up expeditions to explore the world. The expeditions under the command of Captain James Cook in the 1760s and 1770s are the first and the most striking demonstration of the publicly felt urge to explore the geographical world, this time not primarily for profit or power, but to serve the advancement of knowledge. Seventy years later, in the 1830s, the British Admiralty sent Robert FitzRoy around the world on the *Beagle*, to complete the work started by Cook. It was on this expedition that the young Charles Darwin, added to the crew as 'naturalist', conceived of his theory of evolution, later published in his *Origin of Species* (1859). Much like the comparative philology of his day, Darwin combined the expansion of geographical with that of historical horizons.

- *Archaeology and linguistics as daughters of Romanticism*

The historical horizons were widened by the new science of archaeology, which came about at the same time as the new linguistics: both archaeology and linguistics are daughters of Romanticism. A few years before Cook's expeditions, in 1748, a shepherd discovered some Roman statues on the site of the ancient city of Pompei, submerged during a volcanic eruption of Mount Vesuvius in 79 AD. This led to a series of excavations on that site that are still going on at present. In general, from 1750 onward, archaeological expeditions were sent out from various northern European countries to dig up the Classical past of Rome and Greece and establish direct physical contact with that remote era, without the overlay of intermediate centuries. Archaeological collections were formed by wealthy individuals, and museums came into being during the 18th century. The first chairs of archaeology were established in European universities in the early years of the 19th century.

- *The philosophy of the 'Noble Savage'*

Meanwhile, a change of mentality had taken place with regard to coloured, 'primitive' peoples and their cultures. In the earlier period, the coloured races were regarded as inferior, barely human and suitable for exploitation. Access to western education, often even to western languages, was forbidden. In the 18th century, however, more sophisticated elements in Western European societies took the almost opposite view. In their eyes, the 'savages' were fully human and uncorrupted by the wealth and politics of the more civilised European states. The souls of the 'savages' were considered free of sin, needing only baptism and the Christian faith to become examples to morally decadent Europe. This was the philosophy of the Noble Savage (*le Sauvage Noble*).

- *Missionary activities*

Ever since the discovery of the new eastern and western worlds the Catholic Church had taken steps to spread the faith through missionaries who acquired knowledge of the languages spoken by the indigenous peoples and wrote grammars of them. This began as early as the 16th century, just after the discovery of America in 1492 and the penetration of China by the Jesuits. In 1560, to mention just an example, the Spanish priest Domingo de Santo Tomás published a grammar of the South-American Indian language Quechua (*Gramática o arte de la lengua de las Indias de los reynos de Perú*). According to Garza Cuarón (1996), by 1570 'the Franciscan missionaries alone had written more than 80 books about different Indian languages of Mexico'.

This kind of early grammar writing, however, was less inspired by a desire to know more about the languages concerned than by sheer imperialism. The Church acted either in its own political interest or in the interest of the colonizing states, and usually both. It was not until the 18th century that this began to change and indigenous languages were studied more out of curiosity and for their own sake and less in the interest of colonial or religious power. This change coincided with the new philosophy of the Noble Savage.

The first significant initiative to put this philosophy into practice was taken by the United Brethren of the Moravian Church. This church had originated in Moravia, then under Habsburg domination, as a brand of Hussian Protestantism, and had been ousted from the Habsburg empire. In 1722 they found refuge in Saxony, on the estate Herrnhut ('protection of the Lord') of Count Nikolaus von Zinzendorf. Stimulated by the Count, who had met a slave from the Virgin Islands during the coronation of the Danish king Christian VI in 1731, the Moravians organized missions in the Caribbean area and in southern parts of the United States, to preach the gospel to the slaves and improve their lot. These missionaries learned the Creole languages spoken by the slaves, wrote dictionaries and grammars of these languages, and translated parts of the Bible into them. As a result we now have at our disposal a wealth of material about the early history of some Creole languages, in particular Saramaccan, the largely English-based creole of a tribe of runaway slaves in Surinam,[2] and the Negro-Dutch Creole (Negerhollands) of the Virgin islands, which were owned by Denmark but colonized largely by Calvinist Dutch planters (Holm 1988:17-21; 325-328).

2.2 Rationalism versus Romanticism in philosophy

• *Eighteenth Century Enlightenment*
The new Romanticism made itself felt in philosophy as much as in other spheres of life. The philosophical scene in general was characterized by a desire to let insights, opinions and value systems be determined by independent reason as well as by adequate knowledge of facts, and not, as had often been the case in earlier days, by divine revelation or by the authority of tradition and history. The light of reason was meant to shine, together with the light of facts, which gave the philosophy of this period the name of *Enlightenment* (*Aufklärung*, *Philosophie des Lumières*). The greatest achievement of the Enlightenment was perhaps the bringing about of the first major revision of ethical principles since Christianity, with an emphasis on social justice. New theories of state, government, law and society were constructed, not on the basis of divine or imperial authority, but founded on arguments derived from human nature and natural rights. The result was a series of radical political changes and even revolutions by the end of the 18th century.

   Much as philosophy was united around the ideal of the Enlightenment, the new romanticist fervour inevitably led to a split in philosophical opinion. On the Continent of Europe, the split concerned, in rough outline, the role of the formal, deductive derivation of necessary consequences from a priori principles, as against the direct experience of truth based on sensory perception. It was a war between the rationalism of Descartes, Leibniz, Kant and the romanticism of Vico, de Condillac, Humboldt. The British philosophers, with their common sense empiricism, occupied the middle ground, fighting off both rationalism and romanticism in their extreme forms.

---

[2] The exciting publication by Schuchardt (1914) was among the very first to spread knowledge about this intriguing bit of cultural and linguistic history. It contains an Introduction that brims over with information on Saramaccan and other Creole languages, followed by a late 18th century biblical text (from the Acts of the Apostles), then material from the 1880s collected by Schuchardt himself through correspondence, and, finally, the extremely valuable Saramaccan dictionary compiled in 1778 by the Moravian missionary C.L. Schumann.

2.2.1 The paradox of knowledge: two approaches

By the end of the 17th century, the philosophical scene was largely dominated by the paradox of knowledge, which had been forcefully brought to the world's attention by René Descartes during the first half of that century. Descartes had formulated the *cogito*-argument, summed up in his famous phrase *Cogito ergo sum*, which we may render somewhat liberally as 'I experience my own thinking, therefore I cannot deny my own existence'. Beyond that, however, nothing can be proven. It is impossible to prove the reality of the outside world, since the experiences of each individual might be nothing but a prolonged dream of fancies, in which case we would all be thrall to constant deception by false impressions.

Descartes had no principled answer to this problem. All he could say was that God, being intrinsically good and not a liar, could not possibly allow a state of affairs in which large numbers of really existing individuals would be constantly deceived by false impressions. Therefore, one must accept, as an article of faith, that one's impressions are largely reliable and are based on facts really occurring and existing in a real outside world.

But even if we do accept the reality of the world, there is a further problem, posed by the fact that there is no way of knowing the world as it really is, independently of the human categories of knowledge, the world 'an und für sich', as Kant was to put it. These two problems, jointly called the paradox of knowledge, brought about a crisis in philosophy, which is still with us today and is the defining feature of what is known as modern philosophy.

Understandably, in this context, Descartes sought to reduce the role of perception and of empirical data in his philosophical reconstruction of the human capacity for knowledge, placing the weight of explanation on innate cognitive structures, his 'innate ideas'. These were taken to need nothing but a mere stimulus from the, otherwise unknown, outside world, in order to give rise to world knowledge. This way of thinking, which goes back to Plato's dialogue *Theaetetus*, has become known in philosophy as rationalism. Among its most eminent followers we find, besides Descartes, also Leibniz and Kant.

A totally different approach to the philosophical theory of knowledge, or epistemology, was developed in 17th century Britain. Here John Locke (1632-1704), in his *Essay Concerning Human Understanding*, published in 1690, presented the view that all non-mathematical knowledge derives from the experience of sense data, which reflect the world faithfully enough to enable humans to deal with it adequately. All concepts, except those that are purely a priori (as in mathematics), are shaped by the impact of sense data. Locke thus maximizes the role of experience and minimizes that of innate ideas or other innate structures. He became the father of British empiricism.

Locke was well aware of the paradox of knowledge, and acknowledged that the world can only be known through the 'veil of perception', but he refused to doubt the reality of the world, even if only by way of Cartesian 'academic doubt'. Locke was an eminently practical philosopher, who preferred common sense to philosophical dogmatism. Russell put it as follows:

<Locke> enunciates general principles which, as the reader can hardly fail to perceive, are capable of leading to strange consequences; but whenever the strange consequences seem about to appear, Locke blandly refrains from drawing them. To a logician this is irritating; to a practical man, it is proof of a sound judgment. Since the world is what it is, it is clear that valid reasoning from sound principles cannot lead to error; but a principle may be so nearly true as to deserve theoretical respect, and yet may lead to practical consequences which we feel to be absurd. There is therefore a justification for common sense in philosophy, but only as showing that our theoretical principles cannot be quite correct so long as their consequences are condemned by an appeal to common sense which we feel to be irresistible. The theorist may retort that common sense is no more infallible than logic. But this retort, though made by Berkeley and Hume, would have been wholly foreign to Locke's intellectual temper.   Russell (1946:586)

Descartes' argument about the uncertainty of our world knowledge must therefore hide a flaw, or else it could not lead to the absurd conclusion that all experience might be nothing but a long dream. As has been said, one may fairly say that all philosophy since Descartes has tried to find that flaw.

2.2.2 Leibniz and the rationalist tradition

- *Leibniz's stance on the paradox of knowledge: the coherence theory*

The first notable attempt to find a flaw in the Cartesian argument and to formulate an answer was made by the great German philosopher, mathematician and universal scholar *Gottfried Wilhelm Leibniz* (1646-1716). He accepts the Cartesian argument and the whole rationalist tradition it stands in, but finds it incomplete. The incompleteness consists in the failure to realize that our experience forms a coherent system, a theory if you like, which is, by and large, confirmed time and again, and is only occasionally disconfirmed, in which case we are led to improve our 'theory' of the world. Since this game of confirmation and disconfirmation can only be played if there really is something out there, the most rational decision is to accept the reality of something we call the world, that being the best theory. And, as with all theories, the simplest and most coherent one, with the largest coverage of sense data, is to be preferred.

This is the essence of Leibniz's *coherence theory of truth*, which, as is argued by Rescher (1973), is not meant as an alternative to Aristotle's correspondence theory, but as a supplement to it. Whereas Aristotle *defines* the nature of truth, Leibniz provides a *criterion to decide* what is best accepted as true and what is best rejected as false. The criterion, for any given proposition A, lies in the coherence and coverage of the set of propositions (theory) from which A is derivable: the theory that is most coherent and covers the widest range of data stands the best chance to generate true propositions.[3]

---

[3] The reader will notice that this is very much like the principle accepted by modern philosophy of science with regard to the question of how to decide on the truth of scientific theories.

In proposing this answer to the paradox of knowledge, Leibniz took the side of the rationalist tradition, not of the British empiricist movement which, as we shall see, was to become very popular in the context of romanticist thinking.[4] This may have contributed, together with his often arcane style of writing, to the general oblivion he fell into after his death. His writings remained largely unpublished until the beginning of this century, when he was rediscovered in the context of the radical renewal of the machinery of logic brought about by Frege and Russell (see section 5.4).[5]

- *Leibniz as a linguist*

Leibniz's rationalism predestined him to a formalist point of view with regard to the study of language (see section 1.3). And indeed, Leibniz did do the typical thing for a linguistic formalist: in order to improve upon natural language he started devising an artificial formal language, his *Characteristica Universalis*, about which more is said in section 6.1.1. In this respect he was a formalist. On the other hand, however, he was an ecologist, and thus a budding romanticist, in matters of natural language. He saw natural languages as products of nature, and therefore as legitimate objects of systematic scientific enquiry, which would concentrate on the genetic relationships among languages, their historical development and their spread. It is known that Leibniz was in correspondence with persons, mostly diplomats, in various remote parts of the world, asking them to send him information about the languages they heard. On the basis of that information and of what he could lay his hands on in any other way he ventured etymologies and proposed genetic relationships among languages.

In the light of modern knowledge, however, his attempts at getting a science of natural language off the ground were feeble. Though the geographical and historical knowledge of his day was vastly superior to what was available to Plato, the etymologies proposed by Leibniz are hardly less extravagant and fanciful than what is found in Plato's *Cratylus*. And, just as for Plato, onomatopœia should be the leading principle in searching for the 'true' origin of words, though different peoples may have had different ways of rendering experiences in imitative sounds. Humans are endowed with a 'natural urge' (impetus naturalis) to name experiences of things. As words become habitual, their 'true' origin will be quickly forgotten and both word

---

[4] What Leibniz failed to see was that the set of propositions that helps us to cope with the outside world in the safest and most coherent way, making for the best predictions, contains all propositions that express experiences of the outside world, which makes reliance on experience the safest and most rational guide towards truth. Had he given full weight to this observation he would have been closer to Locke's empiricist point of view.

[5] At the end of the 19th century the interest in Leibniz flared up again, owing to the developments that were taking place in mathematics and logic. This led to a number of initiatives to publish Leibniz's writings. Nowadays, a dedicated staff at the Niedersächsische Landesbibliothek in Hannover, formerly the Duke of Hannover's court library, whose librarian Leibniz was from 1676 till his death in 1716, is engaged in the publication of the vast amount of still unpublished written material Leibniz left behind.

forms and word meanings become subject to changes of all kinds. The way in which word forms and word meanings change reveals the history not only of the diversification and spread of the languages of the world but also of the cultural development of the peoples that spoke them.

We thus see that Leibniz' views on natural language, though traditional in that they link up directly with the discussions that went on in Antiquity, held the seeds of what was to become the great historical comparative linguistics of the 19th century. In this respect he presaged the romanticist attitude that led to modern linguistics.

2.2.3 Vico as a precursor of the Enlightenment

In the context of burgeoning Romanticism, Cartesian rationalism, with its relative depreciation of experience, was bound to fall out of favour, and Locke's philosophy, which stressed the value of experience, was bound to gain popularity. This is precisely what happened, even in those philosophical circles that would not be naturally inclined to embrace a point of view coming from the British Isles. Locke's insistence on the value of experience fitted perfectly in a value system that gave pride of place to direct and preferably deeply felt experience, of as wide a range of sense data as could be managed. Locke thus became a celebrated author on the Continent. Locke's popularity did not mean, however, that British empiricism now took root in Europe. On the contrary, Locke was used selectively, only to combat Cartesian rationalism and to bolster the notion that direct experience was to be trusted.

The first clear exponent of this trend was, somewhat surprisingly, a philosopher from Naples, *Giambattista Vico* (1668-1744). Being of humble but respectable origins (his father owned a bookshop), he became a professor of rhetoric at the University of Naples, but his true interest lay in the philosophy of law and of politics, about which he published ideas that were utterly revolutionary for that period. His main work is the *Principi di scienza nuova d'intorno alla comune natura delle nazioni*, published in 1730. His main importance, in the present context, lies in his fierce opposition to Cartesian rationalism, which dominated cultural life in Naples in his day, and in the fact that he was the first to formulate the principles of a romanticist way of thinking which strives to combine sound experience with sound reason, uncluttered by irrelevancies springing from superstition, fear or fancy. The emphasis on experience led to a spectrum of philosophical schools of thought that have since acquired a strong position in western cultural life, often in conflict with what is considered sound science and even sound judgement. Vico's ideas about language were in the same vein as, and helped shape, those of later philosophers of language, in particular Wilhelm von Humboldt.

• *Vico's answer to Descartes' cogito-argument: sense data and nature*
Vico's answer to the paradox of knowledge, in particular Descartes' *cogito*-argument, was, if not downright inept, certainly unimpressive (a fact also noted by his contemporary critics). He begins by saying, without proper foun-

dation, that true knowledge of a fact must imply knowledge of the causes of that fact. Applying this to the *cogito*-argument, he requires that true knowledge of the fact 'I exist' be grounded in knowledge of the causes of my existence. Since Descartes only gives 'I think' as the grounding for 'I exist', and since thinking cannot cause existence, Descartes' argument must be invalid ('t Hart 1979:97-98). Though this argument is logically valid it is useless, since one of the premises, namely that true knowledge of a fact has to imply knowledge of its causes, is unsound. Descartes' *cogito*-argument is likewise valid, because thinking presupposes, and hence requires, a really existing subject. But it differs from Vico's argument in that its premises are sound.

Vico plays down the importance of the problem of the reality of the outside world, positing that it is guaranteed by God who caused the world into being. He thus falls back on God, just like Descartes did, to escape from the paradox, a move that stands in distinct contrast to the ideals of the Enlightenment. But whereas Descartes' appeal to divinity rests on the belief that God cannot deceive, Vico takes God as the cause of the universe, and hence as the epistemological grounding of true knowledge.

- *The nature of science in Vico's philosophy*

The real issue, for Vico, is what comes after the paradox of knowledge, science. He systematically attacks ('t Hart 1979:59-62) the Cartesian view of science as a body of knowledge that follows logically from innate a priori principles, a view that was inspired more by mathematics than by physics. By the end of the 17th century, however, physics, magnificently represented by figures like Newton or Huygens, had upstaged mathematics as the prototypical science.

In matters of science, Vico was a practical man, as was Locke, whom he revered. For him, good science, *Scienza Nuova*, unlike the established Cartesian forms of science as deduction from first principles, is mainly a question of common sense. Principles are fine, but they must never lead to absurdity, and certainly not clash with observed facts. Any reliable 'innate ideas' were implanted into the species at its creation, and must therefore be fetched back from primitive mankind by means of historical reconstruction.

Applying this to the nature of law, Vico maintains that laws, as rule books for the maintenance of justice in social traffic, cannot be derived deductively from eternal a priori principles, but must be regarded as the expression of what is considered just in the context of any given society. Likewise for the best possible organization of the state, which is also not derivable from eternal a priori principles but expresses the historical reality of the community at hand ('t Hart 1979:70-75). To establish what should count, at any moment in history, as a correct law or as an optimal organization of the state one has to consult the people, the 'sensus communis' ('t Hart 1979:84-90).

- *Vico's ideas about language*

The same elements that are manifest in Vico's philosophy are found in his ideas on language. He considers language to be instrumental for the study of primitive societies and their laws. One should reconstruct the mentality of primitive peoples, and from there try to understand how the primitive ideas developed into the sophisticated rational ideas of modern civilisation. The mistake of most scholars, in this respect, has been that they always tried to understand the primitive mind starting from the sophistication of modern learning and scholarship. But one should really travel the opposite way: from the primitive to the modern ('t Hart 1979:143).

In order to reconstruct the primitive mentality one must study language, 'the witness of things' ('t Hart 1979:145), and folklore literature like myths. Both words and myths have preserved much ancient wisdom and reflect primitive forms of thinking. Vico speculates, like so many others, about the way language must have come into being. First, he says, came emotional cries, expressing passion, fear, joy, and the like. Then came deictic expressions, useful for establishing reference. Then individual words that served as names for things. But we shall not go further here into the question of the natural origin of language and the way that question was discussed in the 18th century. That question is taken up again below in section 2.3.4.

- *Romanticist enlightened philosophy strongest in France*

The main stage, however, of 18th century enlightened philosophy was France, where the 18th century is sometimes called 'le siècle de la philosophie'. More than any other city in Europe, Paris was the intellectual centre, attracting the best minds of Europe and even America. It is here that we find the great names: Rousseau, Diderot, de Condillac, Montesquieu, all writing about society, law, the supremacy of the people, commerce, and other issues of social importance, but often also about the natural origin and the general nature of human language. They were extremely influential for the subsequent history of Europe and the rest of the world. It was their ideas about society, the state and law that formed the ideological basis of the French Revolution and of the modern concept of democracy, to say nothing of socialism and even communism. And to some extent also it was their ideas about language that helped to shape the linguistic developments of the 19th century, whether by the positive results gained, as in the study of grammar, or because they were so speculative that they provoked a reaction and made those interested long for a more empirical theoretical basis, as in historical linguistics.

2.3 Linguistics in the eighteenth century

Apart from the more philosophically oriented developments in the 18th century, a fair amount of actual linguistic work was done during that period, not only in France, where the study of grammar flourished alongside heavy speculations about the origin of language, but in other places as well.

2.3.1 Dictionary making in the eighteenth century

It was during the 18th century that the first systematic attempts were made at compiling large dictionaries of the languages of culture, an aspect usually but unjustifiably ignored in handbooks on the history of linguistics. Dictionary making became a recognized activity all over Europe. As regards English, one thinks immediately, of course, of the legendary Dr. Samuel Johnson (1709-1784), the colourful Londoner, who published his *Dictionary of the English Language* in 1755, after nine years of hard work and penury. Yet he was not the first lexicographer of English. Miller (1991:135) mentions three predecessors. An early, and still rather limited, lexicographer was Robert Cawdrey with his *Table Alphabeticall*, 1604, containing a mere 2,500 words. More up to quantitative standards was John Kersey, *New English Dictionary*, 1702, 28,000 words. Nathan Bailey followed, with his *Dictionarium Britannicum*, 1730, 48,000 words. Johnson's 1755 dictionary contained 40,000 words, but with more elaborate descriptions than Bailey's. (The leading modern dictionaries of English contain between 400,000 and 600,000 words.) Somewhat later, in America in 1828, Noah Webster published his *American Dictionary of the English Language*, now one of the leading high quality dictionaries of English. The Englishman Peter Mark Roget (1779-1869) published the first edition of his now famous *Roget's Thesaurus* in 1852.

Similar activities went on in other European countries for other languages (see, for example, Woodhouse (1994) on the tradition of Italian dictionaries; Wooldridge (1994) on French dictionary making). Dictionaries were even made of humble languages such as the Creole language Saramaccan, for which the German Moravian missionary C.L. Schumann wrote a dictionary in 1778 (as was mentioned in note 2 at the end of section 2.1).

2.3.2 Romanticist interest in exotic languages

● *The study of exotic languages in France*

In 18th century France a lively interest developed in exotic languages, inspired by the romanticist urge to explore the world. Whereas the more philosophically oriented linguists remained virtually blind to them, learned travellers visited remote corners of the earth, especially North and South America, and wrote books and papers about them, commenting on the languages and cultures of the communities they visited.

De Clercq & Swiggers (1996:757) mention as a typical example a paper read by Charles Marie de la Condamine, French explorer and mathematician, to the Academy of Sciences in 1745, entitled *Relation abrégée d'un voyage, fait dans l'intérieur de l'Amérique Méridionale*. Commenting on the language of the Peruvian Indians. Condamine observes that no words exist for 'virtue', 'justice' 'liberty', etc., and infers from this that these people must suffer from cultural poverty. A critic in the *Mémoires de Trévoux* (a critical review published by the Jesuits of Trévoux from 1701 to 1775) of 1746 then retorts that:

there is quite a difference between the present state of a people that has been
subjected to servitude for about 200 years and the way it was when it lived in
liberty, governed by its natural principles and its laws.

Moreover, the critic says:

To be certain that they have actually lost these words, or that they have not
supplanted them with equivalents, one has to know their language well. But how
can a passing traveller who encounters new nations every day, always with different languages, manage to learn it? ... Such authors have a great advantage when
they deal with a language that is spoken only at a distance of two or three thousand
miles from Europe. One can do as one likes, make any mistake imaginable, and have
it mean no matter what – one never runs the shameful risk of being exposed.'

Which shows that the paradox of observation, well-known among anthropological and linguistic fieldworkers, is as old as exotic language research itself.

• *The study of exotic languages in America*
During the last quarter of the 18th century America saw the beginning of the
study of American Indian languages. The interest in these languages had been
fired by a number of prominent citizens of the newly founded United States of
America who stayed in Paris for long visits, imbibing the ideas of the
Encyclopedists and the Enlightenment that were popular there. These they
took with them when they returned (together with a great many books),
inspiring others who had not been so fortunate as to have visited Paris. Thus,
many philosophers and amateur historians and antiquarians began to collect
data, especially word lists, from languages spoken by far away nations and
tribes, including the aboriginal peoples of North America.

In 1769 *Benjamin Franklin* founded the American Philosophical Society
(see also section 4.1). This immediately became the centre of a number of amateur linguists, dedicated to the collecting of vocabulary items from Amerindian languages and the drawing up of hypotheses about their genetic relationships. Its most prominent member was *Thomas Jefferson*, the third president of the United States, who was a keen linguist (Andresen 1990:25). Another early member was, interestingly, a Moravian missionary by the name of
John Heckewelder, who became a member in 1797 (Andresen 1990:93). Yet
another was *Pierre Etienne Duponceau* (1760-1844), a Frenchman, who later
took American nationality and renamed himself *Peter Stephen Duponceau*.

Amerindian languages continued to be studied throughout the 19th century
into the 20th. In 1846 the United States' government founded the Smithsonian
Institute, till the present day one of the leading institutes for anthropological
research and the depository of priceless collections of material, data and
library resources. In 1899 the German anthropologist *Franz Boas* was appointed by Columbia University in New York to teach anthropology, not only the
theory but also in the practical sense of fieldwork. He started the 20th
century tradition of American anthropological linguistics, about which more
will be said in section 4.1

• *Exotic languages an avocation for the élite*

The interest in exotic languages was a favourite avocation for the political and social elite. In America, as has been said, we see prominent men like Benjamin Franklin and Thomas Jefferson actively engaging in the study of Amerindian languages. In Europe, Catherine the Great of Russia gave orders to collect vocabularies from all corners of the earth, an enterprise which resulted in the edition of *Mithridates oder allgemeine Sprachenkunde*, published between 1806 and 1817 (Darnell 1994:93). The German aristocrat Alexander von Humboldt, younger brother of Wilhelm (2.6.2), travelled the earth and supplied his brother with all kinds of data on out of the way languages.

2.3.3 The expansion of grammar in eighteenth century France

Although the 18th century saw an enormous increase of grammatical studies, especially in France, the literature on this aspect of the history of linguistics is relatively scarce. A good look at this period reveals that the strict grammarians, those who engaged in the mundane practice of grammar writing, have been neglected by the historians. The philosophers have clearly stolen the show. One also detects a certain antagonism between the philosophers and the grammarians, one party failing to see the merits of the other.

The neglect of the 18th century grammarians by the historians has been such that it has proved difficult to actually trace them. Fortunately, I could consult a unique source of information, the *Courrier de Vaugelas*, a late 19th century bi-monthly periodical devoted to the study, improvement and propagation of the French language, and called after Vaugelas (see below).[6] Right from the first issue, October 1st 1868, the editor, Eman Martin, started a regular column called 'Biography of grammarians', in which he deals extensively with the French grammarians from the 15th to the late 18th century, providing summaries of their works. Contrary to the main stream, Martin obviously favoured the grammarians and disliked 'les philosophes'. He significantly omitted the philosophically oriented grammarians Dumarsais and Beauzée from his column, while giving full attention to many other, minor figures who were more data-oriented.

Despite the neglect by the historians one must recognize the clear fact that the 18th century French grammatical tradition made a major contribution to the terminology and analytical techniques of what is now regarded as 'traditional grammar'. According to De Clercq and Swiggers (1996:763): 'the history of French grammar during the 18th and 19th centuries is marked by renewed standards from the point of view of description, by a methodological expansion, and by an open eye for linguistic reality'. Whereas the 1660 Port Royal Grammar is a booklet of about 150 small pages, the grammars of French that appeared around 1800 were hefty works consisting of many volumes. In between lies the work of the 18th century French grammarians.

---

[6] I am indebted to my colleague Haike Jacobs, who pointed this out to me and lent me his copies of the *Courrier*.

The grammarians were, on the whole, intellectually conservative, continuing the lines set out by the Port Royal tradition. This is in line with the unusually high proportion of priests among the grammarians, as the Church did not, at first, favour enlightened romanticist thinking.

- *Vaugelas, father of French grammarians*

Unlike his 18th century colleagues, *Claude Favre de Vaugelas* (1585-1650), baronet of Péroges, grammarian, lexicographer, and founding member of the Académie Française, is a household name in French history. In his famous *Remarques sur la langue françoise* (1647), which played a key role in establishing the 18th century tradition of French grammar writing, he claims to follow a purely descriptive, non-normative method of linguistic description, based neither on Latin nor on logic. Yet, in spite of his professed descriptivism, he hardly represents the non-normative, descriptive method advocated in modern linguistics. What he intends to describe is the 'good usage' (le bon usage) of the French royal court, supplemented with the 'good usage' of the recognized literary authors. In no way do the people set the norm. The French word *peuple* is, in his view, equivalent with Latin *plebs*, meaning 'lowly folk', and this 'peuple' cannot be taken to set any norm (which is like saying that democracy is a great good but it should not be given to the people). He severely criticizes those authors of the day who show a lack of respect for the purity of the French language, and his actual grammar consists mainly in the pointing out of typical errors made by such writers (and also by Cardinal de Richelieu, who, though close to the royal court, had Vaugelas' royal pension of two thousand pounds per annum cut on account of his political leanings). Vaugelas' 'descriptive' method hardly differs from the normative method practised through the ages from the ancient Alexandrinian grammarians onward. But he is a little clearer than most normative grammarians on the source of his norms. And the emphasis on description of usage is new and will be repeated with greater and greater force by subsequent grammarians.

- *Régnier Desmarais*

We now pass on to the 18th century. It is not possible, given obvious limits of space, to mention all the many French grammarians of that period whose lives and works are discussed in the *Courrier*. We must be selective, even if we run the risk of not making as representative a choice as would be appropriate.

The next notable figure, straddling both centuries, is *Régnier Desmarais* (1632-1713), priest, member of the Académie Française in 1670, and permanent secretary of that august body from 1684 onward. In 1705 he published his *Traité de la grammaire françoise*, summarized in the *Courrier de Vaugelas* 8.7 (October 1st 1877) to 8.24 (June 15th 1878). (Apart from the *Courrier*, the sources on Desmarais are scarce.)

Desmarais is the first grammarian to go through the language with a fine toothcomb and pick up all sorts of details and regularities. His *Traité de la grammaire françoise* is the first work of its kind that will stand comparison with modern works. It starts out with an exposé on proper pronunciation, taking the letters (not the sounds) one by one. Then it passes on to a discussion of the articles, to be followed by nouns and adjectives, comparatives and superlatives, plurals, pronouns, verbal tenses and verb morphology in general, clitic pronouns, adverbs, prepositions, and conjunctions.

It is noteworthy that he recognizes adjectives as a separate, fully fledged lexical category (*Courrier* 8.10, Nov. 15th 1877). His observations are generally acute and subtle, usually still relevant and showing a highly developed grammatical sense.

For example, speaking of the definite article, Desmarais notes the difference between *la noblesse de France* and *la noblesse de la France*, the former referring to the assembled French noblemen, the latter to what is supposed to be the noble character of France (*Courrier* 8.9, Nov. 1st 1877). To take another, more or less random, example (*Courrier* 8.18, March 15th 1878), Desmarais observes that in e.g. *une fortification que j'ay appris à faire* (a fortification that I have learned to build) the past participle *appris* (learned) has to remain uninflected, despite the preceding feminine singular direct object *que*, because *que* depends not on *appris* but on *faire* (build). There is thus a difference with e.g. *la résolution que j'ay prise d'aller* (the decision that I have taken to go), where the past participle *prise* (taken) is inflected for the feminine singular in agreement with the preceding feminine direct object *que*, because *que*, in this case, does depend on *prise*. Observations like these are repeated by later authors, and perhaps couched in more technical terminology. But it was Desmarais who made them first.

- *Claude Buffier*

A slightly younger contemporary, and more properly belonging to the 18th century, was the Jesuit *Claude Buffier* (1661-1737), author of *Grammaire françoise sur un plan nouveau* (for the full title see the bibliography), published in 1709. He contributed to the Jesuit journal *Mémoires de Trévoux* (see 2.3.2), whose editors took pains to promote his views on language and grammar (De Clercq & Swiggers 1996). The *Courrier de Vaugelas* deals with him in the issues 9.1 (March 1st 1879) to 9.9 (July 1st 1879). Buffier has furthermore been studied by the Belgian historian of linguistics Pierre Swiggers (Swiggers 1983; De Clercq & Swiggers 1996).

The *Grammaire françoise sur un plan nouveau* is divided into three parts: a methodological introduction, the actual grammar, and an appendix dealing with pronunciation, orthography, and a few 'bizarreries de la grammaire'. From the point of view of method, this grammar is to some extent a continuation and extension of Vaugelas (1647), yet Buffier seems much more inclined than Vaugelas to accept rationalist deductive principles: a grammar must follow the principles of geometry (i.e. mathematics) in that it should be built up systematically and all terms should be properly defined before being used – something existing grammars badly fail to do, according to him.

Like Vaugelas, he proposes a quasi-descriptive notion of grammar, though it is seductively presented as true descriptivism in the modern sense:

A true and just design of grammar thus can only be one which, accepting a language as established by usage, without wishing to change or modify anything in it, provides only reflections called 'rules', to which can be reduced the manners of speaking customary in this language. It is this collection of reflections that is called 'grammar'. One cannot insist too much on this notion, so as to rectify a misapprehension on the part of various grammarians. One often sees them say: *usage is, on this point, opposed to the grammar*, or: *the language here distances itself from the laws of grammar*, or also: *one speaks of this or that phenomenon, but it goes against the rules of grammar*. It seems to me that one cannot both think in this way and have a correct idea of what grammar amounts to. In fact, if ever grammar finds herself in disagreement with usage, so much the worse for her. It is her fault, and she must reform. For grammar is there only to provide rules or reflections that show one how to speak the way one speaks. If any of these rules or reflections does not agree with the way one actually speaks it can only be false and must be changed.

Buffier (1714[2]:11-12), from De Clercq & Swiggers (1996:765), almost literally quoted in the *Courrier* of March 15th, 1879.

Yet, as with Vaugelas, there is good usage and bad usage. And the difference depends on the linguistic usage of the most distinguished persons in a nation, be it by their quality or authority, or by their prowess in writing well. Again, the royal court is the norm. The 'peuple' does not come into it at all.

A greater modernity is seen in a somewhat romanticist quote from his earlier work (1704), where he advocates the essential equality of all languages, at least from the point of view of 'beauty':

That all languages and jargons spoken in the world have in themselves equal beauty.   Buffier (1704, Proposition VII), from De Clercq & Swiggers (1996:768)

The *Grammaire françoise sur un plan nouveau* repeats this point in less romanticist terms, and restricted to the languages of Europe:

Generally speaking, the perfection of a language consists in three things: abundance, clarity, and brevity. Abundance for the expression of all possible thoughts; clarity for their expression without obscurity; brevity for their brief expression. Given that no particular language of Europe shares any of these properties to any greater extent than any other, one can hardly judge one more perfect than another. And since this has not changed over the past one hundred years, it is a kind of popular error among certain educated people to think that their own language is more perfect than the others. Even so, however, one has to admit that for over a century the arts and sciences have been cultivated in France more than ever, which has made our language richer in terms and expressions, and thus more useful and more abundant, than it was before.   *Courrier de Vaugelas* March 15th 1879

Buffier may have been the first grammarian to reject Latin grammar as the model for all grammar, and to insist on the autonomy of each language's grammatical system. This insight gave rise, in the 18th century, to new notions of universal grammar (grammaire générale), i.e. the universal basis presumed to underlie and restrict all grammars of specific languages and their dialects.

In Buffier's view, every language has its own autonomous system of grammar, a fact not acknowledged by earlier grammarians, who imposed an analysis good for one language (Latin) onto another (French) for which it was not made, and thus produced bad grammars. Yet the different grammars have a strong common element as all languages are instruments for the natural expression of thoughts. And since thoughts obey universal principles, so must, 'by infallible consequence', each language. The main elements of every sentence express (a) the subject, which is what one speaks about, (b) that which is predicated, and (c) modifiers ('circonstances') of either. Language is a little like fashion, which tells every nation how to dress. This they do in ways that depend largely on fantasy or simple coincidence, with hardly any principled reason for this or that mode of dressing. But all fashions obey general functional principles.

- *The grammarians of the Encyclopédie: Dumarsais, Girard, Beauzée*

Of the grammarians that contributed to the *Encyclopédie* three classics will be briefly reviewed: Dumarsais, Girard and Beauzée.

- *Dumarsais*

César Chesnau Du Marsais or *Dumarsais* (1676-1756) was more a philosopher of language and student of literary language than a grammarian in the strict sense of the word. He counts as a 'philosopher-grammarian', the term used in the 18th century for what we now call a theoretical linguist. Yet he did make a good many very interesting and relevant observations on points of grammar, especially in the articles he contributed to the *Encyclopédie*.

His *Traité des tropes* of 1730 is more a stylistic than a grammatical work, dealing with various figures of style, such as metaphor, euphemism, antonomasia, synecdoche, etc., all illustrated with material from the classical Latin authors. His writings on grammar and philosophy of language are scattered over time and were in part left unpublished. These were brought together in Dumarsais (1987), a publication in a philosophical, not a linguistic, series.

Philosophically, Dumarsais was an empiricist, not a rationalist:

> The impressions that we receive of objects, and the thinking we do on these impressions, are the source of all our ideas.   Dumarsais (1977:258)

His main work on the philosophy of language is his *Sur les causes de la parole* (Dumarsais 1987:97-117), an unfinished essay which was never published during his lifetime. Here he voices an opinion on the relation between language and thought and the question of universal grammar that was rapidly gaining ground in the 18th century. Having expounded his views on the origin and formation of linguistic 'signs', i.e. words, he proceeds:

> This brings us to the usage of speech. The articulated sounds, which are very numerous, and to which experience and usage have in the end assigned particular destinations, provide us with the way, so to speak, to clothe our thought, to make it perceptible, to divide it, analyse it, in one word, to cast it in a shape that makes it fit to be communicated to others with greater precision and detail.
>
> Thus, particular thoughts are, so to speak, each a whole, which the usage of speech divides, analyses and distributes in detail by means of the different articulations of the speech organs which form the words. The necessity to analyse our thought so as to be able to pronounce it by the intermediary of the words, makes us observe what we would otherwise never have noticed if we had not been forced to have recourse to this analysis for the purpose of making our thoughts communicable and to make them pass, so to speak, into the minds of others. ...

> But it is not at all the case that all peoples of the world use the same words and the same method for analysing their thoughts and communicating them to others. As each language is a human institution, and they have all been formed in different societies of men assembled in certain lands, who could hardly have constant daily contact with each other, it has been necessary for languages to differ, just as one notices differences in ways of dressing, in habits, tastes and other variables of daily life. The climate and a thousand other factors likewise make for differences on all points. But if we speak of language in general (le langage) we observe that the specific languages (langues) differ among each other:
>
> 1. By nomenclature, that is, by the particular word sounds. . . .
> 2. By the abundance of the words. Some languages are richer in words and even letters than others. In the richer languages the thoughts are analysed in greater detail, more neatly and more precisely. Hebrew, for example, is quite sterile, but Greek is abundant. . . .
> 3. All languages have specific ways of speaking, called 'idioms' or phrases. Thus, *on dit* is a phrase of the French language, but *si dice* is a phrase of the Italian language.   Dumarsais (1987:103-5)

To begin with, we note here that Dumarsais proposes the view that it is language that structures thought, not the other way round. This hypothesis will be encountered again in the work of Wilhelm von Humboldt, who lent his name to it (2.6.2). Furthermore, we see that Dumarsais attributes language differences to the fact that the world is too large for all its inhabitants to communicate with each other on a daily basis, so that differences will have to emerge. What he distinctly fails to account for is the fact that human languages are so like each other that they allow for some categories to be applied generally. If thought is as amorphous and unarticulated as he has it, this fact will remain unexplained.[7]

From a grammatical point of view, Dumarsais' main focus was on Latin, a language he knew intimately. However, in the 149 articles he wrote for the *Encyclopédie* he concentrates on French at least as much as he does on Latin. (The articles run to the beginning of the letter G, as his death occurred in 1756, when the *Encyclopédie* was only half way.) To give an idea of the acuteness of his observations and to let the reader taste the flavour of these writings, let us consider a couple of examples. In his long article called 'Article' (Dumarsais 1987:240-302), he observes, inter alia, that anaphoric pronouns must agree with their antecedent in number and gender. Like all French grammarians of the period he points out violations of this rule in well-known authors:

> Here is an example from The Princess of Cleves, vol. II, p. 119: *Mr. de Nemours would not let any opportunity go by to see Mme de Cleves, without, however, allowing it to appear that he was after them.* Now this *them* of the last phrase is in the plural, and should therefore not be fit to refer back to *opportunity* in the first half of the sentence, which is in the singular.   Dumarsais (1987:293-4)

---

[7] Nowadays the dominant view is that the likeness of languages is explained by the assumption of a highly specific innate predisposition for the acquisition of specifically human languages. The 'language faculty' is thus taken to be a separate autonomous 'module' in the human brain. The otherwise reasonable assumption that the likeness of languages is in part explained by the universality of thought is not very fashionable.

Or again, in the article 'Collectif' he points out:

> One must observe that it is an important principle of grammar that sense is the principal rule of construction. Thus, when one says *An infinity of people support*, the verb *support* is in the plural because, in fact, according to the sense, it is a number of people who support. The word *infinity* is used only to indicate the plurality of people who support. There is thus nothing against the grammar in this kind of construction. That is how Vergil says *Pars mersi tenuere ratem* (a part held the raft, submersed), and in Sallust: *Pars in carcerem acti, pars bestiis obiecti* (a part was thrown into jail, a part was fed to the beasts). Some authors classify these constructions under a style figure called *syllepsis*, others call it *synthesis*. But the name makes no difference to the matter. This figure consists in constructing the words according to their sense rather than their form.   Dumarsais (1987:348)

- *Girard*

Gabriel Girard (1677-1748), priest, man of letters but not much of a philosopher, contributor to the *Encyclopédie*, member of the Académie Française in 1744 (after considerable resistance from jealous members, according to *Courrier* 10.5, August 1st 1880, although his obvious naïveté in intellectual matters may well have contributed to the long delay), wrote a treatise on synonymy and lexical meaning, *Synonymes françois* (1736), which made him famous in and outside France. One year before his death, in 1747, he published his main work on grammar, *Les vrais principes de la langue françoise* (for the full title see the bibliography). He is discussed in *Courrier* 10.5 (August 1st 1880) to 10.12 (Nov. 15th 1880).

Girard is decidedly less empiricist and more rationalist than Dumarsais, but in a rather ingenuous way. In his unsophisticated view, a thought is the union of ideas, which are brought about by the perception of things. Unlike Dumarsais and Beauzée, he is not a 'philosopher-grammarian', as he lacks any depth of philosophical insight, but just a grammarian ('grammatiste'), more data-oriented than theory-oriented (cp. Bartlett 1975:21).

As a grammarian Girard is no more sophisticated, despite his insistence on definitions. Words are forms expressing ideas, with which they are connected by means of their 'value' (valeur). Style is a way of expressing oneself emanating from the genre of the work written or from the author's personality. Voice is nothing but respiratory air in movement. Pronunciation consists in the systematic modification of respiratory air by the speech organs. Every nation has made a specific selection from a universal inventory of possible sounds and articulations. Writing was invented to fix vanishing speech for the purpose of security in matters of law and commerce. Sounds are mixed into words. Languages that mix sounds in a more balanced way, like Italian or French, are easier to pronounce. When the vowels dominate too much, the language becomes effeminate. But if consonants dominate the language becomes harsh and difficult. He then distinguishes long and short syllables, depending on their quantity. He also detects diphthongs, spoken as well as written. All men could have spoken the same language, but they don't, following 'the magnificent plan of the variety of Nature'.

Languages come in three groups. The first is the group of 'analogous' languages, which form their sentences according to the natural order of thought: subject first, then verb, then the objects and modifiers. These languages have articles in their noun phrases. French, Italian and Spanish belong to this group. Languages of the second group, the 'transpositive' languages, follow 'the fire of imagination'. Here any sentence part may come first, but comprehension does not suffer because case endings indicate semantic functions. These languages lack articles. Examples are Latin or Slavonic languages. The third group, exemplified by ancient Greek, shares features of the two preceding groups. These languages do have articles but also relatively free word order.

Grammar is meant to help people learn a foreign language. It is not enough to know the words of a language, one must also know how usage has arranged them in discourse. The arrangement of words is called *syntax*, which means 'construction'. Besides lexical differences among languages, syntactic differences are the most important. Grammar consists of three parts: the knowledge of words, the knowledge of their arrangements in sentences, and orthography.

Government (régime) is 'the concerted action of words to express a sense or a thought'. Some words are higher in rank than others. The more highly ranked words subject the lower words to certain laws and restrictions, such as the obligatory taking on of morphological endings. Other words, however, such as adverbs, do not govern other words but stand by themselves, although they, too, perform a function in the sentence as a whole.

Girard discusses the articles, pronouns, nouns, adjectives, verbs, adverbs, prepositions, conjunctions, and, finally, orthography and prosody. It must be said, however, that he comes nowhere near his predecessor Desmarais in fullness and precision. Girard is at pains to provide definitions of all the technical terms he uses. Thus, a noun is defined as 'a word that has been established simply to name the things or to distinguish them from each other, without any indication of quality, action, or relation' (*Courrier* 10.8, Sept. 15th 1880). The result, however, is not greater precision, since the definitions given are themselves in need of further clarification. What he achieves by this is at best an appearance of precision. Yet later generations have mistaken the appearance for reality, and Girard's definitions have become more or less standard in traditional grammar.

Despite his solemn declaration, at the very outset of his *Vrais principes*, that he does not rely at all on earlier grammarians, we see him copy their observations. Thus he follows Vaugelas and Desmarais in saying that women commonly make the mistake of misusing the anaphoric pronoun *la* with an adjective as antecedent. When it has been said that someone is ill, women often say, incorrectly, *Je la suis aussi* (I am [it] too), instead of saying correctly *Je le suis aussi*, with the masculine pronoun *le* (*Courrier* 10.8, Sept. 15th 1880).

- *Beauzée*

The last French 18th century grammarian we will discuss is *Nicolas Beauzée* (1717-1789).[8] After an initial interest in mathematics he became a philosopher-linguist, with a special concern for education. He taught grammar at the prestigious new Ecole Royale Militaire. After Dumarsais' death in 1756 he was invited to take over the task of writing articles on language for the *Encyclopédie*. In 1771 he became a member of the Académie Française. He was a staunchly conservative Catholic (he wrote a 'proof' of the correctness of the Christian religion in 1747), and his religious conservatism is matched by his conservatism in philosophical matters. As a philosopher he remained true to the rationalist Port Royal tradition in every respect. He was not interested in the romanticist question of the origin of language. For him, language is just the expression of thought, and just as thought was given to mankind by God, so was language (Bartlett 1975:23).

Beauzée is the prototypical 'philosopher-grammarian', philosopher of language as well as theoretical linguist, concerned with theory as well as with data. His main work is his *Grammaire générale* (for the full title see the bibliography), published in two volumes in 1767. It is not so much a grammar of French as a 'grammaire générale', and it stands out among the other 18th century works on grammar because of its high intellectual level and because it provides a principled and highly explicit semantic basis for grammatical classes and constructions. It seems fair to say that he stands out among his contemporaries as regards vision and depth of insight.

In the Preface of his *Grammaire générale* Beauzée almost speaks the language of modern science:

> It is thus with a view to finding an introductory method to languages, which should facilitate and simplify their study, that I have followed, with regard to universal grammar, the research method proposed by Descartes for all philosophical matters, and it would be natural to expect that this method should bring here the same results it has brought in other fields of enquiry. Grammar is in fact a vast area which, so to speak, has only been glimpsed. What we know of it at present is comparable to what the ancient geographers knew about the earth: some of the inhabitable lands, but falsely positioned, their bearings being irreconcilable with the phenomena that have since been observed. Numerous useful discoveries are thus still to be made. Without wishing to single myself out I dare say that I have taken a road not tried before, though there were many indications that it was the best to take. I have made my observations and compared them with each other and with received opinion. I have tried to go back to the fundamental principles of language through the analysis of grammatical facts, and have followed the thread of this analysis, often with difficulty, sometimes in wonder, always faithful to the facts. My system is merely the sincere exposé of my results. Beauzée (1767, I:xxvii-xxviii)

Beauzée studied Semitic, Romance, Germanic and Celtic languages as well as Latin, Greek, Basque, Japanese, Chinese, and Peruvian (Beauzée 1767:xv). Seen in this light, his ideas about universal grammar may not only claim some factual support, they also sound quite modern, as he emphasizes the depen-

---

[8] The best available modern study on Beauzée is Bartlett (1975).

dence of grammars of specific languages on a universal grammar (grammaire générale) that constrains them:

> Grammar, which takes as its object the expression of thought by means of spoken or written speech, thus allows for two sorts of principles. The ones are of an immutable and universal validity. Being connected with the very nature of thought they follow its analysis and thus result from it. The others have only hypothetical validity and depend on fortuitous, arbitrary, and variable conventions, which have given rise to the different languages. The former constitute universal grammar, the latter are the object of the grammars of specific languages.   Beauzée (1767,I:ix-x)

> I believe that one must treat the principles of Language (Langage) as one treats those of physics or geometry or any other science. For there is in effect just one logic, and the human mind, if I may venture this expression, is of necessity subjected to the same mechanism, no matter with what it occupies itself. I have thus, to the best of my ability, been sparing of principles. In order not to multiply them without necessity I have tried, wherever possible, to generalize over usages that appeared to be analogous. I take exceptions to be in grammar what they are in physics: depositions made by experience against the principle to which they are said to be exceptions.
>
> Constantly following this method I found everywhere the same views, the same general principles, the same universality in the laws common to Language. I saw that the differences of specific languages, the idioms, are nothing but different aspects of general principles or different applications of common fundamental laws, that these differences are limited, based on reason, reducible to fixed points, that therefore all the peoples of the earth, despite the differences of their tongues, speak, in a sense, the same Language, without anomalies or exceptions, and that, finally, one can reduce to a relatively small number *the necessary elements of Language*, and the teaching of all languages to a simple, brief, uniform and easy method.
>
> I say 'necessary elements of Language' because they are, in fact, indispensably necessary in all languages to make the analytical and metaphysical deployment of thought perceptible. But I do not mean to speak of individual necessity which would not leave any language the liberty to leave one or more of them unused. What I am speaking of is a necessity of kind, which sets limits to the choice one can make of them.   Beauzée (1767,I:xvi-xviii)

This is talk we understand. We recognize some key words, such as *geometry*, a shibboleth of rationalist philosophers, used by their opponents to disparage them (see 2.3.4, in connection with de Condillac). Of special significance is the term *mechanism* used for the workings of the mind: as is shown in section 3.1 below, the application of the machine metaphor to the human mind did not gain ground till the late 19th century, and is the defining feature of 20th century structuralism in the human sciences. Beauzée must therefore, with Gall, who was mentioned in the Preamble to this chapter, be regarded as an early harbinger of this message. We also notice his explicit application of Ockham's razor: do not multiply principles beyond necessity.

What distinguishes Beauzée's notion of universal grammar from that dominant in our day is mainly that for Beauzée universal grammar simply reflects the structural principles of thought, whereas nowadays most theories see it as a specific innate mental module with its own autonomous principles and processes, which are to a considerable degree independent of the structure of thought (cp. note 7 above). It still remains to be seen which theory will carry the day, the modular one current in the late 20th century, or the not so modular one defended by Beauzée in the 18th century.

- *Beauzée's* 'complément' *and the notion of tree structure*

As regards grammar proper, much of Beauzée's text consists of semantic definitions of word classes, meant to be part of universal grammar. Apart from that, however, there are two notions that stand out from the ordinary (and it was these that Beauzée himself considered his two most significant contributions to the theory of grammar). The first is the notion of *complement*. For Beauzée, a complement 'is an addition made to a word with the purpose of changing or completing its meaning' (1767, II:44). Complements may be considered both from the grammatical and from the semantic point of view (1767, II:53). Semantically, all elements that are called 'modifiers' in present-day terminology are complements, as well as adjectives and adjectival phrases. Lexical argument functions like subject, direct object, indirect object are likewise called 'complements'. The grammatical aspect of complements is expressed by the term *régime* (government), used earlier by Girard. Thus, the same semantic complement may be realized by means of a noun phrase in the dative case in one language and a prepositional phrase in another.

Complements may be nested and ordered hierarchically. Thus, a phrase like *with the care required in circumstances of this nature* (1767, II:55) can be analysed hierarchically as the preposition *with*, combined with the complement *the care required in circumstances of this nature*, and this is again analysable as *the care* combined with the complement *required in circumstances of this nature*, and this again as *required* followed by the complement *in circumstances of this nature*, and this again as *in* with *circumstances of this nature*, and so forth, till one reaches the ultimate words *this* (complement) and *nature*. It is clear that this comes close to the notion of tree structure, which is central in all modern theories of grammar.

- *Beauzée's analysis of verbal tenses*

Beauzée's second important contribution, in his own as well as our estimation, is his masterly analysis of the semantics of verbal tenses and the ways the tenses are expressed in different languages. This analysis is found in (1767, I: 422-513), as part of his discussion of the verb as a word class, to which tense is an 'accessory idea'.

He begins by defining the actual state of affairs described, say A. This can have three possible relations to what he calls the *time of comparison* (époque de comparaison) or C: A can be simultaneous with C, prior to C or posterior to C, giving rise to the present, past and future tenses, respectively.

Then comes a second division of tenses, which can be definite or indefinite, according to whether they are or are not linked up with any identifiable time in history. An indefinite present tense expresses simultaneity with any arbitrary time, as in generic presents ('man is mortal'). But a definite present is anchored in time, as in 'I am in Paris now'. The same distinction is applied to past and future tenses. One thinks, for example, of the difference between the indefinite past in English *I have (once) been in Paris* versus the definite past in *I was (then) in Paris*. For the future one thinks of the definite *It will rain tomorrow* versus the indefinite *Animals will never kill themselves.*

A third division consists in the position of C with respect to the time of utterance U (l'acte même de la parole). Here again, C can be simultaneous with U, or priori or posterior to U. U provides an anchor for identifying historical time, and thus for making a tense definite. If U is disregarded in the semantics of the proposition, the tense will be indefinite. A present tense may be used to express simultaneity with regard to C which is posterior to U, as in *I am leaving tomorrow*. A past tense may be used to express anteriority with regard to a past C, as in *She had left already*.

Not all languages express all possibilities. Greek, Latin, French are particularly rich in tense expressions. French even includes fine nuances of immediacy, as in *je viens de parler* (I have just spoken) or *je vais parler* (I'm going to speak). But in Chinese, for example, most tenses are present only 'potentially' (en puissance – 1767, I:424). In any case, all languages have verbs, whether the tenses are expressed or not.

The informed reader will notice the similarity of Beauzée's tense analysis with that proposed by Reichenbach (1947), which has become standard in modern linguistics (see 7.3.2.2 for further details). It is not generally known, yet worth mentioning, that Reichenbach had an illustrious predecessor in Beauzée. (Bartlett (1975:90) is apparently unaware of this fact.)

- *Beauzée as the crowning achievement of the French grammatical tradition*

It is probably correct to say that Beauzée is the most illustrious of the French 18th century grammarians. He combined deep theoretical insights with an unusual grasp of data from a large variety of languages. He is, one may say, the crowning achievement of a rich tradition, which was centred in France and made, so to speak, grammar come of age. Not only 'traditional' grammar, as it is often called today, but also 'scientific' grammar owes much more to this tradition than is normally realized even among historians of linguistics.

2.3.4 Speculation about the origin of language

With the advent of Romanticism, the old interest in the origin of language and the identity of the 'Ursprache' of mankind was rekindled and became a dominant force. Yet the time had not yet come for a systematic, non-mythological approach to the problem of the origin or origins of the languages of the world. The theories developed in this context were speculative in the extreme and bore all the marks of the 'mythology of language' found in so many western and non-western cultures when a rational approach is not available.

In discussing the 18th century speculations about the origin of language one should realize that, in the orthodox view of that period, the Bible was still the main source of information about the earliest history of the earth and of mankind. It was believed that the earth, and mankind with it, was no older than five or six thousand years. Human language, accordingly, could not be older than that. The Bible, moreover, tells us that language was a gift from God, which would necessarily imply that language, and hence all different languages, have to be perfect. On the other hand, from the perspective of scientific enquiry, it was thought that no means could possibly be made available to investigate the origins of language in anything like an empirically justifiable way. All one could do was consider the oldest extant writings, but it was recognized that spoken language must have antedated written language by a considerable length of time.

- *Romanticism implies an ecologist, not a formalist, view of language*

The new Enlightenment reacted against this orthodoxy, trying to force the issue by speculation. The modern mind is inclined, with some reason, to look upon these speculations with a certain distaste. (In fact, as is well known, the Linguistic Society of Paris decided in 1866 that no papers were to be presented any more about the origin of language, that being too speculative and too fruitless an issue.) Yet one should realize that they also contain an extremely important insight. In considering and explicitly posing the question of the natural origin of language, Enlightenment thinkers like Vico, Herder and many others emphasized the fact that language is a natural phenomenon that must have sprung up spontaneously at some stage during the development of the human race. They thus took what we have called (1.3) the ecologist view of language, as against any variety of a formalist view.

- *Language as a divine gift*

The main formalist view, representing current orthodoxy, was that language came as a gift from God:

> Herder . . . vigorously and successfully attacks the orthodox view of his age . . . that language could not have been invented by man, but was a direct gift from God. One of Herder's strongest arguments is that if language had been framed by God and by Him instilled into the mind of man, we should expect it to be much more logical, much more imbued with pure reason than it is as an actual matter of fact. Much in all existing languages is so chaotic and ill-arranged that it could not be God's work, but must come from the hand of man.   Jespersen (1922:27)

The divine origin view had to be formalist in principle, even though it lacked an actual formal theory to support it, since the naturalist, ecologist view implied human imperfection and the capriciousness of nature, and it would be blasphemous to attribute anything less than perfect to the Creator of heaven and earth.

- *No rationalist theories of the natural origin of language*

Other formalist views on the origin of language were scarce during that period, and have remained so after. A plausible candidate for a formalist position was the rationalist Port Royal tradition, which considered language as the direct expression of presumably perfect and universal rational thought. Here it would have been possible to claim that language must have come about as a direct reflex of the structures and processes of thought, which only needed

vocalization to become language. But only few authors seem to have represented this point of view in any strict sense, probably because it would have been
too blatantly rationalist. Another reason may have been the fact that a
rationalist account of the origin of language would simply pass the bucket of
the divine origin theory, since if language is a direct reflection of thought,
then thought must have been the Creator's gift to mankind, as was observed,
for example, by Herder (1772:61).

In fact, virtually all speculation on the origin of language during the 18th
century and later was of the naturalist kind, assuming that, one way or another, language must have arisen out of some kind of pre-rational, primitive
need for communication and expression.

• *Empirical problems for studying the origin of language*
Formalism and rationalism were in decline, and naturalism or, as we have
called it, ecologism gained the ascendancy. The naturalist attitude manifested itself in two ways. It gave rise, first, to an intense interest in questions
concerning the relation between language and psychological or mental functioning, thought, that is. And secondly, it made philosophers think about the
question of the origin of human language. In both respects, however, there
were serious empirical problems standing in the way of a proper scientific approach. The relation between language and thinking was hard to investigate
due to the absence of any serious psychology. The origin of language was hard
to investigate due to the absence of sufficient empirical data.

Unlike archaeology, linguistics had no empirical access to the past beyond
the oldest written texts in existence. Archaeologists could excavate sites and
find objects, but linguists depended, it seemed, on volatile speech sounds that
could never be retrieved. This was the 'empirical dilemma' of the 18th century philosophers of language, and there appeared to be no way out. Understandably, therefore, the thinkers of that period took refuge in speculation,
and they did so on a grand scale.

• *The oldest language was poetry: Vico, Herder and later*
Remarkably, Giambattista Vico (2.2.3) defended the view that human language originated as poetry. Not the artificial and literary kinds of poetry that
were cultivated in his day, but a natural, folkloric sort of poetry that served
practical needs ('t Hart 1979:146-150). His main argument was that the oldest
known manifestations of language are poetry, in particular the Homeric
poems. (One should take into account that nothing was known, in Vico's day,
about, for example, the very prosaic and much more ancient clay tablets
discovered in Mesopotamia and containing royal edicts or accounts of stocks,
sales and purchases of goods.)

Poetry was, in Vico's view, a necessity for primitive man, who possessed
only a handful of basic words for a handful of basic things. On these words he
depended also when he wanted to talk about a wider variety of things, and
the way to do that was, obviously, to extend the literal meanings by applying
literary techniques like metaphor, metonymy, and the like. (There does seem

to be some truth in this: one does find that a small stock of primitive root forms is used, with various additions, to express a large variety of concepts. The Latin root *fē*, for example, originally meaning 'suckle', is found in *femina* 'she who suckles, woman', but also, by literary extension, in, for example, *felix* 'fruit-bearing, fertile, productive' then 'happy', *fetus* 'brood, progeny', *fenum* 'hay', *fenus* 'interest on capital'.) Vico thus engaged liberally in the activity of etymologizing, much in the spirit of Plato's *Cratylus*, though he criticized Plato for imposing his own sophisticated categories on the old concepts instead of trying to reconstruct these in terms of what one may imagine primitive society and primitive mentality to have been like.

But it was not just the use of literary tropes that made primitive language poetic. It was also the singing that Vico imagined to accompany work in the fields and to develop into articulate sounds and then syllables and words, so that it could be used for memorizing things one had to learn.

We find this view echoed, and expressed in drippingly romantic language, by *Johann Gottfried Herder* (1744-1803), the highly influential German romantic who published a prize essay on the origin of language in 1772. There we read (Herder 1772:87-88), in my best English translation:

> What so many of the old authors have said and so many newer ones have parroted without proper understanding is explained by this living principle: 'that poetry is older than prose!' For what was the first language but a collection of poetic elements? Imitations of the noises, actions and movements of nature! Taken from the interjections of all beings and animated by the interjection of human experience! The natural language of all creatures turned from wit into versified sound, from action, passion and live impact into images! A dictionary of the soul, and at the same time a mythology and a wonderful epic of the actions and reasons of all beings! A constant creation of fables with passion and interest! — What else is poetry?

Herder then goes on, and on, about primitive singing, which was not an imitation of bird song, as some authors had it (how could the raucous human throat even come close to the beauty of the nightingale's love song!), but the natural expression of wonderful human nature.

Wilhelm von Humboldt was apparently charmed by this idea. As is shown in 2.6.2, Humboldt held the view, though he did not express it prominently, that the origin of language lies in the natural urge to produce art. It is commonly said that he derived this idea from Herder's essay. This is no doubt true, but here we see that the idea is older than that and originated most probably with Vico. It lived on till the beginning of the 20th century. Otto Jespersen (1894), repeated in Jespersen (1922:431-7), where he emphatically denies, against all evidence, the romanticist background of this theory, still defends the thesis that language originated as song, in love play and otherwise. Berthold Delbrück (1901) takes over this view, which is then strongly criticized by Wundt (1901:91-7). Nowadays it is entirely forgotten.

• *Further speculative theories about the origin of language*
Speculation about the natural origin of language was particularly fashionable in 18th century France. The first important representative of this fashion is

the philosopher *Etienne Bonnot de Condillac* (1714-1780), who was closely associated with the movement of the *Encyclopédie*. He held, against Descartes
and Port Royal, and very much in the spirit of Locke, that all knowledge is
derived from the senses, and that thought, far from being the main determining factor in the organization of knowledge, is to a large extent shaped by and
dependent upon language. His main work, in this respect, is *Essai sur l'origine
des connaissances humaines, ouvrage où l'on réduit à un seul principe tout ce qui
concerne l'entendement humain* of 1746. In this work he proposes that language
originated as a shapeless mixture of gestures and unstructured sounds and cries.
This would have led to 'artificial', i.e. linguistic, signs, which then became
the basis of articulate thinking. Herder (1772) criticized him for not showing
more explicitly how inarticulate cries could have turned into structured meaningful language, and posited a prior faculty of 'reflection' (Besonnenheit) to
explain that process.

De Condillac's considerable intellectual influence was based on much more
than his speculations on the origin of language. He became a popular and influential figure in Paris during the years 1750 till his death in 1780, owing in
part to his philosophical contributions to Diderot's great project of the *Encyclopédie ou Dictionnaire raisonné des sciences, des arts et des métiers* which
appeared, with numerous interruptions due to political tensions, between 1751
and 1780. As is shown in 2.6.2, Wilhelm von Humboldt was heavily influenced
by de Condillac's ideas during his stay in Paris from 1797 till 1801.

The next important figure was *Jean-Jacques Rousseau* (1712-1778), composer,
writer, philosopher and general genius and adventurer, and for some time also
a contributor to the *Encyclopédie*, for which he wrote on matters of music.
Rousseau's ideas about the origin of language are found mainly in his *Discours
sur l'origine et les fondemens de l'inégalité parmi les hommes* of 1755, and his
*Essai sur l'origine des langues où il est parlé de la mélodie et de l'imitation
musicale*, published posthumously in 1781. He follows, in main outline, de
Condillac on this issue, but places greater emphasis on the social role of
language, and polemicizes sharply with any rationalist ideas about language.

In his *Essai* of 1781 he writes, for example (p. 505 of the Copedith edition of
1970, reproduced from an 1817 edition by A. Belin):

> The genius of the oriental languages, the oldest ones that are known to us, refutes
> absolutely the didactic development imagined in their composition. These languages
> have nothing methodical or rational (raisonné); they are living and figurative. Some
> try to make out the speech of primitive man as languages of geometrists, but we see
> that they were languages of poets. . . .

> All the passions unite the people whom the necessities of life force to separate. It is
> neither hunger nor thirst, but love, hate, pity, rage, that elicited the first vocali-
> zations from them. . . .

> Those are the most ancient words ever invented, and that is the reason why the first
> languages were singing and passionate languages before they became simple and
> methodical. . . .

As the first motivation for making man speak was passion, his first expressions were tropes. Figurative language was the first to come about; the proper meaning was found last.

These passages are significant in that they contain so many telling words. The Oriental languages are said to be the *oldest known*, and are therefore romanticized as belonging to an idyllic world of poetry and love. They are not *methodical* or *rational* – both terms referring directly to the Port Royal tradition – but *living* and *figurative* – terms that evoke Romanticism. Primeval language is not *geometrical* – a term that harks back to Pascal's criticism of Descartes, who, he says, laboured under an 'esprit de géométrie', rather than an 'esprit de finesse'. The oldest language was a language of *poets*, and its expressions were *figurative tropes*: we remember Vico.

Rousseau did not feel, however, that he knew the answer to all questions about the origin of language, and he kept changing his position on details. Considering the view that language may have been part of the *contrat social* which he postulated as the basis of all social order, he wonders how such a 'contract' could have come into being if there was no pre-existing language. Baffled by this paradox he then considers language as the product of cooperative action, such as hunting and fighting, though he still declares himself unable to explain how all this could have led to articulate meaningful language. Later, as is demonstrated by the passages quoted above, he saw language as the product of the passions, not of necessity. Until the end of his life he remained puzzled by the question of how language could have originated, unable to escape from the paradoxes he thought he saw.

Rousseau's ideas on the origin of language found favour with the eccentric Scottish philosopher *Lord Monboddo* (1714-1799), whose principal work, *Of the Origin and Progress of Language*, was published between 1773 and 1792. He, too, sees language as the product of primeval 'animal' cries but, like Herder, he stresses the role of human intelligence and powers of abstraction as necessary prerequisites for the growth of meaningful grammatical language.

A few more names could be mentioned, in this respect. We shall refrain, however, from doing so, mainly because speculations of this kind have not contributed to a better understanding of language in any way whatsoever.

2.4 The beginnings of comparative philology

• *Sir William Jones' speech of 1786 and the birth of comparative philology*
It was in this cultural and socio-economic climate that the foundations were laid of what was to become the great science of historical comparative linguistics, usually called by the name of comparative philology. How comparative philology started is a well-known story. It started with the hypothesis that Sanskrit, the ancient ritual language of India, Latin, Greek, Gothic, Celtic and Persian stemmed from a common source, sometimes believed to be Sanskrit itself. This hypothesis was formulated first by the English lawyer and devoted amateur linguist Sir William Jones (1746-1794). In 1783, Jones was

appointed to the Supreme Court of Justice in Calcutta. He perfected his knowledge of Sanskrit (which he had studied at Oxford) and soon founded the Asiatick Society of Bengal, with himself as president. In 1786 he made a speech to the Society, in which the following famous passage occurred:

> The Sanskrit language, whatever be its antiquity, is of a wonderful structure; more perfect than the Greek, more copious than the Latin, and more refined than either, yet bearing to both of them a stronger affinity, both in the roots of verbs and in the forms of grammar, than could possibly have been produced by accident; so strong indeed that no philologer could examine them all three, without believing them to have sprung from some common source, which, perhaps, no longer exists: there is a similar reason, though not quite so forcible, for supposing that both the Gothic and the Celtic, though blended with a very different idiom, had the same origin with the Sanskrit; and that the old Persian might be added to the same family.

This passage is generally taken to mark the beginning of comparative philology. To some extent, Sanskrit had been known to the West for a long time before Jones made his speech, and the similarities with Greek and Latin had not remained unnoticed. The English Jesuit missionary Thomas Stevens mentioned it in a letter of 1583, but the letter was not published until 1957. Three years later the Florentine merchant Filippo Sassetti wrote about the lexical similarities he noticed between Sanskrit and Italian, but his letters remained unpublished till 1855. Others followed, mostly missionaries and merchants, but they all attributed the similarities to borrowing from Latin or Greek into Sanskrit, or the other way round, not knowing, or wondering, about the lack of historical opportunities for such borrowings (Rocher 1994:3651). In 1767, the French Jesuit missionary Cœurdoux sent a memoir to the Institut Français in Paris calling attention to the lexical and morphological similarities between Sanskrit and Latin, but this was not printed until forty years later (Jespersen 1922:33).

It would be naïve to think that Jones' speech actually caused the birth and rapid expansion of comparative philology. The causes are to be sought in the general climate of romanticist thinking, with the concomitant interest in the natural origin of language, and the 'empirical dilemma', sketched in the foregoing pages, of not having empirical access to the 'ursprache'. What happened was that some people, including the socially influential William Jones, suddenly began to think that such empirical access was possible after all: the systematic comparison of elementary lexical items in different languages formed a workable basis for empirically based theories about some common ancestral language. This discovery was welcomed as a liberation from the bothersome 'empirical dilemma' that had forced linguistic thinkers to take refuge in speculation. We remember that it was commonly thought at the time that human language was no older than about five or six thousand years. And indeed, 'the first generation of comparative linguists ... imagined that the Aryan (Indo-Germanic) language which is the basis of our family of languages (grundsprache) was a fair representation of the primeval language of our earliest ancestors (ursprache)' (Jespersen 1924:31).

It thus seems that the almost explosive success commanded by comparative philology right from the start is to be attributed to a general feeling of liberation, as empirical digging into the unwritten past of at least one family of languages suddenly proved possible, despite the fact that speech sounds disappear as soon as they have been pronounced. The success of comparative philology was so spectacular that it became almost impossible, for more than a century, to look upon language from any other than the historical point of view. 'The chief innovation of the beginning of the nineteenth century was the historical point of view,' writes Jespersen (1922:32). And this remained so till Jespersen's own day, if we accept his opening statement of the Preface of the same book: 'The distinctive feature of the science of language as conceived nowadays is its historical character.' (Jespersen 1922:7).

- *Indo-European posited as a hypothetical source language*

Soon after the year 1800 a small crop of professional linguists sprang up. The key figures of this early period are almost all Germans: the brothers *August Wilhelm* and *Friedrich von Schlegel*, the brothers *Jacob* and *Wilhelm Grimm*, the Dane *Rasmus Rask* (1787-1832), and *Franz Bopp* (1791-1867). The German aristocrat and diplomat *Wilhelm von Humboldt* played an important part as well, but more as a philosopher of language than as a comparative philologist or linguist (see section 2.6.2). Friedrich von Schlegel, Bopp, Rask, and Jacob Grimm were the main, often brilliant, architects of the first attempts at establishing genetic relationships among the languages they compared. A hypothetical source language was postulated, variously called 'Indo-European' or 'Indo-Classic' (Bopp), 'Sanskritic' or 'Indogermanic' (Humboldt). Nowadays the term is 'Indo-European' in the French, English and Scandinavian worlds, and 'Indogermanic' in the German speaking world, although the term 'Indo-European' is gaining ground there, too.

- *The Von Schlegel brothers*

August Wilhelm (1767-1845) and his brother (Carl Wilhelm) Friedrich (1772-1829) von Schlegel were both students of theology and philosophy, with a special interest in Indic and Persian studies. Their study of Oriental languages, especially Sanskrit, opened their eyes to the diversity of the languages of the world. August Wilhelm proposed (1818) a primitive typology for languages which has held up, in principle, till recently, when more sophisticated typological studies took over (see 4.8). His typology was based on morphological criteria, in that he distinguished between languages without any morphology, the *isolating languages*, such as Chinese, and languages with morphology. These were again subdivided into two classes. When the affixes have one meaning and one form and are strung together, as in Turkish or most Amerindian languages, the language is *agglutinative*. When the affixes have composite meanings and differ according to declensions and conjugations the language is *inflectional*, as, for example, Latin and Greek. The younger brother Friedrich laid the foundations for 19th century comparative linguistics with his book *Ueber die Sprache und Weisheit der Indier* of 1808, which directly inspired Bopp, Rask, the Grimm brothers and many others.

• *The Grimm brothers*

The historical importance of the brothers Jacob (1785-1863) and Wilhelm (1786-1859) Grimm far transcends their contributions to linguistics. Both studied law at Marburg and became interested in the antiquarian aspects of law, and then of poetry, folk tales and language. Both fulfilled public offices as ministerial secretaries and librarians in various places, though Wilhelm remained without employment for some time due to bad health. When Wilhelm became secretary to the librarian at Kassel in 1814 Jacob joined him there two years later. From then on they gave up all ambitions of a public career and concentrated on antiquarian and linguistic studies. In 1829 they incurred the displeasure of the Prince Elector of Hessen-Kassel, perhaps for political reasons, and betook themselves to nearby Göttingen, where they were appointed as professors and librarians. There they got into political trouble again, in 1837, when the new king of Hannover, Ernest Augustus, re-pealed the new liberal constitution and re-established despotism. Their public protest led to their dismissal and Jacob was forced to leave the king-dom. After three years of exile in Kassel they accepted an invitation from the king of Prussia to become members of the Berlin Academy with the right to teach at the university. Both died in Berlin.

From about 1816 onward, they produced a stream of publications: collections of folk and fairy tales and legends, often taken from oral tradition, studies on folk literature and mythology, and linguistic works. The works on folk literature have become the basis of a long tradition. In 1828, Jacob Grimm published *Deutsche Rechtsaltertümer*, an as yet unrivalled study of ancient German law practices. The more strictly linguistic works were also written by Jacob, the more active of the two brothers. Between 1819 and 1837 Jacob published his four volume *Deutsche Grammatik* (where *deutsch* is to be taken in the old sense of 'popular': a grammar of the popular Germanic languages), which contains Grimm's law, to be discussed in a moment. In 1838 the brothers started work on the great German dictionary *Deutsches Wörterbuch*, which the longer-lived Jacob saw published only to the letter F. This dictionary set the example for similar enterprises in many other European countries, including Britain. In 1848 Jacob published *Geschichte der deutschen Sprache* ('History of the German Language') in two volumes. They reformed the spelling of German, taking it back to normal roman type without capital letters for nouns. These innovations were gradually reversed later, to the point where gothic type was reintroduced again in the early 20th century. Since 1945 the official spelling uses roman type, but with capital letters for nouns.

Since the 1860s, the Grimm brothers have been a household name all over Europe, mostly due to their immensely popular fairy tale collections: for generations parents have read these marvellous tales to their children. But the general cultural and academic importance of their activities matches their popularity. Without them, Europe would have been different, and not for the better. But we must return to comparative philology.

• *Word-based comparative philology; sound laws but no semantic laws*
Throughout the 19th century, comparative philology was almost exclusively restricted to the Indo-European language family. It was, moreover, entirely word-based: it was words or lexical word stems that were reconstructed from prehistory and followed through history. Morphological elements were taken into consideration, but invariably interpreted as derived from original independent words.[9] The criterion for word identity through time is the coupling of form and meaning: both are changing properties of historical entities called 'words'. As regards meaning, it proved difficult to set up a systematic framework for semantic change. Whatever was observed in the way of lexical semantic change was accounted for largely in traditional and/or intuitive terms, such as specialisation or generalization of meaning, metonymy (transfer by contiguity, as from 'roof' to 'house', or 'fence' to 'garden'), 'bleaching' (e.g. from a literal verb 'go' to an auxiliary verb of futuricity) or metaphor. It was not until much later (e.g. Stern 1931) that a more systematic account of lexical semantic change and development became available, but even with modern taxonomies of types of semantic change nothing like the rigorous method found in the study of form changes has so far been achieved. In particular, it has proved impossible, till the present day, to formulate laws of semantic change applicable to a language or group of languages in the way sound laws could be formulated. And it is unlikely that any such laws will ever be found.

The main thrust in establishing the lines along which words developed and changed through the ages thus came from the study of word forms, not word meanings. Knowledge of phonetics had begun to increase to the point where historical phonology became possible – even though, in the earliest period, the phonetic basis for the description and explanation of the sound changes observed was shaky and 'nowadays cannot but produce a smile' (Jespersen 1922:46). On the whole this meant that the genetic relationships among languages were based mainly on lexical words, and hence mainly on phonological developments through the languages concerned. The concept of *sound law* came to be of central importance in 19th century comparative philology.

• *Grimm's law*
The first sound law that was formulated is known as Grimm's law[10] or the Germanic consonant shift. In its original formulation, which was seriously

---

[9] One must realize that, for most comparative philologists, the notion of grammar was practically restricted to morphology: 'What is grammar after all but declension and conjugation?' said Max Müller in his *Lectures on the Science of Language* (1861:205). What was called 'syntax' was largely a description of the various functions of the nominal cases and of forms of clausal and infinitival complementation.

[10] It is often said, especially by Danish scholars (Otto Jespersen, Holger Pedersen), that it should really be called Rask's law, since the phenomena in question had been noted and

flawed, it says that Greek voiceless plosives (**p, t, k**) changed into the corresponding voiceless fricatives in Old Germanic (**f, y, x**), and again into the corresponding voiced plosives (**b, d, g**) in modern High German. The Greek voiced plosives, in turn, were said to become voiceless plosives in Old Germanic and fricatives in German, and the Greek voiceless fricatives to become voiced plosives in Old Germanic and voiceless plosives in modern German, as shown in fig. 1.

Greek	**p b f**	**t d y**	**k g x**
Old Germanic	**f p b**	**y t d**	**x k g**
Modern German	**b f p**	**d z t**	**g x k**

Figure 1   *Grimm's Law*

Grimm wanted to see a circular movement ('Kreislauf') in the sounds concern-ed, though he had to admit that the modern High German **z** did not fit the pattern. In fact, a great deal more did not fit the pattern. To begin with, what he interpreted as fricatives in Greek, (**f, y, x**) were not fricatives at all but aspirated plosives (**ph, th, kh**). Moreover, modern German often does not have **b** but **f** for Greek **p** (e.g. Greek *poûs* vs. German *fuss*, 'foot'), and often it does not have **g** for Greek **k** but **h** (e.g. Greek *kúōn* vs. German *hund*, 'dog'). Then, in some cases Greek *t* corresponds to German *t*, and not to *d*, as in German *vater* ('father') and Greek *patér*. Yet, in spite of these flaws it was clear that Grimm had captured certain regularities, even if they could not be said to be absolute or exceptionless. For Grimm and his contemporaries, language was not yet an object of rigorous scientific study. They were clearly ecologists, not formalists, and for them this meant that language was subject to the vagaries, whims and weaknesses of the free creative mind and its emotions. All they could see were tendencies, not strict laws.

● *Schleicher*

This began to change soon, however. In the 1850s a debate sprang up on wheth-er the study of language could achieve the degree of precision and rigour found in the natural sciences. The German linguist *August Schleicher* (1821-1868) was one of those who wrestled with this question. Schleicher took the then modern view that linguistics should indeed strive for scientific status, like the natural sciences. But to him this did not mean that, for example, sound change had to be subject to 'laws' in the customary scientific sense. When he advocated a 'scientific' approach to language studies he meant that linguis-tics should be seen as a branch of biology. Just as human individuals walk in virtue of their legs and feet and the whole biological machinery that regul-ates the use of these limbs and the processes that lead up to their proper use,

---

published by Rask well before Grimm published them. On the other hand, it was Grimm who packed the facts together in one general formulation, not presented as such by Rask.

in just that way humans possess a biological machinery that regulates the acquisition and use of language.[11]

- *The family tree metaphor*

In much the same vein, Schleicher saw the spread and diversification of the various Indo-European languages as the result of linguistic evolution parallel in character to the evolution of biological species in natural history. He was a great admirer of Charles Darwin, and transferred the Darwinian view of evolution to language. Just like each species has its place in an evolutionary tree, each language represents a branch in its evolutionary 'family tree' (Stammbaum). This view would soon be challenged by Schmidt (1872), about whom more below.

- *Language as organism*

Schleicher drew the analogy with biology even further. For him, a language is a natural organism leading its own life, with its own mind and propensities:

> Languages are natural organisms that came about independently of the will of man, grew according to certain laws which also determine their development, ageing and death. . . . Glottics, the science of language that is, is therefore a natural science. . . . Its method is identical to that of the other natural sciences.   Schleicher (1863:6-7)

- *The concept of law in comparative philology*

As regards sound laws, Schleicher still held views that bore greater resemblance to the views of older linguists like Jacob Grimm than to modern notions. A great deal of debate went on in those years about the nature and causes of sound laws. Although nobody maintained that sound laws were, in whatever sense, a kind of physical laws, everyone felt the need to deny that view, usually on the obvious grounds that sound laws are restricted in time and space and hence not necessitated by physical nature, but often also with an appeal to the freedom, whims and creativity of human nature. The dominant view was that sound laws are tendencies more than laws, and some proposed, therefore, that the term 'rule' was more appropriate than 'law'. Moreover, the phonetic basis of the sound laws that were proposed was either not taken into consideration at all or only very weakly. For Schleicher this was not good enough. He wanted sound laws to be more precise and, in modern terminology, to be subject to clearer criteria of falsifiability. On the other hand, he also held that all sound change is decay: the pristine language was perfect, and all subsequent change was due to the corruptive influence of generations of

---

[11] Compare also Max Müller (1861:333): 'If we want to gain an insight into the faculty of flying, which is a characteristic feature of birds, all we can do is, first, to compare the structure of birds with that of other animals which are devoid of that faculty, and, secondly, to examine the conditions under which the act of flying becomes possible. It is the same with speech. Speech is a specific faculty of man.' One clearly recognizes here Chomsky's notion of 'language organ', which is but an echo of the views held by Schleicher and Müller.

sluggish and lazy speakers using it without caring to maintain the limpid precision of enunciation and expression as of old.

Schleicher's admonitions regarding the scientific quality of sound laws proved to be a powerful stimulus for his numerous and mostly highly talented students, who did not fail to notice that their teacher fell short of the ideals he defended. He was soon to be criticized violently for certain aspects of his work, in particular for his Stammbaum theory of language genealogy, for his biological leanings, especially his 'natural organism' view of languages, and above all for his idea that all change is for the worse.

- *Indo-European reconstruction*

It was customary in those days to concentrate on the reconstruction of the original 'ursprache' supposed to be the source of all Indo-European languages. Schleicher went so far as to venture an actual reconstruction in the form of a short text, the 'fable of the sheep and the horses', presented at the end of his life (Schleicher 1868):

Avis akvasas ka

Avis, jasmin varna na ā ast, dadarka akvams, tam, vāgham garum vaghantam, tam, bhāram magham, tam, manum āku bharantam. Avis akvabhjams ā vavakat: kard aghnutai mai vidanti manum akvams agantam. Akvāsas ā vavakant: krudhi avai, kard aghnutai vividvantsvas: manus patis varnām avisāms karnanti svabhjam gharmam vastram avibhjams ka varnā na asti. Tat kukruvants avis agram ā bhugat.

[The sheep and the horses

A sheep on which there was no wool saw horses that pulled a heavy cart with a big load, driven by a man. The sheep said to the horses: My heart is in anguish as I see the man driving the horses. The horses said: Listen sheep, our hearts are in anguish as we know: the man, the boss, makes the wool of the sheep into a warm garment for himself and the sheep have no wool left. On hearing this the sheep turned into the field.]

Much as one will admire Schleicher's vast knowledge of Indo-European languages as well as his prowess and courage, it is clear that this fable is more science fiction than science. When one speaks of Indo-European one must be aware that this is not a well-defined language spoken during a well-delimited period in well-delimited places, but more a conglomerate of properties and features supposed to lie at the bottom of masses of linguistic phenomena. Indo-European reconstructions are formulae rather than real words or sentences, as was soon pointed out by the Young Grammarians. Then, the alphabetic rendering of the fable does no justice at all to the refined features hypothetically assigned to the Indo-European sounds, not to mention the total lack of syntactic support. Schleicher's own students realized the futility of such reconstructions and did not hesitate to relegate Schleicher's fable to, indeed, the realm of fables.

• *Max Müller*

Another exponent of this period is the German Sanskritist *Friedrich Max Müller* (1823-1900), who became the first professor of Comparative Philology at Oxford University. In his widely read popularizing *Lectures on the Science of Language*, delivered to the Royal Institution of Great Britain in 1861, he tries to convince his audience that linguistics, i.e. comparative philology, is or should become a physical science, a branch of biology (see note 11). In this he agreed with Schleicher. But more than Schleicher, Müller abhorred 'theories'. He stuck to a strictly positivist view of science, rejecting theorizing and stressing the importance of solid facts:

> But the science of language has nothing to do with mere theories, whether conceivable or not. It collects facts, and its only object is to account for these facts, as far as possible.   Müller (1861:205)

It must be said, however, that the scientific view taken by Müller did not carry much weight. Jespersen gives a correct assessment of Müller's scientific pretensions:

> But his arguments do not bear a close inspection. Too often, after stating a problem, he is found to fly off at a tangent and to forget what he has set out to prove for the sake of an interesting etymology or a clever paradox. He gives an uncritical acceptance to many of Schleicher's leading ideas; thus, the science of linguistics is to him a physical science and has nothing to do with philology, which is an historical science. If, however, we look at the book itself, we shall find that everything that he counts on to secure the interest of his reader, everything that made his lectures so popular, is really non-naturalistic: all those brilliant exposés of word history are really like historical anecdotes in a book on social evolution; they may have some bearing on the fundamental problems, but these are rarely or never treated as real problems of natural science. Nor does he, when taken to task, maintain his view very seriously, but partly retracts it and half-heartedly ensconces himself behind the dictum that everything depends on the definition you give of 'physical science'.
>   Jespersen (1922:86)

• *Müller's brush with Whitney*

Many contemporaries also strongly disapproved of Schleicher and Müller's flirt with biology. A notable critic was the American orientalist and comparative linguist *William Dwight Whitney* (see 4.1), who engaged in a bitter polemic with Max Müller at Oxford. Whitney, a botanist by early training, strongly rejected the biology view of language, especially when it was presented in the guise of the metaphor of language (or a language) as a living organism. For him, language is a human institution, not settled by a prehistoric conclave, but one that has evolved out of the need for sophisticated communication in virtue of a tacit social contract, a 'community of habit'. It is generally agreed that he gave Müller more than his share of criticism, probably because Müller's garrulous style and his tendency to get lost in anecdotal details and often also in loose and somewhat pontificating phrases had an inflammatory effect on the sober American, who strove for neat and well-supported arguments and had an aversion to idle speculations.

If, however, we set the obvious temperamental differences aside we see that Whitney and Müller had a great deal in common. For example, Müller likewise rejected the Schleicherian view of language as an organism, though less emphatically than Whitney, as is shown in the following passage:

> Those who consider that language is a conventional production, base their arguments principally on these formal elements [i.e. affixes, P.S.]. ... This view was opposed by another which represents language as an organic and almost a living being, and explains its formal elements as produced by a principle of growth inherent in its very nature. ... This view was first propounded by Frederick von Schlegel, and it is still held by many with whom poetical phraseology takes the place of sound and severe reasoning. The science of language adopts neither of these views. As to imagining a congress for settling the exponents of such relations as nominative, genitive, singular, plural, active, and passive, it stands to reason that if such abstruse problems could have been discussed in a language void of inflections, there was no inducement for agreeing on a more perfect means of communication. And as to imagining language, that is to say nouns and verbs, endowed with an inward principle of growth, all we can say is, that such a conception is really inconceivable. Language may be conceived as a production, but it cannot be conceived as a substance that could itself produce.   Müller (1861:203-204)

One notices, by the way, that Müller ridicules the conventionalist view of language, as if that view implied some sort of prehistoric convention during which each language was settled. This theme recurs a few times in his *Lectures*, but, as Whitney rightly pointed out, there is also a perfectly reasonable form of conventionalism, which holds that languages arise out of a tacit social contract, following the dynamic processes that we know are very real in communities.

Müller, too, stuck to the family tree metaphor for linguistic genealogy, though he placed greater emphasis than was done before on morphological elements, i.e. grammar:

> ... the founders of comparative philology soon reduced the principal dialects of Europe and Asia to certain families, and they were able in each family to distinguish different branches, each consisting again of numerous dialects, both ancient and modern. ... Genealogical classification is no doubt the most perfect of all classifications, but there are but few branches of physical science in which it can be carried out, except very partially. In the science of language, genealogical classification must rest chiefly on the formal or grammatical elements, which, after they have been affected by phonetic change, can be kept up only by a continuous tradition.
> Müller (1861:165-166)

• *From monosyllables through decay to agglutination and hence to flection*
In Müller's eyes language was originally monosyllabic, each monosyllable or root expressing a definite concept. An original language would thus be totally transparent from the semantic point of view. Through frequent use and concomitant 'phonetic decay' original monosyllables got concatenated into agglutinative constructions of the kind found in, for example, Turkish. Hence, through further 'phonetic decay', the agglutinative morphological constructions coalesced into inflectional constructions as are found in most European languages. Phonetic decay would lead to dialects, and the emergence of new

languages after periods of transition he attributed to 'dialectical regeneration', the process whereby a particular dialect assumed the status of a new language as a result of political and other social factors:

> Now, what we call the growth of language comprises two processes which should be carefully distinguished, though they may be at work simultaneously. These two processes I call,
> 1. Dialectical Regeneration.
> 2. Phonetic Decay.
> I begin with the second, as the more obvious, though in reality its operations are mostly subsequent to the operations of dialectical regeneration. I must ask you at present to take it for granted that everything in language had originally a meaning. As language can have no other object but to express our meaning, it might seem to follow almost by necessity that language should contain neither more nor less than what is required for that purpose. It would also seem to follow that if language contains no more than what is necessary for conveying a certain meaning, it would be impossible to modify any part of it without defeating its very purpose. This is really the case in some languages. In Chinese, for instance, ...   Müller (1861:40)

And here he flies off at one of his lengthy tangents. The idea that language developed from a radical, through an agglutinative, to an inflectional stage is found on p. 318:

> As far as the formal part of language is concerned, we cannot resist the conclusion that what is now *inflectional* was formerly *agglutinative*, and what is now *agglutinative* was at first *radical*. The great stream of language rolled on in numberless dialects, and changed its grammatical colouring as it passed from time to time through new deposits of thought.   Müller (1861:318)

The obvious idea that inflectional morphology would again wear off and lead back to the primitive state of monosyllables is not expressed by Müller, but it is entertained and discussed in later authors, up to Jespersen, who stresses (1922:372) that Chinese is far from the kind of primeval language Müller and others wanted it to be, but that its monosyllabic and analytical character is the result of the wearing off of original morphological elements.

2.5   The Young Grammarians

On the whole, one feels that there was a great deal to criticize in such views as were held by Schleicher and Müller, and some young linguists did precisely that. Though their criticism was no doubt disproportionate, we must say in hindsight that the mere holding up of the mirror of true science to the face of linguistics as it was at the time had a strong beneficial effect. It made the linguistic world realize that historical comparative linguistics as practised around 1875 fell short of what might be considered reasonable standards of scientific rigour and precision.[12]

---

[12] See Amsterdamska (1987:90-143) for a detailed and well-documented account of this remarkable episode in the history of linguistics.

- *The Young Grammarian manifesto: uproar in the halls of academe*

During the second half of the 1870s a few young linguists banded together and, in their youthful enthusiasm, did something unheard of in those days in academic circles: they denounced the older linguists, i.e. their teachers, for sloppiness and an excess of fantasy and proclaimed a new, truly scientific programme for the study of language. The young linguists in question were mainly *Karl Brugmann* (1849-1919), *Berthold Delbrück* (1842-1922), *August Leskien* (1840-1916) and *Hermann Osthoff* (1847-1909), all at Leipzig around that time (Osthoff moved to Heidelberg in 1877). Following Leskien (1876), they proclaimed first of all the 'absolute exceptionlessness of sound laws' (die absolute Ausnahmlosigkeit der Lautgesetze), thereby putting heavy constraints on etymologies. The only class of exceptions admitted were deviations from sound laws on account of 'analogy' (the precise nature of which then became the object of fierce discussions). They moreover advanced the view that sound changes should be studied more systematically in the light of phonetic science, i.e. the science of the articulatory organs and their functioning. Living languages are not corrupted or in decline, but fresh and full of opportunities. In line with that, they argued that greater weight should be lent to contemporary, living languages and dialects, and less to inevitably futile attempts at reconstruction of the presumed original Indo-European language. Finally, they rejected the view that a language was an autonomous organism of some kind, stating instead that languages live only in the individuals using them.

Brugmann, the youngest of the four, was the ringleader. In 1878 he and Osthoff, the one but youngest, published the first volume of *Morphologische Untersuchungen*, with a Preface (pp. iii–xx), written entirely by Brugmann though co-signed by Osthoff.[13] This Preface became the manifesto of the new movement. There we read, for example:

> The reconstruction of the Indo-European source language has so far always been the main aim and the centre of the entire discipline of comparative philology. As a consequence, all research was directed at this language. ... The younger languages were, with a certain disdain, left out of consideration and branded as degenerate, sunken, ageing phases.
>
> It is not on the basis of hypothetical original linguistic structures, nor on the basis of the oldest documented forms of Indic, Persian, Greek, etc., whose earlier forms can only be inferred by hypothesis, that we should, in general, form a picture of the evolution of linguistic forms, but, in accordance with the principle that one should proceed from the known to the unknown, on the basis of those linguistic developments whose earlier phases can be read, over relatively long periods, from available sources so that the starting point is certain and established. The more material is made available to us in well-documented, written form over centuries of historical tradition, the better it is, and of necessity, the longer the stretch of time between the onset of the written tradition till the present day, the more we learn

---

[13] See Brugmann (1900:131-132): 'As far as I can remember, and as Osthoff can remember, he restricted himself to cutting up one or two of my sentences that had become too long and, at my request of course, putting his name to it along with mine.'

from it. The comparative linguist must, therefore, divert himself from the 'ur'-language and direct his gaze at the present, if he wishes to gain an adequate insight into the manner in which language develops, and he must free himself entirely from the idea that the younger phases of the Indo-European languages are of interest to the comparative Indo-Europeanist only to the extent that they throw light on the reconstruction of the old Indo-European language. ...

In other respects as well, the youngest phases of the newer Indo-European languages, the living dialects, are of great importance to the methodology of comparative philology. ...

Only those comparative linguists who manage to leave the hypothesis-laden atmosphere of the workshop where the Indo-European root forms are wrought and to enter the clear air of tangible actual reality so as to gain insight into things that grey theory will never show, only those who once and for all say goodbye to the once widely spread but nowadays still existing method that makes one consider language only *on paper*, that makes everything submerge in terminology, formulae and grammatical schemata and makes one believe that one has understood the essence of the phenomena as soon as a *name* for the thing has been invented, — only those can achieve an adequate picture of how linguistic forms live and change, and master those methodological principles without which no plausible results can be obtained in historical linguistic research and without which, in particular, any progress into the eras that lie behind the historically attested linguistic changes will be comparable to a sea voyage without compass. ...

Despite the deficiencies in methodology indicated above, so many significant and, it seems, for all times permanent results have been gained through the sharp intellect and great industry of the scholars who have so far been active in the field, that one may look back with pride on the history of our science till the present day. But we cannot, on the other hand, ignore the fact that the many good things have been mixed up with much that is deficient and untenable, even if many scholars still hold the untenable elements for solidly established results. Before the building can proceed, the whole construction, as it stands today, needs a thorough revision. Even the foundation walls contain many unsafe spots, and what has been built upon them must of necessity be demolished. Other parts of the masonry, whether or not they reach high up in the sky, may remain, as they stand on solid foundations, or may perhaps need only minor repairs. ...

These principles are based on the immediately obvious twofold thought, first, that language is not a thing that stands outside and above man and has a life of its own, but exists truly only in the individual, and that therefore all changes in its life can come only from the speaking individuals, and second, that the mental and physical activity of individuals when they acquire the language of their forbears and reproduce the acoustic images laid down in their conscience and construct new ones, must be the same for all times.

The two most important methodological principles of the 'Young Grammarian' school are the following:

First, all phonetic change, in so far as it is mechanical, proceeds according to exceptionless sound laws. That is, the direction of the sound movement is identical for all members of a speech community, except when dialect split occurs, and all words in which the sound affected by the change occurs in similar circumstances are comprised in the change without exception. (We speak, of course, only of mechanical sound change, not of certain forms of dissimilation or metathesis, which are founded in the idiosyncrasy of each single word and are always the physical reflex of some mental movement. These have no bearing on the concept of sound law.)

Secondly, as it is clearly so that form association, i.e. the formation of new forms by analogy, plays a significant role in the life of the newer languages, this kind of linguistic innovation certainly has to be acknowledged also for the older and oldest periods. ...

Only he who adheres strictly to the sound laws, the central pillar of our whole science, stands on solid ground in his research. ...

If only someone could succeed in eliminating once and for all the extremely harmful expressions 'youth' and 'old age' of languages, – grammatical terms which, like many others that are in themselves quite harmless, have brought almost nothing but mischief and hardly any blessings!   Osthoff & Brugmann (1878)

The names of the older linguists that were criticized were not mentioned, but anyone in the field would know who were meant, and those who, unlike Schleicher, were still alive took offence, in particular Georg Curtius, who had taught Brugmann and Leskien.

Brugmann's manifesto caused scandal in the strictly hierarchical halls of German academia. With the scandal came the divisions: some young linguists took the side of the uppish young men, others dissociated themselves from the form and manner, though perhaps agreeing in matters of substance.

- *The origin of the name 'Junggrammatiker'*

How the nickname 'Junggrammatiker' came about was made clear in Brugmann (1900). The German term 'Junggrammatiker' was due to be interpreted as a calque of the expressions 'Jungdeutschen', 'Junghellenen' or 'Jungtürken', denoting a series of impetuous nationalistic literary and political movements in Germany, Greece and the Ottoman Empire, respectively. These movements had been coming up in the years prior to the Junggrammatiker's manifesto, and it was obvious at the time that the term 'Junggrammatiker' would be understood as implying a similarity with them, which was not considered a compliment. The term was first used as a private joke by Brugmann's friend Zarncke in a report on a doctoral thesis. Brugmann, not knowing that he thus turned it into a name of pride, defiantly adopted the name 'Junggrammatiker', in quotes, in the Preface to Osthoff & Brugmann (1878). Looking back upon this episode, Brugmann writes (1900:132):

Then I heard from my friend Leskien that my friend Zarncke, in a written report on the PhD-thesis of R. Kögel, had jocularly reckoned him to belong to the school of the "Junggrammatiker". Being still inexperienced and rash, and in need of a suitable expression, I then made use of this gibe [in Osthoff & Brugmann (1878)], not knowing what the consequences would be, and especially not expecting that others, less sympathetic to our way of thinking, would exploit this expression and brand our group as a "sect which had noisily left the main church" and things of that nature, even though I had used the word in quotes and had thus made it clear that it was not of my own making. I bore this, patiently and in silence, as my just and fateful punishment. But what I did experience as unnecessary cruelty was the fact that we had to suffer being told patronizingly by a wise colleague that the name had a negative connotation of notoriety in view of "Young Germany", "Young Hellas" etc. — as though we would not have thought of that ourselves. All this, however, including the name itself, is now, thank God, only history.[14]

Since the English equivalent of terms like 'Jungtürken' is 'Young Turks' etc. it seems appropriate to translate 'Junggrammatiker' as 'Young Grammarians', and not as the commonly used but insipid 'neogrammarians'. We therefore speak of Young Grammarians.

- *Paul*

Despite the provocative stance taken by the Young Grammarians, many linguists at the time shared the feeling that a great deal of then current comparative philology had remained obscure and needed elucidation and improvement. Inevitably, some associated more closely with the angry youngsters than others. A powerful early associate was *Hermann Paul* (1846-1921), who, however, carefully avoided the confrontations and provocations that typified the hard core Young Grammarians. Paul's *Principien der Sprachgeschichte*, first published in 1880, though more an eclectic synthesis than an original study, gained widespread recognition as the most moderate and most considered statement of the Young Grammarians' viewpoints. As such it became highly influential. Each successive edition was heavily modified by Paul. The fifth edition thus reworked appeared in 1920, one year before Paul's death. This is the edition mostly used and quoted. (In 1888 an English translation appeared in London, in 1889 in New York, followed again by a revised Longmans edition in 1890 (Paul 1888-1890).)

Paul insisted on both the historical and the individual psychological nature of language, corresponding to historical and descriptive linguistics, respectively.

He also distinguished between language norm (Sprachusus) and individual speech activity (individuelle Sprachtätigkeit). The language norm, i.e. language, is for him a set of principles that make speech possible, and it is essentially a historical phenomenon that cannot be understood unless historical developments are taken into account. Speech, on the other hand, is not historical in this sense, and can be understood without an appeal to history.

He rejected the idea of a 'social' or 'communal' or 'popular' mind (Volksgeist, or Volksseele) as the repository of language, thereby opposing Steinthal and Wundt, who did defend such a notion. Instead, he insisted, entirely in the Young Grammarian tradition, that language and the speech processes resulting from it cannot be anywhere but in individual minds. The reification of a 'social mind' is, to him, without any justification.

Moreover, speech is a psychophysical activity allowing for infinitely varied use of the language norm. Paul thus envisages, though in a primitive way, language as a generative system making for endless variability in what speakers say. Harking back to Humboldt, he says:

[14] I am grateful to my colleague W. Kloeke who was kind enough to provide me with the text of Brugmann (1900) and sorted out the details of this curious bit of terminological history.

Those formal paradigms (Proportionen) that have gained a certain degree of stability are of eminent importance for all speech activity and for all linguistic development. One fails to do justice to this factor in the life of language when it is called upon only in respect to linguistic change. The old linguistics suffered from the fundamental error of treating all speech, as long as it does not deviate from the existing language norm, as something reproduced merely on the basis of memory. And the result of this has been that the role of the grammatical paradigms in processes of linguistic change was never clearly understood. Though W. von Humboldt rightly insisted that speech is a perpetual creation, one still encounters vivid and often baseless opposition when one tries to draw the consequences from this point of view.

The words and word groups that we use in speech are generated only in part by means of mere memory-based reproduction of what was taken in earlier. Just about as much results from a *combinatorial activity* that is based on the existence of the *paradigms*. The combination consists more or less in the *resolution of a paradigmatic equation*, in that, following the pattern of already habitual analogous paradigms, an equally habitual word is freely provided with a second paradigmatic member. This process we call *analogical formation*. It is an indubitable fact that a large quantity of word forms and syntactic constructions that were never introduced into the soul from outside can not just be generated with the help of the paradigms but can be generated reliably, in such a way that the speaker never has the feeling that he is leaving solid ground. ...

One simply has to admit that only very few sentences produced in speech have been memorized as such. Most sentences are composed at the spur of the moment.
                                                                    Paul (1920:109-110)

The notion of a *generative algorithm* is, understandably, still absent, and Paul is, in a way, still fumbling with the question of how an infinite production can result from a finite set of 'paradigms'. His psychological notion of analogy is clearly insufficient.[15] Yet the structural problem of grammar has been formulated. It will first be ignored by mainstream structuralist linguistics and has to wait to the 1940s to be picked up again by Zellig Harris in America (see 4.5.1).

It is curious to note that Paul was convinced that many of the questions that were posed should be solved in the context of psychological theory. Likewise, those of his contemporaries that invoked a 'social mind' as the repository of language appealed to some sort of social theory. Unfortunately, however, the disciplines of psychology and sociology had not yet developed to the point where they could have provided valid answers. As a consequence, the theorizing of Paul and other linguists at the time remained more speculative and intuition-based than would be deemed acceptable nowadays, despite their often surprising and acute insights into fundamental issues.

---

[15] Morpurgo-Davis (1978:39) and, following her, Graffi (1991:65) observe that Steinthal had also stressed the novelty of speech: 'Sentences do not lie in memory ready for use, as words do, only to be recalled. The mental mechanism, in this case, not only has to reproduce but also to produce. On the basis of remembered words new series, new sentences are formed'. (Steinthal 1860b:142). Steinthal, however, did not appeal to 'analogy', but to 'creation determined by laws' (Graffi 1991:66), and thus appears to have been closer to the algorithmic idea. A more detailed study, however, will be required to establish precisely what Steinthal, and similar authors of the period, had in mind.

- *Many linguists stay aloof*

Other eminent linguists, like Johannes Schmidt, kept a safe distance, though they sympathized with many or most of the ideas put forward by the Young Grammarians. Outside Germany there was less need to declare or decline allegiance, as the personal element was largely absent. Linguists like William Dwight Whitney and Maurice Bloomfield in America, Max Müller and Henry Sweet in England, Michel Bréal in France, Graziadio Ascoli in Italy, Karl Verner in Denmark, and Ferdinand de Saussure in Switzerland easily associated, to varying degrees, with the Young Grammarians' ideas without running the risk of being branded as party members.

- *The critics: Schuchardt*

There were also critics. A prominent, yet only apparent, critic was the classicist Georg Curtius, Brugmann and Leskien's teacher, who fell out with his pupils on personal grounds but still shared many of the Young Grammarians' ideas. The most notable real critic, however, was *Hugo Schuchardt* (1842-1927), professor of Romance philology first at Halle in Germany, then at Graz in Austria, where he stayed till his death. His mild and civil criticism is found in Schuchardt (1885), pointedly dedicated to the Young Grammarian Gustav Meyer.

Schuchardt's criticism is directed especially at the Young Grammarian principle of the exceptionless sound laws. He insists, correctly as we know now, that all speaking individuals show a certain range of variation in their pronunciation, and that the speech of many speakers even deviates systematically from what may be considered the norm. Moreover, contrary to what the Young Grammarians and many of their predecessors maintained,[16] situations of language contact are frequent and often result in real mixing of languages, involving grammar as well as lexical and phonological elements. In fact, linguistic 'mixing' is omnipresent, even in those rare speech communities that have no contact with other groups. For within every group there is always some amount of social stratification, which leads to phonetic and phonological differentiation, and consequently to mixing in the speech of individuals who adapt their speech to different situations and different

---

[16] Müller (1861:71) maintained: 'In the course of these considerations we had to lay down two axioms, to which we shall frequently have to appeal in the progress of our investigations. The first declares grammar to be the most essential element, and therefore the ground of classification in all languages which have produced a definite grammatical articulation; the second denies the possibility of a mixed language.' That is, allowance being made for lexical borrowing on any scale, the grammar (i.e. for Müller: flectional morphology; see above) of a language is never affected. 'We may form whole sentences in English consisting entirely of Latin or Romance words; yet whatever there is left of grammar in English bears unmistakeable traces of Teutonic workmanship' (Müller 1861:74-75). Modern Creolists think of Bickerton's (1981) theory of the innate 'bioprogram' for language, which allows for lexical substrate influences but not for grammatical substrate, i.e. borrowing from one or more native languages into a newly formed Creole. Schuchardt, as we see, was better informed than that.

audiences. Since every form of language is rule-governed, and the rules together form a system, every speaker must have at his disposal a network of interrelated systems, from which he chooses, more or less consistently, while speaking. But let us listen to Schuchardt himself:

> As far as we know from the observation of our own speech or of that of others, no individual speaks without variations, quite apart from successive stages in his speech. This endless language splitting goes hand in hand with endless language mixing. The impact of one dialect upon another, which for the Young Grammarians must lead to a violation of the exceptionless sound laws, and the ironing out of individual differences, which for the Young Grammarians must make exceptionless sound laws possible, these contrary processes are in fact part of the same overall mixing process. There is, however, no reason to assume that the continuous actions of centrifugal and centripetal forces should lead to such a degree of uniformity that no differences are left. True, the Young Grammarians allow for very minimal forms of variation, but they fail to take these into account in their theories, and this is, for a variety of reasons, a grave mistake. For first of all, the mere existence of even the smallest differences contradicts the impossibility of their occurrence, which is required by the Young Grammarian position.   Schuchardt (1885:10–11)

> According to the Young Grammarians, individual differences within a speech community can exist only with regard to the temporal order in which the sound change takes place; never should there be an internal clash within one individual. "As clearly pronounced and thus also conscious opposition," says Brugmann, "old and new can co-exist only in such a way that they are represented by different speech groups, whose mutual interaction is much less intensive than their internal interaction." But how can this be reconciled with Brugmann's earlier assumption of mother and daughter forms within the same dialect, yeah within the same individual? Within one dialect the 'old' and the 'new' appear not just according to age, but also according to sex, education, temperament, in short according to a most diverse set of parameters.   Schuchardt (1885:13)

> How strong is the influence of the school, even where public instruction is at a very low level! How widespread is the wish of the uneducated to speak like an educated person, of the provincial to speak like a city-dweller! Is it not so that with the marches of the military the Berlin *j* for *g* is now penetrating more and more into the heart of Germany? ... Sound change resulting from fashion, whether conscious or not and in any case arbitrary, often brings along further innovations. It can be applied incorrectly, may be stepped up further, or may call forth parallel sound changes. And if, finally, as has been attested historically, a phonetic idiosyncrasy of a socially dominant person, be it a king or a courtier or an actor, is voluntarily copied in their environment, or if it is forcibly imposed, as in the case of a teacher and his pupils, then, clearly, one must accept the possibility of an arbitrary origin of any sound change.   Schuchardt (1885:15)

> As said before, I take it that language mixing occurs even within the most homogeneous communities, and I disagree with Paul who can see such mixing only in the context of ethnic mixing, which, he says, is exceptional. But I object to Paul's view. On the one hand, in every sizeable population centre fluctuations are such that they may be characterized as "mixing" in the strict sense. Far from it "being impossible for differences to arise that are perceived as such," deviant dialects may well leave their clear imprints on the central dialect, which may even lose entirely its original character (as, for example, the dialect of Rome as spoken nowadays is a Tuscan dialect, which was not so five hundred years ago). ... On the other hand, even those cases which Paul accepts as genuine cases of language mixing are far

from exceptional. He accepts only cases "where, as a result of special historical circumstances, larger groups of people were moved out of their original habitat and thrown together with other groups". If we reckon back from the formation of the Romance languages to the first beginnings of the Roman people we see an almost uninterrupted series of manifold mixings, which had their influence not only on the grammars of the Romance languages but also on the grammar of Latin itself.

Schuchardt (1885:16)

Many try to harden the principle of exceptionlessness by creating a false opposition. According to Paul — who, however, assigns it no more than the value of a hypothesis — "whoever rejects it rejects the possibility of a truly scientific grammar". Or, to use the words of Kruszewski, the Young Grammarians put us in the position "either to accept exceptionless sound laws or to reject the possibility of any sound laws at all". To this I wish to observe, first, that deterrents have no place in science, and, secondly, that the dilemma is false, even if it is less crudely formulated. I would like to know who of all the pre-Young Grammarian or anti-Young Grammarian linguists, including my humble self, have ever looked upon and treated sound changes as chaotic. ... Their fundamental fallacy lies in the notion that there could possibly be any area of facts that would not be subjected to laws of some kind. One must, of course, take into consideration that within the various categories of facts there may be great variations in the complexity of the conditions to which the laws are subjected, ranging from the sheer coincidence of a pure chance game to the solid ordering of the mechanical world. ... But more amazing is the fact that they can, on the one hand, perceive so clearly the psychological basis of sound changes, the social character of language, the fluid boundaries of its spatial and temporal manifestations, and, on the other, insist so strongly on the principle of exceptionless sound laws. The Young Grammarians confuse "the very simple concept of law with that of the complex effects produced by a multitude of laws that work in concert and cooperate in a variety of ways" (Merlo). ... Yes, if I were forced to make use of the concept of absolute regularity in my confession, I would apply it not to the sound laws but to the occurrence of sporadic sound change, in the sense that every sound change is sporadic at some stage. If the opposing views are to be characterized by means of contrary expressions, I would say that one can speak of absolute versus relative regularity.   Schuchardt (1885:30-32)

In short, I cannot see the presentation of the Young Grammarians' principle as a radical change of direction in the history of linguistics, which would have placed it on a more secure and faster track. ... The history of this blinding sophism, which has brought about widespread confusion, is remarkable. It has its roots in the old view that separated language from man, gave it a life of its own, and was presented first in a romantic-mystical, then in a strictly scientific garb. The doctrine of the exceptionless sound laws, imposed entirely in the spirit of A. Schleicher if not actually proposed by him, enters the modern period as a remnant of the past. Nowadays we see linguistics as a human science, belonging to the humanities, and we no longer see language as a natural organism, but as a social product.

Schuchardt (1885:33-34)

I have indulged in such extensive quotations in order to show the force and the modernity of Schuchardt's views. In many ways he puts forward considerations and arguments that have a strong modern ring. Present-day advances in sociolinguistics, in particular regarding internal variation in speech communities and the lexical and grammatical effects of language contact,[17] have amply brought out the basic correctness of Schuchardt's views. In this perspective one understands why Schuchardt took such an extraordinary interest in pidgin and Creole languages. Without actually travelling around the world (he was an acknowledged hypochondriac and felt that his, probably largely imaginary, ailments did not allow him to travel), he collected innumerable data by correspondence (most of which awaits editing and publication), and thus became the father of Creole linguistics (Gilbert 1994).

The last of the Schuchardt quotes given above is particularly enlightening. Here Schuchardt actually puts his finger on the following internal contradiction of the Young Grammarian programme. The notion of exceptionless sound laws, conceived in the way they intended, only makes sense in the context of a language as a homogeneous system. But if one looks closely at the minutiae of everyday linguistic usage, as the Young Grammarians insisted one should do, one discovers precisely what Schuchardt saw: no language is a homogeneous system, and every language is a complex network of interrelated subsystems with inbuilt choices at many points, where a selection is made according to factors of situation, personal interaction, dialect background, attitude, emotion, etc. (cp. Seuren 1982). The idealization of an entirely homogeneous speech community may be useful in grammatical and lexical studies (although even there the enormous amount of internal variability within one language community must never be forgotten), it remains an idealization which is, in fact, unrealistic and incompatible with a phonetically realistic description of speech. If the notion of an exceptionless sound change is to make sense it must be limited to a well-defined set of rules within the bounds of a well-defined set of subsystems in the linguistic competence of a well-defined set of speakers. This was way beyond the possibilities of those days, as indeed of ours. But the Young Grammarians never fully admitted these restrictions, even though they were well aware of their stringency. As a result, their principle of exceptionless sound laws dwindled down, in practice, to little more than a statistical preponderance. But then again it must be said in their defence that their first principle, though false as a statement of fact, is useful as a methodological directive, as it forces the researcher to maximize regularity in his rule systems and keep exceptions down to a minimum, i.e. the normal procedure in any branch of scientific enquiry. If only the Young Grammarians had presented their first principle not as a statement of fact but as a guiding principle in setting up hypotheses and theories a great deal of misunderstanding would have been avoided.[18]

---

[17] Cp., for example, Dittmar (1976), which comments amply on the striking new insights gained as a result of Labov's sociolinguistic work, and Myers-Scotton (1993), which is the most convincing proof to date of the far-reaching effects of language mixing.

[18] For Sapir maximally regular sound change is a methodological principle, not a fact (1929:207):

> There are many who would be disposed to deny the psychological necessity of the regularity of sound change, but it remains true, as a matter of actual linguistic ex-

- *Verner's correction of Grimm's law*

At this point the reader will want to see a few examples to have a more lively picture of what the discussion is about. One striking example is a correction of Grimm's law discovered by the Dane *Karl Adolf Verner* in 1875. As was said in section 2.4 above, Grimm's law is seriously flawed. One problem is the fact that old intervocalic *t* is sometimes German *d*, as in *Bruder* ('brother'), which is in accordance with Grimm's law, but sometimes also *t*, as in *Vater* ('father'), which contradicts the law. Verner found that this exception is only apparent, as German intervocalic *t* occurs when the vowel after *t* carried the original word accent, whereas German intervocalic *d* occurs when the original accent was on the preceding vowel. This is no longer visible in German itself since Germanic had variable word accent. Thus, the Greek word for 'father' is *patér*, with accent after *t*; hence German *Vater*, not **vader*. This discovery was hailed as a further confirmation of the Young Grammarian point of view, as it reduced exceptions.

- *From Latin* pōpulus *to Italian* pioppo

Other examples, however, show the weakness of the Young Grammarians' first principle. Consider the following examples taken from Italian. First take the words *pioppo* ('poplar') and *pópolo* ('people'). The former derives from Latin *pōpulus*, with long *o*, the latter from *pŏpulus*, with short *o*. Both forms

---

perience, that faith in such regularity has been the most successful approach to the historic problems of language.

Other, earlier authors are equally critical of the Young Grammarians on similar grounds. Andresen (1990:184) quotes Bréal (1893:21):

> The phonetic laws act blindly if we admit a set of conditions that are never realized anywhere; viz. a perfectly homogeneous population coming into no contact with the outside world, learning everything by living and oral tradition, without any books, without any monuments of religion, — a population in which everyone should be of the same social condition, in which there should be no difference of rank, of learning, nor even of age or sex. No sooner do you leave aside pure theory, to place yourself in presence of the reality, than you see the reasons appear which make the phonetic laws open to exceptions.

She rightly sets this off against Chomsky's (1965:3-4) unrealistic idealized notion of a speech community:

> Linguistic theory is concerned primarily with an ideal speaker-listener, in a completely homogeneous speech-community, who knows its language perfectly and is unaffected by such grammatically irrelevant conditions as memory limitations, distractions, shifts of attention and interest, and errors (random or characteristic) in applying his knowledge of the language in actual performance. This seems to me to have been the position of the founders of modern general linguistics, and no cogent reason for modifying it has been offered.

Chomsky thus appropriates, on historical grounds, the idealization of homogeneity as the only legitimate point of view in linguistic theory. This view is not, however, supported by the facts, which show 'founders of linguistics', like Schuchardt, who regard the tendency towards internal variation as an essential feature of any human language. It is, moreover, harmful to linguistic theory in that the notion of data gets obscured (see 4.6.3).

are irregular, viewed against the background of the majority of cases, which behave like the following:

Latin:		Italian:	
spĕculum	>	specchio	('mirror')
cōpula	>	coppia	('couple')
bāculum	>	bacchio	('stick')
ŏculus	>	occhio	('eye')
auriculum	>	orecchio	('ear')
duplus	>	doppio	('double')
măcula	>	macchia	('stain')

First, the unaccented vowel before *l* is deleted: *spĕclum, cōpla*, etc. Then the voiceless plosive before *l* is geminated and, probably also at this stage, length distinctions in vowels get neutralized and masculine and neuter endings become -*o*: *specclo, coppla*, etc. (The consonantal doubling is the result of a more general rule, as appears from, e.g., *publicus > pubblico* 'public', *labrum > labbro* 'lip', *aqua > acqua* 'water'). Finally, *l* is vocalized into *i*: *specchio, coppia*, etc. Since the length of the accented vowel is irrelevant for this process (in some of the words above it is long, in others short), one would also expect *pōpulus > poppio* and *pŏpulus > poppio*. Instead, we find *pioppo* and *pópolo*, respectively. Is there a reason to be found? Maybe. The word *pópolo* has the appearance of a late scholarly loan from Latin, as, for example, *ostácolo*, not **ostacchio*, from *obstāculum* ('obstacle) or *cúpola*, not **coppia* or **cuppia*, from Latin *cūpula* ('cupola'). But the word for 'people' will hardly have belonged to the elevated sociolect of such scholarly borrowings (in the other Romance languages it clearly did not). Perhaps it was mostly used, in the early Middle Ages, in official Latin texts and not in the emerging vernacular, a factor that may have stood in the way of a regular development. *Pioppo* is clearly the result of a metathesis from *popplo* to *ploppo*, hence *pioppo* (cp. *plenus > pieno* ('full')). It is true that Brugmann excluded metathesis phenomena from the first principle (see the quote above). Yet one wonders what could have been wrong with the expected form *poppio*. Was it farmer's language, or a Northern dialect (since that is where poplars grow most in Italy)? Note that another tree name likewise behaves irregularly: Latin *méspĭlus* ('medlar') became Italian *néspolo*, and not the expected **mespio*. Another, curious, example is the Latin word *cūpa* ('hollow vessel, cup'), which became the Italian noun *coppa* ('cup'), but also the adjective *cupo* ('hollow'). Therefore, if Italian is taken as a homogeneous whole there are no sound laws but only statistically relevant generalizations with exceptions.

• *An example from Mauritian Creole*

Another small but striking example comes from the French-based Creole language of the Indian Ocean island Mauritius, Mauritian Creole (MC). Among the many phonological regularities in the derivation of MC words from French is the following tidy principle: French nasal vowels remain nasal, as in:

French:		Mauritian Creole:	
dans	>	dã	('in')
dance	>	dãs	('dance')
lampe	>	lalãp[19]	('lamp')
pain	>	dipẽ	('bread'; see note 19)
brun	>	brẽ	('brown person, Indian')
tomber	>	tõbé	('fall')

But when the French nasal is followed by a word-final voiced plosive (*d, b* or *g*), the final plosive is dropped, the MC vowel is denasalized and the homorganic *n, m* or *ŋ* (spelled *ng*) becomes a sharply pronounced consonant:

French:		Mauritian Creole:	
bande	>	bàn	('group' → plural prefix)
vende	>	vàn	('sell'; internal VP-form)
Inde	>	Lèn	('India'; see note 19)
tombe	>	tòm	('fall'; internal VP-form)
bombe	>	bòm	('bomb')
langue	>	lalàng	('tongue, language'; see note 19)
ong[l]e	>	zòng	('nail'; < *les ongles*, see note 19)

However, French *main* ('hand') does not give the expected **lamẽ* but *lamé*, French *comment* ('how') does not give **kumã* but *kumá*, and the indefinite article *un* does not become **ẽ* but *èn*, as if the French form had been **inde* (cp. MC *Lèn*, 'India'), and *demain* ('tomorrow') is either *dimẽ* or *dimé*. Why these exceptions? Is it frequency? The answer is that we do not know, and will probably never know. The social fabric that produced Mauritian Creole will have had its unrecorded, and hence irretrievable, chance disturbances, some of which are reflected in what we now perceive as exceptions to sound laws.

- *Labov's study on Martha's Vineyard*
As regards singular sound laws, the remarkable study by Labov (1972) on the centralization of (ay) and (aw) on the island of Martha's Vineyard, Massachusetts, is exceptional in that it provides a minutely detailed and hence realistic description of a process of phonetic change over thirty years. Labov

---

[19] Frequently occurring MC nouns tend to incorporate the French article: *lekor* (<Fr. le corps, 'body'), *lakaz* (<Fr. la case, 'house'). Frequent mass nouns often incorporate the partitive particle: *dilo* (<Fr. de l'eau, 'water'), *disã* (<Fr. du sang, 'blood'), *dipẽ* (<Fr. du pain, 'bread'). Nouns that occur mostly in the plural incorporate the plural article: *zãfã* (<Fr. les enfants, 'child'), *zorey* (<Fr. les oreilles, 'ear').

found a statistical pattern of mean value shift around a target sound, in correlation with age, sex and social attitudes:

> It was concluded that a social value had been, more or less arbitrarily, associated with the centralization of (ay) and (aw): to the extent that an individual felt able to claim and maintain status as a native Vineyarder, he adopted increasing centralization of (ay) and (aw). Sons who had tried to earn a living on the mainland, and afterwards returned to the island, developed an even higher degree of centralization than their fathers had used. But to the extent that a Vineyarder abandoned his claim to stay on the island and earn his living there, he also abandoned centralization and returned to the standard uncentralized forms.   Labov (1972:170)

One may imagine that, after a while, a perceptually distinct acoustic target develops, which in turn has assimilation effects on neighbouring sounds. When that happens we have a real sound change. And if the change in question affects all words that satisfy the phonological conditions stated for it we have an exceptionless sound law in the Young Grammarian sense. But who can trace to such detail the conditions for the innumerable sound laws that have been proposed?

Truly exceptionless sound laws probably do occur, but only within narrowly defined parameters of time, space, sociolect and interactive setting. Unfortunately, for most cases in the past it is now entirely impossible to reconstruct the precise values on all those parameters, which makes checking of the Young Grammarians' first principle practically impossible.

- *Schmidt's wave theory*

The fact that sound changes are spatially limited and do not, on the whole, coincide with the spread of an official standard language made *Johannes Schmidt* realize that Schleicher's metaphor of a 'family tree' (Stammbaum) to describe the development of languages was unrealistic and misleading. In Schmidt (1872) it is shown, with a wealth of examples and in refreshingly clear language, that the sound laws known in those days were all geographically restricted and virtually all of them in different ways. In principle, each sound law has its own 'territory'. This view has become known as Schmidt's *wave theory* (Wellentheorie), as opposed to Schleicher's *family tree theory*. Schmidt thus, in fact, introduced the concept, if not the term, *isogloss*. This would seem to destroy the notion of a single language spoken over a well-delimited area. The best one can make of such a notion, if the territorial point of view is to prevail, is to try and find bundles of isoglosses which would enclose a relatively homogeneous language area.

Schmidt's wave theory, though essentially correct, does not take into account the sociolinguistic fact that, as a result of state-run school education, social prestige of government circles, and other comparable factors, nationally imposed standard varieties of languages tend to develop along with organized states. Often the linguistic status of such national standards is so robust that they have a strong influence on the vernacular dialects. It thus seems that the two views, the dialect view and the monolithic language view, with the corresponding wave theory and the family tree theory, both cover a complementary part of linguistic reality.

Though Schmidt, as was said above, stayed away from the Young Grammarians' movement, his ideas are clearly similar to theirs. The fact that Schmidt's publication antedates the Young Grammarian manifesto of 1878 by six years shows that the angry youngsters were less innovative than they themselves claimed. Other sound laws had been proposed before the Young Grammarian outburst: Grassmann's law on aspirates in Greek and Sanskrit (1863), Verner's correction of Grimm's law (1875), etc.[20] It is, therefore, fair to say that what the Young Grammarians proposed had been on its way for some time and would probably have gained prominence in linguistics anyway.

- *Appraisal of the Young Grammarian movement*

We must agree with Schuchardt that the hue and cry around the Young Grammarian movement was largely unnecessary. The important point is not that the Young Grammarians appeared, but that comparative philology was up against technical and empirical problems of a magnitude that still transcended their powers. An adequate treatment of sound changes requires, besides a solid knowledge of phonetics, a reasonable phonological theory and a sociolinguistic machinery of analysis and description. These were simply not at their disposal, or anyway not to a sufficient degree. In these respects essential progress has been made during this century. Modern phonological theory makes for much improved descriptions of sound changes in terms of sound production and perception, and of their effect on the overall phonological system of the languages concerned. But the Young Grammarians lacked adequate notions of structure and system. It took 20th century structuralism to develop them, painstakingly and still far from satisfactorily. Then, the Young Grammarians lacked sociological insights and techniques. Nowadays, sociology and sociolinguistics have made it possible to produce detailed descriptions of the social and geographical spread of sound changes. They have also provided more detailed and hence more adequate notions of language, dialect, sociolect and idiolect, with the result that 19th century terminology like 'the life of language' (das Leben der Sprache) or 'the popular spirit' (der Volksgeist) now appear as half-mystical reifications of complex processes that are finally opening up to empirical research.

The Young Grammarians were less a break with than the culmination of 19th century comparative philology. In so far as there was a break with their predecessors and those of their contemporaries that did not follow them, it was largely to do with their notions of methodology and philosophy of science. They rejected idle reifications (such as 'the spirit of the people' or 'the organism of language') and speculative reconstructions of 'original' linguistic forms, and proposed greater reliance on actually attested forms and on detailed study of how these changed into the modern ones. They also replaced

---

[20] Collinge (1985), which sums up all the important sounds laws of Indo-European, shows no break at all between the period before and after 1878.

the 'language-as-an-organism' view with the position that a language resides in the individual minds of its speakers. As such they represent a move towards a more positivistic, fact-based conception of science. The causal questions they asked were still largely historical, not functional: 'How did the changes take place?' and not 'How do the forms function?'. The latter question was reserved for the twentieth century.

We will now take leave of comparative philology, though important progress was made after 1900. New Indo-European languages were discovered (Tocharian) or deciphered (Hittite, Mycenaean B), which led to a broader data base for the theories concerned and hence to more solid results. Moreover, significant progress has been made towards a charting of the historical relationships and classification of non-Indo-European languages as well. We will not discuss these matters here because the 20th century advances in comparative philology have, so far, not influenced modern theorizing about grammar and meaning to any significant degree (though one may well feel that they should have). This is not so for 19th century comparative philology, which led straight to 20th century structuralism and hence to the gamut of modern theories of grammar. The study of meaning did not, unfortunately, benefit in the same way from the linguistic achievements of the 19th century. Semantics, 'formal semantics' that is, was destined to grow out of philosophy and logic, and was not to meet up with grammar till quite recently. But before we can begin to discuss these 20th century developments in grammar and meaning we must first look at what the 19th century did for the psychology of language.

2.6 The psychological aspect

2.6.1 Psychological grammar

It is no coincidence that the 19th century had a profound interest in mental phenomena generally, in individuals as well as in groups, and the psychological side of language in particular. Romanticism had brought about a reappraisal of direct experience, and it was therefore to be expected that those who studied language would seek to do so against the background of how language is experienced.

In the beginning, psychology did not exist as a separate institutionalized discipline: that gradually happened towards the end of the 19th century. But a great deal of psychological thinking was going on. The psychological ideas of the 19th century differed in several respects from what is currently held nowadays. First, the mind was equated almost entirely with consciousness. The notion, considered so important now, of automatic computational processes, hidden from introspection or awareness, was virtually unknown. All, or nearly all, that takes place in the mind, also called soul or spirit, was thought to be conscious or readily brought to consciousness. Moreover, the mind, or soul, or spirit, was taken to be non-corporeal, spiritual, of a separate order of being, distinct from concrete matter.

- *Herbartian associationism*

It is not our purpose to write a history of 19th century psychology, but it is important to point to the fact that within this general frame there were, on the whole, two opposing schools of thought. One prominent view, going back to the German philosopher *Johann Friedrich Herbart* (1776-1841), is called *associationism*. It is based on the idea that mental life is governed by associative complexes of representations (Vorstellungen), which are stored in memory and may thus become dormant but never get lost entirely. If there is an unconscious compartment in the mind it is shallow and its contents can be brought back to consciousness by associations (not unlike the Freudian idea of the subconscious). Thoughts were taken to be the result of the coming together of representations.

The Young Grammarians, as well as most linguistic theorists, in particular Steinthal and Paul, favoured Herbartian associationism. For them, the study of grammar was largely based on the idea that whatever combinations of elements are made by speakers are matched by, and perhaps caused by, 'movements of the spirit'. Grammar was thus seen as, in large part, caused by general psychological processes, though room was left also for some amount of feedback from language back to the mind. Grammatical constructions follow patterns and processes of thinking, which may in turn be influenced by them.

For example, if a German speaker places the non-finite part of the verb at the end of the sentence, separating it from the finite verb form, this was taken to reflect a way of thinking whereby a unitary concept is split and one part is held in abeyance. On the other hand, the fact that this kind of construction has become part of the German language could also influence the way German speakers think, vague as that notion necessarily had to remain.

- *Wundtian volitionism*

Another perspective, developed by Wilhelm Wundt by the end of the century and generally called Wundtianism or volitionism, implied that all mental life is by definition conscious, and governed not just by sensations and association of representations but also by other factors such as, in particular, volition, but also sentiments and other affects.

Wundt considered a thought, or 'total representation' (Gesamtvorstellung), to be the primary element, preceding its subsequent division into component parts. This division was taken to proceed in steps – binarily branching steps in intellectually more developed minds and societies, and multiply branching steps in the case of less developed, 'primitive', minds and societies. This idea of decomposition of 'total representations' or thoughts lay at the bottom of his structural analysis of sentences and word groups in terms of hierarchical tree structures (see 4.4.5).

Wundt incorporated some of the central ideas of the Port Royal movement of the 1660s, and his psychology is thus in part rationalistic. But he did modify Port Royal thinking in important respects. In the Port Royal view thinking consists of 'conceiving', 'judging' and 'reasoning', in that order, with logic being the schematic account of these three processes. Wundt, however, saw the judging, or propositional, element as primary, the other two being derived from it. In both theories, the position of logic was secure, as logic was regarded as the formal account of the three elements of thinking, no matter which was considered primary and which derived. Wundtianism, therefore, had the support of logic and had therefore the advantage of being a little more precise than Herbartian associationism, which had no formal theory to back it up.

- *The debate between Delbrück and Wundt in 1901*

In either view, the study of grammar was highly dependent on notions of a psychological nature, which were in part unclear and largely untestable. The drive, during the first half of the 20th century, to make grammar 'autonomous' is to be seen in this light. The idea was that grammar had to stand on its own feet, no matter what psychological theory one might otherwise feel inclined to embrace.

Precisely this issue was part of a highly interesting and relevant controversy between the Young Grammarian Berthold Delbrück and the psychologist Wilhelm Wundt around the turn of the century. In his (1901), Delbrück had mounted a wholesale, but extremely polite, attack on Wundt's linguistic ideas, criticizing him on almost all counts where language was concerned, in particular with regard to the relevance of psychological theorizing to the study of grammar, but also on account of data-collecting from exotic languages (favoured by Wundt), the relevance of sign languages, the psychological basis of sound change, the nature of the sentence, and the origin of language.

What concerns us here is the first of the points mentioned: the relevance of psychological theorizing to the study of grammar. Delbrück's position in this respect was that the (historical) grammarian has no need to choose between different psychological theories, as all that counts to him is the development of grammatical constructions. And for this purpose Herbartian associationism will do as well as Wundtian volitionism. Delbrück thus defends an early version of structuralist 'autonomous' grammar, albeit in historical terms.

Wundt's reply (1901) was immediate, and equally polite. He begins by saying:

> I strongly doubt that Delbrück would feel able to agree with any psychologist making statements to the effect that it makes no difference for the interpretation of a linguistic fact *how* it came into being historically, provided its alleged origin remains within the realm of the possible. He would rightly reply that history does not allow for a double truth, that the historian, and therefore also the historian of language, should rather show how things *really* happened, not how they might have happened in some fictional world. The psychologist must, therefore, show how the real, not any possibly thinkable, historical development should be interpreted psychologically.   Wundt (1901:10-11)

Then he continues, commenting on the practical consequences of a theoretical choice:

Delbrück will no doubt reply that he speaks as a linguist, not as a psychologist. ... In the battle of psychological theories he prefers the role of an impartial spectator, who rejects unjustified psychological claims when they conflict with the history of language, but otherwise tries, in a neutral and possibly sympathetic way, to make the best use of whatever psychological research may have to contribute to the study of language. From this perspective, the question is more likely to be: What is the *practical* use of psychological results? This question is not identical with the other one: What is *true* and what isn't? Wundt (1901:14)

Wundt then gives a few examples, to do with semantic change, and also with the semantics of nominal cases. His comment here is as follows:

I don't doubt that Delbrück himself will acknowledge that his point of view is untenable as soon as he applies to psychology the two fundamental principles that linguistics claims for itself, namely that, first, there can be only *one* truth, not several, ... and, secondly, one has to analyse every complex of facts as thoroughly as is possible, which means that one cannot be satisfied with merely the simplest practically usable solution. Present-day linguistics, however, does not in general do that, a negligence that is no doubt due more to the less than satisfactory state of modern psychology than to any fault on the part of the linguists. Wundt (1901:17)

Claiming relevance for psychology also in matters of history ('For the causes that determine the historical development of language must, essentially and to a large extent, be *mental* powers' (1901:19)), Wundt then stresses the different roles of Herbartian and Wundtian psychology in the study of language:

... put briefly, in the case of Herbartian psychology what is at issue is an application of psychology *to* the facts of language, whereas my efforts are about gaining a psychology *from* the facts of language. Wundt (1901:21)

He also complains about the lack of recognition of his psychology as a proper empirical science:

One recognizes the need for a scientific psychology, but scientific psychology is still not looked upon as an autonomous empirical science that has to occupy itself also, among other things, with the facts of language history. At best it is considered an auxiliary tool that can be used in linguistics whenever that seems useful, just like one uses a Remington or a Hammond typewriter, without that making any difference for the actual purpose of the writing. In the same way one might use Herbartian or any other form of psychology, as long as the linguistic facts are subsumed equally well under this or under that theory. Wundt (1901:17-18)

Although Delbrück, according to the opening words of his preface, directs his comparative essay more to the general public than to philosophers, and has, therefore, striven to keep it as simple as possible, I would wish, on the contrary, that his introductory chapter be read not only by linguists but also, and especially, by philosophers and psychologists. And precisely because his exposé is so elementary that it could not possibly be misunderstood even by a philosopher, I would hope that my closer psychological colleagues would gain from it a better insight into what I take as the basic tenets and goals of psychology. I do not, of course, expect anyone to believe that every single psychological observation I think I have made or every conclusion I have drawn from them is correct. But I would wish that no presuppositions were attributed to me that I consider alien to my work, and that the purely empirical character of my treatment of psychological questions would not be turned into its opposite. Wundt (1901:23-24)

This debate is as topical now as it was a hundred years ago. If we abstract from the historical dimension that permeates the discussion, we see that Wundt advocates realism, in the sense current in the philosophy of science, and hence poses the question of psychological reality, a question that neither he nor Delbrück is able to solve or even elucidate in any empirically profitable way. Delbrück's flight into instrumentalism (the 'practical' use of psychology) fails to convince Wundt, and probably most modern readers as well.

• *The autonomy of grammar in structuralism and in generative linguistics*
It was in this context that the linguistic structuralism of the early 20th century insisted on the autonomy of grammar with respect to the workings of the mind: any appeal to psychology was called the dirty name of 'psychologism', which implied the notion that rules of grammar are a direct reflex of 'mental movements' or thinking processes. Later, with the rise of generative grammar, the question of psychological reality or plausibility came up again (see 4.6.1), but now the concept of mind had changed radically. Now the mind is seen as an enormously complex computing plant, almost entirely hidden from introspection and whose only conscious compartment, accessible to introspection, is afforded by what may be called metaphorically an interface between 'user' and machine (though the nature of the 'user' still remains extremely ill-understood). Modern grammatical theory performs a balancing act between the autonomy of grammar and the claim to psychological reality. In contrast to the 19th century, when grammar and 'mental movements' were thought to go hand in hand, in the late 20th century a safe distance is kept between the two, but it is still largely unclear how they should be related. Nowadays, linguists and psycholinguists alike tend to posit a link between formal grammatical theories on the one hand and psycholinguistic experimental data on the other, the theory being supposed to feed the experiments. Yet in actual practice there is little traffic going on between the two disciplines. One may therefore say with some justification that the status and relevance of grammatical theory with regard to the mental structures and processes involved in speech are still ill-defined. And so are the status and relevance of psycholinguistic experimental results with regard to linguistic theory.

2.6.2 Wilhelm von Humboldt

Outside the specific realm of grammar an extensive literature existed in the 19th century dealing with more general questions of the psychology of language, such as the relation between language and thinking and their possible mutual influence, or the relation between language and culture, or language and logic. We now pass on to a discussion of Wilhelm von Humboldt, whose ideas about some of these questions have been very influential.

The German amateur philosopher-linguist *Wilhelm von Humboldt* (1767-1835) is best known for his voluminous introduction to three hefty volumes entitled *Ueber die Kawi-Sprache auf der Insel Java* (On the Kawi Language on the Island of Java), published posthumously between 1836 and 1840 in the

Proceedings of the Royal Academy of Berlin. The introduction was also published separately, in 1836, as *Ueber die Verschiedenheit des menschlichen Sprachbaues und ihren Einfluß auf die geistige Entwickelung des Menschengeschlechts* (On the diversity of human language-structure and its influence on the mental development of mankind).

- *Life*

Wilhelm von Humboldt, elder brother of the famous scientist and explorer Alexander, was a wealthy man who did not need to work for a living. He studied law in Göttingen and at the same time read much literature, philosophy and history, wishing to cultivate his mind. From 1797 till 1801 he lived in Paris, a city he admired and loved. It was there that he developed his taste for language and languages, strongly influenced by the French intellectual climate of the day, in particular the philosophy of the Enlightenment and the Encyclopédie. Diderot and de Condillac were among his admired authors. From 1802 till 1808 he was accredited to the Vatican as Prussian diplomat, after which he spent many years as a high official in the Ministry of the Interior in Berlin, in charge of the education section. As such he was the main force behind the foundation of the university that now bears his name. He also formulated the principles that have guided classical secondary education, the 'Gymnasium', in Germany till the present day. In 1819, after a brief period as Prussian ambassador to London he retired from public service, to devote himself entirely to his academic pursuits. He wrote an enormous amount but published little, due to what he himself saw as his incapacity to put into orderly writing the complex, many-sided and ever developing stream of thought that went through his mind. In fact, his style of writing is turgid, often vague and imbued with a mysticism that borders on the obscurantist. The many volumes containing his (largely unfinished) writings (Leitzmann 1907) were published long after his death, which occurred in 1835.

- *Language, culture and thought; language as 'energeia'; superior and inferior languages*

Humboldt's main interest was in the relation between the forces of language, culture and thought. For him, this relation is dynamic, with each of the three forces influencing each other and jointly determining as well as being determined by the degree of evolution and civilisation achieved by each language community. His most famous thesis is that a language is not a static product but a living dynamism, or, in his Greek-derived terminology, not an 'ergon' but an 'energeia'. The original impetus for mankind to develop languages was artistic and aesthetic: man's innate creativity had to find an outlet, which was found in language. But each nation developed the language that suited its 'spirit', its socially and racially determined patterns of thought. All languages conform to a 'universal grammar', with universal categories and rules. Yet, at the same time, languages, or rather their speakers, differ in the way they exploit the possibilities afforded by this universal grammar. Some communities, which excelled in intelligence and creativity, developed sophisticated languages with a great deal of morphological inflection and well-determined categories. Other communities delivered inferior linguistic products, due to their inferior intelligence and culture. Chinese, American Indian languages, Malay, for example, may have their charm and possible other merits but they cannot compete with the classical languages of western civilisation as regards clarity, culture, sophistication. Thought and language are inseparable. Yet one often finds that a grammatical construction expresses the underlying thought in a disorderly way. One must, therefore, distinguish between the 'outer form' of a language (its 'surface structure'), and its 'inner form', a difficult and vague term best taken to stand both for semantic structure or thought structure and for the innate language faculty.

- *Humboldt's intellectual roots*

Humboldt's ideas and ideology derived in part from 18th century German philosophers and poets and in part from the Parisian intellectual climate around 1800, which was dominated by the French Encyclopedists and the philosophies of the French Revolution. There is a great deal of literature about Humboldt's intellectual and ideological roots (see for example Heeschen 1977 and Aarsleff's introduction to Peter Heath's 1988 translation of Humboldt (1836)). According to some, he was influenced by Kant (whom he never read), and according to others he wasn't. It is certain that his ideas were shaped by the poet-historian Friedrich Schiller, whom he admired to exaltation, and by the philosopher Johann Gottfried Herder, who, as a young man, published a highly influential romantic essay on the origin of language (Herder 1772). It is equally certain that he was strongly influenced by the French Ideologues, in particular de Condillac (see 2.2.3).

Heeschen (1977) correctly stresses the fact that Humboldt's ideas of language creation were primarily aesthetic: for Humboldt, the first beginnings of language lay in the urge to express and achieve poetic beauty, and likewise for the ultimate end of language, which for him was art. We saw in 2.3.4 above that the idea of the poetic origin of language derives, via Herder, from the early 18th century Neapolitan philosopher Giambattista Vico.

As regards the more mundane aspects of language, Humboldt added a strong evaluative bias, in that he insisted that some languages and cultures are superior to others. In his eyes, languages with flectional morphology were both the expression and the source of superior intellect and civilisation. In fact one may say that his life's work was dedicated to the bolstering of this notion of inequality among languages and peoples.

- *Linguistic prejudice: inflectional languages tend to be superior*

For Humboldt, the languages and cultures that took part in the coming about of the modern culture of Western Europe were the apogee of human nature. He idolized Sanskrit, Greek and Latin, and despised Chinese. For him, Sanskrit was the most perfect language in history, closely followed by Greek, Latin and the Romance languages, all languages with well-developed flectional morphologies. Those Western European languages that shed their flectional morphology were saved by the fact that 'the "staunch and sturdy races" of Western Europe have languages of such energetic maturity that they can cast away inflections without losing their capacity for continued creativity' (Aarsleff in Heath 1988:xxix; cp. also Heeschen 1972:86). The languages of Eastern Europe, on the contrary, found no grace in his eyes, even though many of them have well-developed flectional morphologies as well.

- *Cultural prejudice*

This obvious partiality shows that one can say without exaggeration that Humboldt had a fundamentally chauvinist mind. Despite his extensive studies of exotic languages and cultures (his widely travelled brother Alexander provided him with much of the material he used), his attitude shows a basic Eurocentrism and cultural arrogance. Some (e.g. Aarsleff in Heath 1988) even level the charge of racism. In this context one must not forget that racial and nationalist prejudices were rife in the western world of the early 19th century, not only in Germany but also in other parts of Europe. Yet there were also strong currents of opinion that went the other way: the philosophy of the 'Noble Savage' was omnipresent, and many prominent intellectuals knew perfectly well the hazards of imposing value scales on races or nations. Humboldt's own Prussia was known for the harsh discipline exacted by the authorities within the constraints of a society divided by strict class distinctions and riddled with moral prejudices. In this cultural context Humboldt, for all his knowledge and great international experience, favoured views which are now no longer acceptable in polite society. Colleagues, for example the American students of Amerindian languages *John Pickering* and *Peter S. Duponceau* (see 2.3.2 and 4.1), pointed out to him that his ideas on Western European superiority were morally and intellectually indefensible (Andresen 1990:109, 229). But he would not give in (Aarsleff in Heath 1988:lxii-lxiii). Since he has been such an enormously influential figure both his followers and his critics are visibly finding it difficult to provide a historically correct and unbiassed assessment.

- *Humboldt's main concern ideological*

One probably has to say that Humboldt, unlike his more professional contemporaries in linguistics, did not primarily pursue an empirical goal. It would seem that his main interest did not lie in formulating answers to empirical questions about language development and language structure but in establishing the superiority of European languages and culture. His ultimate aim, one feels, was not scientific but ideological, the shoring up of preconceived mythological, philosophical and ideological notions. This would be a mere detail of history were it not for the enormous influence that Humboldt has had not only in linguistics but, in a much more general sense, in the shaping of the German educational system with its inbuilt values, and thus of German culture in general. If we point a critical finger at certain traits in his views that would ostracize him nowadays, it is not in the first place the historical figure of Humboldt that we aim at but rather the disquieting fact that the Humboldt reception, as a historical phenomenon, has not been more critical.[21] What we do criticise him for directly is his obscure, even obscurantist style of thinking and of writing and his habit of putting forward contrary ideas side by side.[22]

• *The Humboldt-Sapir-Whorf hypothesis*

The famous Humboldt-Sapir-Whorf hypothesis holds that people's thinking patterns are determined at least in part by their language. It is often said, not without reason, that this hypothesis suffers from lack of falsifiability and that no proper empirical access to the questions involved has so far been found. Be that as it may, Humboldt himself was hardly a supporter of the hypothesis that is called after him. For him, it is in the first place the 'inner destiny' of a nation that determines the kind of language that will befall to it by 'an involuntary emanation of the spirit' (Heath 1988:24). After that, the nation in question may pull itself up by an 'uplifting of the spirit which cannot always be explained' (Heath 1988:35), but it will always be constrained by the language it has originally developed:[23]

---

[21] Some authors are still finding it difficult to come to terms with the less palatable aspects of Humboldt's work and influence. For example, Trabant (1990:235-239) is at pains to exonerate Humboldt. While fully admitting Humboldt's Eurocentric élitism and even racism, he defends him by saying (a) that Humboldt's different evaluations of languages are comparable to the normal procedure of assigning different marks to schoolchildren, according to their different achievements; (b) that the rest of Europe, France in particular, was not free either from racist or nationalist prejudices; and (c) that Humboldt's undoubted racism was tempered and counterbalanced by more enlightened ideas about the fundamental equality of mankind. The last point is no doubt correct: Humboldt is capable of changing colour from one sentence to the next (which justifies the charge of inconsistency). Yet one gets the definite impression that he is only covering his tracks, and that his ideas were fundamentally of the unsavoury kind attributed to him by authors like Aarsleff. For the rest, Trabant's defence of Humboldt is a poor one when one considers (a) that Humboldt was strictly partial and favoured the languages of the nations he favoured, overriding his own criteria; (b) that a teacher who assigns bad marks on account of race or ethnic origin does not follow normal practice at all, at least not what we would like to consider normal practice; and (c) that the fact that other nations had their share of racism as well does not obliterate the other fact that nowhere else has such a prominent position been given to a man promoting ideas of racial and national inequality. This is something I think we should accept and recognize calmly and with wisdom.

[22] Even Hovdhaugen provided me with the following quote from Thomsen (1902:56), who commented thus on Humboldt (1836):

> And yet, with all recognition of the work and all admiration for the genial thoughts that we find in his works, one cannot, having put great effort in the attempt to understand his philosophy of language, from a purely linguistic point of view, escape the impression of something that is so far from our more empirical ideas about language and is characterized by something so abstract and unreal, at times even mystical, that one finds it difficult now to understand fully the meaning of it, or even to understand the influence it apparently had on the development of linguistics.

[23] Quotes from Humboldt (1836) are from the 1988 translation by Heath, which, however, frequently needs correction. I have, therefore, felt free to correct where necessary.

It is not just a matter of how many concepts a language designates with its own words. This occurs automatically if it otherwise follows the true path marked out for it by nature, and it is not the aspect from which it must first be judged. Its authentic and essential efficacy in man rests upon his thinking and thinkingly creative power itself, and is immanent and constitutive in a far deeper sense. Questions like whether and to what extent it promotes clarity and correct order among concepts, or puts difficulties in the way of this; whether it retains the inherent perceivable perspicuity of the ideas conveyed into the language from the world-view; whether, through the euphony of its tones, it works harmoniously and soothingly, or again energetically and upliftingly, upon feeling and sentiment – in these and in many other such moods of the whole system of thought and feeling lies that which gives it its true advantages and determines its influence on spiritual evolution ('Geistesentwicklung'). But this rests upon the totality of its original design, upon its organic structure, its individual form. Nor do civilisation and culture, which themselves enter only at a later date, pass over it in vain. The clarity and precision of language gain through the habit of expressing extended and refined ideas, perspicuity is enhanced in a heightened level of imagination, and euphony profits from the judgement and superior requirements of a more practised ear. *But this whole process of improved language-making can only go on within the limits prescribed to it by the original design of the language.* A nation can make a more imperfect language into a tool for the production of ideas to which it would not have given the original incentive, but cannot remove the inner restrictions which have once been deeply embedded therein. To that extent even the highest cultivation remains ineffective. Even what later ages have added from without is appropriated by the original language, and modified according to its laws.

Heath (1988:33-34; italics mine)

This is a far cry from what is now taken to be the Humboldt-Sapir-Whorf hypothesis.[24] In fact, Humboldt stresses the unity of language in general as much as he does the diversity of individual languages, and the influence of the mind upon language as much as the other way round:

Language, indeed, arises from a depth of human nature which everywhere forbids us to regard it as a true product and creation of peoples. It possesses an autonomy that visibly declares itself to us, though inexplicable in its nature, and, seen from this aspect, is no production of activity, but an involuntary emanation of the spirit, no work of nations but a gift fallen to them by their inner destiny. ... It is no empty play upon words if we speak of *language* as arising in autonomy solely from itself and divinely free, but of *languages* as bound and dependent on the nations to which they belong. For they have entered into specific restraints. ... Thus there opens here a glimpse, however dim and weak, into a period when individuals are lost, for us, in the mass of the population, and when language itself is the work of the creative power. Heath (1988:24; italics mine)

For Humboldt there is a feedback between the creation of language and the formation of thoughts, not just a one way influence from language on cognitive structures:

[24] It is true, however, that the Humboldt tradition has always tended to read Humboldt as a representative of the hypothesis called after him. See Christmann (1966) on the ways in which Humboldt, through Dwight Whitney, Max Müller and Franz Boas, exerted an influence on Sapir's thinking and thus on that of Whorf. Christmann (1966) also shows that the notion of a mutual influencing of language and thought was common during the period of 18th century Enlightenment in France, Italy and Germany.

> We must be able to see how [the language of a nation] relates to other languages, not only in the goals prescribed to it, but also in its *reverse effect upon the mental activity of the nation*.
>
> We are to consider the whole route whereby, proceeding from the mind, [language] *reacts back upon the mind*.   Heath (1988:52, 54; italics mine)

The real 'Humboldt-hypothesis' is that language and thought form an inseparable union in the sense that thought is unthinkable without language, in particular the 'vocal apparatus and hearing' (Heath 1988:55). It is through sound-mediated language that thought can constitute itself. A concept comes to full maturity only when there is a pronounceable word to express it. According to Humboldt, articulated sound as the primary medium for language has special qualities that make it an apt and even irreplaceable instrument for the conveyance of thoughts:

> For as living sound it comes forth from the breast like breathing life itself, is the accompaniment, even without language, to pain and joy, aversion and desire, and thus breathes the life it flows from into the mind that receives it, just as language itself always reproduces, along with the object presented, the feeling evoked by it, and within itself couples, in ever repeated acts, the world and man, or, to put it otherwise, the spontaneously active and the receptive sides of his nature.
>
>   Heath (1988:55-56)

- *No thought without language*

Both thought and sound are an activity ('energeia'), not an object ('ergon'). From here on he argues that no clear representation of reality can constitute itself in the mind unless there is a language to shape it. And each different language shapes the burgeoning concepts in a different way:

> The picture of language as designating merely objects, already perceived in themselves, is also disconfirmed by examination of what language engenders as a product. By means of such a picture we would never, in fact, exhaust the deep and full content of language. Just as no concept is possible without language, so also there can be no object for the mind, since it is only through the concept, of course, that anything external acquires full being for consciousness. ...
>
> To learn a foreign language should therefore be to acquire a new standpoint in the world-view hitherto possessed, and in fact to a certain extent is so, since every language contains the whole conceptual fabric and mode of presentation of a portion of mankind. But because we can always carry over, more or less, our own world view, and even our own language view, this outcome is not purely and completely experienced.   Heath (1988:59-60)

(One notes both the circularity of the argument and the escape clause that makes this thesis unfalsifiable.) On the other hand, words are also shackles that prevent the free creation of thoughts:

> The word is the individual shaping of the concept, and if the latter wants to leave this shape, it can only find itself in other words. Yet the soul must continually try to make itself independent of the domain of language, for the word, after all, is a constraint upon its ever more capacious inner sensitivity, and often threatens to stifle the most individual nuances thereof by its nature which in sound is more material, and in meaning too general. The soul must treat the word more as a

landmark for its inner activity, rather than let itself be imprisoned within its boundaries.   Heath (1988:92)

One feels caught up in Hegelian dialectic.

• *Language acquisition by the young child*

In this connection Humboldt has a remarkable passage about native acquisition of language, occasioned, apparently, by his observing his own children while the family lived in Rome: he noticed there that the children spoke better Italian than German (Heeschen 1972:167), which they were not supposed to do, being of German stock and therefore predisposed towards German language forms. Language acquisition, he says, is a process, a 'creative' activity, whereby hidden forces are triggered and whose result is dramatically underdetermined by its input:

> The speech-learning of children is not an assignment of words, to be deposited in memory and rebabbled by rote through the lips, but a growth in linguistic capacity with age and practice. What is heard does more than merely convey information to oneself; it readies the mind also to understand more easily what has not yet been heard; it makes clear what was long ago heard, but then half understood, or not at all, in that a similarity to the new perception suddenly brings light to the power that has since become sharpened; and it enhances the urge and capacity to absorb from what is heard ever more, and more swiftly, into the memory, and to let ever less of it rattle by as mere noise. ... That in children there is not a mechanical learning of language, but a development of linguistic power, is also proved by the fact that, since the major abilities of man are allotted a certain period of life for their development, all children, under the most diverse conditions, speak and understand at about the same age, varying only within a brief time-span. ...
>
> One might wish to object to the foregoing that the children of any nation, when displaced to an alien community before learning to speak, develop their linguistic abilities in the latter's tongue. This undeniable fact, one might say, is a clear proof that language is merely an echoing of what is heard, and depends entirely on social circumstances, without regard for its essential unity, or diversity. In cases of this kind, however, it has hardly been possible to observe with sufficient accuracy how laboriously the native pattern has had to be overcome, or how perhaps in the finest nuances it has still kept its ground unvanquished. But even without paying attention to this, the phenomenon in question is sufficiently explained by the fact that man is everywhere one with man, and the development of the ability to use language can therefore go on with the aid of any given individual.
>
> Heath (1988:58-59)

Unexpectedly, this passage reveals a depth and clarity of insight that is uncharacteristic of the work as a whole, and far ahead of its time (yet no trace of it is found in subsequent linguistic theory till Chomsky (1964:17-21), where this aspect is lifted out of Humboldt's text and used as support for an innatist view of language acquisition). At the same time, as one sees, Humboldt has a knack of making his arguments unfalsifiable. The fact that young children growing up in a linguistic environment different from their own ethnic background acquire the language of the new environment as easily as native children do would speak against Humboldt's thesis that genetic (i.e. racial) endowment or genius and language creation go hand in hand, in mutual reinforcement. To counter this objection Humboldt conjures up possible unob-servables and an appeal to the unity of mankind. Humboldt, it seems, wants to have his cake and eat it.

- *Infinite variety of thoughts, expressed in greatest possible beauty*

Then he passes on to the 'internal and purely intellectual part of language' (Heath 1988:81), i.e. the thought processes that link up with articulate sounds. A few lines down he also includes 'imagination and feeling', which

> … engender individual shapings, in which the individual character of the nation again emerges, and where, as in everything individual, the variety of ways in which the thing in question can be represented in ever-differing guises, extends towards infinity.   Heath (1988:82)

In fact, in its ideal form human language expresses not only perfect thoughts in perfect shapes but does so in the greatest possible beauty. The urge to achieve beauty is, for Humboldt, one of the main driving forces behind the coming about of language. In this connection Humboldt dwells on the notion that thoughts occur in an infinite variety, all of which must be expressible in a language that is worth its salt:

> The artistic beauty of language is not therefore bestowed on it as a casual adornment, but is, on the contrary, an essentially necessary consequence of the rest of its nature, an infallible touchstone of its inner and universal perfection. For the inner work of the mind has only vaulted to its boldest summit when the latter is irradiated by the sense of beauty.
>
> But the procedure of language is not simply one whereby a single phenomenon comes about; it must simultaneously open up the possibility of producing an indefinable host of such phenomena, and under all the conditions that thought imposes. For language is quite peculiarly confronted by an unending and truly boundless domain, the totality of all that can be thought. *It must therefore make infinite use of finite means, and is able to do so in virtue of the identity of the force that engenders both thought and language.*[25]   Heath (1988:91; italics mine)

- *Outer and inner form of language*

Here we touch on the core of Humboldt's ideas of language and languages, the dynamic bond between thought and its expression in linguistic forms. The latter he often calls 'outer form' or 'sound form', the former variously 'inner

[25] The first part of the last sentence of this quote has been brought up repeatedly by Chomsky in support of the notion that a grammar should generate an infinite set of sentences from a finite set of elements and rules. Yet this modern notion of grammar has less to do with Humboldt's idea of making infinite use of finite means than with the mathematical theory of algorithms. Humboldt's notion of generativity is about thoughts, sentences being nothing but their expression, and about artistic creation. In Chomskyan generative grammar this semantic dimension is totally absent. In fact, his grammar is ex-plicitly 'autonomous', i.e. it generates sentences irrespective of any semantic considera-tions (cp. note 25 of chapter 1). Chomsky's notion of generative grammar is reminiscent not so much of Humboldt as of the note scribbled by a medieval monk in his breviary: 'ABCDEFGHIKLMNOPQRSTUVXYZ: per hoc alphabetum notum componitur brevia-rium totum' ('from this well-known alphabet is composed the entire breviary').

form', 'inner laws of language', 'intellectual procedure', 'inner conception of language', etc. In the German tradition of philosophy of language the terms 'outer form' (aüssere Form) and 'inner form' (innere Form) have gained general acceptance.

The last two thirds of the book are taken up with verbose, baseless and inconsistent attempts to show the superiority of the languages of Western Europe, always extolling their virtues compared with the languages of Asia and the Americas, and invariably holding up Chinese as the prototypical case of an inferior language.[26] We shall leave the remainder of the book for what it is and concentrate on the distinction of outer and inner form, as this has had an enormous influence on subsequent thinking about language.

- *Fundamental unclarity of the concepts*

There is a great deal of literature about the precise meaning of these terms. We shall not go into these exegetic questions, since whatever unclarity there is is entirely due to Humboldt himself. There is no reason to suppose that Humboldt's thinking was any clearer, or more consistent, than his writing. From that we gather that his 'outer form' refers on the one hand to what we now call 'surface structure' (and about which we have more precise ideas nowadays), and on the other to the grammar or system of surface language forms. His term 'inner form' is much more enigmatic as it is part of a universe of thought and vision that is not only very different from ours but, without doubt, confused and semi-mystical. It is to do, in a diffuse way, with the total mental machinery behind the production and comprehension of utterances as well as the genesis and the acquisition of language. It includes at least both what we know as universal grammar or the innate language faculty and semantic or logical form of sentences.[27] The fundamental unclarity of this notion may perhaps justify its outright rejection, but that is not what we will do here. Our interest does not lie in the intrinsic value of Humboldt's linguistic notions, which is doubtful, but in the way they influenced later thinking. And from that point of view their importance is considerable. Humboldt's ideas may have been biased by cultural absolutism, but they were influential.

---

[26] This stigmatization of Chinese has its origin in the writings of the 18th century French authors De Condillac and Rousseau, who both thought the Chinese tone system to be a remnant from a primitive stage in the development of human language (Robins 1967:150). The negative appreciation of Chinese is, however, not a necessary consequence of that view. For Rousseau in particular, the assumed primitive stages of language reflected the uncorrupted and free mind of the 'Noble Savage' (an awkward association when one thinks of the Chinese people). Humboldt, however, appears to have jumped on Chinese with eagerness.

[27] Cp. Graffi, who comments, speaking of Humboldt's notion of 'inner form' (1991:32):

> Its value is surely rather difficult to establish in any precise way: we know well what endless, and at times senseless, debates have been conducted on this issue.

Graffi (ibid.) also refers to a comment by Delbrück (1904:47-48):

> One might also say, in Humboldt's spirit if not in his words, that there is a general human inner language form, and a national inner language form.

● *Inner form as semantic form*

We will, from now on, consider Humboldtian 'inner form' mainly from the point of view of the comprehension and production of utterances, i.e. as semantic form. From this angle, one element in Humboldt's texts on inner form is of particular relevance. He repeatedly stresses the *structural aspect* of inner form. Even though he did not have any precise idea of what the structure of inner form could possibly be, other than that it should be 'congruent with' outer form ('Grammatical formation arises from the laws of thinking-in-language, and rests on the congruence of sound forms with the latter' – Heath 1988:140), the very fact that the question of its structure was raised had widespread effects.

● *Is inner form universal or language-particular?*

The first question asked is whether inner form is universal or nation-particular. Humboldt, as usual, does not commit himself either way and answers that it is both:

> It may seem as if all languages would have to be like each other in their intellectual procedure. For the sound-form, an infinite, uncountable multiplicity is conceivable, since the perceptibly and physically unique arises from such differing causes that the number of possible gradations is beyond calculation. But that which rests solely on mental self-activity, as the intellectual part of language does, seems to have to be alike in all mankind, given the similarity of purpose and means; and this part of language does, indeed, preserve a relatively large degree of uniformity. But from various causes there also arises in it a significant diversity. This is brought about, on the one hand, by the numerous levels at which the language-generating force is to any degree operative. But on the other, there are also powers at work here whose creations cannot be measured out by the rational mind and according to mere concepts. Imagination and feeling engender individual forms, in which the individual character of the nation is again expressed, and where, as in everything individual, the variety of ways in which the thing in question can be represented in ever-differing guises, extends towards infinity.
>
> Yet even in the purely intellectual parts, which depend on relations established by the rational mind, one finds differences, though in that case they are almost always due to incorrect or defective combinations. To recognize this, we only have to dwell on the laws of grammar proper. The different forms, for example, which have to be separately identified in the structure of the verb, according to the requirements of speech, should be completely enumerated and correctly distinguished in the same manner for all languages, since they can be found by mere derivation from concepts. But if one compares Sanskrit with Greek on this point, one is struck by the fact that in the former the concept of mood has not only remained obviously underdeveloped but has also, in the very creation of the language, not been truly felt or clearly distinguished from that of tense.   Heath (1988:81-82)

That is, though the sounds of languages may differ indefinitely from language to language, the mental part (inner form) that lies behind them must show greater uniformity. Yet even the mental part differs somewhat from nation to nation, due, first, to the degree to which nations succeed in putting their innate language faculty to good use and, secondly, to the fact that a language expresses more than just thoughts. It also expresses emotions, attitudes, imagination, and these again differ from nation to nation in infinitely many possible ways. Moreover, even from the 'purely intellectual' (which we would call 'truth-conditional') point of view there are differences, as nations make mistakes. It would be futile, of course, to try to find, in Humboldt's text, a set of criteria for correctness in the expression of inner form, or indeed a specification of the structure of inner form itself. But at least the question was raised. Compare also the following passage:

> Speech, therefore, always seeks that arrangement of linguistic elements which contains the liveliest expression of the forms of thought; and hence it is especially given to flection, whose very nature is exactly to consider the concept simultaneously from the outer and the inner point of view, which facilitates the progress of thought, owing to the regularity of the road taken. But with these elements, speech is bent upon achieving the innumerable combinations of winged thought, without any restrictions as to its boundlessness. The expression of all these connections is based upon sentence formation; and this free flight of ideas is possible only if the parts of the simple sentence are put together or separated according to necessary principles that arise from its nature, and not in more or less arbitrary ways. ... The development of ideas requires a double procedure, a representation of particular concepts, and a linkage of them into thoughts. Both also occur in speech.
>
> Heath (1988:109-110)

- *Humboldt as part of the German intellectual establishment*

The Romantic, partly liberal but also starry-eyed and culturally arrogant social value system that prevailed in Prussia during the 19th century and, one has to say, took hold of the whole German world in the 20th century, fitted Humboldt to a tee. Perhaps because of that, perhaps also because he was a man of high social profile, Humboldt was read and admired right from the beginning. This is fully understandable in the cultural setting of German Idealism, where mystical speculation and the cultivation of private experiences of 'deep' or 'true' understanding ('Verstehen') through inner vision ('Anschauung') were considered academically respectable, where wild reifications like 'the popular spirit' or 'the genius of the language' were taken to have explanatory value, where philosophers like Hegel and Fichte were celebrated. Yet the very existence and the long duration of this climate has been, if not a blight for western culture in general, at least a serious setback for the human sciences, including the science of language. The comparative philologists, discussed in the previous two sections, formed a much needed counterbalance to the nebulous world of German Idealism. And it may well have been their deep attitudinal aversion that kept the philologists from going into questions of the general nature of language and thought, as this would have drawn them directly into discussions with the Idealist philosophers. In any case, as far as the philosophy of language and even linguistics itself is concerned, Humboldt has been extremely influential. There is a long tradition of Humboldt exegesis, and many theoretical linguists of today think it edifying to quote him, often, sadly enough, without much knowledge of the wider philosophical or historical context.

We would have dismissed Humboldt as irrelevant, together with the tradition he stood in (and which gave rise to such decadent aberrations as Heideggerian philosophy), had it not been for the fact that the Humboldt tradition has in fact led to developments that are of the greatest relevance and importance, and were not touched upon by the comparative philologists.

2.6.3 The confusion around subject and predicate[28]

- *Incongruity of the subject-predicate distinction in logic, psychology and grammar*

It is not possible to understand the developments in linguistic theory of the 19th and 20th centuries without some knowledge of the great subject-predicate debate that dominated linguistics for almost a century till, roughly, the 1930s. (When we speak of the subject-predicate distinction in this paper we disregard the fact that the predicate may contain further constituents, in particular a direct object and an indirect object. This was certainly known to the main actors in the 19th century subject-predicate debate. However, important as this fact may be in other contexts, it may be neglected here. Following common usage, we continue to speak of the subject-predicate distinction, knowing that it would perhaps be more appropriate to speak of the predicate-arguments distinction.)

Around 1840 a number of linguists and philosophers began to realize, in the wake of the great expansion of grammatical expertise achieved in 18th century France (see 2.3.3), that very often sentence constituents that are grammatically marked as subject do not fit the semantic description of 'subject' provided in Aristotelian metaphysics. It was felt that sentences are often used in such a way that there is a discrepancy between the grammatical subject-predicate division and the way the sentence is understood. The very same propositional content can be presented in different 'modes of presentation', according to how they are to link up with the discourse at hand.

To take an example from Steinthal (1855:199), in a sentence like *The patient slept well* the grammatical subject is *the patient* and the grammatical predicate is *slept well*. However, if the sentence is simply interpreted as the attribution of the property of sleeping well to the individual here described as 'the patient' an important fact is overlooked, namely that often, 'what one wants to say is that the patient's sleep was good'. Therefore, an analysis is wanted, at a different level from surface grammar, in which *the patient's sleep* is the subject and the adverb *well* is the predicate. Steinthal, and many after him, thus realized that many uses of sentences are 'incongruous' in that

---

[28] A useful collection of texts on the subject-predicate distinction in Antiquity and the Middle Ages is Ildefonse et al. (1994) (cp. also Baratin & Desbordes 1981). See also Graffi (1991:121) for a clear and succinct survey of the terminological and conceptual confusion around the terms subject and predicate and their synonyms. A good and informative guide through the 19th century subject-predicate debate is given in Part II of Elffers-van Ketel (1991), from which I have benefited greatly.

the grammatical division between subject and predicate does not coincide with the corresponding semantic, or (psycho)logical, division, and that the same grammatical form may be used to express different semantic forms. If this idea is viable there will have to be two different levels of analysis, a surface grammatical analysis and a semantic, or, as the terminology went at the time, a logical or psychological, analysis, each with their own subject-predicate assignments. Jespersen aptly summarizes the problem as follows:

> The subject is sometimes said to be the relatively familiar element, to which the predicate is added as something new. "The utterer throws into his subject all that he knows the receiver is already willing to grant him, and to this he adds in the predicate what constitutes the new information to be conveyed by the sentence ... In 'A is B' we say, 'I know that you know who A is, perhaps you don't know also that he is the same person as B'" (Baldwin's Dict. of Philosophy and Psychol. 1902, vol. 2. 364). This may be true of most sentences, but not of all, for if in answer to the question "Who said that?" we say "Peter said it," *Peter* is the new element, and yet it is undoubtedly the subject.   Jespersen (1924:145)

The emergence of the subject-predicate problem during this period was a direct consequence of a notional as well as terminological confusion about the term *subject* that goes back to Antiquity, and to the significant advances in grammatical expertise achieved during the 18th century. To investigate the former we must revert to classical Antiquity, and look in greater detail at the history of the terms *subject* and *predicate*.

- *The terms* subject *and* predicate *in Aristotle*

The term *subject* is a Latin translation of the Greek *hypokeímenon*, which was introduced by Aristotle in connection with his theory of truth (see section 1.2.1). For Aristotle, as will be remembered, truth comes about when the facts of the world correspond with what is thought or said. In order to make this correspondence relation specific Aristotle has to resort to a double form of analysis. On the one hand, he has to analyse world facts, i.e. real or possible situations, and on the other he must analyse either what is thought or what is said. And since what is said is more amenable to analysis than what is thought, he opts for sentence analysis, leaving thought analysis in limbo.

For Aristotle, then, a situation or state of affairs, as represented in an assertive sentence, consists of the fact that some entity has a certain property. And a true assertion corresponds with the situation in that it contains a constituent called *predicate*, which assigns the property in question to the entity concerned. In a general sense, therefore, Aristotle's notion of correspondence, as the defining characteristic of truth, consists in an isomorphic relation between entity versus property in the world and subject term versus predicate in the sentence (and is thus a primitive form of model theory; see 6.1.3). The entity is called *hypokeímenon*. The property assigned (if it is an accidental and not a necessary property) is called *symbebēkós* (*accidens* in Latin). The sentence part expressing the property is called *katēgoroúmenon* or *katēgórēma* (Latin *praedicatum*). No specific term, however, is created for the sentence part that refers to the hypokeímenon. Aristotle thus left a terminological gap.

• *Confusion around the term 'subject'*

This gap became the source of a persistent confusion, which lasted for many centuries, between the subject as referent, the thing the sentence is about, on the one hand, and the sentence constituent we now recognize as subject on the other. The 2nd century AD Greek grammarian Apollonius Dyscolus (see 1.4.1) still uses the term *hypokeímenon* in the original Aristotelian sense of the entity in the real or a possible world that the sentence is about. Thus we read, for example (Book. I, ch. 31; Householder 1981:28-29):

> When we look for the identity (*hýparxin*) of some underlying entity (*hypokeiménou*) we say 'Who is moving?' or 'Who is walking?' or 'Who is speaking?', when it is clear that there is (an event of) movement, walking, or speaking, but unclear who the person is that does these things.

But as from the 5th century AD authors begin to use the term *hypokeímenon* also for the grammatical subject term of a sentence. A clear example (despite the not so clear style of writing) is found in Ammonius' 5th century commentary on Aristotle's *De Interpretatione* (Busse 1897:7-8), where Ammonius produces the following somewhat overextended sentence:

> [S]ince some propositions are composed of only two simple words, one being the subject and the other the predicate, as when I say 'Socrates walks' (here the word *Socrates* is called the subject term (*hypokeímenos hóros*) and the word *walks* the predicate, because in every predicative utterance one part is that about which the utterance is and the other part what is said about it, and because that about which the utterance is, i.e. the word *Socrates*, is called the subject as it receives what is predicated of it, while that which is said about it, i.e. the word *walks*, is the predicate as it is said about the subject), since, then, as we were saying, some propositions are composed of just the subject and the predicate, but others may have a third part added to them, as when I say 'Socrates is righteous' (here the subject is the word *Socrates* and the predicate is the word *righteous*, and *is* is simply added), while others again may have a modality added to them, signifying in what way the predicate assigns a property to the subject, e.g. that it is necessary, or impossible, or possible, or well, or clearly, or justly, as when I say 'Socrates may be musical' or 'Socrates explains clearly', and since it is impossible to think of more terms than these that could be combined with each other to form a proposition, the second chapter of the book tells us about the simplest propositions, that is about assertive propositions consisting solely of subject and predicate, the third chapter about the more complex ones that have an extra part [i.e. copula] added to them so that these assertive propositions consist of a subject, a predicate and a third added part, and the fourth about propositions with a modality.

In the sixth century we find Boethius, also in a commentary on Aristotle's *De Interpretatione* (prima editio, 5 (77, 5-15)):

> Now he [i.e. Aristotle] explains what a simple and what a complex proposition is. A simple proposition is one that is composed of two terms. The terms are noun and verb. The latter we predicate in a simple proposition, such as 'Socrates debates', where *Socrates* and *debates* are the terms. The lesser term in the utterance, i.e. *Socrates*, is called the subject (subiectus) term and has to come first. The major term, i.e. *debates*, is predicated and comes second. Thus, a proposition that is composed of one subject (subiecto) and of one predicate is called a simple utterance.

This may well be the first occurrence in the extant Latin sources of the term *terminus subjectus* in the meaning of 'subject term', as distinct from the other main sentence constituent, the predicate. The Greek term *hypokeímenon*, or, more precisely, *hypokeímenos hóros*, had already been used in that sense by Ammonius, as we have just seen.

In roughly the same period the Latin grammarian Priscian, mentioned earlier in 1.4.1, writes (Book 17, ch. 23), translating the passage quoted above from Apollonius Dyscolus:

> When we look for the reality (substantiam) of some underlying entity (suppositi) we say 'Who is moving?' or 'Who is walking?' or 'Who is speaking?', when it is clear that there is (an event of) movement, walking, or speaking, but unclear who the person is that does these things.

Priscian then goes on, still translating Apollonius:

> Therefore, nominative 'subjections' (subiectiones) are made of either proper names or common nouns, the latter conveying also a general reality (substantiam). For we reply 'A man is walking', or 'A horse', or 'Trypho', where it is understood that Trypho is a man. Or a word may be put in (subicitur) which is understood as standing for a noun, a common noun, that is, a pronoun, as when we say 'I [am walking]'.

The last three passages are interesting, especially in conjunction with the text quoted above from Boethius, as they show a tendency in Latin authors to disambiguate the Greek term *hypokeímenon*. About the sixth century a convention apparently began to take hold to translate *hypokeímenon* in the original sense of 'reference object' as *suppositum*, but in the meaning of 'sentence constituent' as *subiectum*. This convention, however, was not universally adopted. In the Middle Ages, although *suppositio* standardly meant 'reference', and the *suppositum* was the reference object, Thomas of Erfurt, as we saw in section 1.4.2, uses the terms *suppositum* and *subiectum* the opposite way. As regards the Renaissance, Percival (1976:240-1) quotes an Italian grammarian of the 14th or 15th century, Giovanni da San Ginesio:

> What is the subject (suppositum)? It is that about which we speak or (vel) whatever precedes the main verb or (vel) is understood to precede it.

The use of the word *vel* for 'or' shows that he saw the two meanings of the term *suppositum* as freely interchangeable alternatives. In the 17th century, however, *subiectum* became the generally accepted term for the sentence constituent denoted by it.

• *No semantics for quantified subject terms*
Besides the terminological confusion, there were other problems as well with regard to both the notion and the term *subject*. As has been said, in Aristotle's original definition, a subject is the entity to which a property is assigned by the predicate of a sentence. This metaphysical or semantic definition applies to assertions with a definite subject term, such as *The man is ill*. Here, the person referred to by the phrase *the man* is assigned the property of being ill

by means of the predicate *ill*, and such an assignment may be true or false. But this definition fails to apply to sentences with a quantified subject term.

Now Aristotle's logic is explicitly restricted to sentences that contain a subject term quantified by the standard quantifiers *all* or *some*. Sentences with a proper name or a definite noun phrase like *the man* or *the men* as subject term are excluded from his logic (ostensibly because they lack metaphysical interest, but in reality (see 6.2.3) because they mean trouble in a strictly bivalent logical system). There is therefore a problem regarding the semantics of subject terms like *all men, every man, some man*, or *some men*. They do not stand for a specific entity, and what they do stand for remained unclear to Aristotle and later generations of logicians. The great master thus had neither an ontology nor a semantics that would define a reference object for a quantified subject term. Yet his theory of truth demanded such a reference object. Aristotle, therefore, also left a semantic gap.

Neither Aristotle nor later ancient and medieval philosophers were able to solve this problem. It remained unsolved until the advent of modern quantification theory, with its quantifiers and substitutional variables (see 5.5). In light of the above it is easy to see what motivated medieval nominalist philosophers to seek a solution in finely grained theories of reference, the well-known medieval *theories of supposition*, with their distinctions between various forms of reference or supposition: personal, simple, material, discrete, communal, determined, confused, distributive, mobile, or immobile, etc. (cp. De Rijk 1967; see also note 15 in chapter 1). These theories were, on the whole, unsuccessful owing to the lack of mathematical and formal sophistication. But they show that the medieval philosophical world was well aware of the unsolved problem of the semantics of quantified (subject) terms.

- *No semantics for subject terms generally*

By the middle of the nineteenth century, as formal grammar had become more sophisticated and linguists had developed a keener sense of the realities of language and speech, a further problem was noticed by a number of linguists and philosophers. They observed that if the Aristotelian definition of subject, to the extent that it applies at all, is applied to sentences in context, very often what should be the subject according to the definition is not the subject recognized in grammatical analysis, and likewise for the predicate. *Heymann Steinthal* (1823-1899), for example, observed (1860a:101-102):

> One should not be misled by the similarity of the terms. Both logic and grammar speak of subject and predicate, but only rarely do the logician and the grammarian speak of the same word as either the subject or the predicate. ... Consider the sentence *Coffee grows in Africa*. There can be no doubt where the grammarian will locate subject and predicate. But the logician? I do not think the logician could say anything but that 'Africa' contains the concept that should be connected with 'coffee grows'. Logically one should say, therefore, 'the growth of coffee is in Africa'. ... Grammatical form is therefore a completely free, subjective product of the popular spirit.

Steinthal is obviously the victim of the widespread misconception that the subject-predicate distinction originated in Aristotle's logic, whereas we know that it originated in his theory of truth. But apart from that, if we apply his definition to the sentence quoted the prepositional phrase *in Africa* should be the predicate since it assigns a locative property to the growing of coffee. (One notices the idea that 'grammatical form' is not subject to rules but a free creation of the 'popular spirit', a concept echoing Humboldt.)

Likewise, we find *Wilhelm Meyer-Lübke* (1861-1936), who also believes that the term *subject* sprang from logic, observing (1899:352):[29]

> I want to stress that 'subject' is used here in a purely grammatical sense, and designates, therefore, the agent of the action. Admittedly, this goes against the original meaning of this term, which, as one knows, originated in logic. From the point of view of logic there can be no doubt that in the sentence *il arrive deux étrangers* ['two foreigners arrive'] the subject is *il arrive* while *deux étrangers* is the predicate, as A. Tobler (Beiträge I, 191) rightly observes. But from the point of view of grammar the relation between Noun and Verb remains unchanged, no matter which comes first in the sentence.

- *Subject and predicate as discourse-related notions*

Around 1900 the distinction between subject and predicate was widely used to account for the way the information contained in an uttered sentence is presented in an ongoing discourse. Thus, elements under contrastive accent, as in *SCOTT wrote Ivanhoe*, as against *Scott wrote IVANHOE*, are considered 'logical' predicates by authors like Wegener, Lipps, Stout or Gardiner, and the uncontrasted parts are, correspondingly, the 'logical' subject. Von der Gabelentz and Paul make the same distinction but use the term *psychological* instead of *logical*.

Georg von der Gabelentz (1840-1893) was the first to use a tripartite terminology. For him, the 'logical' subject does what the constituent corresponding with the Aristotle's metaphysical subject is supposed to do: it represents the thing that the logical predicate says something about. The grammatical subject represents the 'logical' subject and manifests this function by assuming the nominative case. The psychological subject is the representation ('Vorstellung') which comes to mind first:

> What does one wish to achieve when one speaks to another person? The answer is that one wants to arouse a thought in him. In my view this implies two aspects: first, one has to direct the interlocutor's attention (his thinking) to something, and secondly, one makes him think this or that about it. I call that of or about which I want my addressee to think the *psychological subject*, and that which he should think about it the *psychological predicate*. In the sequel it will become clear how much these categories often deviate from their grammatical counterparts.
>
> Von der Gabelentz (1869:378)

---

[29] Notice that Meyer-Lübke falls back on the terms *Noun* and *Verb*, used by the Sophists and Plato, to denote the grammatical subject and predicate, respectively. Notice also that, surprisingly, modern quantification theory teaches us that, indeed, the part *il arrive* represents the subject term, and the part *deux étrangers* the predicate, of the logical analysis of the sentence in question (see 5.5.2).

Thus, in a sentence like *Mit Speck fängt man Mäuse* ('with bacon one catches mice'; Von der Gabelentz 1901:370) the logical subject, expressed through the grammatical subject, is *man* ('one'), but the psychological subject is *mit Speck* ('with bacon'). Von der Gabelentz does, however, signal the difficulty of observational support for his thesis:

> But if one wants to give the inductive proof for all this, one has to be careful with examples. For the phenomena to do with positions in the sentences of different languages are not unambiguous or equivalent.   Von der Gabelentz (1901²:370)

From here it is but a small step to get to the notion of subject and predicate as linked up with a 'context of situation'. The first to bring this to the fore was *Philipp Wegener* (1848-1916), who did not gain much prominence in Germany but was held in high regard by the Englishman Alan H. Gardiner (see 3.5):

> It is the function of the subject ['die Exposition'] to state the position ['die Situation klar zu stellen'], so that the logical predicate becomes intelligible.
> Wegener (1885:21)

Likewise for the German philosopher-psychologist *Theodor Lipps* (1851-1914), for whom, however, logical and psychological subject-and-predicate are identical, while grammar goes its own way. He takes Wegener's view further to a more discourse-oriented notion of subject and predicate:

> The grammatical subject and predicate of a sentence now agree now do not agree with those of the judgement. When they do not, the German language has intonation as a means of marking the predicate of the judgement. The subject and predicate of the associated judgement are best recognized when we bring to mind the question to which the sentence is an answer. That which the full and unambiguous question is about is the subject, while the information required is the predicate. The same sentence can, accordingly, serve to express different judgements, and hence different subjects and predicates.   Lipps (1893:40)

In much the same vein we read the Cambridge philosopher *George Stout* (1860-1944), who, following the lines set out by Von der Gabelentz, Wegener and Lipps, presents a fascinating picture of how specific thoughts arise out of and fit in with ongoing mental activity. We read:

> This relatively indefinite schema, which becomes articulate in the process of thinking, is what logicians call a *universe of discourse*, and what in ordinary language is called a *subject* or *topic*. ...
> The predicate of the subject, in this sense, is the whole discourse through which it receives definition and specification. Predication, from this point of view, just consists in the definition and specification of what is, at the outset, indefinite and indeterminate. It is because this process takes place gradually by a successive concentration of attention, that language is divided into sentences. The predicate of a sentence is the determination of what was previously indeterminate. The subject is the previous qualification of the general topic or universe of discourse to which the new qualification is attached. The subject is that product of previous thinking which forms the immediate basis and starting-point of further development. The further development is the predicate. Sentences are in the process of thinking what steps are in the process of walking. The foot on which the weight of the body rests corresponds to the subject. The foot which is moved forward in order to occupy new ground corresponds to the predicate. ... All answers to questions are, as such,

predicates, and all predicates may be regarded as answers to possible questions. If the statement, "I am hungry" be a reply to the question, "Who is hungry?" then "I" is the predicate. If it be the answer to the question, "Is there anything amiss with you?" then "hungry" is the predicate. If the question is, "Are you really hungry?" then "am" is the predicate. Every fresh step in a train of thought may be regarded as an answer to a question. The subject is, so to speak, the formulation of the question; the predicate is the answer.   Stout (1909, vol.2:212-214)

All these authors distinguish between two kinds of subject-predicate division, one that is mostly called 'grammatical' but sometimes also 'logical', and another that is variously called 'logical' or 'psychological'. The opposition is thus between 'grammatical' and 'psychological', with logic straddling the fence, depending on the view the author in question takes of logic.

• *Logic seen as a cognitive faculty: the art of correct reasoning*
The uncertain status of the term *logical* is probably due to a widely prevailing uncertainty at the time about the status of logic. The fact that logic is by definition a calculus was not widely appreciated. Only some, more mathematically minded logicians, like Boole, De Morgan, Frege, Russell, realized that. For the majority, however, mostly consisting of philosophers and interested linguists, logic was the study of the processes of correct thinking, and hence closely connected with the study of the mind, which was then beginning to be called psychology. These scholars were unaware that Aristotle had grafted his logic on the *verbal* notion of truth as correspondence between what is *said* and what is the case, and not on the *cognitive* version where correspondence is required between what is *thought* and what is the case (cp. Stegmüller 1957:16-17, quoted in 2.6.4). Modern logic has followed Aristotle in this respect and is explicitly non-psychological. But in the nineteenth century matters were less clear. Those who set off a 'logical' subject-predicate division from a grammatical one were, apparently, not troubled by the fact that there was no logical machinery corresponding to their 'logical' subject-predicate division. In this respect, those who preferred the term 'psychological' certainly had good reasons (see also 7.1.3 below for a different perspective).

• *Wundt wants to create order*
Wilhelm Wundt (1832-1920) proposed a reversal to one single subject-predicate division, thereby re-establishing terminological order. He argued that there was no compelling reason for distinguishing between a grammatical and a logical notion of subject and predicate. Why not just follow grammar, he argued, and take the nominal constituent in the nominative case as the subject not only for grammatical but also for logical purposes? What objection is there to consider the grammatical subject of a passive sentence to be also the logical subject? The passive subject simply takes a different predicate from the corresponding active sentence (the fact that the two are, roughly speaking, synonymous should presumably be accounted for by independent principles). And the way information is 'packaged' for presentation should be ascribed to a separate psychological system of 'foregrounding' which interacts with the

logico-grammatical distinction between subject and predicate in various ways. Let us listen to him in some detail:

> Among the less palatable consequences of the mixing up of logical, grammatical and psychological points of view there is hardly one that is more damaging to an adequate view of the facts of language than the transfer of the logical elements of the judgement to the linguistic analysis of the sentence. The fact that the judgement consists of subject and predicate results from an analysis of judgements, and this is an insight that has rightly passed untrammelled from Aristotelian logic (even if present-day scientific thought has otherwise grown out of it) into the more modern forms of logic. The subject is the thing the proposition is about, that which forms the basis, *hypokeímenon*; the predicate is the content of the proposition, the *katēgórēma* , as Aristotle called it. ...

> [Subject and predicate] are present in every judgement, even in impersonal ones, where 'that which forms the basis' is presupposed as something indefinite. And since every assertive sentence can, logically speaking, be regarded as a judgement, the concepts of subject and predicate are immediately applicable to them. ...

> But then, how about those sentences that are not assertive, such as exclamations or questions? And what is the mutual relation of these sentence constituents when the sentence has undergone certain linguistic transformations that do not affect their meaning? Suppose I transform the sentence *Caesar crossed the Rubicon* into *The Rubicon was crossed by Caesar*, does that mean that the subject *Caesar* has become a remote object, and has, conversely, the original object *the Rubicon* now become the subject? And when I say *The crossing of the Rubicon was achieved by Caesar*, has now the original predicate become the subject?

> These are the questions that have led, in our new linguistics, to a kind of distinction that has found a rather widespread acceptance, but which, in my eyes, has increased rather than solved the confusion resulting from the mixing of logic, grammar and psychology. If we are to believe G. von der Gabelentz we should distinguish between a logical, a grammatical, and a psychological subject and predicate. The logical subject and predicate keep the function they have in logic. The psychological subject is seen as "the representational complex that occurs first in the consciousness of speaker and hearer", while "the content that is added to this prior representation" should be the predicate. Or, as v.d. Gabelentz formulates it from the teleological point of view, the psychological subject is "that about which the speaker wants the hearer to think, to which he wants to direct his attention, while the psychological predicate consists of that which the hearer should think about the subject". ...

> Against this we posit that subject and predicate are of themselves logical concepts, and therefore not originally part of grammar, and even less of psychology. One is better advised not to transfer them from their proper domain to different domains as long as no compelling reasons have been presented. This indeed is why some authors have, from time to time and not entirely without justification, objected to a simple identification of grammatical and logical predicate. Yet for assertive sentences, and it is to these that we must restrict ourselves in the present discussion as they are the unique origin of the logical categories, these objections do not apply. When one says that the two sentences *Caesar crossed the Rubicon* and *The Rubicon was crossed by Caesar* have the same logical subject but different grammatical subjects, one has already lost sight of the notion of subject in the Aristotelian sense, namely as that on which the assertion is based, and surreptitiously introduced a psychological consideration, namely that the subject must be an agent. Obviously, the agent in both sentences is Caesar. But only in the first sentence, and not in the

second, is he the basis on which the proposition is grounded. The former is an assertion about Caesar, the latter about the Rubicon. ...

The logical subject of the sentence ... may be foregrounded maximally but also relatively weakly. These are distinctions that must absolutely be denoted by different names, precisely because they always enter into a union with the logical distinctions that occur in thinking and often cut right through them. Or else there will be conceptual confusion.   Wundt (1922[4]:266-271)

In one respect Wundt was clearly right. As long as no answer is provided to the question of what the logical, grammatical and psychological notions of subject and predicate have in common, there is no good reason for identifying or relating them by the use of a single set of terms. In a footnote to p. 268 Wundt says it again: 'This very confusion of nomenclature is a valid reason for insisting on unambiguous definitions for subject and predicate, and for using a different terminology when one is dealing with different concepts.' Wundt then proposes the term *dominant representation* (dominierende Vorstellung) for those elements in sentences that are maximally foregrounded in an information-structural sense, but this term never gained acceptance.

- *Mathesius introduces Functional Sentence Perspective*
Around 1926 *Vilém Mathesius* (1892-1945), professor of English at Prague University, followed Wundt's advice. He introduced (Mathesius 1928) the term pair *thema* and *rhema* for what had counted as psychological subject and predicate, respectively. The two together make up a *functional sentence perspective*, which should account for the discourse-bound foregrounding phenomena mentioned by Von der Gabelentz, Wegener, Lipps, Stout, Wundt and others.

Mathesius founded the Prague Linguistic Circle (see 3.3), where questions of orderly transfer of information have always remained central, even though it proved difficult to supply the new notions with the necessary formal and empirical support.

Contrary to Wundt's term *dominant representation*, Mathesius' term pair, anglicized as *theme-rheme*, has gained wide acceptance. Other term pairs were also introduced, more or less simultaneously, such as *topic-comment*, *topic-focus*, and the like, all fitting into the notion of functional sentence perspective. All theories of functional sentence perspective have in common the view that the subject-predicate division, which they regard as belonging to grammar and/or logic, is nothing to do with functional sentence perspective or information packaging, which is seen as belonging to an autonomous machinery of psychological discourse processing. In principle, subject and predicate have nothing in common with theme and rheme (topic and comment), though in practice it is often the grammatical subject that acts as theme (topic), and the grammatical predicate that acts as rheme (comment). Unfortunately, however, theories of functional sentence perspective have so far suffered from a crippling lack of formal precision and, as is to be expected, a concomitant variety of not always fully coherent notions and definitions.

• *The debate becomes fruitless and stops*

Meanwhile the notions of subject and predicate did not become any clearer. We see, in the period in question, one author after another advancing his intuitive ideas about what subject and predicate should amount to. In the end the confusion was total. Around the turn of the century one witnesses a bewildering game of musical chairs, with authors fighting to occupy the three available chairs of grammar, logic and psychology, some trying to sit on two at a time. The whole debate was blighted by notional confusion and, above all, by a lack of empirical criteria. Even though one is often struck by the courage of and the acute observations made by the participants in this wild debate, the overall impression is that of a fundamental inability to come to terms with the issues. Sciences and theories were invoked that did not exist. Intuitions and sometimes flights of fancy took the place of sober reasoning.

In this context, one can easily understand Theodor Kalepky's exclamation (1928:20): 'Such a confusion simply cries out for relief' (Eine derartige Wirrnis schreit förmlich nach Abhilfe). In fact, Kalepky, like a few others such as Svedelius (1897) and Sandmann (1954:78-81; 105-109), called for a linguistic theory without subject and predicate at all. This call, however, was not followed. The terms and notions of subject and predicate are now firmly established in linguistics, though their status is still unclear.

After 1930 the subject-predicate debate came to an inconclusive end. With the exception of the Prague School, linguistic theorizing moved in other directions. The lack of empirical support and the notional unclarity were taking their toll. Nowadays, most students of linguistics do not even know that there ever was a subject-predicate debate.

• *Subject and predicate accepted but not understood in modern linguistics*

Linguists in the first half of the twentieth century have tended to explicate the notions of subject and predicate in the terms provided by Lipps and Stout, i.e. the subject as that which is up for discussion and the predicate as the new information added. Bloomfield, for example, in his 1914 textbook, explains the terms *subject*, *predicate*, and *attribute* as well, as follows:

> The attention of an individual, – that is, apperception, – is a unified process: we can attend to but one thing at a time. Consequently the analysis of a total experience always proceeds by single binary divisions into a part for the time being focused and a remainder. In the primary division of an experience into two parts, the one focused is called the *subject* and the one left for later attention the *predicate*; the relation between them is called *predication*. If, after this first division, either subject or predicate or both receive further analysis, the elements in each case first singled out are again called subjects and the elements in relation to them, *attributes*. The subject is always the present thing, the known thing, or the concrete thing, the predicate or attribute, its quality, action, or relation or the thing to which it is like. Thus in the sentence *Lean horses run fast* the subject is *lean horses* and the horses' action, *run fast*, is the predicate. Within the subject there is the further analysis into a subject *horses* and its attribute *lean*, expressing the horses' quality. In the predicate *fast* is an attribute of the subject *run*.   Bloomfield (1914:60-61)

This is a curious passage. First, one notices that Bloomfield follows his great example Wundt in assigning a hierarchical constituent structure to sentences (see 4.3; 4.4.5), implicitly defining subject and predicate as main structural components, noun phrase (NP) and verb phrase (VP) in more up-to-date terminology. Then, Bloomfield uses the term *subject* ambiguously: it is either the head of any lower constituent (NP, VP, etc.), a usage that has now been abandoned, or what we call the subject term. Moreover, in his attempt to give a semantic definition for the terms *subject* (in the normal sense) and *predicate* he falls back on the discourse-related notions developed by Wegener, Lipps, Stout and others, which goes very much against Wundt, who explicitly refuses to apply the terms *subject* and *predicate* to what is given and what is new, respectively, in a proposition added to a given discourse.

Hockett, in his *Introduction* of 1958, clearly follows the early Bloomfield. Using Prague School terminology (see 3.3) he says:

> The most general characterization of predicative constructions is suggested by the terms 'topic' and 'comment' for their ICs [i.e. immediate constituents]: the speaker announces a topic and then says something about it. Thus *John | ran away; That new book by Thomas Guernsey | I haven't read yet.* In English and the familiar languages of Europe, topics are usually also subjects, and comments are predicates: so in *John | ran away.* But this identification fails sometimes in colloquial English, regularly in certain special situations in formal English, and more generally in some non-European languages. Hockett (1958:201)

For Hockett the essence of predication is the addition of new information to a given topic. The division between topic and comment he considers to be of a structural nature, expressible in terms of immediate constituents, i.e. as a tree structure. At the same time, however, he makes a distinction between subject and predicate, a distinction that also has a structural counterpart in terms of tree structure. Since the subject-predicate division does not always coincide with the topic-comment division, the question arises as to the relation between the two kinds of tree structure assignment. This question is not answered by Hockett, which shows the embarrassment in modern linguistics regarding the terms *subject* and *predicate*, to say nothing of *topic* and *comment*.

It is only fair to admit that the issue has not so far been brought to a satisfactory conclusion. Linguists operate with the notions of subject, direct object and indirect object without a sufficient basis and without clear notions about the relationship with topic-comment structure. It is now clear that the source of the confusion lies with Aristotle, who *defined* the notions of subject and predicate in terms that we now, with Lipps, Wegener and Stout, recognize as implying discourse-dependency, but who *used* the distinction in a way that we now recognize as grammatical. Aristotle's definition implies dependency on discourse or context as it defines a definite (non-quantified) subject term as denoting an entity that can only be identified with the help of context, including general world knowledge. In non-quantificational sentences the Aristotelian subject term is definite and denotes something *given*, to which the predicate will generally assign a *new* property not so far assigned to it in the discourse at hand. In the 19th century conscientious linguists and philosophers took Aristotle up on his words and found that the definition did not correspond with the use, whether in grammar or in logic. Meanwhile, subject and predicate have become firmly established as syntactic notions. Their definition, however, is still largely up in the air.

- *The insufficiency of semantic definitions, in terms of thematic roles or otherwise*

Attempts have been afoot for a long time to define the notion of subject, and analogously those of direct and indirect object, semantically in terms of *functional* or *thematic roles*. These attempts were revived recently (cp. Fillmore 1968) and, after Jackendoff (1972), found general acceptance in MIT-centered circles of generative grammar. An early comment on these attempts as regards the subject (but it is easily extrapolated to the other argument terms) was given by Jespersen (1909-1949, vol. III, 11.1$_5$):

> The subject cannot be defined by means of such words as active or agent; this is excluded by the meaning of a great many verbs, e.g. *suffer* (he suffered torture), *collapse*, as well as by passive constructions, for in "he is beaten" *he* is the subject, but not the agent. ... How are we to distinguish between the subject and the object (or the objects)? The subject is the primary which is most intimately connected with the verb (predicate) in the form it actually has in the sentence with which we are concerned; thus *Tom* is the subject in (1) "Tom beats John", but not in (2) "John is beaten by Tom", though both sentences indicate the same action on the part of Tom; in the latter sentence *John* is the subject, because he is the person most intimately connected with the verb *beat* in the actual form employed: *is beaten*. We can thus find out the subject by asking *Who* (or *What*) followed by the verb in the form used in the sentence: (1) Who beats (John)? Tom | (2) Who is beaten (by Tom)? John.

This comment seems pretty final. It is, in fact, repeated by Parsons (1995), who adds that the thematic roles themselves are ill-defined:

> One conclusion is agreed upon by all commentators: the various thematic relations have not been specified in accurate ways. But this is well known in part because the authors agree about the classifications that are supposed to result from the specified criteria, and about ways in which the criteria fail to provide them. For example, a typical definition distinguishes two types of Theme (often called "Theme" and "Patient"):
>> The *Theme proper* is the thing that is said to move or remain at rest.
>> The *Patient* is the thing that is said to be affected or acted upon
> But consider the sentence *I play a sonata*. Since the sonata is not said either to move or to remain at rest, that means it can't be the Theme proper. And since it is not said to be affected or acted upon, that means it can't be a Patient. But everyone agrees that the answer we are after is that it *is* the Theme (or Theme/Patient). The criticisms of the criteria are compelling because of agreement about what the right answer is supposed to be.   Parsons (1995:638)

Little seems to be gained, therefore, by these attempts. Even so, it does seem that certain thematic roles appear to gravitate towards certain argument positions with lexical verbs or predicates. And it also does seem that thematic roles are sometimes relevant in the description of syntactic phenomena (cp. Seuren (1996:198-9) with regard to the French *faire*-construction). But they seem neither necessary nor sufficient for the semantic description of the subject and other argument terms.

Other semantic definitions have also been tried. The same Jespersen, as will be remembered from the quote given at the outset of this section (1924:145) defines subject and predicate in terms of discourse-bound topic and comment. A few pages further down, however, in the same book yet another position is defended, namely that 'the subject is comparatively definite and special, while the predicate is less definite, and thus applicable to a greater number of things' (1924:150), as in *The thief was a coward*. This view is virtually identical to the one generally taken in model-theoretic semantics (ch. 6), where the predicate is required to be of a higher order than the subject. Jespersen realized that this semantic notion of subject runs into trouble with identity statements like *Miss Johnson is Mrs. Prendergast,* or, we may add, with statements that assign a value on a parameter, like *The temperature is 50 degrees.* Such problems are discussed in Jespersen (1924:151-4) and (1937:135-7), his last work on theory. But no satisfactory solution is offered. In the light of the foregoing we must, therefore, conclude that no semantic definition is available to date for lexical argument terms.

2.6.4 Logic, thought and language: the eternal triangle

• *Modern predicate calculus interpreted as verbal, not cognitive logic*

It is interesting to compare the 19th century subject-predicate debate with the developments that took place in logic around the turn of the century under the influence of, especially, Frege and Russell, the fathers of modern logic, in particular modern predicate calculus (for biographical details of these two important scholars, see 5.4.1 and 5.4.2). Frege developed most of the ideas but used an awkward formal language, while Russell independently developed many of the same ideas but used a much more appropriate formal language. He devised the language of modern predicate calculus. Modern logic has proved vastly superior to traditional logic, not only because of its formal language of propositional structures, with quantifiers and variables, scope distinctions and *n*-ary predicates, but also because of the model theory that was developed in its wake, supported by the achievements of mathematical set theory (see chapter 5). Never before had logic achieved such a high degree of precision and formal sophistication. As a result, this way of doing logic has become standard and has acquired high prestige. But let us revert to Frege and Russell.

They, too, proposed a 'second face' for sentence structures. Aristotelian predicate calculus, which was based on a surface grammatical analysis of natural language sentences, had collapsed: new formal techniques and notions now provided a solution to certain inherent flaws that had been known since Aristotle but had never been repaired (see 5.1.5). A new predicate calculus had been constructed with the help of entirely new structural elements, such as quantifiers and variables. This new calculus generates propositional structures that may reflect the logic, but do not reflect the grammar, of the corresponding sentences. Yet it is the basis not only of modern logic but also of modern formal semantics, and is thus relevant in the study of linguistic meaning.

The point we want to stress here is that the logical analyses devised by Frege, Russell and later logicians are in fact an explicit account of one version of the Aristotelian truth relation. As was shown in section 1.2.1, Aristotle's notion of truth wavers between two distinct conceptions: on the one hand truth is seen as correspondence between what is *thought* and what is the case, but on the other hand it is also seen as correspondence between what is *said* and what is the case, i.e. the *cognitive* and the *verbal* notion of truth, respectively. It is Aristotle's verbal notion of truth that is made explicit in modern logic. The cognitive truth notion has so far not been made explicit.

• *Cognitive interpretation of logic in the Stoic tradition*
Correspondingly, two currents are detectable in the history of logic. According to the one, truth is seen as a correspondence relation between what is *thought* and what is the case. According to the other, truth is correspondence between what is *said* and what is the case. On the whole, the verbal interpretation, initiated by Aristotle, has scored better from the formal point of view, whereas the cognitive interpretation, first represented by the Stoics, has stronger philosophical and methodological foundations. In the Middle Ages both schools of thought existed side by side, the two notions being identified in Speculative Grammar, while the nominalists opted for the verbal notion. When we come to the 19th century, logic is exclusively interpreted as being cognitive: the Romantic movement had created a climate where anything to do with the mind or the soul was receiving a great deal of detailed attention.

• *The cognitive perspective during the nineteenth and twentieth centuries*
Let us look at a few examples. George Boole, significantly, called his 1854 book *An Investigation of the Laws of Thought on which are founded the Mathematical Theories of Logic and Probabilities*. Russell would soon fight against this cognitive notion of logic, but it persisted till well into the 20th century. A more or less arbitrary selection from logic handbooks, most of which have made no history, will show what the dominant attitude was and how it gradually moved away from the cognitive to the verbal notion (often with some embarrassment).

> If we consider the nature of our Thought, we find that an important part of it is engaged in the attempt to arrive at propositions which are *certain* and *universally valid*, but that it frequently fails to do this when left to its natural development. Hence arises the problem of ascertaining the conditions under which this object can be attained, and of determining in accordance with those conditions the rules to be followed in its attainment. The solution of this problem would place us in possession of a technical science of Thought, directing us how to arrive at certain and universally valid propositions. Such a science we call Logic.
>
> To determine what Thinking in general is, how it differs from other psychical activities, in what relations it stands to these, and what are its different varieties, is primarily the business of Psychology.   Sigwart (1895:1)

The Oxford philosopher Thomas Fowler (1895) takes the cognitive view but has verbal qualms:

> But the more detailed consideration of ... Thoughts or the results of Thinking becomes the subject of a science with a distinct name, Logic, which is thus a subordinate branch of the wider science, Psychology. ...
>
> Logic may therefore be defined as the science of the conditions on which correct thoughts depend, and the art of attaining to correct and avoiding incorrect thoughts. ... Logic is concerned with the *products* or results rather than with the *process* of thought, i.e. with *thoughts* rather than with *thinking*. ...
>
> As all logicians are agreed that we cannot communicate our thoughts without the aid of language, or of equivalent signs, and that practically we do always think by means of language, by sort of internal converse, it will be safer to adopt the terminology of those authors who regard our thoughts as expressed in language rather than that of those who consider or attempt to consider them in themselves as apart from their expression in words. I shall therefore speak of Terms and Propositions, not of Concepts and Judgments.
>
> Sir W. Hamilton and his followers, regarding Logic as primarily and essentially concerned with thought, and only secondarily and accidentally with language, attempt to mark the products of thought by words which do not imply their expression in language. Thus, instead of Terms and Propositions, they use respectively the words Concepts and Judgments. The word Syllogism, owing to the ambiguity of the Greek word *lógos*, stands either for the internal thought or the external expression of it.   Fowler (1895:5-8)

Another Oxford logician, F.C.S. Schiller (1912), falls in with Hamilton and Sigwart:

> The derivation of Logic from the ambiguous Greek word *logikē* would seem to indicate that it is a study either of words or of reasoning. And this ambiguity is significant; for it accompanies Logic throughout its whole career. It is the constant aim of Logic to deal with reasoning, and its perpetual danger to fail to deal with anything more than words, and to substitute classification of verbal distinctions for the study of actual thinking. ...
>
> [Logic] is not concerned with the actual occurrence of processes of thinking and reasoning, but rather with their *products*, the thoughts and reasonings which our intelligence thereby achieves. It is interested not in the arguings but in the arguments.   Schiller (1912:1-2)

The Jesuit A.C. Cotter (1931) has a scholastic touch. He does not show much influence of Russellian logic, or of modern psychology:

> Logic is the science and art of right reasoning. ... Logic is the art of thinking straight. ... The material object of logic is reasoning; the formal object ... is correctness. ... Logic differs essentially from psychology. Logic deals primarily with the objective aspect of our intellectual processes, psychology with the subjective.
>   Cotter (1931:7-9)

Copi's (1961) point of view is both cognitivist and clear. For him logic is a yardstick, a decision procedure for correct reasoning:

> The study of logic is the study of the methods and principles used in distinguishing correct from incorrect reasoning. ...

Logic has frequently been defined as the science of the laws of thought. But this definition, although it gives a clue to the nature of logic, is not accurate. In the first place, thinking is one of the processes studied by the psychologists. Logic cannot be 'the' science of the laws of thought, because psychology is also a science which deals with laws of thought (among other things). And logic is not a branch of psychology; it is a separate and distinct field of study.

In the second place, ... all reasoning is thinking, but not all thinking is reasoning. ...

Another common definition of logic states it to be the science of reasoning. This definition ... still will not do. Reasoning is a special kind of thinking, in which inference takes place or in which conclusions are drawn from premises. But it is still thought and therefore still part of the psychologist's subject matter. As psychologists examine the reasoning process they find it to be extremely complex, highly emotional, consisting of awkward trial-and-error procedures illuminated by sudden – and sometimes apparently irrelevant – flashes of insight. These are all of importance to psychology. But the logician is not in the least concerned with the dark ways by which the mind arrives at its conclusions during the actual processes of reasoning. He is concerned only with the *correctness* of the completed process. His question is always: does the conclusion reached *follow* from the premises used or assumed? ... The distinction between correct and incorrect reasoning is the central problem with which logic deals.   Copi (1961:3-6)

Against this we find the modern tradition of logic, which is explicitly anti-cognitive and verbal. Frege still wavered between cognitive and verbal logic, with a nostalgic preference for the former. He was a little more lenient, also because of his profound interest in natural language. Russell, however, was strongly opposed to the cognitive, 'psychologistic' view of logic. In his day, the fight against cognitive logic seemed an uphill struggle, as virtually the whole of logic was cognitive. That Russellian logic carried the day in the 20th century is mainly due, apart from its intrinsic quality, to the increased importance of mathematics[30] and to the rise of behaviourism and the consequent turning away from 'mentalism' in the human sciences.

● *Lewis Carroll's logic*
A curious exception to the dominant cognitive attitude in logic at the end of the 19th century is the *Rev. Charles L. Dodgson* (1832-1898), of Christ Church, Oxford. In 1896 he published Part I of an eccentric but for a number of years very popular textbook of logic under his literary pseudonym of Lewis Carroll. Part I was written explicitly for children. Part II was not, and remained

---

[30] At least of standard mathematics. With the notable exception of Intuitionism, modern mathematics is entirely non-cognitive. In the widest sense, standard mathematics is perhaps best characterized as the formal calculus of absolute, i.e. metaphysical, necessity to which any possible world is subjected. Intuitionism, on the other hand, founded by the Dutch mathematician L.E.J. Brouwer (1881-1966), is based on the principle that all mathematics is to be constructed by and from the individual mind, very much in the spirit of Plato's dialogue *Meno*, where Socrates makes a young uneducated slave prove the theorem of Pythagoras simply by asking him questions. For Brouwer, mathematics is not so much the formal theory of metaphysical necessity as the formal theory of what is necessary in any form of thinking. In a sense, therefore, Brouwer's Intuitionism is essentially Romantic, contrary to modern standard mathematics, which belongs in the post-Romantic world of the conquest and control of physical nature.

unpublished until William W. Bartley III discovered it and had the whole work published integrally in 1977 (Bartley 1977).

The book starts out with a simple ontological analysis, based on set theory: the Universe is said to consist of *things* and *classes of things*. Each class of things is characterized by an *adjunct*, i.e. an *attribute* or *class of attributes*. A class of things may be real (non-empty) or non-real (empty). Then Carroll proceeds to a discussion of names and propositions (Bartley 1977:67-68):

> The word "Proposition", as used in ordinary conversation, may be applied to *any* word or phrase, which conveys any information whatever. ... But a **Proposition**, as used in this First Part of *Symbolic Logic*, has a peculiar form, which may be called its **Normal form**; and if any Proposition, which we wish to use in an argument, is not in normal form, we must reduce it to such a form, before we can use it. ...
>
> The Subject and the Predicate of a proposition are called its **Terms**.

He thus clearly represents the verbal notion of logic, and is therefore inevitably faced with the problem of the relation between logical analysis ('normal form') and actual sentence structure. He describes this relation as one of 'reduction', which is not very revealing. To stop his youthful readers from worrying too much about such questions he relegates logic to the realm of re-creations and games, but this cannot satisfy his more demanding readers (Bartley 1977:45; 52-53):

> I claim, for Symbolic Logic, a very high place among recreations that have the nature of games or puzzles; and I believe that any one, who will really *try* to understand it, will find it more interesting and more absorbing than most of the games or puzzles yet invented. ...
>
> Mental recreation is a thing that we all of us need for our mental health; and you may get much healthy enjoyment, no doubt, from Games, such as Back-gammon, Chess, and the new Game "Halma". But, after all, when you have made yourself a first-rate player at any of these Games, you have nothing real to *show* for it, as a *result*! You enjoyed the Game, and the victory, no doubt, *at the time*: but you have no *result* that you can treasure up and get real *good* out of. And, all the while, you have been leaving unexplored a perfect mine of wealth. Once master the machinery of Symbolic Logic, and you have a mental occupation always at hand, of absorbing interest, and one that will be of real *use* to you in *any* subject you may take up. It will give you clearness of thought – the ability to *see your way* through a puzzle – the habit of arranging your ideas in an orderly and get-at-able form – and, more valuable than all, the power to detect *fallacies*, and to tear to pieces the flimsy illogi-cal arguments, which you will so continually encounter in books, in newspapers, in speeches, and even in sermons, and which so easily delude those who have never taken the trouble to master this fascinating Art. *Try it*. That is all I ask of you!

Carroll's *Symbolic Logic* is an interesting book from many different points of view, literary, historical, and also logical. The logical ideas expressed are sometimes curiously ahead of their time (though they are also typical of their time in that there is occasional confusion regarding terms and extensions, or object language and metalanguage). But this is not the place to discuss Lewis Carroll's contribution to logic. All we do here is point out the fact that he is an untypical early representative of the verbal notion of logic.

• *Why the verbal concept of logic has been more successful*

There woul;d seem to be a *prima facie* justification for the verbal concept of logic. Logic requires, besides an analysis of that which is or can be the case, an analysis of the structures, whether cognitive or verbal, that carry truth values. And if a choice is to be made between an analysis of cognitive or of verbal structures, then the latter are obviously preferable to the former, thought being unobservable and abstract, whereas sentences are observable as physical utterances. This point of view is clearly expressed by Stegmüller:

> The concept "true" is used as a predicate. But as a predicate of what? ... In principle there are two possibilities. "True" can be regarded as a predicate of sentences as linguistic structures, or as a predicate of that which is expressed by these sentences, i.e. of judgements. At first sight it might seem that the decision should go in favour of judgements. For sentences are there for the judgements, and not the other way round. Sentences are merely linguistic tools; what matters is the judgements expressed in them. Yet it is not advisable to take the judgement option, since one gets immediately involved in a mass of philosophical discussions that have repeated themselves endlessly for a long time without ever leading to any in any way satisfactyory solution and thus to agreement among the investigators involved. When the sentence, as a linguistic expression, is taken as the point of departure such discussions ... can be avoided. We see here a factor that has dominated the whole development of the newer logic. Whenever logical analysis did not take the linguistic expression as its point of departure, three drawbacks could be observed: 1. One got immediately involved in a preliminary discussion on whether this kind of investigation was really logical, and not one that belonged to a different disciplines such as psychology. ... 2. The very reality of the phenomena concerned was often called into question. ... 3. The decisive argument in this context is, however, that only those investigations that sought a connection with linguistic expressions have led to really positive results. The whole development of symbolic logic, and indeed of the modern logic of science, has been possible only because it was a sentence logic and not a judgement logic that took the "cognitive content" of a sentence as its object of enquiry.   Stegmüller (1957:16-17)

• *The problem of the empirical status of logical analysis*

Now that analyses that stay closest to the physical side of utterances had failed from a logical point of view, an alternative, more abstract sentence analysis was needed, and found, in the language of modern predicate calculus. But it was still interpreted by the logicians as *sentence*, not as *thought* analysis. (We must make an exception for Frege, who still took a 19th century view of logic as a formal analysis of *thought.* For him thought was not the actual process of reasoning, which often goes wrong and is subject to all kinds of disturbing influences, but an idealized set of procedures that yield truth if applied correctly. In this respect, therefore, Frege's views did not differ much from those of some of the authors quoted above.) The more abstract analysis of modern predicate calculus was, and is, standardly regarded as a (or the) correct rendering of the logical properties of sentences. Significantly, however, the question of the *empirical status* of logical sentence analysis was never mooted. For a long time logical analysis was never considered to play a role in any explanatory theory. It was just part of an essentially mathematical game without empirical or explanatory import.

Modern predicate calculus has been spectacularly successful and has proved its usefulness in many, often unexpected ways. It can be said to have provided, at least in part, an explicit account of the Aristotelian verbal truth relation between what is said and what is the case, a relation that had remained largely obscure till the advent of modern logic. But it has also complicated matters for itself. Because what has been established is, strictly speaking, no longer a relation between *what is said* and what is the case but a relation between a *logical analysis* of what is said and what is the case. There is, therefore, the new question of the status of logical analysis and of the relation between it and what is actually said. This question is taken up in chapter 7.

• *Ogden and Richards' semiotic triangle*

When we compare the search for logical structure carried out by logicians with the search for semantic ('inner') form conducted by linguists and philosophers of language, we notice that in the latter, but not the former, the main emphasis lies in the role and functioning of cognition. The search for logical form has concentrated on the verbal sentence; the search for semantic form has always, until model-theoretic semantics appeared, concentrated on cognition.

The two searches can be combined into one research programme that would follow the lines of the famous semiotic triangle, drawn by Ogden & Richards (1923:11) (see fig. 2 in section 1.2.1). In this analysis, logical structure hovers, in some ill-defined way, over SYMBOL, and semantic structure, in an equally ill-defined way, over THOUGHT. Now verbal logic, which is what Ogden & Richards had in mind, is an attempt at making explicit the base line of the triangle, the relation between SYMBOL and REFERENT (the world). But, as Ogden & Richards make clear, this base line does not represent a causal but merely an 'imputed' relation, one that can be described by stipulation but is not taken to play a role in the causal processes of uttering and comprehending utterances. A research programme in the sense of Ogden & Richards' analysis of the speech process would investigate the causal relations and disregard the merely 'imputed' relation of Aristotelian verbal truth.

CHAPTER 3

The twentieth century: Europe

3.0 Preamble

This century has seen more linguistic studies carried out than all preceding centuries taken together. Especially after 1950 the increase in numbers of students, professionals and publications has been dramatic. As a result, the field has changed character: numerically and sociologically it has grown from a village into a town. Whether this has brought along improved quality and enhanced scientific status is another question.

The paramount feature of theoretical linguistics throughout the 20th century has been the desire to become a real and autonomous science, after the model of the much-admired natural sciences, in particular theoretical physics. The last sentence in Bloomfield's *Language* of 1933 is but one of the numerous expressions of this wish found in the literature of this period:

> The methods and results of linguistics, in spite of their modest scope, resemble those of natural science, the domain in which science has been most successful. It is only a prospect, but not hopelessly remote, that the study of language may help us toward the understanding and control of human events.   Bloomfield (1933:509)

Modern theoretical linguistics cannot be understood if its struggle for scientific status is not placed at the centre of its history. The main problem in this quest for scientific status has always been that of *empirical access*, that is, some notion of what constitutes reliable data, the formulation of one or more causal questions, and some success at answering these questions by means of an explanatory theory. Accordingly, the central theme pursued in this and the following chapter is the search for this empirical access to language. We shall witness a slow and often uncertain progress towards that end, and we will conclude that some limited access has probably been found. Linguistics, though now recognized as an autonomous discipline called 'general linguistics', is beginning to look like a real science but it hasn't achieved full status yet.

The lines we will pursue are the following. Leaving comparative philology behind as a respected but no longer active force in the shaping of linguistic theory, we will consider the concept of structuralism as a leading force in the human sciences in Europe and in America. As regards Europe, which is the topic of the present chapter, we will look at the late 19th century comparative philologists Baudouin de Courtenay and de Saussure and see how they laid the foundations of a new approach to the study of language in Europe. De Saussure will stand out as the most influential figure, despite serious weaknesses in his work. His influence is traced through the European linguistic schools that flourished between the wars, in particular in Prague, Copenhagen and London. Special attention is paid to the birth of phonology, brought about mainly by the ideas of Jan Baudouin de Courtenay, Ferdinand de Saussure, Daniel Jones, Roman Jakobson and Nikolai Trubetzkoy.

3.1 Structuralism and the problem of mind

Structuralism finds its origin in the gradual realization that the physical world as a whole is a complex and elaborate network of interrelated dynamic mechanisms. At first this insight was applied only to the obviously material world. But when, about a hundred years ago, it became clear that the predicate 'physical' was in certain ways applicable also to the realm of mental phenomena, the mechanization view began to be applied to the products of the human mind as well as to the mind itself. This marked the beginning of what we now call 'structuralism'.

Since the 17th century it had been widely accepted among philosophers and scientists that the world as a whole, and each living body in particular, is an autonomous mechanism, a clockwork, ticking away on its own account till the end comes. The perfection of time pieces was a major achievement of the 17th century, thanks to men like Galileo and Huygens,[1] and they provided a model not only for cosmology, the macroscopic ordering of heavenly bodies, but also for biological organisms. During the latter half of the 19th century the mechanized view of world and body was reinforced and further systematized by the advent and widespread use of machines in industry and in locomotion. Machine technology thus provided an additional model for the interpretation of physical reality, just as clockworks had done in the post-medieval period. Around the turn of the century it became common to see the world as a hierarchy of interrelated objects, starting with individual atomic objects and climbing up through ever higher orders of complexity. Each complex object has an internal structure that governs the interaction of the component parts and ensures a proper functioning.

- *Structuralism as the study of interpretative structures and processes*

It is the application of the machine metaphor to the products of human activity and in particular of the human mind that characterizes *structuralism*. The mind is seen as an information processing machine that fits sense data into a functional structure that serves a purpose and has a meaning. We say that, in so doing, the mind *interprets* the data. Structuralism in the human sciences is the study of the structures that play a role in interpretation processes. The re-

---

[1] The clockwork problem was a central issue in 17th century physics and mathematics. Cogwheel systems had been used to keep the time since the 13th century, but they were not very precise, nor could they be used at sea, where time measurement was essential to determine longitudinal position. By the end of the 16th century the kings of Europe offered large rewards for the invention of a time piece stable enough to keep the time aboard ship. In 1675 the Dutch mathematician and experimental physicist Christiaan Huygens invented the balance wheel with steel spring, as still used in winding watches. This improved longitudinal measurements at sea, but the problem was not solved until a hundred years later by the Englishman John Harrison (Sobel 1996).

lation of these interpretative structures to the physical sense data is often hard to define, owing to the active imposition of overall interpretative wholes upon the data, which are thus forced into a mould of cognitive making. The interpretative structures are functional in the sense that they are embedded in larger networks of purposeful behaviour. This makes the whole more than the sum of the individual parts and thus confers meaning upon them. This general structuralist view is found not only in psychology and linguistics, but also in the study of literature and art in general, and of societies.[2]

In linguistics, structuralism started during the second half of the 19th century. Given the central concern of structuralism with the functional structures occurring in interpretation processes, it is hardly surprising that the first manifestations of structuralism in linguistics concerned the study of speech sounds as physical sense data to be interpreted in terms of a cognitive phonological system that confers meaning upon them.[3] When linguistic structuralism stopped is hard to say and largely a question of definition. One may say that it stopped around 1960, when the computational view of the mind began to take over from behaviourism. But one may also say, with equal justification, that we are still in the middle of it, since the new computational view has not changed the problems that are to be solved. These still revolve around the question of how speech sounds correspond to cognitive structures in such a way that comprehension takes place.

- *Conflict between materialist and functionalist views of language*

The main practical difficulty in applying the structuralist ideas to language consisted in the elusive nature of 'language'. What is the ontological status of language in general, of specific languages in particular? What is a sentence, a word, a meaning? The most concrete, tangible linguistic elements would seem to be the speech sounds. Yet it soon became clear that these, too, were elusive, as they serve their linguistic function of meaning transfer not primarily in terms of their physical reality but in virtue of a system of idealized sound units and their interrelations. Inevitably, those who began to think about these matters were drawn into the realm of the mind. But the mind was an object which had not been subjected to the machine metaphor. On the contrary, owing largely to the still prevailing influence of religious institutions, the mind was seen as

[2] In the case of societies the ultimate purpose was sometimes history and national glory, sometimes also the orderly functioning of the state, which was regarded as the 'sum' taking precedence over its parts, the citizens. In the recent past, as one knows, this has led to a series of totalitarian regimes that subordinated the interests of individuals to those of the state, i.e. the regime. A more humanist balance has now been re-established, as it is now commonly accepted that the ultimate good resides in the well-being of the individuals making up the society, and not vice versa.

[3] Interestingly, there is still no fully formalized theory available that accounts for the recognition of actual speech sounds by listeners. Automatic speech recognition, as opposed to automatic speech production, is still a problem that has no principled solution. The machine recognition systems that are most successful at this moment are all based on statistic analyses of text corpora, not on structuralist principles of interpretation.

something in its own right, of a higher order than physical reality. Given this perspective one understands why the main concern of theoretical linguistics during the first half of this century was to gain *empirical access* to the facts of language, so that some form of explanatory theory, in the full scientific sense, could be set up to answer the causal questions that were beginning to loom.

- *Reductionism: the mind as physical object*

One understands likewise why, from then on, it seemed to make good scientific sense to treat the mind as a physical object so that it could be brought in line with the other physical objects studied in what were considered to be the true sciences, the sciences of physical nature. Thus began the big struggle to subdue all mental structures and processes to the constraints of physical matter. This struggle has lasted till the present day, and the scientific programme behind it is called *reductionism*. Over the decades, this reductionist programme went through many different stages of growth and development. The first serious materialist theory of the mind was behaviourism, which tried to explain the mind by explaining it away, as it was given to an absolutely minimal hypothesis of stimulus association. This gave us grammar without meaning. And when that obstacle had been removed, by the mid-'60s, we were saddled with a semantics without the mind, only because logic, the source of the new semantics, had not caught up with cognitive science, which applies the computer metaphor to mental phenomena.

- *Structuralism in linguistics; Europe and America*

But let us revert to the beginning. The most notable European exponents of the new effort were Jan Baudouin de Courtenay from Poland and Ferdinand de Saussure from Switzerland. In America there were, somewhat later, Edward Sapir and Leonard Bloomfield. In the American variety we see, starting with Bloomfield, a predominance of behaviourist-positivistic methodology, with an emphasis on formulaic analyses. European structuralism was unaffected by behaviourism and preferred introspective and intuitive analyses coupled with a realist interpretation in terms of psychological structures and processes. Both had in common the view that (each) language is an autonomous structure in the mind or brain of its speakers, interacting with other autonomous structures in the mind or brain. In principle, therefore, the structuralist linguists defended what we now call a *modularity concept of language*: language is a self-contained module interacting with other modules in the mind. As a consequence, they declared, both in America and in Europe, the autonomy of linguistics as a science, distinct, in particular, from psychology. It was thus that in the years between the two world wars linguistics established itself, on both sides of the Atlantic, as a discipline in its own right.

One must realize the enormous contrast between the relative ease with which we now speak about these matters and the difficulties experienced by the pioneers of structuralism in casting their thoughts in comprehensible and coherent formulations. There was no accepted terminology. Ideas about the mind were hazy and imbued with dualist concepts of a material mortal body and a non-material immortal soul. The notion of structure was still very abstract. It was unclear what it would apply to or how it could be visualized. For the study of language, in other words, structuralism was a long shot.

3.2   Baudouin de Courtenay and de Saussure

We will now have a closer look at Baudouin de Courtenay and de Saussure, the two key figures of early European structuralism.

- *Baudouin de Courtenay*

Jan Baudouin de Courtenay (1845-1929)[4] was born in Poland as a member of the Polish branch of an ancient aristocratic French family that traced its origins to the Middle Ages. He studied Slavonic languages and historical linguistics in Warsaw, Prague, Jena, Berlin, Leipzig and St. Petersburg, which awarded him his doctorate. For eight years, between 1875 and 1883, he worked at the University of Kazan in Russia in close collaboration with his countryman the psychologist and philosopher M. Kruszewski (1851-1887). While working with Kruszewski, who died young of a neurological disease, Baudouin developed many ideas that were to become highly influential in European structuralist linguistics. In 1893 he was appointed to the chair of Slavonic languages at Krakow. In 1900 he returned to St. Petersburg, but was imprisoned there in 1913 for writing against the state. After the war he returned to Warsaw, where he still did some teaching. He died there in 1929.

Besides a wide interest in general linguistic questions, he concentrated mainly on the psychological aspects of language, distinguishing between the physical and the psychological level of language. There he found a way of applying the notion of structure to language sounds. Together with Kruszewski, during their years at Kazan, he developed the idea that actual physical sounds are the manifestation of psychological sound images in the build-up of words. From the physical point of view speech sounds are infinitely varied, but psychologically there is a relatively small number of structural units in terms of which the actual sounds are realized. These units were called *phonemes*, a term coined by Kruszewski and destined to have quite a career in the 20th century. Baudouin called the study of phonemes 'psychophonetics', which indicates his psychological approach to what we now call phonology. For Baudouin, phonemes were ideal sound images which a speaker would try to approximate as faithfully as possible in producing actual speech sounds.

Baudouin is rightly regarded as the prime founder of phonology, the functional study of speech sounds. Despite the fact that he developed his ideas in faraway Kazan, more than 700 kilometres east of Moscow, and wrote mostly in Russian or Polish, his teaching in Krakow, St. Petersburg and Warsaw was sufficient to make his ideas reach the more influential places in Europe. Daniel Jones (1957:5-6) relates that students of Baudouin whom he met

---

[4] The best source for Baudouin's life and work is Stankiewicz (1972).

in England just before the first world war made him see the importance of the notion of phoneme, with the result that by about 1915 the theory of the phoneme as the psychological principle behind the realization of speech sounds 'began to find a regular place in the teaching given in the Department of Phonetics at University College'.[5]

In Eastern Europe Baudouin was widely read, and it was through Eastern European scholars like Jakobson, Trubetzkoy and many others that phonology as the functional study of speech sounds became a powerful sub-discipline of linguistics. We shall revert to this episode in section 3.3. Now we turn to de Saussure.

- *De Saussure: life*

Ferdinand de Saussure (1857-1913) was born in Geneva in an upper-class family of scientists and politicians. After one year as a student of natural science at Geneva he was allowed to go to Leipzig and study there. He arrived in Leipzig in 1876, and decided to switch over to comparative philology, for which Leipzig was famous. After just a couple of years of linguistic study at Leipzig and two semesters at Berlin he published a 300-page work, *Mémoire sur le système primitif des voyelles dans les langues indo-européennes*, variously dated 1878 and 1879. This work was destined to keep comparative philologists busy for the next one hundred years. It contains the famous laryngeal theory, which postulates two hypothetical sounds for Proto-Indo-European, not attested in any of the Indo-European languages known then, but sufficient to explain a number of puzzling irregularities in the development of certain vowels in a number of languages. Fifteen years after his death it was discovered that Hittite, an Indo-European language deciphered in 1917, contains a sound with precisely the properties predicted by de Saussure's hypothesis. After presenting his doctoral dissertation on the genitive absolute in Sanskrit in Leipzig in 1880 he left for Paris, where he was offered a teaching post at the Ecole des Hautes Etudes in 1881. He stayed there till 1891, when he went back to Geneva to take up the chair of Sanskrit and Comparative Philology. He stayed in Geneva till his death in 1913.

---

[5] Jones had been appointed to teach phonetics at University College London in 1907. He knew (1957:5) that the phonetician Henry Sweet (1845-1912) had developed a notion of 'phoneme' (but not the term) at Oxford during the 1870s (see 3.5). Sweet's notion was psycho-phonetic in that he wanted 'broad' phonetic transcription to reflect the native speaker's intuitions of phonological sound unit (a notion of phoneme also held by Sapir much later). Jones also knew that the French phonetician Paul Passy (1859-1940) had taken the phonemic principle from Sweet and Baudouin and was working with it, urging colleagues in Britain to do the same. Yet it took Baudouin's students to convince him: 'it was some time before we in England realized the full import of the concept' (ib.). It is clear from Jones's account that the theory of phonemes arose out of phonetics and remained within the province of phonetics for a long time. Its autonomy as a branch of the non-physical, or not primarily physical, study of linguistic systems did not come until the late 1920s.

After his thesis of 1880 he never published any more books, just a few articles on topics in historical linguistics. In fact, from 1893 onward he hardly published anything at all. It was then that he began to be depressive and dispirited, seeking refuge, at times, in occult speculations about hidden messages in Greek and Latin poetry, based on occurrences or repetitions of syllables and sounds (Starobinski 1979). He himself attributed his depressions, in a letter to Meillet of 1894, to the overwhelming magnitude of the problems he had started to struggle with. These were the problems of structure, system and method in linguistic studies that he dealt with in the lecture courses on which the posthumous *Cours* of 1916 is based. While still in Paris he had started to develop general ideas about language and the study of language, and he discussed these with a large number of linguists and philosophers, including Baudouin de Courtenay, with whom he later had some correspondence (Godel 1966:480), and in particular Hippolyte Taine, a remarkable cultural figure of the period.

Hippolyte Taine (1828-1893) was a critic, philosopher and historian, a man of great erudition and a correspondingly wide range of interests, a 'généraliste' in the best of French intellectual tradition (he wrote, remarkably, also a history of English literature). Though widely read and quite influential during the *fin de siècle* in Paris and France, he is now largely forgotten. Yet he was among the first to formulate the ideas that underlay the growing structuralist movement, in particular in his main philosophical work *De l'Intelligence*, first published in 1870 and reprinted many times until the first world war. According to Aarsleff (1982:356-71), de Saussure probably derived most of his fundamental ideas from Taine, directly or indirectly, in particular the notions of the linguistic sign and *valeur*, and his now classical distinctions between *langue* and *parole*, and between synchrony and diachrony.

Ordered by the University of Geneva de Saussure gave three courses on general linguistics between 1906 and 1911, although the prospect of having to do this 'simply terrified him: he did not feel up to the task, and had no desire to wrestle with the problems once more' (Godel 1966:493, quoting a friend of de Saussure's who knew him at the time). Although his students and colleagues had hoped that he would write a book on this subject he never did, not only, one gathers, because of his premature death but also because he did not feel ready for it.[6] After de Saussure's death two of his colleagues, Charles Bally and Albert Sechehaye, decided that de Saussure's lecture courses should nevertheless be turned into a book. With the help of a few of de Saussure's students, in particular Albert Riedlinger (who is mentioned as a co-editor), and on the basis of whatever little they could find in de Saussure's own study, a text was compiled, which was published in 1916. This is the famous *Cours de*

---

[6] In their Preface to the *Cours*, Bally and Sechehaye, the two senior editors, politely allude to the possibility that the maître would not have approved of the publication. Godel (1966) is much more explicit: de Saussure felt inadequate and suffered from it. One may infer that he would indeed not have approved the publication.

linguistique générale (henceforth *Cours*), one of the most quoted works in the linguistics literature of this century.

- *The* Cours*: linguistics as a discipline*

The *Cours* is a strange and puzzling book. The first chapter discusses 19th century comparative philology. Here de Saussure[7] addresses severe criticism at pre-Young-Grammarian work, mentioning by name Max Müller, Georg Curtius and August Schleicher, on account of their unrealistic notions of what constitutes a living language. He condemns the 'living organism' metaphor, and praises the Young Grammarians for their effort at establishing a truly historical account of linguistic developments. Yet they, too, have failed to answer the fundamental questions of general linguistics. Chapter 2 begins with a definition of what constitutes data for linguistic theory:

> The subject matter of linguistics is given first of all by all the manifestations of human language, whether of savage peoples or civilized nations, archaic, classical or decadent eras, taking into account always not only 'correct' or 'nice' language but all forms of linguistic expression. And that is not all: as language often escapes observation the linguist will have to take account also of written texts, because these alone can make known to him past or distant idioms.

Then comes the task of general linguistics (note that no causal question is formulated):

> The task of linguistics will be:
>
> a) to make a description and write the history of all the languages that can be reached, which means writing the history of all language families and reconstructing, as far as possible, the lines of parentage in each family;
>
> b) to identify the forces that are at work permanently and universally in all languages, and the general laws to which all language change is subject;
>
> c) to delimit and define itself.

On p. 21 de Saussure briefly sets off linguistics from adjacent disciplines, in particular ethnography, anthropology, social psychology, physiology ('the essence of language, as we shall see, is alien to the phonic character of the linguistic sign') and philology, promising to return to the subject later. When he does so the relationship with psychology turns out to be somewhat troubled. 'All is psychological in language', he says on p. 21. But then, on p. 33:

> One can therefore conceive of *a science that studies the life of signs amidst the life of society*; it would form a part of social psychology, and hence of general psychology. We shall call it *semiology*. ... Linguistics is but a part of this general science; the laws to be discovered by semiology will apply to linguistics as well, which will thus find itself integrated into a well-defined domain in the totality of human facts.
> ...
> Up till now, language has been studied almost always in function of something else, from an alien point of view. First we have the superficial perspective of the general public, who see in language little more than a nomenclature, which suppresses all

---

[7] It must be understood that when we attribute views or quotes to de Saussure we refer to his indirect authorship as it has reached us through the editors of the text.

research into its true nature. Then we have the psychologist's point of view. He studies the mechanism of the sign in the individual. This is the easiest method, but it does not take us beyond the private realization and does not capture the sign, which is by definition social. And when one discovers that the sign should be studied socially all one finds is those traits of language that link it with other institutions, those that depend largely on our free will. Thus one misses the target and neglects the features that adhere to semiological systems in general and to language in particular. For the sign always escapes, to some extent, the individual or social free will. That is its true nature, which, however, is least visible at first glance.

Thus, one gathers, linguistics is part of a yet to be developed semiology, which is part of social psychology, which is part of general psychology. Yet semiology and linguistics seem to form a closer unit than semiology and the rest of psychology do. No reason is given for this difference, and, in general, de Saussure's meaning remains unclear. One feels that he wants to establish a certain autonomy for linguistics but is, in the end, unable to do so in a consistent way.

De Saussure struggles with the threefold terminology of *langage*, *langue* and *parole*. *Langage*, which has no equivalent in English, covers all manifestations of language: physical, physiological, psychological, social. It is best taken as the cover term for both *langue*, the type-level language system, and *parole*, the token-level physical use made of the language system, best translated as 'speech'. The first and foremost principle for the theoretical linguist is (p. 25):

> to take from the very first the point of view of the language system, and take that as the norm for all other manifestations of the 'langage'. ...
>
> The language system ... is a self-contained whole and a principle of classification. Once we assign it pride of place among the facts of 'langage' we introduce a natural order in a complex of facts that admit of no other classification.

- *The langue-parole distinction; the speech circuit*

The distinction between *langue* and *parole* is the first great distinction introduced by de Saussure into the linguistic literature. *Langue* is the language system, or, in his own words (p. 25), 'a social product of the language faculty, a set of necessary conventions adopted by the social body to allow the use of this faculty by individuals, ... a principle of classification'. On p. 30 again: *langue* is 'a treasure deposited by the practice of speech in the members of one community, a grammatical system virtually existing in each brain, or, more exactly, in the brains of a set of individuals. For *langue* never exists completely in one individual, it only does so in a community.' On p. 33: '*Langue* is a system of signs expressing ideas.'

Speech, on the other hand, is the use made of the language system in actual, hic et nunc situations. It involves a circular movement from speaker to hearer and back, whereby sounds are produced and received on both sides, passed through the mind, where the sounds are associated with 'concepts', which leads to new sound productions, etc. The schematic diagram representing this process is given on p. 28, reproduced here as fig. 1.

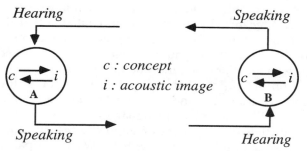

Figure 1 *Schematic representation of de Saussure's 'speech circuit' (p. 28)*

The process starts with a given concept (p. 28)

> triggering in the brain a corresponding acoustic image, a purely mental process, followed by the physiological process of the brain transmitting to the speech organs a set of impulses that correspond with the image. After that there is the purely physical process of the sound waves propagating themselves from A's mouth to B's ears. Then the circuit continues in B in inverse order: physiological transmission of the acoustic image from the ear to the brain, mental association in the brain of this image with the corresponding concept. If B speaks in his turn this new speech act will follow, from his brain to that of A, precisely the same course as was followed by the first.

A host of observations come to mind when we read these passages now, almost a hundred years later. We will consider only a few. First, one notes that de Saussure does not mention the reference objects in the real world that we speak about when our utterances are true, or the imagined reference objects conjured up by fictional speech. The object-directedness of thoughts and concepts is not mentioned.

- *Primacy of the word over the sentence; syntax as part of parole,*
  not of langue

Secondly, and more importantly, one notes that de Saussure speaks of concepts and acoustic images, but never of 'the complete and perfect sense' we encountered in the Speculative Grammar of the medieval modists (section 1.4.2). For de Saussure, the language system is word-centered, while the sentence as the rule-governed expression of a propositional thought is not taken into account. In fact, sentence syntax is for him part of *parole*, not of *langue* (p. 30-31):

> By contrast, *parole* is an individual act of free will and intelligence, in which we distinguish:
> 1) the combinations by means of which the speaking subject makes use of the language code in order to express his personal thought;
> 2) the psycho-physical mechanism enabling him to externalise these combinations.

On p. 172 de Saussure returns to this question. There he says that *parole* is characterized by the freedom of the combinations made by speakers when they express their thoughts. He then wonders whether all of syntax is therefore part of *parole*. His answer is revealing. No, he says, some of syntax belongs to the *langue*, because, first, there are a large number of set locutions, like *What of it?*, or *Let's go*, or *lift a finger*. One understands that these are part of the 'treasure deposited by the practice of speech in the members of one community'. Secondly, (p. 173) all syntagms that are rule-governed belong to the *langue*, and here he mentions first morphological constructions and then word groups formed on the basis of habitual patterning, though for these it is not always possible to draw the line between *langue* and *parole*. We shall see below that this word-based notion of language system was to be a major obstacle to a fruitful further development of linguistic theory.[8] In this respect the European psychologist-philosophers, Wilhelm Wundt in particular, who discussed subject and predicate and always looked at the sentence first, clearly had an advantage. And so had the Americans, who also saw the sentence as the primary unit of analysis in language.

- *De Saussure and phonology: his notion of 'phoneme'*

The following few chapters in the *Cours* deal with less central questions: a division between linguistics of *langue* and linguistics of *parole*, and between external and internal elements of *langue*. External elements are, for example, the geographical extension of a language, its history, its use in various spheres of life, and the like. The internal elements are constituted by 'whatever has an influence on the language system' (p. 43). Then a chapter on writing systems, which we shall leave undiscussed. Next comes a chapter on phonetics, oddly called 'phonology', as he wishes to reserve the term 'phonetics' for what we call historical phonology (pp. 55-56).

This is followed by an appendix (pp. 63-95) based on shorthand notes made of three lectures de Saussure gave in 1897 on the theory of the syllable. Here we frequently encounter the term *phonème*, defined as follows (p. 65):

> The phoneme is the sum of the acoustic impressions and the articulatory movements of the heard and the spoken unit, the one conditioning the other. It is thus a complex unit which has a foot in each chain.

According to Jones (1957:5-6), de Saussure uses the term *phoneme* in the sense of 'speech sound', as it had been used by Louis Havet, one of de Saussure's friends in Paris (Koerner 1994a:3663), in 1876 if not before, and not in the phonological sense of functional sound unit. This does not seem entirely correct. First, de Saussure wishes to distinguish between 'phoneme' and 'sound', though one is left wondering what he actually means (p. 98):

---

[8] On p. 97 de Saussure criticises the view according to which the *langue* is nothing but a nomenclature, a list of terms or words corresponding to as many things. The modern reader pricks up his ears, expecting an argument to the effect that there is also a rule system for the combination of the single units into larger wholes and finally sentences. But no, the criticism is that the link between the word form and that which it denotes is a great deal more complex than just an association of sounds and things. It is true that de Saussure says repeatedly that the *langue* is not only a list of lexical items and locutions but also a 'system'. Yet the 'system' he envisages seems limited to morphological inflections. De Saussure really had no eye for syntax.

It is precisely because the words of the language (langue) are for us acoustic images that we must avoid speaking of them being made up of 'phonemes'. This term implies an idea of vocal action and can therefore apply only to the spoken word, the realisation of the internal image in discourse. We can avoid this misunderstanding by speaking of the *sounds* and *syllables* of a word, provided we keep in mind that we are speaking of acoustic images.

If one compares this with what is read on p. 32 one is puzzled:

In the *langue*, however, we only have the acoustic image, which is capable of being translated into a constant visual image. For if one abstracts from this multitude of movements necessary for a realisation in *parole* each acoustic image is, as we shall see, but the sum of a limited number of elements or phonemes, susceptible in their turn of being evoked by a corresponding number of written symbols.

This would suggest that a phoneme, being part of acoustic images, is a systematic recipe for sound and belongs to the langue. We can only conclude that de Saussure's use of the term *phoneme* is confusing, and probably also confused. On p. 164 we read first that sounds, being material, cannot possibly belong to the *langue*. They are at most elements 'put into action' by the *langue*. In general, each linguistic form ('signifiant') is immaterial and is defined by its being an acoustic image. Then we read:

This principle is so essential that it applies to all material elements of the *langue*, the phonemes included. Each idiom constructs its words on the basis of a system of sonorous elements each forming a clearly delimited unit and whose number is strictly limited. What characterizes them is not, as one might think, their proper positive quality but simply the fact that they are not confused with each other. The phonemes are above all oppositive, relative and negative entities.

We can forgive him the expression 'material elements of the *langue*', as he explains on p. 98 that the term 'material' when applied to the *langue* refers to the form aspect, as opposed the conceptual aspect, of the signs that make up the *langue*. Given this, however, one sees that the phonemes are now part of the *langue*, and no longer of the *parole*.

Secondly, de Saussure did have a notion of the phonological fact that in each language some sound differences serve to distinguish different words (morphemes) while others are in free variation or anyway indifferent. We can infer this not only from the previous quote but also from other passages. On p. 83 he says:

In the act of speaking which we shall analyse we will take into account only the differential elements, those that are salient to the ear and capable of delimiting acoustic units in the chain of speech.

And on p. 72, speaking about sound features, he notes that native speakers of French would not consider the devoicing of *m* after a voiceless continuant 'a differential element'. One suspects that de Saussure had spoken with Baudouin de Courtenay about the notion of phoneme but did not quite know what to do with it, thinking erroneously that the phonemes of a word could be distinguished as such in the acoustic material sound. Jones (1957:5) tells us that the French phonetician Paul Passy knew about the phoneme from Baudouin, with whom he entertained considerable correspondence. We also know that, during his years in Paris, de Saussure taught Passy (Koerner 1994a:3663), who actively promoted Baudouin's notion of phoneme. It would seem almost impossible that de Saussure did not hear about this new concept during that period. Yet, as Jones says correctly (1957:6), although de Saussure 'was beginning to get an inkling of the concept of the phoneme as we know it … his explanation was obscure and of a negative character, and he never reached the point of recognizing the existence of allophones'.

- *The linguistic sign*

We now come to the second major distinction made by de Saussure in his incipient linguistic theory, that between *signifier* ('signifiant') and *signified* ('signifié'), both making up the *sign* as a lexical unit. We shall speak of *form* and *concept*, respectively. The combination of a form and a concept into a sign is a purely mental operation: 'The linguistic sign unites not a thing and a name, but a concept and an acoustic image' (p. 98). And both are purely mental, as signs are. De Saussure warns the reader (p. 99) that he uses the term *sign* not, as is customary, for actual physical forms but for the mental unit in which (mental) form and concept are united. Acoustic images or forms, too, are mental since we can form an image or mental representation of a sound by imagining what it sounds like without any actual physical effect being produced. 'The linguistic sign is therefore a two-faced mental unit' (p. 99), as in fig. 2:

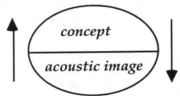

Figure 2   De Saussure's analysis of the linguistic sign

The sign is arbitrary (p. 100) in the sense that there is, normally speaking, no intrinsic reason why this form should combine with that meaning. Only in the case of onomatopoeia does this principle not apply. As we know (see 1.1), the debate about the natural or the conventional character of word forms had started with Plato's *Cratylus*. Like many of his predecessors, de Saussure sides with Aristotle on this issue, adding the consideration (pp. 101, 104) that once a sign has been established it is a social fact that cannot be changed at will by single individuals. He also points out that it is only the primitive lexical elements that are arbitrary: any rule-governed combination yielding a new, complex meaning, is not arbitrary but 'motivated' by the rules. (We have seen that for de Saussure rule-governed combinations are largely limited to morphological constructions.)

• *Diachrony and synchrony; langue as an immaterial system of mere 'values'*
The third major distinction made by de Saussure is that between *diachrony* and *synchrony*, or between the historical and the systematic aspect of language. For us, at the end of the 20th century, this is no longer problematic. But in de Saussure's days it was. The scientific study of language was almost entirely historical (see the quotes from Jespersen on p. 81). Languages were seen primarily as objects in motion through time, and not as machines that function according to structural principles. It was precisely the development of the latter notion that characterizes the period under discussion and led to what we now call structuralism. De Saussure complicates the exposé, however, by presenting the distinction between diachrony and synchrony as part of his idea that 'the *langue* is merely a system of values ('valeurs') that are determined exclusively by the momentary state of its terms' (p. 116). This idea permeates the second half of the book. It is what Jones called the 'negative character' (1957:6; see above) of de Saussure's analytical notions. De Saussure is at pains to drive home his point that the *langue* consists of mutually exclusive abstract units that are definable only by the fact that they are not what the others are. But does he have a point? Is de Saussure's thought coherent in this respect?

In actual use, in *parole*, the abstract units require material realization, but the system governing their use is immaterial. This, oddly, applies also to the acoustic images that form one half of each sign. We have seen de Saussure say, on p. 164, that 'the phonemes are above all oppositive, relative and negative entities', despite the fact that they are also 'the sum of the acoustic impressions and the articulatory movements of the heard and the spoken unit' (p. 65). The text becomes truly enigmatic on p. 166:

> What we have said in the foregoing amounts to saying that *in the langue there are only differences*. And what's more, a difference requires in general a set of positive terms between which the difference holds. But in the case of the *langue* there are only differences without any positive terms. Whether one takes the form or the concept, the *langue* contains neither ideas nor sounds that would have existed before the linguistic system, but only conceptual and phonic differences resulting from the system. Whatever there is in the way of ideas or phonic material in a sign is less important than what is there around it in the other signs. The proof of this is the fact that the value of one term can change without either its sense or its sounds being touched, but only because some neighbouring term has undergone a change.
>
> Yet, to say that all is negative in the *langue* would be true only of the form and the concept taken separately. Once one considers the sign as a totality one finds oneself in front of something which is positive in its own right. ... Although the form and the concept are, each taken separately, purely differential and negative, their combination is a positive fact, the only kind of fact found in the *langue* because what characterizes the institution of language is precisely the maintenance of the parallelism between these two orders of differences.

This passage is difficult to understand. De Saussure cannot have meant that the units in *langue* are defined by negative properties only, since there is no guarantee that something which is not red and not square differs from something which is not green and not round, as it can be blue and trapezoid, for example. The only viable interpretation is that the units of *langue* must be distinct from each other, no matter what material realization they get, as long as they get one. What counts is the 'system', not the substance. De Saussure even speaks of an 'algebra' (p. 168) forming the system of the *langue*. Apparently, he is thinking of an uninterpreted formal system of the kind known in mathematics or logic. But then, to speak of such a 'system' without even giving the slightest indication of its formal properties and the possibilities of interpretation onto the facts of language is vacuous. Moreover, one fails to see why or how the notion of an abstract 'algebra' can be given up and replaced by an interpreted system in terms of 'positive' units once we deal with signs, instead of just form or conceptual stuff. It looks as though de Saussure has allowed himself to be carried away by abstract thoughts while not having them under control. Unfortunately, this flight into abstract units rather spoils his opposition between synchrony and diachrony, unnecessarily because synchrony and diachrony can be distinguished perfectly well without introducing the strange notion of a system of elements that are defined only negatively.

- *Diachronic change like a move in a chess game*

De Saussure likens diachronic language change to a move in a game of chess (pp. 125-6). Before the move, he says, the pieces are defined by their 'values' with respect to each other, i.e. their potential for making the player on their side win. Each new move brings about a change in this 'system of values'. In like manner, the elements of a *langue* are caught up in a web of mutual value relations, and each diachronic change brings about a change in the web. It would have been helpful if de Saussure had been a little more specific about the intended 'oppositions', the web of mutually defined value relations. But he wasn't, and left his readers puzzling.

- *Syntagmatic and associative*

The last great distinction de Saussure draws is between *syntagmatic* and *associative* (later called *paradigmatic* by the English linguist Firth) relations of signs (i.e. words and/or morphemes) with other signs (pp. 170-175). The syntagmatic relations are those they engage in when put together in a syntagm, i.e. a morphological construction or a set phrase or locution. The associative relations exist between a given sign and others that are somehow similar. The 'system' of the *langue* would then consist largely of the associative and the syntagmatic relations of words and morphemes with respect to each other. (One notes that the notion of syntax is entirely absent.)

Well-known is his example of *enseignement* ('teaching') on p. 175, reproduced in fig. 3. This word is taken to have associative relations with its morphological variants *enseigner* ('teach'), *enseignons* ('(we) teach'), etc. Also with synonyms or nouns with similar meaning like *apprentissage* or *éducation*. Then again with other nouns ending in -*ment*, and, finally, also with any other words ending in -*ment*.

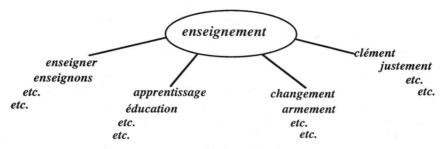

Figure 3   *Associative relations of the word* enseignement *in de Saussure (1916:175)*

- *Overall appraisal of the* Cours

When we look at the *Cours* in hindsight we cannot help but have mixed feelings. Of the four major distinctions drawn by de Saussure those between *langue* and *parole*, between diachrony and synchrony, and between syntagmatic and associative (paradigmatic) have proved constitutive for modern linguistics, though the latter has now been superseded by more sophisticated structural principles. The distinction between signifier and signified has not been influential in linguistics (though it has become something of a household concept in modern French literary criticism and postmodern philosophy).[9] Moreover, his notion of the arbitrariness of the linguistic sign harked back to the ancient debate between Plato and Aristotle, and added little. This notion as well as the distinction between associative and syntagmatic had already been re-introduced by Kruszewski, whose ideas would have been brought to de Saussure's notice by Paul Passy who corresponded with Baudouin de Courtenay (see above).[10] But it is true, the first three distinctions, for all their unclarity, have become an integral part of our present-day thinking about language. To that extent we can acknowledge a real influence exerted by de Saussure on modern linguistic theory, even if not all these distinctions were entirely his own.

Beyond the notions and distinctions mentioned, however, there appears to be little we owe to de Saussure. The *Cours* is badly confused and partly inconsistent. One of the main sources of de Saussure's inadequacy is clear: he failed to see the importance of syntactic structure and took the word, not the sentence,

---

[9] De Saussure's analysis of the linguistic sign is unrevealing in that it fails to show (a) the fact that linguistic signs are used to refer to a non-linguistic and non-conceptual reality, and (b) the fact that the relation between form and corresponding conceptual structure is itself mediated by means of mapping rules that constitute the grammar of the language in question. In these respects, the semiotic triangle presented by Ogden & Richards (1923) is a great deal more informative and more explicit (see 1.2.1 and 2.6.4 above).

[10] The distinction between associative and syntagmatic was taken by Kruszewski from the English 19th century philosopher John Stuart Mill, who placed items in relations of co-existence and similarity (Koerner 1994b).

as the primary unit of linguistic analysis. Bloomfield, significantly, made a point of this in his polite but disparaging[11] review (Bloomfield 1924) of the second (1922) edition of the *Cours*: 'In detail, I should differ from de Saussure chiefly in basing my analysis on the sentence rather than on the word.'

- *Criticism applies to the book, not the man*

It is important to realize that the criticisms we have do not apply to de Saussure as a person. First of all, we do not have his own text but only a text distilled from lecture notes. Then, we have reason to believe that de Saussure would not have approved the publication of the *Cours*, and if this was because he himself saw its inadequacies we can only respect him for not wanting to see it published. What we do see with great clarity is a man struggling to get certain ideas right, trying to find the right concepts for a proper structural linguistic analysis, and design an adequate terminology. He did not succeed, as he himself knew, but he has helped others to make better progress.[12] The linguist who was inspired most by de Saussure and used some of his ideas in a creative and potentially fruitful way (though in combination with the mathematical notion of algorithm) was the Dane Louis Hjelmslev, the originator of the theory called 'glossematics'. Unfortunately, however, glossematics was unsuccessful as a general theory of language (for a full discussion see 3.4).

- *No reference to the Subject-Predicate debate*

One detail, not noticed anywhere in the literature, must be mentioned here: nowhere in the *Cours* is there any reference to the great subject-predicate debate that was central to theoretical linguistics during that period (2.6.3). His editors Bally and Sechehaye did take part in the debate, but de Saussure did not. Why not? Was it because he thought the whole debate too vague and lacking in empirical substance? Or was it because the debate smacked too much of logic and psychology and not enough of his projected semiology? Or did the debate concentrate too much on the sentence, and not enough on the word, as the main unit of linguistic analysis? We do not know, but we do know that de Saussure would have gained a great deal if he had joined in the subject-predicate debate, if only because it might have made him more sensitive to the facts of syntax and have made him see that the sentence, more than the word, provides insight into the system of language.

---

[11] Bloomfield was not alone in this. The brief comment by the Dutch linguist Jac. van Ginniken on the same second edition of the *Cours* in *Indogermanisches Jahrbuch* 1929.5 is revealing: 'Unchanged reprint of the first edition. Of very uneven value. Dilettante extravagancies, next to deep insights into the life of languages.' See also Percival (1981).

[12] After the second world war some scholars, in particular Godel (1957), have tried to reconstruct the 'historical' de Saussure from whatever data could be gathered. Yet even if this reconstruction is feasible and correct what it can add to our knowledge is merely anecdotal. The person who has been present in linguistics since 1916 is the author (or authors) of the *Cours*, not the man who did not want it to be published.

• *Influence of the* Cours *on European structuralism*

Despite all this, the fact remains that the *Cours* became the standard work of linguistic theory in Europe during the years after the first world war. It inspired scholars all over Europe, especially in Prague and Copenhagen, giving rise to new and interesting developments and inspiring eminent linguists like Hjelmslev (3.4) and Gardiner (3.5). Why so many should have been inspired, at the time, so strongly by the *Cours* is an interesting question. There must have been a widespread feeling of frustration about the lack of progress made in the systematic study of language, so that any spark might have triggered a chain reaction. Also, it seems, many professional linguists were beginning to have the feeling that the structures and processes at work in language are not derivable from general psychological or logical principles, but that language is *autonomous* in that it functions according to principles of its own, not shared with or derivable from other areas of physical or mental activity. In more up to date terminology, we should say that a *modular view of language* began to manifest itself. This was happening on both sides of the Atlantic. Around the same time, Bloomfield was growing out of a psychology-derived concept of language manifest in his (1914), and into an autonomous, structuralist concept. In fact, what Bloomfield appreciated in his review (1924) of the *Cours* was what he saw as its emphasis on the autonomy of linguistics as a discipline (he played down the dependence of linguistics on the projected discipline of semiology, although this is very prominent in the *Cours*). Bloomfield's praise in this respect clearly reflects his own efforts around 1924 to establish linguistics as an autonomous discipline (which resulted in the foundation of the *Linguistic Society of America* in December 1924; see 4.3). It is probably correct to say that what European linguists found inspiring in the *Cours*, during the 1920s and after, is traceable, to a considerable extent, to a still implicit desire to see linguistics established as an autonomous discipline, studying the autonomous rules and principles at work in language.

3.3 The Prague School

• *Marty*

The first origins of the Prague School lie with *Anton Marty* (1847-1914), professor of philosophy at Prague and disciple of the German phenomenologist philosopher Brentano. Marty was not a linguist, but as a philosopher he took part in the subject-predicate debate that was going on around the turn of the century. In various writings, many of which were published posthumously, he maintains that no matter what differences can be posited between grammatical and semantic structure, it is misleading to apply the terms 'subject' and 'predicate' to both levels of analysis. In his view, logic does not come into semantics at all: everything semantic is psychological, not logical. Moreover, the grammatical form of a sentence expresses not only its abstract propositional meaning but also its less abstract linguistic meaning or 'inner form', which corresponds more closely to surface structure and intonation and is determined by the way the propositional meaning is to be integrated into running discourse. Like Lipps and Stout (2.6.3), he considers discourse-bound modes of presentation ('inner form') to be guided largely by question-answer structure. The terms 'subject' and 'predicate' are most appropriately used at the 'inner form' level, since what defines a predicate is the attribution of a property to something, which is the subject, and this mental act is achieved when new information is added to what is already there in the discourse.

Marty never carried out any actual linguistic analysis. All he presented was general philosophical argument, and much polemic with contemporary authors, especially Wundt, Steinthal, Paul, Husserl and Meinong. His style of writing was dense, which makes his writings not very attractive to read. It was probably for these reasons that he was less influential than he might have been. But the modern specialist, who reads Marty against the background of present-day analyses and theories, quickly recognizes, despite terminological differences, notions and insights that are not only highly relevant in the current debate on meaning and grammar but also show the balanced and mature judgement underlying his overall approach and ideas.

● *Mathesius and the Prague Linguistic Circle*
Marty's ideas about 'inner form' as discourse-bound mode of presentation were taken up and developed further by the Czech scholar *Vilém Mathesius* (1882-1945), professor of English at Prague University. In 1926 Mathesius and a few others founded the Prague Linguistic Circle or, as it was better known, the Cercle Linguistique de Prague (for a detailed history, see Toman 1995). In this context, Mathesius developed his theory of 'functional sentence perspective', expressed variously in terms of topic and comment (or focus), theme and rheme, given and new. After his death in 1945 these ideas were taken up and further developed by others. The most prominent among these are Petr Sgall and Eva Hajičová, who kept the Prague School going against all odds under the communist regime, and succeeded in officially reviving the Prague Linguistic Circle in November 1992, three years after the downfall of communism.

● *The Prague School: functional sentence perspective and phonology*
The Prague School has made linguistic history because it was the only place where the old subject-predicate debate was kept alive, albeit under the name of functional sentence perspective or the topic-comment distinction. Since the mid-1980s the Prague developments in this respect have merged with work done in various centres in the world, mostly in the United States, on discourse-bound modes of presentation and information structure, where the notions of topic and comment have gained new relevance.

The Prague School has been active on many other linguistic fronts as well. One may say that in its heyday, i.e. between 1926 and 1939, it covered the whole field of general linguistic theory as it existed in Europe in those days. Yet its most notable successes were achieved on two fronts, the theory of functional sentence perspective just mentioned and the pre-war development of phonology, about which we shall say a few things now.

● *Trubetzkoy and Jakobson*

The two central figures of Prague School phonology were the Russians *Nikolai Sergeyevich Trubetzkoy* (1890-1938) and *Roman Osipovich Jakobson* (1896-1982), close friends but very different characters. Trubetzkoy was born in Moscow into a noble Russian family with a long tradition in politics, the military, the arts and in scholarship. His father, Prince Sergei Trubetzkoy, was professor of philosophy and rector of Moscow University. The young Prince Trubetzkoy studied Sanskrit and historical linguistics at Moscow University, and later at Leipzig, where he was taught by Young Grammarians (and found himself in one class with Leonard Bloomfield and Lucien Tesnière). When the October Revolution began to rage he was compelled to flee from Russia. After various professorships here and there in Eastern Europe, he accepted the chair of Slavonic philology at Vienna University, where he stayed till his untimely death in 1938. In 1928 Mathesius invited him to become a member of the newly formed Prague Linguistic Circle, which led to a renewal of his contacts with Jakobson, whom he knew from their Moscow days. His most notable contribution to phonology is his uncompleted and posthumously published general introduction to phonology (Trubetzkoy 1939, 1958²).

Jakobson was likewise born in Moscow, son of a prominent Jewish industrialist and chemical engineer. During his school days he developed an intense interest in modern poetry, especially the experimental poetry current in Russian literature at the beginning of the century. The study of phonological elements in poetic structures led him to the linguistic study of speech sounds and of language in general. He was instrumental in founding the Moscow Linguistic Circle in 1915, of which he became president, as he was instrumental later, together with Mathesius, in founding the Prague Linguistic Circle, of which he became Vice-President. In 1920 he decided to leave Russia and join the Russian expatriates in Prague, where he took his PhD in 1930. He stayed in Prague till 1939, when the Nazi invasion of Czechoslovakia made his further stay in Czechoslovakia ill-advised. Through Denmark and Norway he fled to Sweden, from where he migrated to the United States in 1941. After a couple of teaching positions in New York he was offered the chair of Slavonic languages and literatures at Harvard in 1949, which he combined with the position of Institute Professor at MIT from 1957 on. He died in Cambridge, Massachusetts, in July 1982, at the age of 85, a celebrated figure both in linguistics and in the field of literary studies.

Jakobson and Trubetzkoy jointly determined the main course of Prague phonology till 1939. They were both directly influenced by Baudouin de Courtenay's ideas on the phoneme and on phonology as the functional study of speech sounds. In his later years, Jakobson developed a somewhat coquettish tendency to refer to de Saussure, in particular de Saussure's ideas about an 'algebra' of oppositions without material linguistic substance, as the main source of his inspiration, but in fact there is little to support that claim. The phonetic realizations of phonemes have always played a central role in Prague School phonology, and from as early on as 1926 (Kučera 1983:875)

Jakobson worked on his theory, first published in Jakobson (1941) and more fully in Jakobson, Fant & Halle (1952), of binary distinctive features as the ultimate linguistically functional sound properties for all languages.[13] Clearly, there can be no theory of distinctive features without any reference to their physical correlates, as one sees readily from the title of Jakobson, Fant & Halle (1952). As regards Trubetzkoy, in the first chapter of his *Grundzüge*, where he acknowledges his debt to predecessors, he does mention de Saussure for his *langue-parole* distinction, but stresses the fact (1958:8) that de Saussure made no contribution to phonology, referring emphatically to Baudouin de Courtenay as its real founder.

- *Status of Prague School*

In the early years, the Prague School gained prominence by issuing programmatic statements at three international conferences, the First International Congress of Linguists (The Hague 1928), the First Congress of Slavonic Philologists (Prague 1929), and the International Phonological Meeting (Prague 1930). The statement for the latter contained an appendix proposing a standard terminology for phonology, most of which has indeed become commonly accepted.

The Prague School has been an important station on the road towards improved scientific status for the study of linguistic systems. Throughout the 1930s the regularly appearing *Travaux du Cercle Linguistique de Prague*, the famous TCLP volumes, were the focus of theoretical linguistic activity in Europe. It is true that most of the Prague School work in grammar and semantics has lost prominence as it was superseded by developments taking place in America and grounded in a different tradition. But, on the other hand, the Prague contributions to phonology have proved of lasting value, not least because they were, in the person of Roman Jakobson, transferred to America where they merged with existing American phonology and led to what is now one of the more successful areas of linguistic theory. Moreover, we must acknowledge the fact that for more than fifty years Prague was the only notable place in the world where the theory of topic and comment and of functional sentence perspective was not washed away by the torrential flood of theoretical grammar, in particular transformational generative grammar.

3.4   The Copenhagen School

- *Hjelmslev and his group*

The Copenhagen School was much smaller than its Prague counterpart, and was carried mainly by *Louis Trolle Hjelmslev* (1899-1965). Hjelmslev was born and died in Copenhagen. His father was a prominent mathematician, a fact

---

[13] Nowadays, of course, the distinctive features are an integral part of phonology, though in many phonological theories the features are no longer considered to be binary but, rather, gradient.

which is noticeable in his approach to language (see note 15). He studied comparative philology with Holger Pedersen, whom he succeeded in 1937 in the chair of Comparative Philology at Copenhagen University. He studied in Prague in 1925-26 and then in Paris for another year. Together with *Rasmus Viggo Brøndal* (1887-1942) he founded the Cercle Linguistique de Copenhague in 1931. For the last fifteen or so years of his life his health was gradually undermined by a brain disease, which led to his death in 1965. He planned a method for linguistic description which he called *glossematics*. More will be said about this interesting but inaccessible and highly abstract theory in a moment.

Hjelmslev stood in a long and honourable tradition of Danish philology and linguistics. He succeeded in organizing around himself a small group of interested followers, notably *Hans Jørgen Uldall* (1907-1957), whose international orientation and expansive nature took him to Daniel Jones in London, and then to America, where he worked on an American Indian language. During the second half of the 1930s Uldall lived in his native Denmark and became a close associate and friend of Hjelmslev's. Not finding a tenured university position he went to a British Council teaching post in Athens in 1940. He stayed with the British Council till his final appointment to Nigeria, where he died at the age of fifty. After 1940, his ideas about linguistic theory and description began to deviate more and more from Hjelmslev's, who, for that reason, found it hard to write an introduction to Uldall's main theoretical work (1957).

Eli Fischer-Jörgensen (born 1911) was another critical follower of Hjelmslev's theoretical work. Her main contributions lie in phonology, where she became very prominent, combining her phonological research with extensive phonetic studies. Hjelmslev's work on sounds and phonemes was strongly influenced by what he learned from Fischer-Jørgensen.

The great *Otto Jespersen* (1860-1943) did not belong to the group, feeling that glossematics was far too abstract and speculative, and preferring a more down-to-earth method of language study. Nor did Brøndal, mentioned above, sympathize with Hjelmslev's flight into abstract space. In the end, therefore, the group remained very limited and was carried exclusively by the powerful personality of Hjelmslev himself. After his death glossematics disintegrated.

- *Glossematics*

Glossematics never really became a theory of language. It remained stuck in a preparatory and programmatic phase, which is why Hjelmslev called the work in which he expounds the glossematic machinery (1953/1943) *Prolegomena to a Theory of Language*, rather than simply *A Theory of Language*. Critical exposés of glossematics are found in Siertsema (1954) and de Beaugrande (1991:122-146), both, however, without reference to the wider context of modern theories of language and the philosophy of science. We pay some attention to it because it shows a powerful mind rattling, so to speak, at the empirical gates of language. Hjelmslev had in his grip a number of essential parameters for the setting up of an explanatory general theory of language. He almost gained empirical access, but he failed on a few equally essential counts. Soon after Hjelmslev first presented his *Prolegomena*, in 1943, American developments overtook him. Generative and, later, transformational grammar succeeded where glossematics had failed. The American theory did gain the access Hjelmslev had sought but not achieved.

In the 1953 edition, the *Prolegomena* (PTL) takes up barely 81 pages of text. Much of it we shall discuss only cursorily, as it is not relevant to the present state of linguistic science and only shows the darkness in which European post-Saussurean theoreticians were groping for some opening that would lead to the heart of language. Formulations are sought that are intended to define and encompass human language in every one of its innumerable aspects, and methods for its analysis and description are derived by a priori logical deduction from the general notions. Incapable of coming to terms with semantic phenomena, Hjelmslev sets up a complex structure of abstract formal notions, expressed in weird terminology and lacking any demonstrable relation with any kind of reality, a theoretical house of cards. In addition, Hjelmslev's ideas about the place of linguistics in the totality of science are distinctly proprietary: for him, linguistics is the pivotal discipline around which all science is to be centred (PTL:49). All this we shall leave untouched, as it has only historical interest in that it throws light on the period. We shall, rather, concentrate on those features which, from our perspective, show how close he came to finding a fruitful way of applying the general notion of a scientific theory to language. In doing so we shall try to avoid, as much as possible, any terminological tangle and refer to, or use, Hjelmslev's own terminology only in so far as it is not likely to create misunderstanding.

• *Content plane and expression plane*
Hjelmslev sees language in terms of two broad distinctions. First, following up on de Saussure (1916:155-157), he distinguishes between two independent realms of being ('planes' PTL:37), *content* (or thought) and *expression* in sound or writing (de Saussure's 'ideas' and 'sounds', respectively). Taken by themselves, content and expression are unstructured ('amorphous'), but they crystallize into minimal functional units ('glossemes' PTL:51) through language, which brings content units and expression units into meaningful correlations that vary with each specific language. On either plane, the units thus created can be combined into hierarchically structured complexes, though there is no one-to-one correlation between structures on the expression plane and their correlates on the content plane (PTL:29). Certain configurations of minimal units on the expression plane, i.e. phonemes (or, in Hjelmslev's terms, 'figurae' PTL:29) combine with certain configurations of minimal units on the content plane to form 'signs' (PTL:29). But how the larger structures on one plane are to be correlated to those on the other is left unclear. Even so, Hjelmslev claims (PTL:37) that the content-expression distinction

> proves to result in great clarity and simplification, and it also casts light on the whole mechanism of a language in a fashion hitherto unknown. From this point of view it will be easy to organize the subsidiary disciplines of linguistics according

to a well-founded plan and to escape at last from the old, halting division of linguistics into phonetics, morphology, syntax, lexicography, and semantics – a division that is unsatisfactory in many respects and also involves some over-lapping. But besides, when the analysis is carried through, it shows that expression plane and content plane can be described exhaustively and consistently as being structured in quite analogous fashions, so that quite identically defined categories are foreseen in the two planes. This means a further essential confirmation of the correctness of conceiving expression and content as coordinate and equal entities in every respect.

However, Hjelmslev's claim that the 'analogy' between content and ex-pression is shown when 'the analysis is carried through' is not supported by any actual analysis. In fact, he admits that no analysis in terms of hier-archical structure has so far been presented on the content plane (PTL:42): whatever there is in the way of hierarchical structural analysis is limited to the expression plane. For that reason it is practically advantageous to start linguistic analysis from the expression plane and not vice versa, though there is no a priori reason why it could not be done the other way round (PTL:48).

• *Form and substance*
The second distinction, also derived from de Saussure, is that between *form* and *substance* (note that one must not confuse 'form' with 'expression'). This goes back directly to de Saussure's contention that in the *langue* everything is negative and 'oppositive', without any concrete 'positive' filling or realiza-tion. In 3.2 we expressed our puzzlement at this view. Here we see Hjelmslev taking it over from de Saussure, even to the extent of speaking about an abstract 'algebra' of language (PTL:50), where all that counts is the units, whatever their phonetic (or semantic) realization, and their combinatory possibilities. The abstract units, defined by their algebraic combinatory pro-perties, are the *form*, whereas any conventionally established phonetic (or semantic) realization is the *substance*. The *system* of any language is defined by the formal units, while the more or less arbitrary choice of substance is a question of the *use* made of the system, the actual processes occurring in *parole*.

So far there does not seem to be much in Hjelmslev's theorizing that is original or fruitful enough to deserve special mention. The distinction between content and expression (meaning and form, in more normal terminology) goes back to Antiquity, and that between functional units and their material realization was fashionable in all sciences of the period and found with other linguists as well (e.g. Pike's 'emic' and 'etic' levels of analysis; see 4.4.2).[14] Hjelmslev's ideas about analogous methods of structural analysis on the con-tent and the expression plane, and the interplanar linking up of units into

[14] The distinction is applicable only to grammar, which can be formulated largely without any reference to the actual phonological shape of the units involved. But it fails in phonology, since phonological systems are heavily constrained (though not determined) by the physical properties of the sounds they deal with. Analogously, we now know that the semantic structure of sentences is heavily constrained by the cognitive properties of the elements involved.

'signs' seem, if not untenable, certainly unrealistic. What makes glossematics relevant and interesting is its projected way of specifying the possible combinations of primitive formal units into larger structures, i.e. its notion of algorithmic production of strings of symbols, and the empirical and formal constraints it imposes on any such specification in the light of an evaluation with respect to alternative specifications. Here Hjelmslev's ideas clearly prefigure the theory of generative grammar that sprang up in America a few years later. We shall now have a closer look at this aspect of Hjelmslev's theory of language. In doing so we shall disregard the parallelism between form (i.e. expression) and meaning analysis constantly insisted on by Hjelmslev, and concentrate on the form side only. In practice this is what Hjelmslev himself did, as, by his own admission (PTL:42), no viable analysis or description on the semantic content level had so far been achieved.

- *The term 'theory' in two senses*

Hjelmslev uses the term 'theory' in two senses. On the one hand, a theory of a language is a description of all possible texts in that language. Linguistic theory, on the other hand, is a metatheory of linguistic descriptions. A description (or theory) of a language is subject to a condition which he calls the 'empirical principle' (PTL:6):

> The description shall be free of contradiction (self-consistent), exhaustive, and as simple as possible. The requirement of freedom from contradiction takes precedence over the requirement of exhaustive description. The requirement of exhaustive description takes precedence over the requirement of simplicity.

- *Description as generation, not as analysis; sentences as 'theorems'*

The method of description should not be inductive but deductive (PTL:6-7). That is, it should not proceed from the smallest units (say phonemes) to the largest (texts), but from texts to the smallest units. A text is considered to be built up of smaller units (say sentences), which are again built up of smaller units (say clauses), and so on till the smallest units are reached. (The term 'deductive' is justified (PTL:19) by an analogy with the way logical conclusions are derivable by means of formal logical deduction.) A descriptive theory consists of two parts, a purely mathematical or 'arbitrary' part, which 'includes no existence postulate' (PTL:8) and permits the deduction of theorems, and an 'appropriate' part (ibid.), i.e. an interpretation which applies the theorems to ontologically real observables by means of interpretative 'premisses'. Glossematics is thus an instrumentalist theory.

- *General linguistic theory as universal manual for grammar writing*

The aim of linguistic (meta)theory is described as follows (PTL:9):

> A theory, then, in our sense of the word, may be said to aim at providing a procedural method by means of which objects of a premised nature can be described self-consistently and exhaustively. Such a self-consistent and exhaustive description leads to what is usually called a knowledge or comprehension of the object in question. ...

The objects of interest to linguistic theory are texts. The aim of linguistic theory is to provide a procedural method by means of which a given text can be comprehended through a self-consistent and exhaustive description.

Moreover (PTL:10-11):

If, through this general calculation, linguistic theory ends by constructing several possible methods of procedure, all of which can provide a self-consistent and exhaustive description of any given text and thereby of any language whatsoever, then, among those possible methods of procedure, that one shall be chosen that results in the simplest possible description. If several methods yield equally simple descriptions, that one is to be chosen that leads to the result through the simplest procedure. This principle, which is deduced from our so-called empirical principle, we call the *simplicity principle.*

- *Infinite number of sentences from finite elements*

Hjelmslev realized that an algorithmic description of a language should generate an infinite number of products from a finite number of primitive elements (PTL:26):

When we compare the inventories yielded at the various stages of the deduction, their size will usually turn out to decrease as the procedure goes on. If the text is unrestricted, *i.e.,* capable of being prolonged through constant addition of further parts, ... it will be possible to register an unrestricted number of sentences, an unrestricted number of clauses, an unrestricted number of words. Sooner or later in the course of the deduction, however, there comes a point at which the number of the inventoried entities becomes restricted, and after which it usually falls steadily. Thus it seems certain that a language will have a restricted number of syllables, although that number will be relatively high. In the case of syllables permitting a division into central and marginal parts, the number of members in these classes will be lower than the number of syllables in the language. When the parts of syllables are further partitioned, we reach the entities which are conventionally called phonemes; their number is probably so small in any language that it can be written with two digits, and, in a good many languages, is very low (somewhere about twenty).

- *Simplicity*

The simplicity principle now leads to two further principles (PTL:38):

The principle of economy: The description is made through a procedure. The procedure shall be so arranged that the result is the simplest possible, and shall be suspended if it does not lead to further simplification.

The principle of reduction: Each operation in the procedure shall be continued or repeated until the description is exhausted, and shall at each stage lead to the registration of the lowest possible number of objects.

- *Generalization from clear to doubtful cases*

Finally, one should generalize from clear to doubtful cases in virtue of the principle of generalization (PTL:44), which

has always implicitly played a role in scientific research, although so far as we know it has not previously been formulated. It goes as follows:

If one object admits of a solution univocally, and another object admits of the same solution equivocally, then the solution is generalized to be valid for the equivocal object.

- *Hjelmslev as forerunner of generative grammar*

We can understand why Hjelmslev's contemporaries failed to see the significance of these texts. To anyone not already familiar with the notion of an algorithmically organized generative grammar they must seem arcane, and they are in any case extremely abstract. Although a fair number of isolated examples are provided throughout the text, no actual bit of 'procedural analysis', i.e. generation, is provided, not even in a simplified form by way of example. Yet from the vantage point of modern linguistic theory one immediately recognizes the notion of an algorithmic machinery for the generation of linguistic structures and developed more fully in America a few years later. The terminology strikes us as a little quaint, but so does the terminology of early American generative grammar (Harris 1951:369-370, 372-373; see also 4.5.1). One must realize that no accepted terminology was available in those early years. As in early generative grammar, no systematic distinction is made between phonology, morphology and syntax, all three being considered describable in terms of the same kind of rule system. Both Hjelmslev and Harris were inspired by the mathematical notion of an algorithm as a purely formal production system for a set of strings of symbols. This notion had been developed during the 1920s by mathematical logicians and specialists in the foundations of mathematics,[15] and it is probably accurate to say that Hjelmslev was the first to try and apply it to the generation of strings of symbols in natural language. On the other hand, if European linguists were groping for empirical access to language, so were their American colleagues. The latter, however, had a better sense of practical procedure and clarity, and a greater willingness to do away with speculative clutter.

- *Hjelmslev's projected machinery with, Harris's without meaning*

There are, of course, important differences between Hjelmslev's notion of a generative machinery and its American counterpart. One obvious difference is that Hjelmslev envisaged parallel algorithms for the content and the expression plane, whereas Harris explicitly limited his approach to form, excluding meaning as a matter of principle. We now feel that Hjelsmlev's postulate of form-meaning parallelism was misguided or anyway unrealistic, hampering his efforts rather than helping them. On the other hand, Harris's exclusion of meaning analysis, though practically fruitful for a while, has also proved untenable, as the study of language without taking meaning into consideration is an a priori abomination. The standard view nowadays is that both form and meaning should be studied, but not in double harness.

---

[15] It will hardly have been a coincidence that both Hjelmslev and Harris, the founder of American generative grammar, had mathematical leanings, the former because of his father (see above), the latter by avocation.

- *Hjelmslev's generative universe is texts; no notion of constituent structure*

A further difference lies in the fact that for Hjelmslev the universe of generation consisted of texts, not sentences (though from 1950 on Harris entertained similar views). This choice has proved methodologically unfortunate, since, as we see it today, the rules that govern the grammatical composition of sentences cannot be extended to the composition of texts. Well-formedness as a property of sentences and smaller constructions is considered to be of an essentially different nature from coherence as a property of texts. The former is secured by the separate but interrelated components of syntax, morphology and phonology, the latter by semantics and world knowledge. Moreover, Hjelmslev's ideas about hierarchical constituent structure were much less clearcut and explicit than those presented by Bloomfield and his successors, among whom Harris. As a result, Hjelsmlev was unable to be very specific about the precise form and nature of the 'procedures', i.e. the algorithmic computations or rules, and he remained confined to a mere programmatic phase of the theory envisaged. His later American colleagues were more successful in this respect.

All this, together with his lack of dexterity in promoting his theory, may explain why Hjelmslev failed to achieve the great breakthrough of generative grammar that was to take place in America in the late '50s and was based on largely the same formal-mathematical notions.

It is somewhat disappointing, and even shameful, that glossematics has not received the recognition it deserves. Nowhere in the literature is Hjelmslev mentioned as a close precursor of generative grammar. The few references to glossematics in Chomsky's work (1957:50; 1964:75) are painfully inadequate. As it was, glossematics slid into virtually complete oblivion.

3.5 The London School

Till about 1900 investigations into the nature of language had been definitely underdeveloped in Britain, compared with the main continental countries. A considerable amount of work had been and was being done in lexicography, a field in which Britain excelled. Phonetics was another subject in which Britain held a leading position, largely because of the towering figure of Henry Sweet, about whom more in a moment. Comparative philology was poorly represented, despite the fact that it was the Englishman Sir William Jones who gave the starting shot in 1786 (2.4). Hardly anything was produced in the way of linguistic theory. Max Müller, whom we discussed in 2.4, was a German by birth and remained relatively alien to the British academic establishment. As in France, Belgium and the Netherlands, it was common practice among colonial civil servants, military men and missionaries to write practical grammar books and dictionaries of the languages spoken in the colonies, an activity that went on till after World War II. More than the other countries, however, Britain distinguished itself by incorporating this widespread amateur activity into the university system early on, thus elevating it to a professional level. This led, among other things to the foundation of the *School of*

Oriental and African Studies in London, one of the world's most distinguished institutions for the study of 'exotic' languages and cultures. British linguistics, in other words, was globally oriented, and bent more on practical use and tangible observation than on abstract theory.

When one speaks of the London School of linguistics one thinks primarily of the phoneticians Sweet and Jones, of the general linguist Firth, and, in a special way, of the Egyptologist Gardiner, though, of course a great many more names could be mentioned. Gardiner was by far the most theoretically oriented among them, and it was probably for that reason that he remained more or less a lone figure in the British context. Jones and Firth, one may say, determined the face of British linguistics till the mid-1960s. After that British linguistics went international.

- *Sweet*

Henry Sweet (1845-1912) was the only British 19th century linguist who had an impact outside Britain. Born in London, he made an early start in business. Soon, however, he took an interest in language and studied philology at Heidelberg. He entered Oxford University at the age of 24, and left four years later with a dismal fourth. While at Oxford he discovered his interest in and talent for phonetics, a field in which he soon became a world master. In addition he published a great deal on English grammar and the history of English sounds, and a little also on general linguistic issues. On the basis of earlier work by Alexander Ellis, he developed a broad and a narrow phonetic alphabet, which became the basis for the dual system of phonetic transcription adopted by the International Phonetic Association founded in 1886. As said in note 5 above, he discovered the phonemic principle independently from Baudouin de Courtenay: 'in treating of a single language, it is necessary to have an alphabet which indicates only those broader distinctions of sound which actually correspond to distinctions of meaning' (Sweet 1877:103). He thus combined the philology of English with the general study of speech sounds.

In 1901 he was appointed to no more than a readership at Oxford, where he had hoped for a professorial chair. Until then he had been forced to live on teaching and writing. The British academic establishment's refusal to grant Sweet the official recognition that was obviously due to him in view of his enormous international reputation was caused by his proverbial grumpiness (the tales of which still go the rounds at Oxford). Professor Higgins, the phonetics teacher in Bernard Shaw's play *Pygmalion* (1916) and, later, the musical *My Fair Lady*, was probably modelled on Sweet, though Shaw himself denied any such link.

- *Jones*

More directly relevant to 20th century British linguistics is the figure of *Daniel Jones* (1881-1967), also a Londoner. After a degree in mathematics at Cambridge he turned to the study of language, against his father's wish, who wanted him to become a barrister, like himself. He interrupted his legal training in 1905 to study with the French phonetician Paul Passy. In 1907 he was given a part-time appointment at University College London to teach phonetics. He subsequently became a reader and then a professor at the same institution, where he was allowed, in 1912, to set up the first phonetics laboratory in Britain. He retired from University College in 1950. Jones was fundamentally a phonetician, but with a keen eye for the functional and structural aspects of speech sounds in terms of a linguistic system (see also note 5 above). As befitted a linguist from Britain, he did much phonetic and phonological research in Asian and African languages, paying particular attention to phonological tone. Through his countless students he practically shaped phonetics and phonology throughout Britain and beyond. Outside phonetics and phonology, however, his influence has been minimal.

- *Firth*
John Rupert Firth (1890-1960)[16] read history at Leeds University. During the first world war he entered military service and was sent to Afghanistan, Africa and India, where he became interested in the local languages. From 1920 till 1928 he was professor of English at Lahore. From there he went to University College London as a senior lecturer in phonetics under Daniel Jones, from where he transferred, in 1938, to the School of Oriental and African Studies, which appointed him to the new chair of General Linguistics in 1944. He retired in 1956. At University College he associated closely with the Polish anthropologist Bronislaw Malinowski, who was professor of anthropology at the London School of Economics and left for Yale in 1938. These biographical data are mirrored by the range of his academic interests, which centred on non-European languages, phonetics and phonology (as a result of his work with Jones), and the social aspects of language (Malinowski).

In phonetics and phonology he stressed the importance of prosodic features, arguing that it is not only the substitution of segmental features like nasality or voice that can make a semantic difference but also the substitution of prosodic features of length, tone and stress.

Language he saw as a social product designed for the purpose of social interaction: 'The linguist studies the speaking person in the social process' (57:190). This social perspective, brought into focus by Malinowski's notion of 'context of situation',[17] determined his views on grammar and 'meaning', with scare quotes, as Firth used this term in a highly unorthodox way. For him, 'meaning' was 'function in context', in the widest possible sense (Firth 1957:27):

> The central concept of the whole of semantics considered in this way is the context of situation. In that context are the human participant or participants, what they say, what is going on. The phonetician can find his phonetic context and the grammarian and the lexicographer theirs. And if you want to bring in general cultural background, you have the contexts of experience of the participants. Every

[16] For an excellent survey of Firth's life and academic views see Robins (1961).
[17] See Malinowski's Supplement I in Ogden & Richards (1923). Malinowski's source, though hardly acknowledged, was Wegener (1885; see 2.6.3). Gardiner (1932), on the contrary, gives Wegener his full due.

man carries his culture and much of his social reality about him wherever he goes. But even when phonetician, grammarian, and lexicographer have finished, there remains the bigger integration, making use of all their work, in semantic study. And it is for this situational and experiential study that I would reserve the term 'semantics'.

Thus he speaks of 'grammatical meaning', 'phonological meaning', 'phonetic meaning', and finds it appropriate to say (1957:192) that 'it is part of the meaning of an American to sound like one'. In Firth's view, 'semantics' thus encompasses the structural study of language in all its different facets. In fact, however, Firth never engaged in any structural analysis of language phenomena other than phonetic data. All study of grammar and meaning (in the normal sense) had to be conducted in the Malinowskian frame of a purely social 'context of situation', without any postulate as to underlying mental activity (1957:19):

> As we know so little about mind and as our study is essentially social, I shall cease to respect the duality of mind and body, thought and word, and be satisfied with the whole man, thinking and acting as a whole, in association with his fellows.

Lyons (1966) points out that this method failed to produce any useful or even consistent results in the theory[18] of meaning. One may safely extrapolate this judgement to the theory of grammar: the 'context of situation' approach proved largely sterile.

Yet Firth did advance some illuminating thoughts on grammar and semantics. In a usually crisp and clear-cut style he often drew attention to aspects of language that remained undervalued in the mainstream of theoretical linguistics, largely to do with the social and contextual embedding of speech, in particular the area of what is now called information structure. We see him formulate, for example, what is now called the *principle of informativity* in discourse, which entails that each informative sentence newly added to a given discourse on the one hand enriches the discourse by the information it brings in, while, on the other, it restricts both the range of sentences that can be used intelligibly in that discourse and the set of situations in which the discourse can be true (1957:31-32):

> The moment a conversation is started, whatever is said is a determining condition for what, in any reasonable expectation, may follow. What you say raises the threshold against most of the language of your companion, and leaves only a limited opening for a certain likely range of responses. This sort of thing is an aspect of what I have called contextual elimination. There is a positive force in what you say in a given situation, and there is also the negative force of elimination both in the events and circumstances of the situation and in the words employed, which are of course events in the situation.

These words are now seen to have been prophetic. Yet Firth did not succeed in integrating this insight into a larger explanatory theory.

---

[18] Or, in Firth's terminology, the 'technique': he consistently used 'technique' and 'technical' for 'theory' and 'theoretical'.

On the whole, one may justifiably say that it was less through his theoretical views on language than through his powerful social presence and his organizational activities that Firth put a definite stamp on British linguistics till roughly 1965. His period of office at the School of Oriental and African Studies coincided with the expansion of general linguistics in universities all over Britain. Many of the newly created posts in general linguistics were filled by Firth's students. By the mid-sixties, however, these felt that linguistics as practised in Britain had become too isolated and that closer links had to be forged with what was happening on the international scene.

- *Gardiner*

This conclusion had, in fact, been drawn much earlier by *Sir Alan Henderson Gardiner* (1879-1963), a man of very great standing in his proper profession, Egyptology. In 1927 he published his monumental *Egyptian Grammar*, still a standard reference book. He indulged in general linguistic theory in his spare time (an activity frowned upon by his fellow Egyptologists). He wrote a few articles (and a small book on proper names) on this subject and produced an intriguing theoretical work on language, *The Theory of Speech and Language* (Gardiner 1932/1951[2], henceforth TSL, used here in the second edition of 1951). His father, a prominent businessman, made him financially independent, a privilege which, in his own consideration, imposed on him the duty to advance his subject to the best of his abilities. But for a brief spell as a reader at Manchester University (1912-1914) he never held a university post. In 1948 he was knighted as a reward for his academic achievements. He was widely travelled and spent long periods abroad, especially in Berlin, then an important centre of Egyptian studies. One may assume that it was through his many academic contacts abroad that he understood how insular British linguistics really was. In his theoretical work on language, anyway, he reacted to the leading linguistic theorists of the day, in particular Hermann Paul, Wilhelm Wundt, Ferdinand de Saussure, Karl Bühler and, in the second edition of TSL, also Leonard Bloomfield. TSL is dedicated to Philipp Wegener, 'a pioneer of linguistic theory', who is also frequently quoted.

Due to Gardiner's international orientation as well as to his clear and succinct style of writing, TSL provides us with a good opportunity to discuss general trends and viewpoints in European structuralist linguistics. We will, therefore, devote some special attention to it, even though, at the time of its appearance, TSL was not very well received in Britain and failed to have the influence that works of lesser quality did have.

- *Bühler's 'organon model'*

Like Firth, Gardiner takes single acts of speech as his observable database, his 'primary facts'. He follows the German psychologist Karl Bühler[19] who,

[19] Karl Bühler was Gardiner's exact contemporary: 1879-1963. From 1922 till 1938 he was professor of psychology at Vienna University, where he and his wife Charlotte set up the Psychological Institute, which they ran until they fled from the Nazis in 1938 and emigrated to the United States. Bühler was a leading figure in the German school of

in his 'organon model', provides a general analysis of the way linguistic signs function in their ecological setting of actual speech situations. Bühler and Gardiner distinguish the four factors of (a) the speaker, (b) the listener, (c) the linguistic sign uttered by the speaker and received by the listener, and (d) the 'things-meant', Bühler's 'objects and states of affairs', the real and conceptual things that speech is about. Schematically, the organon model is represented in fig. 4 (Bühler 1934:28):

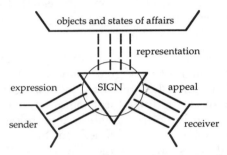

Figure 4   Bühler's Organon model of speech

When a speech utterance takes place, the speaker utters speech sounds, the 'sign', thereby expressing his thoughts and calling on the listener to pay attention ('appeal', Bühler's 'Appell'). The solid lines in the diagram indicate actual physical processes; the interrupted lines from the 'sign' to the 'objects and states of affairs' indicate a process that is mediated by the mind.[20]

- *Back to Gardiner: speech and language*

Having selected speech events as the primary observable facts for linguistic theory, Gardiner then goes on to say that they function in virtue of a *language system* virtually existing in each speaker's consciousness (TSL:5):

> It is my conviction that every adult human being is the living repository of a profound knowledge of language. Not only does he possess a vast store of words, but even the veriest yokel is something of an artist in the matter of their employment.

Gestalt psychology, which considered the role of the component parts of a perceived object subordinate to the perception of the object as a whole, which forms a 'Gestalt'. Applying this insight to language, he developed a notion of the linguistic sign as a Gestalt, a perceptible whole consisting of component parts. He is best known for his 'organon model' of speech, which places the linguistic sign in its context of use. He started working on this model in 1918 and published it in a final form in his book *Sprachtheorie* of 1934. It was this 'organon model' that inspired Gardiner.

[20] It is interesting to compare Bühler's organon model with the 'semiotic triangle' of Ogden & Richards on p. 18, and with de Saussure's 'speech circuit' on p. 149. Interestingly, Bühler's interrupted line corresponds exactly with the dotted line in Ogden & Richards' semiotic triangle. Note also that in the semiotic triangle speaker and hearer are collapsed into the one, mental, factor 'thought'. Bühler treats speaker and hearer as separate factors, justifiably in an analysis of the speech situation. De Saussure's diagram does not assign a separate status to the 'things-meant'.

Here, then, existent in the consciousness of everyone, is an immense treasure of evidence available for the construction of a solid fabric of linguistic theory.

More precisely, the system for each language exists more or less uniformly in the minds of all its speakers as some sort of socially shared 'science' (TSL:21):

> ... speech is fundamentally a social activity. Those who have the patience to read my book to the end will have to admit, further, that language is no personal creation, but a codified science built up by a myriad minds with a view to mutual understandings.

This system, de Saussure's 'langue', is called upon when a speech event takes place: 'Speech is applied language' (TSL:318).

- *Consciousness and introspection*

One notices that Gardiner considers the native speaker's language system to be something existing in his 'consciousness', i.e. accessible to introspection and mental consultation. This idea has proved hard to eradicate. It was not only omnipresent in European linguistics of the 1920s till well after the second world war but existed also in the American school of tagmemics (4.4.2), and, though less overtly, in American psycholinguistics of the 1960s. (The behaviourism that dominated Bloomfieldian linguistics, with its radical elimination of everything mental, had at least the advantage of avoiding this pitfall.) It is in this light that one must understand the widespread conviction in European structuralist linguistics and in tagmemics that the ultimate confirmation of the correctness of a linguistic analysis should lie in the deeply felt agreement by the linguist, preferably the community of linguists, with the analysis in question. The application of this norm for the correctness of analyses has become known in linguistics as the method of introspection.

We now know that this is not only wrong but also a serious obstacle to a proper appreciation of the formal complexity and abstractness of grammatical systems. As long as one thinks that a grammatical system, being mental, must be accessible to introspection and consultation, one will regard proposals involving formally complex grammatical rule systems as psychologically implausible or even impossible, since speakers, obviously, do not go consciously, point by point, through a complex set of rules when they produce or interpret sentences. In the early days of transformational grammar this was indeed a stock objection levelled against it: how could one possibly propose that speakers generate sentences the way transformational grammars generate them! Nowadays, of course, more precise observation and a more adequate survey of the facts have taught us that any empirically adequate rule system describing the well-formed constructions of a natural language, no matter how cleverly reduced to general principles, will always be complex in the intuitive sense of the word. At the same time, however, we are now used to thinking in terms of mental processes that escape awareness, automatic routines locked away in inaccessible compartments of the mind. The computer metaphor of the mind is of good use here as most of the machinery in a computer remains hidden from the user's observation. All the user notices is the interface and epiphenomena like speed or capacity. We now accept more easily that complex grammatical rule systems may be psychologically real yet not be open to awareness. If they were we would not have to venture hypotheses as to their nature.

• *Linguistics as an autonomous science*
Gardiner, like all structuralist linguists, wanted to see linguistics as an autonomous science, dealing with an autonomous object of inquiry, speech and language. But while it was understood that the grammatical system of a language is part of the general psychology of its speakers, he failed to see the possibility of complex *specifically linguistic* rule systems that are, though mentally real, not open to awareness. The failure to see this was an impediment for a full realization of an autonomous linguistics as hoped for and envisaged.

• *Primacy of the word; the sentence is the unit of speech*
For Gardiner, the word is the 'unit' of language, and the sentence is the 'unit' of speech. Here we hit upon another theme in pre-war discussions on language: the question of the 'primacy' of the word or the sentence. What was meant by 'primacy', or by the phrase 'the unit of', was not made clear. But Gardiner insists repeatedly that speech proceeds in chunks which he calls 'sentences' (an 'utterance', for him, is any stretch of uttered speech sound). He even goes so far as to say that a sentence is normally followed by a pause (TSL:208):

> The smallest section or unit of speech is the sentence, marked outwardly by a pause of suitable duration, and inwardly by evincing a communicative purpose recognizable as such – perhaps not the entire purpose of the speaker, but precisely that amount or portion which he thinks fit to accomplish before giving himself and the listener a rest. ... *A sentence is an utterance which makes just as long a communication as the speaker has intended to make before giving himself a rest.*

The idea of a pause after every uttered sentence is, of course, utterly naïve. It has nothing to do with the sentence as such, since speech without pauses after sentences still consists of sentences as much as it would do with them. More important is the fact that Gardiner, and with him the whole of linguistic theory of his day, does not succeed in saying anything specific about the structure and composition of the speaker's 'purpose', or of 'that amount or portion which he thinks fit to accomplish'.

Yet, given the ignorance on this score prevailing in Gardiner's day, his formulation is perfectly sensible and does not pretend to express more than the author can vouch for. This lack of pretension is precisely one of the factors that make TSL such a useful text to show both the strengths and the weaknesses of European structuralist linguistics. Here, in any case, we hit upon a weakness, the inability to assign structure to sentential semantic content. In modern linguistic theory we feel more confident, helped as we are by logic and its predicate calculus. We feel we have pretty precise ideas about the structure of semantic analyses of sentences, and we are beginning to see the possibility of extrapolating from there to what might with some justification be called the structure of thoughts. But in Gardiner's day this was still totally out of sight, in linguistics anyway.

Gardiner thus tries not to assign to the sentence a place in the theory of language, only in the theory of speech. In this he is not entirely successful, as he finds himself inexorably drawn to the unwanted conclusion that sentences have a grammatically defined form and therefore belong to language as well as to speech. Thus we read (TLS:184):

> Thus there is such a thing as 'sentence form', and like all other linguistic forms, it is a fact of language, not a fact of speech.

A little later, however, on the same page: 'It is function, not form, which makes a set of words into a sentence', meaning that the same grammatical form of a sentence sometimes functions as a statement, sometimes as a question, sometimes again as a command, etc. Even so (TSL:199):

> Be this as it may, sentence-form is indisputably the main device by which speakers ensure the right acceptance of their utterances.

And what is meant by 'the right acceptance' we read on p. 195:

> the listener reconstructs the thing-meant by an effort of his intelligence, using the situation as an additional source of inference.

Though it is interesting to see that Gardiner recognizes the fact that sentence meaning underdetermines interpretation, in the sense that often non-linguistic information is required, drawn from the situation or from available world knowledge, for an adequate understanding of what is said, it is equally interesting to see that he fails to grasp the fact that what he calls 'an effort of his intelligence' involves the application by the listener of a complex grammatical and semantic machinery which is entirely independent of general intelligence and functions 'underground', as a strictly linguistic mechanized routine procedure. Yet, like the structuralist linguists in America of the same period, he is working up to that conclusion. Despite his insistence that the sentence is a unit of speech, and not of language, he does begin to see sentence structure as prescribed by grammatical constraints (TSL:200):

> The sentence *Did you go to church yesterday?* exemplifies a familiar type of question-form, of which *Have you been to Rome?* and *Am I ever going to see you again?* provide other instances. But we do not carry about in our minds a stock-example of this outer form of question, as is proved by the hesitation which might be experienced in choosing one. So far as it depends upon words at all, outer sentence-form exists in the mind as a certain aptitude for putting the right words together in the right way so as to yield the appearance appropriate, as the case may be, to a statement, an exclamation, a request, or a question. For the purposes of grammatical teaching, we can exteriorize this aptitude or knowledge in two different ways: either by using a formula, as when we say that French questions for corroboration usually take the form verb+pronominal subject with or without further addition; or else by choosing illustrative examples such as *Vient-il? Iras-tu? Jacques est-il malade?*

Had Gardiner paid closer and more systematic attention to what he called the 'formula' for sentence types, like French yes/no questions, he would have found out that the facts of syntax are not so easily described.

- *Sentence patterns as part of grammar*

Gardiner does not come as close to generative grammar as Hjelmslev did. Yet he does present the notion of sentence pattern, albeit in an altogether off-hand way, in very much the same way that notion was coming up in American structuralist linguistics around that time. All it would have taken to develop it further into a proper theory of syntax was close and precise observation combined with a sensible preliminary analysis of the overall problem of complete and formally explicit syntactic description. Though some European linguists did seriously engage in extensive observation of grammatical facts, including the facts of syntax, they failed, on the whole, to go through the process of a preliminary problem analysis. In section 4.5 we shall see that this is what distinguished American structuralism from its European counterpart: the preliminary problem analysis of the task of syntactic description carried out by Harris and Chomsky showed the intrinsic inadequacy of the sentence pattern model and pointed the way towards the transformational model. In Europe this did not happen, though, as we saw when we discussed Hjelmslev, some came close. Gardiner, writing about 1930, also came close (TSL:85):

> The student of linguistic theory cannot, however, content himself with observing a given series or restricted total of linguistic acts. In search of general principles, he takes all possible utterances as his province, though he not only can, but in my opinion must, use single and particular utterances as his point of departure.

This shows that he did require maximal coverage of facts, but did not grasp the complexity of the task of a full formal description. It would take another twenty-five years for that insight to break through.

- *The Subject-Predicate debate*

Gardiner was among the last to take part in the old subject-predicate debate (2.6.3). Though one may well say that his contribution is relatively unoriginal, as it hardly adds anything new to the debate that had been going on for some eighty years, one must also recognize that Gardiner creates order and clarity in the debate and reduces it to its essential elements. He regards subject and predicate as, literally, parts of *speech*, i.e. of the use of sentences, and not as parts of the language system. He follows the tradition of discourse-bound subject and predicate (Wegener, Lipps, Stout; 2.6.3) in interpreting as subject that part of the sentence that denotes the thing about which something new is said. The new information is expressed by the predicate (TSL:265-273). In this connection he speaks of *logical* subject and predicate, criticising, on unclear grounds, Hermann Paul for the use of the term *psychological* (TSL:272-3; 280-1).[21] He does admit the reality of a *grammatical* subject-predicate distinction,

---

[21] What neither Gardiner nor the other, older, participants in the debate realized is that this notion of logical subject and predicate is precisely what Aristotle had in mind when he defined these terms (though for Aristotle the subject was not a sentence part but the actual reference value, the thing-meant, by the corresponding sentence part). Aristotle, on the other hand, never saw the essential discourse-dependence of his notions of subject and

as advocated by Jespersen (1924), but he rejects Jespersen's view that the grammatical distinction is primary (TSL:274).

It is hard to escape from Gardiner's conclusion that, therefore, there are two types of sentence, the congruent ones where 'logical' and grammatical subject and predicate coincide, and the incongruent ones where they do not. It does indeed seem necessary to distinguish between the grammatical notions of subject and predicate on the one hand, and the discourse-bound notions of what is now currently called topic and comment on the other. Their eventual confusion, in the early 19th century, is due to the long and drawn-out process of establishing an apparatus for grammatical analysis during the preceding centuries.

On the other hand, one sees how underdeveloped Gardiner's notion of grammatical construction still is. But in this respect, as has been said, Gardiner does not differ from what was current in the linguistic theories of the day.

- *Overall appraisal of Gardiner's contribution*

We may perhaps summarize our appraisal of Gardiner's TSL by saying that he did state his primary data, but did not formulate a causal question, and hence did not develop or attempt to develop a formal explanatory theory. His primary data, as has been said, consists of speech events. And he does posit a linguistic system, his 'language', which lies behind every speech event and exists in the 'consciousness' of every speaker. But there is no causal question. The closest he comes to one is on p. 264, where, following a behaviourist lead, he considers the question of what prompts a speaker to produce an utterance. But the question of what enables a speaker-listener to understand and interpret any given speech utterance does not come up in anything like specific terms. Nor, of course, does he see linguistic theory as providing an explanatory answer to such a question. Instead, he expects something quite different from linguistic theory (TSL:8):

> The first benefit that may be expected from a sound general linguistic theory, if attainable, is that it will teach us which of the old-accepted grammatical categories should be retained and which of them are really in need of modification or rejection. ... The second benefit which I anticipate is, however, that the current accounts given of such categories will be substantially changed.

Even though the time had not yet come for the more concerted and more precisely defined effort at setting up an explanatory linguistic theory that we witness in modern theories of grammar, it is easy to see that European theoretical linguistics was definitely moving in that direction. The same holds for what was happening in America at that time. The difference is that the decisive breakthrough was achieved there, not in Europe. We shall now look at the developments that took place on the other side of the Atlantic Ocean.

---

predicate: the subject is that which is up for comment, while the predicate is the new comment.

CHAPTER 4

The twentieth century: America

4.0 Preamble

In this chapter, the American developments in the study of language are traced back to their origins. These are in part indigenous, in so far as they go back to anthropological linguistics on the one hand and to behaviourism on the other. In part, however, they were also inspired by what, over the years, came from Europe. The key figure is Leonard Bloomfield, who incorporated both the American and the pre-Saussurean European tradition. Bloomfieldian linguistics first took hold of the American scene, and then, after World War II, gradually also of much of Europe. By the middle of the century, two main schools had sprung from Bloomfield's teaching, the traditionalists, led by Kenneth Pike, and the formalists, led by Zellig Harris. During the 1940s, Harris developed an early form of transformational grammar, which was systematized and promoted by Noam Chomsky and, after 1957, spread all over the United States and soon after also over Europe and the rest of the world. Since this is now the most influential school of linguistic theory its growth and its general scientific status will be prominently discussed.

One great advantage of the development of transformational generative grammar has been a general deepening of methodological insights. Whereas, up to about 1960, it was common among linguists to think that 'scientific method' consisted largely in systematic data collection and data ordering, after 1960 the notion of 'theory' became prominent, together with questions of explanation and adequacy. On the whole, linguistic theory achieved a much better integration into the overall network of respectable science than before. In general terms one has to say that the much sought-after empirical access to language was realized in a significant way for the first time in the context of transformational grammar. On the other hand, however, we will see that this much praised achievement still leaves much to be desired, as transformational grammar soon began to suffer from poor method: a rather restricted and idiosyncratic choice of research interests, shallow research methods, and, generally, poor contacts with other research groups, most of which pursue their scientific aims in a more balanced way.

The bulk of this chapter is, therefore, devoted to the theoretical developments within transformational grammar. Nothing is said here about the various theories that have sprung up during the past twenty or so years, though their presence is acknowledged in section 7.4. Moreover, due to space limitations, no attention is paid to the developments in sociolinguistics and dialectology, or to the efforts made in psycholinguistics and in computational linguistics to model or simulate natural speakers' linguistic behaviour.

An exception is made for linguistic typology, to which the final section 4.8 is devoted. Linguistic typology or universalist linguistics is a separate branch of language study initiated by Joseph H. Greenberg in the mid-1950s. It tries to stay outside the fracas of the theoretical arena while going about its business in its own way. It is of great interest not only because it provides valuable data on the variety of languages that exist in this world, but also, in particular, because it provides empirical evidence showing that languages do not vary arbitrarily but stay within relatively well-defined patterns.

4.1 Some early history; Whitney, Boas

• *The American Philosophical Society*
The beginning of the American linguistic tradition coincides with independence. The first rallying point of linguistic activity was the *American Philosophical Society*, founded in 1769. As would be expected, linguistic interest in those early years was somewhat nationalistic and focussed on the American Indian languages. As was said in section 2.3.2 above, linguistics was a favourite avocation of the political élite in those days, both in Europe and in America. Among the first persons who took an active interest in American Indian languages and in language in general we find *Benjamin Franklin* (1706-1790), political activist, statesman, physicist, inventor and linguist, and first president of the American Philosophical Society. Next to him we find *Thomas Jefferson* (1743-1826), third president of the American Philosophical Society and third President of the United States. Not a bad start for an academic subject in a new nation.

Both Franklin and Jefferson brought with them, besides a nationalistic fervour, a great deal of European, especially French, culture. Franklin and Jefferson 'frequented the same Parisian *salons* ... as did Wilhelm von Humboldt, and they all three met with the rising group of French intellectuals, who were to be known as the Ideologues' (Andresen 1990:23). Both Franklin and Jefferson possessed extensive libraries, with considerable portions devoted to the study of language and languages, including what was available on American Indian languages (Andresen 1990:25-26). Both insisted that the American Indians and their languages were not 'primitive' or 'savage' but, potentially anyway, equal to their more sophisticated European counterparts. Both formulated empirical questions as well as research programmes regarding the American Indians and their languages. Actual field work in American Indian languages began to be carried out from 1815 onwards. In 1815, writes Andresen (1990:40):

> the American Philosophical Society recognized linguistics by creating the Historical and Literary Committee. This committee chose two objectives: 1) the collection of historic documents; and 2) manuscripts recording Indian languages. ... After this date, the two most important linguists of the first half of the nineteenth century, Peter S. Duponceau and John Pickering, became particularly active.

Thus the foundation was laid for the study of American Indian languages and cultures that is now so much part of the American linguistic and anthropological tradition.

- *Whitney*

The first professional theoretical linguist came somewhat later in the person of *William Dwight Whitney* (1827-1894), mentioned earlier in section 2.4 as one of Max Müller's more forceful critics. Unlike the major American linguists after him, such as Boas, Sapir, Bloomfield, who were immigrants themselves or came from, mostly Jewish, recent immigrant families, Whitney was of traditional protestant American stock. His father was a well-to-do banker; his elder brother was a well-known geologist. During 1849-1850 he studied Sanskrit at Yale, then went to Germany till 1853, whereupon he returned to Yale to stay there till the end of his life. Whitney was the opposite of a field worker. He took no real interest in American Indian languages, and concentrated entirely on comparative philology as it was practised in Europe, combining that with general thoughts on the nature of language.

Whitney stands in the tradition to which we reckon also, for example, de Saussure and Firth, in which a language is considered to be primarily a social product, both a cause and a result of group identity. Every individual is the imperfect and partial repository of the linguistic and cultural tradition of the group to which he or she belongs. A language is primarily a set of word signs and therefore present in the conscious mind, though the mechanism of speech, the use of language, is mostly unconscious. Linguistics, for him, is 'the science of languages or of the origin and history of words; the general and comparative study of human languages and of their elements. Also called comparative philology' (Andresen 1990:165). These views are more conventional than startling. And although Whitney claimed repeatedly that his approach to language was 'scientific' there is no trace either of a delimitation of the observable data or of a causal question, let alone of a theory. Yet he chided German linguistics for not being 'scientific' (Whitney 1875:318-19, quoted in Andresen 1990:165-6):

> [W]hile Germany is the home of comparative philology, the scholars of that country have ... distinguished themselves much less in that which we have called the science of language. There is among them (not less than elsewhere) such discordance on points of fundamental importance, such uncertainty of view, such carelessness of consistency, that a German science cannot be said yet to have an existence.

His fundamental disdain of American Indian languages, which he actively strove to eliminate, is expressed in the following passage (Whitney 1867:181, quoted in Andresen 1990:151):

> As, here in America, a single cultivated nation, of homogeneous speech, is taking the place of a congeries of wild tribes, with their host of discordant tongues, so, on a smaller scale, is it everywhere else: civilization and the conditions it makes are gaining upon barbarism and its isolating influences.

Not quite the attitude of the founding fathers of American Indian studies.

Whitney's importance lies less in his ideas, which were largely unoriginal, than in his social position. Being the first theoretical linguist of note, he controlled for many years virtually all appointments in linguistics throughout the country (Andresen 1990:167). By the time of his death he personified both theoretical linguistics and comparative philology in the United States. It was largely due to his very strong influence on funding and appointments that the descriptive study of American Indian languages was pushed back into a limbo of semi-respectability. Anthropological linguistics thus became separated from the more theoretically oriented study of language. This uniquely American branch of linguistic activity would have been seriously jeopardized had it not been for the foundation of the *Smithsonian Institute* in Washington D.C. in 1846, and the subsequent institution of the *Bureau of American Ethnology* in 1879. It would take a new generation of very different-minded anthropologists and linguists to redress the balance somewhat.

● *Boas*

This new generation came in the person of *Franz Boas* (1858-1942). Boas was a native German from Westphalia. Trained as a physicist and geologist at Kiel he went to Baffin Island in Northern Canada to do a stint of geological field-work. While there, he felt his already nascent interest in ethnology, anthropology and 'exotic' languages awakened and shifted from geology to the study of Eskimos and their languages. Back in Germany he decided around 1885 to emigrate to the United States and devote himself entirely to anthropology and linguistics. In 1899 he was appointed to the chair of anthropology at Columbia University in New York, where he stayed till his retirement in 1937, at the age of seventy-nine.[1]

His main linguistic work is the Introduction to the *Handbook of American Indian Languages*, edited by him and published in 1911 for the Bureau of American Ethnology. This Introduction of barely eighty pages is practically the only piece of writing Boas produced on the general nature of language. Had it been just for this it is doubtful that his name would have stuck in history. In themselves, the ideas expressed in the Introduction are, though on the whole sensible, not very startling or original, and often remarkably similar to those of contemporary linguists in Europe. Like so many others, Boas insisted on the 'scientific' character of linguistics, but meant no more than that linguists should be methodical in their work and collect data that would shed light on the mental and social life of communities. Any kind of explanation would be historical. No notion of 'structure' or of a 'language system' constraining linguistic utterances is found. Unlike most linguists of his day he held that the classifications of any given language are not open to awareness but unconscious:

> It would seem that the essential difference between linguistic phenomena and other ethnological phenomena is, that the linguistic classifications never rise into con-

[1] See Murray (1994:47-65) for a detailed description of Boas's life and work, with an emphasis on his power games in establishing linguistic anthropology as an academic discipline.

sciousness, while in other ethnological phenomena, although the same unconscious origin prevails, these often rise into consciousness, and thus give rise to secondary reasoning and to reinterpretations.   Boas (1911:67)

Other than Whitney before him, he stressed the primacy of the sentence over the word, though no notion of sentence structure as the product of a linguistic system is yet to be found:

> Since all speech is intended to serve for the communication of ideas, the natural unit of expression is the sentence; that is to say, a group of articulate sounds which convey a complete idea.   Boas (1911:23)

(One hears the echo of the Modists, who also spoke of a 'complete sense' generated by a sentence in the listener's mind (1.4.2).) Like de Saussure, and later Hjelmslev, he posited a parallelism between phonetic and semantic structure:

> As the automatic and rapid use of articulations has brought it about that a limited number of articulations only, each with limited variability, and a limited number of sound-clusters, have been selected from the infinitely large range of possible articulations and clusters of articulations, so the infinitely large number of ideas have been reduced by classification to a lesser number, which by constant use have established firm associations, and which can be used automatically.   Boas (1911:21)

It is often thought that this passage is an early expression of the cultural relativism that led to the Sapir-Whorf hypothesis mentioned above in section 2.6.2. Finally, Boas, obviously, held the Indian languages in high esteem and rejected any dichotomy between the great languages of culture and Whitney's 'discordant tongues' showing the 'barbarism' of their speakers.

In no way can one say that Boas represented any form of structuralism in his linguistic work, but he did insist on the autonomy and what to him was the non-universality of the grammatical categories of each individual language – a typical trait of later structuralism:

> No attempt has been made to compare the forms of the Indian's grammars with the grammars of English, Latin, or even among themselves: but in each case the psychological groupings which are given depend entirely upon the inner form of each language.   Boas (1911:81)

(One notes the reference to 'inner form', Humboldt's brain child but reinterpreted in a gamut of different ways by later authors.) Not having been trained himself as a professional linguist he felt more free to define his own position in linguistics. Boas did not belong to any particular school or trend of linguistic thought, but one notices the (sometimes undigested) influence of either historically established or fashionably modern ideas on language.

What is important about Boas's ideas is less their intrinsic value than the fact that they were opposed to Whitney's views, which had slowly become standard in America. Boas's importance in the history of American linguistics lies mainly in the fact that he made the study of American Indian languages regain some degree of respectability, which caused an upsurge in anthropological linguistics. Under Boas's direction, vast collections of actual linguistic data were recorded and stored. He encouraged his students to do field work and record data, which were to be analysed with an uncluttered mind that was open to sensible ideas and perspectives. Boas, moreover, exerted a great deal of influence through the students that were trained by him and through the considerable popularity of the 1911 *Handbook*. The two names that spring to mind in this context are Sapir and Bloomfield, to whom the following sections are devoted.

4.2 Edward Sapir

- *Life*

Edward Sapir (1884-1939)[2] was born in the Northern German-Polish region of Pomerania, where his father was a Jewish cantor. The family emigrated to New York in 1889. While still at school, Edward won a Pulitzer scholarship to Columbia University, where he graduated in 1905 in Germanic Philology. His PhD, which was completed in 1909 and was supervised by Franz Boas, dealt with the Indian language Takelma (spoken in Oregon). From 1910 till 1925 he was the head of the Division of Anthropology of the Geological Survey of Canada. Between 1925 and 1931 he taught at the University of Chicago, and moved to Yale in 1931. There he stayed till his early death in 1939. In December 1924 he founded with Bloomfield the Linguistic Society of America, about which more in the following section. The bulk of his publications is on American Indian languages, especially the Athabaskan and Uto-Aztecan families. A few works (notably 1921, 1925, 1929, 1933; see also Mandelbaum 1961) are devoted to general linguistic questions.

Sapir was the first real structuralist in American linguistics. The way he came to theoretical linguistics mirrors more general trends of the time and shows up the historical roots of American structuralism as it existed between 1920 and 1960. Sapir's interest in and views on language were the blended result of historically oriented comparative philology, of the description of American Indian languages, and of the largely European tradition of reflection on the psychological and logical basis of language, and hence of meaning. It was these three elements that shaped not only Sapir but the whole of American structuralism.

- *Contrast between tradition and modernism; relation with philosophy*

There is a curious contradiction in Sapir's attitude towards language. On the one hand he was a great innovator. The most characteristic feature of Sapir's position and work in general linguistic theory is no doubt the desire to break with the past. Yet the past remains present in sometimes surprising ways. Being somewhat of a romantic, Sapir was impressed with Herder's essay *Ueber den Ursprung der Sprache* of 1772 (so much admired by Humboldt; see 2.6.2), about which he wrote his MA-dissertation in 1907. And he did not, apparently, consider it unscientific to speak about the 'spirit' of a language

[2] I draw on Darnell (1994b) and Murray (1994:77-83) for Sapir's biographical details.

(1921:127). He devotes a whole chapter (1921:157-182) to the somewhat mystic notion of 'drift': 'Language moves down time in a current of its own making. It has a drift' (1921:160). And, as for Humboldt, literary art and aesthetics play a notable part in his theorizing. Against this, however, there is an overwhelming mass of new analytic notions and terms, and a strong desire for clarity and precision. One is inclined to say that Sapir embodies a cross between 19th century German and 20th century American structuralist thinking about language. These two are intermingled in a curious way throughout his writings, which thereby assume a hybrid character.

Sapir wanted a new start to be made, with a new terminology and with greater respect for the autonomy of the systems at work in each individual language (cp. Murray 1994:93-95). The American Indian languages in particular were seen to require new categories that differ essentially from those established for the European languages and go back to the analysis of Latin and Greek. The study of language must disentangle itself from philosophy and logic and be based on formal criteria. Thus we read (1921:125):

> A part of speech outside of the limitations of syntactic form is but a will o' the wisp. For this reason no logical scheme of the parts of speech – their number, nature and necessary confines – is of the slightest interest to the linguist. Each language has its own scheme. Everything depends on the formal demarcations which it recognizes.

Linguistic analysis should precede any sound philosophy, a view to be repeated in the Oxford school of Ordinary Language Philosophy flourishing between 1945 and 1970 (see 6.2.2.2):

> The time is long past when grammatical forms and processes can be naïvely trans- lated by philosophers into metaphysical entities. The philosopher needs to under- stand language if only to protect himself against his own language habits, and so it is not surprising that philosophy, in attempting to free logic from the trammels of grammar and to understand knowledge and the meaning of symbolism, is compelled to make a preliminary critique of the linguistic process itself.   Sapir (1929:213)

- *Only speech 'exists'; language is a hypothesis*

Language itself has no independent existence. What actually 'exists', i.e. is available in physical form, is speech: 'Language exists only in so far as it is actually used – spoken and heard, written and read' (1921:165). If 'exist' is taken here in the sense of actual physical presence, we may infer from this that Sapir had a clear notion of what constitutes 'data'. Then, for him, data is to be found only in actual concrete speech occurrences. 'Language' is an explanatory notion, postulated so as to understand how speech can function:

> The inner sound-system, overlaid though it may be by the mechanical or the irrele- vant, is a real and immensely important principle in the life of a language. ... Every language ... is characterized as much by its ideal system of sounds and by the under- lying phonetic pattern ... as by a definite grammatical structure.   Sapir (1921:57-8)

> Wherever we go we are impressed by the fact that pattern is one thing, the utili- zation of pattern quite another.   Sapir (1921:61)

> Every language has its special method or methods of binding words into a larger unity.   Sapir (1921:116)

• *The sentence as the major unit of speech; subject and predicate*

The primary units of analysis are the morpheme as a minimal element and the sentence as a maximal element, but the notion 'sentence' is described in rather incompatible ways:

> Radical (or grammatical) element and sentence – these are the primary *functional* units of speech, the former as an abstracted minimum, the latter as the esthetically satisfying embodiment of a unified thought. ... The sentence is the logical counterpart of the complete thought only if it be felt as made up of the radical and grammatical elements that lurk in the recesses of its words.   Sapir (1921:33)

In the last sentence we recognize Boas's notion of a 'complete idea' expressed by a sentence. But, like Boas, he fails to specify what makes an idea 'complete', and we are left totally in the dark as regards the criterion of 'aesthetic satisfaction'. Even so, it is historically interesting to see how Sapir is struggling with the concept 'sentence', and how the notion of formal syntax is beginning to shape up, though still loaded with meaningless metaphors like 'lurking in the recesses of words'. In order to reconcile his apparently incompatible notions of sentence he falls back on the old subject-predicate debate discussed in 2.6.3 above:

> We have already seen that the major functional unit of speech, the sentence, has, like the word, a psychological as well as a merely logical or abstracted existence. Its definition is not difficult. It is the linguistic expression of a proposition. It combines a subject of discourse with a statement in regard to this subject. Subject and "predicate" may be combined in a single word, as in Latin *dico*: each may be expressed independently, as in the English equivalent, *I say*; each or either may be so qualified as to lead to complex propositions of many sorts.   Sapir (1921:36)

(We note the difference between what is meant by *existence* here from what we saw on p. 165. We also note Sapir's light-heartedness in saying that it is not difficult to define the sentence!)

Sapir follows here in the footsteps of Wegener, Lipps and Stout (see 2.6.3), who introduced the discourse-related notion of subject and predicate. It is found again, in the context of 'parts of speech', right after the quote from p. 125 given above:

> Yet we must not be too destructive. It is well to remember that speech consists of a series of propositions. There must be something to talk about and something must be said about this subject of discourse once it is selected. This distinction is of such fundamental importance that the vast majority of languages have emphasized it by creating some sort of formal barrier between the two terms of the proposition. The subject of discourse is a noun. As the most common subject of discourse is either a person or a thing, the noun clusters about concrete concepts of that order. As the thing predicated of a subject is generally an activity in the widest sense of the word, a passage from one moment of existence to another, the form which has been set aside for the business of predicating, in other words, the verb, clusters about concepts of activity. No language wholly fails to distinguish noun and verb, though in particular cases the nature of the distinction may be an elusive one. It is different with the other parts of speech. Not one of them is imperatively required for the life of language.   Sapir (1921:125-126)

- *Immediate constituent analysis*

This leads to a further aspect in Sapir's notion of structure. In the one but last quote we saw Sapir allude to the possibility of further elaboration of both subject and predicate, so that quite complex sentences may come about. From the modern vantage point we recognize here the notion of hierarchical tree structure, which Bloomfield had taken from Wundt's works (4.3), and which was in those years taking hold of the American linguistic scene through Bloomfield (1914). A fully worked out example illustrating the hierarchical tree structure principle, though here applied to a word rather than to a sentence, is found in (1921:31-32) (Sapir uses capitals for lexical roots, lower case for grammatical morphemes, and round brackets for elements that cannot stand alone):

> One example will do for thousands, one complex type for hundreds of possible types. I select it from Paiute, the language of the Indians of the arid plateaus of southwestern Utah. The word *wii-to-kuchum-punku-rügani-yugwi-va-ntü-m(ü)* is of unusual length even for its own language, but it is no psychological monster for all that. It means "they who are going to sit and cut up with a knife a black cow (*or* bull)", or, in the order of the Indian elements, "knife-black-buffalo-pet-cut up-sit(plur.)-future-participle-animate-plur". The formula for this word, in accordance with our symbolism, would be (F) + (E) + C + d + A + B + (g) + (h) + (i) + (0). It is the plural of the future participle of a compound verb "to sit and cut up" – A + B. The elements (g) – which denotes futurity – (h) – a participial suffix – and (i) – indicating the animate plural – are grammatical elements which convey nothing when detached. The formula (0) is intended to imply that the finished word conveys, in addition to what is definitely expressed, a further relational idea, that of subjectivity; in other words, the form can only be used as the subject of a sentence, not in an objective or other syntactic relation. The radical element A ("to cut up"), before entering into combination with the coordinate element B ("to sit"), is itself compounded with two nominal elements or element-groups – an instrumentally used stem (F) ("knife"), which may be freely used as the radical element of noun forms but cannot be employed as an absolute noun in its given form, and an objectively used group – (E) + C + d ("black cow *or* bull"). This group in turn consists of an adjectival radical element (E) ("black"), which cannot be independently employed ... , and the compound noun C + d ("buffalo-pet"). The radical element C properly means "buffalo", but the element d, properly an independently occurring noun meaning "horse" ... , is regularly used as a quasi subordinate element indicating that the animal denoted by the stem to which it is affixed is owned by a human being. It will be observed that the whole complex (F) + (E) + C + d + A + B is functionally no more than a verbal base, corresponding to the *sing-* of an English form like *singing*; that this complex remains verbal in force on the addition of the temporal element (g) – this (g), by the way, must not be understood as appended to B alone, but to the whole basic complex as a unit – and that the elements (h) + (i) + (0) transform the verbal expression into a formally well-defined noun.   Sapir (1921:31-32)

Sapir's very precise analysis of this complex word would have been greatly facilitated had he used a tree diagram to illustrate it. In diagrammatic form, Sapir's analysis of the complex Paiute word looks like what is shown in fig. 1: a properly behaved mainly left-branching tree structure.

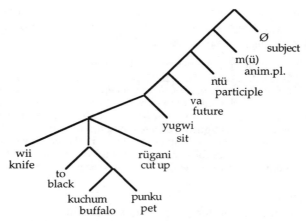

Figure 1   Immediate constituent analysis of the Paiute word
wii-to-kuchum-punku-rügani-yugwi-va-ntü-m(ü)

- *Why no diagrams?*

One wonders why Sapir did not draw a simple diagram like fig. 1 and save himself the trouble of describing verbally the hierarchical constituent structure of the Paiute word in question. The same applies, and with greater force, to Bloomfield and the whole of American structuralism till the mid-1950s: never does one find any constituent structure diagram although constituent structure is at the heart of American structuralism in so far as it applies to grammar (see 4.4.5 for a full discussion). The answer is, I think, that the social code in the humanistic disciplines ('Geisteswissenschaften') simply forbade any schema or diagram representation. In the mathematical and physical sciences this reluctance never existed. Psychology was also more open in this respect (Wundt did draw constituent structure diagrams in his works on language structure). But in the human sciences there existed a curious attitude that this was 'not done'.[3] (Note also that the ancient truth functions of propositional logic were not actually written down as tables until the 1920s, i.e. after logic had gone mathematical.)

- *Meaning as 'thought-before-speech'*

From the point of view of semantics, Sapir does not follow the line we detected in Boas, de Saussure and Hjelmslev, who consider semantic 'matter' in tandem with phonetic matter and leave it to the language system to cut both 'planes' up in units and establish interplanar links. On the contrary, in this respect Sapir is refreshingly old-fashioned and sensible. He distinguishes between a non-linguistic level of language-independent thought and a lower level of

---

[3] When I started to teach linguistics at Oxford in 1970 I was given a lecture room with a minute, cracked blackboard of about four square feet, totally inadequate for my teaching purposes. When I asked for a better board the answer was, first, that one did not need a blackboard for linguistics! Not until I had explained that times had changed was I given a proper lecture hall with all the blackboard space I could possibly want.

thought-before-linguistic-expression. In the latter, the 'pure' thought has been channelled into the categories of the language in question. Language is a procrustean bed. It has, he says (1921:104):

> ... the tendency to construct schemes of classification into which all the concepts of language must be fitted. ... Language ... must have its perfectly exclusive pigeon-holes and will tolerate no flying vagrants. Any concept that asks for expression must submit to the classificatory rules of the game, just as there are statistical surveys in which even the most convinced atheist must perforce be labeled Catholic, Protestant or Jew or get no hearing. In English we have made up our minds that all action must be conceived of in reference to three standard times. If, therefore, we desire to state a proposition that is as true tomorrow as it was yesterday, we have to pretend that the present moment may be extended fore and aft so as to take in all eternity.

- *The tyranny of usage*

Likewise with nominal genders, which have, on the whole, hardly any connection left with natural gender but subject the speaker to 'the tyranny of usage' (p. 103). Modern semantics and psycholinguistics tend to confirm Sapir's view in this matter. Each language does indeed seem to have its own grammatico-semantic 'questionnaire' whose questions have to be filled in before a grammatical sentence can be generated.[4]

- *Incompatibility with the Humboldt-Sapir-Whorf hypothesis*

It is interesting to see that this notion of how language-independent thought is first cast into a more language-specific mould before being expressed as a good grammatical sentence does not tally at all well with what is known as the *Humboldt-Sapir-Whorf hypothesis* (HSW-hypothesis), according to which conceptual structures are seen as the products of a linguistically determined 'construction' of social 'reality'. Sapir is standardly mentioned as the modern source of this idea. The classical passage in Sapir's work expressing the HSW-hypothesis is the following (see also Mandelbaum 1961:68-69):

> Language is a guide to 'social reality'. Though language is not ordinarily thought of as of essential interest to the students of social science, it powerfully conditions all our thinking about social problems and processes. Human beings do not live in the objective world alone, nor alone in the world of social activity as ordinarily understood, but are very much at the mercy of the particular language which has become the medium of expression for their society. It is quite an illusion to imagine that one adjusts to reality essentially without the use of language and that language is merely an incidental means of solving specific problems of communication or reflection. The fact of the matter is that the 'real' world is to a large extent unconsciously built up on the language habits of the group. No two languages are ever sufficiently similar to be considered as representing the same social reality. The worlds in which different societies live are distinct worlds, not merely the same world with different labels attached.   Sapir (1929:207-208)

---

[4] Hence, for example, the well-known difficulty for machine translation programs aiming at automatic translation from, for example, Malay, which hardly expresses any tenses, into English, which has a relatively rich tense system. The Malay questionnaire is less specific on tenses than its English counterpart, which then has to draw the answers from a situational and general knowledge base, rather than from the Malay original.

If this is correct then there is no room for a language-independent level of thought or conceptual structure. Whether it is correct, however, is open to doubt. In Bloomfield we already find a fatal critique *avant la lettre*:

> In Malay the experiences which may be logically defined by us as 'offspring of the same parents' are classed together, and for such an experience is used the word *sudara*. In English we form no such class; we form two classes, according to the sex, and speak of a *brother* or a *sister*. Now, it would be manifestly absurd to say that a Malay does not know his brother from his sister; it would be no less absurd, however, to say that English-speaking people are unable to form the general idea conveyed by the Malay word. Both languages can express the experiences for which no single designation exists by a compound expression which analyzes them, – the Malay by saying *sudara lakilaki* and *sudara perampuwan*, where the added modifying words resemble our terms 'male' and 'female'; and the English by saying *brother or sister* or *child of the same parents*. Bloomfield (1914:85)

The extreme relativism expressed in Sapir's passage just quoted discounts the possibility of strong cognitive universals that largely determine how and in what categories members of the human race interpret the world in which they live, no matter what language, if any, is around. The HSW-hypothesis is also likely to be false for general a priori reasons. How, for example, would human societies have 'construed' reality during all those hundreds of thousands of years when the human race was about but had no articulated language? How do animals cope? Anyone at all familiar with higher vertebrates knows that these creatures have highly specific 'construals' of reality, both social and individual, apparently without any language as the purveyor of their cognitive categories. Add to this the extreme vagueness of the notions involved ('social reality', 'conceptual structures', 'language habits', to mention a few) and the equally extreme lack of convincing data in support of the HSW-hypothesis, and one will see that this hypothesis must, in the end, be considered futile, quite apart from the threat of unfalsifiability. It makes much more sense to assume that language mirrors, to some extent, cultural and social categories, and not the other way round, precisely because language is there to express thoughts, whether individual or moulded by society.

As regards Sapir's position on this issue, it seems fair to estimate that he had not quite made up his mind on it and wavered a great deal between different views. The person who really promoted the HSW-hypothesis was *Benjamin Lee Whorf* (1897-1941), an amateur linguist who, as a mature student, took courses with Sapir during his years at Yale and, for some time, gained popularity with the American anthropological establishment.[5]

- *Sapir's use of the term 'psychological'*

One last observation on Sapir's use of the term 'psychological'. Since, for him, a language is situated in the minds of its speakers, anything to do with the language system is called 'psychological'. This implies that he does not consider a speaker's mastery of a language to be an autonomous ('modular')

[5] For a similar critique of the HSW-hypothesis see Pinker (1994: chapter 3).

compartment of the mind. In Sapir's view, the language system underlying the speech process is on a gradient scale between the conscious and the unconscious:

> When a word (or unified group of words) contains a derivational element (or word) the concrete significance of the radical element (*farm-*, *duck-*) tends to fade from consciousness and to yield to a new concreteness (*farmer*, *duckling*) that is synthetic in expression rather than in thought. In our sentence [i.e. *The farmer kills the duckling*, PS] the concepts of *farm* and *duck* are not really involved at all; they are merely latent, for formal reasons, in the linguistic expression.   Sapir (1921:88)

> Linguistic categories make up a system of surviving dogma – dogma of the unconscious. They are often but half real as concepts; their life tends ever to languish away into form for form's sake.   Sapir (1921:105)

To the extent that Sapir could have an idea of what a language system involves, this halfway view between consciousness and unconsciousness is understandable: words and morphological processes seem to be more open to possible introspection (closer to the 'user interface', one might say using a computer metaphor) than the processes of syntax, which are definitely part of the inaccessible background machinery. Had Sapir realized what the complexities of syntax amount to, he would have taken a position much farther removed from the pole of consciousness. But the syntactic revolution was not yet happening. For that we have to go to Bloomfield.

4.3   Leonard Bloomfield

• *Life*
Leonard Bloomfield (1887-1949) was born in Chicago.[6] His paternal grandparents, originally Austrian Jews by the name of Blumenfeld, had moved to the United States in 1868. In 1896 his parents moved out of Chicago and took over a family hotel at Elkhart Lake in Wisconsin. Unlike Sapir, who was a religious man, Bloomfield was brought up as a humanist, without religion, a fact that gains relevance in the context of his later 'conversion' to behaviourism. The comparative philologist and staunch supporter of the Young Grammarians Maurice Bloomfield was his uncle, an elder brother of his father's. In 1909 Leonard married Alice Sayers. The marriage remained childless, but the Bloomfields adopted two boys as their sons.

Having completed his undergraduate study at Harvard in 1906 he became a graduate student, first at Wisconsin and then at Chicago, where he took his PhD in 1909. The dissertation, entitled *A Semasiologic Differentiation in Germanic Secondary Ablaut*, was philological in the established sense. Both at Wisconsin and at Chicago he made some money as a teaching assistant in German, and also took a variety of courses in Germanic, Slavonic and Indo-European philology and in Sanskrit. His first real academic appointment (1909-1910) was at the University of Cincinnati, where he was an instructor in Ger-

---

[6] For the biographical details I rely mostly on Hall (1990) and Murray (1994:113-135), and incidentally on various contributions in Hall (1987).

man. In 1910 he moved to the University of Illinois, where he became again an instructor in German. It was then that he wrote his first major publication, *An Introduction to the Study of Language*, published in 1914.

- *Year in Germany*

When he was told that a period of study in Europe was mandatory for promotion he went to Germany in the academic year 1913-1914, where he studied at Göttingen and Leipzig. On his return he was promoted to Assistant Professor of Comparative Philology and German. At Göttingen his main teacher was the classicist and Indo-Europeanist Jacob Wackernagel, who introduced him to the secrets of Pāṇini's Sanskrit grammar, a lasting source of inspiration for Bloomfield. At Leipzig he attended lectures on Indo-European by the (then aged) Young Grammarians August Leskien and Karl Brugmann, and also lectures on the psychology of language by Wilhelm Wundt,[7] who was then eighty-one years old. One may surmise that Bloomfield's visit to Germany was more a pilgrimage than a real study trip, as he was already familiar with the views and works of the scholars he went to listen to. All he wanted, one may expect, was to meet in person those authorities whom he revered.[8]

- *First work on Tagalog*

Between 1914 and 1917 Bloomfield made a grammatical analysis and description of Tagalog, the language of the Philippines, using as his informant a native speaker who was a student of architecture at the University of Illinois. The three volumes were published in 1917, 'the first example of a complete, thoroughly structural description performed in American linguistics' (Hall 1990:17). In 1919 he started work on the Algonquian language Menomini. In 1920 and 1921 he visited the Menomini reservation, not far from his paternal home at Elkhart Lake, his first two field trips.

- *Columbus, Ohio: 1921-1927; conversion to behaviourism*

In 1921 he moved to Ohio State University in Columbus, where he took up the chair of German and Linguistics. At Ohio State he met the psychologist *Albert P. Weiss*, with whom he became close friends. Weiss belonged to the new school of behaviourism in psychology. Bloomfield, who had a penchant for positive science, was immediately won over to the new ideology and remained a theoretical behaviourist till the end of his life. In the actual practice of linguistic analysis and description, however, the effects of behaviourism are hardly noticed. More will be said about Bloomfield's behaviourism in a moment, when we discuss his *Language* of 1933.

---

[7] This according to Konrad Koerner in Bloomfield (1983 [1914]:xii).

[8] In the years after his visit to Göttingen and Leipzig Bloomfield occasionally referred, in letters and otherwise, to Leskien and Wackernagel as his 'teachers' (Charles Hockett in Hall 1987:41-42).

● *Foundation of the LSA*

Around this time Bloomfield became convinced that 'linguistic science' deserv-ed its own autonomous place among the sciences, distinct not only from psycho-logy and philosophy but also from comparative philology, dialectology and even from anthropological linguistics. He was not alone in this. Vague and indeterminate as it still was, this feeling was present in many centres of theoretical linguistic activity both in Europe and in America. Bloomfield felt that in order to secure for linguistics the place he felt was due to it a separate society should be founded devoted to the advancement of general theoretical linguistics as an autonomous science.[9] On January 28, 1924 he and two co-signatories of kindred spirit sent around the following circular letter to a large number of possibly interested persons (Hockett in Hall 1987:45):

Dear Sir:

To the undersigned it seems that the study of the linguistic sciences is at present greatly neglected in this country. As an indication of this condition they point to the fact that while we have historical, archaeological, and philological societies and publications in a prosperous condition, there is no important society or publication devoted exclusively or chiefly to linguistics in any of its phases. They believe that the foundation of such a society (to have ultimately its own organ of publication) is the first step necessary to an improvement in the general condition of linguistic studies, and that an improvement in the status of linguistic science will necessarily result in the furtherance of all humanistic studies, and the promotion of the best interests of the existing historical, archaeological, and philological societies.

It is tentatively suggested that such a Society shall hold biennial meetings, devoted to the discussion of linguistic problems and related matters, at such times and places as shall render it conveniently possible for the members to attend also, alternately, the meetings of the A.P.A. or the M.L.A., to one or the other of which it may be supposed that many of the members will belong.

You are respectfully invited to inform the signers whether you approve the idea in substance – indicating any changes you may think desirable. In case you disapprove the idea they would appreciate greatly a statement of the reasons that lead to your dissent.

The next step will be to circulate among those who have approved the plan in substance a preliminary draft of the call in order that it may be criticized by all before issuance.

(Signed)   Leonard Bloomfield
George M. Bolling
E.H. Sturtevant

(The other two signatories were George M. Bolling, professor of Classics at Ohio State University, and Edgar H. Sturtevant, then a junior faculty member at Yale, appointed for Classics and comparative philology, later to become a

---

[9] The idea of a professional society was, of course, not original. The American Philolo-gical Association had been founded in 1869, the Modern Language Association in 1883, and the American Dialect Society in 1889. Boas, moreover, had set up the *International Journal of American Linguistics* in 1917. Europe witnessed the foundation of the Prague Linguistic Circle in 1926 (3.3) and the Copenhagen Linguistic Circle in 1931 (3.4), both devoted to the promotion of general linguistics as an autonomous science.

grand old man of American linguistics.) Sapir was among the first to react enthusiastically. He was one of the signers of the official Call for the Organization Meeting of the Linguistic Society of America or LSA, which was officially founded on December 28, 1924. The LSA, now easily the most prestigious linguistic society in the world, immediately set up a new journal, *Language*, whose first year of appearance was 1925. Bloomfield became an active contributor. His most notable contribution of the first years of the journal was his 'Set of postulates for the science of language' (1926), an echo of an earlier short essay by A.P. Weiss 'Set of postulates for psychology' in the *Psychological Review*, and followed in 1948 by Bernard Bloch's 'Set of postulates for phonemic analysis'.

- *Chicago: 1927-1940; colleague with Sapir*

In 1927 Bloomfield was invited to take up the chair of Germanic Philology at the University of Chicago. He accepted, mainly because at Chicago he no longer had to teach elementary German language courses, which he detested and about which he continuously complained. He stayed at Chicago till 1940. During this period he worked less on native American languages than before and concentrated rather more on Germanic languages and on general theory. It was here that he wrote his epoch-making book *Language*, published in 1933.

Sapir, who had come to Chicago in 1925 and left for Yale in 1931, was therefore his colleague for four years. The two were never close but did maintain mutual respect. Hall quotes Carl Voegelin, the anthropological linguist who studied with both, as follows:

> Sapir admired Bloomfield's ability patiently to excerpt data and collate slips until the patterns of the language emerged, but spoke deprecatingly of Bloomfield's sophomoric psychology. Bloomfield was dazzled by Sapir's virtuosity and perhaps a bit jealous of it, but in matters outside linguistics referred to Sapir as a "medicine man".   Hall (1990:39)

When we set off the religious, romantic, strongly anti-behaviourist Sapir with his artistic and poetic leanings against the non-religious, modernistic, behaviourist Bloomfield with his ideals of improving the world through modern science, it is not difficult to see why they would never become close friends, despite their shared interest in American Indian languages and general linguistic theory.

Meanwhile, in 1933, Bloomfield succeeded in having a linguistics department set up at the University of Chicago. He became chairman of the new department, besides being the professor of Germanic Philology, but it remained small, in fact 'little more than what would nowadays be termed an "interdepartmental program"' (Hall 1990:59), and in constant jeopardy of being abolished.

- *Yale: 1940-1949*

In August 1939 Bloomfield received an offer from Yale to take up the Sterling professorship of Germanic Languages at a considerably higher salary than Chicago was paying him, plus secretarial assistance, which was also denied him at Chicago. When he tried to communicate with the university authorities about this offer he found their reaction inadequate. This, combined with a history of administrative and organizational problems in both the German and the linguistic departments, made him decide, in the autumn of 1940, to leave Chicago and move to New Haven. From a personal point of view this move turned out disastrous. Bloomfield's wife Alice was thoroughly unhappy there, having lost all her Chicago social contacts. She became seriously depressed and had to be institutionalized for a while, which made Bloomfield's life a misery. Probably because of Alice's condition they did not live in a house of their own but stayed in a hotel suite for almost six years, till Bloomfield suffered a stroke in 1946. After that Bloomfield remained crippled and unable to do any work. Three years later he died at the age of sixty-two.

- *Wartime foreign languages programme*

Even before the United States got involved in the second world war the Administration started, for strategic reasons, a programme to promote the knowledge of foreign languages. In 1941 the American Council of Learned Societies (ACLS) sought contact with the LSA to set up an Intensive Language Program (ILP). When the US did step into the war, in December 1941, the ILP was greatly intensified and soon merged with the Army Specialized Training Program (ASTP), which commissioned the writing of materials and crash courses in a number of languages that were considered strategically important, notably Russian, German, Dutch, Spanish, Italian, Japanese, Chinese, Thai, Burmese. (This was the beginning of a period of collaboration between the American armed forces and the linguistic world, which would last for over twenty years, the former playing Dutch uncle to the latter.) Bloomfield took part in the ASTP and produced his *Outline Guide for the Practical Study of Foreign Languages* (1942), and two books on Dutch (1943, 1944-1945) (besides reluctantly putting his name to a Russian course to which he did not actually contribute).

- *Tagalog and American Indian languages again; Yale Linguistics Club;
  Summer Institutes*

At Yale Bloomfield took up again some of the work on Tagalog and on American Indian languages that he had done before in Ohio and had let go of, more or less, in Chicago. He also took an active part in the monthly meetings of the Yale Linguistics Club, a meeting point for the by now numerous linguists of one kind or another at Yale and other universities in the area. Here, and in the courses he gave for the Summer Institutes of the LSA, Bloomfield met and strongly influenced many or most of the younger linguists who were to shape American linguistics in the 1950s and 1960s.

- *The* Introduction *of 1914*

As with Sapir, Bloomfield's views on language originated from three distinct sources: traditional comparative philology, the analysis and description of non-European languages, and the 19th century largely European tradition of reflection on the psychological and logical basis of language and speech, and hence of meaning. It was especially the second of these three elements, the structural study of non-European languages (American Indian languages and the Malayo-Polynesian language Tagalog), that led, after roughly 1920, to those positive innovations and results that have determined the character of present-day theoretical linguistics. It was also in this area that Bloomfield spent most of his energy. Comparative philology only played a minor part in his work. The psychology of language was always there as a factor in the background but he never did any actual research in this area. In fact, the psychological, logical and semantic aspects of language were a constant source of unclarity, and hence of irritation, to Bloomfield, and his whole conversion to behaviourism can be seen as a strategy aimed at not having to bother about them any more. It was his actual descriptive work, and above all the design of a general technical, terminological and notional frame for such work, that mostly kindled his interest and motivated him. It is on account of this work that Bloomfield must be considered the major figure in American structuralism.

His *Introduction* of 1914 was only a run-up to structuralism. In this book, which was meant as an introduction for the general public, the structural study of languages, the major interest of his later life, does not yet come to the fore, although, in hindsight, one detects the beginnings of it in hesitantly innovative grammatical terminology (e.g. 'actor', 'goal'). The two chapters that deal with structural analysis, chapter 5 on morphology and chapter 6 on syntax, are, on the whole, conventional and in no way remarkable. Although the book is liberally sprinkled with examples from all kinds of languages the American Indian languages are still largely absent. The main emphasis in the book, even in the chapters on morphology and syntax, is on the historical and comparative aspects of languages, on phonetics (chapter 2, inspired by Sweet), and on questions surrounding the psychological and logical basis of language. The latter are dealt with explicitly in the relatively short chapter 3, 'The mental Basis of Language', which is, one has to admit, an unconvincing rehash in popularizing terms of some of Wundt's teachings mixed up with ideas that Wundt did not endorse. Taken as a whole the book is largely derivative, a compilation from a variety of existing works, in particular those authored by Sweet, Whitney, Steinthal, Paul, Jespersen, Boas, and, above all, Wundt, all listed in the closing chapter 10. Bloomfield himself says as much in his Preface, which ends as follows:

> I have limited myself to a presentation of the accepted doctrine, not even avoiding well-used standard examples. In a few places I have spoken of views that cannot claim more than probability, of hypotheses, and of problems yet to be solved, but I have done this explicitly and only because I think it fitting to indicate the direction in which our study is at present tending. Consequently the matter here presented is by no means my own, but rather the property of all students of language. It will be found in fuller form and with bibliographic support in the books mentioned in Chapter Ten, and these books I may therefore name as my immediate sources. It will be apparent, especially, that I depend for my psychology, general and linguistic,

entirely on Wundt; I can only hope that I have not misrepresented his doctrine. The day is past when students of mental sciences could draw on their own fancy or on 'popular psychology' for their views of mental occurrence.

It is fair to remember that Bloomfield was barely twenty-seven at the time the book appeared. Its significance lies more in the fact that it apparently filled a gap than in its intrinsic value.

- *First inkling of IC-analysis; subject and predicate*

There is, however, one aspect which has proved to be of overriding importance, the introduction into linguistic theory of the notion of *hierarchical constituent or tree structure* (mentioned above in connection with Sapir's analysis of the complex Paiute word as shown in fig. 1). But for Percival (1976), which states the case very clearly, this aspect is hardly mentioned in the historical literature dealing with this book. In chapter 3, on the mental basis of language, Bloomfield rather dwells on the Wundtian notion that the thoughts ('experiences') underlying uttered sentences are primarily holistic unitary complexes which come in for analysis only secondarily. He then follows Wundt, who proposed the principle of hierarchical constituent structure as the basis of both linguistic and psychological structural analysis in various places (1880:53-71; 1922[1900]:320-355; 1901:71-82). The first division is between subject and predicate, defined in a curiously hybrid way that seeks to strike a balance between Wundt's view on the matter and the discourse view expressed by Wegener, Lipps, Stout and others of the period (see 2.6.3 for relevant quotes) (1914:61):

> In the primary division of an experience into two parts, the one focused is called the *subject* and the one left for later attention the *predicate*; the relation between them is called *predication*. If, after this first division, either subject or predicate or both receive further analysis, the elements in each case first singled out are again called subjects and the elements in relation to them, *attributes*. The subject is always the present thing, the known thing, or the concrete thing, the predicate or attribute, its quality, action, or relation or the thing to which it is like. Thus in the sentence *Lean horses run fast* the subject is *lean horses* and the horses' action, *run fast*, is the predicate. Within the subject there is the further analysis into a subject *horses* and its attribute *lean*, expressing the horses' quality. In the predicate *fast* is an attribute of the subject *run*.

Apart from the odd use of the term 'subject' for what came to be called later 'head of a construction', one clearly sees here the principle of hierarchical constituent structure. The page and a half following this quote are a further elaboration of this idea. Again we read on p. 110:

> **11. The sentence.** When the analysis of experience arrives at independently recurring and therefore separately imaginable elements, words, the interrelations of these in the sentence appear in varied and interesting linguistic phenomena. Psychologically the basis of these interrelations is the passing of the unitary apperception from one to the other of the elements of an experience. The leading binary division so made is into two parts, subject and predicate, each of which may be further analyzed into successive binary groups of attribute and subject, the attribute being felt as a property of its subject.

It is this principle of hierarchical constituent structure, or *immediate con-stituent analysis* (IC-analysis) that was to dominate the whole of American structuralism after 1933 and became a cornerstone of all modern theories of grammar. So let us pursue its career in Bloomfield's *Language* of 1933 and after.[10]

- Language *of 1933*

Bloomfield's *Language* has proved to be the pivot of 20th century linguistic theory. In 1960 one could say that all existing schools of linguistic thought derived, one way or another, from this book. Those that had sought to survive without it, such as most of the European schools mentioned in chapter 3, had either died or been reduced to a private parish. In 1998 this is no longer true, as logic and computer science have introduced new strains from different tra-ditions, but it is still so that within linguistics proper no theory of any note has emerged that stands outside the Bloomfield tradition. It is, therefore, of prime importance that this development should be traced in detail.

First a few words about the book in general. It was originally planned as a second edition of the *Introduction* of 1914. However, as the author had mean-while gone through a theoretical metamorphosis, it had to be rewritten en-tirely. It contains twenty-eight chapters in 550 pages. Chapter 1 gives a sum-mary history of linguistics. Chapter 2 analyses the speech situation in behav-iouristic terms, with Bloomfield's much decried definition of meaning, and discusses other aspects of speech. Chapter 3, 'Speech Communities', discusses the social nature of language. Chapter 4 gives a survey of the languages of the world. The chapters 5-8 deal with phonemes and phonology. Chapter 9 is entitled 'Meaning'. The chapters 10-16 contain Bloomfield's theory of gram-mar, the part that has proved to be most influential. Chapter 17 discusses writing systems and spelling. The remaining chapters are about the compara-tive method, historical reconstruction, language change, dialects and related matters. We shall concentrate on chapters 2 and 9-16.

- *Bloomfield's behaviourism*

But before we can start our discussion of the book we must have a closer look at *Bloomfield's behaviourism*. It will be recalled that Bloomfield was 'convert-ed' to behaviourism while at Ohio State University during the early 1920s, a transition that was triggered by the close and friendly contacts he had with his colleague, the psychologist Albert P. Weiss.

Behaviourism, as a method and a doctrine in psychological research, main-tains that (a) the observable data for psychology consist in the behaviour of living organisms, (b) some forms of behaviour cannot be explained by direct physical causation, and (c) these latter forms of behaviour are the subject

---

[10] Bloomfield provides a useful résumé of his theoretical and practical views on language in his (1939a), an essay written for the Unified Science movement, which was popular in the 1930s and advocated the ultimate unification of all science as an all-encompassing physics.

matter of psychology, which aims at explaining them causally by the assumption of a simple stimulus transfer mechanism ('conditioning'). In fact, however, it was much more than just a theory in psychology. It was a revolt against 'mystic' views of man and mankind and it advertised itself as the embodiment of the new scientific approach to all human phenomena. It was an ideology. As such it fitted in with the brash belief, prevalent in the period between 1920 and 1960, that all social, political, economic and psychological problems would soon be overcome by the results, to be expected shortly, of science and technology. Now, at the end of the century, we have, of course, become a little wiser and a great deal sadder. We realize that the problems are much deeper and more complex than what was thought then, and that scientific understanding barely probes beyond the surface.

After about 1960 behaviourism was abandoned and replaced by the new paradigm of cognitive science. As there is sometimes some misunderstanding about what this actually meant it is useful to be precise about this. The change from behaviourism to cognitive science means exactly that the tenets (a) and (b) remained in full force, but tenet (c) was modified. That is, the delimitation of the primary data as well as the formulation of the causal question remained unchanged, but the kind of theory envisaged as a causally explanatory answer was replaced. Whereas behaviourism put all its money on a simple stimulus transfer mechanism as an adequate explanation, cognitive science makes the much richer assumption of complex and specific (i.e. non-general but purpose-built) computing mechanisms in the mind, totally screened from awareness or introspection and operating autonomously.

For Bloomfield, however, this was not an option. The computer metaphor had not yet appeared on the intellectual scene and he remained convinced that all of human behaviour, including linguistic behaviour, was the result of repeated experiences of stimulus co-occurrences. Not that it mattered very much for his actual method of linguistic analysis, which was untouched by any behaviouristic consideration. It mattered for the way he felt he could now deal with the vexing questions of meaning and of the psychological basis of language. Being a non-religious man and of a modernistic mind he was predisposed to welcoming any claim made by modern science, which he experienced as a liberation from ages of obscurantism. And he felt that the traditional way of thinking about semantic and psychological phenomena was indeed still largely obscurantist and scientifically unsatisfactory. Behaviourism appeared to him to have at least the advantage of showing how, in principle at least, the mists of meaning and psychology could be cleared. No practical answer was provided, since all behaviourism could do was outline a programme of research that would eventually show the regularity between external stimulus occurrences and their linguistic responses on the one hand, and of the linguistic stimulus occurrences and their external responses on the other. This programme being too massive to be undertaken on the spot, it was hoped that future generations would vindicate the behaviourist position. History has meanwhile decided otherwise, of course. But for Bloomfield behaviourism provided an alibi he felt was ideologically acceptable. It opened the way to a form-based analysis of language that still allowed him to speak of semantic phenomena as though nothing had happened while pointing to (and hiding behind) a more scientifically rigorous treatment hoped for in future days.

The most important passage of chapter 2 is the one in which he describes Jack and Jill walking down a lane. Here follow the essential parts of this passage (1933:22-26):

> Suppose that Jack and Jill are walking down a lane. Jill is hungry. She sees an apple in a tree. She makes a noise with her larynx, tongue and lips. Jack vaults the fence, climbs the tree, takes the apple, brings it to Jill, and places it in her hand. Jill eats the apple.
>
> This succession of events could be studied in many ways, but we, who are studying language, will naturally distinguish between the *act of speech* and the other occurrences, which we shall call *practical events*. Viewed in this way, the incident consists of three parts, in order of time:
> > A. Practical events preceding the act of speech.
> > B. Speech.
> > C. Practical events following the act of speech.
>
> We shall examine first the practical events, A and C. The events in A concern mainly the speaker, Jill. She was hungry; that is, some of her muscles were contracting, and some fluids were being secreted, especially in her stomach. Perhaps she was also thirsty: her tongue and throat were dry. ... All these events, which precede Jill's speech and concern her, we call the *speaker's stimulus*.
>
> We turn now to C, the practical events which came after Jill's speech. These concern mainly the hearer, Jack, and consist of his fetching the apple and giving it to Jill. The practical events which follow the speech and concern the hearer, we call the *hearer's response*. The events which follow the speech concern also Jill, and this in a very important way: *she gets the apple into her grasp and eats it.*
>
> It is evident at once that our whole story depends upon some of the more remote conditions connected with A and C. ... The occurrence of a speech (and, as we shall see, the wording of it) and the whole course of practical events before and after it, depend upon the entire life-history of the speaker and of the hearer. We shall assume in the present case, that all these *predisposing factors* were such as to produce the story as we have told it. Supposing this, we want to know what part the speech-utterance (B) played in this story.
>
> If Jill had been alone, she might have been just as hungry and thirsty and might have seen the same apple. ... The lone Jill is in much the same position as the speechless animal. If the animal is hungry and sees or smells food, it moves toward the food; whether the animal succeeds in getting the food depends upon its strength and skill. The state of hunger and the sight or smell of the food are the *stimulus* (which we symbolize by S) and the movements toward the food are the *reaction* (which we symbolize by R). The lone Jill and the speechless animal act in one way, namely   S $\ggg$————→ R ...
>
> Of course, it is important for Jill's welfare that she get the apple. ... Therefore, any arrangement which adds to Jill's chances of getting the apple is enormously valuable to her. The speaking Jill in our story availed herself of just such an arrangement. ... Jack began to make the reactions for her; he performed actions that were beyond Jill's strength, and in the end Jill got the apple. *Language enables one person to make a reaction (R) when another person has the stimulus (S). ... The division of labor, and, with it, the whole working of human society, is due to language.*

We have yet to examine B, the speech-event in our story. ... Thanks to the sciences of physiology and physics, we know enough about the speech-event to see that it consists of three parts:

(B1) The speaker, Jill, moved her vocal chords ..., her lower jaw, her tongue, and so on, in a way which forced the air into the form of sound waves. These movements of the speaker are a reaction to the stimulus S. Instead of performing the *practical* (or *handling*) reaction R – namely, starting realistically off to get hold of the apple – she performed these vocal movements, a *speech* (or *substitute*) reaction, which we shall symbolize by a small letter r. In sum, then, Jill, as a speaking person, has not one but two ways of reacting to a stimulus:

$$S \ggg \longrightarrow R \quad \text{(practical reaction)}$$

$$S \ggg \longrightarrow r \quad \text{(linguistic substitute reaction).}$$

In the present case she performed the latter.

(B2) The sound waves in the air in Jill's mouth set the surrounding air into a similar wave-motion.

(B3) These sound-waves in the air struck Jack's ear-drums and set them vibrating, with an effect on Jack's nerves: Jack *heard* the speech. This hearing acted as a stimulus on Jack: we saw him running and fetching the apple and placing it in Jill's grasp, much as if Jill's hunger-and-apple stimulus had been acting on him. ... When we see Jack doing anything (fetching an apple, say), his action may be due not only, as are an animal's actions, to a practical stimulus ... , but, just as often, to a speech stimulus. His actions, R, may be prompted not by one but by two kinds of proddings:

$$\text{(practical stimulus)}\ S \ggg \longrightarrow R$$

$$\text{(linguistic substitute stimulus)}\ s \ggg \longrightarrow R.$$

It is evident that the connection between Jill's vocal movements (B1) and Jack's hearing (B3) is subject to very little uncertainty or variation, since it is merely a matter of sound-waves passing through the air (B2). If we represent this connection by a dotted line, then we can symbolize the two human ways of responding to a stimulus by these two diagrams:

$$\text{speechless reaction:}\ S \ggg \longrightarrow R$$

$$\text{reaction mediated by speech:}\ S \ggg \longrightarrow r \ldots\ldots s \ggg \longrightarrow R.$$

This brings him to his famous definition of the concept of *meaning* (1933:27):

When anything apparently unimportant turns out to be closely connected with more important things, we say that it has, after all, a "meaning"; namely, it "means" these more important things. Accordingly, we say that speech-utterance, trivial and unimportant in itself, is important because it has a *meaning*: the meaning consists of the important things with which the speech utterance (B) is connected, namely the practical events (A and C).

For a better understanding one must see these passages in a wider context, which Bloomfield provides on pp. 31-3. (Note the curious implication that the linguistic aspect, which 'deals only with the speech signal (r....s)', is already 'fairly well understood'.):

The happenings which in our diagram are represented by a dotted line, are fairly well understood. The speaker's vocal chords, tongue, lips, and so on, interfere with the stream of his outgoing breath, in such a way as to produce sound-waves; these waves are propagated through the air and strike the hearer's ear-drums, which then vibrate in unison. The happenings, however, which we have represented by arrows, are very obscure. We do not understand the mechanism which makes people say certain things in certain situations, or the mechanism which makes them respond appropriately when these speech-sounds strike their ear-drums. Evidently these mechanisms are a phase of our general equipment for responding to stimuli, be they speech-sounds or others. These mechanisms are studied in physiology and, especially, in psychology. To study them in their special bearing on language, is to study the psychology of speech, *linguistic psychology.* In the division of scientific labor, the linguist deals only with the speech signal (r....s); he is not competent to deal with problems of physiology or psychology. The findings of the linguist, who studies the speech-signal, will be all the more valuable for the psychologist if they are not distorted by any prepossessions about psychology. We have seen that many of the older linguists ignored this; they vitiated or skimped their reports by trying to state everything in terms of some psychological theory. We shall all the more surely avoid this fault, however, if we survey a few of the more obvious phases of the psychology of language.

The mechanism which governs speech must be very complex and delicate. Even if we know a great deal about a speaker and about the immediate stimuli which are acting upon him, we usually cannot predict whether he will speak or what he will say. ... Had we been present, we could not have foretold whether Jill would say anything when she saw the apple, or, in case she did speak, what words she would utter. Even supposing she asked for the apple, we could not foretell whether she would preface her request by saying *I'm hungry* or whether she would say *please* or whether she would say *I want that apple* or *Get me that apple* or *I was just wishing I had an apple,* and so on: the possibilities are almost infinite. This enormous variability has led to two theories about human conduct, including speech.

The *mentalistic* theory, which is by far the older, and still prevails both in the popular view and among men of science, supposes that the variability of human conduct is due to the interference of some non-physical factor, a *spirit* or *will* or *mind* (Greek *psyche*, hence the term *psychology*) that is present in every human being. This spirit, according to the mentalistic view, is entirely different from material things and accordingly follows some other kind of causation or perhaps none at all. Whether Jill will speak or what words she will use, depends, then, upon some act of her mind or will, and, as this mind or will does not follow the patterns of succession (cause-and-effect sequences) of the material world, we cannot foretell her actions.

The *materialistic* (or, better, *mechanistic*) theory supposes that the variability of human conduct, including speech, is due only to the fact that the human body is a very complex system. Human actions, according to the materialistic view, are part of cause-and-effect sequences exactly like those which we observe, say, in the study of physics or chemistry. However, the human body is so complex a structure that even a relatively simple change, such as, say, the impingement on the retina of light-waves from a red apple, may set off some very complicated chain of consequences, and a very slight difference in the state of the body may result in a great difference in its response to the light-waves. ... The part of the human body responsible for this delicate and variable adjustment, is the nervous system.

In chapter 9, 'Meaning', we furthermore find the following description of how Bloomfield wishes to see and treat 'meaning' (1933:139-144):

In order to give a scientifically accurate definition of meaning for every form of a language, we should have to have a scientifically accurate knowledge of everything in the speaker's world. The actual extent of human knowledge is very small, compared to this. We can define the meaning of a speech-form accurately when this meaning has to do with some matter of which we possess scientific knowledge. We can define the names for minerals, for example, in terms of chemistry and mineralogy, as when we say that the ordinary meaning of the English word *salt* is 'sodium chloride (NaCl)', and we can define the names of plants or animals by means of the technical terms of botany or zoology, but we have no precise way of defining words like *love* or *hate*, which concern situations that have not been accurately classified – and these latter are in the great majority. ...

The statement of meanings is therefore the weak point in language-study, and will remain so until human knowledge advances very far beyond its present state. In practice, we define the meaning of a linguistic form, wherever we can, in terms of some other science. Where this is impossible, we resort to makeshift devices. One is *demonstration*. If someone did not know the meaning of the word *apple*, we could instruct him by handing him an apple or pointing at an apple, and continuing, as long as he made mistakes, to handle apples and point at them, until he used the word in the conventional way. This is essentially the process by which children learn the use of speech-forms. If a questioner understood enough of our language, we could define the word *apple* for him by *circumlocution* – that is, in the manner of our dictionaries, by a roundabout speech which fitted the same situations as does the word apple. ... Or else, if we knew enough of the questioner's language, we could answer him by *translation* – that is, by uttering a roughly equivalent form of his language. ...

Adherents of mentalistic psychology believe that they can avoid the difficulty of defining meanings, because they believe that, prior to the utterance of a linguistic form, there occurs within the speaker, a non-physical process, a *thought, concept, image, feeling, act of will*, or the like, and that the hearer, likewise, upon receiving the sound-waves, goes through an equivalent or correlated mental process. ... For the mentalist, language is *the expression of ideas, feelings, or volitions*.

The mechanist does not accept this solution. He believes that mental images, feelings, and the like are merely popular terms for various bodily movements. ...

Since we have no way of defining most meanings and of demonstrating their constancy, we have to take the specific and stable character of language as a presupposition of linguistic study, just as we presuppose it in our everyday dealings with people. We may state this presupposition as the *fundamental assumption of linguistics*, namely:

In certain communities (speech-communities) some speech-utterances are alike as to form and meaning.

From here on, Bloomfield proceeds as if no behaviourist thought had ever crossed his mind. All that behaviourism has done for him is provide a shield against further probing in questions of meaning: meaning will be fully understood once the human race has acquired full scientific knowledge of everything. Meanwhile all is as before.

This, in a nutshell, is Bloomfield's behaviouristic account of mind and meaning. It is not very difficult to see through it. Besides many problems of a smaller scale and the obvious and trivial inadequacy of his concept of meaning, the main problem with this analysis is the appeal it makes to the inner neurological workings of the persons ('biological organisms') involved (see Chomsky 1959a for a fatal critique). The kind of habit formation invoked by behaviourism is possible only if, in everybody's early life history, there are a sufficient number of sufficiently similar situations for the habit to have a chance to establish itself. We now know that this condition is not fulfilled:

the utterances young children encounter are so crucially different among themselves, and often so imperfectly presented, that they cannot possibly form a sufficient basis for the remarkably fast, efficient and uniform language acquisition process that children go through. Moreover, the actual linguistic system which they acquire is now known to be so intricate and complex that the notion of 'habit formation' becomes derisory. What is needed for the proper use of a language is a dynamic mastery of the rules and principles of the language system in terms of input and output, an ability to apply rules that form part of a complex machinery. This mastery of the rules is often called 'knowledge' or 'competence', but it must be realized that any such 'knowledge' is instantiated physically as a purely mechanical and totally unconscious specialized computing system. Bloomfield's dilemma between a non-material 'spirit' or 'mind' and a presumed physical device establishing substitution relations among stimuli was a false one. There is another possibility, not thought of by Bloomfield or his contemporaries, that of a physically implemented computing machinery, inaccessible to awareness, capable of generating an indefinitely large set of strings of symbols according to well-defined finite procedures. This third alternative is now generally accepted.

Bloomfield's behaviourism was never really believed in by the linguistic world at large. While there was no rational alternative for it (the old 'mentalistic' approaches had not yielded positive results), it struck most scholars, in America as well as in Europe, as frivolously superficial and implausible to the extreme. This feeling was bolstered when, after 1960, the computational view presented itself as a reasonable alternative. Behaviourism is now universally rejected. Even so, however, it has been of great importance in the recent history of linguistics. Not only did it help linguistics to concentrate more than before on an analysis of forms rather than of meanings, a strategy which has proved extremely fruitful. It also acted as a stepping stone to the computing view of the mind which is current nowadays and is proving its value. It must not be forgotten that the difference between this and the behaviourist view consists only in the kind of theory adopted: instead of a stimulus association theory we now work with a computational theory, but the definition of the primary data and the causal question have remained unchanged. In this, partly negative, way, the behaviourist period can be seen as a, perhaps necessary, first act in the scientific approach to mental phenomena. It is for this reason that it is fundamentally important to know about behaviourism and understand its background. Without such knowledge modern linguistics cannot be understood.

- *Bloomfield's notion of IC-analysis*

The main reason why Bloomfield has become the pivotal figure he is in modern linguistics lies in his sustained and systematic application of the principle of hierarchical constituent structure or *Immediate Constituent analysis*. As we have seen, the principle of IC-analysis figured already, though only weakly, in the *Introduction* of 1914 in the context of Wundt's system of partitioning the unitary thought complex expressed in a sentence. In the light of Bloomfield's radical rejection of Wundtian psychology during the early 1920s one would perhaps expect a concomitant rejection of the IC-analysis principle. Not so, however. Somehow or other Bloomfield (and, as we have seen, Sapir as well) intuited the descriptive potential of this principle. Both saw its usefulness demonstrated in their descriptions of American Indian languages, where IC-analysis made up for the deficiencies of the no longer usable categories of traditional grammar. In *Language* of 1933 IC-analysis has become the cornerstone of grammar, and it has remained so till the present day. Let us have a closer look at the chapters 10-16, which deal with grammar.

Bloomfield's first concern is the definition of the smallest building blocks of grammatical constructions, the *ultimate constituents* or *morphemes*. These combine into hierarchically ordered constructions according to the *immediate constituent principle*:

> A linguistic form which bears no partial phonetic-semantic resemblance to any other form is a *simple* form or *morpheme*. ... From all this it appears that every complex form is entirely made up, so far as its phonetically definable constituents are concerned, of morphemes. The number of these *ultimate constituents* may run very high. The form *Poor John ran away* contains five morphemes: *poor*, *John*, *ran*, *a-* ..., and *way*. However, the structure of complex forms is by no means as simple as this; we could not understand the forms of a language if we merely reduced all the complex forms to their ultimate constituents. Any English-speaking person who concerns himself with this matter, is sure to tell us that the *immediate constituents* of *Poor John ran away* are the two forms *poor John* and *ran away*; that each of these is, in turn, a complex form; that the immediate constituents of *ran away* are *ran*, a morpheme, and *away*, a complex form, whose constituents are the morphemes *a-* and *way*; and that the constituents of *poor John* are the morphemes *poor* and *John*. Only in this way will a proper analysis (that is, one which takes account of the meanings) lead to the ultimately constituent morphemes. ... The total stock of morphemes in a language is its *lexicon*.   Bloomfield (1933:161-162)

- *Bloomfield's reluctance to draw tree diagrams*

Again, as in the case of Sapir's Paiute word, one wonders why Bloomfield does not draw a simple diagram, as in fig. 2. And the answer will again lie in the gentlemanly reluctance to stoop to drawing figures – even though mathematics is called by Bloomfield 'the ideal use of language' (1933:29). It would have been so easy to represent his example *Poor John ran away* as in fig. 2:

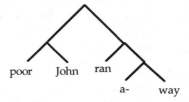

Figure 2   IC-analysis of 'Poor John ran away'

In section 4.4.5 we shall see how long it took for the practice of drawing tree diagrams to become established.

- *The four 'meaningful arrangement' types of forms*

Besides tree constituency, grammar defines other qualitative properties of forms:

> The meaningful arrangements of forms in a language constitute its grammar. In general, there seem to be four ways of arranging linguistic forms.
>
> (1) *Order* is the succession in which the constituents of a complex form are spoken.
>
> (2) *Modulation* is the use of secondary phonemes.
>
> (3) *Phonetic modification* is a change in the primary phonemes of a form. For instance, ... the suffix -*ess* with the meaning 'female,' as in *count-ess*, is added also to *duke* [djuʷk], but in this combination the form *duke* is modified to *duch-* [dʌʧ], for the word is *duchess* [ˈdʌʧɪs]. ... [W]e might hesitate as to the choice of a basic alternant. ... [W]e try, of course, to make the selection of a basic alternant so as to get, in the long run, the simplest description of the facts.
>
> (4) *Selection* of forms contributes a factor of meaning because different forms in what is otherwise the same grammatical arrangement, will result in different meanings.   Bloomfield (1933:163-164)

Modulation is, in principle, what is now covered by the term 'prosodic features'. Phonetic modification is now known as 'morphophonemic alternation'. Selection is the membership of a form in a *form class*, defined as (1933:185):

> The positions in which a form can appear are its *functions* or, collectively, its *function*. All the forms which can fill a given position thereby constitute a *form-class*.

- *Incipient notion of underlying form*

In order to achieve a maximally simple statement of phonetic modification, i.e. of how morphemes may vary according to their immediate environment, it is sometimes useful to assume a 'theoretical basic form' (p. 219) which allows for a simple derivation of the morphemic variants. For example, German has the morphemes conventionally spelled *rund* ('round') and *bunt* ('motley'). But for the initial consonant, however, they are pronounced identically. Yet in combination with the morphological -*e* ending the difference shows up: *runde* versus *bunte*. The simplest way to describe this is to list in the lexicon the 'theoretical basic forms' *rund-* and *bunt-*, respectively (as is the normal practice in German spelling). The rule by which -*e* is added to the basic form can then stand unmodified and in a simple, general form. All that is needed to account for the identical final consonant [-t] is a rule devoicing final voiced stops. The same argument is applied (1933:217) to French adjectives and their feminine forms: *long* vs *longue* ('long'), but *bon* vs *bonne* ('good'), etc. Here and there, e.g. pp. 225, 237, Bloomfield uses the term 'underlying form', suggesting some sort of process whereby the underlying form is changed into its surface manifestation. Some of his followers were keen to reject this suggestion (see the discussion of Hockett (1954) in section 4.4.4). For them there was only a regular alternation of forms occurring in 'complementary distribution', and no devoicing 'process'. After 1957, in the theory of transformational grammar, the notion of underlying form regained respectability and was generalized to cover all kinds of construction, including syntactic ones.

- *Primacy of the sentence; the sentence as the maximum grammatically defined unit of speech*

A stretch of speech consists of one or more sentences (1933:170):

> An utterance may consist of more than one sentence. This is the case when the utterance contains several linguistic forms which are not by any meaningful conventional grammatical arrangement (that is, by any construction) united into a larger form.

One notes that Bloomfield proposes here what came to be known later, in the context of generative grammar, as an 'implicit definition' of the sentence: a sentence is what the grammar of the language defines (generates) as such. The definition is thus as valid as the grammar is successful.

A sentence is a 'free form' in that it can occur alone as an utterance. A sentence may consist minimally of one single word. The word is therefore defined as 'a minimum free form' (p. 178). Free forms are opposed to bound forms, which cannot occur alone, i.e. as a sentence. Morphological suffixes are, normally speaking, bound forms. The distinction between morphology and syntax hinges on that between free and bound forms (1933:183-184):

> In languages which use bound forms, the word has great structural importance because the constructions in which free forms appear in phrases differ very decidedly from the constructions in which free or bound forms appear in words. Accordingly, the grammar of these languages consists of two parts, called *syntax*, and *morphology*. ...There has been considerable debate as to the usefulness of this division, and as to the scope of the two headings. In languages that have bound forms, the constructions in which bound forms play a part differ radically from the constructions in which all the immediate constituents are free forms.

Although the word is assigned 'great structural importance' on account of the 'radical' differences between morphological and syntactic constructions, Bloomfield fails to specify those differences in other than the vaguest possible way. The best he can do is on p. 207:

> In general, morphologic constructions are more elaborate than those of syntax. The features of modification and modulation are more numerous and often irregular — that is, confined to particular constituents or combinations. The order of the constituents is almost always rigidly fixed, permitting of no such connotative variants as *John ran away* : *Away ran John*. Features of selection minutely and often whimsically limit the constituents that may be united into a complex form.

These are gradient, not radical, differences, which vanish into insignificance in the face of the overriding uniformity of the IC-analysis principle that applies throughout the grammar.[11]

---

[11] Yet Bloomfield was probably right, even though he was unable to provide the right reasons. It seems that in modern theoretical grammar the differences between morphological and syntactic constructions are beginning to show up, for example in the fact that, in the European languages at least, syntactic constructions tend to be right-branching while morphological constructions tend to be left-branching.

- *The question of the motivation of IC-analyses*

In the end, when one has made oneself thoroughly familiar with Bloomfield's system of grammatical description, one overriding question stands out: *what determines the choice of constituent structure assignment?* Let us speak here of the *motivation question*. Bloomfield himself did not answer this question in a principled way. He motivates the assignment of IC-structure on purely intuitive grounds, falling back on criteria like 'any English-speaking person who concerns himself with this matter', as we saw above in the quote from p. 161. Interestingly, when Bloomfield feels he is able to visualize the notion of a complete description of the facts he applies the *simplicity criterion.* For cases of morphophonemic alternation (his 'phonetic modification') he obviously can encompass the notion of a complete description of the facts, and here he typically speaks of simplicity as the decisive criterion (italics mine):

> [W]e try, of course, to make the selection of a basic alternant so as to get, in the long run, *the simplest description of the facts.*   Bloomfield (1933:164)

> We have not yet described in terms of phonetic modification, the kinship of the three alternants [-iz, -z, -s] of the bound form that appears in English plural nouns. It is evident that three entirely different statements are possible, according to our choice of one or the other of the three forms as our starting point. Our aim is to get, in the long run, *the simplest possible set of statements* that will describe the facts of the English language.   Bloomfield (1933:211-212)

But there is no indication that Bloomfield had any concrete notion of what a complete description of a whole language would amount to. This was still beyond the powers of imagination of the linguists of those days, who were grappling with notions like 'sentence structure', 'word structure', 'phrase structure', but for whom the notion 'structure of a grammar' was still an unthinkable abstraction. On the evidence of his treatment of morphophonemic alternation we may assume that Bloomfield, had he possessed a notion of the overall structure of a complete descriptive grammar, would likewise have applied the simplicity criterion. This is precisely what Bloomfield's successors did. He himself did not live to see that happen.

4.4 Diversification after Bloomfield

4.4.1 American linguistics after World War II

After the second world war, whose end preceded by little the end of Bloomfield's active life, the American linguistic establishment was thoroughly imbued with Bloomfield's ideas. His prestige was such that he was universally listened to by colleagues and aspiring linguists alike, not only in his own department at Chicago or Yale but everywhere. His followers were, therefore, not primarily his students in the accepted sense of the word, but practising linguists all over the eastern and central parts of the United States (the West Coast was still only of minor importance in linguistics in those days).

• *Linguistic theory as analysis, not as synthesis*

The common concern among all linguists from Bloomfield till roughly 1955 was to determine a method for the establishment of functional units at different levels of analysis. That is, the whole effort was directed at the analysis, not the synthesis, of linguistic material. At the phonological (then called 'phonemic') level, the concern was to determine which and how many phonemes were to be distinguished for the purpose of functional description. Analogously for morphemes on the morphological level. Then came the constructional levels of compound words, phrases and, finally, sentences. Here the constructions had to be determined, i.e. the combinations of lower level elements into higher level elements: morphemes into words, words into phrases, phrases into sentences. When the work was done, each sentence should be describable in terms of an IC-analysis with 'Sentence' as the overarching category, and phrases as immediate constituents, each phrase in its turn to be split up into elements of lower rank, until, finally, the lowest elements of all, the phonemes, were reached.

• *Phonology as the most prominent branch of linguistics*

It was also typical of the period that phonology occupied pride of place among the subdivisions of linguistics. Phonology was seen as the most successful application of the new linguistic science and its techniques and analytical notions were widely applied to morphology and syntax. Since this book is less about phonology than about grammar, we only pay attention to what was happening in phonology during the years concerned if it has a bearing on what happened in grammar, even if that will inevitably result in a somewhat biased picture of the period.

• *Complementary distribution*

One such development in phonology was the introduction, in Swadesh (1934), of the principle of *complementary distribution* as a method for establishing phonemes. The principle says that, on analysis, some phonetic realizations of a phoneme, the so-called allophones, will be found to be conditioned by their environment. For example, English *p, t, k* are aspirated before a stressed vowel, and unaspirated elsewhere. Never will one find, in proper English speech, an unaspirated *p, t,* or *k* before a stressed vowel, or an aspirated one in other positions. The aspirated and unaspirated allophones are therefore in 'complementary distribution', in that they never take each other's place. If such a distribution is found, the linguist is entitled to say that they form one phoneme.[12] This was considered important because it enabled the linguist to estab-

---

[12] It was soon found to be necessary to add a condition of phonetic likeness, since, for example, *h* and N (spelled *ng*) are also, in English, in complementary distribution, the former occurring only at the beginning of a syllable, the latter only at the end. Yet grouping them together as one phoneme is felt to be so counterintuitive as to be unacceptable. This reluctance can be formalized with the help of the Jakobsonian features and a requirement of phonetic naturalness: for two allophones to be reckoned to belong to one phoneme their

lish phonemes without an appeal to meaning differences, a highly valued aim in the context of behaviourism. Harris (1951) extrapolated this principle to the whole of grammatical analysis, as we shall see in a moment.

- *The motivation question as the most fruitful question of the period*

The question of the motivation of particular IC-structure assignments, mentioned at the end of the preceding section, was one of a set of questions discussed in the period concerned. Historically speaking, it stands out as the most fruitful, the one that has led to the most significant developments, as will become clear in section 4.5. We shall, therefore, discuss it first. At the time there were, in principle, two answers to this question.[13] The first answer was that intuition would help to decide. That is, either one asks native speakers how they 'feel' about particular IC-analyses, or the linguist consults his own linguistic 'conscience'. This answer, which rests on *introspection* (see 3.5), was, if favoured, not favoured wholeheartedly in America, as opposed to Europe, where introspection was very popular during that time. The second answer is based on *substitutability* of constituents. In principle it runs as follows. If, having set up a tentative IC-analysis, one finds that a complex form can be put in the place of a simple form while the rest of the construction remains unaffected, then the complex and the simple forms are considered to belong to a substitution class and the tentative IC-analysis is considered confirmed. The substitution of the complex form for the simple form is called *expansion*. Clearly, any decision as to the correctness of the tentative analysis must depend on the eventual simplicity and consistency of the analysis as a whole for the entire language. This answer was provided first by Harris (1946) and elaborated by Wells (1947) and Pittman (1948). We shall see below that it led directly to the principle of generative grammar, a conclusion drawn first by Harris (1951).

- *The main theoretical questions of the period*

Let us now look at the main theoretical questions that occupied the American linguistic establishment between, say, 1940 and 1955. They were roughly the following (cp. Pike & Pike 1955; I leave out the questions uniquely concerning phonology):

1. *Realism versus instrumentalism.* Do the structures assigned by the linguist have neurological or mental reality, or are they an invention 'imposed' by the analyst?
2. *Uniqueness.* Is there one correct structure assignment, or can structures be assigned at will, as the analyst sees fit?

---

phonetic difference must be expressible as a natural, non-ad-hoc rule changing one set of features into another.

[13] Nowadays we have a third option, which we consider to be the correct one. It consists in taking the generative mechanism as the judge for the correctness of the IC-analyses it assigns. If the generative mechanism is adequate, then so are the structures generated by it.

3. *Postulates*. How can the analytical procedure be formalized and axiomatized, as befits a scientific theory?
4. *Distribution of elements as a method for analysis*. Is distribution sufficient
   as a criterion for analysis, without reference to meaning?
5. *Importance and motivation of IC-structure*. Is IC-analysis sufficient for
   structural descriptions? What is the motivation for preferring particular
   IC-analyses over others?
6. *Mixing of levels*. Is it permitted to use information from one level of description to answer questions with regard to another? How do levels relate
   to each other?

These questions are not independent of each other; they are implicationally
related. For example, if question 1 is answered in favour of realism the answer
to question 2 is bound to be positive.

- *Analysis as a formalized procedure; the aims of linguistic theory*

Question 3 illustrates the then widespread feeling that a precise definition of
analytical procedures for the constructions of a language constitutes a *scientific
theory* of the language in question. This is historically interesting since
'causality' and 'explanation' were suspect notions in the days of behaviourism,
but at the same time curious because it shows a tendency to skip the causal
question and jump to the notion of theory without there being a causal question
for the theory to answer. In fact, the structural linguists of the period were
decidedly vague about the aims and purposes of their analytical work and
about the ways the (vague) aims could be achieved. A telling passage, in this
respect, is Harris (1951:3):

> The greatest use of such explicit structural descriptions will be in the cataloguing of
> language structures, and in the comparing of structural types. These descriptions
> will, however, be also important for historical linguistics and dialect geography;
> for the relation of language to culture and personality, and to phonetics and
> semantics; and for the comparison of language structure with the systems of logic.

Typically, this cabinet of possible uses does not include any mention of
explanation or of enhancement of insight. Towards the end of the book, however, as we shall see in section 4.5, Harris has made a few important steps
forward. There he formulates (1951:365) as a possible purpose of the theory
the seeking of

> just enough information to enable anyone to construct utterances in the language
> such as those constructed by native speakers (e.g. in order to predict the utterances,
> or to teach a person how to speak the language).

(One shudders at the prospect of having to learn a language on the basis of
distributional phenomena alone, without learning anything about the meanings of the elements and structures employed.) Here we see the beginning of
generative grammar, about which more in 4.5 below.

- *Level mixing*

Question 6 touches on an issue that came up frequently. It was felt by some that failure to separate the different levels (phonemes, morphemes, words, phrases) might make the analysis circular and therefore invalid. Most linguists, however, accepted level mixing as perfectly legitimate, as long as one distinguished between a tentative analysis at level A, which could be corroborated or disqualified by another tentative analysis at level B. The best (i.e. simplest) match between the two levels was then to be preferred. In the following we will ignore this question; it was a hot issue for a while during the heyday of structuralism but it soon lost its relevance.

- *Bloomfield's followers: the traditionalists and the formalists*

Not all of Bloomfield's followers were equally innovative. Some just followed and did not innovate, such as *Bernard Bloch* (1907-1965, editor of *Language* from 1939 till his death in 1965) and *George Trager* (1906-1992). Both worked in their special fields, Bloch in phonology and Japanese, Trager in anthropological linguistics, but they did not advance the theory of language. Bloch & Trager's booklet (1942) is an anodyne résumé of Bloomfield's teachings, though more systematized and extended here and there with contributions by third parties that had received Bloomfield's *imprimatur*, such as the notion of 'complementary distribution', taken from Swadesh (1934). (See Murray 1994:165-171 for similar but more detailed comments.)

Most, however, got engaged in the paramount questions of the day and strove to make original contributions to the current theoretical questions. In practice, they fell into two main clusters, which will be named the *traditionalists* and the *formalists*,[14] headed by Kenneth Pike and Zellig Harris, respectively. (In discussing these developments we shall not flood the reader with an avalanche of names but limit ourselves to the most influential figures. Those who wish to have a more complete survey of the period will be helped by Hymes & Fought (1975 [1981]) and Murray (1994:137-223).)

4.4.2 The traditionalists: Kenneth L. Pike

Kenneth Lee Pike was born in Connecticut in 1912. He had a lifelong association with the University of Michigan, which he entered in 1948 and left on his retirement in 1978. Being a religious protestant he joined the incipient *Summer Institute of Linguistics* (SIL) in 1935, which had been founded the year before by W. Cameron Townsend, a devoted but linguistically naïve missionary in Mexico, who felt that missionaries should learn to speak the languages of the peoples they wanted to bring the Bible to. Pike accompanied him to Mexico and concentrated on learning Mixtec, a Mexican Indian language. In 1936 he

[14] During the period concerned the traditionalists were often referred to as the *God's truth linguists* (a gibe coined by Householder in his review of Harris (1951)) because many of them belonged to the Wycliffe Bible Translators and engaged in linguistics with a missionary purpose in mind. The formalists, on the other hand, were branded as the *hocus-pocus linguists* in view of the algebraic character of their methods and analyses.

came back and taught at the SIL of that year, where *Eugene A. Nida* was among his students. (In 1937 Nida, in turn, taught at the SIL meeting of that year.) Pike himself attended the Summer Institute of the LSA in 1937. There he was taught by Sapir, who encouraged him to study linguistics professionally. Later he met Bloomfield in a similar context. In 1942 he took his PhD at the University of Michigan, with a dissertation on phonetics. He remained closely associated with SIL, which became a world-wide organization, for the rest of his life, and for a lesser period also with its sister organization, the Wycliffe Bible Translators.

- *Tagmemics*

His main contribution to linguistics proper consists in his theory of grammar, which he called *tagmemics*. It is principally based on a fundamental distinction between a functional or 'emic' level, where structures are found that consist of functional slots, and a material or 'etic' level where one finds the actual phonetic fillers of the slots. (The aesthetically dubious terms 'emic' and 'etic' are derived, by way of generalization, from 'phonemic' and 'phonetic', respectively.) He regards the emic-etic distinction as fundamental for all human behaviour, including, for example, a traditional American breakfast, where the 'eme' of cereals can be filled by Rice Crispies, and the 'eme' of fruit juice by orange juice. Linguistically, the emic level is structured according to the IC-principle, derived from Bloomfield. Tagmemics never evolved very much, although dozens of out-of-the-way languages were described in terms of it. Its use remained limited to SIL-trained linguists (Murray 1994:188). It certainly never became transformational, and it was always characterized by a reluctance to consider the general methodological as well as the formal aspects of the analysis.

- *The answers given by the traditionalists*

What, then, were the answers provided by the traditionalists? These were as follows. Question 1: The structures assigned by linguists, if properly assigned, have *mental reality*. They are 'in some sense to be discovered by the analyst, not created by him' (Pike 1954:20 - § 2.72). This implies a rejection of behaviourism, since mental reality has no place there. Pike writes (1954:79 - § 6.43):

> One of the observable elements of human behavior, however, and an extremely important one, is precisely the fact that participants in that behavior affirm an awareness or knowledge of meaning or purpose, but without analyzing these meanings or purposes as an awareness of that potential for elicitation of responses which we have set forth as the principal component of these meanings. What, then, is the technical awareness of this awareness itself? Or can our theory find room for it, without destroying the objectivity of its approach? Our reply is, first, to accept this fact of affirmed awareness of meanings as an objective observable datum on a par with other observable verbal events; people say things about meanings, and these sayings we collect and study as part of our total corpus of material to be described.

Question 2 must now be answered in the affirmative: structure assignments are *unique* though notational variants may occur. Question 3 is not broached. The traditionalist answer to the important questions 4 and 5 is given in Pike

(1954:155 - § 7.87), an interesting passage where he relates how he came to his 1954 position from work done in 1948:

> To ... make layered structure explicit, I proposed an analysis in a kind of "pyramid-ed" structure, with a chart to show the layerings (... a procedure which in some form or other is now frequently used in the discussion of immediate constituents – e.g. Nida 1949, p. 87 ...). ... I proposed a list of criteria for immediate constituents. ... This list proved incomplete, and not sufficient for a full procedure. Since that time, additional criteria have been suggested by other writers – especially by Wells (1947) and Pittman (1948), but further criteria and theory are still needed. In order to try to solve some of these problems, my colleague Dr. William Wonderley and I attempted in the summer of 1948 to devise a set of formulas which would lead, without reference to meaning, to the immediate constituents of any utterance. ... [W]e repeatedly ran into situations which made the conclusions untenable in the light of grammatical junctures which were obvious from other criteria. In the meantime, however, we noticed that we could with a fair degree of ease and agreement recognize the consistent proportion of one item to its environment and of a sub-stituted item to that same environment and that this recognition occurred long before we could be reasonably sure of the immediate constituents of that utterance. Therefore, in the present theory, I have given the recognition of proportion in substitution an important place in gramemic treatment [i.e. the assignment of struc-ture; P.A.M.S.] ..., and have eliminated from the theory any attempt to determine immediate constituents without reference to structural meaning or proportion.

That is, the main criterion is substitutability of tentative constituents, but helped with and guided by the linguist's intuition about meaning and structure. The simplicity criterion is not mentioned. The traditionalists' 'pack-age' vis-à-vis the questions at issue thus looks as follows:

a. Realism and unique assignment of correct structures.
b. No behaviourism, but mental reality.
c. Substitutability, together with introspective semantic and structural in-tuitions as the criterion for correctness of IC-structure assignments.

4.4.3 The formalists: Zellig S. Harris

As has been said, the protagonist of the formalist school was *Zellig Sabbettai Harris* (1909-1992). Harris was born in the Ukraine, but as a child he came to the United States, where his parents settled in Philadelphia. Harris never left Philadelphia (but for frequent visits to Israel: he was an ardent Zionist). He studied and taught in Philadelphia and never had an appointment else-where. Of all the linguists of his generation he was the staunchest supporter of behaviourism, even though he was strongly influenced by Sapir, whom he mentions frequently. His main influence, however, came from Bloomfield, in particular Bloomfield's IC-analysis. His magnum opus is *Methods in Struc-tural Linguistics*, published in 1951 although the text was finished much earlier, in January 1947, as one gathers from the dating of the Preface.

• *Methods in Structural Linguistics (1951)*
This remarkable book is among the dullest ever published, yet it is carried throughout by a consistent and inspiring idea. The idea is, first, that it should

be possible, in principle, to record a large corpus of actual utterances and then, by careful comparison, set up a tentative inventory of minimal recurrent sound units later to be grouped together as phonemes on the basis of their complementary distribution (but see 7.2.2 below for further comment):

> As the first step towards obtaining phonemes, this procedure represents the continuous flow of a unique occurrence of speech as a succession of segmental elements, each representing some feature of a unique speech sound. The points of division of these segments are arbitrary here, since we have as yet no way of enabling the analyst to make the cuts at precisely those points in the flow of speech which will later be represented by inter-phonemic divisions. Later procedures will change these segmentations until their boundaries coincide with those of the eventual phonemes.   Harris (1951:25)

Then, recurrent phoneme combinations will be recognized as morphs, whose distribution will make it possible to set up an inventory of morphemes. And so on, until all combinations (constructions) have been exhausted. The book consists almost entirely of elaborate descriptions of these operations on all the different levels (and is therefore rather repetitive), laced with a multitude of examples from a wide variety of languages. It is thus one massive discovery procedure for a maximally compact, i.e. simple, statement of all possible constructions of the corpus at the various different levels of phonemes, morphemes, words, phrases, and, finally, the sentence. Put differently, it embodies an axiomatized procedure of what was considered, at the time, a linguistic theory. Like Hjelmslev, Harris had a great interest in mathematics. He was among the very first in America to apply notions and methods from mathematics to linguistic work. The notion of an axiomatized procedure for the discovery of grammars was inspired by what he had found in mathematics. Needless to say, the procedures described in the book are hardly practical: no-one would seriously consider going through a mass of taped material in this way and expect to come out with a grammar in terms of IC-analyses for every sentence in the corpus. Harris was fully aware of that, but he envisaged his discovery method as an idealized procedure that should be applied in an ideal world of science. We shall come back to this book in section 4.5, when we discuss the first beginnings of generative grammar.

● *The answers given by the formalists*
Now consider the formalists' answers to the questions concerned. They were behaviourists and thus, since they denied mental reality, instrumentalists. Structure assignments, for them, are merely constructs, invented by the analysing linguist (Harris 1951:2):

> The methods described here do not eliminate non-uniqueness in linguistic descriptions. It is possible for different linguists, working on the same material, to set up different phonemic and morphemic elements, to break phonemes into simultaneous components or not to do so, to equate two sequences of morphemes as being mutually substitutable or not to do so. The only result of such differences will be a correlative difference in the final statement as to what the utterances consist of. The use of these procedures is merely to make explicit what choices each linguist makes, so that if two analysts come out with different phoneme lists for a given

language we should have exact statements of what positional variants were assigned by each to what phonemes and wherein lay their differences of assignment.

There is thus no question as to their 'correctness' other than that the facts, i.e. the speech material collected in a corpus of utterances, must be covered. The answer to question 3 was given by the whole of Harris (1951), which was intended as a systematic, almost axiomatized, procedure for the discovery of an optimally simple description of the corpus. Distribution is considered virtually the only criterion for setting up tentative analyses, which are further tested on grounds of simplicity and generality of structure assignments:

> The only preliminary step that is essential to this science is the restriction to distribution as determining the relevance of the inquiry. (1951:6)

> It may be noted that distributional procedures do more than offer a rigorous alternative to meaning considerations and the like. Distributional procedures, once established, permit, with no extra trouble, the definite treatment of those marginal cases which meaning considerations leave indeterminate or open to conflicting opinion. (1951:8)

There is, however, a slight concession concerning meaning (more about which in 7.2.2 below):

> In principle, meaning need be involved only to the extent of determining what is repetition. If we know that *life* and *rife* are not entirely repetitions of each other, we will then discover that they differ in distribution (and hence in 'meaning'). (1951:7)

The formalists' 'package' thus looks as follows:

a. Instrumentalism; no unique assignment of structure.
b. Behaviourism, no mental reality
c. Distribution and simplicity as the criteria for correctness of IC-structure assignments. The role of meaning is kept to an absolute minimum.

4.4.4 A linguist in the middle ground: Charles F. Hockett

There were, however, in that period also linguists who preferred the middle ground, perhaps with a preference for one side or the other. An example is provided by *Charles F. Hockett* (born 1916), who studied at Yale with Sapir, and at Chicago with Bloomfield. He held the chair of linguistics at Cornell University from 1946 till his retirement in 1982. Like Harris, he had a penchant for mathematics, and many of the ideas developed by Harris during the late 1940s and early 1950s are also found in Hockett's works of that period. Around 1955 he was regarded as one of the most promising and outstanding younger theoretical linguists of the day. Unfortunately, however, he was unceremoniously eclipsed by Noam Chomsky, who presented the transformational generative model of grammatical description in 1957 and, on the strength of that, sprang to fame.

• *Hockett as an innovator but loyal to tradition*
Hockett was among the first to see how the conception of grammar as an analytical procedure resulting in a listing of all possible functional ('emic')

elements and all possible IC-constructions built up from these elements should be changed into a different conception in which dynamic, generative rules generate underlying structures first, which are then transformed by a different set of transformational rules into the final product. He was probably not the very first to envisage such a development, as Zellig Harris was, in all likelihood, just a little earlier. But Hockett distinguishes himself from Harris, and later Chomsky, in that he remained much more sensitive, and more loyal, to what traditional linguistics had built up over the centuries. Though modernistic in his general outlook, he was much less inclined to do away with the past than his more formalistic colleague Harris and Harris's young student Chomsky. Hockett's most notable contributions to the theory of grammar are his article 'Two models of grammatical description' of 1954, and his well-known and much appreciated *A Course in Modern Linguistics*, of 1958.

- *Hockett's traditional notion of subject and predicate*

Thus, for example, Hockett, like Bloomfield, still adheres to the late 19th century discourse-bound notion of subject and predicate developed by Von der Gabelentz, Wegener, Lipps, Stout and others (see 2.6.3). In his magnum opus (1958:201) we read:

> The most general characterization of predicative constructions is suggested by the terms "topic" and "comment" for their ICs: the speaker announces a topic and then says something about it. Thus *John | ran away; That new book by Thomas Guernsey | I haven't read yet.* In English and the familiar languages of Europe, topics are usually also subjects, and comments are predicates: so in *John | ran away.* But this identification fails sometimes in colloquial English, regularly in certain special situations in formal English, and more generally in some non-European languages.

(Hockett thinks here especially of Chinese, a language he studied intensively.) It is noteworthy that this is the last occasion, in the general theoretical linguistic literature in America, that this notion of subject and predicate is mentioned and supported. In the transformational literature it has entirely disappeared and been forgotten. Likewise in the other developments of formal grammar that have sprung up over the past twenty or so years.

- *Hockett's 1954 article 'Two models'*

In the 1954 article 'Two models' he questions the then standard assumption that linguistic analysis and description should consist exclusively of the setting up of IC-analyses for sentences and parts of sentences. Segmentation and classification, leading to statements of complementary distribution, had been the primary procedures since Harris (1951), and Bloomfield's notion of 'basic' or 'underlying' form (see above) had been rejected. This 'model' of grammatical description Hockett calls the *item and arrangement* or IA model. He demonstrates with great clarity that this model is too restrictive, in that it makes it impossible to express certain relevant generalizations that can be made with regard to the available material. Thus, for example, the English morpheme *took* must be analysed as the past tense of the verb *take*, on pain of losing out on an obvious generalization. In the IA style of description one has little choice but to posit the allomorphs [take] and [t—k] for the verbal stem element, and the allomorphs [-t], [-d], [-Id], [-Ø], and, idiosyncratically, [-u-] for the allomorph [t—k], to be placed in the position between [t] and [k]. Not only does this require a discontinuous morph [t—k], it is also sadly unrevealing. It would be much better, therefore, to reinstate Bloomfield's notion of underlying form and allow for rules as processes. This enables one to posit an underlying abstract morpheme [PAST] which would manifest itself in differing guises according to certain statable regularities, and which, combined with the abstract morpheme [TAKE], would result idiosyncratically in the single 'portmanteau' morpheme *took*. Such a procedure, however, implies a different 'model' or 'style' of grammatical description, which Hockett calls the *item and process* or IP model. This proposal soon gained general acceptance and was generalized into the now current notion of underlying or deep structure for grammar in general. As will be shown in a moment, Hockett himself took this step in his book (1958).

- *Hockett's answers to the questions*

Hockett's answers to the questions listed above were, on the whole, moderate, and sometimes subject to change. One sees him take a middle position between the traditionalists and the formalists, but with a preference for the formalist concept.

- *Realism versus instrumentalism; description must be predictive*

As regards the question of realism versus instrumentalism, and thus of uniqueness or non-uniqueness, his position changed between 1948 and 1958. In (1948) Hockett supports a realist position, combined with the then startling new idea of the predictive power of a linguistic description (Hockett 1948:271):

> The task of the structural linguist, as a scientist, is ... essentially one of classification. The purpose, however, is not simply to account for all the utterances which comprise his corpus at a given time; a simple alphabetical list would do that. Rather, the analysis of the linguistic *scientist* is to be of such a nature that the linguist can account also for utterances which are *not* in his corpus at a given time. That is, as a result of his examination he must be able to predict what *other* utterances the speakers of the language might produce, and, ideally, the circumstances under which those other utterances might be produced.
>
> The analytical process thus parallels what goes on in the nervous system of a language learner, particularly, perhaps, that of a child learning his first language.

In (1958), however, this essentially Chomskyan position has changed to instrumentalism and non-uniqueness, though when different factually adequate solutions are proposed, the differences should be attributed to different levels of description, rather than to the possibility of arranging the available facts differently and still coming to an adequate and simple coverage (1958:252):

> Just as languages differ as to what is assigned to surface grammar and what is handled at deeper levels, so, not unexpectedly, equally competent grammarians often disagree in the analysis of a single language. The disagreements stem from differences of training and previous experience. They should be regarded not as conflicts demanding resolution, but as enrichments in our understanding of the language in

question: both sides can be right in a dispute, in that the apparently conflicting opinions may reflect facts at different grammatical depths.

One notices that here, too, the statement of his position is combined with a startling new thought, the distinction between surface structure and deep structure, about which more in section 4.5.

- *No formalized discovery procedure*

Hockett has no formalized discovery procedure à la Harris. In this respect he is more modern than Harris, in that he allows the analyst to rely on previous experience and grammatical intuitions, as long as the final product fits the facts in a satisfactory way. He refrains, therefore, from the formulation of any set of axioms or postulates.

- *No mention of distribution; no simplicity criterion*

Hockett uses distributional phenomena only implicitly, and not as the only criterion for a proper analysis. One gathers that when the data show complementary distribution it should be taken as a heuristic hint, a suggestion for the setting up of a particular analysis. The ultimate justification of any given analysis lies in the adequate and maximally regular coverage of the facts. The term *distribution* is not used at all in Hockett (1958). Nor is the term *simplicity*. In fact, he politely scoffs at the notion of simplicity (1958:275):

> Even if other criteria are satisfactorily met, one does not assign two morphs to a single morpheme unless the resulting morpheme fits into the emerging grammatical picture of the language in a sensible way. One does not simply strive to see how small a stock of morphemes can be ascribed to the language by clever manipulation of one's data.

This is a rejection not only of the formalists' 'hocus pocus' way of manipulating data into a formally elegant system, but also of the very notion of a formalized discovery procedure of grammars. As has been said, Hockett prefers to judge a grammar by its success once it is there, as is the normal procedure nowadays. One clearly senses here a certain antagonism with respect to Harris's approach, without, however, an identification with the traditionalists' way of doing linguistics.

- *Mildly behaviourist; meaning as a criterion and a heuristic for analysis*

Meaning is considered admissible in linguistic analysis (1958:139):

> [W]e are forced to use semantic criteria in trying to get at the grammatical system, for we have to discover, somehow, whether two utterances or parts of utterances, differing in specified ways as to phonemic shapes, "mean the same thing" or "have different meanings" for the native speaker. It is just in the application of these criteria that we can most easily go astray, vitiating our would-be-description of the central subsystems. No description of a language is free of errors stemming from this source. No description can claim more than a kind of by-and-large accuracy.

Yet, as one sees, scare quotes are used when meaning is mentioned, and the recognition of meaning is ascribed to the native speaker rather than to the linguist. The linguist has to be very careful when dealing with semantic phenomena. He must rely on grammar and avoid mentalistic notions (1958:139):

> It is ... futile to try to analyze a semantic system without understanding the grammatical system to which it relates. ... Anthropologists and philosophers have often attempted the latter, and have found themselves forced to invent pseudo-linguistic "mental" entities such as "ideas" or "concepts", in place of the obvious and empirically discoverable morphemes and larger grammatical forms of a language.

One notices the influence of behaviourism in his terminology and his ideas about language. Thus, for example, language is described as a set of habits (1958:141), just as the behaviourists did. Meaning is described, vaguely, as 'associative ties' (1958:139):

> The meanings of morphemes and of combinations of morphemes are, as has been said, associative ties between those morphemes and morpheme-combinations and things and situations, or types of things and situations, in the world around us. These semantic ties are more or less the same for all the speakers of the language.

- *Hockett's 'package'*

What one finds is thus a 'package' that differs from the traditionalists' and from the formalists' positions. It is behaviourist and generally modernistic, i.e. not traditional, without, however, being very formal either:

a. Instrumentalism; no unique assignment of structure.
b. Behaviourism, no mental reality
c. Distribution and simplicity are not criteria for correctness of IC-structure assignments. Meaning is a prominent criterion (though re-interpreted in a behaviourist sense), together with factual correctness and 'sensible', i.e. intuitively satisfying, solutions.

4.4.5 Tree diagrams in linguistics: from Wundt to TGG

We have repeatedly mentioned the importance of the IC-principle in the tradition of American structuralism, and commented on the curious absence of actual tree structure diagrams in the writings of leading linguists like Sapir and Bloomfield. A few words are in order here about both the origin of the IC-principle and its use in the linguistic literature.

- *The origin of the IC-principle in Wundt (1880)*

As has been said before, we trace the origin of the IC-principle to Wundt (see also Percival 1976):

> The simplest form of a *thought*, i.e. a self-contained apperceptive representational process, occurs when a total representation ('Gesamtvorstellung') falls into *two* parts that are connected with each other. This happens in the *simple judgement*. If we use the sign ∩ for apperceptive connections of successive representations, then A∩B is the psychological symbol of the simple judgement.

> As soon as the total representation, the splitting up of which results in a thought process, is separated into three or more single representations the judgement is no

longer simple but *composite*. In a composite judgement the connection of the single parts is never uniform, in the sense that the form A∩B would extend over a larger number of members, as in A∩B∩C ... . On the contrary, these apperceptive connections always proceed in such a way that first, as with the simple thought, the total representation is separated into two single representations, upon which either or both of these can be subdivided into two further single representations, and so on. Herein lies the essential difference between apperceptive and associative connections. If we use the sign ‾ for the associative connection of successive representations, we see that an associative sequence A‾B‾C‾D ... can contain any number of members. In contrast to this, the apperceptive thought process always proceeds in forms like the following:

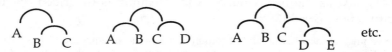

This principle of duality or of binary connection has found its unmistakable expression in the categories of grammatical syntax. For all these categories always reduce to just *two* representations which are connected with each other. Thus we distinguish first the two main representations Subject and Predicate, which correspond with the first division of the thought. The Subject may be divided again into Noun and Attribute. The Predicate, when it is nominal, splits into the Copula and the Predicate proper, upon which the latter, like the Subject, may split into Noun and Attribute again. But if the Predicate is verbal it may split into Verb and Object, or into the Predicate proper and the supplementary Predicate.   Wundt (1880:53-54)

Wundt then continues for a good many pages to write about this notion of hierarchical binary division, allowing, a bit later on, also for ternary divisions, as in the Latin *Socrates venenum laetus hausit* ('Socrates happily drank the poison'), which is represented as in fig. 3 (1880:57):

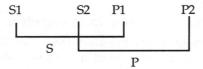

Figure 3   Wundt's analysis of 'Socrates venenum laetus hausit'

where 'S1' and 'S2' stand for 'Socrates', 'P1' for 'laetus', 'P2' for 'venenum hausit', 'S' for 'Socrates laetus' and 'P' again for 'venenum hausit'. (One notes that this analysis reflects some underlying level of semi-semantic analysis, rather than straightforward surface structure. Wundt's text here is so exciting to the modern reader that one is tempted to quote it in full, which, of course, we cannot do. The reader, however, is advised to get the book from a library and look through it.)

- *More on the IC-principle in Wundt (1900)*

Even more extensive is the treatment of the IC-principle in Wundt (1900:320-355). Here, the notation has developed further in that the constituents are now labelled, as shown in fig. 4 (Wundt 1900:329), where 'G' stands for 'Gesamtvorstellung' (=Sentence), 'A' for 'subject' and 'B' for 'predicate':

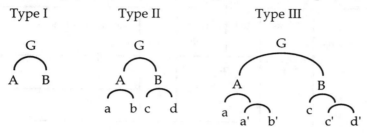

Figure 4   Wundt's labelled trees

It is clear, therefore, where Bloomfield, who in his younger years was a close follower of Wundt, will have found the inspiration for his notion of the IC-principle.

- *The curious reluctance to draw trees*

Strangely enough, however, as we have seen, Bloomfield refrains from presenting any kind of pictorial representation, even though his example, Wundt, makes liberal use of them. It is useful, therefore, to investigate how and when the drawing of tree diagrams became an established convention, which, as was said above, came late. The earliest tree diagram I have been able to find in the linguistic literature is of the kind shown in fig. 3. It is in Nida (1949:87), reproduced here as fig. 5.

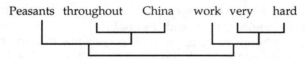

Figure 5   IC-diagram in Nida (1949:87

In the format of an upside down tree (as in figs. 1, 2, and, though with arcs for straight lines, also fig. 4) they occurred first in the mathematical definition of 'phrase structure' in Chomsky ([1956]:181-200), but only applied to mathematical structures as generated by algorithmic rules, not to linguistic structures. Essentially the tree structure notation of figs. 3 and 5, but with categorial labellings, is found in Chomsky ([1956]:229), applied to a linguistic example, as shown in fig. 6:

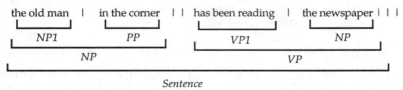

Figure 6   Tree diagram in Chomsky (1975[1956]:229)

A different kind again, more like a box diagram, occurs in Chomsky ([1956]: 258), shown in fig. 7:

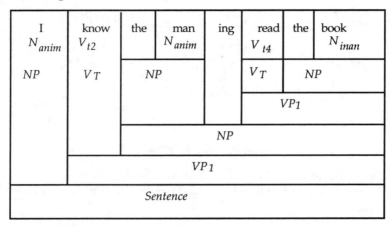

I N_{anim}	know V_{t2}	the	man N_{anim}	ing	read V_{t4}	the	book N_{inan}
NP	V_T	NP			V_T	NP	
					VP₁		

(box diagram: Sentence / VP₁ / NP / VP₁)

Figure 7   Tree diagram in Chomsky (1975[1956]:258)

Hockett (1958) uses the same type of notation, but without the categorial labelling.

- *The problem of discontinuous constituents*

The tree structures of the now familiar kind are generally supposed not to have any crossing lines. This is a point of substance since the problem of discontinuous constituents is all over the American structuralist literature. In a sentence like *I rang him up* the words *rang* and *up* are considered, with some justification, to belong together, and it is natural to declare them one constituent. In that case, however, it is discontinuous since it is interrupted by the word *him*, as shown in fig. 8a. Although discontinuous constituents pose no essential problem, one finds a widespread reluctance to accept them, a reluctance which is as universal as it is badly argued for.

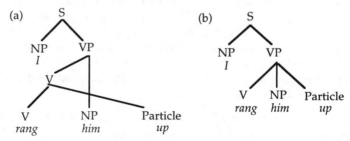

Figure 8   Example of a tree diagram with and without crossing lines

In the context of TGG, the problem was eliminated by the postulation of an underlying structure where the parts that are discontinuous in surface structure are grouped together as a fully continuous constituent. The transformational rule that tears them apart will deliver a derived structure where the parts form separate constituents, as in fig. 8b, their original unity now being accounted for by their unison at a deeper level of representation. In this way no discontinuous constituents need ever be assumed in tree structures. Yet even now no principled answer is given to the question why the derived structure should not also show the unity of the constituent by means of crossing lines.

- *If crossing lines are avoided tree diagrams are representable as strings with labelled bracketing*

As long as discontinuous constituents, and thus crossing lines in the tree diagrams, remain outlawed, any tree diagram is representable as a string of elements that are contained in hierarchically ordered pairs of brackets, each pair being labelled by the appropriate category symbol. Thus, (8b) is representable also as the string:

$$_S[_{NP}[I]\ _{VP}[_V[rang]\ _{NP}[him]\ _{Particle}[up]]]$$

But (8a) cannot be represented in this way, as the reader will quickly find out on trying. The notations in question, by means of a string with labelled bracketing or as a tree diagram without crossing lines, are formally equivalent, but they have different practical advantages and disadvantages. Bracketed strings are easier to print and take up less space. But they are also much more difficult to read and are generally hopeless as a notation when one wants to perform formal operations on IC-structures.

- *An early approach to bracketed structures: Wells (1947)*

The reader will see that figs. 4, 6, 7 are representable as strings with labelled bracketings, but fig. 5 as a bracketed string without labels. In Wells (1947) one finds a notation that is similar to (and formally equivalent with) unlabelled bracketed strings. In this notation the sentence *The king of England opened Parliament* comes out as:

The | | king | | | of | | | | England | open | | | ed | | Parliament

corresponding to the unlabelled tree diagram of fig. 9:

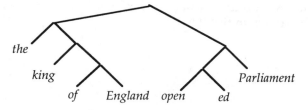

Figure 9   'The king of England opened Parliament'
            according to Wells (1947)

But Wells does not draw any tree diagrams. All he gives is the kind of structure illustrated above.

● *The modern format of tree structure in Chomsky (1957)*

The first tree structure of the kind now universally used and applied to a linguistic structure (and not to a mathematical construct), appears in Chomsky (1957:27), where it is unique: the book contains no other tree structures. It thus seems that it was not until the late 1950s that the convention was established of drawing tree diagrams in the format that is now generally accepted.

● *Derived structure remains underspecified for a long time*

But even when this convention had been established, it took a long time before transformational rules were specified in terms of the effects they have on tree structures. In the literature on transformational syntax it remained the custom to formulate transformational rules in a linear format that heavily underspecifies the tree structures involved. Even nowadays one rarely finds transformational effects fully shown in actual tree diagrams, but this is perhaps less necessary now, at least for the developments led by Chomsky, as the transformational rules have been streamlined to such an extent that tree diagrams are no longer necessary. Until this development took place, however, output structures, in particular, were insufficiently specified, a point noted by Bach (1964:79-81).[15]

The obvious reluctance, in some quarters, to resort to the actual drawing of tree diagrams is not unimportant, as the very notation system has proved a valuable instrument in the formal definition of grammatical rules, structures and constraints.

● *Constituency trees as frames for computation*

An important aspect of tree diagrams consists in the fact that they can be used as an 'abacus', or a framework for a computation procedure. An example from arithmetic will make this clear. Consider the formulas (5 × 6) + 8 and 5 × (6 + 8). Clearly, these differ as to hierarchical constituency in that in the former one must compute first the value of 5 × 6, i.e. 30, and then add 8 to get the final value 38. In the latter formula one must compute first the value of (6 + 8), i.e. 14, and then multiply this by 5, so that one gets the final value 70. The difference between the two formulas is naturally expressed by means of constituency tree diagrams, as shown in fig. 10:

[15] As late as 1975 one finds a book, Kayne (1975), almost 450 pages of French syntax without any tree diagram at all. Since the text does not make up for this deficiency derived structure remains heavily underspecified and the reader has no means of knowing what precise structural claims are made by the author.

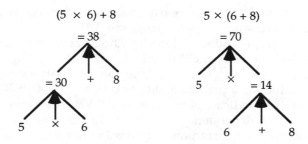

Figure 10   Constituency trees for (5×6)+8 and 5×(6+8)

The principle is simple. The arithmetical operations of multiplication and addition are treated as binary functions yielding a definite value for any input consisting of two natural numbers. In the trees of fig. 10 these functions are flanked on either side by their arguments. The resulting value is passed upward from the function node to the dominating node, where it can be re-used as argument for a further arithmetical operation. As is shown in section 5.5, this can be applied to linguistic IC-structures as well, to compute, for example, the truth-value of a given sentence with respect to a given state of affairs. In natural language sentences it is typically the predicate which acts as the function node. The formal method for doing this is provided by *logical model theory*, the basis of what is known as *formal semantics* (chapter 6).

● *The dependency trees of Tesnière*

The Frenchman *Lucien Valérius Tesnière* (1893-1954) applied a kind of tree structure analysis called *dependency trees.* These differ essentially from IC-analyses. The difference is best demonstrated by using the example from arithmetic again. Like constituency trees, dependency trees can be used for computational purposes. Other than in constituency trees, however, the function node dominates the argument or arguments, as in fig. 11:

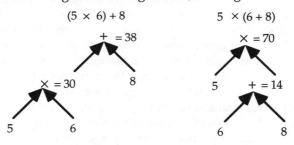

Figure 11   Dependency trees for (5×6)+8 and 5×(6+8)

● *Dependency trees in linguistics*

Dependency trees are standardly used in mathematics and in computer science. In linguistics, however, they are less popular. Most theories of grammar work with constituency trees. Some schools, however, use dependency trees, such as the Prague School (perhaps due to early contacts of Tesnière with Trubetzkoy when they were both students at Leipzig; see 3.3), or the Moscow school of Meaning-Text Theory, founded in 1965 by Zholkovsky and Mel'čuk (see e.g. Zholkovsky & Mel'čuk 1965; Mel'čuk & Pertsov 1987).

A sentence like *The children ate sweets* can be analysed in at least two different ways, either as a predicate with two terms, i.e. as SVO, or as a subject combined with a predicate phrase, i.e. as NP-VP. The former structure can be represented as the dependency tree shown in fig. 12a, the latter as in fig. 12b. The contrast with the corresponding constituency trees is striking, and the question that now poses itself naturally is which of the two structure representation systems is to be considered preferable.

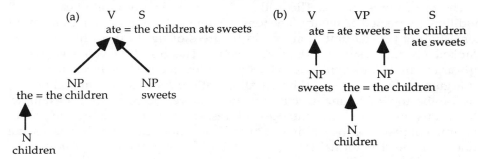

Figure 12   Dependency tree analyses of 'The children ate sweets'

- *Which kind of tree is best for the purposes of linguistics?*

When one looks at actual descriptions in terms of the two systems one is struck by an important difference. In constituency tree descriptions the tree structures themselves play a central role in the descriptive machinery and are an integral part of any explanation provided. In transformational approaches to grammar, which are all based on constituency trees, the tree structure itself is part of the formulation of the transformations concerned. In dependency tree descriptions, on the other hand, the trees appear to play a much more subordinate role. There the actual tree structures tend to be merely auxiliary, a means for representing certain semantic relations in sentences. Dependency tree grammars do not, as a rule, involve operations on trees. From this perspective one may say that constituency tree grammars are richer in explanatory devices than dependency tree grammars, which may have been the main reason why the more influential schools of linguistic thought have opted for constituency trees, even if an explicit argument is hardly ever given. There is also the feeling that dependency grammar, though strong as regards the analysis of predicate-argument structure, has less to offer concerning the analysis of tense and modal systems, and the grammar of adverbial adjuncts of all kinds.

But such considerations are of necessity tentative and provisional. Which of the two approaches should be preferred is to be decided on grounds of the empirical success of a significant body of explicit and successful descriptions. In the eyes of many, the balance of empirical success at present favours constituency tree theory. It is felt that dependency trees have not proved as successful as constituency trees. But one has to admit that it is premature to force a decision on this issue at the present stage of grammatical theory. This book emphasizes constituency trees, thereby reflecting the dominant view. This should, however, not keep any interested student from investigating the possible virtues of dependency tree analyses for the theory of grammar.

4.5   Generative and early Transformational Grammar

4.5.1   Generative Grammar: Zellig S. Harris

• *The origin of Generative Grammar: Harris (1951)*
The origin of generative and of transformational generative grammar (TGG) lies with Zellig Harris. Towards the end of his (1951) (whose text, we remember, was finished in January 1947) he considers the question of how to take stock of the intended results of the whole complex analytical procedure meant to assign IC-structures to all the utterances of the corpus. The obvious thought is to set up charts that specify which combinations are possible and thus rule out the impossible combinations. This is precisely what Harris does. An example is found on p. 350, here reproduced as fig. 13, for the overall phrase structure of English sentences. 'N' stands for 'noun phrase', 'V' for 'verb', 'Vb' for (roughly) 'copula verb', 'P' for 'particle', and 'A' for 'adjective phrase'. The open space to the right of V and Vb allows for the possibility of no material occurring after V or Vb, as in *His old friend departed*, or *God is*.

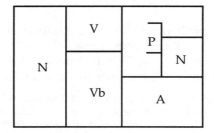

Figure 13   Survey of possible patterns for English sentences (Harris (1951:350))

(A similar chart is found on p. 153 for phoneme combinations in English morphemes up to the first vowel.) It soon became clear, however, that this kind of taxonomic chart quickly becomes unwieldy. An attempt at setting one up for Moroccan Arabic word structure (p. 353) runs into trouble and necessitates the introduction of makeshift devices. Moreover, IC-structure is not indicated in fig. 13, and adding it would make for further notational complications. Therefore, this method of taxonomic charting cannot be considered an adequate way of representing the structural possibilities of sentences, phrases, words, etc., even though it looks intuitively attractive.

Yet the need for a suitable format is there, since the overall purpose of the enterprise remains a characterization of the notion 'sentence in the language' (1951:366-368):

> The over-all purpose of work in descriptive linguistics is to obtain a compact one-one representation of the stock of utterances in the corpus. Since the representation of an utterance or its parts is based on a comparison of utterances, it is really a representation of distinctions. ...
>
> The basic operations are those of segmentation and classification. Segmentation is carried out at limits determined by the independence of the resulting segments in terms of some particular criterion. ... Classification is used to group together elements which substitute for or are complementary to one another. ...
>
> If we were analyzing a corpus without any interest in its relevance for the whole language, we could list all the environments of each tentative segment in all utterances of the corpus, and on this basis decide the segmentation in each utterance. Usually, however, we are interested in analyzing such a corpus as will serve as a sample of the language.

A characterization of the notion 'sentence in the language' is the last station of a series of characterizations of ever ascending rank: from phonemes to morphemes to words to phrases, and, finally, to sentences. The higher the constituent level the smaller the inventory but the larger the class of possible fillers:

> This leads ultimately to sets of few elements having complex definitions but as nearly as possible random occurrence in respect to each other, replacing the original sets of many elements having simple definitions but complexly restricted distribution.   Harris (1951:369-370)

Since the charting method for the representation of the possible combinations yielding well-formed sentences, phrases, words, etc. is not ideal, a different method must be devised. This is found in the formulation of 'statements', the term used by Harris for what we now call 'rules' (1951:372-373):

> The work of analysis leads right up to the statements which enable anyone to synthesize or predict utterances in the language. These statements form a deductive system with axiomatically defined initial elements and with theorems concerning the relations among them. The final theorems would indicate the structure of the utterances of the language in terms of the preceding parts of the system.

Here we have, in nucleo, the concept of *generative grammar*. The system of deductively organized 'statements', or 'rules', forms an algorithm, which generates IC-structured strings of symbols that are interpretable as the 'theorems' of the system. Note that we do not have any notion of *transformational* grammar yet: the rules envisaged here still only generate surface structures directly. But we will not have to wait long before transformational rules are introduced as well.

• *Motivation question now answered in a principled but impractical way*
One should note that the question of the motivation of IC-analyses has now shifted from individual IC-structures to the totality of all IC-structures of the language in question. Any given IC-structure assignment is now motivated by the mere fact that it follows from that generative rule system which is the best available for the language in question: the best rule system generates the best tree structure assignments. And the best rule system is to be found by painstakingly segmenting and classifying, throughout a corpus large enough to be representative of the language as a whole, tentative elements at various levels and establishing their distibutional patterns. It is not hard to see that if this may be reckoned to be a principled answer it can hardly be considered a practical one.

• *The question is now: what is the best theory?*
It is thus not surprising that the question of what makes the best rule system now gains paramount importance. And indeed, the question of how to adjudicate between competing analyses and competing theories has dominated the history of generative grammar from the beginning. One finds it discussed extensively e.g. in Chomsky (1975[1956]:77-103; 1957:49-60; 1965:3-9), but also in, for example, Postal (1972), and many other publications.

• *'High view' of grammar as a whole leads to methodological quandary*
It is important to realize that in those days the notion of a grammar as a whole, a set of rules describing (generating) all the sentences of a language and only those, was well-nigh incomprehensible and unfathomable. Linguists thought in terms of individual IC-structures, or small sets of IC-structures at most, to be motivated on grounds of their individual or group properties. But having to think of the structure of a grammatical rule system as a whole transported them into a totally different realm of thought, way above the myopically close examination of small groups of individual cases. This new 'high view' of a grammar as an organized system of generative rules led to a methodological dilemma. On the one hand, it was the efficacy and simplicity of such a rule system as a whole that should answer the question of the best theory and hence of the best IC-structure assignments. On the other, the procedures indicated by Harris to get at the kind of generative rule system envisaged were totally impractical: no linguist would ever sit down amidst a pile of tape-recordings and start analysing sounds into segments whose distribution should then lead to a tentative phoneme inventory, which would then have to be found to combine into recurrent groups that would be regarded as tentative allomorphs, and so on, till all the constructions of the corpus were exhausted. This being so, the question inevitably arose as to how the as yet abstract notion of a generative rule system could be turned into concrete reality: how can one set up an adequate generative rule system without having to traverse the lethal swamps of Harris's discovery procedure? This question soon forced Harris to adopt a milder attitude with regard to his formal, almost axiomatic discovery procedure and leave more room for structural

intuitions and meaning as determinants of tentative IC-analyses and, in the end, tentative rule systems. These are to be *tested* for adequacy rather than be regarded as resulting more or less automatically from a rigidly defined discovery procedure.

• *Three procedures for settling upon a rule system*

This point of view, which was prepared by Harris, as we shall see in a moment, is expressed with great clarity in chapter 6 of Chomsky (1957:49-60). Here, Chomsky distinguishes between (a) a *discovery procedure*, which is what Harris proposed in *Methods* of 1951 (though Harris is not mentioned in this context), (b) a *decision procedure* which would say of any given grammar whether it is adequate or not, and (c) an *evaluation procedure* which would decide for any two given grammars which of the two is better qualified to generate the sentences of the language and would hence be more adequate. Chomsky (1957:51) presents the diagram given here as fig. 14 to show the difference between the three methods. Option (i) in fig. 14 is a discovery procedure, (ii) is a decision procedure, and (iii) represents an evaluation procedure.

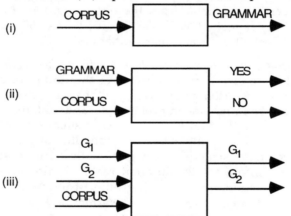

Figure 14   Three ways of settling upon a rule system (Chomsky 1957:51)

• *Evaluation procedure preferred*

Chomsky then decides in favour of (iii), an evaluation procedure, as the most practical way of achieving good quality generative grammars for the language under analysis. This point of view has now been generally adopted. Discovery procedures now only still exist as no more than heuristic guidelines, and any grammar or subgrammar proposed is seen as a hypothesis to be tested on grounds of factual correctness and simplicity (economy of description). As regards decision procedures, no actual formal decision procedure has ever been proposed: the notion of decision procedure is merely an abstraction introduced to fill the gap between a discovery and an evaluation procedure.[16]

4.5.2 Early TGG: Zellig S. Harris

- *PS-rewrite systems*

Rule systems that generate surface structures directly in the sense intended (but not shown) in the last chapter of Harris (1951) later became known as Phrase Structure (or PS) rewrite systems. A PS-rewrite rule is an instruction to 'rewrite' a given symbol into one or more symbols, all symbols to be selected from a given 'alphabet' or 'vocabulary'. The following is a small system of PS-rewrite rules generating a restricted set of English sentences:

System A: Small PS-rewrite system for a restricted set of English sentences

(i)	S	→	NP + VP
(ii)	NP	→	Det (+ A) + N
(iii)	VP	→	V + NP
(iv)	Det	→	{the, a}
(v)	N	→	{mouse, cat}
(vi)	V	→	{ate, caught, chased}
(vii)	A	→	{black, big, quick}

The system is best interpreted as an algorithmic machine. The symbol 'S' (i.e. Sentence) is the starting symbol. When activated the machine prints the symbol 'S' and carries out the instruction associated with it, i.e. rule (i). The arrow symbolizes an instruction to print the symbols to its right underneath the symbol 'S', which is connected with them by straight lines. We now have an *expansion* of S into NP (i.e. Noun Phrase) followed by VP (i.e. Verb Phrase), as shown in fig. 15.

Figure 15   *Expansion of S according to rule (i)*

The symbols 'NP' and 'VP' then activate the rules (ii) and (iii), respectively, leading to further expansions. Rule (ii) contains a bracketed element '(+ A)', standing for the optional addition of the symbol 'A' (i.e. Adjective)

---

[16] In this context, Chomsky discusses the vacuity of the problem of level mixing (see question 6 in 4.4.1), saying (1957:56): 'Once we have disclaimed any intention of finding a practical discovery procedure for grammars, certain problems that have been the subject of intense methodological controversy simply do not arise.' He then proceeds to discuss the old problem of level mixing, as a result of which 'linguistic theory may be nullified by a real circularity' (1957:57). It must be noted, however, that the problem had already been solved in the context of Harris's (1951) discovery procedure, which allows for the setting up of tentative inventories and structures, open to correction in the light of further analytical results. Chomsky's reference to Harris (1951) in note 7 of (1957:57) suggests, incorrectly, that Harris (1951) suffers from the methodological circularity mentioned.

between 'Det' (i.e. Determiner) and 'N' (i.e. Noun). The rules (iv) to (vii) rewrite the symbols 'Det', 'N', 'V' and 'A', respectively, into 'terminal' or 'lexical' elements, which cannot be rewritten by further rules and are taken from the *lexicon* of the language. The braces contain sets of lexical fillers, one of which is to be chosen. One tends to leave out, nowadays, the connecting lines for lexical fillers. System A thus generates, for example, the tree of fig. 16, which corresponds to the sentence *The big cat chased a quick mouse*:

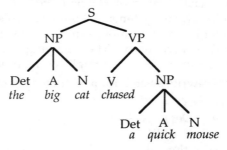

Figure 16   Tree for 'The big cat chased a quick mouse'
according to System A

The lexicon is a proper subset of the total *vocabulary* of the grammar, which consists of the *non-terminal* elements S, NP, VP, Det, A, N, and V, and the *terminal* or *lexical* elements *the, a, mouse, cat, ate, caught, chased, black, big*, and *quick*. The lexical elements form the lexicon. Each lexical element has its *lexical category*, indicated by the *categorial symbol* which it rewrites. The symbols 'Det', 'N', 'V', and 'A' are the categorial symbols of System A.

- *A grammar must generate all and only the well-formed sentences of L*

Once the notion of a PS-rewrite grammar has been made explicit it is easier to take the 'high view' mentioned above. We can now impose general conditions on grammars and ask questions of a general nature. Thus we expect of a grammar that it should generate all and only the grammatically well-formed sentences of the language L it is designed for. If it fails to generate a well-formed sentence of L it is defective, and if it generates a string of lexical symbols that is not well-formed in L it overgenerates. Either way it is factually (observationally) inadequate.

- *Is a PS-rewrite system the only way to generate tree structures?*

We can now also ask the question whether a system of PS-rewrite rules is the only possible, or the simplest, way of generating the sentences of a language, complete with their tree-structures. This leads to the wider question of the formal possibilities of algorithms, discussed more fully in section 4.7.1 below. Here we consider the question historically, to see how, in the early 1950s, it showed Harris the way to Transformational Generative Grammar (TGG).

• *Bloomfield's implicit assumption that grammars are PS-rewrite systems*
Bloomfield had to do without the notion of a generative grammar. But now that the notion has been made explicit we see that, with one exception, his grammatical theory contained the implicit assumption that grammars of natural languages are essentially context-free PS-rewrite systems, since he expects of a grammatical theory that it assign IC-structures to the sentences of a language merely by defining classes of elements and their possible combinations. He thus followed, apart from one exception, the *item and arrangement* or IA-model, as defined in Hockett (1954). The one exception is his postulation of underlying 'basic' forms for morphemes that change under morphophonemic rules. Thus, Bloomfield posits underlying forms for German and French adjectives (1933:217, 219; see 4.3) in view of their phonological shape when combined with suffixes of case or gender. (It was this notion that Chomsky applied in his *Morphophonemics of Modern Hebrew* of 1951.) Obviously, Bloomfield himself was totally unaware of the fact that he was working implicitly with a PS-rewrite system (though supplemented with context-sensitive morphophonemic rules that had, in fact, transformational power), and he was therefore in no position to call this assumption into question. But Harris, in the early 1950s, could begin to query the Bloomfieldian assumption, and he gradually discovered that it was inadequate.

• *Harris discovers the transformational principle through discourse studies*
It is a little surprising that it was by studying discourse phenomena that Harris came to the insight that PS-rewrite systems (supplemented with morphophonemic rules) are insufficient. After 1950 Harris began to see, like Hjelmslev, Gardiner and others before him, that the observational data of linguistic theory consist not so much of isolated sentences (which are already a product of linguistic analysis) but of texts or discourses as found in everyday life. Yet his linguistic theory applied to sentences as maximal units, not to stretches of discourse. In order to bridge this gap he attempted, for the first time in Harris (1952), to apply the distributional method to texts and thus extend it beyond the realm of the sentence. Nowadays this is felt to be misguided. In the modern view the universe of grammatical rules is the sentence, not the discourse. What makes a discourse coherent is a different set of rules and principles, to do more with semantics and pragmatics than with grammar. For Harris, however, this was not at all evident.

He felt that the distributional method should be extended to stretches of text so that we can 'find out all that we can about a particular text' (1981 [1952]:110). To this end, he proposed that one should state the distributional properties of sentences, phrases, words and morphemes within a text and their correlation with what he calls 'social situations', i.e. the meanings of the expressions concerned:

> It remains to be shown as a matter of empirical fact that such formal correlations do indeed exist, that the discourses of a particular person, social group, style, or subject-matter exhibit not only particular meanings (in their selection of morphemes) but also characteristic formal features. The particular selection of morphemes

cannot be considered here. But the formal features of the discourse can be studied by distributional methods within the text; and the fact of their correlation with a particular type of situation gives a meaning-status to the occurrence of these formal features.   Harris (1981[1952]:110)

One must realize that Harris's ideas on these matters are highly speculative. The examples he gives are hardly convincing. In fact, his discourse studies never resulted in any tangible result or further development.

Somehow, however, in the course of his investigations into the structure of discourse, Harris came to think that it would be simpler to apply his discourse programme if the sentences in question could be reduced to some canonical form. Thus, passive sentences should be reducible to their active form (ibid.):

> To this end we would use only those statements of the grammar of the language which are true for any sentence of a given form. For example, given any English sentence of the form $N_1 V N_2$ (e.g. *The boss fired Jim*), we can get a sentence with the noun phrases in the reverse order $N_2 - N_1$ (*Jim - the boss*) by changing the suffixes around the verb: *Jim was fired by the boss*. The justification for using such grammatical information in the analysis of a text is that since it is applicable to any $N_1 V N_2$ sentence in English it must also be applicable to any $N_1 V N_2$ sentence in the particular text before us, provided only that it is written in English. The desirability of using such information is that in many cases it makes possible further applications of the discourse-analysis method. ...

> [S]uch use of grammatical information does not replace work that could be done by the discourse-analysis method, nor does it alter the independence of that method. It merely transforms[17] certain sentences of the text into grammatically equivalent sentences ... in such a way that the application of the discourse-analysis method becomes more convenient, or that it becomes possible in particular sections of the text where it was not possible to apply it before.

What Harris means, apparently, is that if a text contains, for example, the sentences (a) *Jim was fired by the boss*, (b) *The boss fired the secretary*, and (c) *The director wanted to fire the janitor*, then it makes sense to put the NPs *the boss* and *the director* in one category, and *Jim*, *the secretary* and *the janitor* in another, the former being the firers and the latter the ones fired. This cannot be achieved on distributional grounds if the sentences are taken as they are, but if they are reduced to their 'elementary' forms by undoing the effect of the transformations that have acted upon them, the distributional similarities stand out clearly. For then we have the following elementary sentences:

(i)   the boss fired Jim   (the active form of the passive (a))
(ii)   the boss fired the secretary   (=(b))
(iii)   the director wanted X   (the matrix S of (c))
(iv)   the director fire the janitor   (the embedded complement-S of (iii))

The elementary sentences (i), (ii), and (iv) show the NPs *the boss* and *the director* in the position of subject, and the NPs *Jim*, *the secretary* and *the janitor* in the position of direct object.

---

[17] This, incidentally, is the first occurrence of the term *transform* in the technical sense of transformational grammar that I have been able to spot.

One has to admit that the link between the supposed transformational re-lationship of active and passive sentences on the one hand, and discourse struc-ture on the other is tenuous. Yet the fact that this transformational relation-ship was observed and, in addition, made use of in a formal sense meant the beginning of a new era in linguistic theory. It may be considered odd that Harris should have come to this insight in the context of discourse analysis, but this is what we find.

It seems anyway that Harris himself was not entirely happy with the re-striction of transformational equivalents to individual texts or discourses. He soon breaks out of this straightjacket and extends the analysis to the language as a whole (1981[1952]:127-128):

> We raise now the question of advancing further in the same direction by using information from outside the text. The information will be of the same kind as we have sought inside the text, namely whether one section of a sentence is equivalent to another … . It will go back to the same basic operation of comparing different sentences. And it will serve the same end: to show that two otherwise different sentences contain the same combination of equivalence classes, even though they may contain different combinations of morphemes. What is new is only that we base our equivalence not on a comparison of two sentences in the text, but on a com-parison of a sentence in the text with sentences outside the text.

(When reading Harris one is repeatedly struck by his extremely unhappy terminology and his roundabout way of presenting arguments. At the same time, however, it is clear that he is carried by a powerful inspiration sus-tained throughout the almost unreadable text. It sometimes is the fate of great innovators to be held back by a scrupulous sense of duty which makes them feel that their readers should share all the circuitous paths and tracks that they had to cover before hitting on the essentials.)

• *The twelve earliest transformations*

Then follows (1981[1952]:130-131) a somewhat haphazard list of twelve sup-posed transformational relationships, only some of which will be mentioned. Co-ordinated constructions with *and* or *but* are considered to be put together transformationally from their component parts. Then:

$\hat{N}_1 \hat{N}_2$, with primary stress on each *N*, indicates that $N_1 = N_2$; e.g. *The pressure P increases* is equivalent to *The pressure increases* and *P increases.*

Then, *I telegraphed that we'll arrive tomorrow* is equivalent to *I telegraphed: We'll arrive tomorrow.* Passive sentences are transformationally derived from corresponding active ones. Furthermore, '*(They seek) the goal of certainty* is equivalent to some such form as *(They seek) certainty as a goal.' Training in medicine* corresponds to *medical training.* Pronouns repeat a prior noun. *They escaped saving nothing* is a transform of *They escaped: They saved nothing. I bought it for you* is a transform of *I bought it* and *I bought for you.*

Many of these 'transformational relationships' were abandoned in the later developments. Harris is clearly feeling his way about and coming up with some good material but also with worthless stuff, without being able yet to tell the one from the other. Meanwhile, we, as modern readers, are captivated as we watch him proceed.

- *The notion of transformation further refined: Harris (1957)*

Harris (1957) is a much elaborated version of Harris's 1955 Presidential Address to the LSA. It is entitled 'Co-occurrence and transformation', where the term *co-occurrence* refers to what came to be called later 'selectional restrictions'. And this is precisely what this long paper (67 pages in Harris (1981)) is about. The notion of text or discourse has now all but disappeared. Only on the very last page does it recur in a marginal context, and only, one feels, to secure at least some continuity with Harris (1952).

- *The notion of transformation is now based entirely on categorial*
  (selectional) restrictions

The central issue in the paper is the fact that all predicates in a language impose certain categorial restrictions on the kind of object to be denoted by their argument terms. Barring metaphor, a violation of these restrictions results in the necessary falsity, and often also the uninterpretability, of the sentence concerned. Thus, the English predicate *bald* requires of its subject term that it denote an object which (a) has real, physical existence, (b) normally has hair or hair-like pile in prototypical places on its surface.[18] When these preconditions are fulfilled, the sentence (proposition) of which *bald* is the main predicate will be true if the proper satisfaction condition of *bald* is fulfilled, namely that the object in question should lack the hair or pile normally found on its surface. It is commonly agreed nowadays that such phenomena are studied more properly in semantics than in syntax, but in those years, when linguistics was still suffering from a semantic phobia, it was felt that they should be accounted for in the theory of syntax.[19]

The reality of categorial or selectional restrictions and their relevance in the setting up of transformational relationships had already been stated in Harris (1952), in the context of discourse analysis. Now, however, the discourse dimension has faded away, and the full emphasis is on the categorial restrictions. Harris then calls attention to the following anomaly in the sentences of natural languages: the co-occurrence regularities are presumably con-

---

[18] A full semantic description of the predicate *bald* involves a little more. Thus, for example, *bald* enters into a number of idiosyncratic combinations like *a bald tire* or *a bald lie*, and in American English also *a bald rock* or *a bald mountain*. Note also that the German word *kahl*, the nearest equivalent of *bald*, has a wider range of categorial possibilities. *Kahl* can be combined with words for tree, landscape, wall, and so on, the condition being that the object in question be normally covered or adorned with growth or decorations. For such cases, English prefers the adjective *bare*.

[19] The idea that syntax should account for categorial selectional restrictions is still prominent in Chomsky (1965), where the pages 75-127 are devoted to an (unsuccessful) attempt at capturing them in syntactic terms. (One central cause of the failure of this attempt lies in the fact that Chomsky wants his rule system to let the predicate be constrained by the categories of its argument terms, whereas the constraining factor is clearly the predicate, which imposes restrictions on its argument term categories.)

veniently statable in terms of subject, direct object, indirect object, etc., with regard to given predicates or predicate classes; yet in actual sentences they often do not manifest themselves in actual subjects, objects, etc., but in different sentence functions. Having stated, for example, that the English predicate *smuggle* requires a subject term that refers to a human or human-like entity, and a direct object term that refers to transportable goods, one finds that the verbal root *smuggle-* often imposes these restrictions on constituents that do not have the status of subject or direct object, as in (1)-(5), or the predicate is not just *smuggle-* but compounded with one or more further elements, as in (6):

(1)   The whisky was smuggled into the country by some hoodlums
(2)   Smugglers of whisky will be prosecuted
(3)   The smuggling of whisky by hoodlums worries the minister
(4)   Whisky-smuggling is becoming a problem
(5)   The whisky-smuggling hoodlums were arrested
(6)   John smuggles and sells whisky

Since Harris wishes to state the co-occurrence regularities in terms of the distribution of the elements concerned in the sentences of a corpus or, preferably, the language as a whole, there is a problem. Harris now proposes the hypothesis that this problem can be solved by decomposing all sentences into their component clauses or clause-like parts and reduce all these to their 'elementary' form, defined by a handful of hopefully simple PS-rules generating canonical IC-structures. The sentences (1)-(6) are thus reduced to the following elementary forms:

(1')   Some hoodlums smuggled the whisky into the country
(2')   X will prosecute Y AND   Y = any x such that [x smuggles whisky]
(3')   X worries the minister AND   X = the fact that [hoodlums smuggle whisky]
(4')   X is becoming a problem AND   X = the fact that [Y smuggle whisky]
(5')   X arrested the hoodlums AND   the hoodlums smuggled whisky
(6')   John smuggles whisky AND   John sells whisky

Now the categorial restrictions imposed by *smuggle* on its argument terms are distributed over the right constituents.

- *The transformations in Harris (1957)*

The bulk of the paper consists of an extensive discussion of a number of proposed transformational relationships in English, only some of which, again, will be mentioned. Thus Harris discusses nominalizations (e.g. *flight* from either *fly* or *flee*), particle displacement (e.g. *slice up the meat* vs *slice the meat up*), conjunction reduction (e.g. (6) above), pronominalization (antecedent resolution, change of 'I' and 'you' in dialogue, etc.), VP-deletion (e.g. *If you do it I will too*), complementation phenomena (e.g. *I want to leave, I promised him to leave, I ordered him to leave, he stopped speaking, he stopped to speak*, etc., etc.), question formation (e.g. *What did he smuggle?*), adjectival subordination (e.g. (5) above). One sees at once that the transformations concerned are a great deal more relevant, and selected with greater care, than those found in Harris (1952).

- *The notion 'kernel' introduced*

Towards the end of the paper the notion 'kernel' is introduced:

> Given any sentence, we can check it for all transformations; we will then find the sentence to consist of a sequence of one or more *underlying* sentences — those which have been transformed into the shapes that we see in our sentence — with various introductory or combining elements ... We have thus a factorization of each sentence into transformations and elementary underlying sentences and combiners; the elementary sentences will be called sentences of the kernel of the grammar. Any two different sentences will have different factorizations, either the kernel sentences or the transformations being different; but one sentence may have two different fac-torizations, since two one-directional transformations (applied to partly different kernel sentences) may yield the same resultant sentence (homonymy).
>
> The kernel is the set of elementary sentences and combiners, such that all sentences of the language are obtained from one or more kernel sentences (with combiners) by means of one or more transformations. Each kernel sentence is of course a particular construction of classes, with particular members of the classes co-occurring. If many different types of construction were exemplified by the various kernel sentences, the kernel would be of no great interest, especially not of any practical interest. But kernels generally contain very few constructions; and applying transformations to these few constructions suffices to yield all the many sentence constructions of the language.   Harris (1981[1957]:197-198)

Then follows a, perhaps somewhat optimistic, list of seven basic English sen-tence constructions.

- *Transformations change from 'horizontal' relations between sentences to 'vertical' generative operations*

One notes that the elementary sentences are called 'underlying', and that the notion of transformation has shifted from a formally statable symmetrical correspondence relation between pairs of given sentences to an operation per-formed on one or more elementary sentences. The symmetrical 'horizontal' view is in the process of being given up and replaced with an asymmetrical 'vertical' view, which allows for mutual ordering relations among trans-formations. One can see this coming throughout the paper, but it is finally put into explicit words in the quote just given.

The obvious next step was no longer to speak of underlying *sentences* but of underlying *structures*, since it is clearly counter-productive to generate first a full (elementary) sentence, complete with verb agreement and other near-to-surface trimmings, only to have to undo these processes for transformations to apply which will then require a different set of trimmings. This step was not taken by Harris in this paper, but soon became generally accepted in TGG.

The important thing to note here is that Harris is in the process of moving, in Hockett's terms (4.4.4), from an 'item-and-arrangement' to an 'item-and-process' concept of grammar writing, where hypothetical underlying forms are introduced in order to simplify and generalize the description.[20]

- *The kernel is finite; the transformations make the set of sentences of a language infinite*

Then, the kernel sentences form a finite set, but the combinations and extensions afforded by the transformations produce an infinite set of sentences (1981[1957]:201-202; italics mine):

> Finally, as has been mentioned, the kernel (including the list of combiners) is finite; all the unbounded possibilities of language are properties of the transformational operations. This is of interest because it is in general impossible to set up a reasonable grammar or description of a language that provides for its being finite. Though the sample of the language out of which the grammar is derived is of course finite, the grammar which is made to generate all the sentences of that sample will be found to generate also many other sentences, and unboundedly many sentences of unbounded [i.e. unrestricted; P.A.M.S.] length. If we were to insist on a finite language, we would have to include in our grammar several highly arbitrary and numerical conditions — saying, for example, that in a given position there are not more than three occurrences of *and* between N [i.e. NP; P.A.M.S.]. Since a grammar therefore cannot help generating an unbounded language, it is desirable to have the features which yield this unboundedness separate from the rest of the grammar.
>
> Our picture of a language, then, includes a finite number of actual kernel sentences, all cast in a small number of sentence structures built out of a few morpheme classes by means of a few constructional rules; a set of combining and introducing elements; and a set of elementary transformations such that one or more transformations may be applied to any kernel sentence or any sequence of kernel sentences, and such that any properly transformed sentences may be added sequentially by means of the combiners.

[20] Chomsky's comment in (1964) on the concept of transformation, as presented in Harris (1957), fails to take account of the fact that Harris had, by that time, already moved towards 'vertical' transformations:

> A grammatical transformation is defined, from this point of view, as a (symmetrical) relation holding between two sentence forms if corresponding positions in the two forms are filled by the same n-tuples of expressions. This ... is a structural relation holding of sentences and sentence forms generated by a taxonomic, IC grammar (as in Harris, 1951a, chapter 16). The notions of "co-occurrence relation" and "generative transformation" are rather different in formal properties as well as in their role in actual syntactic description, and a great deal of confusion can result from failure to distinguish them. Thus it makes no sense to arrange co-occurrence relations "in sequence", but generative transformations can (and, in practice, must) be ordered and applied in sequence. ... Furthermore, co-occurrence is a relation defined on actual sentences, while generative transformations apply to abstract structures that often bear no close relation to actual sentences. Chomsky (1964:62-63)

As has been shown, it was precisely the notion of what Chomsky here calls 'generative transformation' that was being developed in Harris (1957).

- *The infinity of natural languages used later as an argument against behaviourism*

The mathematical fact, mentioned here by Harris, that the sentences generated by an adequate grammar of a natural language form an infinite set, gains relevance in light of the important debate that sprang up a few years later between proponents of the behaviourist and the cognitivist view of language. The anti-behaviourists, especially Chomsky (1959a), maintained that the kind of rule system required for the generation of an infinite set of sentences cannot be acquired by an organism constrained by the principles of behaviourist conditioning processes. Two further assumptions are necessary: (a) the assumption of an innate cerebral 'pre-wiring' predisposing (young) language learners to expect specific properties in the language of their environment, and (b) the assumption of complex computational processes in the human mind, besides the conditioning processes postulated by the behaviourists. These computational processes must then be assumed to be hidden from awareness and operating as automatic routines given selected inputs. But both assumptions transgress the limits set by the behaviourist paradigm in the study of the causation of human behaviour.

- *No notion of recursivity yet to account for the infinity of the set of sentences of a language*

Moreover, one notices that Harris points at the transformations as the source of the infinity of a natural language but does not mention recursiveness as a possible source, as in early Chomskyan generative grammar.[21] It is probably fair to attribute this to the fact that, at this time anyway, Harris did not yet have a sharp notion of what constitutes a rule of grammar and what the mathematical properties are of rules and rule systems. We shall see in a moment that from this point of view Chomsky was clearly ahead of him.

- *A grammar consists of constructional rules and transformations*

A language is seen as consisting of (a) a set of sentences (kernel or derived), (b) a lexicon, and (c) a grammar consisting of constructional (i.e. Phrase Structure) rules and transformations. This latter point is of interest since this has remained the overall structure of a transformational syntax in most varieties of TGG. In his (1957) Harris is clearly well on his way towards the theory of TGG as developed in different varieties in the '60s and the '70s.

- *Transformations considered necessary in the description of natural languages*

Interestingly, Harris maintains, though only in a cursory way and not as a central point of theory, that natural languages cannot be described in terms of PS-rules alone: transformations are a necessary complement (1981[1957]:167):

---

[21] System A given at the outset of this section generates exactly 768 different sentences. However, the mere addition of an optional rule like "A → A + A" makes the output set infinite, due to the possibility of applying this rule recursively.

Constructions including two V[erbs] (*let go, want to have met, stop going*, etc.) are complicated in their details, and cannot be completely structured without the aid of transformations.

At this point in the development of Harris's notion of transformation, i.e. in the period between 1955 and 1957, Harris clearly advocates a new model of grammatical description where the PS-rule system generating kernel sentences and the transformational rule system are complementary to each other: both are needed and neither has the sole right to legitimacy.

- *Harris's position changed in (1965)*

In Harris (1965) the position has changed. In this paper the basis is laid for what was to become Tree Adjoining Grammar (Joshi, Levy & Takahashi 1975). Harris distinguishes here between a *string analysis* and a *constituent analysis* of sentences, the former being an analysis in terms of transformational adjuncts to a central matrix sentence frame, the latter being a description in terms of IC-structure. He then says (1981[1965]:238)

> To interrelate these analyses, it is necessary to understand that these are not competing theories, but rather complement each other in the description of sentences.[22]

---

[22] A footnote is added here:
> The pitting of one linguistic tool against another has in it something of the absolutist post-war temper of social institutions, but is not required by the character and range of these tools of analysis.

In his Introduction to Chomsky ([1956]), Chomsky obviously takes this footnote as being directed at him personally. He answers by interpreting Harris's position in this respect as a consequence of the instrumentalist, non-realist attitude towards grammars advocated by Harris throughout his life ([1956]:38):

> This effort [i.e. of showing the inadequacy of pure PS-grammars; P.A.M.S] may well be inexplicable to someone who adopts a nonrealist interpretation of linguistic theory. Harris, for example, seems to regard it as a curious aberration, perhaps to be explained in sociological terms [(1965, note 6)]. In his view, there are no "competing theories", and "pitting of one linguistic tool against another" is senseless. Alternative theories are equally valid, as alternative procedures of analysis are equally valid. ... This is, I believe, a faithful interpretation of post-Bloomfieldian structuralism in its more explicit varieties, though, as noted, it leaves much unexplained in the practice of theorists of this persuasion.

It is doubtful, however. whether it is indeed the case that Harris's 1965 position reflects his instrumentalist philosophy of science and stands in contrast to Chomsky's professed realist view. Both positions with regard to grammatical transformations are consistent with both philosophies. What Harris's footnote, if directed at Chomsky personally, does seem to show is Harris's irritation at what he must have perceived as Chomsky's all too radical 'absolutist' political views, parallelled by his pugnacious and divisive style of propagating (his version of) TGG. (Murray (1994:226) quotes Chomsky (1969:22) as saying 'I found that I had political interests in common with him', specifying these as being of a 'leftist' character.) It is obvious that in 1965 the two were, to put it mildly, no longer friends, and one may surmise that by this time Harris felt the need to distance himself from what seemed to be becoming the standard view in linguistics and stake out his own territory. One discerns here the effects of the sociology of the discipline: it is no longer a

In this article, a transformational description (in terms of tree adjunction, i.e. insertion of subtrees either as an addition to, or as a filler of an empty position in a given matrix tree) is a different way of looking at grammatical structures and sentences, on an equal footing with a description in terms of PS-rules but serving different purposes, especially with regard to semantic interpretation. The different properties of a language 'can be used as the basis for a description of the whole language' (ibid.). It is clear that in (1965) Harris has abandoned the idea that transformational rules form an indispensable part of an adequate grammar of a language.

- *Harris prefigures Generative Semantics*

Finally, one notices that Harris places less and less emphasis on a formalized discovery procedure with only the operations of segmentation and classification establishing elements on different levels on the basis of the distributional properties of the segments that have been isolated. Instead, his procedure has become much more heuristic and intuitive. Meaning has also become a great deal more prominent. Not only does Harris make liberal use of semantic criteria as a heuristic means in setting up classifications, he also considers introducing semantic criteria into the grammars of languages (1981[1957]:203):

> When we have transformations which are associated with a meaning change, it is usually possible to attribute the meaning change to the special morphemes (combiners, introducers, subclasses of the primary V[erb]) in whose environment the transformation occurs. To what extent, and in what sense, transformations hold meaning constant is a matter for investigation; but enough is known to make transformations a possible tool for reducing the complexity of sentences under semantically controlled conditions.

In this respect, one has to say, Harris is more daring and more advanced than Chomsky around the mid-1950s. What Harris says here prefigures the theory proposed in Katz & Postal (1964), which led directly to the development known as Generative Semantics and dominated TGG from the late sixties till the mid-seventies (for detailed comment see section 7.3.2 below).

4.5.3 Early TGG: Noam Chomsky

Avram Noam Chomsky was born in Philadelphia in 1928. His father, William Chomsky, who had emigrated from the Ukraine, was principal of a Jewish school in Philadelphia and an authority on early Hebrew grammars. Chomsky confides (1975[1956]:25,50) that, as a young man, he proofread his father's edition of *David Kimhi's Hebrew Grammar*, to which he attributes the fact that he knew some Hebrew when he began to study with Harris in 1947. In that year he read Harris's *Methods in Structural Linguistics* (which was not published until 1951) in proof, and gave 'much-needed assistance with the manuscript' (Harris 1951:Preface). Under Harris's direction he wrote his unpublished MA-thesis *Morphophonemics of Modern Hebrew* (1951), accord-

---

contest between two individuals, but involves claims as to what is considered 'standard', regardless of what is to be considered right.

ing to himself (Chomsky 1975[1956]:25-6, 51) a systematic application to Hebrew of Bloomfield's system of ordered morphophonemic rules specifying the phonemic composition of morphological variants (allomorphs) in terms of underlying morphemes and changes undergone by them.[23]

In 1951 he was awarded a Junior Fellowship of the Society of Fellows at Harvard University, a position he kept till 1955, when he was appointed to the fledgling linguistics department at MIT under Morris Halle. He has stayed at MIT ever since.

During his years as a Harvard Junior Fellow he wrote the first version of *The Logical Structure of Linguistic Theory* ([1956] here, also referred to as *LSLT*), a bulky work of about 500 pages, which remained unpublished till 1975. One chapter of this work was presented as a PhD-thesis at the University of Pennsylvania in 1955 under the title *Transformational Analysis.* While working on [1956] he 'discussed all aspects of this material frequently and in great detail with Zellig Harris, whose influence is obvious throughout', we are told by Chomsky (1975[1956]:4).

As a Harvard Junior Fellow he also wrote a number of articles, mostly of a technical and mathematical nature, reflecting his preoccupation, during those years, with the formal and mathematical aspects of rules and rule systems. In 1957 followed the little book *Syntactic Structures*, published by Mouton, The Hague. This book had the effect of introducing TGG to the linguistic world at

---

[23] In the text just referred to, i.e. (Chomsky 1975[1956]:51), which is the 1975 Introduction to [1956], he criticizes Bloomfield as follows:

> Thus, [Bloomfield's] "Menomini morphophonemics" ... is virtually a generative grammar with ordered rules, but Bloomfield seemed quite skeptical of the notions that he made use of in this study. For example, in his *Language* (Holt, 1933, p.213) he described ordering as an artifact invented by the linguist, as compared with order of constituents, which is "part of language".

He then refers to Chomsky (1964:70), where the same is said, and where Bloomfield's words are interpreted as:

> one aspect of the general antipathy to theory (the so-called "anti-mentalism") that Bloomfield developed and bequeathed to modern linguistics. This tendency fitted well with the operationalism, verificationism and behaviorism that formed a dominant intellectual mood in the early 1930s.

It should be clear that this criticism, as well as its intellectual interpretation, is entirely false. All that Bloomfield said, and meant, in (1933:213) is that the order of elements in a construction is observable data, whereas the ordering of rules in a grammar is part of the linguist's theory or hypothesis (whether realist or instrumentalist, mentalist or behaviourist). In fact, Chomsky gives the correct interpretation of Bloomfield's position in this respect in (1957:81), where he acknowledges that Bloomfield's view in this matter is no different from his own.

One gathers that somewhere between 1957 and 1964 Chomsky decided that he should advertise a radical change in his attitude with respect to Bloomfield. In Chomsky (1964), the appreciation for the grand old man of American linguistics, still obvious in Chomsky (1957), has made way for a totally unfounded attitude of rejection and contempt. What prompted Chomsky to turn on Bloomfield in this manner is probably more a matter of psychological interpretation than of the history of linguistics. See also note 25 below.

large and is therefore regarded as the official beginning of the 'transformational period' in linguistics.[24]

[24] There is an issue concerning Chomsky's position and status in the world of American
linguistics of those years. Chomsky himself likes to stress that he 'was working at the time
in isolation to a considerable extent' (1975[1956]:25), and that he could not 'get [his
work] published' (1969:33). He even went so far as to say (1982a:42-43; quoted from
Murray (1994:246)):

> As I look back over my own relation to the field [linguistics], at every point it has
> been completely isolated, or almost completely isolated. I do not see that the situa-
> tion is very different now. [...] I cannot think of any time when the kind of work that
> I was doing was of any interest to any more than a very tiny fraction of people in
> the field.

Murray's comment is: 'I find it hard not to consider this delusional' (ibid.).

Chomsky's self-appraisal, in this matter, is not supported by Murray (1994: chapter 9),
who presents evidence that Chomsky was held in high regard by his elder colleagues,
including his teacher Harris (who mentioned him regularly and appreciatively in his writings of the period). Murray shows, moreover, that Chomsky's assertion that he could not
get his work published does not bear scrutiny.

As regards [1956], Chomsky informs us (1975[1956]:2-3), that the first version of
[1956] was finished in 1955, but that in early 1956 he started revising it for publication.
Parts of the manuscript were then offered to the Technology Press of MIT but rejected:

> with the not unreasonable observation that an unknown author taking a rather
> unconventional approach should submit articles based on this material to profes-
> sional journals before planning to publish such a comprehensive and detailed manu-
> script as a book. This was no easy matter, however. The one article I had submitted
> on this material to a linguistics journal had been rejected, virtually by return mail.

The article in question had been submitted, unwisely, to the anti-American, anti-formalist,
Europe-oriented journal *Word*, which had been founded during the war by a group of
European refugee linguists, led by Jakobson and centered in New York (Murray 1994:
215-219). It was rejected by one of its editors, André Martinet, on the grounds of its giving
an 'impression ... of utter drabness, unrelieved by any glint indicating some hidden awareness of what a real language is' (Murray 1994:229, quoting from a letter by Martinet).
(But *Word* did publish an article by Chomsky in 1961, and also, in 1959, his review of
Greenberg (1957).) Another article was submitted to *Language* and accepted (Chomsky
1955b). Other articles were published in non-linguistic journals like the *Journal of Symbolic Logic* (Chomsky 1953) or the *Institute of Radio Engineering Transactions on Information Theory* (Chomsky 1956).

In fact, most of the articles Chomsky published before 1957 had been solicited by editors of journals or conference proceedings, including the article that was rejected by *Word*.
As for his *Morphophonemics of Modern Hebrew* and *The Logical Structure of Linguistic
Theory*, according to Murray (1994:230), he himself blocked their publication, contrary to
his own statements, despite the fact that 'two publishers were interested in publishing
[1956] in 1957' (ibid.). *Syntactic Structures* was published by Mouton at the instigation of
Morris Halle, who submitted the manuscript for publication (Murray 1994:230). Chomsky had, moreover, the active support of influential figures like Jakobson and Bloch, and
received a sympathetic hearing from structuralist colleagues in general. Instead of the linguistic establishment marginalizing him, as Chomsky himself has repeatedly suggested, it
was he who insisted on forcing a break with all linguistics prior to 1951 and much of it
after. Regarding his *Morphophonemics of Modern Hebrew* (MMH) of 1951, for example, he
observes (1975[1956]:28):

> Thus the approach of *MMH* represented a sharp break with the procedural theories
> of structural linguistics in any of the clearly formulated versions of this approach.

In view of the widespread yet erroneous belief that the notion of trans-formation in the theory of grammar originated not with Harris (as we saw in 4.5.2) but with Chomsky, we shall now have a closer look at the way Chomsky was introduced to this notion by Zellig Harris, and how Chomsky has been less than generous, in this respect, with regard to his teacher.

- *Chomsky's earliest notion of transformation*

Chomsky became acquainted with the notion of transformation through Harris:

> When I began to investigate generative syntax more seriously a few years later [i.e. after 1951, P.A.M.S.], I was able to adapt for this purpose a new concept that had been developed by Zellig Harris and some of his students, namely, the concept of "grammatical transformation." It was quickly apparent that with this new concept, many of the inadequacies of the model that I had used earlier could be overcome.
>
> Chomsky (1975[1956]:40-41)

There was, however, right from the beginning a difference in the way he approached the notion. In general one can say that Chomsky's early work is characterized much more by an emphasis on the formal and mathematical properties of rules and rule systems than the work produced by Harris in the same period. For him, transformations were rules, formal instructions with an input and an output, not, as they were for Harris, the statement of regular correspondences between pairs of sentences. Chomsky took the 'vertical' view of transformations, with deeper structures transformed into less deep structures by successive transformations, whereas Harris's view was mostly 'horizontal'. It is true that in his article 'Co-occurrence and transformation' of 1957 Harris tentatively presents a 'vertical' view, as noted above, but he never elaborated this the way Chomsky did.

In view of his own statement (1975[1956]:25-6, 51; see above) that MMH is in fact a sys-tematic application of Booomfield's principles, this is hard to understand.

In general, one notices a tendency in Chomsky's autobiographical notes and comments to try to convince the public of both the completeness and the consistency of his thoughts from the beginning to the present day. Thus, in the 1975 Introduction to [1956], he consis-tently calls his 1951 MA-thesis on the morphophonemics of Hebrew a 'generative gram-mar', although 'the syntactic component was rudimentary' (1975[1956]:28). He also main-tains (1975[1956]:7) that [1956], completed in 1955-1956, already contained the distinc-tion between competence and performance (which in fact began to crop up around 1964; in [1956] no mention is made of the distinction and the terms do not occur). It is stated, fur-thermore, that the Cartesian rationalist basis, claimed in the mid-1960s to underlie his work, though 'not discussed in *LSLT*, … [lay] in the immediate background of this work' (1975[1956]:13). Yet no trace of evidence of this claim is to be found in [1956]. Then we read that psychological realism, as opposed to Harris's earlier instrumentalism, 'is not discussed [in [1956]], but … lay in the immediate background of my own thinking' (1975 [1956]:35). Also: 'In *LSLT*, the "realist" position is taken for granted' (1975[1956]:37), and, more strongly: '*LSLT* is devoted to an exploration of this realist interpretation of linguistic theory, primarily in the area of syntax, and to the choice between theories that are plainly in conflict' (1975[1956]:39). Again, there is nothing in the text that would support this claim (see also note 32 below).

- *Chomsky's morphophonemic rules for Modern Hebrew*

It is reasonable to assume that Chomsky's tendency to focus on rules and rule systems found its origin in his MA-thesis of 1951, which was a strongly rule-oriented description of the system of morphophonemic alternations in Modern Hebrew. This work is not available in the normal way, as it was never published, but one gets an impression on the basis of Chomsky (1975[1956]:25-26). Applying Bloomfield's (not Harris's) method of morphophonemic description he sets up underlying forms and formulates ordered morphophonemic rules. In the Introduction to [1956] Chomsky discusses this work (1975[1956]:25-28), presenting as an example the morphophonemics of the Hebrew root *mlk* ('king'). Its treatment is described in words rather than in rules, but the text makes it clear that in the MA-thesis the treatment was in rules and not in words. We can present the following reconstruction of the rules (phonological notation is disregarded; '/ X—Y' stands for 'in the environment X—Y, where either X or Y may be empty; 'C' stands for 'consonant', 'V' for 'vowel'; # is word boundary):

System B: *Morphophonemic rules for Hebrew root* mlk *('king')*

(i)a. mlk → malk- / —i# OR —a#
   b. mlk → malak- / —im# OR —ey
(ii)   k   → x / V—V   (spirantization of intervocalic *k*)
(iii) V   → Ø / —CVCV́   (reduction of antepretonic vowel)

Rule (ia) generates the forms *malk-i* ('my king'), *malk-a* ('queen'), which are not affected by either rule (ii) or rule (iii). Rule (ib) generates *malak-im* ('kings') and *malak-ey—* ('kings of—', i.e. the so-called 'construct state' of Hebrew grammar). Now, however, spirantization of *k* takes place according to rule (ii), yielding, respectively, *malax-im* and *malax-ey—*. Rule (iii) then deletes the antepretonic vowel (Hebrew accent is word-final; construct state structures are considered one word). This gives, respectively, *mlax-ím* and *malx-ey—*. Chomsky argues, correctly, that the ordering of the rules is essential to get the right results. His MA-thesis of 1951 contains '45 general rules, most of which have many subrules' (1975[1956]:26).

- *Chomsky's 1951 morphophonemic rules are transformational and derive from Bloomfield*

It is not difficult to envisage such a system, and it must have been an intellectual pleasure to build it. The question, however, is: do these rules have the format of context-sensitive PS-rules, as is implied by Chomsky, or are they less constrained and therefore transformational? Chomsky himself affirms (1975[1956]):40) that his MA-thesis 'was an explicit generative grammar, but not a transformational grammar'. Yet this cannot be correct for the rules (ii) and (iii) given above.

A PS-rule, whether context-free or context-sensitive, can only take an input, and, in the case of context-sensitive rules, also an environment specification, consisting of symbols actually generated in the output string. Symbols like 'V' or 'C', which function as variables ranging over actual vowels and consonants, respectively, are not admissible, on pain of the system becoming trans-formational. The formal theory of grammatical rule types, set up by Chomsky himself (see 4.7.1), assigns to rules containing symbols that act as variables over actually generated symbols the status of transformations.

Since Chomsky (1951) is, by his own admission (1975[1956]:25-6, 51; see above), a direct application of Bloomfield's (1939) system of morphophonemic description, it follows that, at least with regard to the morphophonemic component of a grammar, Bloomfield already, though only implicitly, operated with transformational rules. It is, therefore, fair to state that Chomsky's concept of transformation, unlike Harris's concept, has its roots in Bloomfield. Harris was, at least till 1955, at pains to avoid Bloomfield's 'underlying' forms and adhered to a strict 'item-and-arrangement' model. Chomsky, apparently, decided early on to deviate from that model and apply a rule system of the 'item-and-process' style (though, of course, Hockett's 1954 article, in which the distinction is put into explicit terms, had not yet been published).

• *Chomsky's 'vertical' transformation concept derived from Bloomfield*
Chomsky probably did not realize straight away, in 1951, that his morphophonemic rule system had the formal properties of a transformational system. When he learned about grammatical transformations in Harris's classes he would not immediately have seen the connection between these and his own work on Hebrew morphophonemics. Yet it is only natural that he should digest and integrate the Harris concept less in a 'horizontal' and more in a 'vertical' way, since he had accustomed himself to thinking in terms of formally explicit, mutually ordered generative rules with hypothetical underlying forms at different levels of depth.

In time, however, Chomsky did link up Bloomfield's principles of morphophonemic description and the concept of transformation. This appears from footnote 6 in (1957:81), which is worth quoting in full:

> In determining which of two related forms is more central, we are thus following the reasoning outlined by Bloomfield for morphology: " ... when forms are partially similar, there may be a question as to which one we had better take as the underlying form ... the structure of the language may decide this question for us, since, taking it one way, we get an unduly complicated description, and taking it the other way, a relatively simple one." (*Language* [New York, 1933], p. 218). Bloomfield continues by pointing out that "this same consideration often leads us to *set up* an artificial underlying form". We have also found this insight useful in transformational analysis, as, e.g., when we set up the terminal string *John - C - have+en - be+ing - read* underlying the kernel sentence "John has been reading".[25]

---

[25] One notes the entirely different tone with respect to Bloomfield. Here Chomsky is still appreciative and friendly, but in (1964) and in the 1975 Introduction to ([1956]) there is bitter hostility (see also note 23). This difference in tone is observable also with regard to his fellow post-Bloomfieldian American linguists during the years following 1957. By 1965, as we have seen (note 22), the references to Zellig Harris have become definitely unfriendly, and many others are subjected to the same treatment.

The last sentence of this quote shows the connection. Given the 'vertical' character of Bloomfield's system of ordered morphophonemic rules, it is only natural that Chomsky should then further develop the concept of transformation as a grammatical rule, to be ordered with respect to other such rules, in the same 'vertical' fashion as Bloomfield's model of morphophonemic rules.

- *In other respects Chomsky's notion of transformation was much like Harris's*

We have seen that the origin of Harris's concept of transformation lay in his observation that selectional restrictions imposed by predicates can only be stated in a regular form if the sentences of a language (or text) are reduced to a canonical, elementary form by means of transformational operations. This is the concept Chomsky encountered in Harris's classes, and which he subsequently moulded into an 'item-and-process' concept with underlying or 'basic' forms and a system of ordered transformational rules as a device to turn them into less basic forms, closer to the surface. How he combined the 'horizontal' and the 'vertical' concepts is shown in chapter 9 of [1956] (the chapter that was presented as his PhD-dissertation in 1955) ([1956]:303-304):

> In the same connection, it seems that certain sentences of presumably different types are related to one another. Thus "he was here" and "was he here", or "John hit Bill" and "Bill was hit by John" seem related in a way in which such pairs as "John hit Bill" and "Bill hit John", "John hit Bill" and "John was hitting Bill" are not. Exactly what this relation is is not clear. It certainly has some connection with meaning. On the other hand, it is not synonymy or logical equivalence. This is clear enough in the case of question and answer, but it is also true in the case of active and passive. We have at present no way of explaining such relations.
>
> A related phenomenon is that in each of these pairs of related sentences, one seems somehow more basic than the other and more central as far as the structure of the language is concerned. A study of the arrangement of English words in sentences will normally treat first such "basic" patterns as subject-predicate (actor-action), using as examples such simple declarative sentences as "John was here" or "I like John", and will discuss passives, questions, imperatives, sentences with relative clauses, etc., only as subsidiary and derived phenomena. ...
>
> The significance of this class of basic sentences, the manner of its construction, and the nature of the relations between basic sentences and "derived" sentences of noncentral sentence types remains to be explored. The process of construction of derived sentences is not an unfamiliar one. It makes intuitive sense to form the passive of a given active sentence, or to construct a question corresponding to a given declarative, active or passive.

This is precisely the notion of transformation as presented in Harris (1957). Since we are told by Chomsky himself that during the years leading up to 1955, when he wrote [1956] and Harris's work was leading towards his 1955 inaugural address to the LSA, published as Harris (1957), he 'discussed all aspects of this material frequently and in great detail with Zellig Harris, whose influence is obvious throughout' (Chomsky 1975[1956]:4), we must conclude that, at least for a few years, the two were thinking along the same lines, mutually influencing each other. As is well-known, it is usually impossible, in such a process of intellectual osmosis, to determine in hindsight exactly who made which contributions.[26]

[26] In many publications after 1960 Chomsky is at pains to emphasize that his 'generative' ('vertical') notion of transformation is essentially different from Harris's 'symmetrical' ('horizontal') concept. We have already observed (note 20) that this is not quite correct. In the 1975 Introduction to [1956] (1975[1956]:42) he supports his view by quoting selectively and out of context from Harris (1957):

> Understood in these terms, transformational analysis is a procedure supplementary to the procedures of structural linguistics, which are complete in themselves. Thus in undertaking transformational analysis, we may assume that the methods of structural linguistics (say, those of Harris's *Methods*) have been applied, along with elicitation techniques if an informant is available. In Harris's original formulation, "we will assume the whole of the usual structural grammar of the language ..." and then turn to "one of the few types of outside questions that are still relevant to it" ("Co-occurrence," pp. 293, 286), namely, determination of co-occurrence sets (these questions are relevant to structural linguistics in that they "are couched in terms of the raw data of structural morphology"). Having applied the procedures of structural linguistics, the linguist can apply the further procedures of transformational analysis and then turn to discourse analysis and other applications, selecting those transformational relations that are useful for the purpose at hand.

One notes that the two references to Harris (1957) are disjointed: one is taken from p. 293 (=1981:154), the other from p.286 (=1981:145). Yet the two are strung together as if they were part of the same passage. This, however, falsifies Harris's intention. On p. 286 Harris is still addressing established structural linguistics, where co-occurrence relations would be regarded as being marginal, a point of view he wishes politely to correct, and not to defend, as is suggested by the way Chomsky quotes him:

> From the point of view of structural linguistics, this amounts to asking one of the few types of outside questions that are still relevant to it, for these are questions which are couched in terms of the raw data of structural morphology (the occurrence of morphemes in sentences), and which lead to additional information about inter-class relations, yet which had not been asked in the original study of class environments.   Harris (1957:286)

On p. 293, on the other hand, the ground is being prepared for the proposed transformational analysis:

> Just how much grammatical knowledge is needed before transformations can be investigated depends in part on how much work is put into discovering the transformations. It may be enough merely to identify the morphemes and to have a constructional analysis of the simpler sentence types. ... For the present formulation, however, we will assume the whole of the usual structural grammar of the language, in order not to have to distinguish parts which are not needed.   Harris (1957:293)

There is nothing in these two passages that would contradict the 'generative' concept of transformations as forming an ordered rule system within the grammar. In section 4.5.2 we saw that towards the end of (1957) Harris explicitly develops that same 'generative' or 'vertical' notion. Yet Chomsky does not refer to those passages at all.

Continuing his attack on Harris's transformation concept, Chomsky then goes on to quote only from Harris (1965), which is indeed different from (1957) but hardly relevant for the question of what the relation is between Chomsky's and Harris's early transformational concepts. Chomsky concludes by saying (1975[1956]:43):

> In *LSLT*, transformations are understood in a very different sense; it probably would have been preferable to select a different terminology instead of adapting Harris's in this rather different context.

• *Chomsky's originality: (1)* Syntactic Structures *created order and clarity in theoretical linguistics*

Even so, looking at the longer lines of development, we may make an attempt to sort out where and how, during the years leading up to 1957, Chomsky's ideas began to differ from Harris's, and what his own, original contributions were. It would seem, then, that his originality lies, first, in the systematic survey and critical evaluation of the positions taken and the notions used by the various structuralist linguists of the day, and in the general conclusions he drew from that investigation. Much of this work is reflected in [1956] and the articles written in the years preceding 1957. *Syntactic Structures*, of 1957, is largely a succinctly formulated synthesis of this work. It had the effect of a formal 'mopping up' operation: the rather motley variety of different approaches and techniques had been charted, ordered and evaluated.

This was a non-trivial exercise which in itself had an enormous influence: before 1957 linguistics was a somewhat messy field, characterized by groping attempts to gain empirical access to linguistic structures and their functioning. Those who studied *Syntactic Structures* seriously, in those years, had the experience of suddenly seeing clarity and system. The 'mopping up' started with *Morphophonemics of Modern Hebrew*, which helped to clarify the formal properties of the rule system devised and employed by Bloomfield for the description of morphophonemic phenomena. It ended, practically speaking, with Postal (1964), which reviews structuralist work by Bloch, Wells, Harris, Pike, Hockett and others, and concludes, with more than a slight bias, that all this work suffered from the fact that it remained constrained within the bounds of PS-rules, stressing the need for a transformational component in syntactic analysis.

• *(2) Greater emphasis on formal properties of rules and rule systems*

Much more than Harris, Chomsky concentrated, in the early years, on the structure of rules and rule systems, and on their mathematical properties. This has proved useful in that greater familiarity with the mathematical space of rules and rule systems helps in taking what we have called the 'high view' and thus in making relevant general formal statements about them (see 4.7.1). On the other hand, however, there is the risk, commonly adhering to mathematical notions in the empirical sciences, that researchers impose mathematical distinctions on the empirical material and strive for analyses that cut the material at mathematical, and not at empirical seams. All too often a system of analysis or description is devised, or preferred, on account of mathematical regularity, whereas more often than not the important restrictions

---

It is now clear that this is contrary to the historical facts, and another manifestation of Chomsky's tendency (cp. note 24) to present himself as a totally new phenomenon in modern linguistics whose roots lie in a much more distant and more dignified past (for which he did not develop an interest until the early 1960s, and then only in so far as it could be used to 'legitimize' his own points of view).

imposed by nature on its products are mathematically uninteresting and derive their interest from their practical functionality.

- *(3) The concept of transformational rule made more precise and integrated into the theory of grammar*

More than any other linguist Chomsky has succeeded in developing a notion of transformational rule that has proved fruitful in that it has led to a host of developments, some of which have given rise to the feeling, whether justified or not, that they produced real insight into central questions of language structure. From our late 20th-century perspective it seems fair to say that it was Chomsky who really pushed through the notion of a transformational rule system as a component of a generative grammar, and that this notion has proved of greater value than Harris's, which was never properly integrated into a model of grammatical description. Chomsky brought together Harris's notion of transformation with Bloomfield's notion of morphophonemic rule and Hockett's notion of 'item-and-process'-style grammatical description. This mix has proved extremely fertile.

Since Chomsky (1957) there has been no essential change in what is considered the overall structure of a formal generative grammar of a natural language. Such a grammar will consist of (a) an ordered set of formation rules of the type exemplified in System A above, i.e. PS-rules, generating deep structures; (b) an ordered set of transformational rules generating surface structures; and (c) an ordered set of morphological, morphophonemic and phonological rules generating, eventually, phonological representations (see, for example, 1957:46). Additions and refinements were introduced later, such as, for example, the principle that the only form of recursion in a grammar is S-recursion, or the principle of cyclic ordering for some transformations (which apply first to the most deeply embedded S-structure, then to the next one up, and so on till the top S-node is reached). Also, after 1963-1964, the addition to the grammar was accepted of a semantic component 'which assigns a semantic interpretation to a deep structure' (Chomsky 1966b:16). But the overall structure of a grammar has remained as specified above, and in accordance with Harris (1957:334-338) – where reference is made to Chomsky (1955a).

- *(4) Behaviourism destroyed*

Then, Chomsky has clearly been an important factor in the destruction of behaviourism. Here, too, Chomsky got his cue from an existing intellectual climate where the issues were discussed with great intensity. In this case he benefited from an atmosphere of anti-behaviourist dissent that existed at Harvard in the mid-1950s, but he soon became a leading figure of this movement:

> There were some murmurs of dissent toward behaviorism in mid-fifties psychology, especially in Cambridge, out of which the new approach was emerging, an approach whose birthday, according to George Miller, is 11 September 1956, the second day of a symposium at Harvard which ended with Chomsky outlining the arguments behind *Syntactic Structures*.   R.A. Harris (1993:55)

His (1959) review of Skinner's *Verbal Behavior* has become proverbial, despite its very serious flaws. MacCorquodale (1970), in particular, has shown that Chomsky misrepresented Skinner's position in many, often essential ways, and that his attack pertained more to behaviourism as a general method and philosophy of psychology than to Skinner's version of it. Yet the rhetoric of the attack was such that Skinner was left more or less by the wayside, defenceless and ridiculed by the younger generation of linguists and psychologists, who now felt free to speak and write again openly of the mind as an object of scientific enquiry.

There can be no doubt that this has had a liberating effect on psychology as well as on linguistics. It was obviously necessary to break out of the behaviourist straightjacket and to embrace the new metaphor of computation, introduced first into psychology and then into all the human sciences after 1960.

- *(5) Linguistics placed in the context of philosophy of science*
Most of Chomsky's work in theoretical linguistics deals with metatheoretical questions, which makes Chomsky a metalinguist rather than a linguist.[27] In formulating metatheoretical questions and providing answers to them he has been able to apply the notions and problems current in modern philosophy of science to theoretical linguistics in a way that had not been achieved before. Questions regarding the nature of linguistic data, realism versus instrumentalism, causality, explanation, criteria of adequacy and the like were now broached in a much more mature and professional way than had been customary among the post-Bloomfieldian structuralist linguists.[28]

---

[27] The paucity of Chomsky's actual grammatical analyses and descriptions is surprising for someone who has written so much on linguistics. Ironically, the only two thorough pieces of analysis produced by Chomsky to date are in morphophonemics (his 1951 MA-dissertation on the Morphophonemics of Modern Hebrew) and, together with Halle, in phonology (Chomsky & Halle 1968). In syntax there is not a single instance of anything approaching a thorough treatment of a construction or set of constructions in English or any other language. Hosts of general principles and constraints have seen the light in endless succession, but no actual analysis or description. All work of that nature produced within the confines of Chomsky-inspired grammar came from others, who then invariably found that the principles and constraints could not be maintained. Cp. Postal in Huck & Goldsmith (1995:142):

> The significant point is then that there is an extraordinary contrast between the paucity of genuine results in Chomskyan linguistics and the forests of paper which have been, and continue to be, devoted to the linguistic ideas involved.

[28] In Huck & Goldsmith (1995:126-127) Postal gives the following accurate account of the methodological views of American structuralist linguists up to the 1950s:

> The linguistics that was being taught at Yale was this really very dogmatic American structuralism – with great pretensions about being scientific, although they really didn't know anything about modern science or the philosophy of science. They had a homemade notion of science as classifying data and being very empirical and were very suspicious of theory or theorizing about which they really knew very little. So Chomsky really shone compared to them.

4.6 Consensus on metatheoretical questions?

4.6.1 Realism in linguistics: psychological plausibility

- *Chomsky's early position was more instrumentalist than realist*

With the advent of more explicit notions about grammatical rules and rule systems, the question of realism versus instrumentalism became more complex and involved. It no longer concerned just the reality, or fictitiousness, of the *structures* assigned to linguistic products, but also of the *rule systems* designed to generate the structures. The answer provided in Chomsky's published works after 1960 is, on the whole, of a realist nature, though there are many ambiguities.[29]

In the early years, however, Chomsky's position was less clear, and appears to have tended more towards instrumentalism than towards realism, contrary to his own statements in this respect: in the 1975 Introduction to [1956] he states repeatedly and emphatically (1975[1956]:35ff.) that, though the issue was not discussed, he had been a realist at heart all the time. This, however, is not what one infers from the available text (see also note 24).

In [1956] a grammar is described not as a reconstruction-by-hypothesis of a native speaker's command of his language, i.e. the rules and principles he must have incorporated to be able to produce and understand uttered sentences, but merely as an algorithmically organized generative rule system generating the infinite set of sentences of a language on the basis of a finite corpus of sentences that are judged well-formed by native speakers:

---

[29] Commenting on Chomsky's realism, the philosopher Harman (1980:21) pointed out that any realist theory in science must distinguish between claims of substance and notational aspects, and that specific categories of data are required for either kind of claim:

> Geography contains true statements locating mountains and rivers in terms of longitude and latitude without implying that the equator has the sort of physical reality the Mississippi River does. ... Sometimes we are not sure about the physical reality of some aspect of a theory, even given strong evidence for the truth of the theory. A different sort of evidence may be needed. The postulation of quarks gives a structure to the proliferation of subatomic particles, but physicists demand a different sort of evidence in order to establish the physical reality of quarks.

There is, therefore, a difference between those data that confirm or disconfirm the general adequacy, or, if one wishes, truth, of a theory on a more abstract level, and those that confirm or disconfirm the more concrete interpretation of certain elements of the theory in terms of actual physical or algorithmic processes. In other words, one may, if one feels sufficiently certain, call a linguistic theory or grammar 'true' in a general sense, but the precise specification of the psychological reality that makes the theory or description true is still another matter, to be decided by specific categories of data, mostly of the kind usually collected in psycholinguistic experiments.

While acknowledging this point in (1980:45), Chomsky has nonetheless continued, in later publications, to insist that no distinction can be made between different kinds of evidence, and that it makes no sense to speak of the general truth of a theory as opposed to, or distinct from, its psychological reality, the latter being a 'mysterious property', which has only led to 'some confusions about the nature and force of the evidence' (1986:274). See Botha (1989:159-164) for a full discussion.

> In a particular grammar, the observable events are that such and such is an utter-
> ance of the language,[30] and the demonstration that this event is a consequence of the
> theory consists in stating the structure of this predicted utterance on each linguistic
> level, and showing that this structure conforms to the grammatical rules, or the
> laws, of the theory. The grammar thus gives a theory of these utterances in terms of
> such hypothetical constructs as the particular phonemes, words, phrases, etc. of the
> language in question. As in the case of any scientific theory, only a certain subset of
> the observable events will have been observed at any given time. In the case of a
> grammar, we have, at any time, only a finite corpus of utterances out of an infinite
> set of grammatical utterances.   Chomsky (1975[1956]:77)

This statement is non-committal as regards the issue of realism versus instrumentalism, though it smacks more of the latter than of the former. The real
issue is explicitly but not very clearly discussed, in [1956], first on p. 81-2:

> There has been some discussion recently as to whether the linguist "plays mathe-
> matical games" or "describes reality" in linguistic analysis of particular languages,
> where the phrase "playing mathematical games" often appears to refer to the con-
> scious development of a theory of linguistic structure for use in constructing and
> validating grammars. If by "describing reality" is meant meeting the external con-
> ditions of adequacy, then in order to give content and significance to the requirement
> that the linguist must describe reality, it is necessary to give independent (i.e. outside
> the particular grammar) characterizations of these conditions, e.g., for sentence-
> hood, by constructing informant response tests to determine the degree of accepta-
> bility or evocability of sequences. But within whatever bounds can be clearly set
> independently, the linguist's goal can only be to construct for each language a simple
> grammar related to other grammars in such a way as to lead to a revealing general
> theory of which all are exemplifications. There seems to be no reason to consider the
> constructs established in pursuit of these goals as being in some sense invalid. If the
> methods developed with these goals in mind lead to unacceptable results, it is im-
> portant to show this. But the alternative to ineffective methods is not abandonment
> of theoretical inquiry.   Chomsky (1975[1956]:81-82)

The general drift of this rather opaque passage seems to be that elements of a
linguistic theory or description may, if one is lucky, have a correlate in mental
reality, but even without such a bonus the theory will still be 'valid' and a
legitimate sample of 'theoretical inquiry'. If this interpretation is correct we
have here a purely instrumentalist position.[31]

Then, on p. 103, the question is taken up again in the context of the ambiguous notion of 'linguistic intuition':

[30] Later on in (1975[1956]:95), Chomsky clarifies this point by saying that 'the speaker
has an "intuitive sense of grammaticalness"', and that it is the goal of linguistic theory to
give 'a rational account of this behavior, i.e., a theory of the speaker's linguistic
intuition'. In other words, the facts or data for grammatical theory consist in the speaker's
acceptance or rejection of given strings of symbols as being grammatical or well-formed. It
should be clear that this does not imply a realist view of linguistic theory, since a theory
may well aim at capturing such 'intuitions' in terms of a formal system without in any
way claiming reality for that system.

[31] One thing is clear in this passage: if a theory is meant to describe psychological reality
it requires specific data (e.g. informant responses) to validate that interpretation, which is
the opposite of what Chomsky claimed in his BBS article of 1980 (see note 29).

In this connection, we can return to the question of whether the linguist "plays mathematical games" or "describes reality" (cf. above, § 11.1). To the extent that this discussion has any meaning at all, it seems to reduce to the question of where between these poles the proper approach lies. In the absence of clear criteria of adequacy and relevance, behavioral or otherwise, for theories, it is difficult to determine a correct position. The danger in the "God's truth" approach is that it sometimes verges on mysticism, and tends to blur the fact that the rational way out of this difficulty lies in the program of, on the one hand, formulating behavioral criteria to replace intuitive judgments, and on the other, of constructing a rigorous account of linguistic structure and determining its implications for particular grammars.   Chomsky (1975[1956]:103)

Again one sees a rejection of a realist point of view in favour of instrumentalism.[32]

- *Moderate realism has become the standard view in linguistics*

In any case, the moderately realist position as defended by Chomsky after 1960, but without its doubtful or controversial edges, is also, by and large, the position that has become generally accepted in theoretical linguistics, with all its remaining unclarities and open questions. It is accurate to say that since 1960 the instrumentalist position as defended by Zellig Harris and other formalists has been abandoned and replaced with a realist position (which is based on a view of the mind as a computational system operating largely below the threshold of awareness and hence not accessible to introspection).

Glossing over the remaining problems we can say that the position now commonly accepted in theoretical linguistics vis-à-vis the question of realism can be summarized as follows:

It is the linguist's task to formulate a principled hypothesis that can reasonably be taken to approximate certain aspects of the cognitive machinery that must be ascribed to the speakers of a language in order to provide a causal explanation of their ability to produce and comprehend well-formed meaningful utterances.

The hypothesis must be *principled*, and not ad hoc. That is, it must maximize generality with regard not only to the phenomena observed in the same language but also to the totality of all human languages. Moreover, the hypothesis can only be taken to *approximate certain aspects* of the supposed mental machinery because it is in principle impossible to provide a complete and de-

---

[32] In the passage quoted above Chomsky even raises doubts as to whether 'this discussion has any meaning at all'. Yet in his 1975 Introduction to [1956] Chomsky insists, as we saw in note 24, that 'In *LSLT*, the "realist" position is taken for granted' (1975[1956]:37). It is difficult to see how this could be the case if the possibility is left open of the discussion not having any meaning. It is, therefore, unlikely that Chomsky never changed his mind on the issue of realism. According to him, the reason why he did not, in [1956], raise this issue explicitly was that it 'seemed to me, at the time, too audacious' (1975[1956]:35). In view of the many highly 'audacious' stances taken not much later by the same Chomsky, one may find this hard to believe. R.A. Harris (1993:269), quoting unpublished work by Iain Boal, points out that in the 1975 edition of [1956] Chomsky actually expunged passages that showed his anti-mentalism and anti-realism of the mid-fifties.

tailed description of the actual machinery itself. This machinery is cognitive, which implies a physical realization, the so-called 'hardware', besides a computational organization, the 'software'. The linguist will have little or nothing to say about the biological hardware. As regards the software, even there he will have to hold back, since it is not always possible, in linguistic descriptions, to separate claims of substance from mere notational aspects (see note 29). In practice, the linguist will have to remain relatively non-specific as to the precise *formula of realist interpretation* he wishes to be applicable to his grammar or theory. But he will always strive for that formula of interpretation that allows for the most straightforward mapping of his theoretical statements onto the intended object of description, i.e. linguistic competence.

4.6.2 Criteria of adequacy

- *There is only one correct description, but how do we know?*

Since structure assignments are meant to reflect mental reality (under some formula of interpretation), it follows that there can be only one correct structure assignment system for the language – provided, of course, all native speakers of the language have essentially the same system of rules. That is, under the assumption of a completely homogeneous speech community only one grammar, and hence only one system of structure assignments, can be correct or 'true'.

This does not mean that we can also *know for certain* that any given grammar is the correct one. All we can do, strictly speaking, is (a) reject a given grammar if it fails to account for relevant facts, and (b) compare the surviving grammars as to their generality and simplicity at different levels. This is standard procedure in the exact sciences, and it is also the procedure considered correct by most modern theoretical linguists.

- *Chomsky's adequacy criteria are confused and unrealistic*

Here, too, as in so many other areas, Chomsky has, on the one hand, stimulated the discussion and been instrumental in bringing the issues out into the open, while, on the other, causing confusion by the opacity of his formulations. Thus we read:

> Within the framework oulined above we can sketch various levels of success that might be attained by a grammatical description associated with a particular linguistic theory. The lowest level of success is achieved if the grammar presents the observed data correctly. A second and higher level of success is achieved when the grammar gives a correct account of the linguistic intuition of the native speaker, and specifies the observed data (in particular) in terms of significant generalizations that express underlying regularities in the language. A third and still higher level of success is achieved when the associated linguistic theory provides a general basis for selecting a grammar that achieves the second level of success over other grammars consistent with the relevant observed data that do not achieve this level of success. In this case, we can say that the linguistic theory in question suggests an explanation for the linguistic intuition of the native speaker. It can be interpreted as asserting that data of the observed kind will enable a speaker whose intrinsic

capacities are as represented in this general theory to construct for himself a grammar that characterizes exactly this linguistic intuition.

For later reference, let us refer to these roughly delimited levels of success as the levels of *observational adequacy, descriptive adequacy,* and *explanatory adequacy,* respectively.   Chomsky (1964:28-29)

This passage is odd in a number of ways. We can live with the notion of 'observational adequacy' of a grammar, provided it means the only thing it can mean, namely that the grammar in question has so far not been falsified by contrary data, i.e. counter-examples. But then it makes no sense to speak of this 'lowest level of success [being] *achieved*', since that would imply the existence of a predetermined corpus of sentences (not utterances), set in advance by some imaginary authority that would sit in judgement over whether or not this 'lowest level of success' has indeed been achieved.

The second 'level of success', descriptive adequacy, is more problematic. This is achieved 'when the grammar gives a correct account of the linguistic intuition of the native speaker, and specifies the observed data (in particular) in terms of significant generalizations that express underlying regularities in the language'. The first condition is strange. To begin with, the term 'intuition' is ambiguous, as is shown below in 4.6.3. In this context it can stand either for a native speaker's judgements as to well-formedness and possible meanings of sentences, or for the mental machinery, his competence, that enables him to use his language according to the norms valid in his speech community. In either sense, however, the condition is strange, though what is meant here is probably the native speaker's competence. Of course, if a description gives a correct account of its object of description it is adequate, true, and generally wonderful. But who is to tell? Again, presumably, a higher authority that is in possession of insights and information not shared with ordinary mortals. The second condition implies that a grammar must strive for maximal generalizations and thus optimize simplicity of description. This is, of course, standard procedure, but to say that this level is 'achieved' when the generalizations are 'significant', presupposes, again, a higher authority that will pronounce on whether or not the generalizations expressed in a grammar qualify for the predicate 'significant'.

Then comes the third 'level of success', explanatory adequacy. This level is achieved, according to Chomsky, 'when the associated linguistic theory provides a general basis for selecting a grammar that achieves the second level of success over other grammars consistent with the relevant observed data that do not achieve this level of success'. But this requires of a general linguistic theory that it provide a procedure to decide whether or not a given grammar 'gives a correct account of the linguistic intuition of the native speaker' and thus presupposes a decision procedure as described and rejected in 4.5.1 above. Again, a supernatural deity or a clairvoyant prophet could perhaps achieve this. In actual fact, all we, earthly mortals, can do is advance cautious hypotheses and test them on factual correctness and degrees of generalization.

- *The notion 'level of adequacy' makes no sense and must be replaced with 'level of elimination'*

In this context it makes more sense to speak of 'levels of elimination' than of 'levels of success'. The lowest level of elimination is observational: counter-examples force the linguist (or should do so, anyway) to revise his analysis. The next level up is that of simplicity relative to rival grammars within the context of the language under description: the grammar with the best generalizations is to be preferred and the others are provisionally discarded. Then there is the level at which possible grammars are eliminated on grounds of relative cross-linguistic simplicity and generalizations. This is where general linguistic theory plays an evaluative role. Finally, a grammar may be compared with a rival and preferred, or discarded, on quite general grounds to do with what is known from adjacent sciences (psycholinguistics, neurolinguistics, etc.) about the actual object of description, i.e. the mental and physical structures and processes involved in the use of language. (This latter level of elimination or evaluation can be applied only under a realist view of scientific theories. This, in itself, is an argument in favour of realism and against instrumentalism, since realism is seen to provide stronger discriminatory means to decide among rival theories than instrumentalism.)

- *The 'official' code not always put into practice*

The accepted view, nowadays, in theoretical linguistics is that the notion 'level of adequacy' is of little use and should indeed be replaced with that of 'level of elimination'. This is the practice officially recognized in evaluating linguistic arguments and theoretical proposals, and, in the context of funding agencies, in adjudicating papers, projects, grant applications and the like. It is accepted as legitimate, nowadays, to appeal to counter-examples or to lack of generality when criticising an argument or a proposal. Conversely, one may boast significant coverage of facts together with absence of falsification, or greater generality when defending one. That the official principle often fails to be reflected in a practical consensus among linguists, many of whom go on acting, teaching and writing along the lines they once established for themselves, in the face of negative evaluation results in comparison to competing theories, must be ascribed, if not to simple human weakness, to what we may call the 'sociological factor' in linguistics.

4.6.3 Empirical access: data, causal question, hypothesis

- *The nature of linguistic data: Chomsky sides with Baudouin and Pike, but only in part*

At this point it is essential that stock be taken of the parameters that determine the notion of empirical access as described in 3.0. The first question is, therefore: Does the present-day community of theoretical linguists agree, by and large, on the nature of linguistic data? The answer is, by and large, affirmative, and, as before, whatever consensus there is has been shaped in large part in the context of the discussions started by Chomsky.

Following up on Baudouin de Courtenay and later European linguists, Chomsky has always stressed that one cannot study language on the basis of physical data alone. His teacher Harris had still built his theory on the neopositivist principle that the data of linguistics consist of physical speech sounds and of observed physical behavioural patterns that correlate with speech sounds. Baudouin de Courtenay, half a century earlier, had defended a very different, more psychological view, accepting as data not simply the physical speech sounds themselves but the attitudes held by native speakers vis-à-vis these sounds. For him, as we have seen (3.2), phonemes were 'ideal' sound images which a speaker would try to approximate as faithfully as possible. Pike, too, takes this view, though he formulates the position with regard to properties of meaning rather than of well-formedness. He accepts native speakers' reports on meanings as valid data: 'Our reply is, first, to accept this fact of affirmed awareness of meanings as an objective observable datum on a par with other observable verbal events; people say things about meanings, and these sayings we collect and study as part of our total corpus of material to be described' (1954:79 - § 6.43; see 4.4.2).

- *Chomsky limits data to judgments of well-formedness and of ambiguity*

Chomsky sides with Baudouin and Pike in this matter. But his notion of data is much more restricted. His view was, and is, that the primary data for linguistic research is provided by the native speaker's assent or dissent with regard to the well-formedness or grammaticality of sentences. Moreover, as has been said, he is willing to consider only highly idealized 'data' meant to be drawn from 'a completely homogeneous speech community' (1965:3), which, as we saw in 2.5, note 18, does not exist. In thus limiting himself to just well-formedness judgements as they seem correct to an idealizing linguist, Chomsky left large areas of possible and more realistic data unexploited and effectively removed both the study of language variation and the study of meaning from linguistic theory.

As regards the study of meaning, tapping native speakers' attitudes of assent or dissent with regard to possible meanings is at least as justified as tapping their intuitions with regard to well-formedness. In fact, since sentence comprehension is a near-to-awareness function directly required of native speakers when they use their language, while this can hardly be said of well-formedness judgements, tapping possible meanings seems a great deal more justified than tapping well-formedness judgements. Yet Chomsky has never relied wholeheartedly on semantic data. When semantic judgements are appealed to, by him or his school, they are virtually always judgements of semantic similarity or dissimilarity. Ambiguity judgements, in particular, have served as data to confirm or disconfirm specific theoretical proposals. But reports on or analyses of actual meanings hardly occur in the Chomskyan tradition of generative grammar. There is a parallel between Chomsky's treatment of meanings and the standard procedure of phoneme specification in American structuralist linguistics, which was to apply the 'pair test': the native speaker was asked whether two chunks of sound were the same or different. Analogously, the native speaker is asked here whether two sentences mean the same or have different meanings. When a sentence A is said to mean the same not only as B but also as C, whereas B and C are not judged to have the same meaning, A is said to be ambiguous.

This diffidence with regard to semantic data is no doubt a belated consequence of the behaviourist period in linguistics. Therefore, if empirical access was gained to language it was partial and pertained only to facts of linguistic form. Semantic facts were still shrouded in mystery, and no progress was made, in the context of TGG, with regard to the setting up of even an incipient semantic theory. Katz, Fodor and Postal called the work they published in 1963 and 1964 'semantic', yet it was in fact syntactic, though it showed a much greater sensitivity with regard to semantic facts than had been customary in the TGG context. A full discussion of this theoretical development is given in section 7.3.

- *Ambiguity of the notion 'intuition'*

Chomsky's position with regard to linguistic data caused some shock among the post-Bloomfieldian structuralists. R.A. Harris (1993:54) quotes the following exchange between Archibald Hill and Chomsky during the *Third Texas Conference on Problems of Linguistic Analysis in English* of 1958:

HILL: If I took some of your statements literally, I would say that you are not studying language at all, but some form of psychology, the intuitions of native speakers.

CHOMSKY: That is studying language.

What, however, was meant by the term 'intuition'?

The early literature suffers from a potentially dangerous ambiguity of this term (cp. Lees 1957:376). This term refers (a) either to the native speaker's alleged ability to discriminate well-formed from ill-formed sentences and to provide semantic reports on them, i.e. to provide the linguist with data,[33] or (b) to the native speaker's competence, i.e. the mental machinery that regulates his use of his language,[34] or (c) to the linguist's (or the more sophisticated native speaker's) pretheoretic, perhaps introspective, sense of plausibility

---

[33] Cp. Chomsky (1957:13; italics mine):

For the purposes of this discussion, however, suppose that we assume *intuitive knowledge* of the grammatical sentences of English and ask what sort of grammar will be able to do the job of producing these in some effective and illuminating way. We thus face a familiar task of explication of some *intuitive concept*, in this case, the concept "grammatical in English", and more generally, the concept "grammatical".

[34] Cp. Chomsky (1965:24) (see also the discussion on levels of adequacy in 4.6.2):

A grammar can be regarded as a theory of a language; it is *descriptively adequate* to the extent that it correctly describes the intrinsic competence of the idealized native speaker. The structural descriptions assigned to sentences by the grammar, the distinctions that it makes between well-formed and deviant, and so on, must, for descriptive adequacy, correspond to the *linguistic intuition* [italics mine] of the native speaker (whether or not he may be immediately aware of this) in a substantial and significant class of crucial cases.

with regard to a given description or analysis.[35] These three senses are, of course, entirely distinct and must not be confused.

When it is said that a linguistic description is meant to give an explicit account of the native speaker's linguistic intuition, we must ask whether what is meant is a grammar that generates all and only the well-formed strings of symbols in a language, or a grammar that provides a true-to-life model of the native speaker's linguistic competence, or a grammar that satisfies the linguist's preconceptions about what linguistic structure ought to be. The answer that is generally accepted nowadays is that what is meant is, first of all, a grammar that generates all and only the well-formed sentences of a language, and, in second place, a grammar that may be deemed to approximate the native speaker's linguistic competence.

- *No objective method of data validation*

Having thus cleared up, to some extent, the ambiguity of the term 'intuition', we must now ask the question of how the purported data can be validated. And here we are in deep water. For no reliable operational method has been developed so far to ensure an objective, verifiable registration of native speakers' intuitions of well-formedness. In most cases no-one will have any reasonable doubts. There is a stark contrast between, for example, *I expected him to come out first* and the clearly ungrammatical **I him first come out expected* – though the latter is perfectly intelligible and could well be said by a foreign learner whose native language has a basic verb-final word order. The difference is less clear, though still clear enough, between, for example, *I have lived in Paris for a long time* and *(*)I have lived for a long time in Paris*, where the place adverbial follows the time adverbial, contrary to common English practice (a mistake also often encountered with non-native speakers). It gets worse when we are called upon to judge the grammaticality of, for example, *I definitely heard the clock nót strike* (said in a post-war English movie by an elderly lady who suddenly noticed that her clock had failed to strike, a prelude to horrible murder). Here we are hard put to decide whether this is ungrammatical or simply unusual given the way auditory perception takes place.

The clear cases pose no serious methodological threat, since one is entitled to expect of any reliable method of data validation that it should discriminate clear-cut grammaticality from clear-cut ungrammaticality. If it fails to do so it is no good as a method. It is the less obvious cases that create problems, real problems. For in the actual practice of syntactic description it often happens that one has to take a decision concerning the grammaticality or ungrammaticality of really doubtful cases, about which opinions differ. We are thus faced with a fundamental underdetermination of the criterion of observational falsifiability. This is a serious methodological flaw, which strikes

---

[35] Cp. Chomsky (1957:56; italics mine):

> One may arrive at a grammar by *intuition*, guess-work, all sorts of partial methodological hints, reliance on past experience, etc.

where it hurts most, since potentially far-reaching differences in theoretical treatment often hinge precisely on the less clear-cut cases.[36]

• *Just asking native speakers does not work*

Theoretical linguists, without any experience or formal training in fieldwork, have sometimes thought that one could simply question any native speaker, on any occasion, about his or her native language so as to collect reliable data. This is extremely naïve. One must realize that in many cultures language is a sensitive topic for conversation. It may even fall under a tabu so that elaborate preparations are required before one is allowed to speak about it, if at all. Moreover, many languages and dialects are felt by their speakers to have an inferior social status. When these speakers are questioned about their language their immediate reaction is likely to be one of fear and shame. They will have the feeling that they are being questioned because they do not speak correctly, and their answers, if any, will be totally unreliable. In some communities, especially among men, talk about language is considered unmanly and whoever starts it will be ridiculed.[37] And so on. If one is not a native speaker oneself of the language under investigation, and has therefore to rely on judgements provided by others who are native speakers, one must take one's time, first to get to know the cultural position of language in the community at hand, and then create the right atmosphere and setting to do the observing. This must sometimes remain restricted to participatory observation, without mak-

---

[36] Chomsky touches on this question in (1957:14). He there provides the answer usually given in circles of Artificial Intelligence when human behaviour is to be modelled:

> That is, we may assume for this discussion that certain sequences of phonemes are definitely sentences, and that certain other sequences are definitely non-sentences. In many intermediate cases we shall be prepared to let the grammar itself decide, when the grammar is set up.in the simplest way so that it includes the clear sentences and excludes the clear non-sentences. This is a familiar feature of explication.

Experience has meanwhile taught us that this does not work: most of the time grammars based on clear cases only simply fail to decide, by dint of extrapolation, on unclear cases, and independent decisions have to be taken. A different answer is given in (1965:19-20):

> Even though few reliable operational procedures have been developed, the theoretical (that is, grammatical) investigation of the knowledge of the native speaker can proceed perfectly well. The critical problem for grammatical theory today is not a paucity of evidence but rather the inadequacy of present theories of language to account for masses of evidence that are hardly open to serious question. The problem for the grammarian is to construct a description and, where possible, an explanation for the enormous mass of unquestionable data concerning the linguistic intuition of the native speaker (often himself).

Here the position that a grammar based on clear cases can be extrapolated to the unclear cases has apparently been abandoned and replaced with the notion that there is no need to consider doubtful cases because the clear cases give us enough to do as it is. But this answer, too, is incorrect, since one cannot restrict one's theoretical questions to those that hinge on clear cases alone without avoiding the charge of arbitrariness. As has been said, theoretical decisions often depend on what one makes of unclear cases.

[37] I have heard stories of an Australian linguist being thrown out of a Sydney harbourside pub as he began asking questions about the variety of English spoken by the patrons.

ing the language the topic of conversation or, worse, of question-asking.[38] And if one is a native speaker of the language under investigation one still has to be careful. Native speakers, even if they are also linguists, are far from reliable as to grammaticality judgements, as experienced linguists know well.

- *Child's 'data' in learning a language and linguist's data are different*

It must also be observed that the much-vaunted parallel between the linguist constructing a formal grammar of a language on the one hand, and the young child learning the language of its environment on the other (see 4.7.3), is seriously flawed, if only by the very different nature of the input data. The linguist collects reports on native speakers' attitudes of acceptability or unacceptability with regard to well-formedness and possible meanings of uttered sentences. The child takes as input a confusing welter of raw sense data that impinge as unique tokens on as yet not fully developed sense organs and cause little more than sensations. Gradually the child begins to order the sensations it has into categories, which leads to incipient type-level recognition and a sense of repetition and similarity. It also begins to separate communicatively significant sense data from the rest. Only then can the first start be made with the construction of a mental lexicon and grammar, on the basis not only of the sounds and gestures made by speaking individuals, but also of situational factors and of whatever has so far been accumulated in the way of general world knowledge. It is, moreover, reasonable to suppose that the process of language acquisition by the young child is strongly guided by what is usually called by the non-committal name of 'innate predisposition towards acquiring a human language'.

It hardly needs comment that the situation of the young child is entirely different from that of the investigating linguist. So much so that it seems frivolous even to compare the two.

- *In practice we just make do*

In the actual practice of grammatical description, the problems caused by the uncertainty regarding the exact delimitation of the data are usually overcome by compromise. A compromise is struck between, on the one hand, validating the purported data as far as it is possible to do so without disrupting the work too much, and, on the other, plain common sense. For the moment and within limits, such compromises work reasonably well, but it must be remembered that we have here a crucial methodological problem that has remained unsolved in principle till the present day and must, therefore, weaken any claim to the status of 'real science' that linguists might entertain.

---

[38] An exception may be made, perhaps, for those communities that are frequently visited by inquisitive linguists and derive some income from that. A colleague once told me that an Australian Aboriginal informant asked him, after an interview, if he would not want to know about the relative clause construction in his language, since all the others had asked him about it.

- *'Ungrammaticality' means 'not well-formed under any interpretation'*

It is useful to realize that the predicate 'ungrammatical' as currently used in linguistics has semantic implications. If this predicate has any meaning at all it must mean that the string of symbols to which it is applied is not a proper expression of any possible meaning whatsoever in the language. It sometimes occurs that a string of symbols is called ungrammatical until it is realized that it ís fully grammatical in some, far-fetched, meaning.

Simple parsing sometimes provides the answer, as in *The young man important places*, which is fully grammatical once it is realized that *man* is the main verb. Sometimes one has to live with an internal contradiction, as in *He is taller than he is*, which can never be true but is fully grammatical in English. Sometimes one has to force an interpretation, as in *He bought two better cameras than his brother*. This is uninterpretable if *his brother* is taken to refer to a person who also bought one or more cameras, but blameless if *his brother* is taken to refer to a particular (type of) camera. Note that *He bought two better cameras than your Kodak* is unproblematic, if, as would be natural, the expression *your Kodak* is taken to refer to a (type of) camera. This, by the way, is an interesting case because *He bought a better camera than X* is easily seen to be ambiguous between 'he bought a better camera than X is (a good camera)' and 'he bought a better camera than X bought (one)'. However, when the indefinite article *a* is replaced with a numeral only the former interpretation remains, and any sentence of the form **He bought two better cameras than X bought* seems to be ungrammatical.

The upshot is that when a string of symbols is qualified as 'ungrammatical' a universal statement is made that generalizes over all possible meanings. This implies the possibility of falsification, since if a meaning is found for which the string of symbols in question can be considered an adequate expression, in the judgement of native speakers, then the qualification must be corrected and the string must be called 'grammatical'.

- *It is better to speak of 'ungrammatical on a reading'*

It is, therefore, legitimate to speak of '(un)grammatical on a reading'. In fact, this notion of (un)grammaticality seems more useful than the blanket notion of ungrammaticality in general, because when 'grammaticality on a reading' is tested it is not necessary to generalize over all possible meanings, as it is with the general notion. Now the testing, whatever form it may take, can concentrate on one specific case of meaning-form association.

- *The causal question of early TGG restricted to well-formedness phenomena*

The limitation to well-formedness judgements current in TGG found a parallel in the causal question that arose with respect to them. All that needed to be explained, in the view of early TGG grammarians, was the native speaker's ability to discriminate well-formed from non-well-formed expressions.

In the chapters that follow we shall see that this is, in fact, an extremely limited perspective. The empirical, causal question that arises with regard to a less restricted view of what constitutes data has a much wider range. If we

accept as data the native speaker's ability to distinguish and produce sentences in the flow of speech, to assign meanings to sentences in such a way that
they link up in relevant ways with existing situations, and to discriminate
well-formed from non-well-formed expressions for given meanings, the question is: what set of mental rules or principles enables the native speaker to do
all this? And the answer to this question will require a theory that is a great
deal richer, and more complex, than the theoretical proposals made in early
TGG. It will in fact, as we shall see in chapter 6, require the postulation of an
organized network of interrelated systems, all contributing to the amazing
feat of human communication by means of speech.

- *The hypothesis: so far no more than a generative grammar*

As it was, however, the causal question asked by early TGG grammarians was
of a much more limited scope. Linguistic communication did not come into it at
all.[39] In the beginning, all that linguistic theory was required to explain was
the native speaker's ability to discriminate well-formed from non-well-formed sentences. And the answer to that question was cast in the mould of a transformational generative grammar of roughly the structure as in fig. 17.

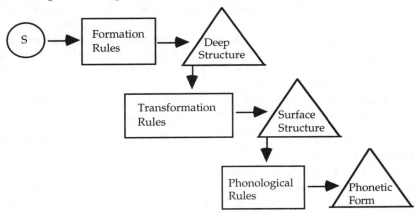

Figure 17   *The overall structure of a Transformational*
Grammar around 1960

The symbol 'S' ('sentence') is input to the Formation Rules, which are of the
ordinary PS-type (see 4.7.1). These generate a deep structure or DS, which is

---

[39] In fact, Chomsky has always denied that the primary purpose of language is communication, and defended the view that language is there to express thoughts (for a vivid
discussion of Chomsky's views in this respect, see Botha 1989:121-124). I can see no conflict between the two views, since one can perfectly well maintain that the kind of articulated expression of thought made possible by language derives its primary motivation
from the need to communicate these thoughts, a basic need in any organized human society.
The point is, rather, that the facts of linguistic communication constitute data for some empirical, explanatory theory, and it seems natural to call that theory 'linguistic', despite
Chomsky's arbitrary refusal to do so.

input to a different set of rules, the Transformation Rules or T-Rules, which transform the deep structure into a surface structure or SS. This is again input to a set of Phonological Rules which generate the final product, the phonetic form or PF.

- *This hypothesis only provides a mathematical answer to the causal problem, not a realist answer*

There was, however, an immediate problem with this proposal. A transformational grammar as sketched in fig. 17 does not, and cannot, answer the empirical question asked. The reason is that, if all goes well, it will *generate* all and only the well-formed sentences of the language L for which it is made. That is, it will provide a formal, algorithmic characterization of the set of well-formed sentences of L. But it will not thereby provide a formal means to *decide* for any given string of symbols (words) whether it is well-formed or not. That is, it will not simulate the native speaker's ability to discriminate well-formed from non-well-formed sentences. What is needed to account for that ability is a formal machinery that will *decide*, given any string of symbols within the lexicon given for L, whether it is grammatical in L or not.

In section 4.7.1 we shall see that, on mathematical grounds, a transformational grammar of the type sketched in fig. 17 allows for a general finite decision procedure, a formal procedure that will tell in a finite number of steps whether any given string of symbols is a sentence of L, only if it is heavily restricted. Unless heavily restricted, a transformational grammar does not allow for a counterpart grammar, a parser, that does the opposite, reduce a surface structure (let alone a phonetic form) to the input symbol 'S'. This problem is known as the *parsing problem* of natural languages.

- *Despite its limited scope, TGG has proved fruitful enough to speak of an empirical opening*

This, together with the all too limited scope of the causal question asked (due to the all too limited scope of the kinds of data recognized as legitimate) forces us to admit that the explanatory potential of a 1960-type transformational grammar was very limited. Yet, contrary to what one would expect given the limitations that have been mentioned, TGG has proved extraordinarily fruitful. On the one hand one has to say that TGG did not achieve the much desired empirical access to the facts of language in any meaningful way. On the other hand, however, experience has shown that Chomsky had an extremely lucky hand when he promoted his version of transformational grammar in the late 1950s. The vast quantities of new positive results and exciting new perspectives, together with the general feeling that these enhanced insights into the way language works, allow one to state that, apparently, some small opening had been forced into the fortress of language, even if one could not speak yet of proper empirical access.

In the following section we shall have a closer look at the formal properties of different types of grammar, and at the mathematical grounds for saying that transformational grammars do not, in general, allow for a parsing procedure.

4.7 Formal aspects of grammars

4.7.1 The Chomsky hierarchy of grammars and languages

- *The value of a preliminary problem analysis*

In the late 1950s Chomsky collaborated with the American psychologist Miller and the French mathematician Schützenberger to work out some mathematical properties of algorithmic production systems. As a result, a hierarchy of grammars was developed, now commonly called the Chomsky Hierarchy (see e.g. Chomsky & Miller 1958; Chomsky 1959b,c; Chomsky & Schützenberger 1963). Though this work was mainly mathematical in character, it is important to realize that it introduced a level of abstraction and generality into the study of grammar that had not been seen before. With the help of these analyses it became possible to carry out a sensible *preliminary problem analysis* specifying the overall nature of the task of writing a grammar of a language, and the conditions this implies for the overall structure of grammatical rule systems. Such a problem analysis had never been carried out before, and it proved extremely useful.

- *Difference between weak and strong generative power*

Before we discuss the Chomsky hierarchy one distinction must be made clear, that between weak and strong generative power. The *weak generative power* of an algorithmic production system or generative grammar is defined by the set of output strings generated by it, regardless of the structure assigned to them by the grammar. Two grammars are weakly equivalent if they produce exactly the same set of output strings.

The *strong generative power* of a production system or grammar is defined by the set of output strings plus the structure assigned to them by the grammar. Two grammars are strongly equivalent just in case they generate the same set of output strings and assign them the same structures. Clearly, two grammars may be weakly equivalent without being strongly equivalent, but not vice versa: two grammars that are strongly equivalent are also weakly equivalent.

- *Four mathematically distinct types of grammar*

The Chomsky hierarchy is based on a few selected mathematical properties of production systems or generative grammars. Four types of generative grammar are distinguished, according to an increasing scale of restrictions imposed on the rules (and hence on the structures generated) by the mathematical rule properties selected. It has been proven that there is a regular correspondence between types of grammar and types of (infinite) language: if a grammar is of type x it weakly generates an infinite language of type x, and conversely, if an infinite language is of type x this means that it cannot be weakly generated by a grammar of type y if this is more restricted than a grammar of type x. (Finite languages are mathematically trivial in that they can be generated by simple enumeration.)

We shall limit ourselves here to only a brief and informal characterization of the four types. For more details the reader is referred to the publications mentioned, and to Levelt (1974 Vol. I, II), which provides a useful survey of all aspects involved.

- *Type-3 or finite state or regular grammars, or Markov systems*

Type-3 grammars, also called finite state grammars or regular grammars or Markov systems, are the most restricted type. The rules are all rewrite rules of the type $\alpha \rightarrow \beta$, where α consists of one symbol only (i.e. $|\alpha| = 1$; the notation '$|x|$' stands for the number of vocabulary symbols in x), and β consists of one or two symbols (i.e. $|\beta| = 1$ or 2), and where, if $|\beta| = 2$, either always (i.e. for all rules) the right hand or always the left hand symbol is rewritable (expandable) by another rule (possibly recursively), and if $|\beta| = 1$, β is either itself a terminal symbol (i.e. a symbol that is not rewritten by any rule) or directly rewritable into a terminal symbol. If, in cases where $|\beta| = 2$, it is always the right hand symbol that is to be expanded, the grammar is monotone right-branching. If it is always the left hand symbol that is to be expanded, the grammar is monotone left-branching.

A simple and trivial example of a regular grammar is System C, a simple algorithm for digitally written natural numbers:

System C: *Algorithm for digitally written natural numbers*

(a)   Initial symbol: **N**
(b)   Vocabulary: {**N**, 0,1,2,3,4,5,6,7,8,9}
(c)   Instructions: (1) **N** → 0(**N**)
                                   (2) **N** → 1(**N**)
                                   (3) **N** → 2(**N**)
                                   (4) **N** → 3(**N**)
                                   (5) **N** → 4(**N**)
                                   (6) **N** → 5(**N**)
                                   (7) **N** → 6(**N**)
                                   (8) **N** → 7(**N**)
                                   (9) **N** → 8(**N**)
                                   (10) **N** → 9(**N**)

System C generates all and only the natural numbers (including 0), and provides them with a monotone right-branching IC-structure, as demonstrated in fig. 18a, or fig. 18b. Both represent the number 2518, though in slightly different arrangements of the tree structure.

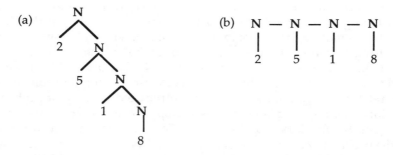

Figure 18   The generation of the number 2518 according to System C

Fig. 18a represents the tree structure in the shape familiar in generative grammar. Fig. 18b shows the same structure, but tilted a little anti-clockwise so that the terminal symbols are horizontal. In itself, this difference in presentation is unimportant, but fig. 18b shows perhaps more clearly that type 3 grammars can do nothing but assign a simple linear or serial structure to any string of symbols in the language.

- *Finite state grammars implicit in 'meaning-as-entropy' theories: statistical approximations*

Modern linguists feel, of course, that this type of uniform structure assignment may do for natural number representations but is bound to be woefully inadequate for the analysis of linguistic structures. Today no linguist will dream of assigning to a sentence like *The old man may have stolen your watch* a structure like that shown in fig. 19 (with 'S' for 'state'):

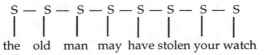

Figure 19   Structure of 'The old man may have stolen your watch' as assigned by a finite state grammar

In the immediate post-war period, however, the structural convictions of linguists were less outspoken. And the notion that a finite state grammar (i.e. a finite system of states connected by transitional paths, each path producing a symbol) might do for natural languages was very much alive, though it was promoted more in non-linguistic than in linguistic circles.

The context in which finite state grammars were favoured was not primarily linguistic, but technological and psycholinguistic, the context of the mathematical theory of communication (Levelt 1974, vol. 2:21). The professional linguists were aware of what was happening among the communication engineers, and considered their notions and techniques with sympathetic interest and even curiosity.

The engineers and mathematical psychologists who developed the mathematical theory of communication started from the assumption that it should be possible to measure the meaningfulness of a given symbol in a serially presented string of symbols or message in terms of the probability of its occurrence given the preceding symbols of the message. If that probability is small, the symbol is significant or meaningful, and conversely, a highly probable symbol will be relatively meaningless. The term introduced for lack of probability or uncertainty, i.e. meaningfulness, was *entropy* (Shannon & Weaver 1949; see also Osgood & Sebeok 1954:35-49; 93-125). For example, given a string *John saw fit* ... the probability of the symbol *to* as the next occurrence must be considered very high, and the addition of *to* should therefore be practically devoid of meaning. On the other hand, given a string *John was* ... the probability of the symbol *walking* as the next occurrence must be considered low, which would make the symbol *walking* more meaningful in this context.

Analogously, the grammar of a language was seen as a system of transitional probabilities given the preceding symbols (words, morphemes, phonemes) in a message or sentence. Only those symbols with a greater-than-zero probability will be grammatical additions. This requires a probability calculus over a suitably large, 'representative', corpus of messages, which will establish statistical probability measures for each symbol in the vocabulary of the language given a sufficiently large number of preceding symbols in a message. One speaks of an *n-th order statistical approximation*, where n stands for the number of preceding symbols in the message minus 1 (Levelt 1974, vol. 2:164-70). A *zero order approximation* generates arbitrary strings of symbols, irrespective of their statistical properties. A *first order approximation* generates strings of symbols according to their frequency of occurrence in the texts of the corpus. A *second order approximation* generates strings of symbols such that every symbol is restricted by its frequency of occurrence in the corpus given one preceding symbol. A *third order approximation* would generate strings of symbols within the bounds of statistical probability given the preceding two symbols, etc.

N-th order approximations with words as symbols are in fact type 3, or finite state, or regular grammars, where the selection of the rule to be applied in each case is restricted by the *n*-th order statistical calculus. One can imagine a grammar like System C where the probability of any of the instructions or rules (1)-(10) being chosen is determined on the basis of an *n*-th order statistical calculus.

One must realize that to achieve even a third order approximation of word sequences given a reasonably large corpus requires an astronomically large number of operations, too large even for most kinds of modern computational equipment. A second order approximation was carried out in the early sixties for a corpus of English sentences. Levelt (1974, vol. 2:164-165) quotes the following results of a zero, a first, and a second order approximation from Miller & Chomsky (1963):

ZERO ORDER: *splinter shadow dilapidate turtle pass stress grouse appropriate radio whereof also appropriate gourd keeper clarion wealth possession press blunt canter chancy vindicable corpus*

FIRST ORDER: *representing and speedily is an good apt or came can different natural here he the a in came the to of to expert gray come to furnish the line message had be these*

SECOND ORDER: *the head and in frontal attack on an English writer that the character of this point is therefore another method for the letter that the tired of who even told the problem for an unexpected*

In order to have an impression of what higher order approximations could look like, the *projection method* was used (Levelt 1974, vol.2 :167-168):

> We present speaker *A* with a *pair* of words (chosen at random from a newspaper or from a sentence composed by another speaker), for example, *family was,* and ask him to form a sentence in which the pair occurs. Suppose that the sentence which he produces is *the family was large.* We then present *was large* to speaker *B,* and request that he in turn form a sentence in which the pair occurs. If this sentence is *the forest was large, dark and dangerous* we present *large dark* to speaker *C,* and so forth. The following string (Miller and Chomsky 1963) was obtained in this way.
>
> THIRD ORDER: *family was large dark animal came roaring down the middle of my friends love books passionately every kiss is fine*
>
> An example of an approximation of English, generated by a 3-limited source, is the following ...
>
> FOURTH ORDER: *went to movies with a man I used to go toward Harvard Square in Cambridge is mad fun for*
>
> ...The following is an example of a fifth order approximation of English (Miller and Chomsky 1963).
>
> FIFTH ORDER: *road in the country was insane especially in dreary rooms where they have some books to buy for studying Greek*

One sees that the productions get better as the order of approximation is raised. (The last text, in fact, has an almost poetical touch about it.) The question is now: will further raising of the approximation order lead to full grammaticality? Are *n*-th order approximations viable grammars for natural languages? One might be tempted to think that they are, provided *n* is set at a sufficiently high level. But Chomsky has argued convincingly that *n*-th order approximations will never be adequate grammars.

- *Chomsky's argument against n-th order approximations as grammars for natural languages*

In *Syntactic Structures,* Chomsky argues that grammars that take the form of an *n*-th order approximation of English are inadequate for any *n*, no matter how high. There are, of course, the obvious queries about what size and quality of the corpus should be required for representativity. But Chomsky's main arguments were the following. He claims, first, that, given the enormous diversity of possible sentences in a language, it makes no statistical sense to speak of measurable differences in probability of occurrence, no matter of what order approximation. The vast majority of probabilities is infinitesimally low, and not calculable in anything remotely like practical terms. His second argument is that the set of sentences in a language is infinite, simply because there is no upper bound to the length of a grammatical sentence: given any arbitrary sentence of the language, there is always another sentence that is longer. This is precisely the mathematical definition of denumerable infinity, just as in the case of the natural numbers, which, for analogous reasons, also form an infinite set: given any arbitrary natural number, there is always another number which is higher.

Of course, there are practical limits to the length of sentences, just as there are practical limits to the size of natural numbers we can operate with. But that is not at issue here: those limits vary from occasion to occasion, and are not, generally speaking, expressible in terms of length or size. To impose any specific limit of length or size upon a production would therefore be arbitrary and theoretically unfounded. For that reason we say that, from a theoretical point of view, the set of sentences of a natural language is infinite, regardless of the practical limits.

If the set of sentences in a natural language were finite then that language could trivially be generated by means of a zero order approximation (by simple enumeration of sentences), and hence by means of a finite state grammar (each sentence would be generated by a separate rule of the grammar). But now that we know that the set of sentences in a language is infinite because of the absence of an upper bound to their length, it follows that there is no upper bound to n when we speak of an n-th order of approximation: for any n, a sentence of length n-1 will need a further approximation since there is no certainty as to what the n-th word will be. This entails that, even if the notion 'order of statistical approximation' were relevant to the definition of grammaticality, no finite apparatus could be built to separate grammatical from ungrammatical sentences. It is, therefore, theoretically unsound to envisage the grammar of a natural language as an n-th order approximation.

- *Chomsky's argument against finite state grammars for natural languages is unsound*

But is it also theoretically unsound to envisage a grammar of a natural language as a finite state or type 3 system, i.e. a statistically unconstrained system of transitional states? Again, Chomsky argues that it is. In *Syntactic Structures* he recapitulates the argument he had given earlier (Chomsky 1956) to show the inadequacy of the finite state grammatical model for the analysis and description of natural languages. Clearly, if finite state grammars are shown to be inadequate, their subspecies, n-th order approximations, will a fortiori be inadequate. Chomsky's argument against finite state grammars is, however, less convincing than that against n-th order approximations. It is, in fact, faulty (Levelt 1974, vol. 2:22-26). The argument runs as follows.

First, it has been proven that regular (finite state) grammars cannot generate all and only the sentences of languages of the type $\{a^n X b^n\}$, i.e. n occurrences of a symbol a, followed by an arbitrary (possibly null) string of symbols

X, followed by again *n* occurrences of symbol *b*. This is a mathematical fact which we shall not call into doubt.

Secondly, Chomsky argues, English contains sentences of the type $\{a^n X b^n\}$. His example is the theoretically unlimited self-embedding property of constructions of the type 'if S_1 then S_2', where S_1 and S_2 are any sentence of English. Given the sentences

S_1 there is smoke

and S_2 then there is fire

there is also a sentence 'if S_1 then S_2', i.e. 'if there is smoke then there is fire'. This sentence can now be substituted for S_1 in 'if S_1 then S_2', giving 'if ['if S_1 then S_2] then S_2'. This can be repeated an indefinite number of times:

[₁ if [₂ if [₃ if there is smoke then there is fire ₃] then there is fire ₂] then there is fire ₁]

In general, English allows for all sentences $\{[\text{if}]^n - [\text{there is smoke}] - [\text{then there}$ is fire]$^n\}$, hence English contains a subset L_{smoke} of the type $\{a^n X b^n\}$.

Chomsky concludes that, since no regular grammar can weakly generate all and only the sentences of L_{smoke}, the grammar of English cannot be a regular grammar.

The error in the argument is quickly detected. If English were totally unconstrained by rules of grammar and contained all arbitrary strings of words from the lexicon of English, it would be weakly generated by a regular grammar like the following:

System D: Regular grammar for unconstrained English, L_{arb}

    (i)   Initial symbol: S

    (ii)   Vocabulary: S plus the lexicon LEX of English words

    (iii) Instruction: S → w∈ LEX - (S)

             (i.e. any word taken from LEX, optionally followed by S)

Since L_{arb} contains all strings of English words, it contains as a subset L_{smoke} defined by the pattern $\{[\text{if}]^n - [\text{there is smoke}] - [\text{then there is fire}]^n\}$. Therefore, System D, which is a regular grammar, weakly generates *all* sentences of L_{smoke}, but not *only* these sentences. The same goes for all languages, including English, containing their lexical variant of L_{smoke} as a proper subset. Since their grammars are not restricted to *only* the sentences of L_{smoke} they may well, for all we know, be regular grammars. Note, moreover, that L_{smoke} can be extended with fully grammatical alternatives that do not follow the $a^n X b^n$-pattern. It is possible, for example, to leave out the word *then* in each consequent clause after the *if*-clause, or to have the consequent clause precede the *if*-clause, which disturbs the regularity of the pattern. Given these complications, one is forced to conclude that so far nothing follows as to the restrictions that must be considered valid for the grammar of English, or of any other natural language.

However, even though Chomsky's (1956) *argument* against the finite state grammar model for the description of natural languages is seen to be faulty, it does not follow that the *conclusion* is false. In fact, it is universally accepted that the conclusion is correct. The assumption that natural languages are regular languages, and can therefore be weakly generated by regular grammars, has proved so hopelessly restrictive that, in practice, no linguist is prepared to go on working on the basis of that assumption. The main difficulty lies in the strong generative power of finite state grammars, which assign a monotone serial structure to any sentence of any language. And serious linguistics requires more sophisticated structure assignments.

What, then, is to be done? It is apparently difficult to find out on formal grounds whether or not finite state grammars can weakly generate precisely, i.e. all and only, the sentences of any given natural language. Levelt's advice (1974, vol. 2:26) is to state as an *axiom*, and not as a *theorem*, the position that natural languages are non-regular but, for example, transformational. If it then turns out that that assumption is fruitful and leads to a host of useful new insights it will always be possible to go back and see if the original assumption can be strengthened (i.e. provided with more restrictions) while the results are maintained.

- *Type-2 or context-free, and type-1 or context-sensitive grammars*

Exit the finite state or type-3 grammar model, though not in a very elegant way. We now pass on to type-2 grammars. Type-2 grammars, also called context-free (CF) grammars, consist of rewrite rules likewise of the type $\alpha \to \beta$, where α consists again of one symbol only (i.e. $|\alpha| = 1$), but where β consists of $1 \leq n$ symbols (i.e. $|\beta| \geq 1$) (and where $\varnothing$ is among the symbols available). As with regular grammars, the application of a rule in a CF-grammar automatically and by definition leads to the generation of a bit of tree structure. But the resulting tree structures are no longer monotone right-branching or monotone left-branching. Instead, CF-grammars impose no restrictions on the trees generated, as long as no crossing branches are allowed to occur. It is easy to see that regular grammars are a specific subclass of CF-grammars, and hence the languages generated by regular grammars, the regular languages, are a proper subset of the languages generated by CF-grammars, the CF-languages.

Type-1 grammars are even less restricted than type-2 grammars. They are called context-sensitive (CS) grammars. Again, they consist of rewrite rules of the type $\alpha \to \beta$, but now $|\alpha| \geq 1$ and $|\beta| \geq 1$ and $|\alpha| \leq |\beta|$. Chomsky (1959c) adds the further restriction (which makes these grammars properly 'context-sensitive') that α must contain precisely one symbol A which is replaced by a substring α_2 of β ($|\alpha_2| \geq 1$). In the Chomsky version, CS-rules can thus be written in the format $A \to \beta \: / \: \alpha_1 - \alpha_3$, or: A can be rewritten as β only if A occurs in the context $\alpha_1 - \alpha_3$ (where α_1 and α_3 can be null). It is, again, easily seen that CF-grammars are a proper subset of CS-grammars, and analogously for the languages generated by them.

Type-2 and type-1 grammars are normally classified together under the heading of phrase structure (PS) grammars. As was said in section 4.3, it was this notion of PS-grammar that implicitly underlay Bloomfield's model of grammar, but for one exception consisting in the fact that Bloomfield assumed that some forms could profitably be taken as *underlying* others. The models of grammatical description developed by the non-transformationalist post-Bloomfieldian structuralists were likewise implicitly of the PS-type, most of them without the notion of underlying form, i.e. of the *item-and-arrangement* style as defined in Hockett (1954).

From the early 1950s on Chomsky has argued that PS-grammars are inadequate as grammars for natural languages. In this case, however, he did not try to set up a formal, mathematical argument that could, so to speak, clinch the issue. In fact, he has never excluded the possibility that PS-grammars may be able to weakly generate a natural language, but any such grammar, he claims, would quickly lose out on a well-conceived type-0 grammar on grounds of simplicity and generality. What then, is a type-0 grammar?

- *Type-0 or transformational grammars*

Type-0 or transformational grammars, finally, are totally unrestricted rewrite systems: any instruction $\alpha \rightarrow \beta$ is allowed, without any restriction on α or β. The languages generated by type-0 grammars have, accordingly, hardly any specific mathematical property other than the minimal property of being *recursively enumerable* or *canonical*, i.e. they are generated by some algorithm. If an infinite language lacks even that property it is undefinable, and hence uninteresting for any purpose whatsoever.

The transformational grammars (T-grammars) that are commonly used in linguistics are 'mixed' in that they consist of a base consisting standardly of context-free formation rules, a set of transformation rules or T-rules, and a set of context-sensitive phonological rules, as shown in fig. 17 above. The T-rules take as input one or more tree structures (generated by the base or already transformed by some T-rule) and deliver one output tree. In most current models of T-grammar (but not, for example, in the theory of Tree-Adjoining Grammar (Joshi, Levy & Takahashi 1975)), each T-rule takes one input structure and delivers one output structure. The structures generated by the base are called Deep Structures (DS). The structures resulting from the T-rules are called Surface Structures (SS). The phonological rules produce Phonetic Forms (PF). T-grammars, in particular those presented in Chomsky (1965), exceed the limits imposed by type-1 or context-sensitive grammars, and are therefore strictly speaking of type 0.

- *The Chomsky hierarchy implies hierarchical inclusion relations*

Since each higher-typed grammar is defined by restrictions not shared by lower-typed grammars, and all restrictions of lower-typed grammars are inherited by higher-typed grammars, it follows that higher-typed grammars are always a proper subset of lower-typed grammars. Type-1 grammars are a proper subset of type-0 grammars, and type-2 grammars of type-1 grammars, just as type-3 grammars are a proper subset of type-2 grammars. The same goes for the languages they generate (see above). This hierarchical relation is shown in fig. 20 (Levelt 1974, vol. 1:12):

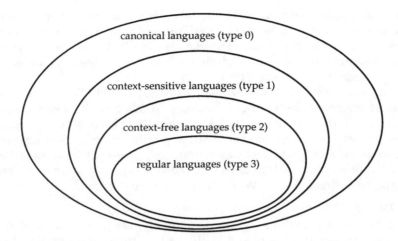

Figure 20   The Chomsky hierarchy of formal languages

(We shall henceforth speak of *pure type-n languages* when we wish to specify the set of type-n languages that are not also more highly typed. Thus, pure type-0 languages are type-0 languages that are not of type 1, and therefore, of course, neither of type 2 nor of type 3.)

- *Theoretical problems with type-0 grammars*

As has been said, Chomsky's main argument with respect to the form of grammars was that grammars of natural languages must be allowed to have the freedom of unrestricted rewrite systems, and thus be of type 0. This, however, gave rise to certain theoretical problems that are grave and, in the eyes of some, fatal. In Levelt's words (1974, vol. 2:39) 'the step towards type-0 models for natural languages must not be taken lightly'. Yet this step was taken in the theory of TGG. These problems were not immediately seen but came to the fore during the late 1960s and the 1970s, and led to a number of different developments.

4.7.2 The parsing problem

- *The problem of undecidability and hence unparsability: TGG less attractive as model for competence*

One problem, adumbrated earlier at the end of section 4.6.3, is the fact that type-0 languages are not all decidable. That is, it is not generally possible, given a string of words in the vocabulary of a pure type-0 language L, to decide in a finite number of steps whether S is a sentence of L. It has been proven that more highly typed languages are all decidable, but type-0 languages are, though recursively enumerable or canonical (i.e. defined by a generative algorithm), not all decidable. It would be simpler if all pure type-0 languages were also undecidable, but that is not so. There are pure type-0 languages that are nevertheless decidable (Peters & Ritchie 1973).[40]

Undecidable languages are also unparsable. A parser is a formal procedure that takes as input a string of symbols (words) in a language and either assigns it a grammatical structure or declares it ungrammatical (Gazdar & Mellish 1989:5; Covington 1994:42). Parsing thus implies a decision procedure, which means that parsing is impossible for an undecidable language.

Therefore, if natural languages are said to need for their description the freedom afforded by a type-0 grammar they run the risk of not being parsable. It is intuitively felt, however, that they must be parsable, given the ability of native speakers to discriminate between grammatical and ungrammatical strings of words, an ability which is informally exercised in the practice of school grammar, and is the basis of what is regarded as empirical data in mainstream TGG (where the data consists of native speakers' judgements as to the (un)grammaticality of individual strings of words). This means that, íf natural languages are of type 0 ánd our intuitions about parsability are correct, then we face the *empirical* problem of specifying a formal parsing (and decision) procedure, but now no longer with the help of the mathematical properties of the rule system (as with more highly typed languages).

Unfortunately, however, solutions to empirical problems are normally not delivered to order, given the surprises reality always seems to have in store. Thus it happened that type-0 grammars came to be widely considered less convenient as models for linguistic competence than more restricted types of grammar, where the parsing procedures are more readily available. Moreover, since it has not been proven that natural languages cannot be adequately described by means of type-1 (i.e. context-sensitive) grammars, while it has been proven that type-1 languages are decidable, most linguists who concentrate on the parsing problem have a preference for the view that the grammars of natural languages should be kept within the boundaries of at least type-1, i.e. context-sensitive, grammars.

---

[40] For example, a language L consisting of precisely the strings $a^n b^n$ ($n \geq 1$) is a context-free (type-2) language defined by the rule $S \rightarrow a(S)b$. But if the symbol c is to be inserted after every mth occurrence of b where m is a prime number, the new language L_c is of type 0. L_c contains the strings *abc, aabcbc, aaabcbcbc, aaaabcbcbcbc, aaaaabcbcbcbbc, aaaaaabcbcb-cbbcb, aaaaaaabcbcbcbbcbbc*, etc. Clearly, L_c cannot be generated by a phrase structure grammar, whether context-free or context-sensitive, but it can be generated by a less restricted and thus more powerful algorithm of type 0, consisting again of the rule $S \rightarrow a(S)b$ plus the rule $b^{pr} \rightarrow bc$, where b^{pr} is any prime-numbered occurrence of b. (Note that b^{pr} is not an actual symbol to be rewritten but a variable ranging over symbols to be rewritten. This makes the latter rule transformational.) Yet, although L_c is a type-0 language there is a simple decision procedure for the sentences of L_c, which, roughly speaking, checks first whether the occurrences of a are initial and successive, then whether their number equals the number of occurrences of b, and finally whether after each mth occurrence of b (m is a prime number) there is a c.

- *TGG is not interested in the parsing problem; computational linguistics is*
Chomsky and his followers have, on the whole, shown little interest in this complication. Others, however, especially computational linguists, have taken it more seriously. For the reasons indicated above they investigate the possibility of treating natural languages as being of a more restricted type, describable by means of a higher-typed grammar such as some form of PS-grammar. Whether this will, in the end, be successful is an open question. Even so, there is a general conviction in computational linguistics that T-grammars are inadequate as a realistic model of linguistic competence. To the extent that these linguists concentrate on parsing procedures, they avoid transformational models and try to make do with more restricted rule systems, even if that means less than complete practical success.

- *Generalized Phrase Structure Grammar (GPSG) takes the parsing problem seriously*
The most notable attempt in this direction has been undertaken by Gazdar, who developed his model of *Generalized Phrase Structure Grammar*. In this model (which we must refrain from commenting on further in this book, due to limitations of space and scope) linguistic structures are all generated by means of PS-rules, and the alleged shortcomings of that type of description are compensated for by a mechanism of metarules generating PS-rules (Gazdar, Klein, Pullum & Sag 1985). This theory has, over the past few years, been developed further into a highly sophisticated computational theory of linguistic analysis and description, with an emphasis on formal parsing procedures. Even though there are remaining doubts as to the capacity of this model to cope adequately with certain types of construction that occur in natural languages (in particular constructions with crossing dependencies), this theory is now regarded as one of the main rivals of TGG, especially on the computational front.

- *Yet type-0 or transformational grammars still stand a chance*
Despite all this, however, one should remember that not all pure type-0 languages are unparsable. The distinction of four types of grammars and languages provides no more than a rough classification in general mathematical terms, and it is realistically possible that natural languages are both pure type-0 languages and fully parsable. In considering this possibility one should realize that natural languages are subject to constraints that are not picked up by the Chomsky hierarchy and may well have the effect of making natural languages parsable. These constraints may be mathematically less interesting, but they have an empirical interest in that they are motivated by the functionality of language as a means of communication. What remains is the purely empirical question of finding the right system that satisfies the conditon of parsability besides being empirically satisfactory in other respects. This was also the opinion expressed by Bar-Hillel:

> It is at this state that the question mentioned at the beginning of this paper arises – *whether there exists a decision procedure for structures in English,* or in other natur-

al languages, for that matter, since it is unlikely that the natural languages should differ among themselves in this respect. Obviously, the answer to our question will depend upon the exact nature of the transformations. Only when we will have a better and more extensive understanding of the kind of transformations at work, will we be in a position to fruitfully attack our problem. At this moment one could only speculate about this answer, and it is doubtful whether such speculations would be worthwhile.   Bar-Hillel (1959:29)

Yet, as has been said, T-grammars are clearly out of favour with computational linguists, who look for parsing procedures for natural languages. The fact that complications are to be expected with a T-grammar as a starting point will have acted as a deterrent. Since the transformational grammarians themselves have, on the whole, stayed away from parsing, the net result is that the parsing properties of T-grammars have so far remained almost totally unexplored.

4.7.3 The constraints problem and post-1970 Chomskyan theory

- *The lack of constraints: a universal 'charter' is needed to adjudicate between rival theories*

The second main problem with type-0 grammars is the lack of constraints. As has been said, a type-0 grammar is totally unconstrained, in that any operation on any input is allowed. For this reason, type-0 grammars are also called 'unrestricted rewrite systems'. They allow the linguist more room for manoeuvre than the more highly typed grammars, but the freedom thus granted soon proved to be problematic.

Peters & Ritchie (1973) called attention to the fact, pointed out in the previous section, that transformational grammars of natural languages are in need of specific empirical restrictions not only for the languages weakly generated by them to be decidable, but also for them to be effectively learnable (though their discussion of the learnability problem remains limited to the mathematical aspects and is based on rather rarified assumptons regarding the actual conditions under which young children go through the language acquisition process).

Transformational linguists of the period, as has been said, were more impressed by the learnability condition than by the condition of decidability. They realized that the transformational literature of that period, including Chomsky's *Aspects* of 1965, suffered from a dangerous lack of constraints on what is and what is not allowable as a transformational operation. Without some kind of charter or constitution for the writing of grammars there is a risk of arbitrariness. A serious linguist will, of course, avoid totally arbitrary transformational operations. But sensible rules or rule schemata may also turn out arbitrary to some extent or anyway underdetermined by the data of the language under analysis. For example, it has been proposed (Koster 1975) that the underlying form of Dutch and German sentences should be taken to be of the type SOV (i.e. subject-object-verb), and a reasonable case has been made out to show that certain significant generalizations in the transformational treatment of Dutch and German can be captured on the basis of that hypothesis. On the other hand, however, it has also been proposed (Seuren 1985, 1996) that the underlying form should be taken to be of the type VSO, a hypothesis that brings a comparable yield of useful generalizations. Which of the two hypotheses is preferable is hard to say on the basis of Dutch and German alone. What is needed is a wider survey of the languages of the world, so that it can hopefully be decided which of the two proposals fits in better with the overall picture. The criterion of cross-linguistic simplicity thus becomes directly relevant to the actual practice of analysing and describing linguistic constructions.

This shows that formal linguistic analyses and descriptions must be constrained by a universal charter, whose interest and importance does not lie primarily in its *mathematical* properties, but rather in the *empirical* restrictions imposed. Knowledge of mathematical properties of rule systems is useful to determine one's position in mathematical space. But inductive delving into the ecological reality of language is necessary if one wants to find out how language is actually shaped.

- *Universal constraints are needed to help explain language acquisition   by the young child*

A prime reason, much stressed by Chomsky and his followers, why a theory of universal constraints on grammars of human languages is required lies in the fact that young children acquire the language of their environment quickly and systematically, according to a relatively rigid plan, regardless of intelligence, social class or other contingent factors. This suggests that the grammars of different languages should be expected to stay within a rigid format of universal parameters that need specific values for the language in question to be defined (with some necessary room for idiosyncrasies), and that the young child is accordingly innately equipped with a highly specific set of (unconscious) expectations regarding the possible forms of grammars for natural languages. This set of narrowly defined expectations is taken to guide the learning process in such a strong sense that the result is uniquely determined and assured within a fixed period of time, on the basis of largely incidental and often less than perfect speech data, and corresponding inferences based on situational knowledge and/or previously acquired world knowledge. The child is thus taken to 'possess', in some appropriate sense, those universal constraints which the theoretical linguist is in the business of detecting when studying the languages of the world and constructing maximally uniform grammars for them. In other words, a necessary but not sufficient condition for it to be comprehensible that the young child acquires the language of its environment quickly and infallibly is that the child be equipped with an innate 'human language faculty' or 'universal grammar'.[41]

---

[41] But one should remember what was said in section 4.6.3 about the essential differences between the linguist's task and the problem faced by the language-learning child.

- *The problem of universal constraints has dominated Chomskyan linguistics since 1970*

Unlike the parsing problem, which has never captured the interest of the Chomskyan school, the problem of universal constraints on grammars has been the dominant driving force in that school since the early 1970s. The emphasis was placed above all on the question of language acquisition by the young child, so much so that Chomsky has declared repeatedly, over the last twenty or so years, that 'the fundamental problem of linguistic theory <is> the problem of determining how it is possible for a child to acquire knowledge of a language' (Chomsky 1975[1956]:12), or statements to that effect.

Since roughly 1970 Chomsky's main concern in the development of grammatical theory has been the search for empirical universal constraints on the form of possible human grammars. However, only some of the wide range of potentially fruitful and serious constraints have been considered. It had been proposed, for example, (Katz & Postal 1964; see section 7.3.1.2), that T-rules should not be allowed to change meaning (should be 'meaning-invariant'), and a strong case had been made out to show that this constraint actually simplifies syntactic descriptions. But this was clearly not the kind of constraint that Chomsky, in the end, deemed worth considering, though for a couple of years he accepted it (Chomsky 1965; see 7.3.1.3), calling the corresponding theory of grammar the 'standard theory'. Chomsky's interest was directed more at formal than at functional properties of rules and rule systems.

- *X-bar theory and the proposed unification of transformational operations*

One particular concern was a uniform expansion system for the main phrases in syntax: Verb Phrase, Noun Phrase, Adjective Phrase, Preposition Phrase, Inflection Phrase (roughly, the auxiliary system), and, depending on the year, one or two more or less. The answer, originally proposed by Jackendoff around 1966 and published in Jackendoff (1977), was sought in 'X-bar syntax', where 'X' is a variable for a main category, e.g. V(erb), N(oun), A(djective), P(reposition) or INFL(ection). In principle, the theory says that each of these categories always has the same type of phrase structure expansion, in more or less the way depicted in fig. 21.

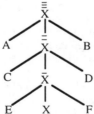

Figure 21   *General structure of a categorial expansion in X-bar theory*

With *V* for *X* we have a V-expansion (a sentence is a V-expansion: the label 'S' is replaced with 'V-treble bar'), with *N* for *X* we have an N-expansion (Noun Phrase), etc. The branches A, B, C, D, E and F may be filled or empty. If filled, they are filled by another X-expansion of any depth (number of bars). The general idea is that this format should accommodate all syntactic phenomena, and, moreover, streamline and simplify transformational treatment. Until recently, X-bar theory was the basis of almost all of the MIT-inspired proposals as to universal constraints on grammar.

- *Methodological problems with Chomskyan grammatical theory since the 1970s*

As was said in the Preamble to this chapter, we will not discuss in any technical detail the theoretical proposals made by Chomsky and his school since the early 1970s and caught under a variety of names. Since the claims made in Chomskyan theory since 1970 are not only highly controversial but also highly ambitious and far-reaching, and since this theory has still not found a final canonical form and is, moreover, on many points not falsifiable or otherwise testable, it seems unwise to attempt a full analysis and discussion in this context. We will, however, devote some attention to the methodological aspects involved. In general, it must be said that these proposals have proved controversial, considered by some to embody whatever scientific progress was made in linguistics during this period, while in the eyes of others they were unwarranted and speculative, labouring under massive amounts of counter-evidence and hence to be ruled inadequate on the first, observational round.

The main driving force, especially during recent years, behind the Chomskyan school has been the urge to reduce the variety of languages and to formulate the strongest and most pervasive possible structural universals for the languages in the world. This has led to a long series of proposals of ever greater abstractness and generality, and with constant but, it must be said, unnecessary changes in terminology. The latest development in this drive for unification is the statement (Chomsky 1995) that there is really only one, abstract, language in the world, and that the differences one observes are all reducible to parametric variation in the lexicon.[42]

---

[42] In a sense this is the main trend in theoretical linguistics. Since Bresnan (1978) linguists have come to see that grammatical processes are, to a very large extent, lexicon-driven, whereas the actual processes involved have a high degree of universality. It seems an obvious thought, therefore, to try to locate linguistic diversity as much as possible in the lexicon, and linguistic unity in the grammar. One is, however, hampered by a vast multitude of facts from all kinds of languages. Chomsky differs, now more than ever, from other linguists by his sweepingly general hypotheses, which are more programmatic than empirical. Cp. for example:

Variation must be determined by what is "visible" to the child acquiring language, that is, by the PLD (=primary linguistic data, P.A.M.S.). It is not surprising, then, to find a degree of variation in the PF (=phonetic form, P.A.M.S.) component, and in aspects of the lexicon: Saussurean arbitrariness (association of concepts with phonological matrices), properties of grammatical formatives (inflection, etc.), and readily detectable properties that hold of lexical items generally (e.g. the head parameter). Variation in the overt syntax or LF (=logical form, P.A.M.S.) component would be more problematic, since evidence could only be quite indirect. A narrow conjecture is that there is no such variation: beyond PF options and lexical

Attractive though such ideas are, they need extremely strong empirical support. And this, one has to admit, has not been forthcoming. To the extent that these proposals are at all testable or falsifiable, they have invariably met with barrages of significant refractory counter-evidence. Critics have, of course, called attention to the empirical weaknesses of the various proposals made by the Chomskyans over the years. They point out that the proposed universal constraints have too often turned out to be assumed too hastily and without serious testing (e.g. Gazdar et al. 1985:3-4; Pullum 1996). In their eyes, this etiolated variety of linguistic theory stands out for its poor contacts with the outside world, its idiosyncratic choice of research interests, and its shallow research methods. The ideological urge to provide backing for whatever unifying principle was being considered at any given time often has led to a selective presentation of data and far-fetched 'explanations' for unsupportive facts that could not be ignored (cp. note 20 in chapter 7). There is, or so it seems to the crititcs, a distinct tendency to be hypersensitive to nuances when that appears useful, but to ride roughshod over data that look subversive.

The Chomskyans have, on the whole, ignored such criticisms. Instead of replying, they have tried to immunize the theory against falsification. Thus, counter-examples were said to be 'peripheral' and not to belong to 'core' grammar. Or they were declared 'contaminated' and not 'idealized' enough, or even 'dialectal'.[43] Or it was ruled that counter-examples should not count

---

arbitrariness (which I henceforth ignore), variation is limited to nonsubstantive parts of the lexicon and general properties of lexical items. If so, there is only one computational system and one lexicon, apart from this limited kind of variety. Let us tentatively adopt that assumption — extreme perhaps, but it seems not implausible — as another element of the Minimalist Program.   Chomsky (1995:169-170)

Note that syntactic evidence (e.g. word order) counts as necessarily 'quite indirect' for the language-learning child, while lexical rule features are taken to constitute primary observable data. Then, the 'narrow conjecture' (deemed 'extreme' but also 'not implausible') is not seriously tested. No attempt is made, for any coherent set of data, to show that the conjecture creates order where chaos seemed to prevail. Note, finally, the total disregard for the massive amount of work done in language typology, where basic word order has proved to be a nontrivial determinant for a host of syntactic phenomena (see 4.8).

[43] In one well-known case a battery of counter-examples in different languages was ruled irrelevant on the grounds of being 'in fact restricted to certain dialects' of Dutch, for which 'there seem to be reasonable alternative analyses' (Chomsky & Lasnik 1977:452). The question at issue is why English should have obligatory *that*-deletion in sentences like *Who do you think (*that) killed the butler?* and not in *Who do you think (that) the butler killed?* This fact was attributed to an allegedly universal '*that*-trace' filter (ibid:451) which would make ungrammatical all *that*-clauses where *that*, or its equivalent in other languages, is immediately followed by a position left empty by a moved constituent. Not only does this filter fail to cover the fact that, in English, *that* is likewise obligatorily deleted when the predicate nominal has been moved, as in *Who do you think (*that) you are?*, but, worse, among the languages that allow for WH-extraction out of a complement clause into the main clause, only English deletes the complementizer in these cases. To say that non-deletion of the complementizer occurs only in 'certain dialects' of Dutch is preposterous. It is also irrelevant as dialects, too, have their grammars. Moreover, the 'alternative analyses' mentioned by Chomsky and Lasnik have so far not seen the light of day.

unless accompanied by a fully fledged alternative theory. And since no other school of linguistics would be prepared to venture into areas of theorizing so far removed from verifiable facts and possible falsification, the Chomskyan proposals could be made to appear unchallenged.

Recently a novel defence was presented in Chomsky & Lasnik (1993:506), whose opening sentence goes as follows:

> Principles and Parameters theory is not a precisely articulated theoretical system, but rather a particular approach to classical problems of the study of language, guided by certain leading ideas that had been taking shape since the origins of modern generative grammar some 40 years ago.

This finally states that what we have here is essentially metagrammar, programmatic rather than empirical. The authors have, as they say, been selective in their choice of the 'certain leading ideas' in generative grammar over the past 40 years. In the original programme, generative grammar was meant in the first place to specify all and only the sentences of any given language and secondly to do so in a maximally uniform way. But what seems to count most, nowadays, is the uniformity, while the precise, empirically adequate specification has gone largely by the board. This means that the uniformity cannot be about adequate linguistic descriptions. Instead, the main concern is with abstract formalisms which express *a priori* hopes for unification but without a prior viability analysis. There is, moreover, a distinct tendency among Chomskyans to suggest that they have special, privileged access to the mysteries of language, a hot line to heaven, so to speak, a tendency which has baffled and often also irritated other linguists. By normal standards, the chances of converting such divine revelation into an adequate theory must be deemed slim (see Pullum 1996 for eloquent and well-informed comment).

To try and reduce all linguistic variety to a handful of abstract universal principles is a laudable but hazardous undertaking which, as has been said, requires an especially solid formal and empirical basis. Without such a basis the theory risks the fate of the earliest pre-Socratic philosophies of nature, which meant to reduce all physical matter to air, or water, or fire, or a non-determinate prime element. As long as it could not be shown in both formal and empirical detail, and falsifiably, how the manifold varieties of physical matter could be derived from whatever prime element was alleged to underlie them, such philosophies had to remain speculative and hence without substance. In like manner, as long as it is not shown in both formal and empirical detail, and falsifiably, how the grammars of the languages of the world can be formulated in terms of the proposed abstract, (meta)grammatical principles, any philosophy proposing such principles has to remain speculative and cannot properly be called a theory.

The fact that no attempts have been made, in the Chomskyan school of linguistics, to provide a full formal description of any natural language or even a relevant part of one is significant. If this were to be tried and the descriptions were to conform to the proposed (meta)grammatical principles, and if, moreover, no data or constructions were to turn up that would show the intrinsic inapplicability of these principles, the proposal would have a case, just as physical theory had a case once it actually provided the formalism to derive all physical matter from a set of elements and ultimately a set of primitive forces. Without those derivations physical theory would not be taken seriously. Likewise, one fears, abstract proposals on linguistic unification will be open to charges of speculation as long as no reasonably adequate, complete and implementable descriptions of a substantial number of natural language constructions are provided in terms of the theory in question. Since this has, so far, not been achieved it seems appropriate to have grave reservations.

We now pass on to a different approach to the question of linguistic universals, one that came about during the same period: linguistic typology or universalist linguistics.

4.8 Linguistic typology

4.8.1 The geographical dimension neglected

Given the fact that the origins of modern linguistics lie in 18th and 19th century Romanticism, which legitimized the desire to get direct experience of both the geographically distant corners of the world and the remote historical and prehistorical past (see 2.1 above), it is decidedly odd and certainly remarkable that the historical dimension got the lion's share while the geographical dimension was kept subservient until only a few decades ago. Sir William Jones's famous speech of 1786 (see 2.4) marked the beginning of the era of comparative philology, the study of historical genetic relationships mainly among the modern and ancient Indo-European languages. In the great centres of linguistic study there was, as the 19th century advanced, little or no interest in non-Indo-European languages. In the beginning this was not so. As we saw in section 2.4 above, August Wilhelm von Schlegel established the first general typology for languages, based on morphological criteria. This work was not forgotten, but not further developed either, during the later 19th and most of the 20th centuries. Linguistic surveys were made from time to time, but they remained merely taxonomic, and that in a primitive sense. A work like *Les langues du monde* (Meillet & Cohen 1924, 1952[2]) stands in this tradition. It still is an invaluable source of information. Yet it is little more than an unsophisticated taxonomic compilation. No attempt is made at a critical evaluation of presumed genetic relationships or at formulating typological generalizations.

If work was done on 'exotic' languages, such as, for example, the work on American Indian languages carried out in America (see 4.1), it remained relatively obscure, and always in the shadow of an anthropological interest. As we have seen above, American anthropological linguistics had a real and direct influence upon mainstream theoretical linguistics through Sapir, Bloomfield and others. Yet this influence did not result in any serious attempt to take stock of what the world has to offer in the way of natural languages and draw general conclusions. The linguistic interest in 'exotic' languages was more incidental and anecdotal than systematic.

Twentieth century linguistic structuralism was less interested in the ecological variety of language than in the in-depth analysis of single languages and the mental mechanisms and structures underlying the use of language (though the dominant position of behaviourism, in the earlier years of this century, was, for a while, an obstacle to any serious investigation of the cognitive aspects of language and speech). Post-bloomfieldian theoretical linguistics kept up and intensified the earlier trend, but it treated mental phenomena in a much more open-minded way than had been customary during the period of behaviourism. In this context, 'exotic' languages were welcome to the extent that they provided useful illustrative material. But no serious attempts were undertaken to go out and actually take stock of the languages of the world with a view to establishing universal principles and constraints on the basis of representative samples. This did not happen till the early 1960s (see Greenberg 1974).

4.8.2 Greenberg's work on typology and universals

- *Joseph H. Greenberg: life*

It is fair to say that the person who made linguistic stocktaking respectable was Joseph H. Greenberg (born in New York, 1915). He studied anthropology at Columbia University and received his PhD from Northwestern University in 1940. After his doctoral dissertation, which was on an anthropological topic concerning Africa (*The Influence of Islam on a Sudanese Religion*), he turned to the study of languages, African languages first, then American Indian and other languages. In 1962 he moved to Stanford University, where, at the time of writing, he is still continuing his research as an emeritus professor. During the 1950s he started on a thorough revision of the genetic classification of African languages, which he divided into four large families, as opposed to the rather haphazard and unreliable classifications that existed before. This new classification (Greenberg 1963a) is now generally accepted, though questions of detail are still the object of discussion. After Africa, Greenberg started classifying the languages of New Guinea and surrounding areas, and then the languages of South and North America (Greenberg 1987). These classifications have proved more controversial, though they are gaining ground. In recent years he has submitted the Indo-European languages to a renewed genetic scrutiny (Greenberg 1993).

In tandem with his work on the genetic classification of languages, Greenberg has laid the foundation of a theory of typological classification of languages, based on structural properties alone, irrespective of historical backgrounds. It is this work that has, or should have, the most direct bearing on contemporary theoretical linguistics. The central publication in this respect is Greenberg (1963b), which lists 45 tentative universals of language, based on a sample (now considered small) of 30 languages. This seminal paper presents a few remarkable innovations.

* *Greenberg's universals*

First, most of the universals proposed are *implicational*, not *absolute*. An absolute universal simply says that all languages have some specific property X. For example, a universal like 'All languages have verbs' (with a proper general definition of the notion 'verb') is absolute. Implicational universals say, rather, that if a language has the property X it also has the property Y.[44] (The implication has to be taken strictly, in terms of standard logic: If X implies Y there is no suggestion that, therefore, Y implies X. Contraposition, however, is valid: if X implies Y it follows that if a language does not have the property Y it does not have the property X either.) For example, the following three Greenberg universals are implicational:

Universal 3   Languages with dominant VSO order have prepositions, not postpositions.

Universal 34   No language has a trial number unless it has a dual. No language has a dual unless it has a plural.

Universal 36   If a language has the category of gender, it always has the category of number.

Most of Greenberg's universals are *categorical* in that they say that if a language has a property X it *always* also has the property Y. The universals just quoted are examples of categorical universals. Other universals are *probabilistic.* These say that if a language has a property X it *usually* also has the property Y. Examples of probabilistic universals are the following:

Universal 4   With overwhelmingly greater than chance frequency, languages with normal SOV order are postpositional.

Universal 17   With overwhelmingly more than chance frequency, languages with dominant order VSO have the adjective after the noun.

The Greenberg universals 1-25 establish a correlation between so-called 'basic word order' of a language and some structural properties. The term 'basic word order' refers to the standard order in declarative surface structure sentences of V(erb), full lexical S(ubject) and full lexical O(bject) in any language with a fixed word order. Greenberg observes that of the possible six permutations VSO, SVO, SOV, VOS, OVS, and OSV only the first three seem to occur regularly, while the latter three are either extremely rare or just not attested. This means that there seems to be a distinct preference in natural languages to have the subject precede the (direct) object, while the verb may be placed initially, medially or finally (Universal 1). Consequently, Greenberg considers only the basic word orders VSO, SVO, and SOV. The remaining

---

[44] According to Koerner (1994c:4815), the notion of implicational universal was proposed in Jakobson (1958).

Greenberg universals (26-45) are indifferent to basic word order and have to do with case, gender and number.

4.8.3 The relation between Greenberg's universals and typology

When Greenberg started his work on linguistic universals the generally accepted typology of languages had progressed little since von Schlegel (1818), which, as we saw in section 2.4, was based on morphology. The presentation of Greenberg's universals raised hopes for a more thorough and more sophisticated typological classification system for the languages of the world.

The type of universal introduced by Greenberg leads to a linguistic typology if there are significant sets of universals that form implicational chains and significant numbers of languages satisfying the chains. Suppose we have the following twelve implicational universals, formulated in terms of the features (properties) *a-p*:

i	$a \rightarrow c$	vii	$b \rightarrow h$
ii	$b \rightarrow e$	viii	$e \rightarrow i$
iii	$c \rightarrow d$	ix	$e \rightarrow j$
iv	$c \rightarrow f$	x	$i \rightarrow m$
v	$d \rightarrow g$	xi	$j \rightarrow o$
vi	$d \rightarrow h$	xii	$j \rightarrow p$

Figure 22   Universals forming implicational chains

Fig. 22 contains the following two significant implicational chains:

$$\text{I.}\quad a \rightarrow c \rightarrow \begin{vmatrix} d \\ f \end{vmatrix} \rightarrow \begin{vmatrix} g \\ h \end{vmatrix} \qquad \text{II.}\quad b \rightarrow \begin{vmatrix} e \\ h \end{vmatrix} \rightarrow \begin{vmatrix} i \\ j \end{vmatrix} \rightarrow \begin{matrix} m \\ \rightarrow \begin{vmatrix} o \\ p \end{vmatrix} \end{matrix}$$

This allows for the distinction of two corresponding types of language, Type I, which is triggered by the feature *a* (the *a*-languages), and Type II, triggered by the feature *b* (the *b*-languages). If both types are satisfied by a significant number of languages we have a typological distinction between *a*-languages and *b*-languages, *a* and *b* being their respective 'root features'. Correspondingly, the features *a,c,d,f,g,h* form a coherent set, and so do the features *b,e,h,i,j,m,o,p*.

The example of fig. 22 is schematic and simplified when compared with reality. It is possible, for example, for features to be related bi-implicationally: $a \rightarrow b$ and $b \rightarrow a$, in which case there is no 'root feature', since from each of these features one can conclude to each of the others. More complicated forms of implicational universals are possible, e.g. universals with a double antecedent, of the type $(a \,\&\, b) \rightarrow c$ (Hawkins 1983).

Greenberg himself made a start with selecting sets of implicationally related universals. He found, in particular, that basic word order features are typical root features in that they imply a number of other features, either categorically or preferentially. The basic word order typology has therefore become a standard way of classifying languages, besides the traditional classification into isolating, agglutinative and synthetic languages. The structural properties taken to correlate with basic word order are to do with the presence of prepositions or postpositions, the placement of adjectives, relative clauses, genitives, inflected auxiliaries, WH-question words, clitic pronouns, and a few more features. For example, if a language has basic word order VSO it has only prepositions (feature: Pr), no postpositions, and qualifying adjectives tend to follow the nouns (feature: N). But if a language has basic word order SOV it has only postpositions (Po), and adjectives either follow (N) or precede (A) their nouns. SVO-languages are mixed but show a preference for prepositions, while, again, adjectives either follow or precede their nouns. This is shown in fig. 23, which shows the results of Greenberg's sample of 30 languages:

	VSO	SVO	SOV
Po-A	0	1	6
Po-N	0	2	5
Pr-A	0	4	0
Pr-N	6	6	0

Figure 23   Basic word order as a typological criterion (Greenberg 1963:77)

Six of the languages in his corpus have basic VSO order, and all six have only prepositions and noun-first NPs. Thirteen languages have basic SVO order, ten of which are prepositional. Eleven languages have SOV order, all of which are postpositional.

It seems likely that other root features are to be found besides basic word order. For example, it may well be the case that the presence or absence of tense and/or mood and/or aspect and/or agreement morphemes on finite verb forms is implicationally related to a significant number of other features in the syntax or morphology of the languages concerned. If so, this leads to a different typology, which may or may not coincide with previously established typologies. We shall return to this problem in section 4.8.5 below.

4.8.4 Areal and historical universals

• *Areal features causing a 'Sprachbund'*
It has been known, or at least intuited, for a long time that sometimes bundles of features are concentrated in languages of one given area, even though these languages are not genetically related. In traditional terminology the languages in question are then said to form a *Sprachbund* ('language confederation'). In English one speaks of *areal features* of the languages in question.

One might say that, in such cases, there is an implicational relationship between the geographical position of a language and some of its linguistic features. Examples are the following rough generalizations, which are almost, but not quite, categorical:

Areal universal I   A language spoken in the Balkans has no infinitives.

Areal universal II   Creole languages spoken in the Caribbean area have serial verbs.

Areal universal III   If a language is spoken in Europe it is SVO, has tensed verb forms, etc.

- *The Balkan Sprachbund*

As regards areal universal I, this is among the prime manifestations of the well-known *Balkan Sprachbund*. The origin of this universal is a much discussed issue (see Joseph 1983:179-212). The most likely explanation seems to lie in complex historical processes of language contact, starting in the early Middle Ages and continuing till well into the 17th century. The first Balkan language to drop its infinitives was most probably Greek (which had had a proliferation of active, middle and passive tensed infinitives in its more classical days). By the fifth century AD ordinary spoken Koiné Greek (not the official literary language) had lost all its infinitives, which had been replaced by finite verb forms (instead of saying 'I want to go' one said the equivalent of 'I want that I go'). The simplified scenario would be that through the political influence and prestige of the Byzantine empire and the intense contacts of travelling tradesmen with adjacent non-Greek areas, in particular present-day Bulgaria, Macedonia and Albania, Greek was widely understood outside Greece proper. The Greek language, moreover, was highly prestigious due to Greek civilisation and Byzantine political power. These factors must have induced non-Greek speakers to copy the salient Greek syntactic construction without infinitive, which thus ended up in the surrounding languages as a structural loan translation. This process spread gradually from Greece proper to almost the entire Balkans, the more remote areas being later in assimilating the loss of their infinitives.

- *The Caribbean Creole Sprachbund*

Areal universal II is likewise widely known. Serial verb constructions are, roughly speaking, infinitival additions to sentences expressing purpose, concomitant circumstance or consequence. A Caribbean Creole language may, for example, have a sentence corresponding to 'he threw the stone *fly* across the yard' or 'the drops were falling *touch* the ground', where the italicized verbs are called serial verbs. They were first spotted in African languages some 40 or 50 years ago, and soon after in the Caribbean Creoles and other languages as well. There is, however, still no generally accepted precise definition available of serial verb constructions: they are recognized largely on intuitive grounds.[45]

---

[45] As a result, the notion of serial verb has occasionally been stretched to include phenomena that are clearly different. Verb composition, for example, as in the French legal expression *saisir-revendiquer* ("impound"), has been branded as verb serialization. In the absence of a formal definition it seems wise to stick to the informal characterization of serial verbs as 'infinitival additions to sentences expressing purpose, concomitant cir-

The explanation of areal universal II is the subject of much debate. Most creolists maintain that this areal feature is due to substrate forces, in that the native speakers of the Caribbean Creole languages descend from slaves that were imported from West Africa during the 17th century and later. Many of the West-African languages spoken by the captured slaves, in particular the Kwa languages, abound in serial verb constructions. The substratists consider it likely that, although the slaves quickly lost command of the ancestral African languages and turned to newly created Creole languages with a simplified grammar and a lexicon largely derived from the European language spoken by their masters, the original (Kwa) languages exerted what is called a substrate influence leaving several traces, including the serial verb constructions.

Against them, Bickerton (1981) claims that serial verb constructions are part of universal grammar in a particular sense. According to him, they will naturally arise when children are born into a community with no more than an improvised pidgin language as the common means of linguistic communication, as one may surmise was the case in the earliest slave communities. These children will then naturally 'create' a fully fledged language, a Creole, out of the pidgin, and, says Bickerton, this language will contain, among other features, also serial verb constructions. The mechanism in universal grammar taken to be responsible for such features he calls the 'linguistic bioprogram'. For Bickerton, areal universal II is therefore due to this 'bioprogram', and it goes with analogous areal universals in regions where Creole languages are spoken.

The debate between Bickerton and the substratists has still not been resolved. For Bickerton to have a case it is necessary that all Creoles that have arisen all over the world should have serial verb constructions, which is what Bickerton claims to be the case, against the opinion of others who claim that serial verbs are absent in many Creoles.[46] The substratists, on the other hand, are open to charges of arbitrariness as long as the only justification for the assumption of substrate influence lies in historical possibility. Within these rather wide limits they are, in Bickerton's words, free to apply the 'cafeteria principle', helping themselves to anything that seems to suit their purpose. The final outcome of the debate will, it seems, depend on the careful collecting of data, and on the development of a reliable statistical measure showing that alleged substrate influences are supported by significant deviations from statistical mean values.

● *'Euro-universals'*

Areal universal III, mentioned above, enumerates, when completed, the alleged 'Euro-universals'. These are considered to form a bundle of features

---

cumstance or consequence', which pretty well covers the phenomena that prompted linguists to speak of serial verbs in the first place.

[46] Cp. the recent discussion between Bickerton (1989, 1990) and Seuren (1990) on the question of whether or not serial verb constructions occur in the French-based Creoles of the Indian Ocean, in particular Mauritian and Seychellois..

exclusively characterizing the languages of Europe, regardless of their historical origin or parentage. To what extent one is justified in speaking of Euro-universals has been the topic of a recent project called 'Eurotype' and financed by the European Community.

- *Differences between Greenberg universals and areal universals*

One should note that areal universals differ from Greenberg-type implicational universals in at least one important respect. The Greenberg universals may conceivably be interpreted as reflecting, probably in an indirect way, a postulated innate language faculty that enables a child to acquire the language of its environment quickly and systematically. Areal universals are in general not open to this interpretation, as it would be absurd to assume that a very young child's language acquisition process would innately be facilitated by knowledge of the geographical position of the language of its environment. Only if areal features are due to a common history and if this history reflects aspects of the innate human language faculty, as in Bickerton's theory of the genesis of Creole languages, can areal universals be interpreted as a reflex of the innate language faculty.

- *Historical universals*

Besides areal universals it makes sense also to think of historical universals. The clearest case in point concerns the origin of the Creole languages. The primary defining feature of a Creole language is historical: any language that has arisen as a result of the (usually forced) migration of sufficiently large numbers of speakers of different languages and their being brought together to form new communities under the direct domination of rulers, masters or slave owners is called a Creole language. Most known Creole languages came into being in the context of the European colonial expansion that took place from the 16th century onwards and led, among other things, to the establishment of plantation colonies in sparsely inhabited (sub)tropical regions like the Caribbean or the Indian Ocean islands. This, however, is no more than a historical description. The question asked by linguists, in this context, is whether these Creole languages are characterized not only by their common history but also by purely linguistic, structural features. The attempt at answering this question defines the subfield of Creole linguistics.

What seems to be the case invariably with languages that have a Creole origin is that they adopt, and adapt, the *lexicon* of the language spoken by the masters. Only few lexical remnants of the ancestral languages are found, mostly to do with magic, religion and food. Creole *grammars* are a different matter. They are, in a sense, simplified in that they lack the more sophisticated features of languages backed by a rich and extended cultural past and a large, well-organized literate society. One never finds, for example, a subjunctive mood, or an elaborate case system, or elaborate classifying systems. Morphology is usually absent or underdeveloped. Interestingly, however, there are also certain positive features common to Creole languages. They seem, for example, to go for basic SVO word order, irrespective of their ancestral substrate languages or the superstrate language spoken by the masters. More-over, in so far as they express tenses, modalities and aspects these tend to turn up as verb-like particles preceding the main verb in that order, the so-called TMA-system. (Bickerton, as has been shown, wishes to include the presence of serial verbs among the features common to all Creoles, but other linguists disagree.) The point is that if there is a substantial bundle of such features that jointly provide a characterization of the group of creole languages, we have a historical universal of the following type:

Historical universal I   If a language has a Creole origin it is SVO, has TMA particles, has virtually no morphology, etc.

This universal will be stronger if it allows reversal of the implication rela-tion. In that case one can say that if a language is SVO, has TMA particles, etc., it is a Creole language. Then this bundle of features characterizes the Creole languages uniquely. Whether this can be done is, however, still a moot point.

To the extent that the Creole historical universal I can be fleshed out with a substantial number of features, the likelihood increases that indeed, more or less as Bickerton has claimed, the universal innate language faculty must be held responsible. It must then be considered to be of such a nature that it will lead, categorically or preferentially, to the kind of phenomena that define the Creole languages given the historical conditions under which they came about. Whether the precise formulation given by Bickerton to his 'bioprogram' can, in the end, be maintained is, of course, a different matter.

4.8.5 Problems in language typology

Since Greenberg (1963) a great deal of work has been done in typology, which is now an increasingly flourishing branch of linguistics. In the course of this work a number of problems have come to light, some profound, others more practical, but most of them quite hard to solve.

• *Conflicting typologies*
One problem is that of conflicting typologies. We have seen (section 4.8.3) that it seems possible to base a typology on the root feature of basic word order. However, as was said at the end of 4.8.3, other root features are likely to be found. It is thinkable, for example, that the presence of morphology implies a host of other features, including the overt expression of tense and/or modality and/or aspect, or that if a language has morphological case marking and a passive voice, it will, besides other consequences, normally assign nominative case to the first nominal argument of the main predicate, accusa-tive case to the last nominal argument, and dative case to any middle term. It is, in short, quite likely that further research into implicational universals will reveal implicational chains that justify further typologies. Perhaps also von Schlegel's early typology may, on closer scrutiny, give rise to one or more implicational chains. The question then is, obviously, to what extent the

various typologies vary from each other. This question has not been broached yet in a systematic way, but when it is, the results will no doubt reveal interesting new perspectives.

- *The typologist's paradox*

From the beginning, typological work has laboured under one overwhelming practical obstacle, the problem of collecting enough relevant data on a sufficient number of languages. One may speak of the *typologist's paradox*. It consists in the fact that the number of languages in the world is far too large to allow anyone, or even any one group, to gain sufficient expert knowledge that would provide solid support for a typology. On the other hand, any serious typology requires more than just superficial knowledge of the languages involved. For example, to decide whether a language has a category 'adjective' takes more than a cursory look and will often require sophisticated in-depth knowledge. A linguist can acquire such knowledge only of a very limited number of languages, whereas the nature of his work demands sophisticated knowledge of a large number of languages. Since there seems to be no practical way out, one speaks of a paradox. Any solution would, ideally, involve close and intensive team work, with each member of the team studying a limited number of languages and testing these for certain well-defined parameters. However, quite apart from the financial implications, linguistics has not so far developed either the theory or the practice to implement such a programme, though steps in that direction are taken here and there.

Existing grammatical descriptions of languages might provide a substitute for direct data gathering by the linguist. Here, however, one has to cope with the scarcity of reliable descriptions and databases available. In practice, typologists still have to make do with little grammars written, mostly during the colonial period, by missionaries or retired government officials with an ecological linguistic interest. Fortunately, many such grammars are available, and some are much better than might be expected of amateur linguists. Yet more often than not they do not contain the information one crucially needs.

- *Languages of mixed type*

A further difficulty consists in the fact that there is no way of knowing whether some given language is of mixed type and how many mixed-type languages there are or could be. It is generally agreed that a language may change type in the course of its history. Proto-Indo-European, for example, is regarded as having had basic SOV word order, yet most of its descendants are no longer of that type. Since languages hardly ever change overnight, the conclusion seems inescapable that allowance must be made for periods when some of the languages concerned are of mixed type. Modern German, for example, seems a mixed-type language: it has basic SVO in main clauses, but SOV in subordinate finite, infinitival and participial clauses. The syntax of German is right-branching, which groups it with the SVO-languages, except in verbal clusters which are predominantly left-branching, as in SOV-languages. And more signs of type mixture could be mentioned. Given the available evidence one will be inclined to say that German is on its way from being an SOV to being an SVO language.

Yet this does not answer the general methodological question of how to determine what makes for a pure type and what makes for a type mixture. In order to answer this question one needs a much richer supply than is available to date of implicational chains and of data from large numbers of languages, and a concomitant statistical measure for the likelihood of grammatical features co-occurring.

- *Explanation of typological universals: functionalism and iconicity*

The main theoretical problem of linguistic typology is posed by the question of what could possibly *explain* the universals, implicational and other, that have been and will be found. While, on the one hand, the universals contribute to our understanding of the innate language faculty and thus help to explain, to some extent, the ways in which languages differ and how young children acquire the language of their environment, they themselves, on the other hand, require some explanation, probably of a functional kind. In this respect, however, functionalism is not a well-defined concept, since not enough is known about the mechanism of language to decide what factors would enhance linguistic communicative processes, and what factors would influence these processes in a negative way and thus be dysfunctional.

Iconicity is often mentioned in this context, as a measure of functionality (Haiman 1985). A linguistic expression or a grammatical construction is iconic to the extent that it 'mirrors', in some intuitive sense, the meaning that is expressed. Sound symbolism (onomatopoeia) is, of course, prototypically iconic. But one may well go a little further. The fact, for example, that subjects tend to precede objects (see 4.8.2) may be considered iconic, since in the many sentences that express a cause-effect relation the subject expresses the cause and the object the effect, and causes necessarily precede their effects. Another example is reduplication. Reduplication is often used as a means for expressing a variety of lexical or grammatical modifications, such as plurality, frequency, intensity or its opposite, mitigation. In Malay, for example, reduplication is regularly used for plurality (*anak-anak* 'children'), and also for the expression of mitigated or non-serious lexical meaning (*jalan-jalan* 'walk around casually', *gila-gila* 'a little mad'). Yet reduplication is also used, though not in Malay, for the intensification of lexical meaning, as in Mauritian Creole *ale-ale* 'go a long way, go with difficulty' or Sranan (the Creole of Surinam) *broko-broko* 'break up in little pieces', or *fon-fon* 'beat up hard'.

There is a problem here, in that one has an intuitive feeling that such reduplicative processes are or should be, in some sense, iconic. Yet how can they be if they can express opposite modifications such as intensification versus mitigation? It would be all too easy to say that, therefore, the notion of iconicity should be considered vacuous, since the paths of psychological association are often inscrutable. Even so, however, the answer is not immediately obvious.

On the whole, one has to recognize that iconicity still remains too poor a factor to explain the whole fabric of linguistic universals. For the moment, the overall conclusion has to be that general linguistic theory is as yet in such a primitive state that a serious explanation, in terms of a general theory, of the few universals that have been established so far is still beyond our grasp.

4.8.6 Typological versus theoretical universals

The typological and the theoretical approaches to linguistic universals ask for a comparison and, if possible, a unifying perspective. They differ in at least one obvious way. The typological universals are explicitly restricted to surface structure phenomena and are, therefore, directly verifiable and/or falsifiable. Greenberg's basic word order parameter, in particular, refers to directly observable surface word order in simple declarative main clauses.[47] The theoretical universals, on the other hand, pertain to the structural properties of the grammatical system of each language. They are much more abstract than the Greenberg universals and have the character of hypotheses that restrict the space within which grammars of natural languages can move. Consequently, they are not directly verifiable or falsifiable on grounds of simple observation, but will stand or fall with the grammars that are restricted by them.

Ideally, the two approaches should be combined to form one coherent general linguistic theory. For example, when a theorist examines the grammatical and/or semantic properties of the possessive complex predicates ('have', 'with', 'without', genitive -s, etc.) or of copula-verbs or whatever, he or she is well-advised to look at what the typologists have to say about these matters. A unified theory would restrict as much as possible the form of possible grammars and lexicons of natural languages and thus have a unifying effect on the notions of grammar and lexicon. This would be a theory in the Chomskyan sense, though with a much more solid empirical base, and not necessarily restricted to just the structural properties of rules and rule systems but relating also to the ways in which a grammar-cum-lexicon links up with the cognitive structures and processes involved in the production and comprehension of speech.

[47] It has been suggested (Koster 1975) that Dutch and German are SOV languages. What is meant there, however, is not that these two languages have basic SOV order in simple declarative main clauses. Such a statement would be obviously false since in main clauses the order is clearly SVO. Nor is what is meant that the surface SOV order in subordinate clauses should be taken to be the standard for basic word order in these languages. What is meant is that Dutch and German have SOV order at the hypothetical level of deep structure, a hypothesis which is as good as its explanatory force.

PART 2

CHAPTER 5

Predicate calculus: from Aristotle to generalized quantifiers

5.0 Preamble

We now turn to the history and development of logic. This may seem ironical, since we argue that logic as such is hardly relevant for the study of language. But we must recognize that logic has led to modern formal semantics, which consists in the application of logical model theory to natural languages.[1] Even if one has doubts about the empirical adequacy of this logical paradigm for natural language semantics, it exists, and we need some knowledge of logic to understand it. But beyond that, it is a fact that the insights and formal techniques offered by formal semantics are an indispensable tool for any proper semantic theory. And finally, as is argued in 7.3, it is gradually becoming clear that the *actual syntax* of modern predicate calculus, though superficially very different from that of natural language, provides not only a sophisticated instrument for the representation of sentence meanings but also, at the same time, a highly explanatory syntactic deep structure from which surface structures can be derived by means of simple and compact grammatical rule systems. Modern predicate calculus thus turns out to be empirically relevant for natural language syntax, an unexpected bonus for the linguists.

This chapter spans the history of logic from the Aristotelian Square of Oppositions to the theory of generalized quantifiers. Yet it is far from a complete history of logic. It pursues only those lines in the history of logic that have turned out to be most relevant to the study of language in our day, and in doing so it focusses on the foundations and the underlying motivations. After an exposé of Aristotelian logic it is shown first why and how, during the late 19th century, Aristotelian logic was replaced by modern formal logic. After that the emphasis is on two aspects: the *structure* of predicate calculus expressions on the one hand, and the associated *model-theory*, what logicians call the 'semantics', on the other. Technical difficulty is kept down to a minimum but some familiarity with the notions and techniques of elementary set theory is presupposed. Mathematical niceties have been avoided and abstract mathematical doubts are ignored unless they prove relevant for the present purpose. Professional logicians and mathematicians may therefore find the treatment given here unusual and selective. They are asked to consider that the study of natural language is not a logical or mathematical but an empirical enterprise. The role played by logic is, though important, merely ancillary.

---

[1] Adequate introductions to standard model-theoretic semantics are Dowty et al. (1981), Gamut (1991).

Although model-theoretic formal semantics has taught us a great deal one must not forget that it was set up, in logic, primarily to create a better logical proof theory, which is something linguists are not interested in (at least not in the present perspective of linguistic studies, which may, of course, prove less durable than we now like to think). But linguists áre interested in the ways logic provides *propositional structures* in order to make explicit the correspondence between what is said and what is the case, the verbal notion of truth, that is. Not that we support the verbal approach to truth and logic. On the contrary, we claim that truth is not primarily a correspondence between what is *said* and what is the case, but between what is *thought* and what is the case, i.e. we uphold the cognitive notion of truth, because words and sentences underdetermine the underlying thoughts. They are messengers that need not bring the whole message to be fully understood, because the receiving party already knows a lot. We argue, therefore, that natural language semantics is to be based on the cognitive, not the verbal, notion of truth. But for the moment we stick to logic as it is, and we have a good look at it, because it teaches us things otherwise unheard of.

During the Middle Ages, logic or, as it was called by the Stoics, *dialectica*, was part of the language-oriented trivium, together with *grammatica* and *rhetorica*, and not of the mathematically oriented quadrivium which comprised *musica, geometria, arithmetica* and *astronomia*. If the liberal arts were to be redistributed nowadays, logic would no doubt come under the quadrivium. The fact that, over the past century and a half, logic steadily drifted away from the study of language to that of mathematics has brought about an alienation. It is to be hoped that this process will be reversed.

Quite apart, however, from the relevance, albeit a limited one, of logic for semantics, there is another way in which logic is making itself felt in linguistics. Over the past fifty or so years, mathematics and logic have become the basic disciplines for formal systems in both the pure and the applied sciences, and as such they now have a diffuse and widespread influence in all spheres of life. And since most language-oriented disciplines have become formal themselves, modern linguistics being a prime example, it stands to reason that even non-semantically oriented linguists have had their interest in logic kindled.

5.1 Aristotelian logic

5.1.1 Semantic and logical consequence

Logic is perhaps best explained if we start with the notion of semantic consequence or semantic entailment and then pass on to the subclass of logical consequence or logical entailment. As before, we take the historical point of view, and will start with the very beginnings of logic in the schools of Plato and Aristotle.

- *Two discoveries, both made in Plato's school, form the basis of logic*

The first foundations for what was to become the discipline of formal logic were laid in Plato's Academy, in the period between 380 and 350 BC. The main figure in this development was Plato's best known student, the Macedonian philosopher Aristotle.

Two discoveries were made in the Academy, which immediately led to the development of the first formal system of logic in the western world. Both concerned the notion of *necessary consequence* of a sentence, also called *entailment*. (In the English-speaking world, the term *entailment* is commonly used for semantic or logical consequence. We will, therefore, speak indiscriminately of entailment and consequence. Other forms of necessary consequence, such as the causally grounded consequences in physical nature, are never called 'entailment': this term is reserved exclusively for semantics and logic.)

- *The discovery of semantic entailment*

The first of these two discoveries concerned the fact that many, if not all, assertive sentences (statements, propositions) of a language allow for inferences solely on the basis of their meanings. For example, when I say *Ben has been murdered*, then anyone who has understood this utterance and accepts its truth will also accept the truth of the statement *Ben is dead*. No independent checking of the situation at hand is necessary: the English language guarantees that if it is true that Ben has been murdered then it is also true that Ben is dead. Anyone unable to make that inference has insufficient knowledge of English, since it is in the meaning of the expression *have been murdered* that whoever has been murdered is dead. We say that the statement (proposition) *Ben is dead* is a necessary consequence of, or follows from, the statement (proposition) *Ben has been murdered*. Likewise, if utterances of (1a, b) are true, then, necessarily, an utterance of (2) is also true:

(1) a. Ben has been murdered
    b. Ali has been murdered

(2)   Ben and Ali are dead

Sentence (2) follows from the set of sentences {(1a), (1b)}, first, because it is in the meaning of *have been murdered* that whoever has been murdered is dead, and second, because in all cases where the same predicate applies to a number of subjects, the subjects can be taken together under the conjunction *and*.

We generalize these observations into a definition of the notion of *semantic entailment* or *semantic consequence* as follows:

> A set of one or more assertive sentences **A** *semantically entails* an assertive sentence B (B is a *semantic consequence* of **A**, or B *follows from* **A**) just in case in all situations where **A** is true B is also necessarily true on account of the meanings of **A** and B.

The following symbolic notation is used for semantic entailment:

$$\mathbf{A} \models B \qquad \text{or:} \qquad \text{'}\mathbf{A} \text{ semantically entails B'.}$$

It is important to observe, at this point, that in order to establish semantic entailment from a set **A** of one or more sentences to a sentence B, it is immaterial, for semantic (and also for logical) entailment, whether an utterance of **A** or B is actually true at the time of the utterance. What counts is that in all cases where **A** is true B must also, necessarily, be true, and that, therefore, no independent checking of the world is necessary. Actual truth or falsity of the sentences in question is not the semanticist's or the logician's concern. They prefer to leave those questions to scientists, the police, the courts, or other investigating bodies. What interests semanticists and logicians is the question of what follows necessarily *in case* the sentences in **A** are uttered truthfully, not the question of *whether* they are actually uttered truthfully.

Clearly, under this definition, any sentence which is necessarily true in virtue of its meaning is entailed by (follows from) any arbitrary assertive sentence in the language in question, even though it is counter-intuitive to use the terms *follow from* or *consequence* in such cases. Thus, for example, the above definition says that a sentence like *No-one is both alive and dead at the same time*, which is necessarily (or: analytically) true, 'follows from' an arbitrary sentence like *Today is Sunday* under the terms of the above definition, since the former sentence is always true, irrespective of whether the latter is or is not. This counter-intuitive result is normally accepted without further comment among logicians and philosophers of language. Yet it makes us wonder if it would not be better to search for a definition that would exclude such violations of one's intuition. One would prefer a definition of semantic entailment more directly based on *lexical* meaning analysis, i.e. on so-called meaning postulates, so that arbitrary consequence relations are avoided. The standard definition is, however, as given here.

• *The discovery of logical entailment and of logical constants*

The second discovery leading up to logic was that of *logical consequence* or *logical entailment*, and the concomitant notion of logic as a formal calculus of semantic consequences of natural language sentences.[2]

> We speak of a *logical entailment* when the entailment is not just based on one's intuitive understanding of the meanings concerned but on a formal calculus enabling one to derive the entailment automatically in virtue of the logical constants and the structure of the entailing statement or statements in **A**.

Logical consequences, or logical entailments, are thus a small subset of the semantic entailments. The usual symbol for logical entailment is ' |– '. Thus:

$$\textbf{A} \;|\!\!-\; B \qquad \text{or:} \qquad \text{'}\textbf{A} \text{ logically entails B'.}$$

---

[2] In the course of the 20th century branches of mathematical logic have been developed that are far removed from ordinary natural language and study truth relations for expressions in highly formalized systems of expression whose relation to natural language is either non-existent or far-fetched. These developments are not discussed here.

That such a logical calculus is possible was discovered by the students and followers of Plato during the first half of the fourth century BC, in particular by the most prominent figure among them, Aristotle, who developed the first formal logical calculus. It was found that sentences of a natural language (Greek in this case, but the discovery extends to all languages) contain certain elements, the so-called *logical constants*, that allow for the automatic, formal derivation of logical consequences. These logical constants were (and are) extremely few in number. In principle, the set contained only the negation *not*, and the quantifiers *all* and *some* (or their Greek counterparts). Somewhat later the elements *and*, *or* and *if-then* were added by Stoic philosophers. The whole of traditional, and a great deal of modern logic is based on this handful of elements.

5.1.2 Aristotelian sentence analysis

• *Sentence analysis as a requirement for logic: the singling out of predicates*
A logical calculus implies a form of sentence analysis. Aristotle's main analytical instrument for the logical analysis of sentences was his singling out of predicates. *A predicate* (Greek: *katēgoroúmenon* or *katēgórēma*) *is a linguistic expression that can be used to assign a property to something given, the subject or substrate* (Greek *hypokéimenon*). Predicates occur as single words, like *run* or *happy* or *dog*, but also as complex expressions, like *read a book* or *be the first man to land on the moon*, or *have a secret bank account*.

• *Two uses of predicates*
A predicate can be used in a number of ways, two of which are relevant here. First it can be used in such a way that the result is truth or falsity. When I say *This is a dog* or *I have a secret bank account*, then the predicates *dog* and *have a secret bank account* are applied to this and me, respectively. The objects referred to by the expression *this* and *I* are what Aristotle calls the 'subject', often also called the 'substrate'. In Aristotle's terminology, this term thus does not denote a sentence constituent but the referent of a sentence constituent (cp. section 2.6.3). The result of applying a predicate to a subject (in the Aristotelian sense) is a proposition which is either true or false.

But a predicate can also be used to make a referring noun phrase, as in *that dog* or *the one who has a secret bank account*. Now the determiner, *that* or *the one who*, combines with a predicate and the result is not a truth value but a referential focussing on a given entity, a given dog or a given holder of a secret bank account. In this case the predicate serves to select the correct reference object, not to make a statement that can be true or false. Let us speak of the propositional and the referential use of predicates, respectively.

These two uses of predicates combine hierarchically to make propositions. Let us make the notion of proposition somewhat more precise by saying that we consider a proposition, in a basic sense, to be the mental act of assigning a property to a given entity in such a way that the assignment is true or false. A proposition is thus the bearer of a truth value.[3] In a simple proposition of the kind we are considering, the property is expressed by means of a predicate in propositional use, and the given entity is, in most cases, referred to by means of an expression consisting of a determiner and a predicate in referential use. In both uses, as has been said, the subject is, in Aristotle's terminology, the thing in the real or an imagined world to which the predicate is applied so that a property is assigned to it, either under the condition of truth or falsity or as a means for fixing reference.

● *Ancient and modern use of the terms* subject *and* predicate

In the course of history, however, the terms *subject* and *predicate* have acquired different but related meanings (see 2.6.3). It has become customary to reserve the term *predicate* for predicates in propositional use, and to use the term *subject* for the constituent in a sentence or proposition that refers to the entity to which the property in question is assigned under the condition of truth or falsity. We now speak of 'subject' and 'predicate' as constituent elements of sentences that express propositions. In Aristotelian terminology, however, only predicates were linguistic expressions, while subjects were reference objects. Given this terminological confusion we must now decide how to use the term *subject*, and we decide to use it in the modern sense, that of the sentence constituent that combines with the predicate to make a proposition.

Here, however, there is a problem, already noted in 2.6.3 above, and never solved by Aristotle himself. The problem is that the Aristotelian notion of subject as *hypokeímenon* applies only to those grammatical subject terms that refer to a real or imagined definite entity, such as 'the man in question', or 'the sword of Achilles' in sentences like *The man was drunk*, or *the sword of Achilles was revered by all soldiers.* But the subject term in Aristotelian logic does not refer to an entity as defined in context, history, mythology, or common knowledge. On the contrary, as we shall see in a moment, the sentence types in Aristotelian logic explicitly exclude such subject terms. In his logic, Aristotle only wishes to consider subject terms like *all men* or *some men*, but not *the man* or *the men*. Yet it is only to the latter that his definition of *hypokeímenon* applies. The grammatical subject in sentences like *All men are mortal* remains unexplained. We have here a problem that was not solved until modern times, when quantifiers and variables were introduced into the logical machinery.

For the moment, however, we shall gloss over this problem, and simply accept that Aristotle divided a proposition into two main constituents, subject and (propositionally used) predicate, both containing predicates in the original sense. He moreover distinguished the logical constants *all*, *some*, and *not*. *All* and *some* are determiners, while *not* combines with either a determiner or a (propositionally used) predicate. A few examples will show how this system of analysis works.

---

[3] This is what the term *proposition* has been meant to stand for through the ages, despite the wildly varying explanations of the term in the theories that have been proposed (cp. Nuchelmans 1973).

- *Aristotle's logical analysis of sentences*

A sentence like *All men are mortal* is separated first into the subject term *all men* and the predicate term *are mortal*, with *all* as the determiner in the subject term. Then the logical structure of the sentence is laid bare by leaving in the logical word *all* and replacing the rest of the sentence by variables ranging over predicates. *All F is G* is thus a formula in Aristotelian Predicate Calculus with the variable *F* replacing a referentially used predicate, e.g. MAN, and *G* standing in for a propositionally used predicate, e.g. (BE) MORTAL. Likewise, in Aristotle's analysis, *Some men are mortal* is represented schematically as *Some F is G*. The negation word *not* can be added either to the logical determiner, as in *Not all men are mortal*, or *No (=not some) men are mortal*, or to the predicate, as in *All men are not mortal*, or *Some men are not mortal*. Both uses can be combined, as in *Not all men are not mortal*, or *No men are not mortal*. The logical structure of these sentences in terms of Aristotelian Predicate Calculus is thus as follows:

(3)a.   Not all men are mortal: not all F is G
    b.   No men are mortal: not some F is G
    c.   All men are not mortal: all F is not-G
    d.   Some men are not mortal: some F is not-G
    e.   Not all men are not mortal: not all F is not-G
    f.   No men are not mortal: not some F is not-G

One rule in Aristotle's logic says that given the truth of a sentence of the type *All F is G* one can automatically derive the logical entailment that the corresponding sentence of the type *Some F is G* is also true: *all* in *All F is G* can automatically be replaced with *some* without loss of truth, or, in logical jargon, *salva veritate*. The same goes for *all* in *All F is not-G*: there as well *some* may replace *all*, according to Aristotle, *salva veritate*.

We can say, therefore, that in Aristotle's logic the following logical entailments hold (are valid):

(4)a.   All men are mortal   ⊢   Some men are mortal
    b.   All dogs do not have wings   ⊢   Some dogs do not have wings
    c.   All mermaids have a bicycle   ⊢   Some mermaids have a bicycle

Logic is thus a calculus of truth relations, or, as is often said, a calculus that maintains or saves truth through a set of statements. When logic allows us to compute, on the basis of logical analysis, that a statement B must necessarily be true if a set of statements **A** is true, then, as has been said, we say that B is a *logical consequence* (*entailment*) of **A**. Semantic entailments, and more specifically logical entailments, derive their validity from the *meanings* of the words and structures employed. That is, if an entailment is valid it is so on *analytical* grounds, in the terminology of Immanuel Kant. What makes a logical entailment special is the fact that it is based solely on the meanings of the logical constants. This makes logical entailments computable on the basis of a schematic sentence analysis that lays bare the logical constants and replaces the elements that are considered non-logical with variables, such as 'F' or 'G'. Since, in this calculus, the variables that stand for non-logical elements range over predicates we speak of *predicate calculus.*

5.1.3 Aristotelian Predicate Calculus and syllogistics

Aristotle's logic consists of a *predicate calculus* and a *doctrine of syllogisms.* The combination of predicate calculus and syllogistics is known in the textbooks as *Aristotelian logic.*

• *Aristotelian Predicate Calculus: the Square of Oppositions*
As has been said, Aristotelian Predicate Calculus works with the logical constants *all, some* and *not,* and with the grammatical distinction between subject and predicate. With these elements and on the basis of his definition of truth (see 1.2.1) and of some basic principles discussed in section 5.1.6, he devised a small logical calculus, Aristotelian Predicate Calculus (APC), for four types of sentences, based on the logical constants mentioned and an analysis in terms of (grammatical) subject and predicate. The four types are:

type **A**:	all F is G
type **I**:	some F is G
type **E**:	all F is not G / no F is G
type **O**:	some F is not G / not all F is G

F and G are *lexical variables* over predicates (expressions for properties): 'man', 'dog' ghost', 'small', 'easy', 'live in London', 'have a bank account', 'wonder where to go', 'hate all men', 'dead and not dead at the same time', etc. Whatever, in each sentence type, stands to the left of *is* is subject, and whatever stands to the right of *is* is predicate. The element *is* (never mind the singular: standard logic has never cared much about the difference between singular and plural) is just a connective (copula) between subject and predicate.

The type names 'A', 'I', 'E' and 'O' are of much later origin. They were introduced by the late Roman philosopher Boethius (480-524 AD) as a teaching aid for beginning students: the first two vowels of the Latin words *affirmo,* 'I affirm', and *nego,* 'I deny', respectively.

Sentences of type **A** and **I** are *affirmative;* those of type **E** and **O** are *negative.* Moreover, sentences of type **A** and **E** are called *general,* while sentences of type **I** and **O** are called *particular.* The particulars distinguish themselves in that they allow for existential generalization: if it is true that some F is G, or some F is not G, then there exists at least one F: in that case the predicate F stands for a non-empty class.

The four types can be combined into a geometrical figure, the famous Square of Oppositions, which serves as an abacus for a small logical calculus. It was again Boëthius who invented this simple notational device:

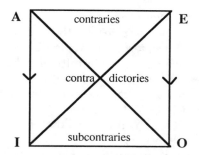

Figure 1 *The Aristotelian Square of Oppositions*

Given truth for a sentence of type **A**, the corresponding sentence of type **I** follows logically, and likewise for **E** and **O**. For example, from *All mermaids have a bank account* the Square allows one to infer *Some mermaids have a bank account*, and from *No mermaid has a bank account* one may deduce *Some mermaid has no bank account*. These two entailment schemata are called the *downward* or, more traditionally, the *subaltern entailments*.

A and **E** type sentences are contraries. They cannot both be true at the same time, but they can both be false. Thus *All bears are smart* and *No bear is smart* cannot, for Aristotle, be true together, but they can, obviously, both be false.

I and **O** type sentences are subcontraries. That is, they cannot, at the same time, both be false, but they can both be true. For example, *Some bears are smart* and *Some bears are not smart* can obviously both be true simultaneously. But, for Aristotle, their negations cannot: *No bear is smart* (= *Not some bear is smart*) and *All bears are smart* (= *No bear is not smart*) cannot, in Aristotle's eyes, both be true at the same time.

Finally, **A** and **O** type sentences, as well as **I** and **E** type sentences, are contradictories: they cannot, at the same time, be either both true or both false. Thus, the truth of an **A**-sentence and the falsity of an **O**-sentence mutually entail each other, and likewise, the truth of an **I**-sentence and the falsity of an **E**-sentence mutually entail each other. Since the negation operator, when placed over a whole sentence, has the property of changing the truth value from 'true' to 'false' and vice versa, we may say that **A** entails **not-O**, **not-O** entails **A**, **I** entails **not-E**, and **not-E** entails **I**.

The Square can be summarized in terms of the following entailment schemata (the symbol '¬' is used for the negation word *not* prefixed to a sentence).

(5)a.	**A**	⊢	**I**	subaltern (downward) affirmative
b.	**E**	⊢	**O**	subaltern (downward) negative
c.	**A**	⊢	¬ **E**	contraries
d.	¬ **I**	⊢	**O**	subcontraries
e.	**A**	⊢	¬ **O**	contradictories
f.	¬ **A**	⊢	**O**	"
g.	**I**	⊢	¬ **E**	"
h.	¬ **I**	⊢	**E**	"

- *The Law of Contraposition*

The *Law of Contraposition* applies to this system. This means that an entailment relation may be inverted, provided both terms of the relation are negated: if X ⊢ Y, then also ¬Y ⊢ ¬X. Intuitively, this is easily understood: X ⊢ Y means 'in all cases where X is true, Y is also true'. Now suppose Y is false, and ¬Y therefore true. In such a case X cannot be true, since if it were true Y would also be, in virtue of X ⊢ Y. Given that there are only two possibilities, 'true' or 'false', for both X and Y, it follows that, if X ⊢ Y, in all cases where ¬Y is true, ¬X is also true, hence ¬Y ⊢ ¬X.

Since two consecutive occurrences of *not* cancel each other out, we may, though superfluously, add the following entailment schemata, based on the Law of Contraposition:

(6)a. (=5c)   **E** ⊢ ¬**A**
  b. (=5d)   ¬**O** ⊢   **I**
  c. (=5e)   **O** ⊢ ¬**A**
  d. (=5f)   ¬**O** ⊢   **A**
  e. (=5g)   **E** ⊢ ¬**I**
  f. (=5h)   ¬**E** ⊢   **I**

- *The Law of Conversion*

Note, furthermore, that *all F is not G* is equivalent with (i.e. mutually entails) *no F is G*, and likewise for *some F is not G* and *not all F is G*. This is due to the *Law of Conversion*, recognized by Aristotle as well as by modern logic, which says that 'all — not' is interchangeable with 'not — some', and 'some — not' with 'not — all'. Hence, in virtue of double negation cancelling, 'not — some — not' = 'not — not — all' = 'all', and, likewise, 'not — all — not' = 'not — not — some' = 'some'. In other words, the quantifiers *some* and *all* are definable in terms of each other. For this reason logicians, who like to minimize specifications, say that one quantifier is sufficient, the other being derivable by Conversion.

- *Aristotle's syllogistics*

The previous section summed up Aristotle's Square of Oppositions, and thus Aristotelian predicate calculus. On top of his predicate calculus, however, Aristotle also constructed what is called his *syllogistics*, the basis of what later, in the hands of the Stoics (Egli 1983), became propositional calculus.[4] The syllogistics, or doctrine of syllogisms, provides entailment relations for pairs of sentences of the types **A**, **E**, **I** and **O**, where the two sentences of each pair share a predicate, whether in subject or in predicate position. The Latin speaking Medieval tradition devised memory aids for students on the basis of the type letters, which gave rise to the traditional names for syllogism schemata like BARBARA, DARII, CELARENT, FERIO, etc. For example (the symbol '∴' is traditional for 'ergo', marking the entailment):

---

[4] For an adequate exposé of Aristotelian syllogistics, see Kneale & Kneale (1962:67-81).

(7)a.	BARBARA:		(7)b.	DARII:	
	all F is G	type **A**		all F is G	type **A**
	all G is H	type **A**		some H is F	type **I**
	∴ all F is H	type **A**		∴ some H is G	type **I**

Each syllogism type was considered axiomatic in the sense that it provides a schema for conducting a logical argument: by applying the schemata one can blindly formulate conclusions, i.e. entailments, from premises. In this sense the doctrine of syllogisms is a form of algorithmic computation. Nowadays, the syllogistic schemata are no longer considered axiomatic. We shall see in section 5.3.2 that the whole of Aristotelian syllogistics is reducible to simple theorems in set theory and computable in terms of Boole algebra. However, the theory of syllogisms, which is a part of logical proof theory, is only of marginal interest in the present context.

5.1.4 Propositional Calculus

Soon after Aristotle's death the Stoics extended Aristotelian syllogistics and developed a *propositional calculus*. The resulting amalgam of Aristotelian and Stoic logic was taught virtually without alterations from Antiquity through the Middle Ages and the Renaissance till well into the 20th century. In the following sections, from 5.2 onwards, it will be shown how and why logic, in particular predicate calculus and syllogistics, went through a series of radical reforms during the 19th and early 20th centuries, leading to modern logic. In modern logic there is no longer any need to teach the syllogisms, as these are easily derived with the help of set theory. Standard modern logic consists largely of a combination of a thoroughly revised predicate calculus and the traditional propositional calculus.

What is now called 'propositional calculus' is essentially a Stoic product. Stoic logic came about in the early third century BC, not long after Aristotle's death, in the philosophy school of Megara, an ancient Greek city situated just West of Athens. Not too much is known about the Stoics, as almost no first hand documentation is available (cp. note 5 in chapter 1). It is known, however, that the Megarian school of philosophy was founded around 400 BC by a man called Euclides (not the mathematician!), who was succeeded by Eubulides, contemporary and critic of Aristotle. (Eubulides is mainly known for his *paradoxes*, including the famous Liar Paradox, which were meant to unsettle Aristotle's logic as taught in nearby Athens. We shall meet Eubulides again in section 6.2.3.1.1, in the context of presupposition theory.) Some time after 300 BC, the Megarian School was headed by a philosopher called Zeno, who died in 264 BC. Zeno is generally regarded as the founder of the Stoic school of philosophy. He and his pupil Philo of Megara distinguished themselves by their contributions to and extensions of existing Aristotelian logic. They added sentences with a definite description or proper name as subject term to the existing machinery of syllogistics, and thus recognized the following as a syllogism:

(7)c.   All humans are mortal
         Socrates is a human

    ∴ Socrates is mortal

They, moreover, discovered propositional calculus.

- *The material implication*

Zeno and Philo realized that the Aristotelian syllogisms can all be schematically rewritten as 'Always, if A and B, then C', where A and B are the
premisses, and C the conclusion. They saw that 'Always, if A and B, then C' is
invalidated only if there is a possible situation such that 'A and B' is true
while C is false. From this Philo of Megara built the notion of the material
implication, expressed by conditional sentences of the form 'At this moment, if
A then B', or, as is usually said, 'If A then B'. Philo stipulated that a sentence
'At this moment, if A then B' is false only when A is (now) true but B is (now)
false. In all other cases the implication is considered true. In particular, when
A is false the implication 'If A then B' is automatically true: the truth value
of B is then immaterial. Thus, both the sentences (8a) and (8b):

(8)a. If the moon is made of green cheese, then Athens is in Greece
   b. If the moon is made of green cheese, then Athens is not in Greece

are considered true if the moon is not made of green cheese (as it isn't). Our best
authority, Sextus Empiricus (2nd cent. AD), explains this as follows, in his
Outline of Pyrrhonic Philosophy II,105:

> For the implication either begins with true and ends with true, as in 'If it is day it is
> light', or it begins with false and ends with false, as in 'If the earth flies the earth
> has wings', or it begins with true and ends with false, as in 'If the earth exists the
> earth flies', or it begins with false and ends with true, as in 'If the earth flies the
> earth exists'. Of these only the one that starts with true and ends with false is
> considered unsound [i.e. by the Stoics], the others, however, are considered sound.

This doctrine of the implication met with fierce resistance throughout
Antiquity on the grounds that it makes little intuitive sense to declare both
(8a) and (8b) true at the same time. During the third century BC the implication debate was apparently a matter of wide public interest, since the contemporary poet Callimachus wrote an epigram saying 'Even the crows on the
rooftops caw about the nature of conditionals' (Kneale & Kneale 1962:128).

The intuitive resistance to Philo's material implication still exists in our
day. It is now commonly accepted that the standard logical account of conditional sentences in terms of the material implication fails to do justice to the
nature of conditional sentences in natural language, and alternative analyses
have been proposed. On the other hand, however, the material implication as
known in standard propositional calculus shows a mathematical regularity
that makes it suitable for formal reasoning both in natural language and in
mathematics. It is for this reason that it has survived in logic, even if it is
under attack in the semantic analysis of natural language.

- *The operators of propositional calculus are truth-functions*

Building on the implication, the early Stoic logicians developed the additional truth functions of *not* (the negation), *and* (the conjunction), and *or* (the disjunction). These are still the backbone of modern propositional calculus, where the logical constants are *not, and, or,* and *if—then*. The standard symbols for *not, and, or,* and *if—then* are, respectively, ¬, ∧, ∨, and →. The variables used to replace non-logical material (usually p, q, r, or A, B, C) stand for propositions, not for predicates. Hence the name *propositional calculus*.

The negation word *not* is not new: it already figured in Aristotelian Predicate Calculus, as shown in 5.1.3. There it functions not only as a propositional operator inverting truth values, but also as an operator on predicates with a different though related semantic function. The negation is thus found both in predicate calculus and in propositional calculus. It will be shown below, in 5.1.5, that this reflects a serious unclarity about the function of negation in ancient logic, an unclarity that had to remain unsolved till the advent of modern logic. Here we just signal the problem, and will be content with looking at ¬ ('not') as a propositional operator which takes a proposition with one truth value ('true' or 'false') and delivers a new, negated proposition with the opposite truth value. Thus, given a proposition A, the negation operator forms a new, negated proposition ¬A with the opposite truth value from A. The negation is thus a unary propositional operator.

The elements *and, or,* and *if—then* are binary propositional operators. They differ from *not* in that they need not one but two propositions to form a new, complex proposition, as in the schematic logical structures:

(9) a.   Ben is in Paris and Ali is in London   or: A ∧ B
    b.   Ben is in Paris or Ali is in London   or: A ∨ B
    c.   If Ben is in Paris then Ali is in London   or: A → B

Sentences like (10a) or (10b):

(10) a.   Ben and Ali are in Paris
     b.   Ben or Ali is in Paris

are analysed logically as, respectively:

(11) a.   Ben is in Paris and Ali is in Paris   or: A ∧ B
     b.   Ben is in Paris or Ali is in Paris   or: A ∨ B

(The reduction of sentences like (11a, b) to their shortened counterparts (10a, b) is known in the theory of grammar as Conjunction Reduction. Linguists know that a full specification of all the possible forms of Conjunction Reduction is far from a simple matter. But we will not go into that question here.)

The logical constants ¬, ∧, ∨, and → are called *truth functions*. A truth function is defined as follows:

> A truth function is a function that takes as input one or more truth values and delivers a new truth value.

In other words, an operator is truth-functional just in case it forms a new sentence out of one or more given sentences and assigns a truth value to the new sentence exclusively on the basis of the truth value (values) of the component sentence (sentences).

Assuming, as Aristotle does, just two truth values, we can make the following matrices or *truth tables* for the propositional operators ¬, ∧, ∨, and →, where '1' stands for 'true' and '0' for 'false':

A	¬A		A	∧ B		∨ B		→ B	
					1	0	1	0	1	0
1	0			1	1	0	1	1	1	0
0	1			0	0	0	1	0	1	1

Figure 2   *The truth-functions* ¬, ∧, ∨, *and* →

This extremely simple propositional calculus has remained essentially unchanged since its invention in the 3rd century BC. Only notational devices are new: the symbols used for the truth-functional operators and the truth values, and the presentation of the truth functions as matrices or truth tables. (The truth tables were not introduced until the 1920s, which is surprisingly late, given that the underlying notions had been around for a few thousand years.)

We shall leave propositional calculus now. It will be taken up again in section 5.3.3, in the context of Boole algebra and set theory. At this point it is more relevant to return to Aristotelian Predicate Calculus, and see to what problems it gave rise.

5.1.5 The defects of Aristotelian Predicate Calculus

The Aristotelian Square of Oppositions leaks. It suffers from a number of major defects, and Aristotle knew it. He was, however, unable to do anything about it, and let the matter rest. It rested till the middle of the 19th century. We shall now discuss three major defects of APC.

• *The first problem: empty F-classes*
First and foremost, APC does not work when the F-variable takes as value a predicate with an empty extension. This is called the *problem of the empty F-class*. The problem is easily demonstrated by making an A-sentence with an F-predicate that has no representatives in the actual world, such as:

(12)   All mermaids have a bank account

The question is: is (12) true or false in the actual world? It has to be one of the two, in virtue of Aristotle's Principle of the Excluded Third (PET), about which more in 5.1.6. Let us assume that (12) is true. In that case the subaltern entailment schema tells us that the corresponding **I**-type sentence:

(13)   Some mermaids have a bank account

must also be true. Now (13), being an **I**-type sentence, is a particular and thus allows for existential generalization, making it follow that there is at least one mermaid. But we had agreed that there are no mermaids in this world. It follows that if we judge (12) to be true, it has an alleged entailment which is false, which means that (12) cannot be true and must, therefore, be false. Well then, let (12) be false. Now, however, in virtue of (5f), the corresponding **O**-sentence must be true:

(14)   Some mermaids do not have a bank account

Now existential generalization applies again, which means that (12) cannot be false either. Therefore, (12) is neither true nor false if the world contains no mermaids, as it doesn't. There goes PET, or else, there goes the Square! (Russell decided, a hundred years ago, that PET should stay but the Square should go. Others now feel that PET should go and the Square should stay.)

The upshot is that APC is valid only for those situations ('models') where the lexical predicate variables range over non-empty sets: the whole of APC has, as the term goes, *existential import*, not just the particulars **I** and **O**.

Aristotle knew this and stipulated that his predicate calculus was valid only for non-empty values of predicate variables. But this is a terrible condition for any logician. It limits the applicability of the logic to the use of certain sentences in certain situations only. This makes the logic dependent on contingent circumstances, which goes against the very nature and purpose of logic. Logic is meant to be a calculus of analytical entailment relations, valid on the basis of the meanings of the expressions used. In other words, logic is meant to be metaphysically valid, and must therefore not be dependent in any way on contingent factors of what may or may not be the case in any world. Moreover, those predicates that have an empty extension by analytical, semantic necessity, such as 'dead and not dead at the same time', would have to be banned from the language. But what grammatical criterion could enforce such banning order?

The situation was, in fact, desperate, and no remedy was in sight. This highly unsatisfactory situation lasted till the middle of the 19th century, when the application of Boole algebra and set theory to Aristotelian logic showed where the fault lay. The remedy, however, destroyed the Square of Oppositions, and with it most of the existing predicate calculus machinery, shifting the main burden of logic on to propositional calculus.

Meanwhile, some philosophers of language and natural language semanticists feel that APC, with its existential import, does more justice to the semantics of natural language than modern predicate calculus. Their problem consists in how to reconcile existential import with the philosophical and mathematical requirements of logic. More is said about this in section 6.2.3.

• *The second problem: lack of expressivity*

The second problem with APC and the Square, the *problem of expressivity*, is to do with the *language* used for the logical analysis. It consists in the fact that the logical expressions *all*, *some* and *not* occur not only in subjects but also within predicates, as, for example, in (15):

(15)   Some children know all football players

Here, the quantified phrase *all football players* occurs inside the predicate of the proposition, and thus cannot be 'factorized out' by the Aristotelian analysis, which recognizes quantifiers only in the subject term. For the purpose of APC, (15) is merely a sentence of type **I**, an affirmative particular, and the fact that there is a logical expression inside the predicate is simply lost. In 5.5 below it is shown how modern predicate calculus has replaced the subject-predicate division of a proposition by an analysis in terms of a more narrowly defined predicate and *n* argument terms, each of which can be independently quantified. This effectively solves the problem of expressivity.

• *The third problem: complications with negation*

The third problem concerns the logical status of the negation. As was shown above, in APC *not* takes scope both over propositions, as in (5d-h) above, and over predicates, as in 'all F is not G' or 'some F is not G'. This makes the status of the negation uncertain and ill-defined. To see the problem more clearly, consider sentence (16), which is a statement about an individual called *Ali*, and is thus of a type that does not figure in APC:

(16)   Ali is not at home

Here we find the logical constant *not*, combined with the remainder ALI IS — AT HOME. Since the remainder makes sense in its own right, as a statement about Ali, we can replace it with a lexical variable, say 'A'. We can now present the logical structure of (16) as:

(17)   not [A]   or: (18)   ¬ A

The lexical variable 'A' replaces the full proposition 'Ali is at home'. As has been said, when the variables used replace full propositions we have a propositional calculus. We say that *not* is a logical constant in propositional calculus. More precisely, we say that *not* is a propositional operator.

We can combine the propositional calculus with APC, for example by constructing the formula:

(19)   not [ALL F (is) G]

where 'ALL F (is) G' is an A-type APC propositional schema. It will be a real proposition as soon as the variables F and G have been given a value (are replaced by real predicates), as in the corresponding:

(20)   Not all humans are mortal

So far the story has been relatively simple. Complications arise, however, when we consider other uses of *not*. Consider the **O**-type sentence:

(21)   Some humans are not mortal

This sentence contains the two logical constants *some* and *not*. For *some* there is no problem, as we can analyse the subject term as 'SOME F'. But what to do with the predicate 'are not mortal'? We could replace it with the lexical variable G, which would result in an **I**-type sentence of the form 'Some F is G'. But this would mean a tremendous loss in logical expressive power, since the element *not* would remain unexploited.

On the other hand, it does not look as though the element *not* can be isolated from sentences like (21) in such a way that the remainder is a full proposition. Of course, the sentence fragment SOME HUMANS ARE — MORTAL is interpretable as a proposition in its own right, and we might be tempted to analyse (21) as:

(22)   not [SOME F (is) G]

But this would be wrong, for (22) means 'it is not the case that some F is G', and would thus be an **E**-type sentence of the form 'no F is G', corresponding to:

(23)   No humans are mortal

which is quite different from the **O**-type sentence (21).

- *Solution not found until late 19th century*

So what to do? Aristotle, and all logicians after him till Frege, did not know the answer. Their solution was to leave the status of *not* undefined: it is used as just a logical constant that occurs in different structural positions in sentences. The proper answer to this question was not found until the 19th century, when the German philosopher of mathematics, logic and language, Gottlob Frege, introduced new technical notions, in particular quantifiers and substitutional variables, and introduced modern quantification theory, where the negation is exclusively a propositional operator. The sophisticated machinery required to keep predicate calculus on its feet is explained in section 5.5 below.

5.1.6 Truth and the axioms of Aristotelian logic

Let us now have a look at the basic principles of Aristotelian logic, as proposed by Aristotle himself. This is important for the study of natural language semantics because all forms of logic, whether Aristotelian or modern, run into difficulties when applied to natural language, despite the fact that the origin of logic lies in the semantic analysis of natural language sentences. Therefore, if the idea of a logic for natural language is to make sense one had better go back to the foundations and the basic principles. This will also make it easier to see that it is erroneous to think that logic is absolute and that there can be only one logic. Although logic is a calculus of analytical and hence metaphysical necessity it does allow for variations, since the necessities that reign supreme in any calculus depend on the underlying axioms and on the defini-tions of the terms used.

- *The Principle of Contradiction*

Logic is based on the notion of truth as correspondence as developed by Plato and, in particular, Aristotle (see section 1.2.1). This correspondence notion of truth entails the *Principle of Contradiction*, which says that no proposition can be true and false at the same time. It must be noted that a *sentence* can easily be true and false at the same time. When this is so, we say that the sentence is ambiguous, i.e. has two or more meanings and thus corresponds to two or more propositions. A proposition, as the bearer of a truth value, is never ambiguous, and cannot be both true and false at the same time. If logic is to apply to sentences instead of propositions, the Principle of Contradiction states that no (assertive) sentence can be both true and false at the same time in one of its meanings. The latter formulation is preferable, since for us, as for Aristotle, the notion of sentence is less mysterious than that of proposition, and the notion of entailment was formulated for (assertive) sentences, not for purely theoretical entities called 'propositions'.

- *The Principle of the Excluded Third (PET)*

Moreover, Aristotle formulated the *Principle of the Excluded Third* (PET), also called the *Strict Bivalence Principle*. If logic operates with (unambiguous assertive) sentences, this principle consists, in fact, of two independent sub-principles, though Aristotle himself did not make this distinction. The two subprinciples are :

(a) the *Subprinciple of Complete Valuation*:
   Every sentence that takes part in the logical calculus always has a truth value

(b) the *Subprinciple of Bivalence*:
   There are exactly two truth values, 'true' and 'false', none in between and none outside.

Neither subprinciple is self-evident the way the Principle of Contradiction is. In fact, both have been challenged.

- *The Subprinciple of Complete Valuation: occasion sentences and eternal sentences*

It is easy to think up a sentence that has no truth value, for example:

(24)   The girl was wearing a beautiful hat

Although (24) is a perfectly meaningful, grammatically well-formed sentence of English, when uttered here and now it makes no sense to ask whether it is true or false. Sentence (24) is, in fact, a sentence *type*, not a sentence *token* (see also section 6.2.3.1.5 below). For it to have a truth value it must be 'anchored' in a given situation and discourse, where it is clear which person is referred to by the expression *the girl* and what time is referred to by the past tense *was*.

Sentences whose utterance tokens need context for the determination of a truth value (or: need context in order to express a proposition) are called *occasion sentences* in the philosophical literature. Some sentences, the so-called *eternal sentences*, do not need context for their utterance tokens to have a truth value. Examples are:

(25)a. Once upon a time there was a king
 b. Anyone mocking animal rights is punishable
 c. Some bears are dangerous
 d. No child knows all football players

No matter where or when they are uttered, sentences like (25a-d) always have a truth value. This is due to the fact that eternal sentences contain no expressions that require any form of contextual 'anchoring'. They lack definite descriptions like *the girl*: all argument terms of the main verb are quantified. Moreover, any past tense is also quantified, as in (25a) by means of *once upon a time*, so that no contextual anchoring is required. Present tenses are considered to be either generic, i.e. in some sense tenseless, or automatically linked up with the time of speaking at any occasion of utterance.

• *Aristotle banned occasion sentences from his logic*
Aristotle did not wish to consider occasion sentences in his logic. The reason he gives is that occasion sentences have no relevance in philosophy, and logic serves only to elucidate philosophical problems. But he may well have had further, less explicit motives for the exclusion of occasion sentences from his logic. It is unlikely that he had a clear view of all the consequences, but we may assume that he sensed danger. We know now, after twenty-three centuries of logical practice, that occasion sentences create havoc in a number of ways, due to precisely their context-dependency. In this respect they are like sentences that carry presuppositions. If occasion sentences are to be incorporated into the logic the basic principles have to be rethought and revised, and Aristotle clearly preferred to avoid such complications, and have a logic that applied equally to propositions, sentences and utterance tokens. The Stoics, as we have seen, were less afraid of occasion sentences. They allowed them into syllogistics and into propositional calculus, where they do little harm. They also thought about the nature of the problem and about what would be required to solve it.

Modern standard logic still has Aristotle's preference for eternal sentences, but at the same time it wishes to account for occasion sentences. The untold problems provoked by this strategy are discussed in section 6.2.3.

• *Sentences about the future are excluded from PET and from the logic: the sea battle*
It was clear to Aristotle that if occasion sentences are let in, the subprinciple of complete valuation no longer holds, since an occasion sentence uttered out of context will lack a truth value. By excluding them from his logic he could

maintain the first subprinciple. Apart from that, however, there is a problem with statements about the future. Aristotle's famous example is:

(26)   There will be a sea battle tomorrow

said, if you like, on the eve of the battle of Salamis, when sailors, soldiers and workmen could be seen to be busily preparing the Athenian fleet for what looked like an imminent heavy clash with the Persian fleet. Here, Aristotle says, there is no actually existing state of affairs that does or does not correspond to what the sentence says. Hence, statements about the future have no truth value and are, therefore, ruled out from logic.

Given all these conditions, one may indeed say that the subprinciple of complete valuation holds. But it also cripples logic so severely that doubts may arise as to its adequacy for natural language analysis. It would seem much better to allow occasion sentences in and let logic operate not with sentence types but with utterance tokens that are properly anchored in their contexts and thus have a truth value. This maximizes the set of propositions, i.e. the set of objects to which logic is applicable, and hence the analytical power of logic. But it also requires a proper theory of contextual anchoring, which is still not available.

• *The Subprinciple of Bivalence*
Now to the second subprinciple, the subprinciple of bivalence. Here, too, there are many complications and uncertainties. Again, the principle is far from self-evident. One can easily imagine different kinds or degrees of truth and falsity. One may think of partial truth, to be set off against partial falsity, and thus posit intermediate values between the extremes of 'true' and 'false'. This is what the modern so-called 'fuzzy logics' are about. These allow for an infinite variety of intermediate values between 'true' and 'false'. They were often constructed with a view to practical applications in cases where gradual transitional values between extreme states are to be computed. Or one may think of different kinds of truth or falsity. In presuppositional logic, for example, it makes sense to distinguish between minimal falsity, which is the ordinary, unmarked form of falsity, and radical falsity, arising when a sentence is asserted while one or more of its presuppositions are false (see section 6.2.3 for further discussion).

• *PET not to be confused with the Principle of the Excluded Middle (PEM)*
The Principle of the Excluded Third should not be confused with the Principle of the Excluded Middle (PEM), even if they are often confused in the literature. Whereas PET requires that all propositions dealt with in the logical system have one of two truth values, PEM only excludes any intermediate values. PEM thus covers only part of the ground covered by PET. It is part of the more general Principle of the Excluded Third, but not identical with it.

The 'fuzzy' logics of our day violate both PET and PEM, but logics with, for example, different kinds of falsity, as developed in presupposition theory, only violate PET, not PEM. Their point is not the introduction of intermediate truth values, but the splitting up of one truth value into different kinds.

Aristotle placed a great deal of emphasis on PEM because he wished to classify the adjectival pair 'true-false' with the class of absolute, strictly binary, all-or-nothing oppositions, toggling between 'yes' and 'no', such as 'alive-dead' or 'locked-unlocked'. Most other adjectival opposition pairs are not like that. They have gradual transitional states between the extremes named by the adjectives. For example, pairs like 'light-dark', 'easy-difficult' or 'full-empty' allow for infinitely many intermediate states where the referent is neither entirely the one nor entirely the other. Such pairs are contraries, in that they cannot both apply, but they can both fail to apply.

In Aristotle's view, the pair 'true-false' does not belong to this class of gradable oppositions. This pair is of the all-or-nothing type, and thus obeys PEM: there are no half truths. Adjectival pairs of the gradual type do allow for half values, as a bottle can be half full, which then makes it also half empty. But to say of a bottle which is half full that it is full is simply false, not half false, if we follow Aristotle.

- *PET jealously guarded throughout the history of logic*

Aristotle was adamant with respect to PET, though he was fully aware of its debatable status. One senses an almost emotional edge to his attachment to PET, as if he feared that the proud, though small, edifice of logic might collapse if PET were not strictly enforced. In any case, both the Principle of Contradiction and PET are still considered basic to logic, the former for obvious reasons which few will want to doubt, the latter on much more obscure grounds. PET is somehow sacrosanct in modern logic, and those who tinker with it are considered either marginal or just not serious. This is, however, quite unjustified, and also counter-productive for a better understanding of language.

- *The Aristotelian and the Stoic tradition*

One should keep an open mind as to which of the following two courses is preferable. One course is to replace the actual machinery of Aristotelian logic but maintain the basic principles, i.e. the Principle of Contradiction and PET. The other course is to reconsider the basic principles on the basis of detailed observation of the semantics of natural language sentences, and reconstruct the logical machinery accordingly. The former course is the one followed by modern logic, where the Aristotelian axioms are jealously guarded. This is what we might call the Aristotelian tradition. The latter course may be called the Stoic tradition. In modern times it is more popular with philosophers of language. Those who follow the Stoic tradition tend to find much of value in the original Aristotelian Square of Oppositions, complete with its existential import. In order to escape the undesirable aspects they propose to extend logic in ways that violate the Principle of the Excluded Third.[5]

5.2 Nineteenth century formalization

It took almost twenty-two centuries to remedy the faults of Aristotelian predicate calculus, while maintaining the Aristotelian axioms. And the rescue came not from the philosophers, who had been in charge of logic during the intervening period, but from the mathematicians. Since the 17th century, mathematics had been going through a period of radical change and renovation, providing the necessary instruments for the new physics, chemistry, astronomy and other physical sciences. Mathematicians, in the 17th century, were rarely just that. Normally they would also be philosophers, like René Descartes or Blaise Pascal in France, or Gottfried Wilhelm Leibniz in Germany, or they would also be physicists, like Isaac Newton in England or Christian Huygens in the Netherlands, often combining their theoretical talents with engineering skills. Pure mathematicians began to appear towards the end of the 18th century. It was then also that there was a notable increase in the interest, already manifest in Leibniz much earlier, in the relations between logic and mathematics, and even between language and mathematics.

• *Logic turns mathematical*
The big change, however, occurred around the middle of the 19th century. It is difficult to draw an adequate picture of the historical forces that led to the formalization of logic. The mathematical aspects of logic had attracted the attention of a small group of scholars since the Renaissance, including Leibniz, (see Kneale & Kneale 1962:345ff.), but the 18th century saw an increasing number of logicians and philosophers (Immanuel Kant among them) trying to fit the Aristotelian theory of syllogisms into more regular frames, most of which were, unfortunately, logically unsound and did more harm than good to logic. It was not until the middle of the 19th century that the mathematical aspects of logic began to be exploited seriously and competently.

For some reason the lead was taken by England, or anyway the British Isles. Why this should be so is not clear. The Utilitarian movement, then powerful in Britain, may have been a factor. Utilitarianism was the philosophy that went with the new industrial revolution and new ideas about social justice. It underlined the importance of calculus ('the greatest good for the greatest number' had to be computed), and thus stimulated, in a general sense, the interest in any kind of application of computing techniques to philosophy, not just ethics. The main Utilitarianist philosopher John Stuart Mill (1806-1873), published his *System of Logic* in 1843. This influential book is full of logical (and philosophical) confusion, but it does put forward the idea that

---

[5] A prime example of this trend is Strawson (1952), much derided by mathematically-oriented logicians, yet a powerful source of inspiration for philosophers of language and semanticists.

the Aristotelian syllogistic figures should be considered consequences of a more abstract system of inference.

- *De Morgan and Boole: the first wave*

In the 1840s mathematically trained *Augustus de Morgan* became professor of logic at University College London, a Utilitarianist institution. His mathematical background quickly made him see that logical entailments are a variety of formal proofs such as are found and constructed in mathematics. He rediscovered the fact that logic is a calculus, and therefore subject to the general laws and principles of calculi, a sister of mathematics. Around the same time, *George Boole* was developing a general theory of algebras and found that the Aristotelian syllogisms could be shown to follow directly from a specific algebra, now called Boole algebra, made for calculations on sets rather than on numbers. This led to the first wave of logical formalization, the application of algebra to logic, which concentrated mainly on constructing improved calculi for the derivation of entailments, i.e. logical proof theory. This movement has been carried on without interruption till our own day: logical proof theory is a strong and thriving field, though, it seems, of less direct interest to the study of language.

- *Frege and Russell: the second wave*

The second wave began to occur some thirty or forty years later, with *Gottlob Frege* in Germany, and then with *Bertrand Russell* in England. Here the emphasis was more on the structural properties of the language used to express logical propositions. Without delay this interest in the language of logic led directly to an interest in the language of humans. Frege, even more than Russell, was a philosopher of language (though he did not wish to consider himself a philosopher) as much as he was a logician and mathematician. This is where logic caught on to natural language, with formal semantics as the main product.

- *Rift between logic and linguistics*

It is hardly surprising, given the totally different backgrounds of the linguists and the logicians, that there was enmity between the two groups. We have seen, in the preceding chapters, what occupied the minds of the 19th and 20th century linguists, and it is clear that, but for a few rare exceptions like Hjelmslev and Harris, logic was not among their concerns, let alone mathematics. The logicians, on the other hand, took no professional interest in either comparative philology or structuralist theories of grammar. The new logical ideas and techniques dismayed linguists and linguistically-oriented philosophers. It was felt that the new logic did language an injustice. Kneale & Kneale, discussing early attempts at formalization of logic, comment:

> Ordinary language may seem cumbrous in contrast with a symbolism specially designed for talking about relations of extensions and nothing else, but it has the very great merit of being useful in indefinitely many different contexts.
>
> Kneale & Kneale (1962:352)

This certainly accords with what the Cambridge philosopher Alfred Sidgwick wrote in 1895:

> The chief habit of thought antagonistic to a regard for special context is, beyond dispute I suppose, that due to the attempt to make Logic formal, or (worse) symbolic. Whatever value these developments of Logic undoubtedly have is bought at a cost which deserves to be reckoned rather than ignored. But ... there is hardly a suspicion in the minds of formal logicians that they have any cost to pay.
>
> Sidgwick (1895:282)

The linguists and the logicians thus became totally alienated from each other, a situation that lasted till about 1970, when, on the one hand, the philosopher Donald Davidson, soon followed by the logician Richard Montague, began to apply new logical techniques to the semantic analysis of natural language sentences, while, on the other, some linguists, especially those who contributed to the Generative Semantics movement, began to study logic. But the new *rapprochement* between the two groups was not without problems. First there was the practical difficulty of learning to understand each other's way of thinking and arguing, not to mention the technical details of the disciplines involved. But then it also became clear that there are fundamental differences of view and insight, not to be ironed out by any amount of goodwill and open-minded contact, but concerning real, substantive issues in the analysis and description of natural language. It is one of the aims of this book to present these issues in a clear and uncompromising manner, in the hope that a clearer view will make it possible to find a fruitful solution.

5.3 The first wave: the application of algebra to logic

The most significant development from the point of view of turning logic into an algebraic calculus is due to *George Boole* (1815-1864), born in the North of England, self-educated and appointed to the chair of mathematics at the newly founded Queen's College at Cork in Ireland in 1849. In 1847 he published a little book *The Mathematical Analysis of Logic*, stimulated by the polemic between Sir William Hamilton of Edinburgh and Augustus de Morgan of London about quantifiers and predicates. This controversy attracted a great deal of public attention, with Sir William accusing De Morgan of plagiarism, meanwhile making derogatory statements about mathematics and its influence in education.[6] As the controversy was raging Boole thought that it might help if he developed further and put into writing certain ideas on the relation between mathematics and logic which had occurred to him first when he was, as a young man, employed as an usher at a private school in Lincoln (Kneale & Kneale 1962:404). He wrote about this to De Morgan in London, who replied that it might be better not to compare notes for the time being and wait till

---

[6] See the Appendix in De Morgan (1847:297-336) for a full documentation on this famous infamous episode in the history of logic.

both had published their books. This happened in 1847, when De Morgan published his *Formal Logic* and Boole his *Mathematical Analysis of Logic*.

- *Boole algebra to compute syllogisms*

Boole's original idea was that the Aristotelian syllogisms were in fact consequences of a special algebra which need not be applicable to numbers but to other entities, properties or classes. Such an algebra would share certain properties with the algebra of numbers but it would also differ from it in important respects. The algebra he developed with this aim in mind is now known as *Boole algebra*. It is, as all algebras, an abstract and purely formal system. It lends itself, in a general sense, to an interpretation on sets of objects.

From this, Boole saw a number of possible special interpretations. The first special interpretation Boole attached to his algebra was a formalization of the Aristotelian syllogisms, explained in 5.3.2. Soon, however, he discovered that propositional calculus could likewise be reduced to Boole algebra (with only the values '1' and '0' for the variables). This is explained in section 5.3.3. And thirdly, he found that his logic was applicable to the sets of situations in which a given proposition is true — that is, to what we now call *valuation spaces* of propositions. In this third special interpretation, explained in section 5.3.4, Boole algebra produces the classical truth tables in the context of modern model-theory. All these applications of Boole algebra are based on the basic principle that Boole algebra is most naturally interpreted as being not about numbers but about sets. But let us first look at the actual mechanics of Boole algebra.

5.3.1 Boole algebra as a formal system

Taken by itself, Boole algebra is simple.[7] Boole algebra has two *constant symbols*, '1' ('unity') and '0' ('zero'), and a set of *variables*: $a, b, c,...$, ranging over 1, 0, and any other symbols that may be needed for any given interpretation (in particular sets). It has, furthermore, two binary operations, *addition* and *multiplication*, defined as follows ('=': 'mutually substitutable in all contexts'; '≠' not mutually substitutable in all contexts):

addition: (1) $a + 0 = a$ multiplication: (1) $a \bullet 0 = 0$
          (2) $a + 1 = 1$ (2) $a \bullet 1 = a$
          (3) $a + a = a$ (3) $a \bullet a = a$

These two operations are:

symmetrical (or *commutative*): $a + b = b + a$, and: $a \bullet b = b \bullet a$
associative: $(a + b) + c = a + (b + c) = a + b + c$, and: $(a \bullet b) \bullet c = a \bullet (b \bullet c)$
          $= a \bullet b \bullet c$
distributive: $a + (b \bullet c) = (a + b) \bullet (a + c)$, and: $a \bullet (b + c) = (a \bullet b) + (a \bullet c)$.

There is also a unary operation of *complement* defined as follows:

---

[7] In the theory of algebras, Boole algebra is a distributive lattice with Zero (0) and Unity (1), in which every member has a complement that is itself a member. This aspect, however, is not discussed here.

complement: (1) $\bar{1} = 0$ (4) $\bar{a} \cdot a = 0$
               (2) $\bar{0} = 1$ (5) $\bar{\bar{a}} = a$
               (3) $\bar{a} + a = 1$

It is convenient to define a further operation of *subtraction* in terms of either addition or multiplication:

subtraction: (1) $a - b = \overline{\bar{a} + b}$ or: (2) $a - b = a \cdot \bar{b}$

We can now add the following three theorems:

Theorem 1: $\bar{a} = 1 - a$

Proof: $1 - a = \overline{\bar{1} + a}$ by subtraction (1);
          $\overline{\bar{1} + a} = \overline{0 + a}$ by complement (1);
          $\overline{0 + a} = \bar{a}$ by commutativity and addition (1).
          Hence: $\bar{a} = 1 - a$.

Theorem 2: $a - 0 = a$

Proof: $a - 0 = a \cdot \bar{0}$ by subtraction (2);
          $a \cdot \bar{0} = a \cdot 1$ by complement (2);
          $a \cdot 1 = a$ by multiplication (2).
          Hence: $a - 0 = a$.

Theorem 3: $a = 1 - \bar{a}$

Proof: $1 - \bar{a} = \overline{\bar{1} + \bar{a}}$ by subtraction (1);
          $\overline{\bar{1} + \bar{a}} = \overline{0 + \bar{a}}$ by complement (1);
          $\overline{0 + \bar{a}} = \bar{\bar{a}}$ by commutativity and addition (1);
          $\bar{\bar{a}} = a$ by complement (5).
          Hence: $a = 1 - \bar{a}$.

Addition and multiplication are definable in terms of each other. That is: $a + b = \overline{\bar{a} \cdot \bar{b}}$ and $a \cdot b = \overline{\bar{a} + \bar{b}}$. The proofs run as follows:

Theorem 4: $a + b = \overline{\bar{a} \cdot \bar{b}}$

Proof: $\overline{\bar{a} \cdot \bar{b}} = \overline{\bar{a} - b}$ by subtraction (2);
        $\overline{\bar{a} - b} = \overline{\overline{\bar{a}} + b}$ by subtraction (1);
        $\overline{\overline{\bar{a}} + b} = a + b$ by complement (5).
        Hence: $a + b = \overline{\bar{a} \cdot \bar{b}}$.

Theorem 5: $a \bullet b = \overline{\bar{a} + \bar{b}}$

Proof: $\overline{\bar{a} + \bar{b}} = \bar{a} - \bar{b}$ by subtraction (1);

$\bar{a} - \bar{b} = \bar{a} \bullet \bar{\bar{b}}$ by subtraction (2);

$\bar{a} \bullet \bar{\bar{b}} = a \bullet b$ by complement (5).

Hence: $a \bullet b = \overline{\bar{a} + \bar{b}}$.

It is easy to see that Boole algebra formalizes set theory. Let the symbols *a*, *b*, *c*, ... be taken to denote sets, while 0 is the null set Ø and 1 stands for the universe of objects. Interpret multiplication as set-theoretic intersection ($\cap$), addition as set-theoretic union ($\cup$), subtraction as set-theoretic difference (-), and complement as set-theoretic complement ($\bar{x}$). Boole algebra now computes all set-theoretic operations.

5.3.2 Application to APC and syllogisms

The Aristotelian Square of Oppositions is entirely expressible in terms of set theory, and hence in terms of Boole algebra (for a clear account of this application see Lewis & Langford (1959:51-77)). In fig. 3 all ten possible configurations of two arbitrary non-empty sets F and G are given within a universe of individuals *I* (note that the cases where F = Ø or G = Ø are excluded in APC):

1. F is contained in G
2. G is contained in F
3. G and F coincide
4. F coincides with *I*
5. G coincides with *I*

6. G is the complement of F
7. F is the complement of G
8. both G and F coincide with *I*
9. G and F partly coincide
10. G and F are totally disjoint

For each of these ten possible states of affairs exactly two Aristotelian sentence types are true, and, therefore, exactly two sentence types are false. The ones that are true are specified for each situation in fig. 3.

We recall from 5.1.3 that APC is restricted to the four sentence types **A**, **I**, **E**, and **O**, defined as follows:

type **A**:	all F is G
type **I**:	some F is G
type **E**:	all F is not G / no F is G
type **O**:	some F is not G / not all F is G

Fig. 3 now shows that whenever there is **A**, there is also **I**, and likewise for **E** and **O**, respectively. This takes care of the subaltern entailments. Moreover, whenever **A** is present, **E** is absent and whenever **E** is present **A** is absent: **A** and **E** are contraries. Then, whenever **I** is absent, **O** is present and whenever **O** is absent, **I** is present: **I** and **O** are subcontraries. Finally the contradictories: whenever **A** is present, **O** is absent and vice versa, and likewise for **I** and **E**, respectively.

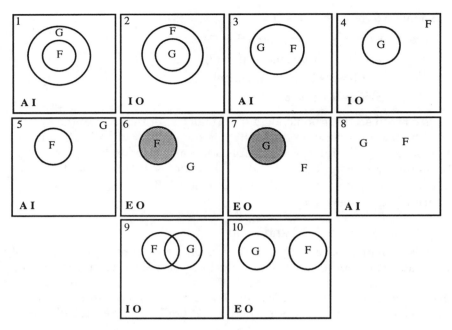

*Figure 3   Venn diagrams representing the cases where **A, I, E** and **O** are true*

More technically, the Aristotelian entailment schemata can be demonstrated as follows, making use of the notion 'valuation space' (Van Fraassen 1971; see section 5.3.4). The *valuation space* of a sentence (type) X is the set of cases where X is true.The notation we use for the valuation space of X is: /X/. For the Aristotelian sentence types the valuation spaces are as follows, in terms of fig. 3:

$$/\mathbf{A}/ = \{1,3,5,8\}$$
$$/\mathbf{O}/ = \{2,4,6,7,9,10\}$$
$$/\mathbf{I}/ = \{1,2,3,4,5,8,9\}$$
$$/\mathbf{E}/ = \{6,7,10\}$$

Let **U** be the total set of all possible siuations $\{1,2,3,4,5,6,7,8,9,10\}$. Now we see that $/\mathbf{A}/ \cup /\mathbf{O}/ = \mathbf{U}$ and $/\mathbf{I}/ \cup /\mathbf{E}/ = \mathbf{U}$, and also $/\mathbf{A}/ \cap /\mathbf{O}/ = \varnothing$ and $/\mathbf{I}/ \cap /\mathbf{E}/ = \varnothing$. This shows again that **A** and **O** are contradictories, and so are **I** and **E**. Moreover, $/\mathbf{A}/ \cap /\mathbf{E}/ = \varnothing$, which shows that they cannot be simultaneously true, i.e. are contraries. Then, $/\overline{\mathbf{I}}/ \cap /\overline{\mathbf{O}}/ = \varnothing$, which shows that they cannot both be false at the same time, i.e. are subcontraries. Finally, we see that /**A**/ is contained in /**I**/, and likewise /**E**/ is contained in /**O**/, which means that **A** ⊢ **I** and **E** ⊢ **O**, i.e. the downward or subaltern entailments.

This allows us to translate the Aristotelian sentence types into Boolean formulas, where the predicate variables *F* and *G* are replaced by the Boolean variables *f* and *g*, respectively:

(27)	**A:**	all F is G	$f \bullet g = f$
	I:	some F is G	$f \bullet g \neq 0$
	E:	all F is not G	$f \bullet \bar{g} = f$
	O:	some F is not G	$f \bullet \bar{g} \neq 0$

To see this, consider the set-theoretic translations of the Boolean expressions: $F \cap G = F$ is true for all members of /**A**/, i.e. {1,3,5,8}, and likewise, $F \cap G \neq \varnothing$ for /**I**/, i.e. {1,2,3,4,5,8,9}, $F \cap \bar{G} = F$ for /**E**/, i.e. {6,7,10}, and $F \cap \bar{G} \neq \varnothing$ for /**O**/, i.e. {2,4,6,7,9,10}.

Now we come to the main point, the fact that Boole algebra calculates the Aristotelian syllogisms. The syllogisms turn out to be theorems in Boole algebra (i.e. set theory). We will not show this for all syllogisms, only, by way of demonstration, for BARBARA and DARII.

Consider the syllogism BARBARA again: all F is G; all G is H; ergo: all F is H. This is computable as follows. BARBARA now reads:

(28)	(1)	$f \bullet g = f$
	(2)	$g \bullet h = g$
	(3)	$\therefore f \bullet h = f$

The proof is straightforward: We read (28.1) as $f \bullet (g \bullet h) = f$, in virtue of (28.2). Then, by associativity, $(f \bullet g) \bullet h = f$, and finally, in virtue of (28.1), $f \bullet h = f$.

A similar proof is provided for DARII: all F is G; some H is F; ergo: some H is G. Translate 'some H is F' as '$h \bullet f \neq 0$'. DARII then reads:

(29)	(1)	$f \bullet g = f$
	(2)	$h \bullet f \neq 0$
	(3)	$\therefore h \bullet g \neq 0$

The proof is: We read (2) as $h \bullet (f \bullet g) \neq 0$, in virtue of (29.1). It follows that $h \bullet g \neq 0$, because, if it were so that $h \bullet g = 0$ then $h \bullet (f \bullet g) = 0$, quod non. Hence: $h \bullet g \neq 0$.

The interest of this result lies in the fact that the old syllogisms are no longer to be viewed as axiomatic, posited in order to construct a viable logic, but as mathematical consequences from set-theoretic constructions. These consequences are formally, algorithmically, computable in precisely the sense announced by Leibniz some one hundred and fifty years earlier but not put into practice.

- *The problem of the empty F-class now solved, but at a considerable cost: hardly any logic remains*

Remarkably, the problem of the empty F-class now turns out to be solved. For if the F-class is empty a type **A** statement of the form 'all F is G' translates as $0 \bullet g = 0$, which is true for any arbitrary g in virtue of multiplication (1). Moreover, 'some F is G' will turn out false, since $0 \bullet g \neq 0$ is false for any arbitrary g. Therefore, under the Boolean interpretation, predicate calculus no longer has existential import as a whole. Only the particulars, i.e. the type **I** and type **E** statements, now have existential import.

This was, of course, very gratifying. Yet the cost was high, since the Square of Oppositions had collapsed. The downward entailments are no longer valid if empty extensions are taken into account. The contraries are cancelled, since **A** and **E** are both true if the F-class is empty. The subcontraries are both false with an empty F-class, so they, too, have to go. Only the contradictories remain. But these are each other's negations and are therefore valid on account of the negation's truth-functional property of inverting truth values, and thus belong to propositional calculus. All that is left now of predicate calculus is the fact that 'all F is not G' is interchangeable with 'no (= not some) F is G', and 'not all F is G' with 'some F is not G', i.e. quantifier conversion with the help of negation. But this is hardly enough to build a predicate calculus on. It would take Frege and Russell, and their new theory of quantification, to rebuild predicate calculus while not neglecting empty predicate extensions.

- *The problem of expressivity and the status of negation still unsolved*

The second problem, the problem of expressivity, was still unsolved, as was the question of the status of negation. The algebraic formalization shed no light on these issues. Here, too, it was the new language of quantification, developed by Frege and Russell, that would bring relief.

5.3.3 Application to propositional calculus

- *Boole algebra also applicable to propositional calculus*

Boole algebra also provides a natural algebraic formalization for propositional calculus (see 5.1.4). In propositional calculus, as has been said, the lexical variables do not stand for predicates but for whole propositions. Commonly used variable symbols are A, B, C, ..., standing for propositions. Propositional calculus contains the operators ¬ for 'not', ∧ for 'and', ∨ for 'or', and → for 'if—then'. These operators turn one or more given propositions into a new proposition, and assign the new proposition a truth value on the basis of the truth value(s) of the given proposition(s). The functions, which were represented as a matrix in fig. 2 above, can also be written, in a mathematically more current notation, as follows (where, again, '1' stands for truth, and '0' for falsity):

(30)   ¬ : {⟨1,0⟩,⟨0,1⟩}
        ∧ : {⟨⟨1,1⟩,1⟩,⟨⟨1,0⟩,0⟩,⟨⟨0,1⟩,0⟩,⟨⟨0,0⟩,0⟩}
        ∨ : {⟨⟨1,1⟩,1⟩,⟨⟨1,0⟩,1⟩,⟨⟨0,1⟩,1⟩,⟨⟨0,0⟩,0⟩}
        → : {⟨⟨1,1⟩,1⟩,⟨⟨1,0⟩,0⟩,⟨⟨0,1⟩,1⟩,⟨⟨0,0⟩,1⟩}

Note that the three binary operators are expressible in terms of each other (mutually definable), with the help of negation. Strictly speaking, only one of the three is required, as appears from the following theorems ('≡' stands for mutual entailment):

(31)   (1)   A ∨ B ≡   ¬ (¬ A ∧ ¬ B)
        (2)   A ∧ B ≡   ¬ (¬ A ∨ ¬ B)
        (3)   A → B ≡   ¬ A ∨ B

The proofs, as usually given, are easy: under all possible truth value assignments the resulting value of the formula on the left hand side of the equivalence is identical to that of the right hand side formula. Let us show the proof for A → B ≡ ¬ A ∨ B:

(32)

A → B	¬ A ∨ B	A → B	¬ A ∨ B	A → B	¬ A ∨ B	A → B	¬ A ∨ B
1 1	1 1	1 0	1 0	0 1	0 1	0 0	0 0
1	1	0	0	1	1	1	1

A different type of proof is provided by a simple form of Boolean formalization. Take a Boole algebra with only two constant symbols, '1' and '0', to be interpreted as 'truth' and 'falsity', respectively. (This is, in fact, the origin of the now standard convention to use '1' for 'truth' and '0' for 'falsity'.) If conjunction (∧) is mapped onto Boolean multiplication, disjunction (∨) onto Boolean addition, and negation (¬) onto Boolean complement, we can formulate the following equations corresponding to the truth tables for negation, conjunction and disjunction (see Van Fraassen 1971:89-91):

(33)   Negation   Conjunction   Disjunction

          $\bar{1} = 0$ $1 \bullet 1 = 1$ $1 + 1 = 1$
          $\bar{0} = 1$ $1 \bullet 0 = 0$ $1 + 0 = 1$
                              $0 \bullet 1 = 0$ $0 + 1 = 1$
                              $0 \bullet 0 = 0$ $0 + 0 = 0$

Each of these ten equations is valid in Boole algebra, as is easily checked. The isomorphism with the functions enumerated in (30) and in fig. 2 for negation, conjunction and disjunction is obvious. (33) is also expressible in a matrix form which is isomorphic with the truth tables of fig. 2:

(34)   Negation   Conjunction   Disjunction

—		•	1	0		+	1	0
1	0	1	1	0		1	1	1
0	1	0	0	0		0	1	0

We can now define implication as the addition (disjunction) of b and the complement of a: A → B computes as ā + b over the constants 1 and 0:

(35)   Implication   or: Implication

          $\bar{1} + 1 = 1$
          $\bar{1} + 0 = 0$
          $\bar{0} + 1 = 1$
          $\bar{0} + 0 = 1$

→	1	0
1	1	0
0	1	1

(31.1) now computes as $a + b = \overline{\bar{a} \bullet \bar{b}}$, i.e. as Theorem 4 of section 5.3.1 on Boole algebra. And (31.2) computes as $a \bullet b = \overline{\bar{a} + \bar{b}}$, i.e. as Theorem 5 of 5.3.1. The proofs of these theorems are therefore also proofs of (31.1) and (31.2). Note that (31.1) and (31.2) are, in fact, the Laws of De Morgan, usually presented in the equivalent form of (36.1) and (36.2), respectively:

(36) (1) $\neg (A \vee B) \equiv \neg A \wedge \neg B$
      (2) $\neg (A \wedge B) \equiv \neg A \vee \neg B$

5.3.4 Application to valuation spaces

• *A third application of Boole algebra: valuation spaces*
Besides the application to propositional calculus shown in the previous section, in particular in (33)-(35), there is another, more interesting and more fruitful,[8] way in which Boole algebra can be seen to apply to propositional calculus. Boole himself did see this, though not very clearly, and the formal elaboration had to wait for well over a century. In his own words (Boole 1847:49-50; quoted from Kneale & Kneale 1962:413-14) he says:[9]

> To the symbols X, Y, Z, representative of Propositions, we may appropriate the elective symbols x, y, z, in the following sense. The hypothetical Universe, 1, shall comprehend all conceivable cases and conjunctures of circumstances. The elective symbol x attached to any subject expressive of such cases shall select those cases in which the Proposition X is true, and similarly for Y and Z. If we confine ourselves to the contemplation of a given Proposition X, and hold in abeyance any other consideration, then two cases only are conceivable, viz. first that the given Proposition is true, and secondly that it is false. As these two cases together make up the Universe of the Proposition, and as the former is determined by the elective symbol x, the latter is determined by the elective symbol $1-x$. But if other considerations are admitted, each of these cases will be resoluble into others, individually less extensive, the number of which will depend on the number of foreign considerations admitted. Thus if we associate the Propositions X and Y, the total number of conceivable cases will be found as exhibited in the following scheme.

	Cases	Elective expressions
1st	X true, Y true	xy
2nd	X true, Y false	x (1-y)
3rd	X false, Y true	(1-x) y
4th	X false, Y false	(1-x) (1-y)

Unfortunately, Boole's terminology is not entirely consistent. His use of the terms *case*, *circumstance* and *consideration* is imprecise and may therefore lead to confusion. There is no confusion as long as he uses these terms for specific situations for which a given proposition may be true or false. Then the

---

[8] Kneale & Kneale (1962:413-414) speak of a 'different and perhaps more interesting' interpretation, and of a 'very promising suggestion'.
[9] In Boole's own notation, 'xy' stands for what we write as '$x \bullet y$'.

'elective symbol' x stands for the set of situations in which the proposition X is true. Nowadays, following Van Fraassen (1971), we speak of the *valuation space* of X, which we decide to symbolize as /X/. Further down, however, Boole speaks of the 'case' in which X is true and the other 'case' in which it is false. This is a different, and confusing, use of the term *case*. Here we should read 'sets of cases'. Moreover, the term *consideration* should be read as *proposition*. With these amendments we now read:

> If we confine ourselves to the contemplation of a given Proposition X, and hold in abeyance any other Proposition, then two sets of cases only are possible, viz. first those in which the given Proposition is true, and secondly those in which it is false. As these two sets of cases together make up the Universe of the Proposition, and as the former is determined by the elective symbol x, the latter is determined by the elective symbol 1-x. But if other Propositions are admitted, each of these sets of cases will be resoluble into others, individually less extensive, the number of which will depend on the number of foreign Propositions admitted. Thus if we associate the Propositions X and Y, the total number of possible sets of cases will be found as exhibited in the following scheme.

	Sets of cases	Elective expressions
1st	X true, Y true	. . . . . xy
2nd	X true, Y false	. . . . . $x(1-y)$
3rd	X false, Y true	. . . . . $(1-x)y$
4th	X false, Y false	. . . . . $(1-x)(1-y)$

Now the passage is a great deal clearer, and lends itself to a formal elaboration. It is perhaps the element of unclarity in Boole's thoughts, plus, of course, the fact that model-theory was still to be developed, that is responsible for the long delay in putting this interpretation to good use.[10]

• *The notion of valuation space*

In order to see how this third application of Boole algebra to propositional calculus works we must get used to the rather abstract concept of 'the set of possible situations in which a given proposition is true'. Modern formal semanticists prefer to speak of 'possible worlds' rather than of 'possible situations', but other semanticists and philosophers have pointed out that the notion of 'possible world' is ill-defined and unconstrained, and therefore not really useful. So we shall speak of situations rather than of worlds. And we say, as above in 5.3.2, that each proposition that can be formulated as a well-formed sentence in a natural or formal language is associated with the set of possible situations in which it is true, i.e. with its *valuation space* (Van Fraassen 1971). We express this as follows: /A/ is the valuation space of the proposition A.[11]

---

[10] This interpretation of Boolean algebra is mentioned, but not elaborated, in Lewis & Langford (1959:50) and in Van Fraassen (1971:88).

[11] Formal semanticists use the term *intension* for /A/, but many critics of formal semantics feel that this use of the term *intension* is counter-intuitive and that the term had better be

• *Boolean constants as valuation spaces*

We now consider an interpretation of the constant symbols in Boole algebra as valuation spaces of propositions. In this interpretation the Boolean operations 'complement', 'multiplication', and 'addition' translate, again, as the truth-functional operations of negation, conjunction and disjunction, respectively. There is no commonly used truth-functional equivalent in propositional calculus of 'subtraction', nor is there a common Boolean equivalent of truth-functional implication, but this does not affect the parallelism, since, in Boole algebra as in propositional calculus, the three binary operations are expressible in terms of each other, with the help of negation/complement. For Boole algebra this has been shown in the descriptions of multiplication, addition and subtraction. For propositional logic this has been shown above. It is easy to see that A → B corresponds to Boolean ā + b. Why Boole algebra should have an extra operator of subtraction, and propositional calculus one of implication, is merely a question of convenience. We now pass on to a more formal treatment, demonstrating the model-theoretic generation of the classical truth tables.

Let **U** (depicted as the outer rectangle in figs. 4-7) be again the set of all possible situations. Then the valuation spaces /A/ and /¬A/ are as indicated in fig. 4, where the shaded area is /¬ A/. /A ∧ B/ is the shaded area in fig. 5. /A ∨ B/ is the shaded area in fig.6; /A → B/ is the same in fig. 7.

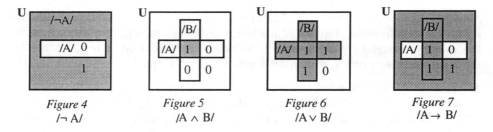

Figure 4	Figure 5	Figure 6	Figure 7
/¬ A/	/A ∧ B/	/A ∨ B/	/A→ B/

In each case, the shaded area represents the valuation space of the compound proposition in question. That is, if a given situation is an element of the valuation space, the proposition in question is true, when it is outside the shaded area, it is false. The representations in figs. 4-7 enable us to reconstruct the truth tables given above by placing the symbol '1' for truth in the shaded areas that correspond to the matrices of fig. 3, and the symbol '0' for falsity in the corresponding blank areas.

On the basis of all this the reader will have no difficulty proving for himself that all Boolean operations correspond entirely to their counterparts in propositional calculus. For example, De Morgan's laws, which, as we saw earlier, allow for mutual conversion of conjunction and disjunction with change

---

reserved for something else. It was certainly not Frege's use of this term, as will become clear in chapter 6.

of polarity (i.e. negative becomes positive and vice versa) corresponds to its Boolean analogue:

De Morgan: $\neg A \wedge \neg B \equiv \neg (A \vee B)$ Boolean: $\bar{a} \bullet \bar{b} = \overline{a+b}$
                 $\neg A \vee \neg B \equiv \neg (A \wedge B)$ $\bar{a} + \bar{b} = \overline{a \bullet b}$

After Boole, logic was in a bad way. Those few who realized the importance of the algebraic innovations knew that predicate calculus had virtually collapsed. Predicate calculus had been widened so as to cover also cases (situations) where predicates have a null extension. This millennia-old birth defect of Aristotelian logic had been repaired, but the cure was amputation, and the patient barely survived. All that remained of logic was propositional calculus, and the logical power of the quantifiers had been lost. Two things were necessary to allow the patient to grow to full health and vigour. First, the notion of quantifier had to be redefined in set-theoretic terms, and secondly, a suitable formal language had to be devised for the adequate expression of the set-theoretic properties of the quantifiers. The first task was fulfilled by Frege, the second by Russell.

5.4 The second wave: the formalization of logical language

The two towering figures in the second great formalization wave of logic are the German *Gottlob Frege* (1848-1925) and the Englishman *Bertrand Russell* (1872-1970), two very different characters. Not too much is known about Frege as a person. Apparently, he was a rather colourless and, as far as is known, introvert man, though with strong conservative and nationalistic views. Russell, on the contrary, was a flamboyant, outgoing man, radiating self-confidence, with a lot of panache and wit, a pen as sharp and masterly as his mind. Also, not unimportantly, he was a leading anti-authoritarian and pacifist, though of very high English nobility. Frege never wrote about himself, Russell filled volumes with autobiographical material.

5.4.1 Gottlob Frege

Frege taught mathematics at Jena in Germany. Like Leibniz, he is one of those figures in history who did not get recognition till some time after their death. In the 1870s he developed ideas leading to new foundations for mathematics, set theory and logic. He formalized the notion of mathematical function, giving it the set-theoretic interpretation which is now standard. He generalized and sharpened the notion of variable, and shaped the modern concept of quantifier, thus perfecting logical language (though using an awkward notation). Unlike Russell and many other logicians, he never wanted to be seen as a philosopher, though he studied and was influenced by Leibniz, and held certain essentialist views that are reminiscent of Plato's theory of Ideas.

● *Frege and Russell's paradox*

Frege contributed to the axiomatization of set theory, now a standard instrument in logic and mathematics. But Georg Cantor, the main founder of set theory, refused to take his contributions seriously, which embittered Frege. Among the few who saw the importance of Frege's work was Bertrand Russell, who wrote to him in June 1902, expressing his admiration for the older man, and pointing out to him what would soon be known as Russell's paradox, contained in the question of whether the set of all sets is or is not a member of itself. Here follow some passages from Russell's letter, published in Van Heijenoort (1967:124-125):

> I find myself in complete agreement with you in all essentials, particularly when you reject any psychological element in logic and when you place a high value upon an ideography for the foundations of mathematics and logic, which, incidentally, can hardly be distinguished. With regard to many particular questions, I find in your work discussions, distinctions, and definitions that one seeks in vain in the works of other logicians. ...

> Let *w* be the predicate: to be a predicate that cannot be predicated of itself. Can *w* be predicated of itself? From each answer its opposite follows. Likewise there is no class (as a totality) of those classes which, each taken as a totality, do not belong to themselves. From this I conclude that under certain circumstances a definable collection does not form a totality. ...

> The exact treatment of logic in fundamental questions, where symbols fail, has remained very much behind; in your works I find the best I know of our time, and therefore I have permitted myself to express my deep respect to you.

Frege replied promptly. The following are passages from his letter to Russell (Van Heijenoort 1967:127-128):

> Your discovery of the contradiction caused me the greatest surprise and, I would almost say, consternation, since it has shaken the basis on which I intended to build arithmetic. ...

> I must reflect further on the matter. It is all the more serious since, with the loss of my Rule V, not only the foundations of my arithmetic, but also the sole possible foundations of arithmetic, seem to vanish. ...

> In any case, your discovery is very remarkable and will perhaps result in a great advance in logic, unwelcome as it may seem at first glance. ...

> Incidentally, it seems to me that the expression 'a predicate is predicated of itself' is not exact. A predicate is as a rule a first-level function, and this function requires an object as argument and cannot have itself as argument (subject). Therefore I would prefer to say 'a concept is predicated of its own extension'. ...

> The second volume of my *Grundgesetze* is to appear shortly. I shall no doubt have to add an appendix in which your discovery is taken into account. If only I already had the right point of view for that!

Russell's, at first tentative, solution to the paradox was published first in (1903a:104-105), elaborated in Appendix B of the same book (1903a:523-528). It consists of the Theory of Types, which sets up a hierarchy of sets: sets of individuals (1st order sets), sets of sets (2nd order sets), sets of sets of sets (3rd order sets), etc. This way it makes no sense any more to speak of 'the set of all sets', as such a set is undefined. After a series of subsequent rejections he final-ly settled for this solution in (1908). This solution has since been considered standard. It must not, however, remain unnoticed that Frege, in his letter quoted from above, already presents this solution, when he says that 'a predi-cate is as a rule a first-level function', which 'requires <a name for> an object as argument and cannot have itself as argument'.

When Van Heijenoort asked Russell's permission to print the 1902 corres-pondence in his *Source Book*, Russell replied, in a letter dated 1962 (Van Heij-enoort 1967:127):

> Dear Professor Van Heijenoort,
>
> I should be most pleased if you would publish the correspondence between Frege and myself, and I am grateful to you for suggesting this. As I think about acts of integrity and grace, I realise that there is nothing in my knowledge to compare with Frege's dedication to truth. His entire life's work was on the verge of completion, much of his work had been ignored to the benefit of men infinitely less capable, his second volume was about to be published, and upon finding that his fundamental assumption was in error, he responded with intellectual pleasure clearly submerg-ing any feelings of personal disappointment. It was almost superhuman and a telling indication of that of which men are capable if their dedication is to creative work and knowledge instead of cruder efforts to dominate and be known.
>
> Yours sincerely,
>
> Bertrand Russell

● *Frege the father of modern semantics*
Frege also applied his new mathematical and logical insights to natural lan-guage, generalizing the notions of extension and intension in such a way that a real semantic theory became viable (see chapter 6 for a full discussion). He is, more than anyone else, the father of modern semantics, even though present-day formal semantics has taken a course that he would have strongly disap-proved of. His handling of natural language issues was delicate and subtle. Frege had a feel for the fine points of language, more than for its elegant use: his style of writing was somewhat turgid. In this respect, too, he differed from Russell, who possessed great literary gifts, though his way of dealing with linguistic issues was positively hamfisted.

● *Frege's genius not recognized till about 1950*
During his lifetime Frege did not get the recognition he deserved either in logic and mathematics or in the philosophy of language, his ideas being con-sidered outlandish and far-fetched. In logic and mathematics he was upstag-ed by the brilliant Russell. In the philosophy of language, whose main de-velopments took place in the Anglo-Saxon world, Frege was not read, until Peter Geach and Max Black published a volume with an English translation of some of his writings (Geach & Black 1952). It was then that Frege began to exert real influence. On the one hand, he influenced philosophical thinking about language (in particular presupposition theory). On the other, he stimu-

lated new attempts by logicians to devise a model-theoretic formal semantics of natural language. His full recognition came with the monumental work by Michael Dummett, *Frege. Philosophy of Language* (1973). In the following chapters we shall come across Frege repeatedly, especially in section 6.1.2 on the beginnings of modern semantic theory, and section 6.2.3 when we discuss presupposition theory.

5.4.2 Bertrand Arthur William Russell

Russell's is a very different story. Born in 1872 into an old aristocratic family, high up in government, the military and society, he grew up in the care of his grandparents, as he had lost both his parents at an early age. He never went to school but received all of his scholastic education at home (the English Public Schools were considered too common by the very highest aristocracy). His first opportunity to measure himself against 'able contemporaries' (Russell 1967:56) came when he went to Cambridge to sit for the entrance examination to Trinity College at the age of seventeen (Alfred North Whitehead was one of his examiners). At Cambridge he studied mathematics and philosophy from 1890 till 1894. He remained associated with Cambridge for the rest of his life. Like Wittgenstein much later, he became a life fellow of Trinity College.

His pursuit of an intellectual career somewhat disappointed his family, and his class. But it was not only by his mathematical and philosophical interests that they were disappointed. Having become interested in politics at an early age – his first book (1896) was on politics – Russell soon developed social and political ideas that were considered highly inappropriate, becoming a pacifist and publicly opposing Britain's belligerent role during the first World War. This landed him in prison for a period of six months towards the end of the war. There he wrote his *Introduction to Mathematical Philosophy* (1919). He remained a pacifist and opposed to the supremacy of the National State till his final days. After 1918 he hardly did any logic, and past the age of seventy-five he hardly did any philosophy either (though he did publish, in 1957, a wry little article directed at the Oxford philosopher Peter Strawson). Instead he devoted himself entirely to political causes, setting up, amongst other things, the well-known Russell tribunal to pronounce judgement on persons and institutions considered guilty of crimes against humanity. The post-war Labour government awarded him the Order of Merit in 1949. In 1950 he won the Nobel Prize for literature. When he died, in May 1970, at the age of almost ninety-eight years, the press obituaries were, though admiring, generally sour, as it was felt that he had betrayed his class and had been less than loyal to his country. A few days after his death a long letter appeared in The Times, written by Russell and opposing the American programme of sending manned flights to the moon, this being a waste of good money that had better be given to the poor and needy.

- *Russell's first philosophical book was on Leibniz*

His first philosophical book, published in 1900, was, significantly, a study of Leibniz. It was no doubt Leibniz's theory of truth finding, the Coherence Theory of Truth, that made Russell embark on his programme of logical atomism, meant to find a formal philosophical way of reconstructing bare reality from atomic logical propositions.[12]

- *Russell's philosophy of man*

In Russell's philosophy of man, rational thought held pride of place (Russell 1903b). Where man was originally rude and uncouth and slavishly submissive to the brute forces of nature, he has elevated himself to a higher plane of culture and virtue, not by the grace of a God or Gods, nor simply in virtue of being human, but by using and developing his powers of thought, which make him master, not slave, of the inevitable. It is through his intellect that man can free himself and become master of all evil in the world.[13] Russell considered it his duty to impart some of this freedom to the less privileged of this world, which made him write a number of popular books advising the populace about matters of life and knowledge.

- *Russell and Whitehead: modern Predicate Calculus*

Between 1900 and 1910 Russell developed modern predicate calculus, replacing the Aristotelian Square of Oppositions. The underlying idea was that mathematics should be reduced to logic, a programme that has found many followers as well as opponents during the 20th century. Together with the mathematician-philosopher *Alfred North Whitehead* (1861-1947) he wrote, between 1900 and 1910, the monumental *Principia Mathematica*, published between 1910 and 1913, presenting the foundations of modern logic. Whitehead later dissociated himself from Russell, disapproving of his political and social views, as well as his unconventional libertarian way of life. Whitehead left Cambridge in 1910, to take up a teaching position and then a professorship in London. In 1924 he accepted a professorial appointment in philosophy at Harvard, where he turned to central philosophy and the study of religion.

---

[12] During the years leading up to the first World War a rich young student from Vienna, by the name of Ludwig Wittgenstein, presented himself to Russell insisting to be admitted as his student. In spite of young Wittgenstein's strange and at times infuriating behaviour (Russell wrote about him almost daily to his lady-friend Ottoline Morrell who lived in Oxford — see Clark 1975:170-2, 192-4; Monk 1990:36-47), Russell took him on. This is how Wittgenstein became familiar with logical atomism, of which he created his own, extreme version. Russell soon distanced himself from Wittgenstein, for both intellectual and personal reasons. See 6.2.2.1 for more on Wittgenstein.

[13] In note 8 of chapter 1 we quoted the following statement by Russell made in a speech to a lay audience (Russell 1956:197): 'I am allowed to use plain English because everybody knows that I could use mathematical logic if I chose. Take the statement: "Some people marry their deceased wives' sisters". I can express this in language which only becomes intelligible after years of study, and this gives me freedom.' The last few words are, of course, arrogant. Yet they are more than just that: they reflect Russell's deep-seated conviction that rational thought bestows freedom on mankind.

- *The complex problem of definite descriptions*

One of the issues Russell wanted to settle once and for all, during the first years of the century, was the question of definite descriptions in natural language. As we saw in section 5.1, Aristotle had excluded occasion sentences from logic, a decision Russell understood but regretted. In 1905 he published his Theory of Descriptions, meaning to include sentences containing definite descriptions in the logic. Neglecting the condition of contextual referential anchoring that comes with definite descriptions, he concentrated on descriptions that fail to refer as the intended referent does not exist. His celebrated example was *The present king of France is bald*, where the definite description *the present king of France*, though well-formed and well-equipped for reference, fails to denote any real existing individual in this world. The solution proposed by Russell for this problem is discussed in section 6.1.2.3, where its inadequacy is shown. Due to the great prestige of Russellian logic, his Theory of Descriptions was considered inviolate by logicians during the whole of this century, thereby forming a formidable obstacle to the development of more empirically adequate ideas about the semantics of natural language.

5.5 Modern predicate calculus: quantification theory

Oversimplifying somewhat, one may say that modern predicate calculus is cast in the language of Russell, expressing Frege's ideas. It rests on two principles, that of n-ary predicates and, above all, that of quantification.

- *The Principle of n-ary Predicates*

The principle of n-ary predicates implies that a proposition (sentence) is no longer analysed in terms of subject and predicate, where the predicate encompasses the whole remainder of the sentence, but in terms of a more restricted predicate (verb, adjective, noun) and its n argument terms. A sentence like *Helen loves Bert* is no longer analysed as (37a) but as (37b), usually written as 'Love(Helen,Bert)':

(37)a.   sentence[subject[Helen] predicate[Loves Bert]]

   b.   sentence[predicate[Loves] subject[Helen] object[Bert]][14]

This is less trivial than it seems, for the following reasons.

In the Aristotelian subject-predicate mould, a proposition (logical sentence) has a binary overall division (in the terms of Bloomfield (1933): two immediate constituents), representable as the tree structure (38a). Given a particular situation where some people love some other people and where the person called *Bert* is loved by a number of individuals, we can set up the class L_B of people that love Bert. This class L_B is called the *extension* of the predicate in the given situation: [[*Love Bert*]] = L_B (double square brackets are standardly used to specify extensions). Now we look up where the person called *Helen* is:

---

[14] For the notation with labelled bracketing, see section 4.4.5.

is she or is she not a member of L_B? The person called *Helen*, i.e. Helen, is the extension of the subject term: [[*Helen*]] = Helen. Now, if Helen is a member of L_B the sentence is true in the situation at hand; otherwise the sentence is false.

Analogously, but differently, with (38b), which has a ternary structure: the binary predicate *Love* and its two terms. Now we first find who the persons called *Helen* and *Bert*, respectively, are. That is, we determine the values of [[*Helen*]] and [[*Bert*]]. Then we look up the extension of the predicate *Love*, i.e. [[*Love*]]. But note that [[*Love*]] is not now a set of individuals but a set of pairs <x,y> such that x loves y. (It is customary to interpret the first co-ordinate of the pair as the subject, the second as the direct object of the predicate in question.) When it is found that the pair <Helen,Bert> is indeed an element in [[*Love*]], the sentence is true, and otherwise it is false.

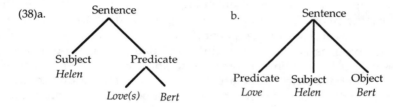

The point is that the *n*-ary analysis makes it possible to quantify over each of the terms, which is something the Aristotelian analysis could not do. In other words, this new method of *n*-ary analysis is intended to solve the problem of expressivity mentioned in section 5.1.5. And to all intents and purposes it does look as though this problem has indeed been eliminated.

- *Categorial calculus*

Note, incidentally, that this method of computing truth values in a model is called *categorial calculus*. The principle stems from Frege. The term is due to the Polish school of logicians flourishing in the 1930s. Categorial calculus is the basis of *model theory*. It uses the tree structure as some kind of abacus or computational frame, starting with the extensions of the terminal elements at the bottom of each branch, the 'leaves'. Then it composes the extensions of the higher constituents by means of the functions that must be available at every level, until it finally produces a truth value for the whole structure. In section 5.5.1 below we will say more about model theory and the associated categorial calculus.

5.5.1 Variables, functions and some model theory

- *Substitutional and lexical variables*

We are now ready to look at quantification, the central element in modern predicate calculus. To understand quantification one must first understand the nature of a *(substitutional) variable*. We have already encountered variables here and there. But now is the time for a more principled definition.

In general, a variable is a symbol in a (natural or formal) language that does not refer: it has no extension of its own. It just fills a syntactically defined position and implies an instruction or agreed procedure to look for the correct substitution by a term that does refer, a so-called *constant*. Some lexical words in natural languages are variables, for example the word *local*. Take the case of John wanting to ring the police. He takes the phone book and looks up 'Police', only to find 'see local police'. He then looks under *local* but finds nothing. What was his mistake? Clearly, the word *local* is not a constant, the actual word that has to be looked up, but a variable. What John should have done is first think and remember what village, town or district he was in, and then look thát up. If John is in Petersfield he should look up *Petersfield police*: the name *Petersfield* is, in this case, the *value* of the variable. And likewise for any other locality. We say that the variable term *local* has a *range*: it ranges over the set of all villages, towns and districts in the area covered by the phone book, and the (implicit) instruction is to determine the locality one is in and substitute its name for the word *local*. The usefulness of such variable terms is obvious: in this particular case the variable makes it unnecessary for the telephone company to specify for the entry *police* every village, town and district in the area. But a little thinking on the part of the user is required. A variable, in other words, does not refer, but wants to be replaced, according to a well-defined procedure, by an expression that does.

Formal languages have variables as well, and more systematically. We have already made the acquaintance of *lexical variables*, which stand for the non-logical part of sentences, i.e. predicates in predicate calculus or propositions in propositional calculus. Frege has taught us, however, that there are also *substitutional variables*. It is these that we shall now concentrate on.

Consider the ordinary arithmetical formula '$x < 5$'. It makes no sense to ask if this is true or false, because the term x is not a constant: it does not refer to a number. It just occupies a syntactic position that can be filled by a number name: x ranges over the set of natural numbers. To make sense of '$x < 5$' an instruction is needed that specifies what is to be done with the variable x. Sometimes the value of x is to be retrieved from outside, for example when x is the number of students in a class. Then the instruction is: 'count the students in the class and substitute the name of the number found for x'. This is an instruction for substitution, allowing us also to say, for example: 'if $x < 5$ the class will be cancelled'. But if no instruction is given the expression '$x < 5$', strictly speaking, makes no sense.

In some cases, the instruction is to replace the variable by the names of all the members of its range, in this case the names of all natural numbers. This is so, for example, when a propositional structure containing a variable term stands under a quantifier that binds the variable. In such cases we say that the instruction is to *rotate the variable over its range*, even if this operation is infinite. In the case of '$x < 5$' each such substitution results in a proposition that is either true or false. Given this, we can assign a precise meaning to the expression 'x < 5': we say:

the extension of the expression 'x < 5', or $[[x < 5]]$, is the set of those numbers whose names, when substituted for x, result in a true proposition.

For x < 5 this is the set $\{0,1,2,3,4\}$. Therefore, in this context:

(39) $[[x < 5]] = \{0,1,2,3,4\}$

In other words: the extension of 'x < 5' in this context is the set of natural numbers $\{0,1,2,3,4\}$ – where we consider $0, 1, 2, 3$ and 4 to be numbers, whose names are '0', '1', '2', '3' and '4', respectively.

If no context is specified or available, the default assumption is that the variable should be rotated over its range. In this sense it is said that, default-wise, 'x < 5' expresses a *propositional function,* a function from the variable range, in this case the set of natural numbers, to propositions with a truth value, since for each natural number name put in the position of the substitutional variable there is a truth value. *Any function from a set of objects X to truth values is a propositional function.* If we use the symbol '**1**' for truth and '**0**' for falsity, $[[x < 5]]$ constitutes the following infinite propositional function, expressed by 'x < 5':

(40) $[[x < 5]] = \{\langle 0,\mathbf{1}\rangle, \langle 1,\mathbf{1}\rangle, \langle 2,\mathbf{1}\rangle, \langle 3,\mathbf{1}\rangle, \langle 4,\mathbf{1}\rangle, \langle 5,\mathbf{0}\rangle, \langle 6,\mathbf{0}\rangle, \langle 7,\mathbf{0}\rangle, \langle 8,\mathbf{0}\rangle, ...\}$

Rotation of x over all natural numbers thus gives both (39) and (40). This is no problem because (39) and (40) are considered equivalent: the set $\{0,1,2,3,4\}$ is precisely the function from all natural numbers to the two truth values **1** and **0** such that $0,1,2,3$ and 4 are associated with the value **1**, and all other natural numbers with the value **0**. The equivalence of (39) and (40) rests on the Fregean notion of variable as a non-referring symbol that needs to be rotated over its range, which gives rise to the notion of propositional function.

- *Characteristic functions*

A different term for 'propositional function' is 'characteristic function'. *Any function from a set of objects X to truth values is a characteristic function.* A characteristic function F that delivers the value '1' for the members of a subset Y of X is said to *characterize* Y. Characteristic functions are thus an alternative way of characterizing sets within a universe of individual objects. The term 'characteristic function' is used in contexts where it is important to characterize sets (it will become clear in a moment that characteristic functions are a central ingredient in the machinery of model theory). One speaks of 'propositional function' when one refers to an expression in a logical language that has the syntactic structure of a proposition but one of whose term positions is filled by a variable.

- *Predicates denote characteristic functions*

Yet another name for a function from a set of objects X to truth values is 'predicate'. Again, *the name for any function from a set of objects X to truth values can be regarded as a predicate.* The term 'predicate' is preferred when one refers to a linguistic expression made up of elements from the lexicon of a natural or formal language.

- *Unbound substitutional variables merely fill a syntactic position*

We now see what Frege meant when he stressed that it makes no difference for the extension of a propositional function expression whether the variable is inserted or not. The only difference consists in the syntactic form: '< 5' is a predicate, 'x < 5' is a propositional function: all the substitutional variable does is to specify the syntactic position of the constant terms that will combine with the predicate '< 5' to make a proposition. What links the two is the fact that both $[\![x < 5]\!]$ and $[\![< 5]\!]$ are the same set or characteristic function: $[\![x < 5]\!] = [\![< 5]\!] = \{0,1,2,3,4\} = \{\langle 0,\mathbf{1}\rangle, \langle 1,\mathbf{1}\rangle, \langle 2,\mathbf{1}\rangle, \langle 3,\mathbf{1}\rangle, \langle 4,\mathbf{1}\rangle, \langle 5,\mathbf{1}\rangle, \langle 6,\mathbf{0}\rangle, \langle 7,\mathbf{0}\rangle, ...\}$.

- *Application to language: some elementary model theory*

This machinery is transferable to language (whether natural or logical), provided we insert substitutional variables into sentence structures. To show this we shall indulge in a bit of primitive model theory, anticipating further discussion in chapter 6.

Let there be a situation with the set of individuals $\mathbf{I} = \{H,J,K,A,B\}$. There are two subsets of $\mathbf{I}$ (one-place relations), viz. $\mathbf{G}^1 = \{H,J,K\}$ and $\mathbf{B}^1 = \{A,B\}$. There is a language $\mathbf{L}$ which has the following names for the individuals in $\mathbf{I}$: *Helen, Joan, Kate, Alex* and *Bert*, for H, J, K, A, and B, respectively. Then $\mathbf{L}$ has the two predicates *Girl* and *Boy*, with the extensions $[\![Girl]\!] = \mathbf{G} = \{H,J,K\}$ and $[\![Boy]\!] = \mathbf{B} = \{A,B\}$.

A more precise formulation, of the kind that is current in model theory, is given in (41), which defines the model $\mathbf{M}$, which consists of a world $\mathbf{W}$, a language $\mathbf{L}$, and an interpretation $\mathbf{Int}$ specifying the extensions of the lexical expressions of $\mathbf{L}$ in $\mathbf{W}$:

(41) $\mathbf{M} = \langle W, L, Int \rangle$ (W is a world; L is a language; Int is an interpretation)

   $\mathbf{W} = \langle I,R,TV \rangle$ (I is a set of individuals; R is a set of relations in I; TV is a set of truth values)

   $\mathbf{I} = \{H, J, K, A, B\}$

   $\mathbf{R} = \{G^1, B^1\}$ (the superscript stands for the number of places in the relation)

   $G^1 = \{\langle H,1\rangle, \langle J,1\rangle, \langle K,1\rangle, \langle A,0\rangle, \langle B,0\rangle\}$

   $B^1 = \{\langle H,0\rangle, \langle J,0\rangle, \langle K,0\rangle, \langle A,1\rangle, \langle B,1\rangle\}$

   $\mathbf{TV} = \{1,0\}$

   $\mathbf{L} = \{S \mid \langle Lex,G \rangle \text{ generates } S\}$ (**Lex** is a set of expressions; **G** is a set of rules)

   $\mathbf{Lex} = \langle Pred,N \rangle$ (**Pred** is a set of predicates; **N** is a set of terms)

Pred = {Girl^1, Boy^1} (the superscript stands for the number of term places)

N = ⟨**N**$_c$, **N**$_{var}$⟩   (**N**$_c$ is a set of names; **N**$_{var}$ is a set of variables)

N$_c$ = {Helen, Joan, Kate, Alex, Bert}

N$_{var}$ = {x,y,z}

G = [**Pred**(**N**)] is an **S**   (any member of **Pred** followed by any member of **N** is an **S**)

Int = [[Girl^1]] = **G**^{1} = {⟨H,1⟩, ⟨J,1⟩, ⟨K,1⟩, ⟨A,0⟩, ⟨B,0⟩}

[[Boy^1]] = **B**^{1} = {⟨H,0⟩, ⟨J,0⟩, ⟨K,0⟩, ⟨A,1⟩, ⟨B,1⟩}

[[Helen]] = H	[[Alex]] = A
[[Joan]] = J	[[Bert]] = B
[[Kate]] = K	x, y, z are variables ranging over **N**$_c$.

One notes that **W** contains, besides the set of individuals **I** and the set of relations **R**, which are covered by terms and predicates, respectively, in **L**, also the set **TV** of truth values. But **L** has no expressions denoting the members of **TV**. (In fact, **L** is not allowed to contain expressions like *true* or *false*, to denote 1 and 0 respectively, as this would admit metalanguage predicates into the object language.) Yet **TV** is needed for the categorial calculus when truth values are assigned as values of characteristic functions, since all values have to be part of **M**. Later, when we introduce the truth functions (see (50)), the members of **TV** will also have to act as input to the truth functions, which makes them all the more indispensable.

- *A simple example sentence in L*

Now consider the **S** 'Boy(Joan)', generated by ⟨Lex,G⟩, i.e. the lexicon and the grammar of the language **L**. We represent this **S** as the tree structure in (42a):

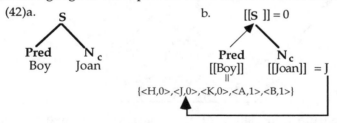

(42)a.   b.   [[S]] = 0

In (42b) the S-structure is repeated, but the extensions of *Joan* and *Boy*, as specified by **Int** for **W**, have been added. Then J (=[[Joan]]) is fed into the function [[Boy]]={⟨H,0⟩, ⟨J,0⟩, ⟨K,0⟩, ⟨A,1⟩, ⟨B,1⟩}, which specifies the value '0' for the input 'J'. This value is passed on to the dominating node **S**, which now receives the extension '0': [[S]] = 0. That is, **S** is false in **M**.

What we have done amounts to a simple application of the Fregean *categorial calculus* to (42a). Languages in models that allow for a categorial calculus to compute the truth value of the sentences generated by the grammar are called *compositional*. The notion of compositionality derives from Frege.[15] It has acquired an enormous importance in formal semantics, which wants to uphold the principle that natural languages are compositional in this sense. We shall see in chapter 6 that this position is untenable.

- *Full sentences have a truth value as their extension*

It is important to realize that Frege generalized the notion of extension to truth values. That is, when we say that a sentence (proposition) is true, then, according to Frege, the extension of that sentence is '1', and when it is false the extension is '0'. Following Frege we can now say: $[[(42a)]] = 0$. This practice, of treating the truth value of a sentence as its extension, has become more or less standard in model theory and formal semantics. Yet most practitioners feel that there is something artifical and counter-intuitive about it, a feeling that is strongly shared by non-logicians. To justify this generalization, Frege invoked an almost Platonic form of essentialism, saying that a true sentence denotes 'the true', while a false sentence denotes 'the false', as if these could be considered real entities. But it is widely believed that Frege's real motive for this step was the fact that it streamlines the model-theoretic categorial calculus, which is a purely formal motive with no empirical impact. In fact, as will be shown in section 6.1.5, the streamlining is deceptive and leads ultimately to an insoluble quandary. There can be no doubt that one of the things that have to be done in an adequate semantic theory of natural language is to undo this Fregean step and find a better candidate, for example 'fact', for the notion 'extension of an S'. For the moment, however, we will follow the convention established by Frege.

- *The computation of a propositional function*

Now consider the S-structure (43a), likewise generated by ⟨**Lex,G**⟩:

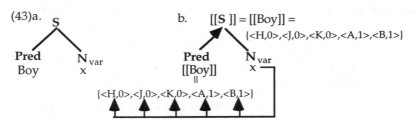

(43a) has no truth value, since **Int** does not specify an extension for the variable x. But when x is replaced by the name of an individual a truth value will result. That is, if we rotate the variable over the set of individuals, by placing their names one by one in the position of x, and keep account of the resulting truth values for each individual, the result is:

---

[15] See Frege (1906:302): '[Definitions] presuppose knowledge of certain primitive elements and their signs. The definition puts together a group of those signs according to certain principles, so that the meaning of this group is determined by the meanings of the signs used.'

Boy(Helen)	false:	⟨H,0⟩	Boy(Alex)	true:	⟨A,1⟩
Boy(Joan)	false:	⟨J,0⟩	Boy(Bert)	true:	⟨B,1⟩
Boy(Kate)	false:	⟨K,0⟩			

If we now put together the pairs that specify the truth value for each substitution we get the set of pairs {⟨H,0⟩, ⟨J,0⟩, ⟨K,0⟩, ⟨A,1⟩, ⟨B,1⟩}, which is precisely the function that gives the extension of the predicate *Boy*, i.e. the set {A,B} or the characteristic function {⟨H,0⟩, ⟨J,0⟩, ⟨K,0⟩, ⟨A,1⟩, ⟨B,1⟩}. In other words, rotation of a variable assigned as a term to a predicate P results in precisely the set of individuals denoted by P. In this case: [[Boy]] = [[Boy(x)]] = **B** = {A,B} = {⟨H,0⟩, ⟨J,0⟩, ⟨K,0⟩, ⟨A,1⟩, ⟨B,1⟩}. This way the categorial calculus is made to work for variables as well.

5.5.2 The notion of quantifier and more model theory

- *What is a quantifier?*

We are now ready for the quantifiers. The point is that substitution of an appropriate referring expression (name) for a variable is not the only way to produce a truth value for a propositional function. There is another way as well: we can *generalize over admissible substitutions*. For example, we can say that for all, or some, or most, or less than half, of the admissible substitutions truth will follow. This is what quantification amounts to. *To quantify is to generalize over those admissible substitutions that yield truth.* Moreover, *a quantifier is a particular way of generalizing over those admissible substitutions that yield truth.*

- *Two standard quantifiers in logic*

For the purpose of logic, i.e. for the purpose of computing entailments, two quantifiers, have proved most useful: 'for all admissible substitutions' and 'for at least one admissible substitution' (or: 'for some admissible substitutions': plurals have never been the forte of standard logic). The former is the *universal quantifier*, written '∀', the latter is the *existential quantifier*, written '∃'. Thus, 'everyone is a boy' can be written in a logical language as:

(44)   ∀[Boy(x)]

and likewise for 'someone is a boy', or 'there is at least one boy':

(45)   ∃[Boy(x)]

(44) means 'for all admissible substitutions of the variable x in "Boy(x)" we get truth', while (45) means 'for some (at least one) admissible substitutions of the variable x in "Boy(x)" we get truth'. Russell , in his article 'On denoting' (1905), at a time when he did not yet have his notation ready, used the expressions *always* and *sometimes* to render the universal and the existential quantifiers, respectively: 'always[Boy(x)]' and 'sometimes[Boy(x)]'.

- *More quantifiers in one proposition: variable binding*

More than one quantifier may occur with predicates that take more than one term, but then it must be indicated which quantifier specifies which term, or, more technically, which quantifier *binds* which variable. This is done by indexing the quantifier for the variable that is bound by it, '$\forall_x$' or '$\exists_x$', usually written '$\forall x$' and '$\exists x$', respectively. Thus we have formulas like (46):

(46) $\forall x \exists y [Love(x,y)]$

This is normally read as: 'for all x there is at least one y such that x loves y', but the full paraphrase is:

for each admissible substitution of x in 'Love(x,y)' there is at least one admissible substitution of y in 'Love(x,y)' such that 'Love(x,y)' is true'.

Likewise we may have, for example:

(47) $\exists x \exists y [Love(x,y)]$

which is normally read as 'there is at least one x such that for some y, x loves y', but more properly as:

for at least one admissible substitution of x in 'Love(x,y)' there is at least one admissible substitution of y in 'Love(x,y)' such that 'Love(x,y)' is true',

- *The model M extended with quantifiers: M'*

To show how this works in a toy model we extend the model **M** (=(41)) to **M'** (=(48)). **M'** has an additional two-place relation **Lo²**, denoted by the binary predicate *Love²* with the extension {⟨J,A⟩,⟨K,B⟩,⟨B,H⟩}. (The superscripts indicate the number of terms a predicate takes. They are usually not written when the model is put into action.) **G** is reformulated in such a way that the quantifiers are also properly generated.

(48) **M'** = ⟨**W, L, Int**⟩ (**W** is a world; **L** is a language; **Int** is an interpretation)

$\quad\quad$ **W** = ⟨**I,R,TV**⟩   (**I** is a set of individuals; **R** is a set of relations in **I**; **TV** is a set of truth values)

$\quad\quad\quad$ **I** = {H, J, K, A, B}

$\quad\quad\quad$ **R** = {**G¹, B¹, Lo²**}$\quad\quad$(the superscript stands for the number of places in the relation)

$\quad\quad\quad$ **G¹** = {⟨H,1⟩, ⟨J,1⟩, ⟨K,1⟩, ⟨A,0⟩, ⟨B,0⟩}

$\quad\quad\quad$ **B¹** = {⟨H,0⟩, ⟨J,0⟩, ⟨K,0⟩, ⟨A,1⟩, ⟨B,1⟩}

$\quad\quad\quad$ **Lo²** = {⟨⟨H,H⟩,0⟩, ⟨⟨H,J⟩,0⟩, ⟨⟨H,K⟩,0⟩, ⟨⟨H,A⟩,0⟩, ⟨⟨H,B⟩,0⟩,
$\quad\quad\quad\quad\quad$ ⟨⟨J,H⟩,0⟩, ⟨⟨J,J⟩,0⟩, ⟨⟨J,K⟩,0⟩, ⟨⟨J,A⟩,1⟩, ⟨⟨J,B⟩,0⟩,
$\quad\quad\quad\quad\quad$ ⟨⟨K,H⟩,0⟩, ⟨⟨K,J⟩,0⟩, ⟨⟨K,K⟩,0⟩, ⟨⟨K,A⟩,0⟩, ⟨⟨K,B⟩,1⟩,
$\quad\quad\quad\quad\quad$ ⟨⟨A,H⟩,0⟩, ⟨⟨A,J⟩,0⟩, ⟨⟨A,K⟩,0⟩, ⟨⟨A,A⟩,0⟩, ⟨⟨A,B⟩,0⟩,
$\quad\quad\quad\quad\quad$ ⟨⟨B,H⟩,1⟩, ⟨⟨B,J⟩,0⟩, ⟨⟨B,K⟩,0⟩, ⟨⟨B,A⟩,0⟩, ⟨⟨B,B⟩,0⟩}

$\quad\quad\quad$ **TV** = {1,0}

L = {**S** | ⟨**Lex,G**⟩ generates **S**}   (**Lex** is a set of expressions; **G** is a set of rules)

Lex = ⟨**Pred,Qu,N**⟩   (**Pred** is a set of predicates; **Qu** is a set of quantifiers; **N** is a set of terms)

Pred = {Girl^1, Boy^1, Love^2}

Qu = {∀$_\alpha$, ∃$_\alpha$}   ('α' is any member of **N**$_{var}$)

N = ⟨**N**$_c$, **N**$_{var}$⟩   (**N**$_c$ is a set of names; **N**$_{var}$ is a set of variables)

N$_c$ = {Helen, Joan, Kate, Alex, Bert}

N$_{var}$ = {x,y,z}

G = (1) [**Pred** (N*)] is an **S** (N*: as many terms as there are term places for **Pred**)

(2) [**Qu** (S$_{[\alpha]}$)] is an **S**   (α is any member of **N**$_{var}$; 'S$_{[\alpha]}$': at least one term place of the **Pred** under S must be filled by α)

Int = [[Girl^1]] = **G**^{1} [[Boy^1]] = **B**^{1}

[[Love^2]] = **Lo**^{2}

[[Helen]] = H   [[Alex]] = A

[[Joan]] = J   [[Bert]] = B

[[Kate]] = K   x, y, z are variables ranging over **N**$_c$

Note that though the relation **Lo**^{2} consists of the set {⟨K,B⟩, ⟨J,A⟩, ⟨B,H⟩}, this set has been characterized in **M'** by means of a characteristic function that yields truth only for the pairs ⟨J,A⟩, ⟨K,B⟩, and ⟨B,H⟩.

• *Some examples*

The S-structures (46) and (47) given above are generated by **M'**. Intuitively one will have no difficulty in seeing that (46) is false in the extended model **M'** but (47) is true.

All S-structures generated by **M'** are representable as tree diagrams. Just as we did for (42a) and (43a) above, we can represent (44) and (45) as tree diagrams, generated by ⟨**Lex,G**⟩ of **M'** (the subscripts to the Ss have been added for ease of reference):

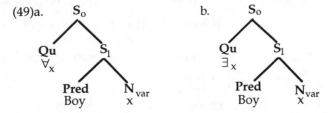

(49)a.   S$_0$ b.   S$_0$

Qu   S$_1$ Qu   S$_1$
∀$_x$ ∃$_x$

Pred   N$_{var}$ Pred   N$_{var}$
Boy   x   Boy   x

Note that in the format of (49a,b) the predicate comes first, followed by the required number of argument terms, just as in (38b) above. In (38b) there are two argument terms under the binary predicate *Love*: the subject term *Helen* and the direct object term *Bert*. Here, we have a unary predicate, *Boy*, follow-

ed by the variable x that acts as subject term. It is customary in logical notation to let the predicate precede its terms, whereby the first term corresponds
to the subject, the second to the object. Logical languages thus normally follow
the format known in linguistics as VSO (see section 4.8).

Note also that $[\![S_1]\!]$ is well-defined here. S_1 stands directly under a quantifier which binds the variable x. In this position the instruction for the variable is to rotate it over its range, in this case the total set I of individuals in
the model, yielding the set {A,B} of all boys in I.

- *Quantifiers as higher order predicates*

At this moment we see something interesting. In both (49a) and (49b) the extension of S_1 is the set of boys in the model, i.e. the boys A and B, named *Alex*
and *Bert*, respectively. That is, $[\![S_1]\!] = [\![Boy(x)]\!] = \{A,B\}$. This being so we may
just as well treat the quantifiers, $\forall x$ or $\exists x$, as predicates that say something of
the set {A,B}. The universal quantifier says of $[\![S_1]\!]$ that it equals the total set
of individuals in the model, i.e. {M,H,J,A,B} or I, while the existential
quantifier says of $[\![S_1]\!]$ that it is non-empty. Clearly, the former yields falsity
and the latter truth. The S-structure S_1 is now considered to be the subject term
of the predicate.

It pays in many different ways to treat the quantifiers as 'abstract' (non-
lexical, logical) predicates.[16] However, they are not predicates over individuals but over sets of individuals, just like the ordinary lexical predicates
disperse or *congregate*, or *numerous*, which cannot be used for individuals but
only for groups of individuals.

- *Model M' reformulated with quantifiers as predicates: M "*

Accordingly, we modify **M'** into **M"** in such a way that the category **Qu** is
eliminated and $\forall_\alpha$ and $\exists_\alpha$ are made elements of **Pred$_{\log}$**, listed as $\forall^1_\alpha$ and $\exists^1_\alpha$,
with the superscript '1' because they are one-place predicates. For good
measure we also add the truth-functional operators $\neg$, $\wedge$, $\vee$ and $\rightarrow$ as members
of the set **Pred$_{\log}$**, the first as a unary predicate, the others as binary predicates. They are not predicates over individuals or sets of individuals but,
entirely in the spirit of logical model-theory, over truth values. The set **N**
now also comprises the subset **N$_{\log}$** which contains the symbol **S**:

(50)   **M"** = **M'** except that **L** is replaced by **L"** and **Int** is extended with **Int"**:

$\qquad$ **L"** = {S | <**Lex,G**> generates S}   (**Lex** is a set of expressions; **G** is a set
$\qquad\qquad\qquad\qquad\qquad\qquad\qquad\qquad\qquad\qquad$ of rules)

$\qquad$ **Lex** = <**Pred,N**> (**Pred** is a set of predicates; **N** is a set of terms)

---

[16] The treatment of variables and quantifiers given here differs from what is normally
found in textbooks (see, for example, Dowty, Wall, Peters 1981). Normally, quantifiers are
introduced syncategorematically, i.e. as special elements outside the categorial calculus
that determines truth values. Now that generalized quantifiers (see 5.5.5) have become
standard the treatment of quantifiers as predicates is also becoming more and more
accepted.

Pred = ⟨**Pred**$_{lex}$, **Pred**$_{log}$⟩
    Pred$_{lex}$ = {Girl^1, Boy^1, Love^2}
    Pred$_{log}$ = {∀$^1_\alpha$, ∃$^1_\alpha$, ¬^{1}, ∧^{2}, ∨^{2}, →^{2}} ('α' is any member of **N**$_{var}$)
N = ⟨**N**$_c$, **N**$_{var}$, **N**$_{log}$⟩
    N$_c$ = {Helen, Joan, Kate, Alex, Bert}
    N$_{var}$ = {x, y, z}
    N$_{log}$ = {S}
G = (1) [**Pred**$^*_{lex}$(**N**$^*_{c/var}$)] is an **S** (* is a variable for the number
                                            of term places)
      (2) [**Pred**$^*_{log}$(**S***)] is an **S** (if **Pred**$_{log}$ = ∀$^1_\alpha$ or ∃$^1_\alpha$ then the
                                    argument-**S** = **S**$_{[\alpha]}$: at least one
                                      term place of a **Pred**$_{Lex}$ under **S**
                                      must be filled by α)

Int'' = [[¬]] : {⟨1,0⟩,⟨0,1⟩}
      [[∧]] : {⟨⟨1,1⟩,1⟩,⟨⟨1,0⟩,0⟩,⟨⟨0,1⟩,0⟩,⟨⟨0,0⟩,0⟩}
      [[∨]] : {⟨⟨1,1⟩,1⟩,⟨⟨1,0⟩,1⟩,⟨⟨0,1⟩,1⟩,⟨⟨0,0⟩,0⟩}
      [[→]] : {⟨⟨1,1⟩,1⟩,⟨⟨1,0⟩,0⟩,⟨⟨0,1⟩,1⟩,⟨⟨0,0⟩,1⟩}

Technically speaking, predicates over individuals, i.e. most lexical predicates, are *1st order predicates*, while predicates over sets of individuals are *2nd order predicates*. And, of course, predicates over sets of sets of individuals are *3rd order predicates*, etc., but this does not have to concern us right now. Since the predicates in the range of lexical predicate variables in predicate calculus, such as F, G and H above, are meant to be 1st order predicates, the predicate calculus under discussion is standardly called *1st order predicate calculus*. In 1st order predicate calculus the only 2nd order predicates are the quantifiers. Likewise, in a 2nd order predicate calculus the quantifiers will be 3rd order predicates, etc.

- *Examples revisited: a whole lot of computation*

Let us now, by way of exercise, represent (46) and (47) as the tree diagrams (51a) and (51b), respectively, and see how their truth values are computed.

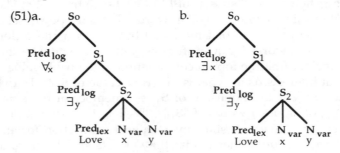

(It would be more regular to have the symbol **N**$_{log}$ above the S-terms of the logical predicates, but we have left it out so as not to overburden the trees.)

We cannot, at this stage, formally compute the truth values of (51a,b) since **M"** does not specify the extension of the quantifiers $\forall_X$ and $\exists_X$. But we know intuitively that (51a) is false and (51b) true in **M"**. These values are produced when we stipulate that $[\![\forall_X]\!]$ requires of its argument-S that it be identical with the total set of individuals **I** in **M"**, and that $[\![\exists_X]\!]$ requires of its argument-S that it be a non-empty set.

More formally, we provide $[\![\forall]\!]$ and $[\![\exists]\!]$ with the following general definitions, which remain unchanged no matter what model they occur in:

(52)a. $[\![\forall]\!] = \{X \mid X \subseteq I \text{ and } X = I\}$ or: $[\![\forall]\!] = \{I\}$

   b. $[\![\exists]\!] = \{X \mid X \subseteq I \text{ and } X \neq \varnothing\}$ or: $[\![\exists]\!]$ is the set of non-empty subsets of **I**

Strictly speaking, what is needed for the purpose of categorial calculus is characteristic functions. As characteristic functions, both (52a) and (52b) are the sets consisting of all the pairs made up of a subset of **I** as the first coordinate and the value '1' as the second. The application of (52a) to **M"** is as in (53a) or, more completely, as in (53b):

(53)a. $[\![\forall]\!] = \{\{H,J,K,A,B\}\}$ (i.e. $\{I\}$)

   b. $[\![\forall]\!] = \{\langle\varnothing,0\rangle, \langle\{\langle H,1\rangle,\langle J,0\rangle,\langle K,0\rangle,\langle A,0\rangle,\langle B,0\rangle\},0\rangle,$
   $\langle\{\langle H,0\rangle,\langle J,1\rangle,\langle K,0\rangle,\langle A,0\rangle,\langle B,0\rangle\},0\rangle,$
   $\langle\{\langle H,0\rangle,\langle J,0\rangle,\langle K,1\rangle,\langle A,0\rangle,\langle B,0\rangle\},0\rangle, \ldots ,$
   $\ldots ,\langle\{\langle H,1\rangle,\langle J,1\rangle,\langle K,1\rangle,\langle A,1\rangle,\langle B,0\rangle\},0\rangle, \ldots ,$
   $\ldots , \langle\{\langle H,1\rangle,\langle J,1\rangle,\langle K,1\rangle,\langle A,1\rangle,\langle B,1\rangle\},1\rangle,\}$

And (52b) applied to **M"** is as in (54a) or, more completely, as in (54b):

(54)a. $[\![\exists]\!] = \{\{H\},\{J\},\{K\},\{A\},\{B\},\{H,J\}, \{H,K\},\ldots,\{H,J,K,A,B\}\}$

   b. $[\![\exists]\!] = \{\langle\varnothing,0\rangle, \langle\{\langle H,1\rangle,\langle J,0\rangle,\langle K,0\rangle,\langle A,0\rangle,\langle B,0\rangle\},1\rangle,$
   $\langle\{\langle H,0\rangle,\langle J,1\rangle,\langle K,0\rangle,\langle A,0\rangle,\langle B,0\rangle\},1\rangle,$
   $\langle\{\langle H,0\rangle,\langle J,0\rangle,\langle K,1\rangle,\langle A,0\rangle,\langle B,0\rangle\},1\rangle,$
   $\langle\{\langle H,0\rangle,\langle J,0\rangle,\langle K,0\rangle,\langle A,1\rangle,\langle B,0\rangle\},1\rangle, \ldots ,$
   $\ldots , \langle\{\langle H,1\rangle,\langle J,1\rangle,\langle K,1\rangle,\langle A,1\rangle,\langle B,1\rangle\},1\rangle,\}$

i.e. as the function from all subsets of **I** to 1 or 0 such that only $\varnothing$ is paired with 0 and all other subsets with 1 (in other words, $[\![\exists]\!]$ is the power set of **I** minus $\varnothing$, while $[\![\forall]\!]$ is the power set of **I** minus all but **I**). With these definitions the categorial calculus works for quantifiers as well, as will now be shown.

Let us consider first the formal computation of the truth value of (51a). The question that interests us is 'what is the truth value of S_0?' To determine that we need to know if the extension of S_1 is a member of the extension of the predicate $\forall_X$, or, in other words, if $[\![S_1]\!] \in [\![\forall_X]\!]$. But what is $[\![S_1]\!]$? In (51a), S_1 denotes a set of individuals since the standard instruction for an S-structure acting as term to a quantifier is that the variable should be rotated over its range. S_1 would be a proposition (sentence with a truth value) were it not for the variable x. In this context S_1 expresses a propositional function.

Therefore, we must begin by rotating the variable bound by the highest quantifier, in this case the *x*-variable. This gives five variants of S_1, one for each *x*-substitution:

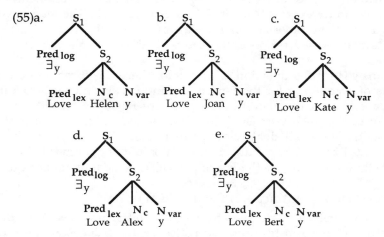

(55)a.

b.

c.

d.

e.

But now, to find out the truth value for each of (55a-e), we must determine $[\![S_2]\!]$ for each case. That is, for each of (55a-e) we must now, in turn, rotate the *y*-variable and determine the corresponding truth value, while keeping track of the substitutions and the values found. Rather than drawing 25 tree diagrams for S_2 in (51a), we shall use tables. For each *x*-substitution we list the *y*-substitutions with the corresponding truth values. This gives a set Y of individuals for each *x*-substitution. Remember that $[\![Love]\!] = \{\langle J,A\rangle,\langle K,B\rangle,\langle B,H\rangle\}$.

(56)

x	Y	x	Y	x	Y	x	Y	x	Y
H:	⟨H,0⟩	J:	⟨H,0⟩	K:	⟨H,0⟩	A:	⟨H,0⟩	B:	⟨H,1⟩
	⟨J,0⟩		⟨J,0⟩		⟨J,0⟩		⟨J,0⟩		⟨J,0⟩
	⟨K,0⟩		⟨K,0⟩		⟨K,0⟩		⟨K,0⟩		⟨K,0⟩
	⟨A,0⟩		⟨A,1⟩		⟨A,0⟩		⟨A,0⟩		⟨A,0⟩
	⟨B,0⟩		⟨B,0⟩		⟨B,1⟩		⟨B,0⟩		⟨B,0⟩
	0		1		1		0		1

Since S_1 is existentially quantified, non-emptiness of Y is sufficient for the truth of each *x*-substitution. The tables in (56) show that there is truth for the *x*-substitutions J, K and B, since for these substitutions the Y-class is non-empty, but falsity for H and A: H(elen) and A(lex) love nobody. The extension of S_1 is thus: $\{\langle H,0\rangle,\langle J,1\rangle,\langle K,1\rangle,\langle A,0\rangle,\langle B,1\rangle\}$, or $\{J,K,B\}$. Since $[\![S_1]\!] = \{J,K,B\} \neq \{H,J,K,B,A\}$, $[\![S_1]\!] \notin [\![\forall]\!]$ and thus sentence (51a=47) is false in the model $\mathbf{M}''$.

The truth value of (51b) is now quickly established. Up to S_1 everything is the same as for (51a). Only for S_o, the last step, the conclusion is different. S_o is existentially quantified, which means that non-emptiness of $[\![S_1]\!]$ is sufficient for truth. Now $[\![S_1]\!] = \{J,K,B\} \neq \varnothing$. Therefore, $[\![S_1]\!] \in [\![\exists]\!]$, which means that (51b=47) is true.

- *How do we express the Aristotelian sentence types?*

Meanwhile, we are still not able to translate a simple sentence of any of the four Aristotelian types into the language of modern predicate calculus. In particular, how do we express 'All F is G' and 'Some F is G'? The reason we cannot do this is that we have as yet no way of giving the F-predicate, i.e. the predicate that is used referentially (see 5.1.2 above), a place in the syntactic structure.

The answer to this question is threefold: there are three, closely related, methods of accounting for the F-predicate in logical sentence structures. The first is called restricted quantification theory or RQT, the second is unrestricted quantification theory or UQT, the third is generalized quantification theory or GQT. We shall deal with them in that order. Two of these three methods, RQT and GQT, require an adaptation of the grammar **G** in the model **M"** of (50); for one of the methods, namely UQT, no adaptation is required.

5.5.3 Restricted quantification theory (RQT)

The difference between these two forms of quantification lies in the definition of the range of the substitutional variables. In 1st order RQT the range of a variable is restricted to the set denoted by the Q-predicate, i.e. the predicate quantified over (the F-predicate in Aristotelian logic). This brings about a number of consequences, which we shall discuss in a moment.

- *Russell's early rejection of RQT*

RQT was considered by Russell and Whitehead for their *Principia Mathematica*, but rejected in favour of UQT for reasons that will be explained presently. Yet RQT has always appealed to language-minded logicians and philosophers (and linguists, to the extent that they took notice of logic at all) because RQT analyses of natural language sentences are intuitively much more attractive than UQT analyses. For Russell and Whitehead this was of no concern. In fact, Russell (1905) prided himself on the fact that his logical analysis actually *destroyed* the grammatical structure of the sentences concerned. But we feel that this pride was inappropriate. For if one of the aims of logical analysis is to specify what sentences mean, then the logical analyses had better stay as close to the actual sentences of the language as possible, as any claim to the effect that logical analyses differ from surface syntactic structures implies a theory relating the logical analyses to the corresponding surface sentences of the language in question. And any such theory had better be kept as simple as possible. Therefore, far from feeling proud of the distance he had created between language and logic, Russell should have regretted it. In the end, as we shall see in 5.5.5, RQT did win, also on the purely logical front. The language of GQT, the quantification theory which is now universally recognized as the most adequate, is structurally identical to, or anyway a variant of, RQT. What distinguishes GQT from RQT is not the logical language used but the model-theoretic semantics associated with it. It is, in fact, the new development of GQT that has brought logic and language closer to each other again, after many years of separation.

• *Some examples in terms of RQT*
How does RQT work? We will not specify the full formal details of an RQT model (the reader may find it amusing to do that for himself). We will, rather, demonstrate how it works by giving a few representative examples. Consider the sentence (57a) with its analysis in terms of RQT (57b):

(57)a. All boys are asleep
    b. ∀x:Boy[Asleep(x)]

(57b) is read intuitively as: 'for all *x* such that *x* is a boy, *x* is asleep'. *Boy* is the F-predicate in Aristotelian predicate calculus. We shall henceforth call it the *Q-predicate*, i.e. the predicate of the term that is quantified over. The predicate *Asleep* we no longer call the G-predicate, but the *M-predicate*, i.e. the predicate of the matrix sentence. The range of the variable *x* is the extension of the Q-predicate *Boy*, i.e. the set of boys in the model. If we take up the model **M"** again as defined in (50), [[Boy]] = {⟨H,0⟩,⟨J,0⟩,⟨K,0⟩,⟨A,1⟩, ⟨B,1⟩} or {A,B}. We add the predicate *Asleep*, with the extension: [[Asleep^1]]= A^1 = {⟨H,1⟩,⟨J,1⟩,⟨K,0⟩,⟨A,1⟩,⟨B,0⟩} or {H,J,A}, saying, in effect, that Helen, Joan and Alex are asleep while the others are not. **L** must be changed so that it generates structures like (57c), which corresponds with (57b). We shall not specify, at this point, the formal rules for the language of RQT. Never mind, therefore, the label '**Pred$_{log}$**' for the complex quantifier [∀x:Boy]. We shall come back to this detail later, in 5.5.5, when we deal with GQT.

(57)c.

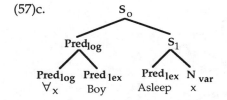

The principle of RQT is that the rotation of the *x*-variable is restricted to the set denoted by the Q-predicate, in this case the set of boys, i.e. {⟨H,0⟩, ⟨J,0⟩, ⟨K,0⟩, ⟨A,1⟩, ⟨B,1⟩}. There are therefore only two substitutions to make for the M-predicate in **S$_1$**, *Alex* and *Bert*. Since the extension of *Asleep* has been defined as {⟨H,1⟩, ⟨J,1⟩, ⟨K,0⟩, ⟨A,1⟩, ⟨B,0⟩}, only the name *Alex* will yield truth, not the name *Bert*. This fixes the extension of **S$_1$** as just {A}, or: {⟨H,0⟩, ⟨J,0⟩, ⟨K,0⟩, ⟨A,1⟩, ⟨B,0⟩}:

(58)   Asleep(Alex)   true, hence   ⟨A,1⟩
        Asleep(Bert)   false, hence   ⟨B,0⟩

In RQT the general condition for the universal quantifier to yield truth is that the extension of the Q-predicate equals the extension of the **S$_1$**-term. The extension of **S$_1$** in (57c) is the set of those individuals that are both boy and asleep. The condition for the universal quantifier ∀x:Boy to yield truth is, therefore, that the set of boys be equal to the set of boy-sleepers, or: $[\![Boy]\!]$ = $[\![S_1]\!]$. This condition is not fulfilled, since, for (57c), $[\![Boy]\!]$ = {A,B} and $[\![S_1]\!]$ = {A}. Therefore, (57) is false.

Analogously for the same sentence with the existential quantifier:

(59)a.   Some boys are asleep (At least one boy is asleep)
    b.   ∃x:Boy[Asleep(x)]
    c.

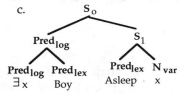

Again, the rotation of the *x*-variable is restricted to just the set of boys, i.e. {A,B}, resulting in (58), as before: $[\![S_1]\!]$ = {A}. The condition for the existential quantifier to yield truth, in RQT, is that the extensions of the Q-predicate and the M-predicate in S_1 have a non-empty intersection. For (59c) this means that the condition is that $[\![S_1]\!] \cap [\![Boy]\!] \neq \varnothing$. This condition is fulfilled since {A} ∩ {A,B} ≠ ∅. Hence (59) is true.

This is easily extended to sentences with more than one quantifier, like (60a), written now as (60b), with the corresponding tree diagram (60c):

(60)a.   Some boy(s) love(s) some girl(s)
    b.   ∃x:Boy ∃y:Girl [Love(x,y)]
    c.

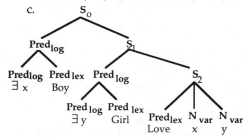

To determine the value of $[\![S_1]\!]$ we have to substitute the members of {A,B}, i.e. A and B, for *x* under S_2, and then, for each substitution, find out the resulting truth value, based on the set Y constructed for each substitution. The set Y is found, each time, by rotating the *y*-variable in S_2 over just the set of girls, i.e. {H,J,K}. The difference with (51) above is, therefore, that only two *x*-substitutions are now required, and only three *y*-substitutions. The extension of the predicate *Love*, one remembers, is: $[\![Love]\!]$ = {⟨J,A⟩,⟨K,B⟩,⟨B,H⟩}. The computation goes as in (61), where for each *x*-substitution σ there is a (possibly empty) set Y of girls loved by $[\![σ]\!]$:

(61)   x   Y   x   Y
          A: ⟨H,0⟩   B: ⟨H,1⟩
               ⟨J,0⟩   ⟨J,0⟩
               ⟨K,0⟩   ⟨K,0⟩
               ‾‾0‾‾   ‾‾1‾‾

This gives {⟨A,0⟩,⟨B,1⟩}, or {B} for $[\![S_1]\!]$, and since {B} ∩ {A,B} ≠ Ø (60) is true.

- *The problem of expressivity now solved, but not the problem of the empty F-class*

As it operates with *n*-ary predicates, each of whose terms can be quantified, RQT provides an answer to the *problem of expressivity*, mentioned in section 5.1.5. But, with the semantics presented here, it fails to solve the *problem of empty F-classes*. This is because when the extension of the Q-predicate is empty, substitution of the variable by the name of an individual in the model (i.e. rotation), which is required by the system, is impossible, which effectively blocks the assignment of a truth value. For example, if we add the predicate *Monkey* to the language of the model but do not introduce any monkeys into **W** there is no individual whose name could stand in for the *x*-variable in a sentence like *All monkeys are asleep* or *Some monkeys are asleep*, and no truth value assignment can take place.

This is the main reason why Russell decided not to use this form of quantification theory, and to use UQT instead. What Russell did not realize is that RQT works perfectly well, also for Q-predicates with an empty extension, even better than UQT, provided the variables are allowed to rotate over the total set **I** of individuals in the model. This will become clear in section 5.5.5, when the generalized quantifiers are discussed.

5.5.4 Unrestricted quantification theory (UQT)

UQT was the standard form of quantification theory till the 1980s, when, at least for the purpose of language analysis, it was modified into generalized quantification theory (GQT). In 1st order UQT all substitutional variables always range over **I**, the total set of individuals in the model, just like what we had in section 5.5.2 above. To express the Q-predicate help is sought from propositional calculus: a sentence like (62a), *All girls are asleep*, is translated as (62b), with the associated tree diagram (62c), while (63a), *Some girls are asleep*, is translated as (63b), with the tree structure (63c). Note that in the tree diagrams the truth-functional operators → and ∧ are treated as predicates, just like the quantifiers. This has been done because, as was shown in section 5.3.3 above, the truth-functional operators all have truth values as output, which makes it possible to treat them as special abstract predicates over truth values, thus streamlining the categorial calculus. Accordingly, the truth-functional operators are assigned the syntactic position of a predicate, to the left of the terms, which are **S**-structures.[17]

(62)a. All girls are asleep
　　b. $\forall x[\text{Girl}(x) \rightarrow \text{Asleep}(x)]$
　　c.

(63)a. Some girls are asleep
　　b. $\exists x[\text{Girl}(x) \wedge \text{Asleep}(x)]$
　　c.

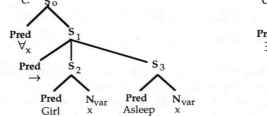
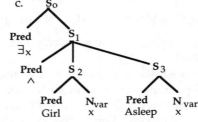

Similarly for (64) and (65):

(64)a. All boys love some girl(s)
　　b. $\forall x[\text{Boy}(x) \rightarrow \exists y[\text{Girl}(y) \wedge \text{Love}(x,y)]]$

(65)a. Some boys love all girls
　　b　$\exists x[\text{Boy}(x) \wedge \forall y[\text{Girl}(y) \rightarrow \text{Love}(x,y)]]$

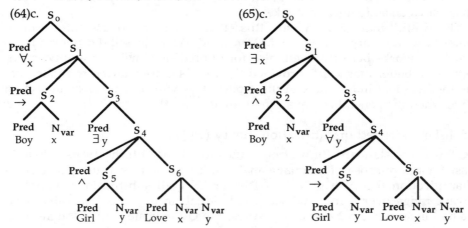

• *Application of the categorial calculus: traffic rules must be observed*
Let us apply the categorial calculus to (62c). In UQT, the condition for the universal quantifier is that $[[S_1]] = \{I\}$, as in section 5.5.2. So we ask: what is $[[S_1]]$? And here we must be careful to avoid mistakes. One might think that, as is normally the case, the extension of S_1 consists of the output of its predicate

[17] This means that we are adopting so-called Polish notation. In Polish notation a sentence (proposition) like $p \rightarrow q$ is written $\rightarrow (p,q)$. Our decision to adopt Polish notation is nothing to do with the logic. It is motivated entirely by linguistic considerations: Polish notation naturally suits the grammar that transforms the logical structures into natural language sentences (see Seuren (1996) for details).

function, in this case the propositional operator →. But this is wrong, as will become clear when this procedure is followed.

What value is passed on by the predicate of S_1, i.e. the operator → ? To answer this we need the extensions of its argument terms S_2 and S_3, i.e. [[S_2]] and [[S_3]]. And these must be truth values, since all the operator → can do is take two truth values and deliver a new one. But S_2 and S_3 in (62c) do not have an extension. Both contain the unbound variable x, which means that an instruction is needed that specifies what is to be done with the variable. In this case there is no instruction as the operator → does not bring along any instruction for variables: all it can do is receive two truth values and pass on a third one. Here the categorial calculus stalls. What was the mistake?

The mistake was that the instruction issued by the very highest predicate, $\forall_x$, has been ignored. The instruction is: rotate the variable x in S_1 (and, of course, rotate over **I**). We start, therefore, with the substitution of the name *Helen* for all occurrences of x in S_1, as shown in (62c1). Then we substitute *Joan* for x, as shown in (62c2), then *Kate*, then *Alex*, then *Bert*.

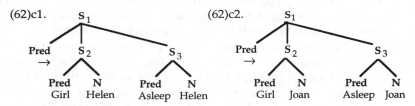

All these substitutions deliver a truth value. When x is replaced by *Helen*, as in (62c1), the truth value of S_1 is '1', because the antecedent clause of the implication operator, S_2, is true and, moreover, the consequent clause S_3 is true (remember: [[Asleep]] = {H, J, A}), which gives truth for the whole implication. Therefore we write up for [[S_1]]: <H,1>, i.e. for the individual H S_1 yields truth. For the other four substitutions we get the results: <J,1>, <K,0>, <A,1>, and <B,1> (the latter two because neither A nor B is a girl, which ensures truth for the whole implication). Therefore, [[S_1]] = {<H,1>,<J,1>,<K,0>,<A,1>,<B,1>}, or {H,J,A,B}. But this set is not a member of {**I**}. Therefore, sentence (62) is false.

- *More computation*

Let us do this again, but more precisely, this time. We substitute all occurrences of x in S_2 and S_3 by names for all members of **I** in turn. There are five admissible substitutions: *Helen, Joan, Kate, Alex* and *Bert*, referring to H, J, K, A and B, respectively. Each substitution yields a truth value for S_1. The pairs of substitutions and truth values yield the set that forms [[S_1]]:

(66)

x → S_2,S_3	x → S_2,S_3	x → S_2,S_3	x → S_2,S_3	x → S_2,S_3
H: 1 1,1	J: 1 1,1	K: 0 1,0	A: 1 0,1	B: 1 0,0
$\overline{1}$	$\overline{1}$	$\overline{0}$	$\overline{1}$	$\overline{1}$

[[S_1]] = {<H,1>,<J,1>,<K,0>,<A,1>,<B,1>} = {H,J,A,B} ≠ **I**. Hence, (62) is false.

For (63c) the categorial calculus is largely similar, but the predicate of S_1 is $\wedge$, not $\rightarrow$:

(67) $\begin{array}{llll} x & \wedge S_2, S_3 \\ H: 1 & 1,1 \\ \hline & 1 \end{array}$ $\begin{array}{ll} x & \wedge S_2, S_3 \\ J: 1 & 1,1 \\ \hline & 1 \end{array}$ $\begin{array}{ll} x & \wedge S_2, S_3 \\ K: 0 & 1,0 \\ \hline & 0 \end{array}$ $\begin{array}{ll} x & \wedge S_2, S_3 \\ A: 0 & 0,1 \\ \hline & 0 \end{array}$ $\begin{array}{ll} x & \wedge S_2, S_3 \\ B: 0 & 0,0 \\ \hline & 0 \end{array}$

Now $[[S_1]] = \{\langle H,1\rangle,\langle J,1\rangle,\langle K,0\rangle,\langle A,0\rangle,\langle B,0\rangle\} = \{H,J\} \neq \varnothing$. Hence, (63) is true.

Let us now do the same for (64c). That is, both occurrences of the x-variable in S_1 are replaced, subsequently by the names *Helen, Joan, Kate, Alex* and *Bert*. Each substitution will yield a truth value, but this time not immediately. The procedure is, in fact, quite longwinded.

Let us consider first the result of substituting *Helen* for x in S_1, as in (64c1). Now we can take the easy way out and say that this substitution leads to truth for S_1 simply because the antecedent clause of the implication operator $\rightarrow$ is false (Helen is not a boy), so that the whole implication is automatically true. But that is too easy, since, for one thing, we want to know whether S_3 yields a truth value as well. For if it does not the categorial calculus will stall. Therefore, knowing that S_2 is false we still want to establish the truth value of S_3 (for the substitution *Helen*). Now to find out whether S_3 is true for the substitution *Helen* we must, again, go over all five individuals in **I**, now for the y-variable, and see what we get for S_4. The first such y-substitution is, again, *Helen*, as shown in (64c2), and it yields falsity, since, though Helen is a girl, she does not love *Helen* (herself). And for the operator $\wedge$ both the argument propositions must be true to get truth. The second substitution, shown in (64c3), yields again falsity since, though Helen is a girl, she does not love *Joan*.

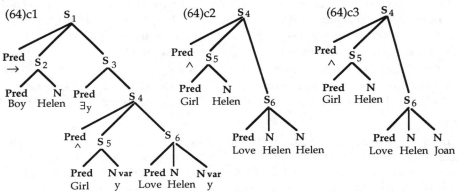

When we carry on this way for *Kate, Alex* and *Bert* as substitutions for the y-variable we get the value 0 for each substitution. So, in determing $[[S_4]]$ for the substitution *Helen* in S_1, we can now write up (remember: $[[$Love$]]$ = $\{\langle J,A\rangle,\langle K,B\rangle,\langle B,H\rangle\}$):

(68)a.   x → S_2, S_3

H:	0, y	$\wedge S_5, S_6$	y	$\wedge S_5, S_6$	y	$\wedge S_5, S_6$	y	$\wedge S_5, S_6$	y	$\wedge S_5, S_6$

H: 0,y $\wedge S_5, S_6$ y $\wedge S_5, S_6$ y $\wedge S_5, S_6$ y $\wedge S_5, S_6$ y $\wedge S_5, S_6$
   H: 0 1,0   J: 0 1,0   K: 0 1,0   A: 0 0,0   B: 0 0,0
    ‾0‾   ‾0‾   ‾0‾   ‾0‾   ‾0‾

This gives: $\{\langle H,0\rangle, \langle J,0\rangle, \langle K,0\rangle, \langle A,0\rangle, \langle B,0\rangle\}$ as the value for $[\![S_4]\!]$ for the substitution *Helen* in S_1. Now, in the given model, $\{\langle H,0\rangle, \langle J,0\rangle, \langle K,0\rangle, \langle A,0\rangle, \langle B,0\rangle\} = \varnothing$, and the quantifier (predicate) $\exists_y$ in S_3 requires that $[\![S_4]\!] \neq \varnothing$. That is, for the substitution *Helen* in S_1 $[\![S_3]\!] = 0$. Now we have both $[\![S_2]\!] = 0$ and $[\![S_3]\!] = 0$, which means, under →, that, for the substitution *Helen* for the *x*-variable, $[\![S_1]\!] = 1$. So we can write: $\langle H,1\rangle$ as the first of the five members of $[\![S_1]\!]$.

Likewise for the *x*-substitutions *Joan, Kate, Alex* and *Bert*. This gives, respectively:

(68)b.   x → S_2, S_3

J: 0, y $\wedge S_5, S_6$ y $\wedge S_5, S_6$ y $\wedge S_5, S_6$ y $\wedge S_5, S_6$ y $\wedge S_5, S_6$
   H: 0 1,0   J: 0 1,0   K: 0 1,0   A: 0 0,1   B: 0 0,0
    ‾0‾   ‾0‾   ‾0‾   ‾0‾   ‾0‾

That is, with *Joan* for *x*, $[\![S_3]\!] = 0$, and, again, since $[\![S_2]\!] = 0$ (Joan is not a boy), $[\![S_1]\!] = 1$. Therefore, we can add $\langle J,1\rangle$ as the second member of $[\![S_1]\!]$. Next we substitute *Kate* for *x*, and get the same result. So we add $\langle K,1\rangle$ as the third member of $[\![S_1]\!]$:

(68)c.   x → S_2, S_3

K: 0, y $\wedge S_5, S_6$ y $\wedge S_5, S_6$ y $\wedge S_5, S_6$ y $\wedge S_5, S_6$ y $\wedge S_5, S_6$
   H: 0 1,0   J: 0 1,0   K: 0 1,0   A: 0 0,0   B: 0 0,1
    ‾0‾   ‾0‾   ‾0‾   ‾0‾   ‾0‾

Now we get the names of the two boys to stand in for *x*. For them, $[\![S_2]\!] = 1$, so it now depends on $[\![S_3]\!]$ what value is to be added to $[\![S_1]\!]$.

(68)d.   x → S_2, S_3

A: 1, y $\wedge S_5, S_6$ y $\wedge S_5, S_6$ y $\wedge S_5, S_6$ y $\wedge S_5, S_6$ y $\wedge S_5, S_6$
   H: 0 1,0   J: 0 1,0   K: 0 1,0   A: 0 0,0   B: 0 0,0
    ‾0‾   ‾0‾   ‾0‾   ‾0‾   ‾0‾

So, with *Alex* for *x*, $[\![S_4]\!] = \varnothing$, hence $[\![S_3]\!] = 0$. Therefore, $[\![S_1]\!] = 0$. This adds $\langle A,0\rangle$ as the fourth member of $[\![S_1]\!]$. Finally we substitute *Bert* for *x*:

(68)e.   x → S_2, S_3

B: 1, y $\wedge S_5, S_6$ y $\wedge S_5, S_6$ y $\wedge S_5, S_6$ y $\wedge S_5, S_6$ y $\wedge S_5, S_6$
   H: 1 1,1   J: 0 1,0   K: 0 1,0   A: 0 0,0   B: 0 0,0
    ‾1‾   ‾0‾   ‾0‾   ‾0‾   ‾0‾

Now $[\![S_4]\!] \neq \varnothing$, hence $[\![S_3]\!] = 1$. Therefore, with *Bert* for *x*, $[\![S_1]\!] = 1$. This adds $\langle B,1\rangle$ as the fifth and last member of $[\![S_1]\!]$. We now know the value of $[\![S_1]\!]$ since all five *x*-substitutions have taken place. The accumulated result is:

$$[\![S_1]\!] = \{\langle H,1\rangle, \langle J,1\rangle, \langle K,1\rangle, \langle A,0\rangle, \langle B,1\rangle\}$$

This shows that (64) is false, because the universal quantifier in S_o requires that $[[S_1]] = I$, which is not the case.

Analogously for (65). The reader will see that $[[S_1]] = \emptyset$, which means that (65) is false, as $\exists_x$ in S_o requires that $[[S_1]] \neq \emptyset$, which is not the case.

As has been said, the procedure is longwinded. In fact, a full computation is even more drawn out, since we have taken a short-cut over the quantifiers. We have said that the extension of the universal quantifier $\forall$ is $\{I\}$, or $[[\forall]] = \{I\}$, which is simple enough. But if we write out the full characteristic function we have to associate a truth value with each of the subsets of I, all of which are paired with 0, except I itself, which will get 1. Analogously for the existential quantifier $\exists$, which associates the value 1 with each of the subsets of I except $\emptyset$, which receives $\emptyset$ (cp. (52a,b) above). For the little model at hand, with only five individuals, this means that we have to construct a function of $2^5 = 32$ members, and it is easy to see that the system will quickly explode when I gets larger. (In fact, when I is infinite the procedure cannot be carried out effectively. All one can hope for then, if one wants to establish a truth value, is that one hits upon a falsifying counter-example for the universal quantifier, or upon a verifying instance for the existential quantifier.)

- *Categorial calculus psychologically real?*

Obviously, this raises questions as to the possible cognitive reality of the categorial calculus in the semantics of natural language. Such questions need not worry logicians, who only want to provide a mathematical specification of the Aristotelian truth relation, the correspondence between a formula and a state of affairs. Our aim, however, is to specify what goes on in the brain when a sentence is understood, and it is at least open to doubt whether anything like a full categorial calculus is in any way involved in that process. A more likely hypothesis is, perhaps, that the cognitive processing of a sentence like *All boys sat on an elephant* involves an obligatory association, for the discourse at hand, of any mental boy-representation with the property 'sitting on an elephant', so that the discourse will reject any boy-representation without that property. Such questions, however, need not occupy us here. It is too early yet to worry about the cognitive aspects of the process of comprehending uttered sentences, even if comprehension is necessarily a cognitive process. What interests us here is the secondary, ancillary problem of how to specify the truth relation in mathematical terms. And here we notice, with interest, that a precise calculus of the truth relation for such apparently simple sentences as (64a) or (65a) is in fact quite a circumstantial matter.

- *The problem of empty F-classes no longer an obstacle*

It should be clear now that in UQT the first problem of the Aristotelian Square of Oppositions, the *problem of empty F-classes*, does not stall the calculus, as it did in RQT. Let us add the predicate *monkey* to L and define [[monkey]] as the empty set, $\emptyset$. Now take the sentence *All monkeys are asleep*, translated as (69b), with the tree diagram (69c):

(69)a. All monkeys are asleep
   b. ∀x[Monkey(x) → Asleep(x)]
   c.

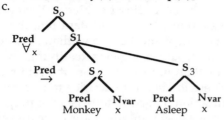

The categorial calculus gives truth for all substitutions, due to the fact that the implication gives truth whenever the antecedent clause, i.e. S_2, is false (remember: [[Asleep]] = {H,J,A}):

(70)   x → S_2,S_3 x → S_2,S_3 x → S_2,S_3 x → S_2,S_3 x → S_2,S_3
       H: 1 0,1   J: 1 0,1   K: 1 0,0   A: 1 0,1   B: 1 0,0
       ───────   ───────   ───────   ───────   ───────
          1   1   1   1   1

[[S_1]] = {⟨M,1⟩,⟨H,1⟩,⟨J,1⟩,⟨A,1⟩,⟨B,1⟩} = {M,H,J,A,B} = I. Therefore, (69) is true. But note that (71a), *All monkeys are not asleep,* is also true:

(71)a. All monkeys are not asleep
   b. ∀x[Monkey(x) → ¬[Asleep(x)]]
   c.

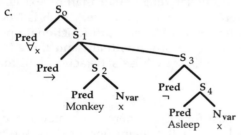

(72)   x → S_2,S_3 x → S_2,S_3 x → S_2,S_3 x → S_2,S_3 x → S_2,S_3
       H: 1 0,0   J: 1 0,0   K: 1 0,1   A: 1 0,0   B: 1 0,1
       ───────   ───────   ───────   ───────   ───────
          1   1   1   1   1

Since the Q-predicate *Monkey* has an empty extension the truth value of the consequent clause, S_2, of → is immaterial. As we found for (69), [[S_1]] = I.

- *The problem has in fact been limited to the marginal condition that I must be non-empty*

In modern quantification theory, whether UQT or GQT, universal quantification over an empty Q-predicate yields truth, as long as I is non-empty. For if I is empty no substitution can take place at all and no predicate calculus is possible. The problem has thus been shifted to the extreme case of an empty I.

While this may be acceptable for mathematical language, there is a problem for natural language. Natural linguistic intuition does not seem to agree with the judgement that both (69) and (71) are true if there are no monkeys.

Logicians tell us that both (69) and (71) are true precisely *because* there are no monkeys, but this is hard to accept for an ordinary speaker. For example, if a mechanic who has serviced my car, which has a diesel engine, tells me that all spark plugs have been renewed so as to justify an exorbitant bill, the man lies, *because* a diesel engine has no spark plugs, and he knows that. Any court of justice will agree with this assessment, and a logician testifying for the defence that modern logic has taught us that, in this situation, the sentence is true, will be dismissed as irrelevant. There is, therefore, a price to pay for the Frege-Russell solution, and not all natural language semanticists are prepared to pay it. How to avoid paying it and yet have an adequate logical system besides an adequate semantics is a different matter. It would seem that presupposition theory contains the possibility of an answer to this problem, but that discussion must wait till chapter 6.

5.5.5 Generalized quantification theory (GQT)

- *Other quantifiers than* all *and* some *cannot be handled in UQT*

There is a further problem with the applicability of UQT to natural language. Every natural language has more quantifiers than just the standard quantifiers *all* and *some*. Quantifiers like *most, half, less than half, exactly two, enough,* etc. are common if not universal. The problem with UQT is that it cannot translate these non-standard quantifiers into its language other than by extremely circuitous means. Consider the sentence *Most girls are asleep*, which is true in the toy model at hand. Now, no matter which binary truth-functional operator is used under S_1, $[[S_1]]$ will always be a set of individuals, and there is no way a condition can be formulated for this set whose satisfaction will make *Most girls are asleep* true.

- *But they can be handled in RQT*

Interestingly, the problem does not exist for RQT, where the sentence can be translated as (73b), with the symbol 'Ω' for the quantifier *most*, or the tree diagram (73c). In RQT, the condition for *most*, i.e. Ω, can be given as: $|[[S_1]]| >$ $|[[Q\text{-pred}]]|/2$, where '$|A|$' stands for the cardinality (the number of elements) of the set A. Now, in (73c), $[[S_1]] = \{H,J\}$ (note that the x-variable is allowed to rotate only over $[[Girl]]$), so that the condition is fulfilled: $|\{H,J\}| >$ $|\{H,J,K\}|/2$, or: $2 > 3/2$. Since this is the case, sentence (73) is true.

(73)a. Most girls are asleep
   b. $\Omega x{:}Girl\ [Asleep(x)]$
   c.

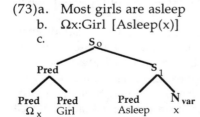

- *In GQT the quantifiers are binary higher order predicates*

We now see why UQT cannot handle non-standard quantifiers. In UQT the quantifiers are *unary* 2nd order predicates, assigning a property to a set. But in RQT the quantifiers can be seen as *binary* 2nd order predicates, expressing a relation between pairs of sets (in (73c), the sets [[Girl]] and [[Asleep]]). This was first discovered by Mostovski (1957), who showed that all quantifiers, standard and non-standard, are best regarded as two-place operators, i.e. as binary predicates expressing a relation between pairs of sets. The standard *universal* quantifier says that the Q-set (i.e. [[Q-pred]]) is contained in the matrix set or M-set (i.e. [[S_1]]), or: [[Q-pred]] $\subseteq$ [[S_1]] (or: [[Q-pred]] $\cap$ [[S_1]] = [[Q-pred]]). The standard *existential* quantifier says that the Q-set and the M-set have a non-empty intersection, i.e. [[Q-pred]] $\cap$ [[S_1]] $\neq$ $\varnothing$. The non-standard quantifier *most* (Ω) in GQT is satisfied just in case: | [[Q-pred]] $\cap$ [[S_1]] | > | [[Q-pred]] | /2.

Thus, in GQT, quantifiers are binary 2nd order predicates, i.e. predicates over pairs of sets of individuals. They are called *generalized quantifiers* because they form one general category for both the standard and the non-standard quantifiers.

- *Generalized quantification theory not recognized till about 1980*

Unfortunately, Mostovski's discovery was left unused by the logical world, probably because it was felt that the two standard quantifiers are likely to be sufficient to specify any thinkable state of affairs and are certainly sufficient to express mathematical propositions. In formal semantics not much attention was paid to the problem of the non-standard quantifiers, until Barwise and Cooper (1981) unearthed the Mostovski solution and thus made it known to the formal semantics community. From then on it has been generally recognized that the natural language quantifiers are best represented in the language of logical analysis as, indeed, higher order binary predicates.

- *The RQT notation better replaced with a notation expressing quantifiers as binary predicates*

In Barwise and Cooper (1981) the old format of RQT analyses was still maintained. That is, sentences like (59a), *Some boys are asleep*, were still assigned the structure (59b), i.e. $\exists$x:Boy[Asleep(x)], with the tree structure (59c), but interpreted differently from RQT, i.e. with a different model-theoretic 'semantics'. This means, as has been said, that the range of the variable is not restricted to the Q-set but equals **I**. Therefore, the extension of **S_1** is established by rotation of the variable over all of **I**, just as in UQT. And likewise for the extension of the Q-predicate, which is, therefore, also best considered to be expressed as an **S**-structure, i.e. with a variable, delivering a characteristic function.

Given these considerations it seemed more convenient and more systematic to abandon the customary RQT notation and switch to a representation of the quantifiers as genuine binary predicates, i.e. the quantifier predicate followed by two **S**-structures denoting sets, that is, as:

Quantifier$_{variable}$ [S$_1$,S$_2$]

where both S$_1$ and S$_2$ are propositional functions whose variable is bound by the quantifier.

• *Some examples*

This is shown in (74) for the sentence *Some boys are asleep*, expressed in RQT as (59b,c), and in (75) for *All boys are asleep*. We deviate from normal practice in that we place the Q-term, i.e. 'Boy(x)', *after* the matrix term or M-term, i.e. 'Asleep(x)', and not, as is the custom, *before*. We do this for purely linguistic reasons, since the grammar that translates the logical structures into natural language sentences gains in simplicity and regularity if the order is reversed.[18] From the point of view of logic, however, the order is irrelevant, provided it is well-defined. One notes that in GQT it is no longer necessary to use the implication to factorize out the universal quantifier, and the conjunction to factorize out the existential quantifier. In GQT, the same syntactic analysis applies to all quantifiers.

(74)a. Some boys are asleep
  b. $\exists x[\text{Boy}(x),\text{Asleep}(x)]$
  c.

(75)a. All boys are asleep
  b. $\forall x[\text{Boy}(x),\text{Asleep}(x)]$
  c.

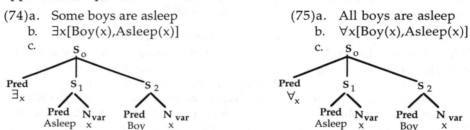

Now the condition for $\exists x$ in (74c), namely $[\![S_1]\!] \cap [\![S_2]\!] \neq \varnothing$, is fulfilled, since $[\![S_1]\!] = \{H,J,A\}$ and $[\![S_2]\!] = \{A,B\}$. The intersection, $\{A\}$, is non-empty. Therefore, (74) is true. Analogously for (75). Here the condition is: $[\![S_2]\!] \subseteq [\![S_1]\!]$, and it is not fulfilled since $\{A,B\} \not\subseteq \{H,J,A\}$.

Sentence (73a) is now re-analysed as (73c'):

(73)c'

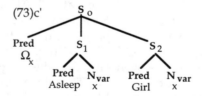

---

[18] From the point of view of natural language syntax, the RQT structure is regarded as the result of the incorporation of the object term into the predicate: the S-structure Boy(x) has been made part of the quantifier predicate. Object incorporation is a common phenomenon in natural languages, where the new, compound predicate is sometimes lexicalized, as in *keep tabs, take care*, etc. Since object incorporation is normal in natural languages, while subject incorporation hardly ever occurs, and then only under the most stringent conditions, it seems preferable to treat the S-structure that contains the Q-predicate and is incorporated into the quantifier as its object term, and not as its subject term (see Seuren 1996:300-9).

Now, the x-variable rotates over I, so that $[[S_1]] = \{H,J,A\}$. The condition set by Ω in GQT is: $|\,[[S_1]] \cap [[S_2]]\,| > |\,[[S_2]]\,|\ /2$. For (73) the condition of Ω is: $|\,\{H,J,A\} \cap \{H,J,K\}\,| > |\,\{H,J,K\}\,|\ /\ 2$, or $|\,\{H,J\}\,| > |\,\{H,J,K\}\,|\ /\ 2$, or $2 > {}^3/2$. This being sound arithmetic, sentence (73) is true.

How, then, are sentences with multiple quantifiers represented? Consider again (60a) *Some boy(s) love(s) some girl(s)*, translated into GQT as (76b), with the tree diagram (76c):

(76)a. Some boy(s) love(s) some girl(s)
    b. $\exists x[\exists y[Love(x,y),Girl(y)],Boy(x)]$

    c.

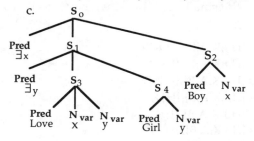

$[[S_2]] = \{A,B\}$. Now we must establish $[[S_1]]$ (i.e. the set of all individuals x such that x loves at least one girl). To that end five substitutions must be carried out, in the usual way. A truth value must be established for each substitution depending on whether or not the set of girls loved by x is empty. Those for which the truth value is '1' are members of $[[S_1]]$. The computation is shown in (77) (remember that $[[Love]] = \{\langle J,A\rangle,\langle K,B\rangle,\langle B,H\rangle\}$):

(77)

x	$[[S_3]] \cap [[S_4]]$	x	$[[S_3]] \cap [[S_4]]$	x	$[[S_3]] \cap [[S_4]]$	x	$[[S_3]] \cap [[S_4]]$	x	$[[S_3]] \cap [[S_4]]$
H:	$\langle H,0\rangle\ \langle H,1\rangle$	J:	$\langle H,0\rangle\ \langle H,1\rangle$	K:	$\langle H,0\rangle\ \langle H,1\rangle$	A:	$\langle H,0\rangle\ \langle H,1\rangle$	B:	$\langle H,1\rangle\ \langle H,1\rangle$
	$\langle J,0\rangle\ \langle J,1\rangle$		$\langle J,0\rangle\ \langle J,1\rangle$		$\langle J,0\rangle\ \langle J,1\rangle$		$\langle J,0\rangle\ \langle J,1\rangle$		$\langle J,0\rangle\ \langle J,1\rangle$
	$\langle K,0\rangle\ \langle K,0\rangle$		$\langle K,0\rangle\ \langle K,0\rangle$		$\langle K,0\rangle\ \langle K,1\rangle$		$\langle K,0\rangle\ \langle K,1\rangle$		$\langle K,0\rangle\langle K,1\rangle$
	$\langle A,0\rangle\ \langle A,0\rangle$		$\langle A,1\rangle\ \langle A,0\rangle$		$\langle A,0\rangle\ \langle A,0\rangle$		$\langle A,0\rangle\ \langle A,0\rangle$		$\langle A,0\rangle\langle A,0\rangle$
	$\langle B,0\rangle\ \langle B,0\rangle$		$\langle B,0\rangle\ \langle B,0\rangle$		$\langle B,1\rangle\ \langle B,0\rangle$		$\langle B,0\rangle\ \langle B,0\rangle$		$\langle B,0\rangle\ \langle B,0\rangle$
	$\varnothing$		$\varnothing$		$\varnothing$		$\varnothing$		$\{H\}$
	0		0		0		0		1

Therefore, $[[S_1]] = \{\langle H,0\rangle,\langle J,0\rangle,\langle K,0\rangle,\langle A,0\rangle,\langle B,1\rangle\} = \{B\}$. The final question is whether or not $[[S_1]] \cap [[S_2]] \neq \varnothing$, and we see immediately that this is so. Therefore, (76) is true.

Note that it makes no difference for the old Aristotelian problem of empty F-classes whether we use UQT or GQT: in both cases universal quantification over an empty class results in truth. For UQT this is because of the implication, in GQT because $\varnothing$ is a subset of any set. Model-theoretically, therefore, there is no difference between UQT and GQT. They differ only syntactically. RQT and GQT, on the other hand, are syntactically (virtually) identical, but they differ model-theoretically.

We may, finally, ask what the extensions are of the universal and existential quantifiers in GQT. This question is answered as follows. The universal quantifier delivers truth for all pairs of sets $\langle X,Y \rangle$ such that X and Y are both subsets of I and $Y \subseteq X$. The existential quantifier delivers truth for all pairs of sets $\langle X,Y \rangle$ such that X and Y are both subsets of I and $X \cap Y \neq \emptyset$. By comprehension (not by enumeration), $[\![\forall]\!]$ and $[\![\exists]\!]$ are defined as follows:

(78)a. $[\![\forall]\!] = \{\langle X,Y \rangle \mid X,Y \subseteq I \text{ and } Y \subseteq X\}$

   b. $[\![\exists]\!] = \{\langle X,Y \rangle \mid X,Y \subseteq I \text{ and } X \cap Y \neq \emptyset\}$

Writing out the extensions in full, i.e. defining $[\![\forall]\!]$ and $[\![\exists]\!]$ by enumeration for a given model, is tedious, even for the small model that we have used. To give an idea:

$[\![\forall]\!] = \{\langle\{H,J,K,A,B\},\{H,J,K,A,B\}\rangle$, $\langle\{H,J,K,A,B\},\{H,K\}\rangle$,
   $\langle\{H,J,K,A,B\},\{H,J,K,A\}\rangle$, $\langle\{H,J,K,A,B\},\{J,K\}\rangle$,
   $\langle\{H,J,K,A,B\},\{H,J,K,B\}\rangle$, $\langle\{H,J,K,A,B\},\{K,A\}\rangle$, ...,
   ..., $\langle\{H,J,K,A,B\},\{H,K,A,B\}\rangle$, $\langle\{H,J,K,A,B\},\{H\}\rangle$,
   $\langle\{H,J,K,A,B\},\{J,K,A,B\}\rangle$, $\langle\{H,J,K,A,B\},\{J\}\rangle$, ...,
   ..., $\langle\{H,J,K,A,B\},\{H,J,A,B\}\rangle$, $\langle\{H,J,K,A,B\},\emptyset\rangle$,
   $\langle\{H,J,K,A,B\},\{H,J,K\}\rangle$, $\langle\{H,J,K,A\},\{H,J,K,A\}\rangle$,
   $\langle\{H,J,K,A,B\},\{H,K,A\}\rangle$, $\langle\{H,J,K,A\},\{H,K,A,B\}\rangle$, ...,
   ..., $\langle\{H,J,K,A,B\},\{H,K,B\}\rangle$, $\langle\{H,J,K,A\},\emptyset\rangle$,
   $\langle\{H,J,K,A,B\},\{K,A,B\}\rangle$, ..., $\langle\{H,J,K\},\{H,J,K\}\rangle$, ..., $\langle\emptyset,\emptyset\rangle\}$

Any reader with masochistic tendencies is welcome to write out the complete extensions for $\forall$ and $\exists$. An even more severe punishment consists in the task of writing them out completely as characteristic functions, i.e. all pairs of members of the power set of I, each paired with a truth value. For an I of five members this amounts to a function with $2^5 \cdot 2^5 = 1024$ members.

CHAPTER 6

The study of meaning

6.0 Preamble

Like logic, semantics has suffered from neglect in linguistics, due not only to the inhibiting influence of behaviourism but also to the fact that the basic notions were lacking. Much semantically oriented work has been done in psychology, but that work has been largely experimental, touching on aspects of mental machinery, especially the storage of and access to lexical items, and hardly relevant to questions involving the place and function of meaning in relation to sentences and utterances. The main thrust in the development of modern semantics has come from philosophy, in two very different ways.

The main and foremost contribution came from logic, especially from the formalized versions it adopted under the influence of mathematically oriented thinking, as sketched in the sections 5.2 to 5.5 of the previous chapter. This development, known as formal semantics, is a further elaboration of the simple model theory described in the sections 5.5.1 and 5.5.2. In 6.1 a closer look is taken at this basically *formalistic* theory (cp. section 1.3 above).

It is then also shown in what respects it falls short of meeting essential requirements of empirical adequacy. The main points on which standard model-theoretic semantics is seen to fail are the following. It lacks an adequate account of reference, especially reference to non-existing entities. Russell's attempt (1905) to remedy this weakness is criticized and rejected. Secondly, it has been unable to account for the typical discourse function of anaphora. In 6.2.5 it is shown how this problem comes to a head in the so-called donkey sentences. Then, model theory has proved unable to cope with presuppositions. And finally, it has been unable to account for intensionality phenomena, owing to the very notion of possible world that was given such a central place in the theory.

The second major contribution came from the school of Ordinary Language Philosophy, which flourished at Oxford between 1945 and 1970. Here the general attitude was *ecologistic* (cp. section 1.3), and the emphasis was, right from the start, on the shortcomings of the mathematically inspired developments in formal logic regarding the semantics of natural language. Though the Oxford-bred ideas did not lead to a fully fledged, formally and empirically adequate theory of natural language semantics, they did give rise to several new developments that are now helping to shape such a discipline. The Ordinary Language philosophers pointed at phenomena of anaphora (mainly inspired by Peter Geach), of presupposition (Peter Strawson), and of speech acts (John Austin), showing in each case how these phenomena meant trouble for the established logical paradigm of model-theoretic formal semantics. During the 1960s and 1970s, anaphora theory, presupposition theory, and speech act theory linked up, each in its own specific way, with ongoing work in theoretical linguistics, leading to a radically new approach to meaning phenomena, known as incremental, or discourse-oriented semantics. This new development, which has only just begun, is sketchily described in section 6.2.

6.1   Logical and model-theoretic semantics

In this section we will concentrate on logical model theory and its application to natural language semantics as conceived and introduced by Montague. In the sections 5.5.1 and 5.5.2 we already encountered some simple model theory. Now we will look at it in a wider historical and methodological perspective. We will look first at Leibniz's attempt at defining a semantically 'pure' language, his *Characteristica Universalis*. From there we will move on to Frege, the father of modern semantics, and then to Montagovian model-theoretic semantics, which, despite its undoubted great merits for semantic theory, will be rejected as a suitable paradigm for the study of natural language meaning.

6.1.1   Leibniz's *Characteristica Universalis*

Leibniz (see also 2.2.2) was both a child of his age and a giant producer of daring and creative new insights, next to being an extraordinarily talented mathematician. In matters of natural language he was, on the one hand, an ecologist, but on the other he also took a dim view of the quality of natural language for the purpose of precise reasoning and exact science. His views on the general nature of language are largely traditional and still belong essentially to the old period. Yet there are interesting pointers to the future, in particular to the later development of comparative philology.[1] For him, natural languages are unreliable as vehicles for correct reasoning:

> Natural languages, though generally used for the purpose of reasoning are never-theless subject to innumerable equivocations and cannot fulfill the office of calculus. Sometimes reasoning errors can even be seen to arise from the very formation of the words and the constructions in which they are used, as if they were solecisms and barbarisms.[2]   Gerhardt (1890:205e)

Therefore, a formally precise language, *Characteristica Universalis*, is needed enabling anyone not only to produce semantically exact, unambiguous propositions but also to conduct faultless arguments. The idea that reasoning is a formal operation with linguistic or mental signs is omnipresent in his largely programmatic writings[3] on the *Characteristica Universalis*. For example:

---

[1] See Heinekamp (1975) for a detailed discussion and appraisal of Leibniz's views on natural and formal languages.

[2] The terms *solecism* and *barbarism* were current in Antiquity for errors in syntax and phonology, respectively.

[3] Leibniz provides only a small specimen of what a *Characteristica Universalis* should look like, to be found in (Gerhardt 1890:218-247). According to Gerhardt, the manuscript was worked over intensively by Leibniz, and one part bears the gloss (crossed out later)

All our reasoning is but the putting together and substitution of characters, whether these are spoken or written words or even images.   Gerhardt (1890:31)

But to revert to the expression of thoughts through characters, I feel that controversies will never come to an end nor will sects ever be brought to silence unless we are called back from complex reasonings to simple calculi, from words with a vague and uncertain meaning to well-defined characters. The purpose in this all must be to show that every faulty argument is nothing else but a computational error, and that a sophism, once it is expressed in this kind of new script, is really nothing but a solecism or a barbarism, easily detectable from the laws of this philosophical grammar.   Gerhardt (1890:200)

That is, the propositions of the *Characteristica Universalis* are not only meant to be just true or false, but also provably entailed or not entailed by propositions given earlier. Leibniz's *Characteristica Universalis* was thus meant not only as a syntactically, semantically and logically well-defined artificial language but also as a machinery for the derivation of entailments from axioms *salva veritate*. Although we may assume that Leibniz did not grasp the full consequences and the enormity, if not the impossibility, of his enterprise, we must grant him the honour of being a great visionary and a genius of unusual proportions, who foreshadowed a series of research programmes that did not begin to be realized until two centuries later. We see here, inter alia, the first modern and detailed attempt to provide a formal language that is better suited to logical and semantic interpretation than surface structures of sentences, which have been thought suspect from that point of view since Plato and the Stoics.

Leibniz's *Characteristica Universalis* is, moreover, an attempt at providing scientific theories with an algorithmic machinery for the formal derivation of entailments from given axioms *salva veritate*, beyond the means afforded by logic and making use of formal analyses of the meanings of individual lexical items. How realistic this second aim of his *Characteristica* is, is not for us to decide. But it is relevant, in the present context, to observe that in recent years, a number of linguistically minded logicians and logically minded linguists have sought explanations for certain classes of linguistic facts precisely in the syntactically derivational properties of formal logical languages, that is, in the syntactic variety of logical proof theory. We shall now, by way of deviation, have a brief look at one such attempt.

6.1.1.1 Proof theory in linguistics?

Proof theory or the theory of formal derivation of entailments is, of course, the backbone of logic. As was explained in section 5.1.1, it is the business of logic to devise formal calculi for the derivation of entailments. The theory behind such formal systems is called proof theory. Like Leibniz's *Characteristica*

'Non elegans specimen demonstrandi in abstractis'. Here we also find (p. 228) one of the formulations of Leibniz's famous Principle of Substitutivity (see 6.1.2.1): 'Eadem sunt quorum unum potest substitui alteri salva veritate.' It is quite clear that Leibniz's project of a *Characteristica Universalis* never got beyond the programmatic phase.

Universalis, the first attempts at constructing a sound proof theory for logic were *syntactic*, in that they were based exclusively on the syntactic properties of the expressions (formulae) employed. The later development of logical model theory came about as an attempt to provide what logicians call a *semantic* proof theory, meant to be stronger than the existing syntactic theories.

All this would not be our concern had not some linguists and logicians conceived the idea that proof theory, in one form or another, might be useful for the explanation of linguistic facts. But how can it be? Let us first look at an example to show how, in the eyes of some, it can be.

The example of *any* versus *some*

Consider the conditions under which the English word *any* is allowed to occur and compare these with the conditions for the corresponding word *some*. *Any* (at least the *any* that stands in for *some*, not the so-called 'free choice' *any*, as in *Anyone will tell you*) is a member of the class of Negative Polarity Items (NPIs) which, roughly speaking, require what is called a 'negative context'.[4] For example, *any* occurs in main clauses under negation, as in *She did not buy anything*. But also in main clauses under semi-negative adverbs like *hardly*, as in *She hardly bought anything*. It occurs, furthermore, in questions (*Can anyone help me?*), in *if*-clauses (*If she buys anything she will receive a free gift*), and also in the context *every A who ...*' (*Every student who had done any work passed*), or *only* (*Only multinationals take any unemployed graduates*), and similarly for quite a few more contexts. The question now is: what is the general principle that licenses the occurrence of the NPI *any*? To answer this question (which is, by the way, one of the many puzzles still unsolved in linguistics), the proof-theoreticians have attempted to make use of the logical distinction between upward and downward entailment.

A sentence *A* has the property of *upward entailment* with respect to the expression *e* in *A* when it is always possible to form a sentence *B* which is entailed by *A* and is identical with *A* but for the substitution of the expression *f* for *e*, where *f* denotes a class that contains the denotation of *e*. For example, the sentence *Jim has been murdered* is upwardly entailing with respect to the expression *has been murdered* since a sentence like *Jim is dead* is entailed by it and the expression *be dead* has a larger extension than the expression *have been murdered*, and likewise for all other sentences that fulfill this condition, like *Jim has been killed*.

Downward entailment is the opposite. It is like upward entailment, except that *f* must denote a class that is contained in the denotation of *e*. Negative sentences have downward entailment with respect to their predicate expression. *Jim has not been murdered* does not entail *Jim is not dead* but vice versa: *Jim is not dead* entails *Jim has not been murdered*.

The point that proof-theoreticians now wish to make is that *any* is licensed by the property of downward entailment. Thus, *She did not buy anything* entails *She did not buy any flowers*, and *If she buys anything she will receive a free gift* entails *If she buys any flowers she will receive a free gift*, and *Every student who had done any work passed* entails *Every student who had done any serious work passed*.

The problem is, however, that this condition fails to account adequately for the facts observed. *She hardly bought anything* does not entail *She hardly bought any flowers*, and *Only multinationals take any unemployed graduates* does not entail *Only multinationals take any unemployed graduates with a criminal record*. Moreover, the condition fails to account for the fact that *any* is sometimes excluded in downwardly entailing contexts. For example, **Each student who had done any work passed* is ungrammatical, despite the fact that *any* is part of an expression with

---

[4] For literature on the vexed question of polarity items, see, for example, Klima (1964), Ladusaw (1979), Linebarger (1980). For a criticism of the proof-theoretic approach to the problem, see Giannakidou (1997).

respect to which this sentence is downwardly entailing. And sometimes, for example in *if*-clauses, both *any* and *some* are possible, though with a subtle semantic distinction which is hard to define, as in *If she buys anything she will receive a free gift* versus *If she buys something she will be caught* (cp. Robin Lakoff 1969b).

It thus seems that the proof-theoretic property of downward entailment fails to account adequately for the occurrences of *any* versus *some*. It is both too narrow and too wide. This does not mean that one should reject any such attempts out of hand, since one never knows what surprises are in store (especially since no theory, whether logical, syntactic or semantic, has so far been able to account for the facts at hand). But it must be observed that the proof-theoretic entailment machinery called upon as a basis for explanation has no clear empirical status. Prima facie one is inclined to expect that some form of psychological reality for the machinery of logic would have to be assumed, which is a little disturbing given the fact that some psychologists (e.g. Johnson-Laird 1983) feel that the assumption of a logic machine as part of the human cognitive equipment stands very little chance.

The problem is compounded, and made more interesting, by the curious fact that proof-theoretic explanations often look successful initially but almost always fail later in the light of counter-examples, as here with *any*. That this should be so is, in itself, intriguing. For why should it be that proof theory so often appears to have some nontrivial grip on the facts but never seems to grasp them quite adequately? The answer to this question is not known, but the question itself should be a warning not to reject this approach too easily.

- *Does logic have any other role to play in linguistics?*

Does this mean that modern logic has no role to play in linguistics? Not at all. As was explained in chapter 5, modern predicate calculus has proved convincingly successful, perhaps not so much on account of the proof theory associated with it as on account of its structural linguistic properties. It is the *language* of modern predicate calculus, more than its *proof theory*, that has scored best. Predicate calculus, enriched with some extra elements that do not affect its status, has proved to be the best instrument available to date for the systematic rendering of sentence meanings. Moreover, predicate calculus expressions are seen to have a tree structure very much in the way sentences are assigned tree structures, which means that the relation between sentence structures and the corresponding logical structures is transformational in the accepted sense. But a full discussion of these issues will have to wait till section 7.3.

As has been said, besides *syntactic* forms of proof theory, logicians have also devised what they call *semantic* forms, in particular logical model theory. Logical model theory, too, has been applied to the study of language, but in a different, much more ambitious way, not in order to explain sets of linguistic facts but to provide a general notional and formal framework for a theory of natural language meaning. We shall now concentrate on the development of model-theoretic formal semantics, which, though probably not sufficient for the purpose of an empirically adequate theory of natural language meaning, has proved immensely instructive in a number of ways and must therefore be given the prominence it deserves.

6.1.2   Frege and Russell at the cradle of modern semantics

Any account of modern formal semantics has to start with Frege and Russell. We have already encountered them several times, especially in 5.4. What needs to be stressed here is the fact that both were among the first philosophers[5] in modern times to take a detailed and formal look at the central question inherent in the classical Aristotelian correspondence theory of truth, according to which truth comes about when there is 'correspondence' between what is said (or thought) and what is actually the case (see 1.2.1). As such they prefigure model-theoretic semantics, which is a detailed formal theory of that correspondence.

We shall first discuss the two problems Frege (1892) presented for the Aristotelian concept of truth, namely (a) the problem of identity statements and (b) the problem of intensional contexts. These two problems have proved fundamental for the whole of 20th century semantics. Both arise from the fact that Aristotle's truth theory entails *the principle of substitution of co-referring terms salva veritate*, also called *the principle of substitution salva veritate* (SSV), the *principle of substitutivity*, or *Leibniz's Law*.

This principle amounts to the following. The truth or falsity of the proposition contained in an utterance should never be affected if a term *a* is replaced by a term *b* as long as both terms refer to the same object. What matters is the property assigned to an object by the predicate: only if that property is in fact a property of the object in question can the utterance be said to be true, and otherwise it is false. It is therefore irrelevant what term is used to name the object. If the sentence *The morning star is inhabited* is false, so is the sentence *The evening star is inhabited*, because the terms *the morning star* and *the evening star* refer to the same object, the planet Venus, and that object, whatever you call it, is not inhabited. From this follows the principle of SSV:

> If two terms refer to the same object they can always stand in for each other salva veritate (i.e. without any change in truth value).

We will then pass on to Russell's solution to the equally fundamental problem of reference, in particular reference to non-existing entities. We shall find that Russell's Theory of Descriptions, presented in Russell (1905), is ingenious but untenable.

6.1.2.1 Frege's first problem: identity statements

Frege surprised the world by setting out to test the principle of SSV empirically, trying it out on natural language sentences. As he did so he hit upon the two

---

[5] Frege himself did not wish to be considered a philosopher, just a mathematician. Yet his importance for semantics is so enormous that we may feel fully entitled to call him a philosopher.

problems mentioned above. The first, as has been said, is that of identity statements ('Gleichheiten'). His example is:

(1)   The morning star is the evening star

The problem is that sentence (1) is not true a priori and therefore necessarily, but a posteriori: its truth was discovered a few centuries ago, and it could have been otherwise. But how can it be an a posteriori truth? For it is a central axiom of any ontology that every entity is identical with itself. Therefore, one would expect sentence (1) to be a vacuous platitude, a necessary truth not worth mentioning. Moreover, substitution of one of the terms by the other results in either (2) or (3), both of which are the kind of platitude we expected (1) to be, true yes, but now a priori and therefore necessarily:

(2)   The morning star is the morning star
(3)   The evening star is the evening star

What brings about this change in truth quality? This may not be an immediate threat to Aristotle's truth theory but it suggests that there is more to the correspondence relation than meets the eye.

Frege answers as follows. If the extensions of the referring terms *morning star* and *evening star* were given by a simple interpretation function for terms of the language ('name stickers', as in the toy models of 5.5.1 and 5.5.2), then the language itself would cause necessary truth for (1): (1) would be true in virtue of the language. Sentence (1) shows, however, that such a theory is incorrect. Frege then introduces the assumption that referring terms, in particular the so-called *definite descriptions*, far from being simple name stickers, bring along an 'intension', 'meaning', 'sense' or, as he says, 'Sinn', which is a method for getting at the reference object, the 'extension' or, in his terminology, 'Bedeutung'.[6] For referring terms, the Sinn is a search procedure that will produce the object referred to if properly followed and successful (cp. Dummett (1973:281): 'In Frege's theory, the sense of a name consists of the means we have provided for determining an actual (existent) object as its referent.'). If not successful the procedure will come up with a negative answer: there is no such reference object, or, if there is more than one, with an indeterminacy. Thus, the term *the present queen of England* leads the interpreting subject first to England, then to its head of state. How language users succeed in doing that is an empirical problem that Frege did not consider. [7]

---

[6] In (1892) Frege's terminology does not yet reflect modern German, where *Bedeutung* stands for 'meaning', not for 'reference'. Later he adapts to modern usage. Husserl, who adopted Frege's theory of sense and reference, uses the modern terminology of *Bezeichnung* ('denotation') for reference, and *Bedeutung* for meaning (1900:49): ' ... daß es also mit Recht heißt, der Ausdruck bezeichne (nenne) den Gegenstand mittels seiner Bedeutung' (... that one says correctly that the expression denotes (names) the object via its meaning).

[7] One must realize that this notion of search procedure is an oversimplification. Modern lexical studies, in particular work relating to the variability of lexical meaning and the criteria used by speakers in selecting particular lexical items given their communicative intention and the contextual and interactive setting, have shown that the success of a lexi-

Different descriptions may be assumed to embody different search procedures. If these turn out to lead to the same object there is cause for surprise. But
if the same search procedure is followed twice it is hardly surprising that the
same object will be produced again. The case of the two co-referring terms *the
morning star* and *the evening star* can be represented schematically as in fig. 1.

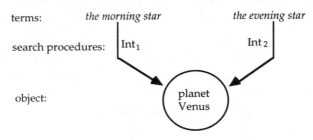

terms: *the morning star*   *the evening star*

search procedures: Int$_1$ Int$_2$

object: planet
                               Venus

Figure 1   Different intensions leading to the same object

- *Frege generalizes the traditional distinction between intension and
  extension*

Let us have a closer look at Frege's solution. First we observe that he made use
of the traditional philosophical distinction between the intension and the
extension of predicates. Traditionally, the *intension* of a predicate is its cognitive content as defined by the set of necessary and sufficient conditions any entity must satisfy to qualify for that predicate, or, in other words, the concept
associated with the predicate. Intensions can often be analysed with the help
of other predicates (concepts) that are considered more fundamental. Thus, the
intension of the predicate *bachelor* is the set of conditions jointly posed by the
concepts 'male', 'of marriageable age', and 'unmarried'. Many predicates,
however, defy an exhaustive analysis in terms of other predicates or concepts
because they express a property that is unique to a natural kind, like *apple*. In
all cases the intension is considered to be a cognitive filter that helps one to
decide whether a given entity does or does not satisfy that predicate's conditions. The *extension* of a predicate, on the other hand, is traditionally the set
of entities that satisfy its conditions in a given setting or 'world'.

In traditional philosophy, a referring term or definite description occurring
in a sentence (proposition) is considered to have as its *extension* the entity or
entities the term refers to when the sentence is used appropriately, i.e. in
relation to an existing state of affairs where the term has a reference value.
The notion of *intension* is traditionally not defined for referring terms.

Frege, however, generalized, and thereby changed, the two notions, applying them throughout to predicates, terms and sentences. His generalized distinction between 'Sinn' (sense, intension) and 'Bedeutung' (extension) is
represented in fig. 2.

---

cal item in helping to identify the intended referent is subject to heavy restrictions imposed
by context, cognitive machinery and factual knowledge (cp. Geeraerts et al. 1994).

type of linguistic expression	categorial type	extension (Bedeutung)	intension (Sinn)
term	e	individual	search procedure
predicate	(e,t)	set of individuals	concept
sentence	t	truth value	thought

Figure 2 Frege's system of extensions and intensions for extensional sentences

We see here that the extension of a term is what it is in traditional philosophy: the entity (or individual) selected by the term in question as its reference value. But terms now also have an intension, which is the search procedure, in Frege's terms 'die Art des Gegebenseins' or 'mode of presentation', associated with the description contained in the term.

As regards predicates, Frege follows the tradition: a predicate's extension is the set of entities (individuals) that satisfy its conditions, and its intension is the concept that corresponds with the predicate and can be made explicit by formulating the set of satisfaction conditions associated with it.

- *Frege defines the extension of a sentence as its truth value*

The application of the intension-extension distinction to sentences is entirely new. For the intension of a sentence ('Satz') Frege follows the pattern set by terms and predicates, in that he places it in cognition: the intension of a sentence is defined as the cognitive content or thought expressed by it. But then, surprisingly, he takes the actual truth value of a sentence as its extension. This has struck many as strange, even counter-intuitive, yet it has become absolutely standard. All formal semanticists, or almost all, accept that the best, or correct, decision to take when we want to define the extension of a sentence is to say that it is its truth value. We did the same when we presented the toy models of 5.5.1 and 5.5.2.

Frege's reason for doing so was not at all philosophically profound. On the contrary, he took this decision simply because it appeared to facilitate the categorial calculus yielding truth or falsity for sentences in a model (see in particular Frege 1892:31-36). We shall argue that this may well be so, up to a point, for the purpose of defining truth or falsity in an Aristotelian sense, but that it is questionable whether it is a wise step to take in the context of natural language semantics. It is a fact, in any case, that the fatal crash of model-theoretic semantics explained in section 6.1.5.1 below was caused by the way it applied the Fregean notion of truth values as extensions of sentences.

- *Categorial types*

A column has been added in fig. 2 for the so-called categorial type of the expressions concerned: e, t, or (e,t). These symbols stand for 'entity', 'truth value', and 'function from entities to truth values', respectively. They indicate the 'type' of the expressions concerned, in that they indicate the general ontological category of their extensions in the simplest cases: terms stand for entities, sentences for truth values, and simple, unary predicates are characteristic functions from entities to truth values, as explained in section 5.5.1: an element of type e is fed into a function of type (e,t) which delivers a truth value of type t. The truth values are 'true' and 'false', denoted by '1' and '0', respectively, according to the convention introduced by Boole (see 5.3). Truth functions can be regarded as a special kind of predicate in that they take truth values as input and deliver truth values as output. (This system can be extended from unary to n-ary lexical predicates, and to quantifiers as well, which are naturally regarded as higher order predicates, as shown in 5.5.2.)

This typing goes back to Frege, but was further developed by Ajdukiewicz in the '30s and Montague in the '60s. It is based on the assumption that in a categorial truth calculus for extensional sentences no categories are needed beyond 'entity' (e) and 'truth value' (t) and functions in terms of these. This typing thus reflects the condition of mathematical or set-theoretic manageability of the ontology adopted in model theory discussed in 6.1.3 below.

- *Identity statements in the light of simple extensional model theory*

Let us look at identity statements in terms of the simple toy models presented in 5.5.1 and 5.5.2 above. We note, first, that the language **L** in these models contains no provision for definite descriptions: the terms that refer to individuals are all simple names, or, in Kripke's terminology, rigid designators: *Helen, Joan, Kate, Alex* and *Bert*. Now suppose two names in **L** refer to the same individual: we introduce the new name *Lofty*, which, like the name *Bert*, takes the individual B as its extension. Thus, [[Bert]] =[[Lofty]] =B. Now it will never make any difference for the truth value of a sentence in **L** which name is used: SSV applies freely. In fact, the unrestricted applicability of SSV has become the main criterion for what is called the extensional character of a language. The language **L** is thus fully extensional, and its terms are all rigid designators.

Now let **L** be extended with a binary predicate of identity '='. In terms of the model as it is now, the identity statement '= (Bert,Lofty)' ('Bert is Lofty') must be true a priori and not a posteriori as in natural language. This is because **L** lacks definite descriptions and has only rigid designators for terms. If we were to introduce definite descriptions in **L**, which would then be of the form illustrated in fig. 3, there is a problem for the interpretation function **INT**.

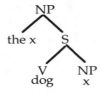

Figure 3   *The presumed logical structure of the definite description* the dog

The problem is that there exists no general formal method to relate definite descriptions to their intended reference object. The S-constituent in fig. 3 takes the set of all dogs as its extension, and the functor 'the x' will have to select from the set of all dogs the one specific dog that is the intended object of reference in the case at hand. It has so far proved beyond the powers of logical model theory to define such a function, for the simple reason that in real life that function needs information from discourse and situation to select the intended individual. And such information falls outside the scope of model-theoretic systems.

- *The problem of identity statements still unsolved*

This means that the reference function is not compositional (see 5.5.1), and that Frege's 'search procedure' of fig. 1 has not been made explicit. It also means that although Frege's distinction between sense and reference points the way towards a solution of his first problem it does not solve it. This explains in part why Russell and others were so keen to get rid of definite descriptions in the formal treatment of language. We shall see, however, in 6.1.2.3, that Russell's alternative is fundamentally inadequate, so that we must conclude that Frege's first problem is still wide open. All we have is a principle, the distinction between sense and reference, but no formal solution.

- *What kind of predicate is the identity predicate?*

Then there is still the unsolved problem of the nature of the identity predicate. If we introduce the predicate '=' into the extensional language **L** of the models in 5.5.1 and 5.5.2 we must define its extension in the models. Suppose we do this by defining '=' as a binary predicate over individuals. Then [[=]] can only be the set of all pairs <a,a> of identical individuals *a*, since every individual is identical with itself and no two different individuals are identical with each other. This is a fundamental axiom of any workable ontology. The relation [[=]] will then be reflexive, symmetrical and transitive, and thus trivial. More importantly, the predicate '=' can then only be used to express a trivial ontological necessity.

At the very outset of his (1892) Frege considers the possibility of treating the predicate '=' as a predicate over pairs of *names*, not pairs of *individuals*, but he rejects this proposal immediately:

> If we want to regard identity statements as expressions of a relation between the referents of the names 'a' and 'b', then it would seem that *a* = *b* could not differ from *a* = *a*, provided *a* = *b* is true. It would express a relation between an entity and itself, a relation, that is, which every entity has to itself and no entity to another. What one wants to express by means of *a* = *b* appears to be that the signs or names 'a' and 'b' have the same referent. But then the statement would be about those signs, it would assert a relation between them. However, such a relation between names or signs could hold only in so far as they mention or signify something. The relation would be mediated by the link that each of both signs has with the same referent. But this would be arbitrary. One can forbid no-one to appoint any perceptible process or object as a sign for something. A sentence like *a* = *b* would then no longer be about the entity itself but about our way of signifying. And it would not express a cognitive content, although that is what we want it to do in many such cases. If the

sign 'a' differs from the sign 'b' only as an entity in itself (in this case by its shape) and not as a sign (i.e. not by the way in which it refers to something), then the cognitive content of $a = a$ would not differ essentially from that of $a = b$, provided $a = b$ is true. A difference can come about only if the difference between the signs corresponds to a difference in the mode of presentation of the reference object.

Frege (1892:26)

And indeed, the idea that the identity predicate is about names is highly unsatisfactory. The extension [[=]] of the predicate '=' would then be defined as the set of all pairs <a,b> such that a and b are names and both refer to the same individual. The sentence *The morning star is the evening star* must then be taken to say 'the name "morning star" has the same extension as the name "evening star"'. But if this were so we would expect it to be correct to write (4), just as it is correct to write (5):

(4)   'The morning star' is 'the evening star'
(5)   'Rome' consists of four letters

where the quotes make it clear that the terms of the predicates refer to names, not to entities. But whereas (5) is both natural and true, (4) is not only unnatural, it is also false since the two names are not identical.

- *Intensional entities seem inevitable*

So the extension of the identity predicate cannot be a set of pairs of names: it is not a metalinguistic predicate. But it cannot be a set of pairs of entities either, since it yields truth precisely for single entities, which are always and trivially identical to themselves. So we have reason to ask what the extension of the identity predicate consists of, if it is neither names nor entities. Frege fails to answer this question. His appeal to a separate intension or 'mode of presentation' may be correct, it does not answer this question.

In fact, Frege's ontology made it impossible to answer it. His ontology, like that of model theory, had no room for intensional entities which have *being* but no existence in any physical way. If we want to escape from this undesirable dilemma we must enrich our ontology with such entities, which is what we will do in section 6.2.6.1 below, where we accept the reality, though not the existence, of intensional entities, which can then act as referents.

6.1.2.1.1 Kripke's theory of proper names[8]

At this point a few words are in order about Kripke's (1972) rejection of Frege's treatment of identity statements, which, according to Kripke, fails to apply to proper names as terms. For Frege's *The morning star is the evening star* he uses the parallel sentence

(6)   Phosphorus is Hesperus

Phosphorus being a traditional proper name for the morning star and *Hesperus* for the evening star.

---

[8] For a thorough and lengthy criticism of Kripke's theory of proper names see Dummett (1973:110-151). The conclusion reached by Dummett does not essentially differ from the one reached here.

For Kripke, proper names are *rigid designators*: their reference is fixed by the interpretation function of the language, as if they were labels stuck on to their reference object by the rules of the language. Hence, he argues (following John Stuart Mill), they have no intension but only an extension, and Frege's distinction between intension and extension cannot be used to solve the problem of identity statements when proper names function as terms. A different solution is therefore called for.

Varying on Kant, he believes he has found one in a new philosophical category, that of necessary a posteriori truth: a sentence like (6) is necessarily true, since every entity is identical with itself, yet it is also true a posteriori, which is possible, he says, because many necessary truths (like most truths of mathematics) are not given in advance but are to be discovered. Kripke thus rejects Frege's dilemma: according to him it is possible to express a necessary relation of identity without thereby asserting a trivial tautology.

This may be so, but is it so in the case of identity statements? The answer, one has to fear, will have to be negative. Kripke, like Frege, fails to specify what the extension of the identity predicate amounts to. The implication is that the extension consists of single entities (individuals). But then Frege's question of what makes the difference when identity is stated comes up again. For Frege, the difference is brought about by the different 'modes of presentation' or search procedures associated with the linguistic terms. For Kripke, one assumes, it must, in the case of proper names, be the different events of name-giving or 'baptism' associated with the terms that causes the difference. But how can such a difference be discovered a posteriori?

The problem is best illustrated in terms of model theory. We have said above that if a model contains only proper names as terms (as the models in 5.5.1 and 5.5.2 do), then identity statements are true in virtue of the model, in particular the interpretation function of the model. Clearly, knowledge of a language implies knowledge of this interpretation function, as one cannot maintain that someone knows a language if he or she has no interpretation for the sentences of the language. But then it is hard to assume that an identity statement can express an a posteriori discovery, since the assumption that a competent speaker has to search his or her own linguistic competence for a reference relation is hardly plausible. In fact, it is highly implausible to assume that referential anchoring is part of natural language at all. Language is made to be used in any situation whatsoever and therefore does not contain any terms that link it by rule to particular real or imaginary entities. Referential anchoring always takes place via a procedure involving the assignment of referential values to non-linguistic cognitive parameters.

Therefore, if identity is not to be discovered from linguistic knowledge it must be discovered from historical and other facts, precisely the way Frege has it. Frege's intension is, as has been said, a cognitive search procedure that may or may not yield a result in the shape of an actual reference object. It is not clear in what way Kripke's proposal improves on the Fregean position.

But, Kripke says, proper names cannot have an intension, only an extension: they can only be 'rigid designators'. The question is: is Kripke right in this? And again, our answer is negative. Proper names cannot be rigid designators, as they sometimes travel from one reference object to another. A case in point is the name Calabria, which in Antiquity referred to the 'heel' of Italy (now Apulia), but is the name of Italy's 'toe' nowadays, due to a medieval warlord who was master of Calabria, conquered the whole of Southern Italy and subsequently lost all except the toe, keeping the name *Calabria* for his territory. This did not bring about a change in the language, only in the political power structure of the day.[9]

Then, proper names are sometimes given to hypothetical individuals (Jack the Ripper), or to fictitious individuals, as in mythologies. Obviously, hypothetical or fictitious individuals cannot be actually baptized. Some proper names also have variable reference, such as Christmas or Easter, which take recurrent tokens as reference objects, not one token. In other words, the semantic behaviour of proper names differs from that of definite descriptions only in that proper names are relatively stable and less dependent on discourse and context for their reference value, whereas ordinary definite descriptions vary more across situations.[10]

Proper names are not rigid designators at all, but descriptions of the form 'the x such that x is called "Hesperus"', just like ordinary definite descriptions, which, as shown in fig. 3, have the form 'the x such that P(x)', where 'P' is a predicate. In the case of proper names the predicate P is 'be called "N"', where 'N' is a proper name. This view was expressed in Kneale (1962) but, if not ridiculed, given short shrift by Kripke. According to Kripke, an analysis of a name like *Socrates* as 'the x such that x is called "Socrates"' is circular:

> Someone uses the name 'Socrates'. How are we supposed to know to whom he refers? By using the description which gives the sense of it. According to Kneale, the description is 'the man called "Socrates"'. And here, (presumably, since this is supposed to be so trifling!) it tells us nothing at all. We ask to whom does he refer by 'Socrates' and then the answer is given as, well he refers to the man to whom he refers. If this were all there was to the meaning of a proper name, then no reference would get off the ground at all.   Kripke (1972:284)

It is easily shown, however, that this is a fallacy. The predicate 'be called "X"' expresses a property acquired in virtue of the referent's position in a community (like e.g. the property of being rich, or of being without a name). Like any other property it can be used to select a unique individual for the

---

[9] Cp. Dummett (1973:151): 'There is therefore no room in Kripke's account for a shift of reference in the course of a chain of communication: the existence of such a chain, accompanied all the time by the required intention to preserve reference, must be taken as guaranteeing that reference is in fact preserved. Intuitively, however, there is no such guarantee: it is perfectly possible that, in the course of the chain, the reference has been unwittingly transferred. Once this is conceded, the account crumbles altogether.'

[10] In many languages, some or all proper names for certain categories of objects (e.g. rivers, countries, mountains) require the definite article: *the Rhine, the Gambia*. Some languages (e.g. Modern Greek) require or allow the definite article for all proper names.

purpose of reference, provided the property is known or accessible to speaker and hearer, as with all properties used for the purpose of reference.

Kripke's notion of proper names shows with painful clarity the neglect of cognition in logically oriented accounts of natural language comprehension. We conclude that the whole problem of rigid designators is to be dismissed as contrived. Kripkean rigid designators do not occur in natural language. They are an artifact of those philosophies that feel awkward in the presence of minds.

6.1.2.2 Frege's second problem: intensional contexts

Frege's second problem is an even more serious threat to the classical concept of truth, as it shows up cases where SSV really does not seem to apply. And as with the first problem, Frege only provided a principle, but no full formal answer. The problem is that SSV runs into trouble when applied in a clause that is argument to a predicate relating to thought processes. For example, in (7) the term *the morning star* cannot always be replaced by the term *the evening star* salva veritate. For if John does not believe that the two are identical he may believe that there is life on the one but not on the other:

(7)   John believes that there is life on the morning star

SSV appears not to apply in such cases, which jeopardizes the classical notion of truth.

• *Frege's second problem formulated by Eubulides around 330 BC*
It is not usually recognized that we have here the ancient paradox of Electra, formulated by Aristotle's contemporary Eubulides of Miletus (about whom more will be said in section 6.2.3.1). Eubulides took this paradox from Greek mythology. The story is as follows. When Agamemnon, king of Mycenes, returned from Troy his wife Clytaemnestra had set up house with a lover. So as not to lose this man she murdered Agamemnon in his bath the day he returned. His son Orestes now had the duty to avenge him. His father's murderer, however, happened to be his own mother, and in ancient Greece, as in most other cultures, one was not supposed to kill one's mother. Facing a moral dilemma Orestes goes away for a while to think. He then returns to Mycenes resolved to avenge his father by killing his mother. Fearing to receive the kind of welcome his mother gave to his father, he disguises himself as a beggar and knocks on the gate. He is let in, and his sister Electra has him shown into the kitchen and given some soup. Eubulides now enters the scene and asks: is the sentence *Electra knows that her brother Orestes is in the kitchen* true or false? It should be true, if we apply Aristotle's truth definition to the letter, but it clearly is not. It is known that Aristotle was embarrassed by this complication and had no reply. Here we see Frege rediscover the problem over 2000 years later, as is demonstrated in (7). So we are curious to see what answer he gives.

• *Frege's answer to his second problem*
Frege answers as follows. Some predicates assign to a person the property of entertaining a thought, expressed as a complement clause (i.e. in 'indirect

speech'). Such a clause refers to a thought and does not have a truth value as its extension. The thought referred to by such a clause is precisely the thought that is its intension (Sinn) when it is used independently. As it is assumed that the intension of a complex expression is built up compositionally from the intensions of the component parts, it follows that substitution of term *a* in the embedded clause by a co-referential term *b* changes the Sinn of the corresponding free sentence, and hence the Bedeutung in indirect speech. Therefore, SSV does not apply to terms in indirect speech (intensional contexts) even though the terms in question are in reality co-referential. Substitution of co-referential terms changes the thought underlying a sentence or clause. If an argument clause refers to a thought, SSV is blocked. The matrix provided in fig. 2 must therefore be extended with a new class of expressions, clauses as argument terms of intensional predicates, and their type, extension and intension have to be defined. This Frege does, but only in part, as is shown in fig. 4.

type of linguistic expression	categorial type	extension (Bedeutung)	intension (Sinn)
term	e	individual	search procedure
predicate	(e,t)	set of individuals	concept
independent sentence	t	truth value	thought
clause as argument term of intensional predicate	?	thought	?

Figure 4   Frege's system of extensions and intensions for extensional sentences and sentences in intensional contexts

• *Problems with Frege's answer*

However, Frege's solution, though intuitively appealing, has some formal problems. First, a type and an intension are required for thoughts, and Frege fails to provide them, as is shown by the question marks in fig. 4. Then, more importantly, the compositional truth calculus applies only to extensions, not to intensions. Frege did not develop a compositional calculus for meanings, although the notion of compositionality of meaning is present in his work.[11] Frege's notion of what intensions amount to for the different types of linguistic expression did not seem to lend itself naturally to any kind of compositional calculus to be integrated into a formal theory.

---

[11] For example in Frege (1906:302): 'Of course, <definitions> presuppose knowledge of certain primitive elements and their signs. The definition puts together a group of those signs according to certain principles, so that the meaning ('Bedeutung') of this group is determined by the meanings of the signs used.' By this time Frege has conformed to standard German usage and uses *Bedeutung* for 'meaning', no longer for 'extension'.

For this reason, model-theoretic semantics resorted to a different way of handling intensions. The notion of 'possible world' was called in and the extensional calculus as exemplified in the models of 5.5.1 and 5.5.2 above was generalized to the set of all possible worlds while the language **L** was kept constant. What this amounts to, and why this treatment of intensional phenomena came to nothing, is discussed in the sections 6.1.4 and 6.1.5 below. But before we can pass on to model-theoretic semantics we have to see first what Russell had to say about reference.

6.1.2.3 Russell's Theory of Descriptions

We have concluded, in 6.1.2.1.1, that natural language has no rigid designators: all definite terms refer via a cognitive procedure that is to some extent dependent on the history of the discourse at hand and on situational and background knowledge. Three main problems present themselves here, that of identification, that of non-existing referents, and that of reifications. It was to solve these three problems that Russell proposed his famous Theory of Descriptions (1905), which we will discuss now.

6.1.2.3.1 *The problem of identification*

In natural language, the basic structure of a definite description contains at least a definite determiner and a predicate. The corresponding logico-semantic analysis of a simple definite description like *the dog* is usually given as in fig. 3 above, provided, that is, one is prepared to recognize the logical reality of definite descriptions and does not adopt Russell's analysis. For in Russell's logical analysis of natural language sentences the definite descriptions that occur in them are dissolved into a complex formula so that they are no longer a single constituent in the logical analysis, as we shall see in 6.1.2.3.2.

- *The definite article is not a compositional function*

As was shown in 6.1.2.1, the operator *the x*, if it is not spirited away by a Russellian sleight of hand, must denote a function from the set of all dogs to one particular dog. That is, it must be of the type $((e,t),e)$: a definite description can only get through to its reference object by means of a function computation with a set of individuals, i.e. (e,t), as input and an individual, i.e. e, as output. The problem is, however, that no principled formal method is available to select one particular individual from a set of individuals, unless the set contains just one member.

Russell, in his famous article 'On denoting' (1905), saw this problem coming:

> It remains to interpret phrases containing *the*. These are by far the most interesting and difficult of denoting phrases. ... Now *the*, when it is strictly used, involves uniqueness; we do, it is true, speak of '*the* son of So-and-so' even when So-and-so has several sons, but it would be more correct to say '*a* son of So-and-so'. Thus for our purposes we take *the* as involving uniqueness.   Russell (1905:481)

Nowadays, instead of reprehending natural language we try to find out how it works. And we observe that definite descriptions ('denoting phrases') are regularly and naturally used in cases where the set in question contains many members. It is easy to imagine a man receiving a note from his friend saying that they will meet in the pub at five. Although there may be many pubs around it need not be specified which pub is meant, as both know precisely where they are supposed to meet. This knowledge, however, transgresses the powers of self-contained compositional models, and cannot, therefore, be captured in the sort of model current in model-theoretic semantics.

- *Non-linguistic knowledge is required for reference*

Normally, definite descriptions in natural language will not find the individual(s) they refer to without the help of available *non-linguistic knowledge*, which can be of any kind whatsoever. It may be strictly contextual knowledge, as in *I saw a man. The man was drunk.* It may be private knowledge, as in *Let's meet in the pub at five*, said among friends. It may involve inferential knowledge, as in *A prisoner escaped last night. The pathological murderer is still at large.* Or whatever. For normal definite descriptions the reference function requires a complex cognitive machinery that extends way beyond the parameters of model theory. This means that the hope of a strictly compositional calculus for the extension of sentences, nurtured by Frege, Russell and by the model-theoretic semanticists, must be considered unrealistic.

6.1.2.3.2   The problem of non-existing referents

The second and main puzzle that occupied Russell in his 'On denoting' of 1905 is that of non-existing referents. Definite descriptions are often used in meaningful utterances that are informative and possibly even true although there exists no object that can serve as their extension. The identification problem and also, to some extent, the problem of reifications, were taken into the bargain but his main interest was in solving the problem of non-existing referents.

Russell denied any ontological status to non-existing objects (1905:483), attacking Meinong who distinguished between really existing objects and objects that lack real existence but 'are there' as imagined 'intensional' entities (see 6.1.3.4).[12] Since intensional entities have no place in Russell's ontology the question arises: how can a truth calculus work for sentences containing a definite term that lacks a reference object?

Russell's example was the now hackneyed:

(8)   The present king of France is bald

Since France has no king the sentence must be false, and its negation true:

(9)   The present king of France is not bald

The difficulty is: how are these truth values computed? If the subject term lacks an extension there is no input to the function [[bald]] and hence no output, so that both (8) and (9) will lack a truth value, which violates the sacrosanct

---

[12] Unfortunately, Russell's critique of Meinongian ontology plays on terminological equivocations: he makes Meinong say (1905:483) that virtual objects do and do not exist or may both have and lack a property, which is a travesty of the view held by Meinong and like-minded philosophers.

Aristotelian Principle of the Excluded Third. But there is another problem as well: why do people tend to take (9) as implying (10)?

(10)   There is a king of France

Sentence (9) is taken by most people to imply that there is a king of France and that he has a hairy scalp. This is a logical problem because if people accept that (9) entails (|=) (10), then (10) must be a necessary truth: (8) |= (10), but if also (9) (i.e. ¬(8)) |= (10) then (8) |= (10) ánd ¬(8) |= (10), hence, by contraposition, ¬(10) |= (8) ánd ¬(8), which means that ¬(10) cannot possibly be true, so that (10) must be a necessary truth, which is absurd. Or, in Russell's own, less technical, words (1905:485):

> By the law of excluded middle, either 'A is B' or 'A is not B' must be true. Hence either 'the present King of France is bald' or 'the present King of France is not bald' must be true. Yet if we enumerated the things that are bald, and then the things that are not bald, we should not find the present King of France in either list. Hegelians, who love a synthesis, will probably conclude that he wears a wig.

• *Russell's solution in terms of quantification*

To solve this problem along with that of identification and that of reification, Russell proposed an analysis for definite descriptions in terms of existential quantification: in logical analysis definite descriptions are dissolved into the existential quantifier and a few propositional functions, — his famous Theory of Descriptions. (8) is now analysed as follows:

(11) $\exists x [KoF(x) \wedge Bald(x) \wedge \forall y [KoF(y) \rightarrow x=y]]$

or 'there is an x such that x is king of France and bald, and such that for all y, if y is king of France, x is identical with y'. This amounts to saying that there is one and only one king of France and that he is bald. In the actual world (11) is false, and its negation true, if only because KoF(x) is false for all values of x:

(12) $\neg \exists x [KoF(x) \wedge Bald(x) \wedge \forall y [KoF(y) \rightarrow x=y]]$

Now (10) does not follow from (12), so that no awkward consequences have to be faced with regard to (10) being a necessary truth.

6.1.2.3.3   *The problem of reifications*

A further problem for the theory of reference, also noted in Russell (1905), is that of reifications. A reification comes about when a mental construct of some complexity is captured, more or less by way of definition, in a single nominal expression. Reifications come in different kinds. Nominalizations are reifications: *the destruction of the village, the difference between A and B, the rotation of the earth.* So are expressions like *the average Boston cabdriver* or *the military-industrial complex.* Also names for property parameters like *temperature, colour, length, weight, number* (as in *The number of planets is nine*). They are problematic, obviously, because if they are definite descriptions they are in search of a reference object, and no sound ontology could possibly provide entities corresponding to such expressions.

Natural speakers are in no doubt that reifications do not directly refer to specific objects or individuals. Every speaker knows that the average Boston cabdriver is nowhere to be found. He is an abstraction, based on some more or less precise calculus of values on selected parameters. Adequate interpretation of sentences containing reifications requires knowledge of the conditions under which reifying expressions are to be applied to the objects of the world. If one really wants to know if the military-industrial complex oppresses the working classes one must know first what conditions must be fulfilled for it to be legitimate to identify a political and economic structure as 'the military-industrial complex'. Only then can one check if this structure is guilty of oppressing the working classes, provided the conditions are fulfilled for identifying a social structure as 'the working classes' and an activity as 'oppressing'.

Russell (1905) proposed to apply his Theory of Descriptions also to reifications, which would then be treated not as definite descriptions requiring a referent but as part of the propositional content of the sentences in which they occur. However, Russell omitted any demonstration of how this could be done.

6.1.2.3.4   *The untenability of the Theory of Descriptions*

Russell's analysis, though very widely accepted as correct throughout the 20th century, does not agree with native intuitions about the meaning and use of definite descriptions and anaphoric pronouns. These intuitions are so strong and stable that they may be given the status of data. That being so we must conclude that the Theory of Descriptions is inadequate on empirical grounds.

• *Uniqueness and anaphora*

First, definite descriptions do not logically or otherwise imply uniqueness of the object referred to. Two friends can agree to meet in *the pub* even if there are many pubs around, as we have seen. Moreover, while the uniqueness clause may be taken to account for the inconsistency of e.g. (13a) or (13b) it fails to account for the consistency of (14):

(13) a. The king laughed and he did not laugh
     b. There was a king and he laughed and he did not laugh

(14) There was a king and he laughed, and there was a king and he did not laugh

For in Russell's analysis, the sentences (13a), (13b) and (14) are all equivalent.

• *Geach's analysis of anaphora in conjunctions*

Geach's answer (1969; 1972:115-27) to this objection is that a sentence like

(15) There was a king and he laughed

should not be analysed as a conjunction of the type A ∧ B, but as:

(16) ∃x [King(x) ∧ Laugh(x)]

i.e. with the conjunction within the propositional function under the existential quantifier. However, it is shown in Seuren (1977; 1985:319-21) that this analysis founders on scope problems in cases like:

(17) Beryl was glad there was a king and she hoped that he laughed

For if the anaphoric pronoun *he* is to be bound by an existential quantifier there are only two possible analyses, both of which are semantically inadequate on account of incorrect scope assignments:

(18)a. ∃x [King(x) ∧ Glad(Beryl,[Hope(Beryl,[Laugh(x)])])]
    b. Glad(Beryl,[∃x [King(x) ∧ Hope(Beryl,[Laugh(x)])]])

In (18a) a specific king is mentioned, of whom it is said that Beryl was glad that she hoped he laughed. (18b) says 'Beryl is glad that there is a king and that she hopes he laughs'. But (17) means neither. Geach's analysis, therefore, lacks generality, and we have no choice but to fall back on the analysis of (15) as, indeed, being of the logical form A ∧ B. But if this is so a special provision is needed to account for the use of anaphoric pronouns like *he* in (13)-(15), since these pronouns are neither bound variables nor full definite descriptions. The point is taken up again in 6.2.5 below.

- *Russell's analysis fails as a theory of reference*

We have diagnosed two respects in which the semantic analysis of natural language sentences transcends the boundaries of established logic. First, (14) implies the existence of at least two kings, one who laughed and one who did not, whereas its logical analysis does not. Secondly, the analysis of (15) shows that a separate category of anaphoric pronouns must be assumed.[13]

Furthermore, in Russell's terms a sentence like:

(19)a. Beryl was glad there was a king and she hoped that the king
        laughed

cannot be analysed in such a way that the term *the king* relates anaphorically to the king whose presence made Beryl happy. For the term *the king* requires a new use of the existential quantifier, which destroys any binding by the first.

One easily finds further cases where Russell's theory is inadequate. For example, in Russell's analysis, (19b) should mean 'Beryl hoped that there was exactly one king and that he had a good time', which, of course, it does not:

(19)b. Beryl hoped that the king had a good time

We conclude that Russell's Theory of Descriptions is fundamentally inadequate for the analysis of definite descriptions.

- *Donkey sentences*

This conclusion is not new. Since Geach (1962) the problem of the so-called *donkey sentences* has dogged the theory of reference. These are sentences such as (20a,b), with anaphoric pronouns that cannot be bound in logical analysis because of scope problems:

(20)a. Every farmer who owns a donkey feeds it
    b. If a farmer owns a donkey he feeds it

---

[13] Groenendijk & Stokhof (1991) develop a logic that captures these two features of natural language.

Despite the vast literature on this subject, the conclusion must inevitably be that no solution can be provided without a fundamental revision of the standard Russellian approach.[14] We have just seen that the threat is more comprehensive than just the donkey sentences: anaphora goes wrong on any number of counts in the Russell analysis.

- *Russell's analysis fails on grammatical grounds*

Finally, Russell's Theory of Descriptions destroys grammatical structure, as he himself recognized (1905:488): 'If I say "the author of Waverley was a man", that is not a statement of the form "x was a man", and does not have "the author of Waverley" for its subject.' He does not consider the empirical question of how natural speakers relate the surface form of sentences to their presumed logical analysis. If Russell's analysis provides the basis of a proper interpretation of the sentences concerned, speakers must have internalized a set of rules relating the two classes of structures. But there is not a shadow of empirical support for the extraordinary and extremely ad hoc rule system that would be required to make Russell's analysis grammatically viable.

So we take leave of Russell's Theory of Descriptions and revert to the traditional analysis of definite NPs as sentence constituents in their own right at all levels of analysis. This means that we are saddled again with the three problems of identification, of non-existing referents, and of reifications. We argue that they can be solved only in the context of a cognitive theory that takes into account factors of background knowledge, context of utterance and preceding discourse.

6.1.3   Logical model theory: problems with possible worlds

The origin of logical model theory lies in logical proof theory: it was developed, during the 1930s and after, in order to provide a better tool for proof theory than the purely syntactic tools available till then. We shall, however, not be concerned here with the proof-theoretic qualities of logical model theory. We will concentrate instead on a secondary use that has been made of it, namely its application to the semantics of natural language.

Logical model theory is based directly on the Aristotelian concept of truth as correspondence between the propositions in some language L and states of

---

[14] In the many discussions of donkey anaphora one fact is invariably overlooked: the pronouns in question do not represent bound variables at all but are external anaphoric pronouns. This appears, for example, from the fact that the pronoun *it* in (20a,b) can be replaced by an epithet:

    (i)   Every farmer who owns a donkey feeds *the wretched animal*

    (ii)   If a farmer owns a donkey he feeds *the wretched animal*

Pronouns that represent bound variables never allow for such replacement:

    (iii)   Everyone$_i$ thought that he$_i$/they$_i$ would die

    (iv)   *Everyone$_i$ thought that [the wretched man]$_i$ would die

Unfortunately, there is no place for external anaphoric pronouns in logic or indeed in standard model-theoretic semantics. We shall revert to this question in 6.2.5 below.

affairs. Neither Aristotle himself nor any later logician until Frege and Russell investigated the exact nature of that correspondence in detail, no doubt because of the daunting difficulty of that task (though, as explained in 2.6.3 above, Aristotle's distinction between subject and predicate did amount to a primitive form of model theory). Only after the 1930s did logical model theory come into being as a formal definition of the Aristotelian notion of truth, and hence as a method for proving logical theorems.

- *Analysis on two fronts: propositions and states of affairs*

In order to define in a formal way what the correspondence between the propositions of a language and a given state of affairs consists in, it is necessary to apply a twofold analysis, one of the propositions and one of the states of affairs concerned. The logicians of the 20th century found that, on the propositional side, the best language available for that purpose is the language of modern predicate calculus as prepared by Frege and devised by Bertrand Russell. As for the states of affairs, they decided to stick to mathematically manageable states of affairs, fully definable in terms of set theory.

- *Model-theoretic ontology: possible worlds*

In fact, logicians do not like to speak of 'states of affairs'. They prefer to speak of 'worlds' and 'sets of worlds'. Each world is treated as consisting exclusively of truth values and individuals, and sets of (sets of sets of ...) individuals, i.e. functions from (functions from ... (functions from individuals to truth values) ... to truth values) to truth values, i.e. $((...((e,t),t),...,t),t)$ (see 5.5.2).

Moreover, worlds can themselves be arranged in sets of worlds. Only one world, at any given point in time, is the real world. The real world is also a possible world, as reality entails possibility, but all the other, non-real, worlds are merely possible. There are, however, a number of formidable problems, conceptual as well as empirical, connected with the notion of possible world, some of which we will now review.

- *Truth values as part of reality: an ontological anomaly*

Curiously, the ontology of model-theoretic semantics requires the existential reality of truth values, which function as extensions of sentences. (It was for that reason that the truth values 1 and 0 were listed as elements of **W** in the models of 5.5.1 and 5.5.2 above.) Given the prevalence of nominalism in model theory and related brands of philosophy (see in particular 6.1.3.4 below), this is, to say the least, an anomaly. But it is required by the computational system envisaged by Frege and implemented in the modern theories.

6.1.3.1 Problems with the set of all possible worlds

- *The infinity of the set of all possible worlds*

The total set of all possible worlds must be infinitely large, but it must be so in a way that is more complex than by simple denumerable infinity. One cannot, in an ideal sense, count these worlds one by one and then find that there is always a new world to be defined, which would make the set of worlds denumerably infinite. On the contrary, possible worlds differ in myriads of ways, all criss-crossing with each other. The possible world that is identical to the present world but for the fact that I was born one second later than I actually was, is a different world from the real one. The same goes for any possible world in which my birth took place any fraction of a second later than it actually happened. Thus, if any ordering is to be imposed it must be the ordering of real, not natural, numbers. But that is not enough, for each alternative world has such a set of alternatives of its own, as any fact may be somewhat different, or just absent. The sad truth is that the set of all possible worlds is unfathomably infinite and mathematically either unmanageable or extremely difficult to manage. The notion of possible world thus defeats one basic purpose of logico-mathematical model theory: mathematical manageability. It certainly defeats any attempt at realistic interpretation, as it is totally unrealistic to postulate a mental machinery that carries out its computations at such an elevated level of abstraction and still comes out with very precise results about usually extremely mundane matters.

6.1.3.2 Reifications again

One further empirical problem is that the down-to-earth ontology adopted in this framework will make it hard if not impossible to operate with quasi-entities like *the military-industrial complex*, or *the interest taken by the general public in scandals involving politicians*, or *the average Englishman*. Even mathematically well-defined 'entities' like *the average age of blue-collar workers in the American car industry* are beyond the grasp of model theory. Yet they are treated linguistically as if they were entities, since they are referred to by referring terms (see 6.1.2.3.3). The same goes for economic quasi-entities like earnings, profits, losses, and for parameters like temperature, number, name, colour, salary, size, etc., etc.

The ontology that goes with model theory may make sense from a purely ontological or from a purely logical point of view (although on that score, too, there are serious objections, as we shall see in a 6.1.3.4), it is no good for a semantic analysis of language. Language is a product of the mind and any link between language and whatever one takes real or possible worlds to be, must necessarily be mediated by the mind, which performs much more than a simple one-to-one mapping function.

The mind maps reality in surprisingly complex ways. It creates, among other things, abstract quasi-entities that it, or the cognizing subject, knows do not exist as such in material form though they may 'exist' via a more or less exact formula of interpretation, thus maintaining a link of correspondence with reality. In the philosophical literature such quasi-entities are called *reifications*, and the cognitive process by which they come about is known as *reification*. Cognitive constructions are set up and given the status of representations of entities that can have properties and take part in relations. In language such mental constructions function as anchoring points that mediate in referential processes, and their grammatical reflex is a noun phrase. Model-theoretic semantics has so far failed to provide a semantics for such noun phrases, and it stands very little chance of doing so as long as it ignores the role played by the mind.

6.1.3.3 Identity across worlds

Apart from this, there is a great deal of philosophical literature querying the notion of possible worlds on grounds of conceptual clarity, in particular the question of establishing identity of entities across different possible worlds. For example, what guarantees that you are you in all other worlds where you are meant to be you, and what about worlds where you never existed? An important issue concerns the parameter time: what mathematical system can guarantee identity through time where that is called for? It would take us too far to discuss these problems here. We will instead proceed as if the notion of possible world were well-defined, and concentrate on other problematic aspects of model-theoretic formal semantics.

6.1.3.4 Intensional entities

An issue of paramount importance is the philosophical question of levels of reality, or different categories of being. This is a sensitive issue in philosophy as well as in logic, and the dominant attitude is to reject any ontological distinction between really existing entities and entities that do not materially exist but have some form of virtual existence on account of having been thought up or imagined by someone. Entities of the latter kind are often called 'intensional entities'.

This is an old and vexed question in philosophy. Most philosophers in the Anglo-Saxon world prefer to stick to an ontology with only really existing entities. For them, when you speak about non-existing entities like the abominable snowman, the monster of Loch Ness, Pegasus, the god Apollo, or the present king of France, there is nothing you speak about, and therefore, you speak about nothing.

Some philosophers, however, find this too terse a view of reality. They take it that you do speak about something in such a case, even though that something has no existence in the actual world. These philosophers can be roughly divided into two classes. First, there are those, mostly of Continental European origin, who defend the notion of an intensional entity that has some form of being, but not of actual existence in substance (i.e. subsistence) in the actual world. For them, intensional entities have what is called 'virtual' being. This view is often associated with the Austrian philosopher Alexius Meinong (1853-1920), and attacked by Russell in his 'On denoting' of 1905.

On the other hand, philosophers with possible world leanings, in particular the formal semanticists (who follow Montague), though also ready to accept intensional entities, accept them not as virtual inhabitants of the actual world but as denizens of other, merely possible worlds. When we speak about an intensional entity, they say, we speak about an entity occurring in a class of non-actual possible worlds, not an entity in the one and only real world, which can only contain objects endowed with solid reality.

This view, however, which is widely respected in philosophical circles, raises the issue of the *truth value* of a sentence that contains an expression referring to an intensional entity, like Russell's famous *The present king of France is bald*. Is such a sentence true or false with respect to the actual world? And if it is false, then its negation must be true. Russell saw this difficulty clearly, though when he wrote about it in (1905) model-theoretic semantics did not yet exist. Despite Russell's Theory of Descriptions and despite model-theoretic semantics, this problem just will not go away. In section 6.2.3 below we shall take it up again, and find that this is a nasty problem both for established bivalent logic and for established forms of ontology.

• *Quine rejects all forms of virtual being*
The first, terse view has been defended with particular rhetorical vigour by the American philosopher Willard Van Orman Quine (born 1908). In his famous essay 'On what there is' (1953:1-19) he introduces the fictitious philosophers McX and Wyman, who engage in a philosophical discussion with Quine himself. McX is made to defend the position that what we talk about when we talk about Pegasus is the mental Pegasus-idea. This position is given short shrift, and rightly so: nobody will deny the reality of the Pegasus-idea, but most will deny the reality of Pegasus, so talk about one cannot be the same as talk about the other. Then Mr. Wyman is made to maintain the Meinongian position that Pegasus may not *exist* yet he *is* as an unactualized possible. But this too meets with Quine's strong disapproval:

> This tangled doctrine might be nicknamed *Plato's beard*; historically it has proved tough, frequently dulling the edge of Occam's razor.   Quine (1953:2)

> Wyman's overpopulated universe is in many ways unlovely. It offends the aesthetic sense of us who have a taste for desert landscapes, but this is not the worst of it. Wyman's slum of possibles is a breeding ground for disorderly elements. Take, for instance, the possible fat man in that doorway; and, again, the possible bald man in that doorway. Are they the same possible man, or two possible men? How do we decide? How many possible men are there in that doorway? Are there more possible thin ones than fat ones? How many of them are alike? Or would their being alike make them one? Are no *two* possible things alike? Is this the same as saying that it is impossible for two things to be alike? Or, finally, is the concept of identity simply inapplicable to unactualized possibles? But what sense can be found in talking of entities which cannot meaningfully be said to be identical with themselves and distinct from one another? These elements are well-nigh incorrigible. By a Fregean therapy of individual concepts, some effort might be made at rehabilitation; but I feel we'd do better simply to clear Wyman's slum and be done with it.   Quine (1953:4)

On the basis of this analysis Quine advertised his famous slogan 'No entity without identity'. Needless to say, when, after 1970, possible world semantics came into being Quine fulminated as vigorously against possible worlds as he did against possible entities.

- *We reject Quine's view and accept Meinongian intensional entities*

Despite Quine's flaming prose, however, we cannot join his herd. Our taste is for lusher landscapes than deserts, and we do not share Quine's horror of Wyman's slum. The point is that Quine fails to reckon with the constraining factor of cognition. When he summons us to imagine 'the possible man in that doorway' and we do so, we have a mental representation of a man in that doorway, even though there is no such man.

Not being real but only imagined, the man lacks values for most of the parameters that any real persons must have values for. Imagined entities are by definition incompletely defined. A real man has a precise age, weight, size, and a unique life history. An imagined man may well be undefined for a great many parameters, just like a fictitious character in a story or in a picture. Yet he has his identity, which is conferred upon him by the mental representation of which he is a part. When I decide to make him bald he is bald, and when I then imagine him as fat he, the same man that is, is fat. In other words, the identity of intensional entities is secured by the cognitive representations in which they figure, not by anything in the physical world. Intensional entities derive their being from cognitive representations, not from physical reality. (This makes it odd to say that I have imagined two different men but do not know that they are the same. It takes something as powerful as Freudian psychology to solve that tangle.)

How cognition is able to create intensional entities is one of the unsolved problems in the philosophy of mind and psychology. Yet the inability of philosophers and psychologists to account for the human ability to create cognitive representations of 'virtual' beings and states of affairs cannot stop us from accepting the fact that that is what humans do. We accept that the world is populated not only by what exists but also by what there is as a result of cognitive representations, which may materialize as paintings or movies, and also as verbal texts consisting of sentences that contain references to non-existing entities. Humans invent non-existing situations, to which they apply the same processes of abstraction and subsumption they apply to their representations of what they take to be the real world. Ultimately, all semantics is intensional (see 6.2.6.2).

In 6.2.6.1 below we will opt for the Meinongian view on the grounds that we have no choice but to accept the reality, though not the existence, of thought-up intensional entities. This choice is forced by the rejection of possible worlds as a viable notion in semantics, and by the utter untenability of the Quinian position that we speak about nothing when we speak about Santa Claus. All we can do is take the one remaining option, which is the Meinongian one. The decision to accept the reality of intensional entities will also help us out of the truth value dilemma that tripped up Bertrand Russell.

6.1.4 The model-theoretic treatment of intensionality

Perhaps the most outstanding feature of model-theoretic semantics is its treatment of intensionality phenomena. Spurred by Frege's formulation of the problems connected with intensional contexts (see 6.1.2.2), Montague, who rejected Frege's appeal to cognitive structures and processes, expected to find a solution in a model theory involving sets of possible worlds. The point of departure was the insufficiency of Frege's matrix for the intensions and extensions of various categories of expressions as given in fig. 4 above, due not only to the cognitive notions involved but also to the impossibility of an extensional categorial calculus for sentences whose predicates create intensional contexts.

• *Intensional contexts under modal operators*

An example involving the modal predicate *possible* will make this clear:[15]

(21)   It is possible that there is life on the morning star

This involves a structural analysis of the following kind:

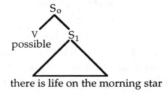

Figure 5   The logico-semantic position of the possibility operator

If the extension of S_1 is a truth value and the extension of S_0 is again to be a truth value, the predicate *possible* must be a function from truth values to truth values, i.e. of the type (t,t), just like *not*. However, the predicate *possible* does not correspond to any of the four mathematically possible unary truth functions:

(a)	$\{\langle 1,1 \rangle, \langle 0,0 \rangle\}$		(c)	$\{\langle 1,1 \rangle, \langle 0,1 \rangle\}$
(b)	$\{\langle 1,0 \rangle, \langle 0,1 \rangle\}$		(d)	$\{\langle 1,0 \rangle, \langle 0,0 \rangle\}$

(a) corresponds to 'it is true that ...'; (b) is the model-theoretic extension of the standard logical operator *not*; (c) makes every proposition true: 'it is true or false that ...'; and (d) makes every proposition false: 'it is true and false that ...'. Most readers will agree that *possible* does not do any of these things.

So what can be done? Montague and his school of model-theoretic semanticists reasoned as follows. Sentence (21) is true, they say, if there is at least one possible world in which its argument clause S_1 is true, that being the intended purpose of the very notion of possible world. If this idea is to be formalized we must define the extension of S_1 as the set of all possible worlds in which the

[15] It was Quine who introduced the idea that modal predicates belong to the class of predicates that create intensional contexts (1953:139-159), not Frege, as is incorrectly stated in Dowty, et al. (1981:142). In fact, one may assume that Frege shied away from modalities, being all too aware of the difficulties involved. (Cp Dummett (1973:281): 'It may be objected that Frege's theory has in fact made no contribution to the development of modal logic; that the idea which proved effective in providing a semantics for modal logic was the totally different one of possible worlds.')

sentence 'There is life on the morning star' is true. The predicate *possible* must then denote a function from sets of possible worlds to truth values.

- *Intensions as functions from possible worlds to extensions*

In order to turn this idea into a formal system a few drastic operations must be performed on the simple kind of model theory exemplified in 5.5.1 and 5.5.2 above. The first step to be taken is to define the *intension of a sentence A* as 'the set of possible worlds in which sentence A is true'. Each sentence thus gets associated with a set of possible worlds, i.e. the set in which it is true. The intension of a sentence A can thus be represented as a characteristic function (see 5.5.1) from possible worlds to truth values. If we introduce a new categorial type w for possible worlds, the intension of a sentence is thus of type (w,t).

Then the predicate *possible* must be defined as denoting a function that has as input not the extension of the argument-S but its intension. It is therefore of the type $((w,t),t)$: it takes sets of possible worlds and delivers a truth value. The condition under which it delivers truth, i.e. the value '1', is simply that the set denoted by its argument-S be non-empty. Other predicates of that type are, for example, *necessary* and *probable*. The condition for *necessary* is that the set of worlds denoted by its argument-S be equal to the set of all possible worlds, and for *probable* it is, presumably, that any arbitrarily chosen world stand a greater than 50 per cent chance of being a member of the set of worlds denoted by its argument-S. The modal predicates *possible* and *necessary* are thus treated analogously to the existential and universal quantifiers.

To finish the job it would be necessary to integrate these new notions and techniques into the formalism of existing extensional model-theory. This we shall not do, as it will become clear below (in 6.1.5.1) that the model-theoretic approach runs to ground anyway. This makes it unnecessary to go through the complex motions required to achieve formal precision in all respects.

All we do here is mention Montague's notation for expressions in **L** denoting intensions:

'For any expression a in **L**, there is an expression ˆa denoting the intension of a.'

This means that the language **L** in any model is extended with expressions denoting the intension of any expression already given in **L**. (This process is recursive: for any expression E, **L** will contain not only ˆE but also ˆˆE, ˆˆˆE, etc. These higher order intensionalities, however, have played no role in model-theoretic semantics as it has been applied to natural language.)

The machinery makes it necessary to define intensions not only for S-structures (whether main clauses or embedded under an intensional predicate), but also for terms and predicates. Every type of expression gets its intensional counterpart, and every corresponding extension gets a corresponding intension, which is always a function from possible worlds to the extension type at hand.

All intensions are thus functions from possible worlds to something. Term intensions assign a unique individual to each possible world. Unary predicate intensions assign a unique set of individuals to each possible world. And sentence intensions assign a unique truth value to each possible world. Sentence intensions can thus be seen as sets of possible worlds. The intension of an expression, thus defined, is considered to correspond to what is intuitively called the 'meaning' or 'sense' of that expression.

- *The Montague system of extensions and intensions*

For every predicate it must be specified whether it takes intensional or extensional terms: extensional terms take their value in one world, intensional ones from all possible worlds. An S embedded under *not*, for example, is extensional: its truth value in one world is fed into it, and it produces a new truth value. But an S embedded under, say, *possible* is intensional and must therefore be written ^S, which takes the intension of S as its extension. Now the extension-intension matrix need not suffer from undefined slots, as was the case with the matrix of fig. 4 (except that there is no recognized standard name for the intension of a proposition, but that slot is never used anyway). The possible world semantic matrix looks as in fig. 6.

type of linguistic expression	extension and type	intension	
		standard name and type	description: function from possible worlds to:
term	individual e	individual concept (w,e)	individuals
predicate	set of individuals (e,t)	property $(w,(e,t))$	sets of individuals
independent sentence	truth value t	proposition (w,t)	truth values
sentence as argument term of intensional predicate	proposition (w,t)	$(w,(w,t))$	propositions

*Figure 6   Montague's system of extensions and intensions
(partly based on Dowty et al. 1981:149)*

- *The Montague solution to Frege's second problem*

We now see what the Montague solution to Frege's second problem amounts to. Since it is a contingent fact that the morning star is identical with the evening star, there is a set of possible worlds in which the two are distinct. Consequently, the set of worlds in which there is life on the morning star differs from the set of worlds in which there is life on the evening star. This blocks SSV of *morning star* and *evening star* in sentence (7) above. The fact that these two terms in fact refer to the same entity is no longer relevant. What is relevant is that the clausal term *that the morning star is inhabited*, the object term of the main verb *believe*, is not co-extensive with the clausal term *that the evening star is inhabited*, which means that these two clausal terms cannot stand in for each other salva veritate. This solution is analogous to Frege's, but it avoids notions like 'thought', which are ontologically awkward in philosophies with an underdeveloped philosophy of mind.

● *The extensionalisation of intensionality*
The essential element in the Montague treatment of intensional phenomena is its way of generalizing the purely extensional model theory illustrated in 5.5.1 and 5.5.2 to all possible worlds and, with it, of creating an abstract computational schema indicating how the computations would proceed if they were effectively computable. This programme is generally called the extensionalisation of intensionality. It aims at making intensionality phenomena mathematically as transparent as extensionality phenomena.

There is no doubt that this programme is the result of profound and consummate mathematical thinking. Yet, in spite of its formal superiority to Frege's theory, which still fumbles about to find workable formalisms, it fails eventually. One may say that it is precisely due to its great formal precision that the argument leading to its failure is so clear and inescapable. This argument will be discussed in the following section.

6.1.5 Where model theoretic semantics comes to grief

What contribution can model-theoretic semantics make towards answering the empirical question of how successful communication is achieved by means of language use? Or, in other words, how do we evaluate model-theoretic semantics as a scientific theory providing an explanatory answer to the causal question of why speakers understand the uttered sentences of their language in certain and not in other ways?

Let us, in trying to comment on this question, refer to the distinction between *specifying*, and *procedural* theories. Specifying theories aim at merely defining the object of inquiry without providing a causal explanation, while procedural theories try to answer the question of how the phenomena under investigation come, or have come, about. Being a branch of linguistics, natural language semantics is expected to aim at a procedural theory, which reconstructs as closely as possible those structures and processes that causally underlie the events of successful interpretation of verbal messages. That is, we want a theory that is psychologically plausible.

In this section we argue that model-theoretic semantics is intended as a specifying theory of natural language interpretation, and that as such it fails to come to adequate grips with the facts. Given its failure as a specifying theory we may conclude that it also fails as a procedural theory.

The central reason for the empirical failure of model-theoretic semantics as a theory of meaning lies in the systematic neglect of the cognitive factor. The famous semiotic triangle drawn by Ogden & Richards (1923:11), reproduced on p. 18 in section 1.2.1, shows precisely where the fault lies. In this triangle the roles of speaker and hearer are merged, an acceptable idealization, since successful communication implies total identity between the relevant mental representations of speaker and hearer. Given this idealization, the triangle correctly represents the relation between the 'symbol', i.e. the linguistic expression, and the 'referent', i.e. the extension or 'world', as an 'imputed' relation, not part of the actual causal machinery that links expressions with the world, but stipulated by definition. The relations between expressions and the mind and between the mind and the world, on the other hand, are causal and thus the object of a procedural theory.

Model-theoretic semantics aims at making explicit the base line in the triangle, constituting the 'imputed' relation of truth. It was shown in 1.2.1 that if truth is taken, in the Aristotelian way, as a relation of correspondence, there are two notions of truth, the verbal notion according to which truth is correspondence between what is *said* and what is the case, and the cognitive one, according to which truth is correspondence between what is *thought* and what is the case. Adherents of the verbal notion will say that the base line in the Ogden & Richards triangle correctly represents the truth relation. But adherents of the cognitive notion will say that the base line should be taken away altogether as truth is to be defined on the line connecting thought and world.

However, whether one believes that the cognitive or the verbal notion of truth is correct, is a mere philosophical issue. What counts for the semantics of natural language is rather how mental representations, which may or may not represent the world as it really is, are adequately expressed in the shape of verbal messages and how verbal messages lead to the intended representations. From this point of view, model-theoretic semantics does not seem to be the right answer, though it has given us some very useful instruction in formal precision and some much-needed notional clarity.

Let us now look at a few points where model-theoretic semantics fails as a specifying theory, starting with the most central and most fatal objection.

6.1.5.1 Predicates of propositional attitude

The most fundamental obstacle for model-theoretic semantics lies in its treatment of predicates of propositional attitude. The term *propositional attitudes* is generally used, in model-theoretic semantics, for the expression of a speaker's subjective attitude with regard to some propositional content. The standard predicate expressing a propositional attitude is *believe*, but others, such as *hope*, *expect*, and even factive[16] predicates like *know* or *realize*, count as well, even if they hardly figure in the relevant literature.

We have just seen how model-theoretic semantics solves the problem of non-substitutivity of co-extensional definite descriptions in clauses embedded under a propositional attitude predicate. This solution implies the notion that such embedded clauses take as their extension not a truth value but the set of possible worlds in which they are true, that is, their intension. Alternatively one can say that a verb like *believe* is intensional with regard to its clausal object term. It is taken, in model-theoretic semantics, to express a relation between a believing subject and a set of possible worlds. If a person says *I believe*

---

[16] For the notion of factivity, see 6.2.3.2.

that the morning star is inhabited he or she is taken to hold, on subjective grounds, that the actual world is a member of the set of worlds in which the morning star is inhabited.

One may or may not find such an analysis intuitively convincing, it certainly carries some prima facie conviction from a formal, mathematical point of view. Yet it also leads to a serious problem that has so far proved insurmountable. The problem (Dowty et al. 1981:170-175) consists in the fact that logically equivalent sentences take the same set of possible worlds as their intension and should therefore be synonymous as well as mutually substitutable salva veritate in intensional contexts, whereas, in fact, they are often neither synonymous nor mutually substitutable. For example, *John is ill* is logically equivalent with *John is ill and either all dogs are black or not all dogs are black*: the conjunction of any sentence A with a necessary truth is logically equivalent with A. Also, any inconsistent sentence or set of sentences takes the empty set as its intension, since, by definition, inconsistency implies falsity in any possible world. And the intension of a tautology equals the set of all possible worlds, as tautologies are true in any world. But this means that an inconsistent sentence embedded under a propositional attitude predicate takes the empty set as its extension, and a necessary truth the set of all possible worlds. Now Leibniz's Law applies: SSV should be allowed under the predicate in question.

This creates empirical problems for the predicates of propositional attitude, such as *believe, hope, wish, suggest*, which are intensional with respect to their object S-term. For it may be true that *Stuart believes that John is ill*, but false that *Stuart believes that John is ill and that either all dogs are black or not all dogs are black*, since Stuart may not have any beliefs about dogs at all. Likewise, Stuart may believe, both that every human has two human parents and that Darwinian evolution theory is correct,[17] but according to model-theoretic semantics he should then also believe that, say, some humans are both dead and alive, as both beliefs are inconsistent. One inconsistency is worth any other, and the same for tautologies, in this framework. Yet humans are, on the whole, not logically omniscient. A number of authors have called attention to this fact, e.g. Lewis (1973:46):[18]

> But one part of the tradition about propositions must be given up: propositions understood as sets of worlds cannot serve as the meanings of sentences that express them, since there are sentences — for instance, all the logical truths — that express the same proposition but do not, in any ordinary sense, have the same meaning.

Dowty et al. (1981:175) admit that

---

[17] Example borrowed from Barbara Partee (personal communication).

[18] The philosopher most determined to solve this problem has no doubt been Cresswell (see in particular Cresswell 1985). For a detailed discussion of Cresswell's proposal the reader is referred to the review by Israel (1987), whose verdict is, in the end, cautiously negative (see 1.2.1).

the problem of propositional attitude sentences is a fundamental one for possible world semantics, and, for all we know, could eventually turn out to be a reason for rejecting or drastically modifying the whole possible world framework.

So far, this problem of propositional attitude predicates has not been solved in the framework of possible world semantics. It is therefore not surprising that there is now a growing conviction, even among formal semanticists, that some drastic reorientation is called for. Apparently, the equation of propositions with sets of possible worlds makes for too coarse a grid. What is needed is a specification of the *content* of thoughts expressed in embedded clauses. In 6.2.6. we argue that the notion of cognitive representation is of greater use, in this respect, than that of sets of possible worlds.

6.1.5.2 Lexical dependency on a knowledge base

There are, however, other problems as well. We know, for example, that certain natural language predicates have incomplete meanings. To decide whether their satisfaction conditions are fulfilled an appeal must be made to contextual or world knowledge. Linguistic knowledge alone is insufficient for adequate interpretation. This is most obviously so for the class of *gradable predicates* (*small, big, old, ugly*, etc.), which imply a yardstick of prototypical normalcy: something is small when it stays below what is considered the norm for this kind of case. This norm depends on cognitive factors and escapes modelling in terms of possible world semantics.

A less well-known but equally interesting case is the *possessive complex*, consisting of verbs like *have* and *lack*, the prepositions *with* and *without*, the genitive morphemes or case endings, and perhaps a few more. Consider the following examples (already mentioned in 1.2.1, taken from Seuren 1985:21):

(22)a.   Each of the 25 rooms in the hotel has a shower
     b.   Each of the 25 students in the class has a supervisor

(22a) is false if different rooms have to share a shower, even if there is a note pinned on the inside of each hotel room saying that its shower is at the end of the corridor. For rooms to have showers a one-to-one mapping is required. Not so with students and supervisors: (22b) is true if several students have to share a supervisor, since for students to have supervisors a many-to-one mapping is sufficient. The meaning description of the English predicate *have* therefore contains an open parameter referring the user to his or her knowledge base. *Have* expresses an association between an individual and something else, but the precise nature of the association must be 'looked up' in every speaker's world encyclopedia, which will specify the way it is with hotel rooms and showers, or with students and supervisors, etc. If the language user does not know 'the way it is' with this or that he cannot interpret the utterance in question. For example, an expression like *the room's front wheels* requires either a world picture in which rooms have a known standard relation to front wheels, or otherwise at least a context where this room's relation to front wheels has been explained.

The consequences of this observation are far-reaching. It destroys semantic compositionality in terms of a calculus computing sentence meanings from the meanings of the component parts and their structural position. It also means that sentences are sometimes not true or false per se but only against the background of available world or contextual knowledge (which would seem to have serious consequences for the base line in the Ogden & Richards triangle).

6.1.5.3 Topic-comment modulation and information structure

A further difficulty with regard to model-theoretic semantics is to do with what is currently often called information structure. Sentence structures can carry their propositional information in different ways, depending on how the sentence is made to fit onto preceding discourse: sentence structures often differ according to their mode of presentation in discourse. Observations to this effect have been made since about 1850, but it has proved difficult to integrate them into an adequate overall theory of grammar and meaning.[19]

Model-theoretic semantics has traditionally maintained that differences in modes of presentation have no effect on the truth conditions of sentences and are, therefore, irrelevant to semantics and should be studied in pragmatics. Below we argue that sentence meaning is more than mere truth conditions. But apart from that we see that topic-comment differences may well affect truth conditions, which makes the model-theoretic position untenable. Consider, for example, (23a,b), where contrastive accent marks the comment under an intensional operator, or (24a,b), which has different nuclear sentence accents. Clearly, it is possible for (23a) to be true while (23b) is false, and likewise for (24a) and (24b): (24a) brands John as a bad worker, whereas (24b) suggests that he is a workaholic:

(23) a.   She was surprised that SCOTT wrote Ivanhoe
    b.   She was surprised that Scott wrote IVANHOE

(24) a.   John SLEEPS, in his office
    b.   John sleeps in his OFFICE

Given these truth-conditional differences it is mandatory for any theory of natural language meaning that it account for them. Since model-theoretic semantics is in principle unable to do so, it must be considered inadequate.

6.1.5.4 Viewpoint

One further problem for model-theoretic semantics to be discussed here (and already mentioned, though in a different context, in section 1.2.1) covers a range of phenomena generally caught under the term 'viewpoint'. In general,

---

[19] See Sasse (1987) for an excellent survey. An important structural principle appears to lie in the fact that new sentences are typically meant to provide an answer to a question the speaker implicitly assumes will have arisen with his audience: the comment is thus seen as the answer provided by the speaker to the assumed implicit question. As was shown in 2.6.3 above, the original idea goes back to 19th century scholars like Lipps, Wegener, Stout.

the relevant facts involve a position, decided on by the speaker, with respect to what is being said, sometimes with truth-conditional consequences. The issue is of recent origin and has attracted a great deal of attention in psycholinguistics (mainly regarding spatial expressions), less in linguistics, and none in formal semantics. The latter is to be expected since viewpoint phenomena are clearly cognitive, and model-theoretic semantics has no place for cognition. Discourse-based varieties of semantics, which posit cognition as an intermediary station between language and any 'world', are clearly better qualified. Yet here, too, there is almost total silence. Only Mitchell (1986), which follows Barwise & Perry (1983), takes up viewpoint phenomena from the linguistic literature (there is no mention of psycholinguistics), placing them in the context of propositional attitudes. The scarce linguistic literature (mainly Bierwisch 1967; Cantrall 1969, 1974; Lyons 1977:690-703; Leech 1969:156; McCawley 1971:107; Kuno 1987) stays at an impressionistic level of analysis, with hardly any operational criteria or precise analysis. Only Bierwisch and Lyons concentrate on the issues raised in the psycholinguistic literature, i.e. on spatial expressions.

- *Non-truth-conditional cases*

For many cases where viewpoint plays a role there is no truth-conditional difference corresponding with the viewpoint taken. Some examples (Cantrall 1969; Kuno 1987) deal with the use or avoidance of reflexives in picture NPs:

(25)a.   I saw pictures of me all over town
     b.   I saw pictures of myself all over town

In (25a), there is more distance, detachment, on the part of the speaker. In (25b), on the other hand, the use of the reflexive expresses a greater personal, even emotional, involvement.

Phenomena of the 'come and go'-type show an orientation towards or away from a speaker's viewpoint:

(26)   A few men were waiting to be shown into the office. The door opened and one of them went in. After two minutes another man *went in / came in.*

The difference between the two versions is clear, though hard to express in other than metaphorical terms. With *went in*, the 'camera', so to speak, has remained in the corridor. With *came in*, it has moved along with the first man and is now inside the office. Such phenomena are clearly semantic, in that they reflect meaning differences even though they do not correspond to different sets of truth conditions.

- *Truth-conditional cases*

There are, however, also cases that do involve truth conditions. These are well-known in psycholinguistics (see the references given in note 2 of 1.2.1), though no mention of the truth-conditional aspect is made in the psycholinguistic literature. These cases concern largely the use of spatial prepositional expressions. Consider the sentences (27a,b) in connection with fig. 7 (repeated here from 1.2.1):

(27)a. The ball is to the right of the man
   b. The ball is in front of the man

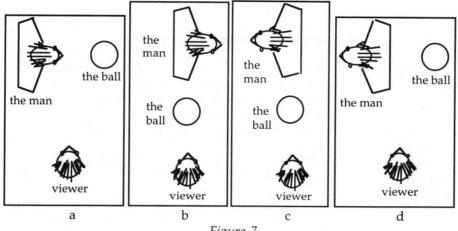

Figure 7

In this case there are clear truth-conditional differences corresponding with the viewpoint taken. As one can read from fig. 7, sentence (27a) is true for the models a, b and d, but from different viewpoints. Likewise, (27b) is true for the models a, b and c, again from different viewpoints. In the 'deictic' reading, i.e. if the viewpoint coincides with the viewer (who may or may not be identical with the speaker), (27a) is true for a and d, and false for b and c, while (27b) is false for a and d and true for b and c. But if the man is taken as viewpoint (the 'intrinsic' reading) (27a) is false for a, c and d and true for b, while (27b) is true for a and false for the others. (If these sentences are not about a man but, say, a tree, with no front or back, then, as the tree cannot take on the viewpoint role, the only possible viewpoint is the viewer.)

Observations of this kind show that truth values may be sensitive to subjective factors like 'point of view', a fact that model-theoretic semantics, with its Aristotelian concept of truth and falsity, is in principle unable to account for.[20] This fact is of prime importance not only for the question of whether model-theoretic semantics provides an adequate approach to the

[20] A little reflection will show that a proper formulation of the lexical meanings (satisfaction conditions) of the expressions *to the right of* and *in front of* is not trivial (see Levinson 1996), as the following stab may show. Let *to the right of* be defined as follows: 'If V(iewer) faces North, O(bject), i.e. the ball, is East of S(ubject), i.e. the man'. Clearly, if V and S are distinct the deictic reading arises, and if they coincide one has the intrinsic reading. Not so, however, for *in front of.* Here such an analysis is impossible. Instead, the following seems viable: 'The shortest line from O to S touches S on the front side. The front of S is either the side of S facing V or its intrinsic front (if it has one).' The reader is invited to try this out.

study of natural language meaning, but also, in a more profound sense, for the Aristotelian concept of truth as correspondence. It thus touches on a basic philosophical issue: it looks as if the scientific study of natural language meaning will lead to a position that is ultimately irreconcilable with the age-old Aristotelian concept of truth.

6.2   Cognitive semantics: discourse-dependency

• *Discourse as a central parameter in the semantics of natural language*
The notional and empirical problems enumerated in 6.1.3 and 6.1.5, especially the most obviously fatal one of propositional attitudes (discussed in 6.1.5.1), are basic and affect the core of model-theoretic semantics. As no principled reply came forth from those quarters, a few researchers felt, during the late 1970s and the early 1980s, that an entirely new approach was called for. The main names are Kamp (1981), Kamp & Reyle (1993), Heim (1982, 1983), Barwise & Perry (1983), Fauconnier (1985), Seuren (1972a, 1975, 1985), Groenendijk & Stokhof (1991).

These authors come from different traditions. Kamp, Reyle, Heim, Groenendijk, Stokhof, and many others, have a background in logic and model-theoretic semantics (as appears, for example, from the title of Kamp & Reyle 1993). They tend to minimize the break with model theory and prefer to depict the new, discourse-oriented forms of semantics as a direct continuation of the old model-theoretic approach. Barwise and Perry are primarily philosophers and as such closer to the world of logical model-theory than to that of linguistics. Fauconnier and Seuren are primarily linguists and thus more inclined to link up linguistic analysis with semantic theory. Despite the different backgrounds and preferences, however, they all agree that no adequate semantics of natural language is possible unless discourse is taken into account.[21]

By 'discourse' is meant, first, the set of relevant preceding utterances produced by the discourse participants, or, for some, the corresponding mental construct that contains, in some form or other, a systematic file of whatever has been established or excluded as the basis of interpretation for newly produced utterances. The term 'discourse', however, is often extended to include also the actual setting of any utterance, what has been called the 'situation' or 'pragmatic context' (cp. the sections 3.3, 3.4, and 3.5 above). Some theorists, moreover, take any available fund of world knowledge as belonging to the 'discourse' as well.

Different authors have had different grounds for assuming that semantics must be discourse-oriented. Some took their cue from psycholinguistics, where discourse-dependency had been taken seriously and studied for some time, though never from the point of view of truth-conditional semantics. Others

---

[21] Remarkably, there are no psycholinguists among the discourse-oriented innovators of semantic theory, despite the fact that psycholinguistics was the first discipline where discourse-dependent phenomena were studied systematically.

were driven by the inability of model-theoretic semantics to cope with definite reference (the Russell problem) and/or phenomena of pronominal anaphora (donkey sentences), and realized that a successful theory of reference must take discourse factors into account. Some came to discourse semantics on account of presupposition phenomena. In all cases, however, it was realized that, generally speaking, sentence meanings are made in such a way that they make the sentences in question fit for use in certain contexts or discourses and unfit in others. This made discourse a central parameter in the study of natural language semantics.

6.2.1 Semantics and pragmatics

● *Relation between meaning, truth conditions, and possible worlds*
Another issue arising out of the critique of model-theoretic semantics is the relation between meaning, truth conditions and sets of possible worlds. The party line in model-theoretic semantics is that the three are identical:

Equation A: sentence meaning = truth conditions = sets of possible worlds

But early on in the piece many voices were raised to protest against the equation of meaning with either truth conditions or sets of possible worlds. We saw in 6.1.5.1 that the philosopher David Lewis cuts into this equation by saying that 'propositions understood as sets of worlds cannot serve as the meanings of sentences that express them' (Lewis 1973:46). The most notable attempt, however, to repair or uphold Equation A came from pragmatics.

● *Friction between logical analysis and actual language use: pragmatics*
Until quite recently all those with a professional interest in semantics would subscribe to the view that logic is the backbone of semantics. Yet no-one could deny that natural semantic intuitions are often at odds with what would be expected on grounds of logical analysis. All standard truth-functional propositional operators, for example, behave in ways they shouldn't if they were purely logical operators. Negation is terrible, as one will gather from 6.2.3 below. The *and*-operator is ill-behaved, as there is a clear and even truth-conditional difference between sentences like:

(28)a. She got rich and went to Spain
    b. She went to Spain and got rich

whereas the ∧-operator in logic is symmetrical. *Or* is even worse, as it often implies exclusivity: when we say 'A or B' we usually mean 'either A or B but not both', thus excluding the possibility that both disjuncts are true. And the implication operator *if ... then* in conditional sentences of the type 'if A then B' is the worst of all: not only is it often taken to imply 'if not-A then not-B' but it also usually involves some form of causality or reasoning from A to B, not to mention other anomalies.

Natural language quantifiers are also accused of irregular conduct. Most people, for example, take a sentence like *Some children laughed* to imply that not all children laughed, whereas all logical analysts since De Morgan's and

Hamilton's acrimonious polemic (see 5.3 above) have agreed that such an implication cannot be logically valid. Universal quantification in language is likewise terrible not only because there are so many different varieties of it but also because most varieties seem to presuppose the non-emptiness of the set of entities quantified over, a presupposition that does not fit at all into Russell's predicate calculus (see 5.5.4).

- *Pragmatics to fill the gap between language and logic*

This tension between language and logic gave rise to the idea that those aspects of linguistic usage that do not seem to fit the logical mould should be accounted for by a separate theory of language use called *pragmatics*.[22] The main instigator of this idea was the philosopher Herbert Paul Grice (1913-1988), whose William James Lectures, given at Harvard in 1967, were extremely influential (see Grice 1989). Grice introduced the term *implicature*, which stands generally for anything inferred from given utterances that is not semantically or logically entailed. Oxford philosophers had already used the term *invited inference* for non-necessary conclusions, but Grice's term won the day.

- *Grice's conversational maxims: the Co-operative Principle*

The central principle behind Grice's analysis is the consideration that logic is not the only system underlying linguistic comprehension but that there is also a system of mutual expectations, some sort of 'social contract', in operation between speaker and listener, knowledge of which allows discourse participants to draw certain inferences to do with rational communicative behaviour. This is known as Grice's *Co-operative Principle*. Discourse, or, as Grice says, conversation, is guided by maxims that form part of a universal code of rational behaviour in communication. Observance of this code makes discourse participants assume that, until otherwise proven, interlocutors will stick to the topic at hand and will be generally helpful in that they will provide just the relevant information, neither less nor more.

For example, the logical meaning of a normal sentence like *John has two children* is, according to Grice and most model-theoretic semanticists, 'John has at least two children', and thus leaves open the possibility that John has more than two children. But listeners may rationally expect that anyone uttering such a sentence will observe the conversational maxims, which means that (s)he will maximize relevance. Suppose John has in fact three children, then, in some settings, the speaker may be regarded as not having told the whole truth, which goes against the code and may thus justify a charge of deviousness. Analogously, when one says *Some children laughed*, the listener may tentatively infer that not all children laughed because, if all children had laughed, a maxim-observing speaker would have had to say so.

---

[22] The term was borrowed from the American philosopher Charles Morris (1938), but in Grice's hands it took on a quite different meaning. See Levinson (1983:1-5) and Gazdar (1979:1-5) for synopses of the history of the term.

- *Is pragmatics a limbo between logic and language?*

This is not the place to go into the countless questions that have arisen in connection with Gricean pragmatics. All we wish to point out here is that Gricean pragmatics was created essentially to fill the gap between formal logic and living language. Gazdar used this birth certificate to define pragmatics in a way that may be clear and succinct, yet is considered misleading by many. According to Gazdar, pragmatics is 'meaning minus truth conditions':

> Put crudely: PRAGMATICS = MEANING – TRUTH CONDITIONS.   Gazdar (1979:2)

If taken literally this means that pragmatics is concerned with the study of linguistic meaning, and should thus be considered a part of semantics. But not many pragmatists subscribe to that view: they believe in Equation A. For them pragmatics is separate from semantics, since semantics is to do with truth conditions and pragmatics is concerned with other aspects of linguistic comprehension and communication.

Be that as it may, in actual practice pragmatics has staked out a certain territory for itself. It is concerned mainly with phenomena of situation-bound deixis, with Gricean implicatures, with presuppositions, with speech acts, and with the structure of texts and discourses (as is witnessed by the list of contents in Levinson 1983). Some areas border on sociolinguistics, such as, for example, politeness phenomena, power and solidarity symbols. Only some of these topics come under Grice's Co-operative Principle, others do not or only partially so. Deixis straddles the fence between grammar and cognition, and does not seem to have many links with Grice's Co-operative Principle. Implicatures and presuppositions are usually taken to be core phenomena of conversational co-operativity. Speech acts are to do with entering commitments of various kinds by the speaker with regard to the listener. They are connected with the Co-operative Principle to the extent that such commitments are part of the kind of 'social contract' or 'code of conduct' that Grice envisaged. Text structure, finally, has no more than tenuous links with Gricean pragmatics. Its study has now developed into a more or less separate field called 'rhetorical studies'. In practice, therefore, pragmatics is held together more by a sense of belonging and solidarity ('leave the logicians to their job; we will do the cleaning up') than by a clear statement of problem, data, and theory, the general set-up for a scientific discipline.

- *Pragmatics suffers from formal shyness*

In actual practice, also, pragmatics has found it difficult to define its place among the disciplines and subdisciplines that take natural language as their object of investigation. And it has found it difficult to achieve the degree of formal precision considered desirable in the linguistic sciences nowadays.

To the extent that pragmatics rests on Grice's Co-operative Principle, its force lies in the fact that one can hardly deny that there is indeed a set of natural expectations between speaker and listener, a code of communicative conduct, which must explain, or help explain, certain phenomena. Its weakness lies in its exclusive reliance on the Co-operative Principle, without taking into account alternative sources of explanation, and in its persistent inability to come to terms with formal systems and provide formal explanations.

Both defects seem to be the result of a certain shyness with regard to formal systems. Most pragmatists (Gazdar emphatically excepted) feel awkward in the presence of a formal system. Without that shyness, formal explanations might have come forth. And pragmatists might have realized, as Gazdar did, that the equation of meaning with truth conditions and with sets of possible worlds, i.e. Equation A given above, is not an a priori necessity but open to doubt and correction.

- *The burden of explanation is too heavy for the Co-operative Principle*
They might also have realized that the phenomena they attempt to tackle are unlikely to be tamed by no more than the Co-operative Principle. A more detailed analysis of the phenomena in question strongly suggests that the bulk of the explanation is to be sought in specific cognitive, grammatical and semantic structures and processes, whose functionality may ultimately have been motivated by the need for sensible co-operative communication but whose functioning is a matter of precise formal scrutiny.

- *The example of quantity implicatures:* John has two children
The questions involved are too complex and too manifold to be given a full treatment in the present context. But we can, by way of example, have a somewhat closer look at the sentence presented above:

(29)a.   John has two children

As has been said, the assumption is that the logical analysis of this sentence should be something like 'there are at least 2x such that x is a child of John's'. Other than the logical analysis makes one expect, however, this sentence is commonly interpreted as implying that John has exactly two children, not less and not more. The Gricean answer to this dilemma is that the 'exactly' interpretation comes on top of the 'literal' logical meaning as a result of the Co-operative Principle (cp. Horn 1989:213-16). In this view, the 'exactly' reading is not truth-conditional but a mere implicature (a so-called 'quantity implicature') since, it is said, it can be 'cancelled', as in:

(29)b.   John has two children, in fact he has three.

This answer has been widely accepted, in part because it leaves the logicians in peace, and in part because it is felt to have an intuitive appeal.

There are, however, serious objections to the Gricean solution (see Seuren 1993; Scharten 1997). First, one may well query the assumption that the logical analysis standardly assigned to (29a), let us call it *the existential reading*, is the only possible one. Logicians tend to think in terms of quantification. And it is not in doubt that the existential reading is possible. But there is another reading as well, let us say *the cardinality reading*, which runs as follows:

'the cardinality of the set of John's children is 2'

This very plausible second reading needs no pragmatic rectification, and it is, moreover, perfectly well formalizable, even if propositional structures involving the assignment of a value to a parameter (as in *The temperature is 90 degrees*, or *My name is Pieter*) have not enjoyed much popularity with logicians.

That (29a) is indeed ambiguous in the way indicated is supported by the observation (Horn 1989:251) that a question like (30a) can be answered truthfully as both (30b) and (30c) when the addressee has three children:

(30)a. Do you have two children?
    b. No, I have three
    c. Yes, in fact I have three

The proposition questioned in (30a) thus satisfies Quine's classic criterion for ambiguity (even though Quine speaks only of lexical meaning):

> Ambiguity differs from vagueness. Vague terms are only dubiously applicable to marginal objects, but an ambiguous term such as 'light' may be at once clearly true of various objects (such as dark feathers) and clearly false of them.
>
> Quine (1960:129)

If a proposition is at once clearly true of a situation and clearly false of it, we may say, following Quine, it is ambiguous. This now does appear to be the case with the proposition questioned in (30a), and hence with the proposition expressed in (29a). Horn makes the observation but fails to draw the conclusion.

It is clear, moreover, that the context of utterance will normally decide which reading is intended. Suppose John has (exactly) three children. Then if (29a) is an answer to the question *How many children does John have?*, it is false in the full truth-conditional sense. No court of justice and no ordinary conversationalist would accept the excuse that (29a) merely means that there are two individuals that are both children of John's, and should therefore be considered true. But if (29a) is an answer to the question *Who has two children?*, for example in a context where 'one of the welfare benefit eligibility criteria is having <two> children' (Gazdar 1979:138), the answer is true.

There is also an intonational difference between the two readings of (29a). In the cardinality reading the main sentence accent is on TWO, since that is the information required. In the existential reading the main accent will fall on JOHN, again because that is the information asked for.

Finally, and perhaps most fatally, if the English word *two* meant 'at least 2' the English expression *exactly two* should mean 'exactly at least 2', which would prevent any 'exactly' reading getting off the ground. It seems much more plausible to assign to the English word *two* (and analogously to all other numerals) the cardinality reading, which, as has been said, is perfectly well definable in mathematical terms. The cardinality reading will then be basic, and the existential reading 'at least 2' will be derived: 'there is at least one set with cardinality 2 such that ...'.

This solution, however, necessarily involves a fair amount of formal machinery. It also involves a sharp deviation not only from established logical and formal semantic doctrine but also from established practice in pragmatics. In particular, it requires a further integration of the questions at issue in the wider contexts of grammar, cognition and discourse, rather than putting everything down to the Co-operative Principle.

• *Pragmatics fails to make up for deficiencies of model-theoretic semantics*
The most obvious weakness of pragmatics, however, lies in its failure to do
what it was set up to do, bridge the gap between logic and logical, i.e. model-
theoretic, semantics on the one hand and the facts of language on the other.
We have seen that model-theoretic semantics has proved unable to account for
propositional attitude phenomena, for cognitive dependencies in the lexicon,
for information structure and viewpoint phenomena. We shall see in 6.2.5
below that the language of predicate calculus lacks the power to account for
certain forms of anaphora. If pragmatics had been up to its task it would have
tackled these issues with some success. In fact, one must conclude, it has not.

• *Semantics breaks loose from Equation A*
There is a growing awareness, nowadays, that Equation A should be abandoned and replaced by a different equation:

Equation B: sentence meaning **>** truth conditions **>** sets of possible worlds

where '**>**' stands for 'is underdetermined by' or 'is richer than'.

The evidence against Equation A and in favour of Equation B is massive. A
crude but immediate argument is provided by the sentences (31a) and (31b),
whose truth conditions are identical but whose meanings obviously differ:

(31)a.   The man drove a car
    b.   The driver of the car was a man

But a more detailed analysis shows the same. Propositional attitudes (6.1.5.1)
show that sentence meaning transcends sets of possible worlds and also truth
conditions. Definite descriptions (6.1.2.3) show that reference, a precondition
for the assignment of truth values, requires discourse and world knowledge,
which makes truth conditions contingent upon cognition and thus richer than
sets of possible worlds. Lexical meanings may likewise depend on world knowledge (6.1.5.2). Topic-comment modulation (6.1.5.3) may influence truth conditions, as illustrated in (23) and (24), and thus shows that sentence meaning is
richer than truth conditions and, a fortiori, richer than sets of possible worlds.
Viewpoint phenomena (6.1.5.4) may codetermine truth values in a way not expressible in terms of sets of possible worlds. And presuppositional facts, discussed in 6.2.3, show that sentence meaning is codetermined by discourse
acceptability conditions, and thus underdetermined by truth conditions. In
general, the reasons for which Equation B holds, all derive from cognition as a
factor in the build-up of meanings and, though more rarely, of truth conditions.

The delimitation of sets of possible worlds may approximate a definition of
truth conditions, but it is insufficient. Then, the definition of the truth
conditions of a sentence is necessary but not sufficient for a description of its
meaning. A command of the truth conditions of a sentence is insufficient for a
command of its meaning. Testing knowledge of truth conditions may be useful
for checking (e.g. in foreign language teaching) whether a subject understands
the meaning of a sentence, but it has to figure along with other tests that focus
on non-truth-conditional aspects of sentence meaning.

6.2.2 Ordinary Language Philosophy

The reservations we have expressed with regard to a strictly logical analysis of language, and which pragmatics sought to alleviate by an appeal to conditions of use, have been felt and expressed by philosophers ever since logic became a mathematical discipline. By the end of the 19th century the Cambridge philosopher Alfred Sidgwick had serious qualms about the mathematical formalization of logic that was taking place in his day:

> Logical doctrines are seldom errors to be refuted; ... rather, they are truths that need supplementing now and then, — truths with a blemish which from various motives we are often led to overlook.   Sidgwick (1895:282)

And, as we also saw in section 5.2, his main objection was the neglect of context by the logicians, and hence their lack of subtlety when analysing meanings:

> ... the 'logical character' of any name and of any proposition is to be sought not merely in that name or proposition taken as an independent entity, but as influenced by the special context in which it happens to be used.   Sidgwick (1895:281)

We must not forget, in this connection, that George Stout, another Cambridge philosopher, was writing profusely, in those days, about the context-sensitivity of the notions subject and predicate (see 2.6.3 above), thereby implicitly challenging linguistic analysis in terms of logic alone.

This attitude of distrust with regard to logic was inherited by Wittgenstein, some forty years later (after an initial period of total faith in logic), and then by the Oxford school of Ordinary Language Philosophy. Let us turn our attention first to the singular and striking figure of Wittgenstein.

6.2.2.1 Ludwig Wittgenstein

One curious figure in the history of philosophy stands out particularly in this respect, the Anglo-Austrian philosopher Ludwig Wittgenstein, already mentioned in section 5.4.2, note 12.[23] Born in Vienna in 1889 as the eighth and last child of an extremely wealthy but nouveau riche family (his father was a steel magnate who favoured the arts in a grandiose manner), he was sent to study engineering, first, from 1903 till 1906, at a technical college (Realschule) in Linz (where he overlapped for one year with Adolf Hitler), then, from 1906 till 1908, at the Technische Hochschule in Berlin. After that, he went to Manchester University to study aeronautics, in those days probably an exceedingly eccentric, but to those who saw ahead also a most promising branch of engineering. There he became interested in pure mathematics, and became a great admirer of Russell and Frege, who had been writing on the foundations of mathematics. In the context of his study of aeronautics he made a new design for a propeller, which was patented in 1911 as 'Improvements in Propellers applicable for Aerial Machines' (Monk 1990:34).

---

[23] For a splendid biography and analysis of the man Wittgenstein see Monk (1990).

- *Wittgenstein at Cambridge*

In the autumn of 1911 he decided to go to Cambridge and study with Russell, on the advice of Frege whom he had visited during the summer. At Cambridge he proved an eccentric and extremely demanding student, yet considered by most, not least by himself, to have genius. As was said in section 5.4.2, Russell frequently mentioned him in his daily correspondence with Ottoline Morrell, his lady friend at Oxford, telling her of Wittgenstein's exasperating behaviour. The following excerpts from this correspondence (Monk 1990:39-40) will give an idea:

> My German friend threatens to be an affliction, he came back with me after my lecture & argued till dinner-time – obstinate & perverse, but I think not stupid.
> [19 Oct. 1911]

> My German engineer very argumentative & tiresome. He wouldn't admit that it was certain that there was no rhinoceros in the room . ... [He] came back and argued all the time I was dressing.   [1 Nov. 1911]

> My German engineer, I think, is a fool. He thinks nothing empirical is knowable – I asked him to admit that there was no rhinoceros in the room, but he wouldn't.
> [2 Nov. 1911]

> My lecture went off all right. My German ex-engineer, as usual, maintained his thesis that there is nothing in the world except asserted propositions, but at last I told him it was too large a theme.   [13 Nov. 1911]

> My ferocious German came and argued at me after my lecture. He is armour-plated against all assaults of reasoning. It is really rather a waste of time talking with him.
> [16 Nov. 1911]

Then, after a while, Russell takes to him and writes about him in a more sympathetic and appreciative fashion (Monk 1990:43):

> His disposition is that of an artist, intuitive and moody. He says every morning he begins his work with hope, and every evening he ends in despair — he has just the sort of rage when he can't understand things that I have.   [16 March 1912]

> I have the most perfect intellectual sympathy with him — the same passion and vehemence, the same feeling that one must understand or die, the sudden jokes breaking down the frightful tension of thought.   [17 March 1912]

> His attitude justifies all I have hoped about my work.   [22 March 1912]

In the end, however, both discovered that they were too different, temperamentally, morally and intellectually, to remain friends. By 1922 they broke off whatever remained of their friendship, and went on to lead entirely separate lives.

- *Wittgenstein's struggle with the paradox of knowledge*

Russell admitted to Ottoline that he often had the feeling that he did not quite understand what Wittgenstein was up to. And one can hardly blame him for that. For we now know, in hindsight, that Wittgenstein was struggling with the paradox of knowledge (or Kantian dilemma; see section 2.2.1), which shows all empirical knowledge to be based on faith and unprovable. This struggle with the paradox of knowledge is the key to all of Wittgenstein's thoughts and to his entire professional life. He never came to a satisfactory solution, neither in his radical, uncompromising and quasi-logical *Tractatus* nor in his later more language-oriented *Investigations* and other collections of sayings. One may say that he fell victim to the deepest and most dangerous question in philosophy, that of the foundation of knowledge, a question so dangerous that, I am told, it is forbidden to meditate about it in Buddhist mysticism as it may make one lose one's sanity. No wonder Russell told him 'it was too large a theme'.

- *Wittgenstein in the Austrian army*
In June 1914 Wittgenstein happened to be in Austria on a family visit. When the First World War broke out, by the end of that month, he volunteered for military service, and was sent first to the Eastern front in Poland, then, in 1918, to the Italian front. At the end of the war he was captured by the Italians and kept as a prisoner of war till August 1919.

The first thing he did upon his return was dispose of his very considerable wealth. He was one of the richest men in Europe, due to his father's decision, before the war, to transfer the whole family fortune into American bonds (Monk 1990:171). Against the stiff resistance of his family he had his whole estate donated to his sisters Helene and Hermine, and his brother Paul.

- *The post-war years in Austria: 1919 - 1929*
He then enrolled in a teachers' training college, resolved to become an ordinary school teacher. And a school teacher he did become, though not an ordinary one. His first post was at the mountain village of Trattenbach, which was poor enough for his taste (in that period he professed a contempt for wealth). There he applied modern teaching methods, which were apparently successful with the better pupils but left the poorer ones in despair, despite rather severe manually-administered discipline. After a year he was distrusted and shunned by the villagers to such an extent that he felt he had better leave. A few more abortive attempts at village school teaching followed, which were invariably unsuccessful for always the same reasons. He had to abandon his career as a school teacher when he was summonsed on criminal charges for severely beating up a young school girl. The court case was settled without him having to go to gaol, mainly owing to intervention by the powerful Wittgenstein family.

Throughout this time he suffered from periodic depressions, continually considering taking his own life, an example that had been set by a few of his brothers. In early 1926 he decided that he wanted to become a monk but was, sensibly, refused. Instead he became a gardener in a monastery just outside Vienna. This lasted for three months, after which he resettled in Vienna.

There he collaborated with the architect Paul Engelmann in the building of a large house for his sister Gretl. Other than common lore has it, 'his role in the design of the house was concerned chiefly with the design of the windows, doors, window-locks and radiators' Monk (1990:236-7). In supervising these works he proved himself a demanding customer:

> During discussions with the engineering firm responsible for the high glass doors which Wittgenstein had designed, the engineer handling the negotiations broke down in tears, despairing of ever executing the commission in accordance with Wittgenstein's standards. The apparently simple radiators took over a year to deliver because no one in Austria could build the sort of thing Wittgenstein had in mind. Castings of individual parts were obtained from abroad, and even then whole batches were rejected as unusable. But, as Hermine Wittgenstein recalls:
>> Perhaps the most telling proof of Ludwig's relentlessness when it came to getting the proportions exactly right is the fact that he had the ceiling of one of the rooms, which was almost big enough to be a hall, raised by three centimetres, just when it was almost time to start cleaning the complete house.
>>   Monk (1990:236-7)

The house itself was also rather unique:

> The house was designed with little regard to the comforts of ordinary mortals. The qualities of clarity, rigour and precision which characterize it are indeed those one looks for in a system of logic rather than in a dwelling place. In designing the interior Wittgenstein made extraordinarily few concessions to domestic comfort. Carpets, chandeliers and curtains were strictly rejected. The floors were of dark polished stone, the walls and ceilings painted a light ochre, the metal of the windows, the door handles and the radiators was left unpainted, and the rooms were lit with naked light-bulbs.   Monk (1990:237)

Meanwhile his *Tractatus* (see below) had been published and was widely admired. In the eyes of many, Wittgenstein was now an important philosopher. One of his early admirers was Moritz Schlick, philosophy professor at the University of Vienna and founding member of the Vienna Circle. Schlick was keen on having Wittgenstein as a member of the Circle, but the young Maestro was too aloof and too abrasive to fit into any circle. The most he could offer the Circle was an occasional benevolent attendance at their meetings.

In those days, also, contact was re-established with John Maynard Keynes, whom he knew from his pre-war days at Cambridge (see Von Wright 1974). Keynes was bursar of King's College Cambridge, and an economist of world-wide renown, who regularly assisted and advised governments in Europe and America on economic matters. It was Keynes who persuaded Wittgenstein to return to England and take up philosophy again.

He arrived in England in January 1929. Keynes ran into him on the London train, and on arrival at Cambridge he wrote to his wife, who lived in London:

> God has arrived, I met him on the 5.15 train.   Monk (1990:255)

Keynes had hoped to introduce Wittgenstein into his social circles, especially the Apostles, an exclusive society of young brilliant Cambridge intellectuals (counting among its members the later spy Anthony Blunt), and the London Bloomsbury group. His behaviour, however, was such that both groups found it impossible to keep him on. Keynes soon got tired of Wittgenstein, and the only friendship he enjoyed during this period was with the brilliant, then twenty-five year old mathematician-philosopher Frank Ramsey, one of his greatest admirers, whom he had met in Vienna and with whom he had been in correspondence. Unfortunately for the world of learning, Ramsey died in 1930, at the age of twenty-six.

- *The Tractatus Logico-Philosophicus*

During the last years of the war Wittgenstein had compiled a manuscript, consisting of strings of pronouncements or 'propositions' on the basic questions of being, knowing and saying. Upon his return he tried to get it published in Germany or Austria, but it was systematically turned down.

He sent copies of it to a few friends, including Frege and Russell. Frege's reply rather disappointed him. Frege had obviously not been able to read beyond the first page (Monk 1990:163-4), and in his letter to Wittgenstein he pointed out the many confusions and mystifications one finds in that text. Wittgenstein's reaction was, not unexpectedly, that Frege had failed to understand him. Despite a subsequent correspondence which lasted for a few years, neither man changed his opinion.

Russell's reaction was more temperate than Frege's, yet he too expressed his puzzlement over certain central issues. In any case, Wittgenstein was not sufficiently put off by Russell's reply to refuse to meet him. In December 1919 the two men, one a British and the other an Austrian national, met in The Hague, on neutral ground. There Russell promised to write an introduction to the little book, with a view to publication in Germany. Wittgenstein, however, later found Russell's introduction inadequate, and without it the book could not be published (as Russell was a best-selling author, but Wittgenstein was not).

In the end, the book was published twice over. In 1921 a sloppy German edition appeared (on the strength of Russell's introduction) under the title 'Logisch-Philosophische Abhandlung', in the *Annalen der Naturphilosophie*. The editor had apparently not even taken the trouble to glance through the manuscript, with the result that the printed text was full of misprints. Wittgenstein did not even receive an offprint, and when he discovered, almost a year later, how it had been printed he considered it a pirated edition and disowned it. In 1922 it was published properly by Kegan Paul in London, at the instigation of C.K. Ogden, who was then the editor of the series in which it appeared. Its new title, approved by Wittgenstein, was *Tractatus Logico-Philosophicus*. The English edition was bilingual, the translation was made by Charles K. Ogden, and the book contained Russell's introduction.

This book has fascinated and puzzled countless philosophers and non-philosophers ever since its appearance. I take it to be essentially an attempt at coming to terms with the paradox of knowledge. In strange but perhaps not altogether unexpected contrast to his obvious emotional instability, his attitude towards the paradox is one of impatience and apparent absolute self-confidence. In the Preface he writes:

> On the other hand the *truth* of the thoughts that are here set forth seems to me unassailable and definitive. I therefore believe myself to have found, on all essential points, the final solution of the problems.

It seems to me, however, that a dispassionate inspection of the text shows that the book is fundamentally confused, just as Frege thought it was. Being the fin-de-siècle Viennese uncompromising radical he had grown to be, Wittgenstein could not resign himself to the idea that all our dealings with the outside world, and with other human beings in particular, are based on an intellectual compromise, on faith rather than on solid argument. His way out appears to be one of extreme solipsism. To the extent that one can make sense of the many unsettling leaps of thought, one gains the impression that he is trying to develop the idea that all so-called 'things' in the world are intensional entities, created by thought and cognitive representations.

Already in the early days of his study with Russell, as we have seen, he had developed the idea that all that really exists in the world is 'asserted propositions'. Now, in the *Tractatus*, he insists, right at the beginning, that the world exists only in 'logical space'. His terminology is confusing. The ordinary reader will take terms like *fact, thing, world, state of affairs, what is the case, reality, existence*, to refer to what is 'out there', a reality which is there no matter what we think or know about it, and which makes what we say or think true or false. Most commentators and interpreters of the *Tractatus* have indeed read the text this way. For Wittgenstein, however, facts, things, states of affairs etc. exist in 'logical space', whatever that can be:

> The world is the totality of facts, not of things. (proposition 1.1)
> The facts in logical space are the world. (prop. 1.13)
> We picture facts to ourselves. (prop. 2.1)
> A picture is a fact. (prop. 2.141)
> If a fact is to be a picture, it must have something in common with what it depicts. (prop. 2.16)
> A picture represents a possible situation in logical space. (prop. 2.202)
> A propositional sign is a fact. (prop. 3.14)

An attractive aspect of this approach, it seems, is the attempt to confer some kind of reality upon thought-up entities and states of affairs, an attempt that has our full sympathy, though 'logical space' hardly seems a satisfactory abode for them. One big problem, however, seems to remain, one which he appears to be unable to solve. Nowhere does he succeed in making the distinction between really existing and merely thought-up facts. Although he states that they are different he fails to provide the ontological basis. Yet this distinction is necessary for any correspondence view of truth.

We shall, however, not get lost in this tricky maze, and press on.

● *The later Wittgenstein*

When Wittgenstein arrived back in Cambridge in 1929 his official status in the university was that of a graduate student, with Frank Ramsey, his junior by fifteen years, acting as his supervisor. It was then that the unique episode occurred in which Wittgenstein allowed himself to be convinced that he was wrong in assigning 'logical structure' to things. This episode, together with his discussions with the exiled Italian Marxist economist Piero Sraffa (Monk

1990:260-1), was probably responsible for Wittgenstein's 'conversion' to ordinary language, away from logic.

In order to secure him a position as a fellow of Trinity College, the philosopher G.E. Moore submitted the *Tractatus* as Wittgenstein's PhD-thesis. The examination took place in June 1929, with Moore and Russell as examiners, the latter being more than a little embarrassed at having to meet his one time friend again. Monk describes the situation as follows:

> As Russell walked into the examination room with Moore, he smiled and said: 'I have never known anything so absurd in my life.' The examination began with a chat between old friends. Then Russell, relishing the absurdity of the situation, said to Moore: 'Go on, you've got to ask him some questions – you're the professor.' There followed a short discussion in which Russell advanced his view that Wittgenstein was inconsistent in claiming to have expressed unassailable truths by means of meaningless propositions. He was, of course, unable to convince Wittgenstein, who brought the proceedings to an end by clapping each of his examiners on the shoulder and remarking consolingly: 'Don't worry, I know you'll never understand it.'
>
> In his examiner's report, Moore stated: 'It is my personal opinion that Mr Wittgenstein's thesis is a work of genius; but, be that as it may, it is certainly well up to the standards required for the Cambridge degree of Doctor of Philosophy.'
>
> Monk (1990:271-2)

In the years that followed, Wittgenstein lectured and travelled a great deal, seeking happiness and satisfaction but never achieving any. His thinking moved away rapidly from the doctrinaire position of the *Tractatus* to a no less doctrinaire anti-logical and anti-scientific relativism. Not being able to find a foundation for truth and falsity in an Aristotelian correspondence between what is the case and what is said or thought, he began to think and teach that truth and falsity have no other foundation than mere convention, expressed mainly in language. Not only are propositions not true or false on account of any objective correspondence with what is the case, words themselves have no fixed meaning. An analysis of language will show, he thought, that there is no fixity in it, just habits and vaguely delimited focal areas.

In February 1939 Wittgenstein was appointed professor of philosophy at the University of Cambridge, succeeding Moore who had retired. A few months later he gained British citizenship, thus avoiding legal and other complications that were certain to present themselves in view of the impending war.

During 1939 he lectured, among other things, on the foundations of mathematics. Among those attending was Alan Turing, the great mathematician. Since Wittgenstein insisted that mathematics has no metaphysical necessity but is made by man, and that contradictions do not matter in mathematics, or, for that matter, in logic, Turing engaged in heated discussions with him. After a few of those lectures, however, he ceased to attend, feeling they were a waste of time (Monk 1990:421).

When the war broke out Wittgenstein quickly became sceptical about academic life. In the autumn of 1941 he left Cambridge and took on a humble job as a porter at Guy's Hospital in London, in an area frequently hit by German bombs. He had found the job through the good offices of John Ryle (brother of the Oxford philosopher Gilbert Ryle), who was then Regius Professor of Physics at Cambridge but temporarily attached to Guy's Hospital for reasons to do with the war. When, during the following winter, Wittgenstein visited the Ryles' home in Sussex, Wittgenstein met John Ryle's wife, two bombed-out working-class boys from Portsmouth they had taken in out of social concern, and the son Anthony, then fourteen years old. Anthony's diary notes about the meeting are priceless:

> Daddy and another Austrian (?) professor called Winkenstein (spelling?) arrived at 7.30. Daddy rather tired. Wink is awful strange – not a very good English speaker, keeps on saying "I mean" and 'its "tolerable"' meaning intolerable. ...
>
> Witkinstein spent the morning with the evacuees. He thinks we're terribly cruel to them. We spent the afternoon argueing – he's an impossible person everytime you say anything he says 'No No, that's not the point.' It probably isn't his point, but it is ours. A tiring person to listen to. After tea I showed him around the grounds and he entreated me to be kind to the miserable little children – he goes far too much to the other extreme – Mommy wants them to be good citizens, he wants them to be happy.   Monk (1990:434-5)

In April 1943 Wittgenstein moved to Newcastle-upon-Tyne, to work as a laboratory assistant in the Clinical Research Laboratory at the Royal Victoria Infirmary. After a long stay in Swansea he returned to Cambridge in October 1944, to resume his professorial duties, much against his inclination. In 1947 he gave up his chair and settled in Ireland, writing and thinking. After a visit to America in 1949 it was found that he suffered from an incurable cancer. Two years later he died in Cambridge, at the home of his doctor.

• *The Philosophical Investigations*

Between 1929 and 1949 Wittgenstein wrote a great deal, always in the form of numerically ordered short notes or remarks, longer than those in the *Tractatus* but hardly ever exceeding a printed page's length. One manuscript thus composed was published posthumously, in 1953, under the title *Philosophical Investigations*. It was translated into English by Miss G.E.M. Anscombe, his only female student.

This book reflects Wittgenstein's long struggle with the same questions that haunted him in the *Tractatus*, but he now approaches them from an entirely different angle. Whereas in the *Tractatus* he still hoped to solve the paradox of knowledge by the rigorous application of logic, he had now given up all such hope and sought refuge in the way humans, as speakers of their languages, experience concepts, expressed in words, and use these words just as they use tools, more or less appropriately for the purpose at hand. It is here that we find Wittgenstein's famous simile of language as a game, and his statement that we must not look for the meaning of a word, because there is none to be found, but only for its use.

The Preface, dated January 1945, tells the reader about his philosophical volte-face, which began in 1929, and about Ramsey's and Sraffa's influence:

The thoughts which I publish in what follows are the precipitate of philosophical investigations which have occupied me for the last sixteen years. They concern many subjects: the concepts of meaning, of understanding, of a proposition, of logic, of the foundations of mathematics, states of consciousness, and other things. ...

For since beginning to occupy myself with philosophy again, sixteen years ago, I have been forced to recognize grave mistakes in what I wrote in that first book [i.e. *Tractatus*]. I was helped to realize these mistakes – to a degree which I myself am hardly able to estimate – by the criticism which my ideas encountered from Frank Ramsey, with whom I discussed them in innumerable conversations during the last two years of his life. Even more than to this – always certain and forcible – criticism I am indebted to that which a teacher of this university, Mr. P. Sraffa, for many years unceasingly practised on my thoughts. I am indebted to *this* stimulus for the most consequential ideas of this book.

We shall not go into the details of this remarkable book, as its influence upon linguistic thinking has largely remained limited to literary studies. The linguistic world proper was never impressed, though philosophers of language have at times gone out of their way to detect profundity in it.

- *Why has Wittgenstein fascinated so many people?*

The incredible fascination that so many people have had with Wittgenstein as a philosopher was never fed by an urge for scientific method and empirically valid results, whether in linguistics or any other branch of scientific inquiry. Wittgenstein is appreciated most by those who value the effort more than the results. To those who measure intellectual or philosophical endeavour in terms of devotion and struggle Wittgenstein is a hero, whose philosophy is as relevant as his biography. But when it comes to results Wittgenstein cuts a poor figure. It is fair to say that none of his thoughts have led to any research programme that has proved of lasting value. The only important influence detectable is his role in the coming about of the Oxford School of Ordinary Language Philosophy. This school did achieve results and has had a lasting influence, but less on account of any of Wittgenstein's thoughts than on the grounds of their own original contributions.

6.2.2.2 The Oxford School: Ryle, Austin, Strawson

When the second world war was finally over and the academics who had served their country in the war effort had returned to their universities to resume normal work, a group of Oxford philosophers decided that the basic questions of metaphysics and epistemology, including the paradox of knowledge, should be looked at afresh from the point of view of 'ordinary language', the language spoken by people in their normal daily business (we prefer to speak of 'natural language'). Without wishing to diminish the other philosophers of this school, we single out Gilbert Ryle, John Austin and Peter Strawson, as these have been of particular relevance for the study of language.

The Oxford philosophers' interest in ordinary or natural language sprang from Wittgenstein's teachings at Cambridge during the 1930s and 1940s, to the extent that he was still active then, but there was also a strong admixture originating from, in particular, Gilbert Ryle who had been developing kindred thoughts since the early 1930s.

- *Metaphysics is linguistic trickery*

It was felt that a careful analysis of the ways words are used would reveal that most or all of the age-old metaphysical questions of being and knowing are not real questions at all but are in fact due to the very ways in which words are used. It was hoped that all metaphysical questions would turn out to lack substance, being merely of a verbal nature, and that a further, more precise analysis of language would reveal this linguistic trickery.

- *Yet natural language is the best available witness of the world*

On the other hand, it was also thought that the best we can achieve when trying to penetrate Locke's 'veil of perception' is to break down our conception of the world, or whatever it is that we take to be 'out there', to the smallest, most primitive elements. In order to do that one has to rely on some form of language, not, as in Russell's logical atomism, on an artificial formal language, but on natural language, since the questions at hand are between cognitively functioning man and whatever he experiences as the world outside.

Natural language was thus seen both as an object of criticism and a source of insight, a witness, yes, but not one to be trusted too much, of the world outside. Over the years, however, this double-faced attitude began to worry most of the Oxford philosophers, with the result that during the 1960s much greater emphasis was placed on the wisdom bred into language by nature. What was at first taken to be misleading was now re-interpreted as a sign of superior sagacity, whose secrets were to be discovered by painstaking observation and analysis. The Oxford philosophers looked to language for help.

- *Gilbert Ryle (1900-1976)*

In his article 'Systematically Misleading Expressions' of 1931-2, Ryle still sides with Russell and the younger Wittgenstein in accusing natural language of philosophical deception: a sentence like *Mr Pickwick is a fictitious person* does not entail that Mr Pickwick is a person, and *Jim and Harry are friends* does not entail that Jim, or Harry, is a friend, although the grammatical form of these sentences may make one think that these entailments should hold. Yet he already suggests that the deception is discovered by an analysis of the very same language that is under suspicion.

- *The mind as a reification*

Later, in his famous and for some time very influential book *The Concept of Mind* of 1949, Ryle applies this method to an analysis of what we refer to when we speak of 'the mind'. Against Cartesian dualism, which considers man as consisting of a body and a soul (the theory of the 'ghost in a machine'), Ryle defends a strictly unitary theory, with only one kind of entity. He denies that his theory is materialist. In fact he refuses to take a stance on the issue:

> [T]he hallowed contrast between Mind and Matter will be dissipated, but dissipated not by either of the equally hallowed absorptions of Mind by Matter or

of Matter by Mind, but in quite a different way. For the seeming contrast of the two will be shown to be as illegitimate as would be the contrast of 'she came home in a flood of tears' and 'she came home in a sedan-chair'. The belief that there is a polar opposition between Mind and Matter is the belief that they are terms of the same logical type. ... It would be like saying, 'Either she bought a left-hand and right-hand glove or she bought a pair of gloves (but not both)'.   Ryle (1949:23-4)

Despite the telling similes, however, Ryle's basic ontology remains unclear. Without having to commit himself to a right-on statement that all that exists is material, he could have said that existence can only be defined in the same terms as are used to define the existence of those things we call 'material'. But he prefers to stay aloof. In practice, however, his approach is materialist, and it has always been interpreted as such.

What appears to us as a separate entity 'mind' is in fact an ensemble of dispositions of the (material) body to behave in certain ways, just as the brittleness of glass is not an entity but a property to be described as a disposition to break under impact. The mind is thus a complex property of the body. The fact that we, like Descartes, are inclined to regard the mind as a non-material entity with an independent existence is the result of typical manners of speaking, which the philosopher must reduce to talk about observables (much in Wittgenstein's vein).

We would say, nowadays, that the mind is a reification, whose reduction to ontological primitives constitutes a long-term reductionist programme. Ryle's book marks the beginning of the philosophical aspects of that programme, which is still in full swing in what is known as 'the philosophy of mind'. Scientifically, the reductionist programme had started much earlier, in the behaviourist movement. Ryle recognizes this, but he does not seem to care too much about it: 'The general trend of this book will undoubtedly, and harmlessly, be stigmatized as "behaviourist"' (1949:308). But he does express doubts as to the philosophical foundations of behaviourism (1949:308-11).

- *Notional and empirical shortcomings*

Yet the foundations of his own philosophy also leave much to be desired. His philosophical method is of the 'ordinary language' kind: locutions and common expressions in natural language use are 'scanned' for terms that denote mental phenomena, which are then paraphrased with the help of other terms that seem to Ryle to be more explanatory. For example, the fact that a person may have a tune or a visual image in mind, or 'in the head', or that he can do mental arithmetic without using pen and paper, is no evidence for a ghostlike soul or mind. He is 'merely imagining' (1949:37) the noises, visions or figures:

It is merely the convenient privacy which characterizes the tunes that run in my head and the things that I see in my mind's eye.   Ryle (1949:35)

I suggest, then, that the phrase 'in the head' is felt to be an appropriate and expressive metaphor in the first instance for vividly imagined self-voiced noises, and secondarily for any imaginary noises and even for imaginary sights. ... It is an interesting verbal point that people sometimes use 'mental' and 'merely mental' as synonyms for 'imaginary'.   Ryle (1949:39)

But what is gained by the reduction of 'mental' or 'in the head' to 'convenient privacy' or 'imaginary' remains unclear. There are much better ways to get rid of the 'ghost in the machine'.

Ryle's ideas about the empirical aspects of the mind's workings are under-developed. He displays an almost total lack of familiarity with what was actually going on in experimental psychology in those days. To him, learning and the development of perception processes are simply 'practice'. The following passage is one of many where this view is aired:

> There is no more of an epistemological puzzle involved in describing how infants learn perception recipes than there is in describing how boys learn to bicycle. They learn by practice, and we can specify the sorts of practice that expedite this learning.   Ryle (1949:219)

Yet despite the many criticisms and doubts one may well have regarding this book, it must be recognized that it signalled the start of the philosophical programme of reductionism. Generations of psychology students had to study this book, to be informed about the philosophical aspects of their subject. Nowadays, that function is fulfilled by more adequate and more up-to-date books, which are better informed about what actually happens in cognitive psychology and related fields of inquiry. But Ryle's *The Concept of Mind* still remains a momument in the history of the programme of reducing mental to physical phenomena.

- *John Langshaw Austin (1911-1960)*

Austin was one of those who publish little but do a lot.[24] Most of his publications appeared after his untimely death. Although he was a philosopher with a wide range of interests, his main and no doubt lasting contribution to philosophy and to the study of language was his theory of speech acts.

In a paper called 'Other Minds', read to the Aristotelian Society in 1946 (Austin 1961:76-116; esp. pp. 99 ff.) he points to the difference between saying, for example, 'I promise' and 'I firmly and irrevocably intend', or between 'I know that p' and 'I am absolutely sure that p'. The former of these pairs entail a commitment, a putting oneself on the line, in a way the latter of these pairs do not. This notion is further elaborated in the William James Lectures he delivered at Harvard in 1955 (Austin 1962), and in his paper 'Performative Utterances', read on the BBC Third programme in 1956 (Austin 1961:233-252).

In section 6.2.4 below we shall be a little more specific about the notion of speech acts. At this point we merely point out that sentences such as *I swear that I will be back in five minutes* cannot be said to be either true or false in the normal way. If it can be said at all that such sentences, which embody the entering of a commitment on the part of the speaker, have a truth value they do not have it on account of an existing state of affairs. There is no question of a possible 'correspondence' between a state of affairs and the uttered sentence that would make the sentence true. If it can be said to be true it is so because

---

[24] For a biographical sketch of John Austin, see Warnock (1963).

the speaker has made it true by pronouncing it in an appropriate situation. Such utterances Austin calls 'performative utterances' (a term for whose ugliness he apologizes in the paper of that title), and the theory that deals with them is called 'speech act theory'.

Performative utterances are a problem for the Aristotelian theory of truth. For they have the structure of normal sentences, yet they do not have a normal truth value, if they have any at all. This would seem to be in conflict with Aristotle's Principle of the Excluded Third, or the Bivalence Principle. We shall see in 6.2.4 below that performative utterances also pose serious problems, most of which are far from solved, for the grammatical and semantic analysis of sentences. We shall see, moreover that the theory of speech acts has important consequences for an appraisal of the position of language in social life.

- *Peter Frederick Strawson (1919)*

Unlike Austin, Strawson has been a prolific author. This is not the place to discuss his many contributions to philosophy. We shall single out his work on presuppositions, as that has contributed directly to linguistics, in particular semantics. Being intent on respecting natural language, he sympathised with those philosophers who felt that modern Russellian logic fails to do justice to the facts of language. He did not oppose the notion that language should be subjected to a formal analysis, but he did feel that Russell's analysis, especially his Theory of Descriptions (see 6.1.2.3), was too crude as it overlooked the essential semantic ingredient of presupposition. In the early 1950s he wrote two articles (Strawson 1950, 1954), and a few pages in his book on logic (1952:170-6), attacking Russell's analysis of definite descriptions and proposing the notion of presupposition. This proposal entailed a direct violation of Aristotle's venerated Principle of the Excluded Third, and therefore met with vehement resistance on the part of the logicians, Russell in particular. We note that this was the second attack on Aristotelian bivalence after Austin had come up with his performative utterances.

In Strawson's view, Russell tinkered with the facts of language. The logicians, however, felt that Strawson tinkered with good logic. In a bitter little article called 'Mr Strawson on Referring', in *Mind* of 1957, Russell retaliated, backed by the majority of logicians. Strawson's defence, in (1964), was weak and unconvincing, and he thus left the floor temporarily to the logicians. Yet his criticism was not only justified, it was also carried by a powerful intuition about presuppositions in language. That Strawson, for the time being at least, lost out against the logicians may be ascribed to the fact that his alternative analysis was too weak, not only from an observational point of view but also because it lacked logical sophistication as well as the backing of sufficiently developed notions of discourse semantics.

- *The end of Ordinary Language Philosophy in 1970*

Ordinary Language Philosophy flourished between 1945 and 1970. It lived mainly at Oxford but, owing to the very great prestige of the Oxford philosophers, it exerted a strong influence all over the Anglo-Saxon world, including Australia, New Zealand, and the English-speaking parts of America. During that period virtually all English-speaking philosophers of note passed through the Oxford machine. Around 1950 Gilbert Ryle had started a (still very popular) special two-year postgraduate BPhil course for philosophers, and this was what everyone came to Oxford to follow. Ordinary Language Philosophy thus came to be a household word in philosophy after the second world war.

Yet, although there had been significant successes, such as Ryle's reductionist programme of all things mental, presupposition theory and speech act theory, there was an ever stronger feeling that Ordinary Language Philosophy was leading nowhere. The main objective, which was to show that all metaphysical questions resulted from wrong verbiage, was likely to prove unrealistic, and the meticulous analysis of the usage of philosophically important terms such as 'good' or 'true' or 'ought to' was proving interesting but shallow. There was a general neglect of and even, occasionally, some contempt for formal systems and analyses, both in linguistics and in logic.

Thus, in order to prevent ruin it was decided, in the late 1960s, that the best way to preserve whatever good had come of Ordinary Language Philosophy and to avoid its downfall was to call a halt to it and become more traditional again and more evenhanded. The University instituted a chair of formal logic and a lectureship in linguistics in 1970, which is thus a convenient year to mark the end of the period of Ordinary Language Philosophy.

● *Russell's acrimonious reaction*

However, Ordinary Language Philosophy did not reign supreme in England during that period. For Russell looked down upon it with great contempt. In the little article in *Mind* of 1957 mentioned above he gave short shrift to Strawson's critique of his Theory of Descriptions:

> Suppose (which God forbid) Mr Strawson were so rash as to accuse his char-lady of thieving: she would reply indignantly, 'I ain't never done no harm to no one'. Assuming her a pattern of virtue, I should say that she was making a true assertion, although, according to the rules of syntax which Mr Strawson would adopt in his own speech, what she said would have meant: 'there was at least one moment when I was injuring the whole human race'. Mr Strawson would not have supposed that this was what she meant to assert, although he would not have used her words to express the same sentiment. Similarly, I was concerned to find a more accurate and analysed thought to replace the somewhat confused thoughts which most people at most times have in their heads.
>
> Mr Strawson objects to my saying that 'the King of France is wise' is false if there is no king of France. ... This is a purely verbal question; and although I have no wish to claim the support of common usage, I do not think that he can claim it either. ... I agree, however, with Mr Strawson's statement that ordinary language has no exact logic.   Russell (1957:388-9)

Earlier, in an essay entitled 'The Cult of "Common Usage"', published in Russell (1956), he writes:

The doctrine, as I understand it, consists in maintaining that the language of daily life, with words used in their ordinary meanings, suffices for philosophy, which has no need of technical terms or of changes in the signification of ordinary terms. I find myself totally unable to accept this view. I object to it:

(1)   Because it is insincere;
(2)   Because it is capable of excusing ignorance of mathematics, physics, and neurology in those who have had only a classical education;
(3)   Because it is advanced by some in a tone of unctuous rectitude, as if opposition to it were a sin against democracy;
(4)   Because it makes philosophy trivial;
(5)   Because it makes almost inevitable the perpetuation among philosophers of the muddle-headedness they have taken over from common sense.

(1) *Insincerity.* I will illustrate this by a fable. The Professor of Mental Philosophy, when called by his bedmaker one morning, developed a dangerous frenzy, and had to be taken away by the police in an ambulance. ... It happened that I, who live on the professor's staircase, overheard the following dialogue between the bedmaker and the policeman:

Policeman.   'Ere, I want a word with yer.
Bedmaker.   What do you mean – – 'A word'? I ain't done nothing.
Policeman.   Ah, that's just it. Yer ought to 'ave done something. Couldn't yer see that the pore gentleman was mental?
Bedmaker.   That I could. For an 'ole *hour* 'e went on something chronic. But when they're mental yer can't make them understand.

In this little dialogue, 'word', 'mean', 'mental', and 'chronic' are all used in accordance with common usage. They are not so used in the pages of *Mind* by those who pretend that common usage is what they believe in. ... What they believe in is the usage of persons who have their amount of education, neither more nor less. Less is illiteracy, more is pedantry – so we are given to understand.   Russell (1956:154-5)

Russell clearly had a deep and personal aversion to what he perceived as the anti-logical and anti-scientific attitudes displayed by culturally arrogant middle-class Oxonians with merely a classical education. To him, their claim to supremacy for 'ordinary language' was as ridiculous as any such claim put forward by really 'ordinary' people such as bedmakers or char-ladies.[25]

- *The Oxford School represents ecologism; Russell and formal semantics represent formalism*

In terms of the opposition, sketched in section 1.3, between analogism and anomalism, or their modern counterparts formalism and ecologism, it is clear that the Oxford School of Ordinary Language Philosopy is an outspoken representative of the ecologist approach. The formalist stronghold was located at Cambridge, in the person of Bertrand Russell.

It is interesting to see the ancient opposition re-emerge in modern times. Modern linguistics, with its Romanticist origin, is clearly ecologistic, though some recent developments smack more of formalism. Model-theoretic seman-

[25] Peter Strawson told me once that Quine, who considered Ordinary Language Philosophy a mixed blessing and was inclined to side with Russell, having spent a sabbatical at Oxford during the early 1950s, concluded his table speech at the farewell dinner given in his honour with the following words: 'From now on in future, whenever I hear ordinary language spoken, I shall think of Oxford.'

tics, its origins being firmly in logic, is clearly formalistic. Ordinary Language Philosophy is ecologistic again, and thus found it relatively easy to see eye to eye with linguistics. Formal semantics, on the other hand, has always suffered from the fact that it belongs in a totally different tradition from linguistics, the tradition of logic and formal analysis. It is also interesting to see that in Classical Antiquity it was the philosophers (especially those belonging to the Stoa) that were ecologists whereas the formalists were to be found among the grammarians from Alexandria and elsewhere. In modern times the roles are practically reversed. Nowadays the philosophers, but for the Ordinary Language Philosophers, are the formalists and the linguists (with the Ordinary Language Philosophers) are the ecologists.

6.2.3 Presuppositions

We shall now pass on to a discussion of presuppositions, a phenomenon in the semantics of language that does not fit at all into the established logical mould and is a prime example of how an ecologistic method of analysis can supplement, and to some extent supplant, the purely logical analysis.

6.2.3.1 History of the presupposition problem

6.2.3.1.1 *Eubulides of Megara*

• *The Megarian school of philosophy*

Presuppositions already caused Aristotle trouble. The trouble came from Megara, a town about thirty miles west of Athens. Megara had a small philosophy school that had been founded by a follower of Socrates called Euclides (±450-380 BC). His successor at the school was Eubulides, who originated from Miletus in Asia Minor. Little is known about Eubulides' life. He is said to have offered hospitality to Plato and some of his fellow Socratics immediately after Socrates' death in 399, when, for political reasons, they thought it safer to leave Athens (Plato, in fact, exiled himself from Athens till 387). It is also said that he took over the Megarian school in 380. Tradition has it, moreover, that he taught rhetoric to Demosthenes (384-322), the great Athenian public orator and politician who was the main obstacle to Macedonian power over Athens. If these reports are reliable he must have been Aristotle's senior by at least thirty-five years.

The links with Socrates, Plato and Demosthenes are relevant in that they show a political affiliation. Eubulides apparently sided with the Athenian nationalist party, who opposed Macedonian domination and were thus set against Alexander's reign, and also against Aristotle's presence in Athens.

• *Eubulides' paradoxes*

Eubulides is known in the history of philosophy for his so-called paradoxes, four in number. The most famous one is the *Liar Paradox*, which comes about, in its simplest form, when a sentence says of itself that it is false, or when two sentences say of each other that they are false. The paradox is that when such sentences are true they are at the same time false, and when they are false they are at the same time true. This paradox was a well-known riddle in Antiquity, and a frequent source of worry to Medieval as well as modern logicians. Tarski considered it important enough to set up his famous distinction between object language and metalanguage to get rid of it, adding the injunction that the two should never be mixed.[26]

The paradox is also found in St. Paul's Epistle to Titus (I. 12-13). In a diatribe against the evil Cretans, he writes, apparently unaware of the paradox:

> One of their own prophets said: 'Cretans always lie, the wicked beasts and lazy bellies', and he spoke the truth.

The 'prophet' in question is usually identified as the half-mythical Cretan poet Epimenides (6th century BC), which is why the paradox is also often called the *Epimenidan Paradox*.

Another paradox is the *Electra Paradox*, also called the *Paradox of the Hooded Man*. We have already discussed this, in 6.1.2.2, and we have seen that it constitutes Frege's second problem with regard to Aristotle's truth definition and the principle of Substitutio Salva Veritate.

Then there is the *Paradox of the Heap*, or the *Sorites* (from the Greek word *sōrós* 'heap'). It runs as follows. One grain of sand in an hourglass does not make a heap. Two grains do not make a heap. Ten grains do not make a heap. Five hundred grains, however, do make a heap. At what stage does it become true to say that there is a heap of sand? The implication is that there is an intermediate 'grey' area where it is neither entirely true nor entirely false to say that there is a heap. This paradox would seem to call into doubt the Aristotelian Principle of Bivalence, in particular the Principle of the Excluded Middle. It is a plea for recognition of the inherent vagueness of many common predicates.

Finally, we have the *Paradox of the Horns*, expressed as a somewhat salacious joke about cuckolds (unappreciated by Aristotle, one presumes):

> What you have not lost you still have. But you have not lost your horns. So you still have horns.

If this reasoning were correct one could argue that every person who has never worn horns wears them. It is this paradox that will occupy us in the present section. Kneale & Kneale's comment is as follows:

> [Paradoxes] of the fourth type show that if a statement (e.g. 'You have lost horns') involves a presupposition (e.g. that you once had horns) it may be negated either in a

---

[26] According to Kneale & Kneale (1962:228-9), late Medieval treatises on logic abounded with all kinds of solutions to the Liar Paradox. The solutions centered mainly around the concepts of *cassatio* (meaninglessness) and *restrictio* (restriction). Cassatio implied that sentences suffering from this paradox are meaningless (but no precise reason could be given why they should be so). Restrictio implied an injunction not to use such sentences. Clearly, Tarski's answer is a kind of restrictio. Kneale & Kneale (l.c.) observe correctly that this is 'too restrictive, since it wrongly excludes harmless self-reference such as that of the sentence "What I am now saying is a sentence of English".'

restricted way with acceptance of the same assumption or in an unrestricted way
without acceptance of that presupposition.   Kneale & Kneale (1962:114)

We shall see below that this comment is precisely right.

• *Why were the paradoxes not taken seriously until now?*

One by one these paradoxes have proved of the utmost importance for the
semantics of natural language. One may even say, without undue exaggeration,
that Eubulides formulated, in the 4th century BC, the central questions of natural language semantics as it has been practised in the 20th century (and will
be after, no doubt). In view of this fact it is odd, to say the least, that Euclides
should be depicted as merely one who 'wrote a lampoon against Aristotle'
(Cary et al. 1953, s.v. Eubulides). Kneale & Kneale are likewise puzzled:

> All [these paradoxes] are interesting, and it is incredible that Eubulides produced
> them in an entirely pointless way, as the tradition suggests. He must surely have
> been trying to illustrate some theses of Megarian philosophy, though it may be
> impossible for us to reconstruct the debates in which he introduced them. We shall
> find that even in the mangled form in which it was transmitted this part of Megarian
> teaching has been of some importance in the later history of logic.
>   Kneale & Kneale (1962:114-15)

Perhaps the answer is to be found in academic sociology, which existed then
as it does now. What the paradoxes have in common is that they all attack
the classic axioms of Aristotelian logic, the Principles of Contradiction and of
Bivalence (see 5.1.6). We know that Aristotle was rather prickly about these
matters and that there was considerable animosity between the two men, not
least because of their opposite political allegiances. We also know that
Aristotle had no real answer to his Megarian colleague's paradoxes. There are
some attempts at refutation in his *De Sophisticis Elenchis* (On Fallacies), but
they do not amount to much. Could it be that he was so enraged about these
frustrating paradoxes that he, or his followers, tried to write Eubulides out of
history? If so the attempt was almost successful.

• *Interesting parallel with Oxford versus Russell*

It is fascinating to see how history can repeat itself, even in irrelevant details. In Greece of the 4th century BC we see Aristotle, the creator of the first
system of formal logic, being attacked by the ecologist Eubulides, at a distance
of some thirty miles to the west, on account of the axioms of logic. In 20th
century England we have the Cambridge philosopher Bertrand Russell, the
major reformer of Aristotelian logic, attacked by the Oxonian Ordinary Language Philosophers, at a distance of some sixty miles to the west, again on
account of the Aristotelian axioms of logic. In both cases the ecologists had no
alternative formal system to offer, or anyway not to the extent that the
formalists had developed their formal systems. In both cases there was considerable irritation on the part of the formalists. There is one difference, however: whereas Aristotle was never known for any sense of humour, Russell
clearly was. Another difference, hopefully, is that perhaps this time the conflict will be brought to a satisfactory solution.

6.2.3.1.2 *Peter of Spain and Walter Burley*

Not much is known about work in presupposition theory during the remainder of Antiquity and the Middle Ages. If we are lucky we catch an occasional glimpse, but no systematic survey exists. One wonders if any such survey can be made at all given the scarcity of the sources available.

One such glimpse is granted us in the work of the Medieval Portuguese logician Peter of Spain (see Mullally 1945), who died in 1277 at the age of about sixty-five as Pope John XXI, having been elected to the papal throne in 1276.

In his *Tractatus Exponibilium* he deals with 'exponible' propositions, propositions containing words that are not parts of terms and thus need special explanation, such as *only, begin to, but for*. One class of 'exponibles' is found in the *propositiones exclusivae*, which contain words like *tantum* (only) or *solus* (alone). Perhaps following Abelard (Mullally 1945:lxxv) he divides these into two component propositions, a *propositio praeiacens*, literally 'proposition that lies before', and the actual predication. The *praeiacens* is what we call presupposition, but that term could not be used given the established use of *suppositio* as 'reference' (see 2.6.3).[27] The term *praeiacens* clearly expresses the intuition, elaborated in 6.2.3.3, that a presupposition is somehow temporally prior to its carrier sentence. A sentence like *Tantum homo est rationalis* (only man is rational) is divided into the *praeiacens* (presupposition) 'man is rational' and the predication 'no thing other than man is rational'.

Another author we have been able to unearth is Walter Burley (or Burleigh), who lived from ±1275 till after 1344, during the heyday of Speculative Grammar (see 1.4.2). Probably born in Yorkshire, he taught 'Artes' at Oxford as early as 1301, left for Paris in 1310, where he became Magister in Theology. In 1327 he was appointed by King Edward III to the papal court in Avignon. Several treatises by Burley on logic and on the theory of reference ('suppositio') have survived the malign neglect of the Middle Ages. Two of these, *De Consequentiis* (On Entailments) and *De Exclusivis* (On Propositions Containing Exclusive Terms), are of particular interest here (Stuart 1986:22-3).

In these he deals with the logical properties of the 'exclusive terms' *tantum* and *solus* mentioned above, closely following the analysis of Peter of Spain. Both the *praeiacens* and the predication must be true for the whole proposition to be true, which means that presuppositions are entailed:

> If the whole proposition is true both component propositions are true. If either is false, the whole proposition is false. ... From the whole proposition to its *praeiacens* is a valid conclusion.   Peter of Spain, *De Consequentiis*, from Stuart (1986:22-3)

Unfortunately, too little is known about Medieval presupposition theory. The sources are scarce and hard to get to, and it is extremely difficult to find out what influence it may have had on later generations.

---

[27] According to Horn (1985:123), referring to Mullally (1945), Peter of Spain 'employed the verb *praesupponere* in approximately the modern sense'. This is erroneous: Peter of Spain does not use the verb *praesupponere* at all, presumably for the reason indicated.

6.2.3.1.3   *Frege's approach to presuppositions*

The modern history of presupposition theory probably starts with a footnote in Frege (1884), quoted in 6.2.3.1.4, but anyway with Frege (1892), already discussed in 6.1.2 above. For Frege, the use of a definite term normally presupposes ('setzt voraus') the real existence of its reference object. When we say *The moon is smaller than the earth* we presuppose that there is a real moon and a real earth, and we say of the former that it is smaller than the latter (Frege 1892:31). Only if this presupposition is fulfilled can the sentence have a truth value. If it is not fulfilled the sentence may still have a sense or meaning, as happens in fictional, often literary, contexts but it lacks a truth value. Most sentences in Homer's Odyssey, for example, are without a truth value:

> Why is the thought not sufficient for us? Because and to the extent that we care about its truth value. This is not always the case. When we listen to an epic poem, for example, it is, besides the euphony of the language, only the sense of the sentences and the images and feelings evoked by them that will captivate us. But as soon as we ask if it is all true we take leave of the artistic pleasure and embark on a scientific investigation. For that reason it is a matter of total indifference to us whether the name *Ulysses*, for example, has a reference as long as we take the poem to be no more than a work of art. It is, therefore, the effort to achieve truth that pushes us forward everywhere from the sense to the reference.   Frege (1892:33)

This argument is part of Frege's vision of a compositional calculus. In a model (see 5.5.1 and 5.5.2), the truth value of a simple sentence is computed by feeding the term extensions into the function denoted by the predicate. Since predicates denote characteristic functions, the resulting value is a truth value. Now, clearly, if one of the terms lacks an extension there is no, or a deficient, input to the predicate function and no truth value can result.

The notion of presupposition is not at all prominent in Frege (1892). The term *presuppose* ('voraussetzen') is not a technical term in that article. It is used in its ordinary, natural meaning, only to support the thesis that truth values can be computed compositionally by means of a categorial calculus. It is not until Strawson takes up the issue again, more than half a century later, that presupposition theory takes off as a serious part of semantics.

Meanwhile we note that Frege and Strawson discussed only *existential presupposition*. The presupposition that Eubulides presented in his Paradox of the Horns was of a different kind, to do with the lexical predicate *have lost*. And the presuppositions associated with terms like *only*, as studied by Peter of Spain and Walter Burley, are different again. Whether we are entitled to group all these phenomena under the common denominator of 'presupposition' is a natural question which, however, we cannot go into here (see Seuren 1994). Here we observe that in recent years the reverse process has taken place. After Strawson had put existential presuppositions on the map, some linguists (re)-discovered lexical and other types of presupposition. Fillmore (1971) raised the issue of the presuppositional properties of the predicates *accuse* and *criticize*. Kiparsky & Kiparsky (1971) introduced the notion of factive presupposition (see 6.2.3.2 below). Horn (1969) called attention to the presuppositions induced by words like *only* and *even*.

6.2.3.1.4 *Geach on presuppositions*

There is a curious little article of 1950, written by Peter Geach, then at Cambridge, where the concept of presupposition is used in, let us say, the old-fashioned way, not restricted to existential presupposition. The article is a critique of Russell's Theory of Descriptions (see 6.1.2.3), first on account of its failure to recognize presuppositions in ordinary language, then on account of Russell and Whitehead's defective definition of the iota operator in *Principia Mathematica*. About the former, Geach writes:

> On Russell's view 'the King of France is bald' is a false assertion. This view seems to me to commit the fallacy of 'many questions'. To see how this is so, let us take a typical example of the fallacy: the demand for 'a plain answer – yes or no!' to the question 'have you been happier since your wife died?' Three questions are here involved:
>
> 1.   Have you ever had a wife?
> 2.   Is she dead?
> 3.   Have you been happier since then?
>
> The act of asking question 2 presupposes an affirmative answer to question 1; if the true answer to 1 is negative, question 2 *does not arise*. The act of asking question 3 presupposes an affirmative answer to question 2; if question 2 does not arise, or if the answer to it is negative, question 3 *does not arise*. When a question does not arise, the only proper way of answering it is to say so and explain the reason; the 'plain' affirmative or negative answer, though grammatically possible, is *out of place*. (I do not call it 'meaningless' because the word is a mere catchword nowadays.) This does not go against the laws of contradiction and excluded middle; what these laws tell us is that *if* the question arose 'yes' and 'no' would be exclusive alternatives.
>
> Similarly, the question 'Is the present King of France bald?' involves two other questions:
>
> 4.   Is anybody at the moment a King of France?
> 5.   Are there at the moment different people each of whom is a King of France?
>
> And it does not arise unless the answer to 4 is affirmative and the answer to 5 is negative.   Geach (1950:84-5)

We shall see below that Geach is wrong in saying that this does not violate the law of excluded middle. What Geach has in mind is a gapped bivalent logic, which does violate PET, and hence the law of excluded middle. But the interesting thing about this article is that it takes us back to Peter of Spain and Walter Burley, with the additional benefit that the existential presupposition is brought in line with other kinds of presupposition. Whether there is a historical path from the Medieval authors to Geach or Frege is unclear, but there is a footnote in Frege (1884:87-8), mentioned by Geach, which runs as follows:

> The expression 'the largest real fraction', for example, has no content because the definite article has a claim to the possibility of pointing at a unique object. ... If one were to determine, by means of this concept, an object that falls under it, two things would no doubt have to be shown first:
>
> 1.   that there is an object falling under this concept;
> 2.   that there is no more than one object falling under it.
>
> Since the first of these assertions is already false, the expression 'the largest real fraction' makes no sense.   Frege (1884:87-8)

Somehow, therefore, there is a connection, whether historical or simply because of parallel ways of thinking, between the Medievals, Frege and Geach.

6.2.3.1.5   *Strawson's analysis of presuppositions*

At Oxford, meanwhile, Peter Strawson worked at his own critique of Russell's
Theory of Descriptions. In 1950 he published his article 'On Referring', the
title a clear echo of Russell's 'On Denoting'. His attack on Russell's theory has
the form of an alternative analysis which, Strawson claims, agrees better
with the facts of natural language. We have already seen that Russell treats
this alternative with outright contempt. Yet we shall argue that Strawson,
and not Russell, was on the right track, even if we are compelled to point out
some flaws in Strawson's analysis.

- *Occasion sentences restored*

Strawson begins with restoring occasion sentences (see 5.1.6) to their rightful
position. Russell had undertaken to make them disappear by analysing definite descriptions in terms of quantifiers. His basically Aristotelian programme, which was later continued by Quine, consisted in reducing all occasion
sentences to eternal sentences. Strawson pointed out that it is much more sensible to say that sentences as such, that is as types, do not have a truth value
and should not be expected to have one. Only assertive sentences that are
actually uttered, or conceived, in an appropriate context, statements in his
terminology, can be expected to have a truth value.

The normal or prototypical sentence has to be anchored in discourse to acquire a truth value. Suppose I produce the sentence (to hark back to Geach's
example) *He has been happier since his wife died* out of the blue, for example
in an English language class to discuss its grammatical and semantic properties. I would make myself look ridiculous if I asked the students if this sentence is true or false. I can ask what the subject is, what the meaning is of the present perfect tense *has been*, etc. But I cannot reasonably ask whether the sentence is true or false. That is possible only if the sentence is properly anchored
in discourse, so that it is known who is meant by *he* and in such a way that it is
also understood that that person is a widower. Or, as Strawson has it, if the
sentence is used as a statement.

There are, of course, also eternal sentences. These need no special contextual
anchoring. Consider *Once upon a time there was a wicked queen*. This sentence,
regardless of any special context, is no doubt true when uttered now, but must
have been false once, before there were any wicked queens. Such cases, however, Strawson maintains, are marginal cases of occasion sentences. Their contextual anchoring happens to be unrestricted. Strawson thus makes use of the
common mathematical ploy to reduce marginal cases to proper cases. Just as in
mathematics every set is a subset, but not a *proper* subset, of itself, in semantics
eternal sentences need to be anchored, though not, if you like, *properly* anchored, in discourse to receive a truth value. Whereas Russell wished to reduce
occasion sentences to eternal sentences, Strawson does the opposite.

- *Unanchored 'proper' occasion sentences have no truth value*

It is thus possible to have unanchored 'proper' occasion sentences, like *He has been happier since his wife died* produced out of the blue. And it follows that such products do not have a truth value. This consequence, however, is relatively trivial and unimportant. Defenders of the Bivalence Principle are free to retort that such sentences do not express or contain a proposition, and that the Bivalence Principle, and logic in general, applies to propositions, which can be asserted to express a commitment with respect to the way the world is, not to sentences as abstract grammatical objects.

- *Does a false anchoring point also lead to a lack of truth value?*

Strawson, however, like Geach quoted above, goes further. It may be found that one of the anchoring points of a well-anchored occasion sentence is unsound, or false. If such falsity passes undetected nothing happens: the story goes on untrammelled, as when I spin a yarn about a non-existent duke of Lombardy, saying all sorts of things about him, and am believed by my gullible audience. But the moment I introduce the fictitious duke my story radically departs from reality in that subsequent sentences will fit into a context that has long lost its correspondence with the world as it is.

In Strawson's (and Geach's) view a sentence which is otherwise well-anchored but whose contextual anchoring is false in one or more respects, also lacks a truth value, no matter whether the falsity of the anchoring point or points in question is known or unknown to the discourse participants. Strawson thus makes no distinction between, on the one hand, an unanchored occasion sentence presented out of the blue and therefore not expressing a propositional commitment, and, on the other, a well-anchored occasion sentence which does express a propositional commitment but whose contextual anchoring does not correspond with reality.

The former kind of sentence is not a statement and does not express a commitment with regard to the way the world is. It lacks a truth value for the simple reason that it is not the kind of object that can bear one. To say that it has a truth value is a category mistake, just as it would be a category mistake to say that my son's motorbike is true or false.

The latter kind of sentence, which is well-anchored but with a faulty context, is normally said to suffer from presupposition failure. For these sentences it is not obvious at all that they lack a truth value. They can be used to express a propositional commitment, and the question of their truth or falsity, therefore, most certainly does arise.

- *Now the Bivalence Principle is affected*

Strawson's argument is not about unanchored occasion sentences but about sentences suffering from presupposition failure. He does recognize that they express a propositional commitment, and concludes that they must be taken into account in propositional logic, unlike motorbikes or unanchored sentences. Yet he also stresses repeatedly that 'the question of their truth or falsity simply does not arise', which is odd given the fact they do contain a real well-anchored proposition.

It seems that we must accept that the question of the truth or falsity of sentences suffering from presupposition failure does arise. The very history of presupposition theory, where this question keeps arising, proves the point. But if we disregard this detail and look at Strawson's analysis as it is, we see that he envisages a logic where propositions are allowed to lack a truth value, besides being either true or false. This idea makes perfect sense and is implementable as a system of propositional logic, known as a *gapped bivalent logic*. Now a gapped bivalent logic violates the Aristotelian Principle of the Excluded Third or Bivalence Principle. Geach's reassuring statement, quoted above, that this Principle is not at issue is therefore incorrect. The question of truth and falsity does arise, and the lack of a truth value is a third option, not admitted by the Aristotelian principle.

• *Strawson's analysis of existential presuppositions fits into Frege's calculus* It must be observed that, to the extent that existential presuppositions are concerned, the Fregean concept of compositional categorial calculus automatically leads to the conclusion, as we have seen, that sentences suffering from reference failure for one or more of their terms lack a truth value. This is inherent in the Fregean programme. For Strawson, reference failure is the same as failure of an existential presupposition, and as long as the analysis remains restricted to existential presuppositions he can claim support from Frege. But how about other kinds of presupposition, like the one induced by the predicate *have lost*, or by *only*? Here Frege's analysis says nothing about the loss of a truth value.

If Strawson's theory of presupposition is to cover not only cases of existential presupposition but all other cases as well, which is certainly what is intended, there are questions to answer. One serious question certainly arises if the other, non-existential presuppositions resist treatment in terms of a truth-value-gap. If for those cases it appears more fruitful to set up, for example, a three-valued logic, with the third value for sentences with presupposition failure, a way will have to be found to escape from the Fregean conclusion that failure of existential presupposition necessarily leads to the lack of a truth value. We shall see in 6.2.6.1 that the assumption of the reality, but not the existence, of intensional entities will answer that question.

• *Presupposition and negation in Strawson's analysis: Eubulides' paradox still unsolved. The Bivalence Principle is now seriously at risk.* Quite apart from the logical aspects of non-bivalent logics, which must remain undiscussed here, let us consider Strawson's analysis of negation. Natural language negation, in Strawson's view, is presupposition-preserving. That is, if a sentence *B* presupposes, and therefore entails, *A* (that is, $B \gg A$ and $B \models A$), then *not-B* still presupposes, and therefore entails, *A* (*not-B* $\gg A$; *not-B* $\models A$). Thus, let *B* be the sentence *You have lost your horns*, which presupposes *A*: *You had horns before*, and asserts that the possession of horns by the addressee has come to an end. For Strawson, the negation of *B*, *You have not lost your horns*, still presupposes *You had horns before* but asserts that the possession of horns by the addressee has not come to an end: *not* negates only the assertive content of a sentence, but leaves the presuppositional entailment intact.

Since this goes for anything one may have lost or not lost, Strawson can say, with Eubulides, *What you have not lost you still have*. But the minor of Eubulides' Paradox of the Horns runs: *You have not lost your horns*. If this preserves the same presupposition *You had horns before*, the paradoxical conclusion that the addressee still has horns will hold. In order to undo the paradox it is necessary to accept that the negation in *You have not lost your horns* is not presupposition-preserving. Hence the comment by Kneale & Kneale (1962:114), quoted in 6.2.3.1.1, that 'if a statement involves a presupposition ... it may be negated either in a restricted way with acceptance of the same assumption or in an unrestricted way without acceptance of that presupposition.' In order to solve the paradox we must accept that the negation in *You have not lost your horns* is of the 'unrestricted' kind.

Strawson's presupposition theory is thus unable to solve the Paradox of the Horns. To solve that it seems necessary to assume a distinction between a 'restricted' and an 'unrestricted' negation, as proposed by Kneale & Kneale. If that distinction is incorporated into the logic any variety of bivalence, whether strict or gapped, must be given up.

- *Does the definite article induce an existential presupposition?*

Another problem with Strawson's presupposition theory is the following. If the definite article *the* and the universal quantifier *all* (as is proposed in Strawson 1952:174-6) carry with them an existential presupposition, then it should not be possible to deny the existence of a supposed entity by using a sentence of the form *The so-and-so does not exist*. Let us agree that there is nothing in this world that corresponds to the Monster of Loch Ness. It follows from Strawson's theory that the sentence *The Monster of Loch Ness exists* not only asserts but also presupposes the existence of that mysterious entity, ánd must be deemed to lack a truth value because *The monster of Loch Ness exists* is false! Likewise, the sentence *The Monster of Loch Ness does not exist* asserts its non-existence but presupposes its existence, ánd should suffer from a lack of truth value because it is true! But these sentences are simply false and true, respectively, if the Monster of Loch Ness does not exist, and the theory should account for that (see Atlas 1989:91-119 for a perceptive discussion).[28]

- *Strawson's analysis under heavy attack from logicians*

Whereas the linguistic world, to the extent that it was taking notice, was rather enthusiastic about Strawson's analysis of presuppositions, the logicians growled. Strawson's publications on presupposition (mainly Strawson 1950,

---

[28] A solution to this problem is given if it is assumed that the definite article does not induce a presupposition of existence but requires uniqueness of the discourse address to be selected by the definite description at issue. Then real existence does not follow from the word *the* but from the extensional character of the predicate in question with regard to the term in question.

1952, 1954, 1964) released an avalanche of mostly angry reactions by logicians decrying what they saw as his irresponsible handling of established logical principles. On balance, however, one must say that Strawson took no greater liberties with logic than Frege did, and his handling of logical issues was, if perhaps not presented in the clearest possible way, certainly competent. The real question is not whether Strawson's logic is sound but whether his analysis fits the facts of language. There is still no generally accepted answer to this question.

6.2.3.2   The projection problem and the entailment analysis

After Strawson's publications on presupposition there have been some developments, which, however, are considered too recent and still too open to controversy to deserve a full treatment in the present context.[29] We will, therefore, merely point at some major proposals.

- *Karttunen's treatment of the projection problem*

Around 1970 the Finnish-American linguist Lauri Karttunen drew attention to what has since been called the 'projection problem' of presuppositions (see esp. Karttunen 1973, 1974). The problem consists in determining under what conditions, in what form and why a presupposition P carried by a carrier sentence C is 'projected' upwards when C is placed under a higher operator.

Some operators are 'holes': they preserve the presupposition P in an undiminished, fully entailing form. These operators generally preserve entailments, and hence also presuppositional entailments. The factive predicates, such as *know, realize, have forgotten, regrettable*, fall under this category. They induce the presupposition that the embedded *that*-clause if true. But other entailing operators, such as the conjunction *and*, belong to this group of operators as well.

Other operators are 'filters'. These generally let presuppositions of embedded clauses through but in a weakened form, no longer as full entailments but as more or less strong suggestions, invited inferences, or default assumptions (DAs). For example, a sentence like:

(32)   Joe believes that his son lives in Kentucky

does not entail, but it strongly suggests that Joe has a son. This suggestion can be undone by preceding context, for example when (32) is uttered in a context where it has been established that Joe has no son. In such a case the listener will draw certain conclusions about Joe's mental soundness.

The predicate *believe* is thus a filter. So are *or, if, not*. The sentence:

(33)   Either Joe's son lives in Kentucky or Joe doesn't like travelling

does not entail but does suggest that Joe has a son. Yet the operator *or* does not always let presuppositions of its argument propositions through as DA's. In:

(34)   Either Joe's son lives in Kentucky or Joe has no son

---

[29] See Seuren (in prep.) for a full discussion of the notion of presupposition.

no suggestion is left that Joe has a son. Similar phenomena occur with implications, and with *not* (as we shall see in an instant).

A third category of higher operators is called 'plugs': they stop all presuppositions of the embedded clause C, even in the weakened form of a DA. Examples are predicates like *try to convince, suggest* or *say*. A sentence like:

(35)   Joe says that his son lives in Kentucky

does not even suggest that Joe has a son, since he may spin any yarn he likes.

For about ten or fifteen years the projection problem of presuppositions dominated the literature on presupposition theory. No satisfactory solution, however, was presented. The 'filters', especially, proved resistant to all attempts at getting them under control. Nowadays it is felt that a solution to the projection problem will have to be an integral part of a general discourse-oriented theory of presupposition. Attempts at treating it in isolation have met with failure.

• *The entailment analysis of presupposition*
Meanwhile, around 1975, an attempt was made to ban presupposition from semantics altogether and relegate it to pragmatics. The main authors were Wilson (1975) and Boër and Lycan (1976).

Taking Strawson's thesis that presuppositions are preserved under negation as their point of departure, they argued that this is not so, since negation is, in Karttunen's terms, a filter: it lets presuppositions through merely as a DA and not as a full entailment. This is shown by the consistency of sequences like:

(36)a.   The King of France is NOT bald. There ís no King of France!
    b.   David is NOT divorced. He has never been married!

Admittedly, there is a suggestion or DA that France has a king and that David once entered matrimony, respectively, but these are not entailments.

Since suggestions or default assumptions are not the business of logic, logic has nothing to do with presuppositions and can carry on as before, unperturbed. Logically speaking, presuppositions are just entailments. Whatever is presuppositional is to be accounted for by pragmatics, one way or another. This analysis was dubbed the entailment analysis of presupposition.

This analysis would have a great deal going for it had it not suffered from two serious weaknesses. First, the pragmatic part of the bargain has never been honoured: pragmatics has so far been conspicuously unable to provide a rational account for presuppositional phenomena. Secondly, and more seriously, although in most cases the negation word *not* can, apparently, override the DA whereby the presupposition is left intact, there are uses of sentence negation where the presupposition of the non-negated sentence cannot be overridden and is left intact as a full entailment. Consider, for example:

(37)a.   Only Trevor was caught   ≫   Trevor was caught
    b.   Not only Trevor was caught   ≫   Trevor was caught

The standardly accepted analysis is that (37a) presupposes, and thus entails, that Trevor was caught, and asserts that no-one else was. The normal negation of (37a) is (37b).[30] But (37b) still presupposes, and entails, that Trevor was caught. It is grossly incoherent to say, for example, (38), no matter how strong an accent is placed on *not* to make it cancel the presupposition:

(38)   !Not only Trevor was caught, he wasn't caught at all!

It seems that there is a connection between the presupposition-preserving character of the negation in (37b) and (38) and its position at the beginning of the sentence. What has transpired (Seuren 1985:230-2) is that negation in 'non-canonical' position is necessarily presupposition-preserving, where 'canonical position' is defined as 'in construction with the finite verb'.

The same is found when sentence negation is morphologically incorporated (and not standing immediately over an existential quantifier, as in *nobody*, *never*). In such cases, too, presuppositions are preserved. Turkish, for example, normally incorporates negation, and such negations preserve presuppositions:

(39) !Ben Kemal-ın araba-sı-nı   al- ma- dı- m.   Kemal-ın araba-sı yok
       I   Kemal's   car-his-ACC buy-not-PAST-1sg. Kemal's car-his is-not
       'I didn't buy Kemal's car. Kemal has no car.'

The presupposition is that Kemal had a car. If he did not have one (39) cannot serve as a corrective answer to the inappropriate question (40), no matter how much emphasis is given to the negation morpheme *-ma-*:

(40) Sen Kemal-ın araba-sı-nı al- dı - n - mı?   'Did you buy Kemal's car?'
      you Kemal's   car-his-ACC buy-PAST-2sg-question particle

Turkish has no direct translation of *I did NOT buy Kemal's car: he hád no car.* The Horns Paradox, in other words, does not translate into Turkish.[31]

Thirdly, factive clauses and nominalizations in subject position keep their presuppositions:

(41)a. That Trevor died did not surprise her   »   Trevor died
     b. Trevor's death did not surprise her   »   Trevor died

The conclusion must, therefore, be that there are natural language sentences where the negation does preserve presuppositions as full entailments, without the presuppositions in question being necessary truths (which are entailed by any sentence). This conclusion is fatal for the entailment analysis, which claims the adequacy of standard logic for the logical analysis of natural language, and it necessitates a revision of standard ideas about the logic of natural language. Such a revision will have to bear on the very foundations of the logical system, as it involves a violation of the age-old Aristotelian Bivalence Principle.

---

[30] Note that *Only Trevor was not caught* is not the negation of (37a): it presupposes that Trevor was not caught, and asserts that every-one else was. Curiously, Peter of Spain and Walter Burley deny the validity of (37b), no doubt because they saw trouble ahead.

[31] According to Horn (1985:164) 'The normal Turkish negation *-mA-* is similarly restricted, with the suppletive periphrastic form *değil* showing up in contrastive and other contexts.' I have, however, not been able to find an informant producing a sentence with *değil* in the presupposition-cancelling sense.

6.2.3.3 The discourse nature of presupposition

- *Presupposition is not a logical phenomenon*

But will such a major revision solve the presupposition problem? In an ancillary way it may help, but a logical analysis stands little chance of revealing the true nature of presupposition in language. Presupposition does not seem to be a phenomenon that can be adequately captured in terms of logical entailment. Even if natural language *not*, or a particular use of *not*, is such that it preserves presuppositional entailments, such a fact cannot be used to define the phenomenon we wish to recognize as presupposition. The reason is simple. If presupposition is defined as follows, in terms of a non-bivalent logic:

Def-1 $B \gg A =_{Def} B \models A$ and not-$B \models A$

then all necessary truths must be taken to be presupposed by any arbitrary sentence. This is so because necessary truths are vacuously entailed by any arbitrary sentence, and therefore by any sentence B and its negation not-B. Moreover, any sentence B that is necessarily never true will presuppose anything, for the well-known reason that a sentence that is necessarily never true vacuously entails anything. In such a case B is either necessarily false in the sense that not-B is necessarily true, or B has by logical necessity fallen into the third option, the *tertium* disallowed in strictly bivalent logic, in which case both B and not-B are necessarily never true. All this according to Def-1.

In logic, such vacuous entailments are taken to be harmless. But as soon as the entailment relation is treated as an empirical phenomenon vacuous entailments become a major nuisance. This is what is happening here: as was observed by Peter of Spain, Walter Burley, Frege, Geach, Strawson and many others, presuppositions are an integral part of the meaning of what is said. A purely logical definition, which would allow us to say that *I like ice-cream* presupposes *All bachelors are unmarried*, would deprive the notion of presupposition of all its empirical content.

We may, if it is found that natural language *not* preserves presupposition, regard this as a logical property of presupposition in the following way:

Logical Property: If $B \gg A$ then $B \models A$ and not-$B \models A$

But this means that the notion of presupposition is still to be defined.

- *Presupposition is to be defined as a discourse phenomenon*

The defining feature of presupposition seems to be the fact that a sentence B_A (i.e. B presupposing A) is fit for use only in a discourse that already contains the information carried by A. A discourse or, more properly, a discourse domain is seen as a cognitive 'working space' for the interpretation of new incoming utterances. The information carried by each new utterance is added to the information already stored in the discourse domain. The technical term for this specific form of 'adding' information to a given discourse domain is *incrementation*. How exactly incrementation is best considered to take place is still very much a question of ongoing investigation: hypotheses and mechanisms are being tried out in various quarters (see 6.2.6). What counts here is that a sentence B_A is considered unusable in a discourse not allowing for the incrementation of A.

• *Negation is presupposition-preserving: the Negation Principle*
When a sentence B_A is fit for a given discourse **D**, then not-B_A is likewise fit for incrementation in **D**, where *not* is the normal unmarked sentence negation of natural language and not the highly marked radical negation (see e.g. Seuren 1988) or Horn's (1985) metalinguistic negation. That is, we establish the Negation Principle:

Negation Principle: If B ≫ A then also not-B ≫ A

thereby matching the Logical Property just given. When not-B is incremented to **D** this means that B's papers, so to speak, are in order yet it is rejected because that is how the speaker chooses to tell his story. Given the defining property of presupposition, which says that a sentence B_A is fit for use only in a discourse that already contains the incrementation of A, and given the Negation Principle, which says that if B presupposes A then so does not-B, it follows that if A is disallowed in the discourse at hand, then both B and not-B must likewise be considered disallowed.

• *Criteria of usability of sentences in a discourse*
As far as can be judged at the present state of the enquiry, there are two possible reasons for the incrementation of a sentence A, or of a sentence B entailing A, to be disallowed in a discourse **D**, a logical and a cognitive reason. A is blocked for logical reasons if **D** already contains information entailing the non-truth of A, in which case the incrementation of A would make **D** inconsistent. A is blocked for cognitive reasons if **D** fails to represent a recognizable state of affairs that makes functional sense in a given context. For example, many fully grammatical sentences express a relation of possession or belonging, but not all such sentences 'make functional sense'. If I say:

(42)   Harry's living room has a very nice front page

there is cognitive protest as long as the listener has not been told what the functional relation is between a front page and a living room. Therefore, unless such contextualization has been provided, a sentence like (42), or any other sentence that entails (42), will be refused for incrementation.

In any actual discourse where a sentence B is used, the presuppositions of B thus restrict the 'universe of interpretation' or 'setting' in terms of which B is to be interpreted. In this respect presupposition differs radically from ordinary entailment. For there is no requirement for ordinary entailments to precede their carrier sentences in discourse, whereas for presuppositions there is.

• *Accommodation or post hoc suppletion of presuppositions*
The fact that presuppositions restrict the 'setting' in terms of which their carrier sentences are to be interpreted makes for a hugely important phenomenon in verbal communication. The point is that it is not necessary for A to be explicitly pronounced before B can be uttered. What happens normally is that a sentence B_A is uttered without A having occurred yet in the discourse. A is

then quickly slipped in post hoc, so as to make B_A interpretable. This process is known as *accommodation* (Lewis 1970) or *post hoc suppletion* (Seuren 1985).

To use an example given in Karttunen (1974), a speaker may say:

(43)   We regret that pets are not allowed in the precinct

He may do so without first having to actually utter the factive presupposition that goes with the verb *regret*, which would have resulted in the stilted:

(44)   Pets are not allowed in the precinct, and we regret that

Post hoc suppletion is extremely common. It is made possible by the fact that presuppositions are systematically retrievable from the sentences that carry them. Although there is as yet no generally accepted analysis of the structural source of presuppositions in their carrier sentences, enough is known to trace them back to so-called presupposition inducers, which are often lexical verbs, sometimes expressions like *only* or *even*, and sometimes constructions like clefts or pseudoclefts. This means that anyone with a sufficient command of the language in question will grasp the presuppositions of a sentence on hearing or reading the sentence. If one or more of its presuppositions have not been actually uttered in preceding discourse the competent listener will simply supply them cognitively post hoc. This makes it unnecessary for a presupposition to be pronounced in full: owing to the fact that sentences carry presuppositions, a speaker may say things without actually saying them. Not only does this make for an enormous saving of energy in the verbal transmission of information, it also opens the way towards all kinds of communicative and literary devices, ranging from the coarse to the extremely subtle. This, however, is an aspect we must regrettably leave undiscussed in this context.

6.2.4   Speech acts

Speech act theory is fraught with problems, most of which are still unsolved. In fact, most problems of speech act theory have proved so stubborn that not much progress can be reported over the past thirty or so years. That speech act theory is crucial to an adequate understanding of language is generally agreed. But few researchers seem inclined to try and do something about it.

The speech act character of (utterances of) sentences is problematic for the logical analysis of sentences and thus for model-theoretic semantics. For that reason speech act theory was relegated, for some time, to pragmatics. Nowadays, however, it is generally recognized that the speech act quality of a sentence is part of its meaning, so that speech act theory should be considered part of semantics, not of pragmatics.

The semantic aspect of a speech act is not realized in the truth-conditionally defined relation a sentence may have with respect to a given real or imagined situation, and is thus not part of truth-conditional, model-theoretic semantics. But if semantics is redefined as discourse semantics, speech act theory is clearly part of it, since speech act qualities manifest themselves in the many forms of communicative verbal interaction that we call discourse.

- *Performative utterances*

As was said in section 6.2.2.2 above, one of the major and probably lasting achievements of Ordinary Language Philosophy was the discovery of speech acts by John Austin. As a latter-day Eubulides, Austin succeeded in disturbing the Aristotelian dream of Bivalence. He did so by asking simply: is a sentence like (45) true or false if pronounced seriously and on an appropriate occasion:

(45)   I hereby promise to return your book by tomorrow

What could make it false? And if it is true it is not so in virtue of an existing state of affairs that makes it true. In fact, if it is true it is so in virtue of the fact that it has been pronounced seriously and on an appropriate occasion, i.e. well-anchored. As Austin says, sentences of this kind make themselves true by being uttered 'felicitously'. For that reason he decided to call them *performative utterances*: they bring about their own truth – a situation not catered for in Aristotelian truth theory or in 20th century model theory.

An important caveat is in order here. One may produce a performative utterance felicitously, i.e. seriously and appropriately, without being sincere. One may make a promise and never intend to keep it. If one does, the promise is no less valid, as is proved by the fact that a person making an insincere promise can nevertheless be held accountable for the promise made. Sincerity, in other words, plays no role in the theory of speech acts, despite the confusion sometimes found in the literature (in particular Austin 1962:9-11) on this score.

- *Performative utterances parade as ordinary assertions*

Performative utterances are tricky. Sometimes the listener is alerted to them by the use of the first person singular (occasionally also plural) and the simple present tense, together with the word *hereby*. But the word *hereby* must be token-reflexive, that is, it must refer to the very act of speaking, not to anything else occurring at the same time. For example, suppose Alexander had said, while raising his axe in order to cut the Gordian Knot:

(46)   I hereby cut this knot

he would not have produced a performative utterance, despite his use of the word *hereby*. For here, *hereby* is not token-reflexive but refers to the action of raising the axe and letting it come down on the knot. By uttering (46) Alexander would not have had to worry his teacher Aristotle.[32]

So even totally explicit performative utterances such as (45) are not uniquely characterized by their grammatical form. But many performative utterances are not entirely explicit. Sometimes the result is simply stated, with or without *hereby*. Consider the following cases:

(47)a.   I hereby declare you husband and wife
   b.   You are hereby husband and wife

---

32 It is interesting to note, in this connection, that standard model-theory, following Russell's and Tarski's ban on mixing object language and metalanguage, forbids token-reflexivity absolutely. As was noted by Kneale & Kneale (see note 26 above), this modern 'restrictio' places unreasonable constraints on natural language use.

c. You are now husband and wife
d. You are husband and wife

Sometimes a performative utterance is not even a statement, as in:

(48)   Praise be to our Lord!

which by itself bestows praise on the Lord. The effect caused by a performative utterance may even be brought about without any utterance at all, as when a brave soldier takes a step forward, thereby offering himself for a dangerous mission, or when a police officer, instead of saying *You are free to go*, simply waves his hand in a gesture of dismissal. It is thus clear that there is no safe grammatical criterion for identifying performative utterances. There may be indications, but these are neither sufficient nor necessary.

• *Impossibility of drawing up a list of performative verbs*

It has likewise proved impossible to define performative utterances on lexical grounds. Austin (1962:149-163) made an attempt, what he called (1962:150) 'a flounder around', at listing the verbs that can be used performatively, but added immediately that he was 'far from happy about all of them'. This has not changed since Austin gave his William James Lectures in 1955. What makes a performative utterance performative, as we shall see presently, is not the selection of a particular lexical predicate from a list but the bringing about of an element of social reality. And just as an object can be named by a virtually limitless variety of nominal expressions (a picture can be called a picture, but also a work of art, a piece of trash, Susanna's cherished treasure, that thing over there, etc., etc.), an act that brings about an element of social reality can be characterized by a virtually limitless variety of verbal expressions.

• *Performative utterances and speech acts. What is a speech act?*

Performative utterances play an important part in the theory of speech acts. A speech act is an utterance act (an act of speaking or writing) whereby the speaker (or writer) creates a socially valid effect of some kind with regard to the proposition expressed in the utterance. It is a remarkable fact about language that it does not allow one to utter a 'pure' proposition. One cannot express a mere mental picture of a state of affairs, like 'Mary making pies' (Lewis 1946:49), without adding some kind of social commitment. Language is not just a system for the representation of states of affairs, but necessarily involves socially valid effects, usually commitments. This fact says something about the intrinsically social and communicative function of language.

Every utterance of a sentence is thus a speech act. Moreover, every (uttered) sentence can be ponderously rephrased as a performative utterance by making the social commitment explicit. Thus, instead of saying (49a), one might utter the performatively explicit (49b), and likewise for (50)-(52):

(49)a. Joe was washing his car
    b. I hereby assert that Joe was washing his car

(50)a. Was Joe washing his car?
    b. I hereby ask if Joe was washing his car

(51)a. Joe was washing his car, wasn't he?
  b. I hereby suggest that Joe was washing his car

(52)a. Joe, wash your car
  b. I hereby order you, Joe, to wash your car

Each of these sentences, when uttered seriously and appropriately, establishes a committal relation, in these cases between speaker and audience, and thus an element of social reality. Mostly, in daily life, the commitment relates to trivial matters, but there is no telling whether it may not gain greater relevance in the context of important issues. Any lawyer will have stories about apparently trivial utterances that turned out crucial in the context of some big criminal or civil case. A trivial commitment may assume legal proportions.

Since the type of commitment is encoded in the grammatical form of the (a)-sentences, which have the grammatical form of an assertion, a question, a suggestion and an imperative, respectively, it came as a natural thought to Ross (see Ross 1970) that the grammatical analysis of sentences should contain a performative verb as the highest sentential operator. This proposal, however, was strongly criticized in Fraser (1974). After that the question has been allowed to rest: there is still no general agreement on the question of the grammatical treatment of speech act operators.

● *What is a performative utterance?*

Quite apart from this grammatical question, there is the question of the relation between performative utterances and speech acts. The sentences in (49)-(52) are all speech acts when uttered seriously and appropriately (even if the (b)-sentences hardly represent what people would normally say). But they are not all performative utterances: the (a)-sentences are not performative utterances when uttered seriously and appropriately. So we ask: what distinguishes a performative utterance from a speech act?

Austin himself never came round to answering this question (which may be why he did not publish his thoughts on speech acts). In principle, a performative utterance is defined by the fact that it brings about the associated socially valid effect by actually saying so. Thus, (45) brings about the promise to return the addressee's book within a day by actually saying so. The (b)-sentences in (49)-(52) bring about the assertion, question, suggestion, and order concerned by actually saying so. (47a) brings about, and says it does, the declaration that the addressees are now husband and wife, a declaration considered by society to be sufficient for establishing a matrimonial bond. In contrast, (47b-d) also bring about such a declaration but do not say so explicitly. (48) bestows praise on the Lord but does not say how. Performative utterances are thus explicit speech acts, which allows us to say that they bring about their own truth. This may perhaps do as a definition, it leaves the grammatical problem unsolved. Do we have to say that all sentences contain an underlying speech act operator, which may or may not be made explicit in surface structure? We do not know.

We note, furthermore, that the effect brought about by a performative utterance may in all cases be an element of social reality, but it does not always have to be a commitment entered into by the speaker in relation to his audience. In (47b-d), for example, the effect brought about is a matrimonial bond between two addressees, with whom the speaker has no further committal relationship.

But is it necessary for a performative utterance to bring about an element of social reality? Could it not simply be required, generally, that a performative utterance brings about the effect described, whatever it might be? (53a) trivially makes itself true whenever it is actually pronounced. Or imagine a sorcerer setting a person on fire by uttering (53b):

(53)a.   I hereby produce sound
     b.   I hereby set you on fire

These utterances are in the first person singular and in the present tense, and *hereby* is token-reflexive, but the effect produced is physical, not social. What happens if we treat (53a,b) as performative utterances? Not much, presumably. It seems a question of mere definition. But whether or not we extend the category of performative utterances in this way, we must uphold the principle, it seems, that speech acts create social effects and thus bring about social reality. Even if we are prepared to regard (53a,b) as performative utterances they cannot be considered to constitute a speech act of producing sound or setting-on-fire, or else speech act theory loses most of its relevance.

• *Literal and non-literal speech acts*

Austin (1962:94-107) distinguished between locutionary acts, illocutionary acts, and perlocutionary acts. A locutionary act is merely an act of speaking (or writing) seriously and appropriately. In performing a locutionary act the speaker (writer) is also performing an illocutionary act, i.e. an act of asserting, questioning, suggesting, ordering, or of pronouncing a verdict, establishing a bond of matrimony, opening a meeting, etc. An illocutionary act is by definition literal. A perlocutionary act, also often called 'indirect speech act', is non-literal: by uttering it the speaker tries to achieve an ulterior aim to be inferred by the listener. For example, if I am in a room with a draught due to an open window, I may say to another person also in the room:

(54)   I hate draughts. They make me ill.

and the other person will then infer from my utterance that I would like him or her to shut the window. Likewise, if I am having breakfast and ask for the salt by saying:

(55)   Could you pass me the salt?

I do not expect the answer *Yes* but the salt being moved my way.

Indirect, or perlocutionary, speech acts are standardly used for reasons of politeness or social grace. They avoid a directness of approach which, in some cultures, is considered rude. The politeness consists in allowing the other party to draw their own conclusions so that they feel respected.

6.2.5   Anaphora

● *What is anaphora?*

Anaphora, in the traditional and commonly accepted sense of the term, is a linguistic device that makes it possible not to repeat a full referential expression in order to re-establish a referential link that has been made just before in a discourse.[33] The usual means for such an abbreviated pick-up of a recently made reference is the use of a personal or possessive pronoun, as in:

(56)a.   The woman in the red hat came in. *She* sat down.
    b.   The woman in the red hat came in. The maid took *her* coat.

In these sentences *the woman in the red hat* is the antecedent, and *she* and *her* are anaphoric pronouns.

● *Anaphoric epithets*

It is also possible, however, to use a full nominal description containing a qualifying noun that expresses the speaker's attitude or opinion:

(57)a.   The woman in the red hat came in. *The poor creature* sat down.
    b.   The woman in the red hat came in. The maid took *the poor creature's* coat.

Evaluative expressions like *the poor creature, the hateful animal, the old bum*, etc., which add no or hardly any new information about the matter at hand but mainly serve to allow the speaker to express his opinion or attitude, are usually called *epithets* (see note 14, in section 6.1.2.3.4 above).

● *Sentence-external and sentence-internal anaphora*

An anaphoric expression does not have to be external, i.e. to occur in a different sentence from its antecedent. It may also occur within the same sentence, but then there must be a clause or adjunct boundary between the anaphoric expression and the antecedent, as is shown in (58a-c). In these cases it is not always necessary for the antecedent to precede the anaphoric expression: in (58b) the anaphor precedes the antecedent. Yet there are structural constraints which may prohibit an anaphoric relation, as is demonstrated in (58c), where anaphora between *John* and *him* or *the poor guy* seems problematic:

(58)a.   Because John was ill, *he* (*the poor guy*) had to stay in bed
    b.   Because *he* (*the poor guy*) was ill, John had to stay in bed
    c.   ?Because of John's illness I gave *him* (*the poor guy*) a present
    d.   Because of *his* (*the poor guy's*) illness, I gave John a present

The exact nature of the constraints that hold for anaphora within a sentence is a topic of much debate among grammarians, and we shall not try to solve that problem here, as it is not directly germane to discourse semantics.

---

[33] In circles dominated by Chomsky it has become customary to use the terms *anaphora* and *anaphoric pronoun* for what is normally called *reflexive binding* and *reflexive pronoun*. The advantage of this terminological change is not clear; the disadvantages are.

● *Non-anaphoric pronouns: bound variable pronouns*

But it must be pointed out that not all uses of pronouns are anaphoric. One class of non-anaphoric pronouns are the bound variable pronouns. In the case of a bound variable pronoun the logical analysis of the sentence shows a quantifier binding a variable which appears in the surface structure as the pronoun in question. This is the case in, for example:

(59) a. I told everybody that the doorman will park *their* car
     b. To some people the idea that *they* will lose is unbearable

Note that bound variable pronouns cannot be replaced with an epithet: the use of an epithet destroys the binding relation:

(60)   !I told everybody that the doorman will show *the bums* in

In fact, the possibility of using an epithet as an anaphoric device provides a test for anaphoricity: epithets can only function as anaphoric expressions; they cannot stand in for variable binding or other non-anaphoric pronouns.

● *Reflexive pronouns*

A further category of non-anaphoric pronouns is formed by the reflexive pronouns. These express the reflexivization of the predicate with respect to the subject (or, occasionally, the indirect object). A reflexive pronoun can, therefore, never stand in subject position. In (61) the reflexivized predicate is something like 'self-hurt', as appears from the VP-anaphor *so do*:

(61)   John hurt *himself*, and so did Harry

This sentence can only mean that Harry also hurt himself, not that he also hurt John.

Reflexive pronouns are often, but not always, characterized morphologically. In English, some reflexive pronouns are marked by the suffix *-self*, but others are not marked at all and look like ordinary pronouns, as in (62a):[34]

(62) a. In *his* office John never smokes
     b. !In John's office *he* never smokes
     c. In *his* office John's wife is not allowed to smoke
     d. In John's office *his* wife is not allowed to smoke

In (62a) the pronoun *his* is best considered reflexive, controlled by the subject term *John*. This explains why in (62b) there can be no co-referentiality between *John* and *he*, since in this sentence *he* occupies the subject position. It also explains why *his* in (62a) cannot be replaced with an epithet. In (62c,d), where the subject term refers to John's wife, there is no reflexivity. As a conse-

---

[34] Languages differ as regards the conditions for morphological marking of reflexivity. English *his*, for example, may be reflexive but is not marked. But Swedish and Latin use *sin* and *suus* for the reflexive third person singular possessive pronoun, as opposed to the non-reflexive *hans* and *eius*, respectively. In some languages, especially Creole languages, there is no marking of reflexivity at all. And those Creole languages that do mark reflexivity often do so only optionally and then use a so-called 'body' reflexive: 'he washed his head/body/skin' for 'he washed himself'. (The etymological origin of Germanic *-self* is unknown.)

quence, co-reference is possible in both versions, and the use of an epithet anaphor seems possible.

- *Focus on primary anaphora: inadequacy of predicate calculus analysis*

We shall, however, not be concerned here with non-anaphoric pronouns, and concentrate on genuine anaphora, in particular the special form of anaphora that occurs when the anaphor picks up reference to an entity that has just been introduced by means of an existential quantifier. Let us call this *primary anaphora*. The reason for our special interest lies in the fact that primary anaphora shows up cases where an analysis in terms of standard Russellian predicate calculus gets into deep trouble, and where the new notion of discourse semantics seems to bring relief.

Consider the cases (63a-c). The possibility of using an epithet shows that we have genuine cases of anaphora here. Normally, it makes no difference for sentence-external primary anaphora whether the conjunction *and* or, if appropriate, *but* is used, or even no conjunction at all, as is shown in (63a). (63b) is incoherent as the first conjunct forbids the introduction into the discourse domain of a representation for any car of Tom's, whereas the second conjunct requires such a representation. (63c) is both interesting and puzzling for a variety of reasons. It is usually explicated as *Tom does not own a car, or he owns one and it's red*, which, if correct, imposes, among other things, heavy demands on a theory of natural language disjunction:

(63) a.   Tom owns a car, (and/but) *it* (*the thing*) is red
 b.   !Tom does not own a car, (and/but) *it* (*the thing*) is red
 c.   Tom does not own a car, or *it* (*the thing*) is red

- *Complement anaphora*

A first complication arises with what has been called (Moxey & Sanford 1986/7) *complement anaphora*, illustrated in (64a). The reader will notice that in this sentence the pronoun *they* is most naturally interpreted as referring to those members who were not at the meeting. This phenomenon is most surprising and has not found an explanation in any existing theory of anaphora. It is even more surprising when it is noticed that the use of the conjunction *and*, as in (64b), makes complement anaphora impossible: (64b) can mean only that the few members who were at the meeting were also in the pub:

(64) a.   Few members were at the meeting. *They* were (all) in the pub.
 b.   Few members were at the meeting and *they* were (all) in the pub.

- *Geach's problem; his solution is not tenable*

The main point, however, is that sentences like (63a) pose a fundamental problem for an analysis in terms of predicate calculus. This discovery was prompted by Geach (1969; 1972:115-27), who observed that (65a) is consistent with (65b). If both sentences are true at the same time Tom must own at least two cars:

(65)a.   Tom owns a car and it is red
   b.   Tom owns a car and it is not red

Geach then argues as follows. The fact that (65a) is consistent with (65b) shows that the logical analysis of these sentences cannot be of the form A ∧ B and A ∧ ¬B, respectively, since that would create inconsistency. In order to save standard predicate calculus as the language of logico-semantic analysis he proposes a solution in terms of (restricted) existential quantification over the whole sentence, so that *it* becomes a bound variable pronoun:

(66)a.   ∃x:car [own (Tom,x) ∧ red (x)]
   b.   ∃x:car [own (Tom,x) ∧ ¬[red (x)]]

This maintains consistency, and requires that Tom owns at least two cars.

Geach's solution, however, is not tenable. A first problem is that an epithet can stand in for *it*, which suggests that it is not a bound variable pronoun:

(67)a.   Tom owns a car and *the thing* is red
   b.   Tom owns a car and *the thing* is not red

More importantly, however, as was pointed out in section 6.1.2.3.4 (see also Seuren 1977; 1985:319-21), Geach's solution lacks generality. For the problem crops up again when intensional operators are inserted, as in:

(68)a.   I was told that Tom owns a car, and they said it was red
   b.   I was told that Tom owns a car, and they didn't say it was red

This pair is again consistent but requires that I was told at least twice about a car owned by Tom. But these sentences do not allow for an analysis à la Geach, owing to scope conflicts. In terms of Geach's analysis, which sticks to standard predicate calculus, (68a) must be analyzed as either (69a) or (69b):

(69)a.   ∃x:car [was told (I,[own (Tom,x)]) ∧ say (they,[red (x)])]
   b.   was told (I,[∃x:car [own (Tom,x) ∧ say (they,[red (x)])]])

Yet either analysis fails to correspond to the natural meaning of (68a). (69a) reads 'there is a car such that I was told that Tom owns it and such that they said that it was red'; (69b) reads 'I was told that there is a car such that Tom owns it and such that they said that it was red'. But in reality (68a) means 'I was told that there is a car such that Tom owns it, and they said that *that car* was red'. And analogously for (68b): 'I was told that there is a car such that Tom owns it, and they did not say that *that car* was red'.

• *Basic problem: predicate calculus lacks a reference function for anaphors*
The conclusion must be that these meanings cannot be rendered in terms of standard predicate calculus (no matter whether restricted or unrestricted quantification is used; see 5.5). And the reason is that predicate calculus only allows for two kinds of (non-sentential) argument terms to predicates in full propositions: constants and bound variables. The constant terms must refer to an entity in the model (and we have seen, in 6.1.2.3.4, that standard model theory can only achieve this by stipulating fixed reference relations); the bound variables are part of a machinery that allows for constant terms to substitute for the variables (see 5.5.1).

Given this restriction to constants and bound variables, the tendency has always been for formal semanticists and philosophers of language to interpret pronouns either as constants or as bound variables. For a long time it had been the standard opinion that pronouns like *it* in (65a,b) (i.e. pronouns of primary anaphora) are some sort of constants, even though there was an everlasting uncertainty about the precise formulation of their reference function, until Geach proposed that they should be interpreted as bound variables, which, as we have seen, is not a viable analysis either.

It does seem, on balance, that primary anaphoric pronouns should be treated as a special kind of constant terms, and not as bound variables. The question is then how to define their reference function. All researchers who have looked at the problem from this point of view agree that the reference function of primary anaphoric pronouns must be defined in relation to preceding context.[35]

● *Donkey sentences*

The problem comes to a head in the so-called donkey sentences.[36] They are of the following types:

(70)a. If this farmer owns a donkey *he* feeds *it*
    b. Every farmer who owns a donkey feeds *it*
    c. Either this farmer does not own a donkey or he feeds *it*

(Note that (70c) has the structure of (63c).) The problem is that the pronoun *it* can be interpreted neither as a constant referring term nor as a bound variable. If it is interpreted as a constant term there is a reference problem in cases where no farmer owns a donkey. For in such cases the sentences in question are true, but *it* fails to refer which should result in the lack of a truth value.

On the other hand, if *it* is interpreted as a bound variable it cannot be properly bound owing to scope problems. In standard unrestricted quantification (70a) should read as something like:

(71) $\exists x$ [donkey(x) $\land$ own(this farmer,x)] $\rightarrow$ feed (this farmer,x)

But, as one sees, the term *x* of the consequent clause 'feed(this farmer,x)' is not bound by any quantifier.

An often heard reply is that (71) is not the correct analysis and that universal quantification should be applied, leading to (72):

(72) $\forall x$ [donkey(x) $\land$ own(this farmer,x) $\rightarrow$ feed (this farmer,x)]

Now all variables are properly bound, but this analysis lacks generality, and is therefore ad hoc, for the same reason that Geach's solution to (67a,b) was ad hoc. This is clear when one considers sentences like:

(73)   If it's a bad thing that this farmer owns a donkey it's a good thing that he feeds it

---

[35] Groenendijk & Stokhof (1991) propose an enrichment of predicate calculus, called dynamic logic, which allows for variable binding across propositional boundaries.

[36] They are called 'donkey sentences' on account of the fact that in Geach (1962), where the problem is raised for the first time, the example sentences all involve a donkey.

The antecedent clause allows only for existential, and not for universal quantification: an analysis like 'for every donkey, if it's a bad thing that this farmer owns it, it's a good thing that he feeds it' fails to capture the meaning of (73), which is more like 'if it's a bad thing that this farmer is a donkey-owner, it's a good thing that he feeds the donkey he owns'. This being so the same old scope problem rears its head. In (74) the *x*-term in the consequent clause is unbound:

(74)   bad thing [∃x [donkey(x) ∧ own(this farmer,x)]] →
         good thing [feed(this farmer,x)]

And similarly for the types (70b) and (70c):

(75)a.   Every farmer who is thought to own a donkey is expected to feed *it*
    b.   Either this farmer no longer owns a donkey or he still feeds *it*

It thus seems a hopeless undertaking to try to interpret the problematic pronouns as bound variables. Since they cannot be referring expressions either (in standard model theory), predicate calculus has a problem. We note, meanwhile, that the pronouns in question behave like anaphors, since they allow for epithet substitution, as was shown in note 14 above. This weakens the hypothesis that they should, after all, be treated as variables bound across propositional confines, as is suggested by Groenendijk & Stokhof. Assigning them the status of constant terms is more likely to meet with success.

This can be done in discourse-oriented semantics. There, the reference function is mediated by a cognitive machinery that operates between the constant term and the world or situation to which the discourse applies. Instead of letting constant terms refer directly (an impossible task anyway, as we saw in 6.1.2.3, given the context-dependency of the reference function), we let them select or 'denote' cognitive representations of real or imagined entities. The relation between the cognitive representations and any real world or situation is then a matter of independent concern, to be sorted out in a new theory of truth conditions not for sentences vis-à-vis the world, but for discourse representations vis-à-vis the world. This is what is done in Kamp's Discourse Representation Theory (Kamp 1981; Kamp & Reyle 1993), which took the donkey sentences as its starting point, and in Seuren's Discourse Semantics (Seuren 1972a; 1975; 1985), which is based on the analysis of presuppositions.

6.2.6 Discourse-oriented theories of meaning

• *Modern semantics is an exemplar of paradigm change in science*
The developments in formal semantics over the past half century have, in a way, been exemplary. Although formal semantics was formally precise and made important headway initially, it was plagued by continuous and on the whole successful attempts by critics showing why and how its methods were basically flawed. These attempts have gradually gained recognition, with the result that it became increasingly clear that drastic and fundamental changes were called for. Only rarely in the human sciences does one see a struggle of this nature fought out so neatly and within the span of one lifetime.

- *Standard model-theoretic semantics could not be salvaged*

The basic problems faced by standard model-theoretic semantics are legion. Some, like the imperfect 'fit' of the truth-conditional operators, in particular *or* and *if*, are obvious and have been known since the very beginning. Others came to light later, starting with the Middle Ages but for the most part during the second half of the twentieth century. Some of these have allowed for a formally precise formulation and have, perhaps for that reason, also proved most influential, in particular the problem of reference, especially reference to non-existing entities, the problem of intensional contexts, presupposition, and the problem of primary anaphora, especially donkey sentences. But the objections raised by viewpoint phenomena, topic-comment modulation and speech acts, which proved more difficult to formalize, have also contributed significantly to the now widely accepted view that model-theoretic semantics must be enriched with a cognitive dimension.

The salvaging operation called 'pragmatics' did lead to the introduction of a cognitive dimension, but in a way that was too informal and not integrated into the formal semantic machinery: common sense applied to an outside processing machine. What is needed is a semantic processor that is a functional part of the same overall cognitive machinery that also makes for common sense, and which, in addition, links up organically with the machinery of grammar.

We shall conclude with some remarks about non-existing entities and about intensional contexts.

6.2.6.1 The reality of non-existing intensional entities

We have seen on several occasions, especially in 6.1.2.3.2 and 6.1.3.4 above, that reference to non-existing entities is a major problem in model-theoretic semantics. Put simply, the problem is that in such cases there is nothing to refer to, which creates insurmountable problems for the assignment of truth values, as well as for the specification of the extension of intensional predicates: a predicate like *imaginary*, for example, would have a zero extension.

We have also seen that a discourse-oriented semantics implies the postulation of a cognitive 'working space', normally called 'discourse domain' or 'discourse representation', which contains mentally constructed representations or 'addresses' that are supposed to correspond to possible entities or data of any kind in any real world that may come our way. The mind is thus considered to be endowed with the power to generate situational representations that may or may not correspond with what is the case in the real world.

- *Discourse representations solve the structural, not the ontological problem*

In principle, the problem of reference to non-existing entities is solved if it is assumed that so-called referring expressions in sentences do not immediately refer to world entities but first select and denote addresses in the cognitive discourse domain at hand. Only secondarily do they refer to real world entities, depending on the relation of the discourse domain at hand with that part of the real world the discourse is about. From a structural point of view, therefore, the problems associated with reference in model-theoretic semantics can be solved by an appeal to mental constructs.

- *Imagination creates non-existing entities as objects of aboutness*

But the ontological problem remains. For the *point* of using language is not to discuss each other's mental constructs but to interact with each other in matters regarding the real world and our position in it. The mental machinery involved is, though indispensable, ancillary to that purpose. It is in this sense that we speak *about* things. We speak *about* things in the real or any imagined world, in much the same way as we depict a dog when we draw or paint one. If the dog depicted is the product of fantasy it does not represent anything really existing, yet one cannot say that it represents nothing because to make a picture without representing anything is to produce abstract art, which, by definition, a dog-picture is not. In the same way, when we speak about the king of France being bald, we do not speak about nothing, which is impossible to the extent that 'abstract speech' is impossible, but about the non-existing king of France. As a consequence, non-existing entities must be given a place in ontology as those entities that would be real (and thus defined by a full set of properties) if the mental representation in which they occur corresponded to a real situation. To create a representation is to create possible entities.

6.2.6.2 Intensional contexts

How discourse-oriented semantics can solve the problem of intensional contexts is an obvious question. In answering it we must first emphasize that the particular problem discussed in section 6.1.5.1 above does not arise for discourse semantics, as it is a direct consequence of the notion of possible world and the view that a predicate like *believe* expresses a relation between persons and sets of possible worlds. Since possible worlds do not occur in discourse semantics this particular problem does not arise. But Frege's second problem (see 6.1.2.2) remains: why is substitution salva veritate not allowed in intensional contexts? There is, moreover, a set of empirical observations and questions directly related to intensional contexts, which require an empirical answer as well.

- *Projection of presuppositions and anaphora across intensional contexts*

One example is the projection behaviour of presuppositions (see 6.2.3.2): presuppositions tend to 'climb up' into the main clause, where they are preserved as default assumptions. Another example is the possibility of pronominal anaphora across intensional contexts. In (76), for example, the pronoun *him*, which occurs in the context under *expect*, is anaphoric with regard to *someone* even though that someone occurs in the context under *imagine*:

(76)   Kim imagined that someone was following her, and she expected me to grab *him*

Quite apart, therefore, from the particular problem confronting possible world semantics, there is the independent empirical problem of how to deal with intensional contexts.

* *Intensional and extensional subdomains*

Although this is not the right place to go into formal and theoretical details, it can be pointed out how discourse semantics should, in principle, be able to deal with intensional contexts. The answer consists in the setting up of *subdomains* as a specific kind of discourse address. A subdomain is defined as the discourse representation of a propositional term that acts as argument term to a given predicate or operator (e.g. the object term of *believe*, or the two arguments of the disjunctive operator *or*, or the antecedent clause of the conditional operator *if*) in the utterance of a given sentence. It has the same internal structure as the overarching discourse domain (also called 'truth domain'), i.e. with addresses and properties assigned to them, but it is subject to 'traffic rules' regarding the importation and exportation of discourse addresses with respect to the truth domain and other subdomains.

A subdomain need not be intensional, it may also be extensional and allow for substitution salva veritate, as in the case of the disjunctive operator *or*, which is incremented as two alternative and mutually exclusive subdomains. Each of these is suitable for incrementation to the truth domain, but the speaker has not made up his mind which to choose. Most subdomains, however, are intensional in that they disallow substitution salva veritate.

* *The negation* not *does not introduce a separate subdomain*

Although it is postulated that *or* introduces two alternative subdomains the operator *not* is not taken to introduce a separate subdomain but to brand a particular incrementation unit, though otherwise suitable for incrementation, as undesirable and hence to be excluded from the discourse domain. The difference is shown in (77). (77a) is a disjunction whose first disjunct shows primary anaphora with the help of *and*, which suggests that a separate subdomain has been set up. Analogously for the second disjunct in (77b). (77c), however, cannot mean 'it is not the case that he has a car and takes care of it', i.e. with a separate subdomain for *not*. The negation cannot be taken to set up a separate subdomain, as primary anaphora under *not* is impossible:

(77)a. Either he has a car and he takes care of it, or he doesn't have one
     b. Either he has no car or he has one and takes care of it
     c. !He does not have a car and he takes care of *it*

* *The principle of downward percolation*

The first general principle is that of *downward percolation*. It allows addresses to trickle down from the truth domain into lower subdomains, unless the subdomain in question contains material forbidding the introduction of a higher address. For example, if the address for Marion's brother in (78) is located in the truth domain, it is free to re-appear in the subdomain of what Marion dreamt, unless it has been said that she dreamt that she had no brother:

(78)   Marion dreamt that her brother had had an accident

But an address that has been introduced in a subdomain and not in the truth domain, such as the address set up by *someone* in the subdomain of *imagine* in (76), is confined to the subdomain in question and its cognate subdomains.[37]

A given SD can also be continued, provided cognitive consistency is maintained. In that case the continuation of the subdomain is the preferred option. Thus, in the interpretation of (79a) there will be one single SD of possibility, but in (79b) there will be two different such SDs:

(79)a.   Harry may be rich, and he may be happy (as well)
     b.   Harry may be dead, and he may be alive (!as well)

The conjunctive structure of (79a) may be reduced to (80a), but for (79b), taken literally, such a reduction is less natural:

(80)a.   Harry may be rich and happy
     b.   !?Harry may be dead and alive

As a consequence, primary anaphora is possible within one single SD, as in (81a), but not across two alternative and mutually incompatible SDs, as in (81b) or (81c):

(81)a.   Harry may have a pen and (he may) use *it*
     b.   !Harry may have a pen, and he may not have *it*
     c.   !Harry has a pen, or he does not have *it*

Non-primary anaphora is all right in such cases, because with non-primary anaphora the antecedent has been introduced before the subdomain was established, so that downward percolation applies:

(82)a.   Harry may love his wife, and he may hate *her*
     b.   Harry either loves his wife, or he hates *her*

• *The principle of projection*

The second general principle is *projection* (see 6.2.3.2). This ensures that normally a presupposition supplied post hoc (by accommodation) will be filled in not just in the particular subdomain where its carrier sentence belongs but will percolate upwards into higher subdomains and eventually into the truth domain, unless it is stopped by logical or cognitive inconsistency, or even by a lack of 'cognitive sense' in the spirit of 6.2.3.3.

---

[37] The notion of a cognate subdomain is not easy to define formally. But the general idea is that a subdomain SD_2 associated with the predicate Q is cognate with a subdomain SD_1 associated with the predicate P if Q is different from P, and P and Q have the same subject (in case they take a subject), and the ontology of SDs associated with Q presupposes the ontology of SDs associated with P, or both presuppose the ontology of SDs associated with a third intensional predicate R. For example, the SD associated with *expected* in (76) is cognate with the SD associated with *imagined* because they share the subject *Kim* and there is a predicate, for example *believe*, such that whatever a person A has imaginations or expectations about A must also believe to exist. The point is that addresses may move freely between cognate subdomains, so that anaphoric relations can be established, as shown in (76).

The typical behaviour of Karttunen's 'holes', 'plugs' and 'filters' should simply follow from the machinery of truth and subdomains and post hoc suppletion, and the constraints of consistency and cognitive backing. The operator *or*, for example, requires that both disjuncts be independently suitable for incrementation, each leaving open the possibility of post hoc suppletion. Thus, a sentence like (83a) should make good sense in a discourse where the question of Harry's having children has just been mooted but not answered. The second disjunct will, for the purpose of comprehension, be extended to *or Harry has children and they are all asleep*. And (83b) should make sense in a discourse where it is clear that Harry is not working now. Here both disjuncts are extended by post hoc suppletion, but the presuppositions supplied, i.e. *Harry worked before* and *Harry did not work before*, are each other's contradiction:

(83)a. Either Harry has no children or they are all asleep
   b. Harry has either stopped working or he hasn't started yet

Factive presuppositions (see 6.2.3.2) must be passed on to the domain where the factive predicate is incremented, since factive clauses are entailed. Thus, the presupposition *Harry had a criminal record* must be supplied to the subdomain of Harry's dream and will be supplied by default to the truth domain, unless it has been said there that Harry did not have a criminal record:

(84)   Harry dreamt that everybody knew that he had a criminal record

- *Viewpoint presuppositions may be accommodated directly in the truth domain*

Some presuppositions, however, seem to be able to skip the subdomain that their carrier clause is incremented to, and jump straight into the truth domain. These presuppositions seem to be related more to the cognitive state of the speaker than to the state of affairs described. For example, the presuppositions that come with words like *even, too, (not) yet*, say little about the state of affairs described in the proposition in which they occur. Instead they reveal a belief or expectation pattern on the part of either the speaker or the subject of the intensional predicate. This kind of presupposition has been neglected in the literature. We speak of *viewpoint presuppositions*. They do not contribute to the truth conditions of the sentences in which they occur, and the inferences they admit are not about the 'world' but about certain aspects of the speaker's or the subject's mental state. Consider:

(85)a. Kate had the impression that *even* Joe laughed
   b. Kate says that the letter has *not yet* been posted

In (85a) Kate may merely have had the impression that Joe laughed while the surprise expressed by *even* is the speaker's contribution. Likewise in (85b), where the expectation that the letter will shortly be posted need not be Kate's but may be the speaker's.[38]

---

[38] Fauconnier (1985:105-6) made similar observations which, however, go way beyond viewpoint presuppositions. To the extent that they do, however, they appear less convincing.

• *The maximization of unity in discourse domains*

The functionality of the principle of downward percolation and of the projection principle is clear: both principles maximize the unity of the discourse domain as a whole. Subdomains are like truth domains unless otherwise specified, and to the extent that they are otherwise specified, subdomains ensure maximal suitability for incrementation to other domains as well, in particular the truth domain. One may speak of the *ceteris paribus* condition. The sentence content is added, and all other domains that may be affected are adapted so as to keep differences down to a minimum. For example, for:

(86)   Sue believes that her brother lives in Ohio

the default interpretation will be that Sue has a really existing brother (owing to the projection principle), and that she believes of this person that he lives in Ohio, where the principle of downward percolation allows the subdomain of what Sue believes access to the representation of her brother in the truth domain. This ensures that, in the default interpretation, the clause *Sue's brother lives in Ohio* is itself suitable for direct incrementation to the truth domain, so that it makes sense to ask whether it is true that Sue's brother lives in Ohio.

• *Extensional and intensional term positions*

Predicates are lexically marked for intensionality with respect to their argument terms. Unmarked terms are simply extensional. For example, the predicate *touch* takes two terms, a subject and a direct object, both of which are extensional. That is, given a proposition with *touch* as main predicate it is a necessary (but not sufficient) condition for its truth that both the subject term and the direct object term refer to really existing entities. Discourse-semantically, this means that the incrementation of such a proposition requires that the truth domain contain representations for the intended reference objects of the subject and the object term.

However, a predicate like *talk about* is extensional with respect to its subject term, since only really existing entities (persons) can talk, but intensional with respect to its prepositional object term, since one may very well talk about non-existing things. Consequently, the incrementation of a sentence like:

(87)   The old man kept talking about the Abominable Snowman

requires previously created addresses both for the old man and for the Abominable Snowman, but the former has to be in the truth domain, whereas the latter may be in any intensional subdomain.

• *The predicates of existence and of identity*

This provides a straightforward semantics for the predicate *exist*. We say that *exist* is intensional with respect to its subject term, so that the incrementation procedure for a sentence like:

(88)   The Abominable Snowman does not exist

is free to look for the Abominable Snowman address in any intensional subdomain. The discourse-semantic effect of the non-negated sentence then consists in the insertion of that address into the truth domain (leaving, of course, a copy in the original subdomain), whereas for the negated sentence (88) the effect consists in the prohibition of any such insertion into the truth domain.

Analogously for the predicate of identity. When it is said that:

(89)   The Greek goddess Athena is the Roman goddess Minerva

two addresses are required, one for Athena and one for Minerva, but neither has to be in the truth domain, though, of course, they may be. The discourse-semantic effect of the sentence is that the two addresses are collapsed into one.

- *Substitutivity in extensional and intensional contexts*

Frege's second problem is now also solved, and placed in a wider context. Since a definite description in an intensional context requires an address in the corresponding subdomain there is no guarantee that this address also occurs in the truth domain (if not there is reference to a non-existing entity), or that it has undergone the same unifications with other addresses in virtue of identity statements. Thus, in (90) substitution salva veritate of *Evening Star* for *Morning Star* is disallowed, since Archie may well believe them to be distinct:

(90)   Archie believes that the Morning Star is inhabited

On the other hand, however, if Archie believes, contrary to fact, that Jones and Smith are the same person going under different names, *Jones* and *Smith* are mutually substitutable salva veritate in sentences like:

(91)a.   Archie believes that Jones is a thief
    b.   Archie believes that Smith is a thief

This is a valid consequence not drawn by Frege.

- *The intensionalisation of semantics; the definition of 'sentence meaning'*

The whole enterprise of discourse semantics amounts to an overall intensionalisation of semantics. Whereas Montagovian model-theoretic semantics consists essentially in the extensionalisation of semantics, in that simple extensional model-theory (of the type shown in 5.5.1. and 5.5.2) is generalized to all possible worlds, discourse semantics generalizes the notion of incrementation into a domain, whether the truth domain or some intensional or non-intensional subdomain. It was in this sense that, at the end of section 6.1.3.4, it was said that ultimately, all semantics is intensional.

Consequently, the result of the categorial calculus through the constituent tree of an uttered sentence is not a truth value but an actual incrementation. And we say, generally, that the meaning of a sentence as type, not as uttered token, is a schematic specification of the increment value of that sentence given any suitable discourse domain.[39]

---

[39] This definition of sentence meaning is now widely accepted. It was presented first in Seuren (1975:237):

> We can now say that the meaning of a proposition or a semantic representation or a transformationally related sentence can be described as the kind of change that the proposition in question can bring about in any given thought complex.

CHAPTER 7

Meaning and grammar

7.0 Preamble

After our expeditions into the history of grammatical and semantic studies we now naturally face the question of how these two branches of enquiry stand in relation to each other. At the moment there exists a large variety of widely diverging opinions and approaches, all of which have their roots in one or more of the historical traditions that we looked at in the previous chapters. It is our purpose, in the present chapter, to unravel the tangle of traditions that have led to the present complex situation, even if we must realize that this purpose can be achieved only very partially. Our strategy will be to identify the issues that have been of all times, and to show how, through the centuries, they became more and more visible and explicit. This will bring us to the present time where most of these issues have indeed become highly explicit but where lines of research have become so institutionalized that the overall view is obscured and often even shut out. The historical perspective is, accordingly, considered a threat which is preferably ignored or, at best, used in the opening sentences of pieces of writing as a source of selective allusions that are often ill-informed but confer an aura of culture and urbanity. Not surprisingly, the research conducted under such conditions is often blinkered and thus fails to link up with wider areas of knowledge and insight.

The key notions in the history of the relation between meaning and grammar are those of structure and analysis. And the perennial frame in terms of which this process of explicitation worked itself out is the semiotic triangle, splendidly made visible in Ogden & Richards (1923:11), and discussed earlier in 1.2.1 and 2.6.4. Both the notions of structure and analysis, and the semiotic triangle remained hazy and opaque for many centuries. Not until the twentieth century did they gain an acceptable degree of clarity and explicitness, though, as has been said, in a highly compartmentalized way: the clarity gained has remained restricted to a series of relatively closed chambers.

Against the background of the semiotic triangle we revert to the distinction between the Platonic and the Aristotelian traditions, both forming a large stream of thinking throughout the history of the western world and both providing a general way of looking at things. Plato and Aristotle themselves were no doubt largely unaware of the wider implications of their basic stance. One may say that their thinking has proved to possess an immanent generative power bringing forth products that could not have been foreseen by their originators but which it is the historian's prerogative to interpret and classify as belonging to the one or the other paradigm.

We shall see that the Platonic tradition is generally characterized by a deeper insight into the nature of the issues involved and, inevitably, by a relative incapacity to provide adequate formal analyses, whereas the Aristotelian tradition typically shows great formal prowess, but, equally inevitably, at the expense of adequate insight and coverage of facts. Representatives of the Platonic tradition are therefore typically forced into the position of a critic who can offer general notions and criticisms but no alternative formalism, while the 'Aristotelians', with their clever formal systems, can claim temporary success but are invariably overtaken by the facts they have proved unable to account for. In a way, it is the old story all over again of the opposition between ecologism and formalism discussed in section 1.3 above.

Naturally, in this context, the interesting developments occur when a 'Platonist' succeeds in bringing the complexity of things closer to a reduction in terms of a formal system, thereby making the best of the strong points of the two traditions and diminishing their weaknesses. This appears to be the kind of process we feel to be at work, even if full formal success is rarely achieved, in the Stoa, in the works of Sanctius, the Port Royal grammarians, the participants of the great 19th century debate on Subject and Predicate structure, in some manifestations of 20th century European structuralism, in transformational grammar and, in particular, generative semantics.

Closely parallel and equally interesting are attempts by 'Aristotelians' to extend the power and coverage of existing formal systems so as to take care of certain hairy data that have come to light and pose a challenge. Sometimes it is hard to say *prima facie* whether a particular piece of work is Platonic or Aristotelian in spirit, since what it tries to achieve is a better agreement between facts and formal theory. But on closer inspection one usually sees the difference. When the primary aim is to save (or salvage) a formalism by adapting it a little so as to make it fit one or two new data, one has to do with an Aristotelian, or formalist attempt. When the primary aim is to save the facts while existing formalisms are considered useful only to the extent that they help doing so, there is a Platonist, or an ecologist, at work.[1]

It is from this overall perspective that we discuss, in the present chapter, the relation between grammatical and semantic studies through the centuries (even though we realize well that it is, of course, not the only valid point of view to be taken). While unfolding this perspective we have to pay renewed visits to some of the historical facts and figures discussed in earlier chapters. The reader will no doubt find that this is not repetitious but, on the contrary, adds to the knowledge gained earlier and is an incentive to further reflection. On the whole it will lead to a better insight into the historical roots of the theories and theoretical adumbrations that have come into existence over the past fifty or so years, and thus provide a better basis for their description and evaluation.

---

[1] Sometimes, as with Chomskyan post-1970 grammar, we witness a transition from a Platonic or ecologistic to an Aristotelian or formalistic methodology.

7.1 Until 1900: all linguistic structure is meaningful

* *What is structure?*

The first question we have to ask is 'What is structure?' In section 3.1 above we discussed the notion of structuralism in the human sciences, and we saw that there structuralism means the application of the machine metaphor to mental structures and processes. But we did not discuss the notion of 'structure' as such. This we shall do now.

Generally we speak of 'structure' when we are faced with a complex entity consisting of parts that have been put together in such a way that they make a functional contribution to the complex entity in question. The entity as a whole can do more than either each of the parts or an unstructured heap of the parts can do. In this sense the complex entity, the whole, is more than the simple sum of its parts. It is the sum of its parts only after they have been put together according to certain structural principles. The entity is then said to be a structure, or to have one. A class of similar structures is called a construction.

It is difficult to separate the perception of a structure from the purpose that the complex entity involved is supposed to serve. That purpose may seem far-fetched, as when psychologists find that subjects detect a structure in, for example, a face, which is considered to be built up from elements such as a chin, a mouth, eyes, a nose, ears, eyebrows, etc., even when faces as such do not seem to serve specific purposes. In this case, however, the structure is assigned not with a view to any purpose served directly by the face in question but, more indirectly, in order to enable subjects to recognize and distinguish individual faces. Since each face is attached to a unique person and since individual persons may have great functional value, the indirect purpose of face recognition is the identification of the person concerned – an important factor in everyday life. So important, in fact, that face recognition patterns seem largely innate.

* *Naïve and culturally acquired structure assignment*

The recognition of structures can be naïve and part of the natural acquisition of knowledge, as when a child begins to detect structure in a toy car and is driven by curiosity to take it apart, usually finding itself unable to put it together again. In science, however, the analysis of a complex entity and the subsequent assignment of structure can be a longwinded process extending itself over centuries. The assignment of structure is then a cultural achievement, which may be integrated into the education system of a community to such an extent that the members of the community find it difficult to say whether these structure assignments are natural or culturally-acquired. Something of the kind seems to occur in the case of phoneme recognition in function of alphabetic writing. In modern societies people find it the most normal thing in the world to distinguish a *p, r, o* or *u*, or whatever other sound may occur in their language. But one should realize that it took, roughly speaking, two and a half millennia to get from ideographic to syllabic to alphabetic script, and, one may assume, the concomitant recognition of individual phonemes as structural units in a word.[2]

- *Only a dim notion of sentence structure in Plato and Aristotle*

The detection of sentence structure is a clear case of scientific, and thus culturally acquired, knowledge. We therefore prefer to speak of the *assignment* of sentence structure, rather than of its *perception*.

As we saw earlier, especially in 1.1, 1.2 and 2.6.3, the distinction between subject and predicate as main sentence constituents emerged very slowly indeed. It first arose, in the works of Plato and Aristotle, as a means for the systematic determination of truth and falsity: if the property expressed by the predicate is indeed a property of the referent of the subject term the proposition expressed in the sentence is true, and otherwise false. The sentence was thus seen as a complex entity whose purpose it is to express truth or, perversely, falsity, and its subject-predicate structure was seen as subservient to that purpose. No notion of 'meaning' was involved (indeed no term existed for what we call meaning). Subject and predicate, to the extent that they were recognized, were conceived of as sentence parts to be put together for the purpose of truth speaking. This much is common ground between Plato and Aristotle. Soon, however, profound differences became visible.

7.1.1 The Platonic tradition: Stoa, Sanctius, Port Royal

- *Plato's ideal world of stable and perfect being*

As will be remembered from section 1.1, Plato's notion of truth was wider than what we consider acceptable nowadays. For him, truth is as much a property of words as of sentences. In his dialogue *Cratylus* Plato seeks the 'truth' of words in a hidden 'reality' behind the actual word, and in an 'ideal' word form, which is a faithful and regular expression of the things it stands for. The largely mystical notion of an ideal universe where everything is stable and true and which confers substance and system to the changeable and fickle world we live in, which derived, as we saw in 1.1, from Heraclitus, permeates all of Plato's thinking.

---

[2] Words, on the other hand, seem much easier to recognize 'naturally' as structural elements in a sentence, if one may go by Sapir's famous footnote (1921:35):

> Twice I have taught intelligent young Indians to write their own languages according to the phonetic system which I employ. They were taught merely how to render accurately the sounds as such. Both had some difficulty in learning to break up a word into its constituent sounds, but none whatever in determining the words. This they both did with spontaneous and complete accuracy. In the hundreds of pages of manuscript Nootka text that I have obtained from one of these young Indians the words, whether abstract relational entities like English *that* and *but* or complex sentence-words like the Nootka example quoted above [Sapir obviously refers to the complex Paiute word we discussed in 4.2 and whose structure is given in fig. 1 there; P.S.], are, practically without exception, isolated precisely as I or any other student would have isolated them. Such experiences with naïve speakers and recorders do more to convince one of the definitely plastic unity of the word than any amount of purely theoretical argument.

Although Plato never evolved a theory of grammar or of meaning, it is entirely in his spirit to see the 'truth' of sentences also expressed in a separate, ideal structure where language and states of affairs are linked in perfect and systematic harmony. Subsequent, less mystically inclined thinkers have anyway attempted to apply Plato's vision of an 'ideal world' to sentence structure, postulating for each sentence a 'deeper' structure of greater fixity and systematicity and more reliable as an expression of truth. The often erratic nature of sentence structure, keenly observed by followers of the Platonic tradition, together with the diversity of the languages of the world, confirmed the idea of a more unified reality hidden behind the surface of the sentence as such.

- *Anomalism is Platonic in spirit*

Against this background it becomes clear why the tradition called 'anomalism' in Hellenistic times, and which we have dubbed 'ecologism' (see 1.3), fits well into the Platonic frame of mind. The irregular and seemingly capricious nature of linguistic surface phenomena is an invitation to postulate an 'ideal' system that is somehow related to the surface phenomena and does in a regular way what the irregular surface phenomena cannot do, forge a systematic link with those as yet mysterious structures and processes that make the use of language effective.

- *What is the 'ideal being' of a sentence? Deep structure theories*

However, what this 'ideal' and hopefully explanatory structure should amount to and what its exact ontological counterpart should be remained unanswered questions for many centuries. Yet in spite of this uncertainty the notion of a hidden sentence form never ceased to exert a powerful influence on thinking about language, precisely because it was realized that the observable form of sentences is too variable and too irregular to link up directly with whatever function they fulfil in the daily use of language.

The first attempts, after Plato, to fill in the uncertain notions concerned were made in the great Ancient tradition of the Stoa. Unfortunately, as was said in chapter 1, our knowledge of the Stoa is, for the most part, based on secondary documents and much is still to be sorted out. Yet we do know that the Stoics made notable progress in formulating theories about the semantic function of language. They developed a notion of linguistic sign, distinguishing linguistic form from the world structures thought to be reflected in cognition. They even designed, as was shown in chapter 1, a notion of transformation relating word structures to the, presumably cognitive, underlying forms reflecting the structure of the world in a direct and transparent fashion.

Later, in particular in the work of the 16th century linguistic scholar Sanctius (see 1.5.2), this notion of transformation was extended to sentences, thus forming the platform on which 20th century transformational grammar could be built. Sanctius' aim was to 'regiment' natural language sentences in such a way that the irregularities disappear and all information conveyed in a sentence is cast in a uniform propositional mould, some sort of 'deep structure'. These underlying propositional structures are his answer to Plato's 'ideal' sentence form. They are certainly to be interpreted as cognitive structures, whose relation with the actual or any possible world was left out of account, not being within the linguist's province.

Sanctius, as was shown in 1.5.3, exerted a strong influence on the immensely important 17th century French treatise on grammatical theory, the Port Royal grammar of 1660, where, again, sentences were meant to be 'translated' into a more complete and semantically more systematic language by means of a system of paraphrastic translation rules. We saw in section 2.3.3 how the 18th century grammarians, especially in France, kept the Port Royal tradition alive, against the clamorous and sometimes vicious opposition of the more trendy Romanticist philosophers, who preferred to indulge in wild specula-tions about the natural origins of language and had no business with the mun-dane details of linguistic analysis and description.

Although, as was shown in 2.3.4, the 18th century Romanticist speculations about the origins of language prepared the ground for the monumental edifice of comparative philology erected during the 19th century, they did little for the analysis of the relation between grammar and meaning. For that we must turn to the professional grammarians, who completed that other edifice of traditional grammar, and prepared the ground for the great 19th century debate on subject-predicate structure to which we revert in section 7.1.3 below.

• *The Platonic tradition interpreted in terms of the semiotic triangle*
To discern the lines of history more clearly it may be of help to try and define the Platonic tradition in terms of Ogden & Richards' semiotic triangle, refer-red to repeatedly in previous pages. In fig. 1 one sees the three basic elements in the use of language: linguistic, cognitive and world structures.

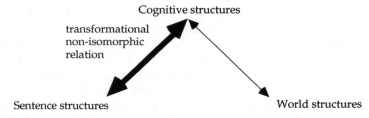

Figure 1   The Platonic tradition in terms of the semiotic triangle

The important fact here is that it is assumed that at least the linguistic and the cognitive structures are not isomorphic. The relation between world struc-tures and their cognitive counterpart is left to the philosophers to investigate. Thus, if structure is to be assigned to perceptible sentence forms it is in virtue of their primary purpose or function, i.e. to express the non-perceptible cognitive content underlying them.

7.1.2 The Aristotelian tradition: Priscian and the Modists

The Aristotelian tradition is a different story altogether. Even though Aris-totle accepted in principle the tripartite division of the semiotic triangle his interests lay elsewhere. For him, a sentence was primarily a bearer of a truth value, not the expression of a thought. Accordingly, sentence structure was to be seen in the perspective of his theory of truth, in particular his metaphysical categories and his logic, which, as we saw in 1.2.1 and 2.6.4, was based on the verbal, not the cognitive, notion of truth.

His primary interest was thus with the base line in the semiotic triangle, not with the sides. He probably realized, as Ogden and Richards did, that the base line has no causal status and can be no more than an 'imputed' relation. But he also assumed the basic isomorphism of the three kinds of structure. Cognitive structures are considered a direct reflex of world structures through the Aristotelian categories, which, as we saw in section 1.4.1, embody the most general possible cognitive categories in terms of which any world can be interpreted. Sentence structures, moreover, are considered a direct reflex of the corresponding cognitive structures.

Consequently, if sentences mirror cognitive content which mirrors the world, we may assume that sentences mirror the world, and we may study sentences in direct relation to what we take the world to be, i.e. as logical structure in terms of the metaphysical categories. The more so since logical structure assignment proves much more successful than the Platonic search for deeper structures. Whereas the Platonists were constantly at a loss to define their postulated underlying structures, the Aristotelians had their answer ready: sentence structure ís logical structure, and linguistic predicates are generated by metaphysical categories. Little else need be assumed. We thus have fig. 2 as a schematic rendering of the Aristotelian way of thinking about language.

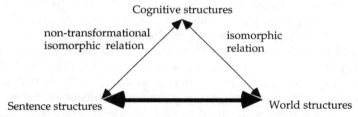

Figure 2   The Aristotelian tradition in terms of the semiotic triangle

• *Analogism is Aristotelian in spirit*

Neither Aristotle nor his followers were impressed with the irregularities and quirks of natural language sentences that were so important to the followers of the Platonic tradition. Such apparent irregularities were attributed to the natural weakness of human nature, which had lost most of its original moral fibre, and to the fallibility of cognition. Much better to apply Ockham's razor *avant la lettre* and avoid assuming distinctions, unless one is forced by the facts. Aristotle strongly disliked the mystical elements in Plato's thinking. He preferred the clarity and simplicity, and the controllability, of Quine's 'desert landscapes' (see 6.1.3.4), and this clarity he found more than anywhere else in his logico-metaphysical analysis of sentences. The Aristotelian way of thinking thus agrees naturally with the tradition known as analogism in Antiquity and renamed 'formalism' here.

- *The central question: isomorphism or no isomorphism?*

It is crucial to realize, in this context, that the principal and defining difference between the Platonic and the Aristotelian ways of dealing with language lies in the assumption or rejection of an isomorphic relation between linguistic and cognitive structures. For the Aristotelians this relation is isomorphic, for the Platonists it is not.

- *This question need no longer be speculative: it has now become empirical*

Until recently it was not possible to decide on independent grounds which view is to be preferred, the Aristotelian or the Platonic view, with the result that discussions about these matters were bound to be speculative. Nowadays we have better tools for deciding on such matters, owing to advances in the philosophy of science, the philosophy of mind, and the disciplines of linguistics and psychology. We can now say that the matter is empirical to the extent that theories formulated in terms of either tradition meet accepted standards of adequacy.

The clouds that for many centuries enveloped notions like 'sentence structure', 'cognitive structure', and indeed the very notion of 'mind', have now cleared up sufficiently for us to be able to formulate incipient scientific theories about them. Modern psychology has set the stage for a scientific treatment of cognitive phenomena, and linguistics has made some headway towards doing the same for linguistic phenomena. Both language and the mind are now beginning to be empirically accessible, with partially formalized theories generating predictions and thus inviting the challenge of counter-examples and of alternative, more unified theories.

In the old days, however, this was not so. For those who are familiar with present-day thinking about language and the mind it is difficult to imagine the opacity, vagueness and even mysticism surrounding the notions and phenomena concerned. When one begins to realize how things were in this respect one also begins to appreciate the intellectual power and courage of the principal thinkers of the past, who, gropingly and little by little, created all those concepts and insights that we take for granted but without which we would be back to square one.

- *Priscian and Speculative Grammar are part of the Aristotelian tradition*

As we saw in section 1.4.1, the 6th century Latin grammarian Priscian aimed at casting word classes and word meanings into the mould of the ten Aristotelian categories of substance, quantity, quality, relation, place, time, position, state, action and affection. The point of this enterprise was to demonstrate that linguistic categories are really a direct reflex of cognitive categories (which in turn are assumed to reflect ontological categories in a straightforward way). We can see now that this places Priscian firmly in the Aristotelian camp.

Much the same can be said about the Modists and their Speculative Grammar. In 1.4.2 we defined Speculative Grammar as an attempt at establishing a relation of regularity between the ontological and metaphysical categories taken to structure the real world, the mental categories of thought, and the grammatical categories of language. This again is entirely Aristotelian in spirit, but also as speculative as the name Speculative Grammar suggests.

7.1.3 The Subject-Predicate debate revisited

The Platonic tradition entered a new phase of life when it was realized, around the middle of the 19th century, that the Aristotelian isomorphism does not hold. The grammatical subject-predicate division of a sentence and the cognitive structuring of a thought as a mental act of assigning a property to a given entity most of the time do not run in tandem. As we had ample occasion to see in section 2.6.3, this new insight led to the postulation of a separate cognitive or psychological subject-predicate division, which thus played the role of the hidden underlying structure of the Platonists.

Although it had become clear, towards the end of the 19th century, that the psychological division is closely linked up with the step by step progress of a given discourse, precious little emerged in the way of precise theory formation.The form and nature of the cognitive structures postulated remained totally unclear, to say nothing of the rule systems by which the grammatical and the cognitive structures should be thought to be connected with each other.

In this essentially Platonic perspective, the position of logical structure with regard to grammatical sentence structure had to be ill-defined. For Wundt, the notions of subject and predicate are essentially of a logical nature as they are taken to be the prime elements of a 'judgement', i.e. of a propositional thought that has a truth value. This logical distinction is, in his view, reflected isomorphically in the grammatical structure of a sentence. He does recognize a psychological side to things in that he admits that within a judgement one element, which need not be the subject term, can be a 'dominant representation', but that is psychology, not logic. The obvious question is, of course, why it should be the logical, and not the psychological, structure that is reflected in grammar. This question Wundt fails to answer, no doubt because he was, at heart, an Aristotelian, not a Platonist. Those who, like Von der Gabelentz, proposed a tripartite division of a grammatical, a logical, and a psychological subject-predicate structure did so without being specific about the role and status of the logical leg of the tripod.

On the whole, one must conclude that the entire subject-predicate debate was Platonic in spirit but that the participants in the debate were largely unaware of that fact. They allowed themselves continuously to be diverted by elements of Aristotelian thinking precisely because they failed to see the overall structure of the problem. Wundt was the only unambiguous Aristotelian amongst them, but he, too, appears insufficiently aware of the general and wider implications of his position.

Little wonder that, in the end, a number of authors, such as Svedelius, Kalepky, Sandmann (see section 2.6.3), proposed that linguistic theory should do without the notions of subject and predicate at all. This proposal never led to anything much but it demonstrates the hopeless frustration of the scholars concerned. As we saw in 2.6.3, Kalepky called out (1928:20): 'Such a confusion cries out for formal relief'. But the relief that followed consisted in a simple ignoring of the whole issue, which has now all but disappeared from linguistic theory. Varying on Sidgwick (1895:282), quoted in 5.2 above, we may say that whatever value the developments of modern linguistics undoubtedly have is bought at a cost which deserves to be reckoned rather than ignored; yet there is hardly a suspicion in the minds of theoretical linguists that they have any cost to pay.

7.2   After 1900: the autonomy of linguistic structure

Up till the beginning of the 20th century it was inconceivable to discuss structure without at the same time taking into account the purpose, function, or meaning served by the structure in question. Structure for the sake of structure had never entered the discussions. Yet this began to happen after the first world war in America.

7.2.1   European structuralism: structure still with 'meaning'

• *The autonomy of linguistics and of linguistic structure ('form')*
The first steps towards 'structure without meaning' were taken in Europe around or just after the year 1900, in the work of Hippolyte Taine and Ferdinand de Saussure (see 3.2). Although they were far from claiming that structure could be studied without any appeal to its function or 'meaning', they did propose the autonomy of grammatical structure, distinct from psychological and/or ontological structure. De Saussure, as we saw in 3.2, had a troubled relationship with the psychology of his time, in that he wished to consider linguistics to be both a branch of psychology and distinct from it. He did not engage in the debate on subject and predicate structure, which is a remarkable fact. But we may infer that he implicitly opted for the Platonic view: no strict isomorphism between grammatical and cognitive structure.

Consequently, the Saussurian view of linguistics implied the autonomy of linguistics as against psychology and logic. There is no denying that it was the central aim of incipient theoretical linguistics in 20th century Europe (and America) to establish the autonomy of their discipline. This meant the legitimacy of attempts to investigate linguistic structure ('form') for its own sake, or, as was said by many in those days, to study language as it is and in its own right. Linguistics was no longer to be the servant of psychology or of logic.

• *Autonomous linguistics is Platonic, not Aristotelian*
This is clearly a Platonic attitude. In the Aristotelian tradition, which was embodied in the new developments in logic, such views were never aired. There natural language was either treated with disdain or forced into the mould of logical analysis.

● *European structuralism was confused about meaning*

The ideal of an autonomous linguistics did not imply full independence. The European structuralists never claimed the legitimacy of studying structure without any reference to function or meaning. They only claimed, or implied, the non-isomorphism of linguistic and cognitive or logical structure. But they failed to see that it was a necessary consequence of their attitude that they should try to define the relation of linguistic structure to the other structures involved, and therefore also to define those other structures precisely enough to define an exact formal relationship.

Instead, European structuralism remained stuck in imprecise notions of linguistic structure. As we saw when discussing de Saussure in section 3.2, the Saussurian notion of structure is fatally vague, and his notions of function and meaning heavily underdeveloped. It was an almost miraculous turn of events that Hjelmslev (see 3.4) achieved such formal clarity and power as he did in his theory of glossematics on the marshy foundations of Saussurian linguistics.

European linguistics was thus in the predicament of, on the one hand, not wishing to give up the semantic dimension in linguistic theory while, on the other, being unable to give any substance to the semantic dimension that was postulated. This weakened European linguistics to such an extent that, after World War II, it was largely taken over by the developments that had meanwhile taken place in America.

7.2.2 American structuralism: structure without meaning

● *Behaviourism cut the semantic knot with brute force*

The same predicament existed in American linguistics around the turn of the century. Linguistic structure should be studied for its own sake, but not without reference to its function or meaning. Yet no workable notion of function or meaning was in sight. This was the situation in which Bloomfield wrote his *Introduction to the Study of Language* of 1914, and there can be little doubt that Bloomfield, and others with him, felt frustrated by it.

It is legitimate, therefore, to see Bloomfield's sudden 'conversion' to behaviourism in the early 1920s in this light. By rejecting the possibility of a scientific study of meaning and proclaiming not just the autonomy but the total independence of linguistics from cognition and logic, Bloomfield severed all ties with the semiotic triangle and thus placed himself outside the dichotomy of the Platonic and the Aristotelian traditions.

The reactions of his contemporaries and the remarkable success of Bloomfieldian linguistics in America suggest that this was widely welcomed as a liberation from the shackling darkness and obscurity of past ages.

● *Yet linguistic structure cannot be studied without an appeal to meaning*

The question, however, was whether this daring enterprise was sustainable. The task now was to study linguistic structure without any appeal to function or meaning. But that must be an impossible task, since linguistic structure is not to be found in the physical speech data available. As with all structure assignment in sense data, linguistic structure is projected onto the physical data by the interpreting subject in virtue of the meaning attributed to them.

- *The vicious circle of structure assignment*

It is true that this involves a vicious circle, in that the data cannot be interpreted without an appeal to their meaning, whereas their meaning can be established only after the structure has been assigned. Much of the research in the psychology of perception and some of the research in linguistic semantics is devoted precisely to the undoing of this vicious circle. It is said, in particular, that the interpreting subject starts from a hypothesis about the probable meaning of the data in the context given, and then puts this hypothesis to the test. If it is confirmed the subject accepts that he has understood the data, if not, he will try again. It is in this light that one has to see the recent development of discourse-oriented semantic theories: the comprehension of new utterances is guided and restricted by preceding context, not in the purely statistical way proposed in entropy theory during the 1950s (see 4.7.1), but in more cognitively integrated ways that are the object of intensive research nowadays.

- *Zellig Harris hit the hard bottom of structure without meaning*

The question came to a head in the work of Zellig Harris, who insisted in his (1951) that structure should be discovered and assigned without any appeal to meaning or function, and indicated a procedure for doing so (see 4.4.3 above). True, in a footnote at the very beginning of the book he admits that native intuitions are required when it must be decided whether two sounds count as 'the same' or 'different' in the native speaker's language, thus letting at least certain intuitions about the functionality of sounds into the methodology, but this is considered a blemish that can hopefully be removed in the future, when distributional measurements are more precise and more complete:

> In principle, meaning need be involved only to the extent of determining what is repetition. If we know that *life* and *rife* are not entirely repetitions of each other, we will then discover that they differ in distribution (and hence in 'meaning'). It may be presumed that any two morphemes *A* and *B* having different meanings also differ somewhere in distribution: there are some environments in which one occurs and the other does not. Hence the phonemes or sound features which occur in *A* but not in *B* differ in distribution at least to that extent from those which occur in *B* but not in *A*.
>
> Harris (1951:7)

It is now generally recognized that the method proposed in Harris (1951) for the discovery and assignment of structures to sentences is fundamentally flawed. We saw in section 4.5 how it was superseded by a method where semantic considerations are recognized as, at least, a criterion of adequacy, in that the grammar must, at some level of description, disambiguate ambiguous expressions. Even so, however, the central question of how and to what extent semantic considerations can or must play a role in the discovery and assignment of structure has remained unanswered till the present day.

7.2.3 Surface semantics and deep structure semantics

Up till the mid-1950s, the lack of interest in questions of meaning in American structuralism was such that it is impossible to find out what ideas the linguists concerned had about the nature and status of meaning and meaning representations. Since Bloomfield had taken linguistics out of the semiotic triangle, the question of whether or not there is isomorphism between grammatical, cognitive and logical structures simply did not arise.

- *Semantic considerations were let in again after 1957*

But it came back when semantic considerations were let in again after 1957. Linguistic theory, in other words, was put back into the semiotic triangle, or vice versa, depending on how one looks at it. Not long after 1957 questions began to be asked about the way semantic content and semantic distinctions could or should be represented. The emphasis was not so much on lexical content as on structural semantic properties, such as the semantic subject status of *John* with respect to *please* in *John is eager to please*, but its semantic object status with respect to *please* in *John is easy to please.* Such observations, together with a few now very well-known ambiguities like *the shooting of the hunters*,[3] were used to argue that a grammar should, at some (surface or deeper) level of analysis, account for these facts by assigning structures to the sentences and phrases in question in such a way that the semantic properties at issue are transparent and leave no room for ambiguity. Somehow, for reasons that were as yet unclear, such arguments appealed to large sections of the linguistic community.

Despite the cloudiness that hung over semantic notions in the early days of transformational grammar, one thing did stand out with relative clarity. If it is required of a grammar that it disambiguate any ambiguity arising in a sentence or phrase and if that disambiguation often requires a deeper, underlying level of analysis, it follows that surface structure alone is insufficient for the rendering of all semantic content. This conclusion naturally made one wonder if another level of representation should not be postulated where all (non-lexical) meaning is rendered precisely and adequately.

- *But what was their role in determining structure?*

The general trend in theoretical linguistics after 1960 was to answer this question in the affirmative. In other words, theoretical linguistics sided with the Platonic and rejected the Aristotelian tradition. But this did not mean that the assignment of structure was now firmly based on semantic criteria again. On the contrary, apart from the requirement that grammars (and

---

[3] It must be said, in this connection, that the range of semantically relevant examples that were being discussed was extremely limited, and geared to the formal possibilities that were available at the time. Potentially interesting observations, such as the ambiguity of (i) as against the non-ambiguity of (ii), noted in De Rijk (1974) (which was written in 1967), were largely ignored, probably because existing theory had no grip on them:
    (i)   I no longer remember the names of my students
    (ii)   I have forgotten the names of my students

lexicons) should disambiguate ambiguities, everything remained as it was. As we saw in section 4.6.2, the criterion for the selection of a grammar was the degree of overall simplicity and the conformity with similar rule systems for other languages. The role of meaning remained marginal and ill-defined.

This was inevitable for a very simple reason. If it is assumed that surface structure is insufficiently specific with regard to meaning it becomes very difficult to use meaning as a criterion for the assignment of grammatical structure. Meaning, in other words, remained an awkward presence, even though the atmosphere of taboo surrounding it was beginning to dissipate. A more principled answer to this predicament came in 1964, with the influential book by Katz and Postal, which is discussed in 7.3 below.

- *Why not surface structure semantics?*

In this context one is fully entitled to ask why the world of theoretical linguistics was so quick in accepting the basic tenet of the Platonic tradition and rejecting the notion of surface structure as the primary bearer of linguistic meaning. Logicians, in those days, also began doing grammar, in particular Montague and his school. And it was their opinion that no separate level of meaning representation is required: surface structure, for them, provides a good enough grid for the computation of the truth value of a given sentence S given a 'world', and, once the program of intensionalization is put into motion (see 6.1.4), for the determination of the set of possible worlds in which S is true.

One may reply that Montague grammar makes systematic use of 'translations' of natural language expressions into the language of predicate calculus, and that the Montagovian truth calculus depends to some extent on the structure of these logical translations, so that a separate level of semantic analysis is surreptitiously introduced after all. Such a criticism may be well-founded, but other logically inspired forms of surface semantics, such as categorial grammar in all its varieties, are clearly not guilty of any such form of 'semantic bootlegging', and yet the arguments against surface semantics apply equally to them. So the question is: what are the observations that make it unlikely that surface semantics will succeed?

We note, to begin with, that surface semantics has the clear *prima facie* advantage of Ockham's razor: why should one assume a level of analysis if it is not necessary to do so? That is, the burden of proof rests undoubtedly with those who propose a separate level of semantic representation. They have to show cases where any adequate semantic treatment will involve highly ad hoc provisions if no separate level of semantic representation is admitted.

In this author's view, the opponents of surface semantics have a strong case. It is not difficult to present a large array of examples suggesting the need for a separate level of semantic representation (see e.g. Seuren 1985:61-86), but the following examples of copying (or 'spread') may serve as sufficient illustration here. Consider the copying of negation, common to varying degrees of intensity in many languages and dialects. For example, if in the Cockney sentence

(1)   'E ain't never been no good to no woman, not never

the negations were all interpreted as sentential negations of the normal, un-marked kind (according to the Negation Principle of section 6.2.3.3), then the sentence would mean 'he has at some time been some good to some woman', which is clearly not what it means. Its real meaning involves an emphatic denial that the person in question has ever been any good to any woman whosoever, in proper English. But in proper Cockney the expression is as in (1). As we saw in 6.2.2.2, Russell (1957:389) attributed negation copying to 'the somewhat confused thoughts which most people at most times have in their heads', to the lack of intelligence of common folk, that is, but we know enough about language nowadays to say with confidence that Russell's explanation cuts no ice. Negation copying is not only widespread in the languages of the world, and not at all restricted to population strata with a presumed consti-tutional lack of intelligence, it is also subject to very precise rules and restric-tions. The rule for (1) is, roughly speaking, that the one and only sentence negation has been copied, presumably for greater emphasis, for every subse-quent existentially quantified phrase and once again, in *not never*, in its own right. It is, in other words, a fact of the language in question. And it shows that language apparently feels free to manipulate forms, for whatever reason, in such a way that the literal meaning gets obscured, without the speakers of the language in question being fooled.

Another striking example, also of copying or 'spread', is the following sen-tence observed by the American linguist Paul Schachter in a study on serial verbs in the West African Kwa language Akan. The sentence quoted is in the Akuapem dialect, said by a speaker who described the washing of the corn in the river:[4]

(2)   Me-de   aburow   mi-gu   nsu-m
       I-take   the corn   I-flow   water-in
       'I pour the corn into the water'

and comments (Schachter (1974:258-9):

> We see from this example that, whatever the semantic subject of the second verb may be, its syntactic subject is identical with that of the first verb. Thus in [(2)], there is no doubt that *aburow* 'corn' is the semantic subject of *gu* 'flow' (as well as both the syntactic and the semantic object of *de* 'take'); for clearly it is the corn, and not the speaker, that is being poured into the water. Confirmation of this is provided by [(3a)], which shows that there is a selectional incompatibility between a subject like *me-/mi-* and the verb *gu* (*gu* requires a mass or plural subject as in [(3b)],

[(3)]a.   *mi-gu   nsum
           I-flow water-in

  b.   aburow gu   nsum
        corn   flow   water-in
        'corn is flowing into the water'

[4] I tested this sentence on a native speaker of Akan, who replied that it was correct in the Akuapem dialect, but that only older and more dignified people (his aunt, for example) would use that dialect. He was, he said, sufficiently confident about Akuapem to confirm Schachter's observation.

If the surface structure of (2) were taken as the grid for the determination of the meaning of this sentence the result would be starkly incorrect. The sentence would then appear to imply that the speaker 'flows into the water', and not the corn, as is intended by the speaker.

The grammatical machinery behind sentence (2) is clear enough: the original semantic subject 'it' of the verb *gu* (flow), anaphorically resuming the object *aburow* (the corn) of the main verb *de* (take), has been deleted (under standard control conditions) and the original subject *mi* (I) of the higher verb has been copied for the subordinate verb. This is a case of syntactic Subject Copying, clearly a rule without any semantic import, but syntactically necessary for a proper description of this dialect of Akan.

- *Deep structure semantics requires a rule system connecting surface*
  structures with semantic representations

Since observations like these are easily multiplied for any language, it seems sound strategy to reject surface semantics and to accept the Platonic view that meanings tend to hide behind semantically misleading surface structures. This implies, however, that to describe a language it is necessary to define, for each sentence, a semantic representation, ánd to define a rule system relating semantic representations to surface sentences and vice versa. This conclusion had already been drawn in principle by Sanctius, as was shown in section 1.5.2, but its full impact was only now beginning to hit the world of theoretical linguistics. It was time, some linguists of the early 1960s felt, to become serious about the nature of semantic representations, and of the rule systems required to relate them to surface structures. The assignment of structure to sentences and phrases would then be determined by the criterion of what rule system provided the simplest overall mapping procedure between the two levels of representation, the surface level and the semantic level.

Not surprisingly, after decennia of semantic neglect and given the basic unclarity of existing notions of meaning and related articles, such insights and convictions grew slowly and hesitantly, and often against fierce resistance. In the following section we shall see how this question was dealt with and what resulted from it.

7.3   Deep structure in Transformational Grammar

When behaviourism was abandoned, around 1960, it became respectable, and desirable, again to talk about meaning. The problem was, however, that linguists did not know how. Meaning proved to be elusive and no way was seen to gain empirical access to semantic phenomena. Even so, Katz & Fodor (1963) and Katz & Postal (1964) attempted to break through the semantic barrier. These attempts were made in the context of the then current form of transformational grammar. In this section we discuss these developments, and see how they led to the birth, in the second half of the 1960s, of what became known as *generative semantics*. Generative semantics was less a theory of meaning than a contribution to the theory of syntax, in that it made syntax more sensitive to semantic phenomena than had been the case before. In particular, the way appeared to have been found towards an organic integration of the study of grammar into the wider context of semantics, cognition and language use. Virtually all of that work was still to be done, but the beginnings were there, and so were the inspiration and the enthusiasm. The first priority, so it seemed at the time, was the development of a theory of linguistic meaning. In this context the discovery was made, in the late 1960s, that the language of modern predicate calculus is non-trivially relevant to the study of syntax in a way hitherto unsuspected, which made many generative semanticists turn to logic, a new experience for linguists. By 1970 generative semantics was the dominant trend in theoretical linguistics, and it looked as though grammar was going to be generative semantics for some time to come. McCawley in particular was developing new and inspired insights, which were having a profound effect on the theory of syntax and supported the view that syntax stood to gain significantly from the hypothesis that syntactic deep structures should be formulated in terms of an enriched variety of predicate calculus.

This new development was, however, nipped in the bud (see 7.3.3 for a more detailed analysis). About 1968 Chomsky took sides against generative semantics, having gone along with it for a few years. In the most generous view, his objections derived chiefly from his aversion to the generative semanticists' somewhat stormy manifestations of joy at the re-introduction of meaning into the study of grammar and the rapprochement to logic, which had been painfully separated from grammar since the late 19th century. Though he himself had been instrumental in the downfall of behaviourism, Chomsky found no inspiration in semantic considerations and felt more comfortable with purely syntactic structures and principles. Starting in 1970 he and his followers effectively destroyed the generative semantics movement in a few years, strategically concentrating the attack on where it was most vulnerable. And vulnerable it was, first because of the generative semanticists' lack of familiarity with the relatively unknown territories of logic and semantics which they were enthusiastically exploring, and secondly because of their *laissez-faire* attitude as regards the acquisition of funds for research students. As the young generative semanticists were trying to find their feet they had no defence against sudden attacks meant to destroy them.

This episode in the recent history of theoretical linguistics is odd in that no academically relevant arguments were brought to bear. The onslaught on generative semantics was based entirely on claims to prestige and on other sociological factors, leading to wholesale rejection and even utter derision. It was a clash of personalities and ambitions, more than of academic issues.

A further, minor, factor contributing to the disintegration of the generative semantics movement was the advent of logic-inspired formal semantics (see 6.1). Whereas generative semantics was poised to start developing a theory of linguistic meaning, the Californian logician Richard Montague introduced a form of semantics entirely alien to the linguists' way of thinking and born from

the totally different tradition of logical model theory. The generative semanticists, who were not or hardly trained in this tradition, were caught by surprise and, for the time being, lost the initiative to the formal semanticists.

7.3.1 No competence without meaning: the semantic component

7.3.1.1 Katz and Fodor (1963)

* *Linguistic competence necessarily implies knowledge of meanings*

In section 4.6.3 we observed that the theoretical aims and the coverage of the
theory of transformational grammar as it was around 1960 were unnecessarily
restricted and too impoverished to serve as a basis for an integrated causal
theory of language structure and language use. The data considered were
limited to well-formedness judgements elicited from native speakers (usually
linguists themselves), while no adequate attention was paid to semantic and
other data. Around 1962 Chomsky began to speak of 'linguistic competence' as
the object of enquiry, the mental processing unit deemed to be the underlying
cause of the observable data and to be reconstructed by hypothesis. But this
notion of competence was still limited to the native speaker's ability to separate well-formed from unwell-formed strings of symbols (words).

It was at this point that the philosophers Jerrold J. Katz and Jerry A.
Fodor, both working in Chomsky's immediate environment, realized that this
notion of competence was actually rather strange. Imagine a speaker who is
capable of separating well-formed from unwell-formed strings of symbols in
his language but has no inkling of what the strings of symbols mean. Could one
possibly say that such a speaker is in any way *competent* in his language? Of
course not. In fact, such a speaker would be an unnatural monstrosity never
encountered in real life. If there is any point to the notion of linguistic competence it must encompass the speaker's ability to grasp the meaning of any
given sentence and to express any given meaning adequately, that is, in a
grammatically and lexically correct way, in his language.

In practical terms this implies that, given a statement S and an appropriate situation A, a competent speaker should be able to answer at least two
questions. First, he should be able to judge whether or not S is true with respect
to A. This is the truth-conditional test. Knowledge of meaning implies a few
more things besides the ability to satisfy the truth-conditional test, but this
much was known and accepted in philosophical circles around 1960. Secondly,
a competent speaker should be able to say whether S, as understood, is an
adequate or correct expression for the intended meaning. This is the grammaticality test, discussed above in section 4.6.3.

* *Introduction of a Semantic Component to complement the existing
Syntactic Component*

Katz and Fodor thus felt that it was necessary to extend the notion of competence to cover also the semantic aspect of sentences, not just their well-
formedness or grammaticality. The problem was how. They reasoned that for

every sentence there should be, besides a syntactic representation at different levels of syntactic analysis, also a *semantic representation* (SR), specifying the meaning of the sentence at hand. This was a bold step to take, especially since they lacked any precise notion as to what such a semantic representation could or should look like. Even so, however, they proceeded with courage, putting forward the idea that an integrated description of a language should contain not only the generative machinery devised for the specification of grammatical well-formedness, but also a machinery for the derivation of SR's from given syntactic structures. Hence, they argued, a separate interpretative *semantic component* should be added to the grammar, consisting of so-called *projection rules*, which were meant to take syntactic structures as input and to produce SRs as output.

- *The transformational model current during the early 1960s*

At this point it is useful to say a few words about what a transformational grammar was meant to look like during the period at hand, that is, the early 1960s. The syntactic deep structures, generated by the formation rules, would contain a specification of tense, of modality (if any), and of the lexical predicate-argument structure of the sentence under generation. The transformational rules came in two kinds, the *singulary transformations*, which operated on a single underlying S-structure, and *generalized transformations*, which operated on sets of two (or more) underlying structures. The singulary transformations would turn an underlying S-structure into a negative sentence, or a question, or an imperative, or a passive. Or they would transpose a verbal particle (e.g. from *He rang up the girl* to *He rang the girl up*). Or they would delete the subject-NP of an embedded clause (e.g. from *John wanted [John go away]* to *John wanted to go away*). Or they would turn an underlying S-structure into a nominalization (later to be re-integrated into a sentence by means of a generalized transformation), and a few other operations of that nature. Generalized transformations would combine two (or more) underlying structures, not necessarily deep structures but possibly already transformed structures themselves, into a new combination, as with sentences conjoined by *and* or *or* or *but*, or with subordinate clauses headed by a subordinating conjunction like *because* or a relative pronoun, or with nominalizations to be re-integrated into a matrix sentence. It should also be noted that both the notation of the transformational rules and their actual descriptive content were intolerably sloppy.

- *The 1963 version of a Semantic Component*

In this context, the proposal made in Katz & Fodor (1963) amounted to the following. The actual generative machinery for sentences remained embodied in a transformational grammar, now called the Syntactic Component. The new Semantic Component was conceived as a set of rules taking syntactically defined structures as input and delivering a semantic representation. In the 1963 version the syntactic deep structures (SDS) produced by the formation rules on the one hand, and the surface structures (SS) produced by the transformational rules (T-rules) on the other, were both input to projection rules. These were thus divided into two classes, the P1 rules acting on deep structures, and the P2 rules acting on surface structures. Jointly they were meant to produce the intended SRs. The P1 rules would cater mainly for lexical predicate-argument relations, and perhaps also for tenses and modalities. The P2 rules would specify the semantic effects of the singulary and generalized T-rules devised for the introduction of negation, for passivization, for question and imperative formation, conjunction reduction and similar jobs.

The overall architecture of the theory would thus be as shown in fig. 3, where the rectangular boxes represent sets of rules and the triangles linguistic tree structures. The intended SR-output is placed in a non-descript oval owing to the unclarity as to its nature and format. Note that the model shown in fig. 3 (where the phonological rules and the phonetic form have been left out) is an extension of the model shown in fig. 17 of section 4.6.3.

- *The semantic notions involved remained hazy and underdefined*

One should realize that no precise notions existed at the time as to the nature and format of either the semantic representations or the projection rules. The examples given by the authors to illustrate the working of the projection rules were limited to lexical disambiguation on the basis of selection restrictions.

For example, to select the correct meaning of the ambiguous word *ball* the P1 rules would have to look at the governing verb and at the argument function of the NP in which the word *ball* occurs. Thus, if it is (head of) the object-NP of the verb *kick* then the meaning 'round object used for playing purposes' would be selected on the basis of the lexical selection restrictions of the verb *kick*. But as (head of) the object-NP of a verb like *organize* the meaning 'social occasion at which dancing takes place' would be chosen.

Not much later McCawley (1968) showed that such a task description for projection rules is woefully inadequate if one wishes to get semantic representations of any significance, and also that this method of lexical disambiguation, though based on notions that are sensible enough in themselves, fails in many instances. For example, given a sentence like *The king is made of plastic* it is impossible to decide on the basis of just the words used in this sentence whether the NP *the king* is intended to refer to a chess piece, a toy, a representation of a king, or even a real king uncharitably described by a non-king. It is clear, in other words, that Katz & Fodor (1963) represents a brave but immature attempt at integrating semantics into the theory of grammar.

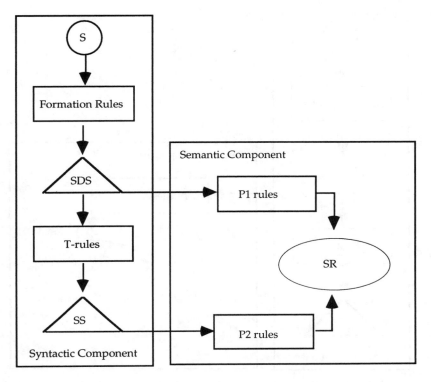

Figure 3   *Overall architecture of an integrated linguistic description according to Katz & Fodor (1963)*

7.3.1.2 Katz and Postal (1964)

- *The 1964 version of a Semantic Component: the principle of Semantic Invariance of T-rules*

Katz & Fodor (1963) was soon overshadowed by Katz & Postal (1964), a book written by the same Jerrold J. Katz and the transformational linguist Paul M. Postal. This book, proved of great importance for subsequent developments. In it the authors proposed a radical restriction on the function of transformational rules, and thus on the form of grammars generally, the restriction being that T-rules should not be allowed to change the meaning of the sentence under generation. This restriction, the *Semantic Invariance of T-rules*, implies that there is only one class of projection rules, which take SDSs as input and deliver SRs. Moreover, the SDSs are now taken to be semantically complete in the sense that they express the full meaning of the sentence under generation. In this view, an integrated linguistic description (but for the phonology) has the overall structure as shown in fig. 4.

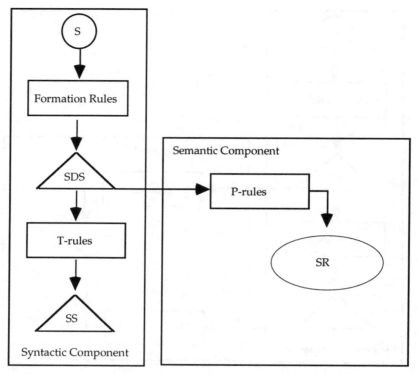

Figure 4   *Overall architecture of an integrated linguistic description according to Katz & Postal (1964)*

- *The argument was strictly syntactic*

Katz and Postal argued that if one adheres to the principle that T-rules should be kept semantically invariant, the grammar as a whole will gain in simplicity and generality, and will thus have to be preferred over grammars that do not abide by this principle. Since the argument was directed at the improvement of syntactic descriptions it was, strictly speaking, a syntactic argument, though it made use of semantic notions and criteria. Against the background of linguistic theory of the early 1960s this is not surprising, since one had just learned how to set up syntactic arguments. Setting up semantic arguments was still beyond the grasp of the theoretical linguists. In fact, in Katz & Postal (1964) the notions of P-rule and of semantic representation were still as hazy and underdefined as they were in Katz & Fodor (1963).

The bulk of the book (pp. 71-156, out of a total of 174 pages) is taken up with a discussion of cases where it might seem that T-rules should be allowed to change meaning. In all these cases the argument is that these T-rules had better be changed in such a way that they do not change meaning. This part of the book is therefore purely syntactic theory, albeit in the interest of semantic integration. The argument also deals with singulary and generalized transformations. As regards the latter, it was suggested (1964:120-148) that they should be replaced by a system with dummy elements indicating the positions where embeddings could take place, and that only S-embeddings should be allowed. This proposal was soon universally accepted (see also 7.3.1.3 below). As for the singulary transformations, the authors concentrated on passives, negatives, imperatives and questions, the main meaning-changing singulary T-rules in the literature of those days.

- *The Passive argument*

Chomsky (1957:100-101) had already observed the semantic difference between sentences like:

(4)a.   Everyone in the room knows two languages
   b.   Two languages are known by everyone in the room

Sentence (4a) is preferably interpreted as saying that everyone in the room is bilingual (reading (a)), whereas (4b) seems to say that there are two specific languages, say Swahili and Turkish, known by everyone in the room (reading (b)). The difference is one of scope: in reading (a) the universal quantifier *everyone* takes scope over the existential quantifier *two languages*, whereas in reading (b) the relation is inverted. It is easy, of course, to imagine a situation where the one is true while the other is false. It would thus seem that the passive transformation is capable of changing the meaning of the sentence at hand. Katz & Postal, however, argue (1964:72) that there is no semantic difference here, since both sentences can be interpreted both ways. Hence, they say, the passive transformation poses no threat to the principle of Semantic Invariance of T-rules.

Quite independently, and in a totally different context, this view was also taken by Richard Montague who, at about the same time but across the country in California, was shaping his theory of formal semantics. Yet it is based on defective observation. While it can still be maintained for the sentences (4a) and (4b) that they can be used to express both meanings, though there appears to be a clear preference for reading (a) in (4a) and for reading (b) in (4b), this is no longer so when negation comes into play. The following active-passive pair does indeed have different meanings, depending on the scope relations of the quantifiers involved and the negation operator. It does seem that (5a) can only be read as (6a), while (5b) can only be read as (6b). To try and impose (6a) on (5b), or (6b) on (5a), is so hard that one must accept that this is not on:

(5)a.   Not everyone in the room knows two languages
   b.   Two languages are not known by everyone in the room

(6)a.   not - $\forall x$:persons in the room - $\exists 2y$:languages [know (x,y)]
   b. $\exists 2y$:languages - not - $\forall x$:persons in the room [know (x,y)]

Therefore, the answer given by Katz & Postal must be judged inadequate. Yet this does not weaken their hypothesis, since it has proved advantageous on independent grounds to eliminate the passive transformation from the list of T-rules and to have passives generated at deep structure level by the formation rules.

- *The Negation argument*

As regards negation, one cannot, of course, deny the semantic import of any T-rule inserting *not* into a given S-structure. Here, Katz & Postal were fortunate in that they could fall back on the monumental study on negation in English by Ed Klima which had just appeared (Klima 1964). Here Klima argues, on grounds that were entirely independent of Katz & Postal's Semantic Invariance hypothesis, that the grammar of English would gain if the negation word *not* were generated by the formation rules and not inserted transformationally. This cuts the argument short in that Katz & Postal can now simply refer to Klima (1964). They write (1964:74):

> The more recent treatment does not mean that there is no longer a negative transformation. There is. But instead of introducing a morpheme it now only repositions the morpheme, and instead of being optional it is now obligatory.

- *The Imperative argument*

As regards imperatives, Katz & Postal propose (1964:74-79) that their syntactic deep structure should be generated by the formation rules in such a way that it contain an imperative 'marker' *I* as a high sentential operator, indicating that the sentence in question is to be interpreted as an imperative and triggering the transformational chain that will lead to grammatically well-formed imperatives.

It had already been argued by transformational grammarians that imperatives should not be derived by simply deleting whatever tense, modality and subject-NP the S-structure might have. It had been recognized as counter-productive to derive an imperative like *Kill the duckling* from something like, for example, *The farmer killed the duckling*. This must be judged inadequate in view of facts like the following:

(7) a.   Don't hurt yourself/yourselves
    b.   *Don't hurt myself/ourselves/themselves
    c.   Leave me alone, will you
    d.   *Leave me alone, must you

The grammaticality of (7a) as against the ungrammaticality of (7b) shows that it pays to assume an underlying second person singular or plural for imperatives. This conclusion is reinforced by the tag *will you* in (7c), which, moreover, makes it plausible to assume an underlying modal auxiliary verb *will*, and not, for example, *must*, as in the ungrammatical (7d). Yet, the authors argue, it is not enough to posit an underlying *you will ...* for imperatives since the modal auxiliary *will* is ambiguous between a predictive-declarative meaning and an imperative meaning, in virtue of which the speaker imposes his will on the addressee. The Semantic Component would thus not have anything to go by if it were to disambiguate between the two readings.

The reader will see that this, by itself, is no argument, since one can always reply that a sentence like (10a) is simply ambiguous between a predictive-declarative and an imperative meaning, and that therefore the Semantic Component will have to come up with two different readings. But then Katz &

Postal go further and exploit the parallelism between imperatives and corresponding sentences starting with 'I request that ...' as regards the possibility of (a) sentence adverbials, and (b) the selection of the main verb. Thus, there is a strict parallelism between the grammaticality status for the sentences in (8) and those in (9), not matched by the sentences of (10) which contain the ambiguous modal auxiliary *will*:

(8)a. Leave the house now
 b. *Undeniably leave the house
 c. *Leave the house yesterday
 d. *Perhaps leave the house
 e. Moreover, leave the house

(9)a. I request that you leave the house now
 b. *I request that you undeniably leave the house
 c. *I request that you leave the house yesterday
 d. *I request that you perhaps leave the house
 e. Moreover, I request that you leave the house

(10)a. You will leave the house now
 b. You will undeniably leave the house
 c. *You will leave the house yesterday
 d. You will perhaps leave the house
 e. Moreover, you will leave the house

The authors then argue that whatever explanation will account for the facts of (9) can be applied to account for (8) as well, if the grammar derives sentences like those in (8) from semantically equivalent sentences under the imperative operator *I*, whose semantic translation is 'I request that'. The grammar can do so by replacing the imperative operator *I* with the imperative modal *will* at some early transformational stage.

There is, furthermore, a parallelism between ungrammatical imperatives like (11a-d) and the corresponding *request*-sentences in (12), again not matched by the *will*-sentences in (13). Here the ungrammaticality of the sentences in (11) and (12) is caused by the fact that the main verbs used denote a mental state that falls outside the subject's control:

(11)a. *Believe the claim
 b. *Understand the answer
 c. *Want more money
 d. *Hope it rains

(12)a. *I request that you believe the claim
 b. *I request that you understand the answer
 c. *I request that you want more money
 d. *I request that you hope it rains

(13)a. You will believe the claim
 b. You will understand the answer
 c. You will want more money
 d. You will hope it rains

Finally, the authors compare the grammatical (14a) with the ungrammatical (14b), and conclude that for an imperative to figure as the second element in a conjunction the first element has to be an imperative as well:

(14)a.   Come here and I'll give you a dollar
   b.   *I'll give you a dollar and come here

Their conclusion is that the grammar is improved if it is assumed that the syntactic deep structure contains an imperative marker *I* triggering the transformations needed to get a well-formed surface imperative and at the same time providing the semantic specification required for imperatives.

- *The Question argument*

The most extensively elaborated syntactic argument concerns questions (Katz & Postal 1964:79-117). Here the authors are much more specific than in their presentation of the other arguments, and they do, in fact, present a concrete example of a projection rule for questions (Katz & Postal 1964:115-116). Again, the authors query the correctness of existing treatments. Transformational treatments of questions, in those days, were indeed too primitive. For yes/no (or polar) questions there was a machinery consisting of a set of operations on assertive sentences to turn them into polar questions. WH-questions were mostly generated by inserting a WH-element at the beginning of the sentence and having that attract any indefinite pronominal NP ('someone', 'something') in the S-structure.

The authors start out by re-applying the adverbials argument used for imperatives, observing that high sentence adverbials tend not to occur in questions, as they do not occur in imperatives, and showing the parallelism with full speech act paraphrases for questions, as they did for imperatives. The paraphrase they use for questions is 'I request that you answer ...', but a better fit is obtained with, for example, 'I ask you to tell me if/WH ...', as in (15a-e), which corresponds exactly with the polar and WH-questions in (16a-e). Again, the argument is that whatever will explain (15) will explain (16):

(15)a.   I ask you to tell me if Harry has left the house
   b.   I ask you to tell me if Harry has perhaps left the house
   c.   *I ask you to tell me if Harry has surely left the house
   d.   *I ask you to tell me what Harry has unforgivably written
   e.   *I ask you to tell me why Harry has undeniably left the house

(16)a.   Has Harry left the house?
   b.   Has Harry perhaps left the house?
   c.   *Has Harry surely left the house?
   d.   *What has Harry unforgivably written?
   e.   *Why has Harry undeniably left the house?

One notices that the adverbials that cannot occur in questions form a more restricted class than in the case of imperatives. Moreover, some adverbs, like *perhaps*, may occur in polar questions but not in WH-questions.[5] Nevertheless, the authors conclude that, as for imperatives, a high operator should be assumed, in this case the question operator Q, whose semantic translation would amount to something like 'I request that you answer ...' (or perhaps better 'I ask you to tell me if ...'). This operator would then set in motion the transformational chain required for polar questions.

The authors subsequently argue that the existing way of treating WH-questions is inadequate. In their view, there must be a high sentence operator Q to attract the WH-element, and the WH-element attracted should be marked as such in the S-structure. This argument is based on the consideration, which was being tentatively explored at the time in transformational circles, that every deletion and substitution resulting from a transformational rule should be *uniquely recoverable*. The unique recoverability criterion requires that any lexical material to be inserted or deleted by a T-rule should be specified as such in the rule or else be a non-specific Pro-form. The authors defend this principle as follows:

> The motivation for this principle requiring unique recoverability, which receives its formulation in the general theory of linguistic descriptions, is both syntactic and semantic. The syntactic motivation comes primarily from evidence about particular natural languages which shows that the simplest grammars of the transformational type for these languages conform to the requirement of this principle. Of course, there is not enough evidence of this kind to settle the issue decisively. But the best hypothesis at this stage is clearly the one which says that deletion and substitution rules of any syntactic component must permit unique recoverability. This is the best hypothesis because it is the narrowest constraint on the form of syntactic components consistent with the available evidence, and thus it is the strongest claim about the nature of human language. ... The semantic motivation for this principle will be discussed later.   Katz & Postal (1964:79-80)

(One notices the early concern with universal constraints on grammars and the requirement that the empirical effects of a proposed universal constraint should be tried out on the description of a variety of natural languages.)

If the principle of unique recoverability is applied to WH-questions the existing treatment is inadequate as it fails to distinguish between, for example, *Who saw someone?* and *Who(m) did someone see?* The authors propose, therefore, that WH-questions should have an underlying form as in (17a) (Katz & Postal 1964:89), with the question operator Q at the beginning of the sentence and any WH-element in the sentence marked as such. The syntactic status of Q is specified more clearly on pp. 115 and 154, which show that Q is treated as an operator with a nuclear S-structure as its argument. The 'Nucleus' is meant to consist of an optional sentence adverbial followed by a constituent called 'Theme', which expands into the then usual NP and VP, as shown in (17b).

Then the authors proceed to argue (p. 96) that polar questions are in fact a subtype of WH-questions, where the questioned WH-element is an underlying

[5] It should be observed that the question of which adverbials can and which cannot occur with questions and/or imperatives has remained unanswered to the present day.

either-or disjunction, as in (17c). Both disjuncts are S-structures, and the second disjunct is the negation of the first, so that the two S-structures form a polar opposition. It will be noticed that the disjunction operator *either...or* is treated as a sentence adverbial and placed over the NP-VP structure called 'Theme'. This implies that subsequent transformational operations will have to assign the elements *either* and *or* their proper position in the sentence.

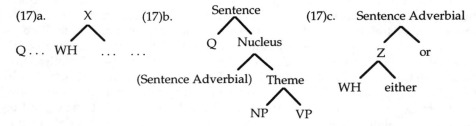

This analysis of polar questions is defended by the observation (Katz & Postal 1964:96) that a simple polar question like *Has Harry left the house?* has alternative synonymous forms like *Has Harry left the house or not?* or *Has Harry left the house or hasn't he?* The same goes for dependent questions: *She asked if/whether Harry had left the house (or not)* or *She asked if/whether Harry had (or had not) left the house.* The authors might have added the observation that a question like (18a) is ambiguous as long as no account is taken of intonation. But with rising tone on *English* and a somewhat higher tone on *French*, and a falling final tone, the sentence is equivalent to (18b). On the other hand, with flat tone on *English* and *French*, and a rising final tone, (18a) is equivalent to (18c):[6]

(18)a. Did the English or the French win the war?
    b. Was it the English or was it the French who won the war?
    c. Did the English or the French win the war, or didn't they?

The actual transformational machinery required for the correct surface forms of questions is presented on pages 104-105, and further elaborated and illustrated in the subsequent pages.

---

[6] There is an anecdote about Bertrand Russell, who reputedly, when asked by a stewardess on a plane whether he wanted tea or coffee, replied 'Yes', thereby wishing to make it clear that the disjunction operator *or* does not indicate mutually exclusive alternatives but is inclusive in that it yields truth when both disjuncts are true. Whether the anecdote is historically correct or not, it reflects Russell's attitude towards natural language, which he regarded as messy and corrupted by the general lack of intelligence of the human race as a whole. However, the implicit criticism of natural language contained in the anecdote is inappropriate. Had Russell been more open to intonational phenomena, like those shown in (18a-c), he would perhaps have felt more lenient towards the stewardess and indicated his preference for tea or for coffee. But then, the intonational features of stewardesses' endlessly repeated questions as they work their way down the aisle often tend to deteriorate.

- *Katz & Postal (1964) immediately proved highly influential*

We will omit a discussion of other syntactic issues in this book, in particular those connected with generalized transformations. Suffice it to say that the book presents a sample of syntactic reasoning that must be considered highly sophisticated for its day. As we said at the outset, the book proved very influential right from the beginning. Chomsky, and with him the whole group of transformational grammarians, were immediately swayed. The principle of Semantic Invariance of T-rules was universally accepted.

7.3.1.3 The *Aspects* model (1965)

It was also, at the time, accepted by Chomsky, who put it into practice in his very widely read book *Aspects of the Theory of Syntax* of 1965. The overall grammatical model in this book is precisely that of fig. 4 above, except that no effort was made to fill in any detail of the Semantic Component. *Aspects* is not about meaning representations or about projection rules, but about syntax and its relation to the lexicon.

- *The principle of cyclicity: some T-rules are ordered cyclically*

Apart from long discussions on questions of general methodology, adequacy and evaluation of alternative theories (1965:3-62; see 4.6 above), and apart from a tedious and still-born proposal regarding the treatment of selection restrictions (1965:63-106; see 4.5.2, 4.5.3), the book essentially follows up on the hypothesis put forward in Katz & Postal (1964). The only substantial new idea in *Aspects* is the proposal that some transformational rules, the cyclic rules, should be taken to apply cyclically and bottom-up, where each embedded S forms a cycle until the top-S is processed. We shall now see how this extremely important proposal grew out of Chomsky's way of incorporating the Katz & Postal hypothesis.

- *Chomsky takes over the principle of semantic invariance of T-rules*

Having mentioned one or two proposals made by Robert Lees and Ed Klima in the early 1960s regarding the introduction of abstract markers triggering certain transformations relating to negations or to questions – proposals that were also extensively quoted in Katz & Postal (1964) – , Chomsky then continues:

> Katz and Postal (1964) have extended these observations and formulated them in terms of a general principle, namely that *the only contribution of transformations to semantic interpretation is that they interrelate Phrase-markers* (i.e., combine semantic interpretations of already interpreted Phrase-markers in a fixed way). It follows, then, that transformations cannot introduce meaning-bearing elements (nor can they delete lexical items unrecoverably ...). Generalizing these remarks to embedding transformations, they conclude also that a sentence transform embedded in a matrix sentence Σ must replace a dummy symbol of Σ. ...
>
> Katz and Postal point out that the principle just stated greatly simplifies the theory of the semantic component, since semantic interpretation will now be independent of all aspects of the Transformation-marker except as this indicates how base structures are interrelated. They have also succeeded in showing that in a large variety of cases, where this general principle has not been met in syntactic

description, the description was in fact incorrect on internal syntactic grounds. The principle, then, seems very plausible.   Chomsky (1965:132-3)

- *Chomsky takes over the elimination of generalized T-rules*

Following up on Katz & Postal's suggestion that dummy elements should indicate the positions where embeddings are to take place and that only S-embeddings should be allowed, Chomsky writes:

> These observations suggest a possible simplification of the theory of transformational grammar. Suppose that we eliminate the notions "generalized transformation" and "Transformation-marker" altogether. In the rewriting rules of the base ... the string #S# is introduced in the positions where in the illustrative example we introduced the symbol S'. That is, wherever a base Phrase-marker contains a position in which a sentence transform is to be introduced, we fill this position with the string #S#, which initiates derivations. We now allow the rules of the base to apply cyclically, preserving their linear order. ...
> We have thus revised the theory of the base by allowing #S# to appear on the right in certain branching rules, where previously the dummy symbol S' had appeared, and by allowing the rules to reapply (preserving their order) to these newly introduced occurrences of #S#. A generalized Phrase-marker formed in this way contains all of the base Phrase-markers that constitute the basis of a sentence, but it contains more information than a basis in the old sense since it also indicates explicitly how these base Phrase-markers are embedded in one another. ...
> In addition to the rules of the base, so modified, the grammar contains a linear sequence of singular transformations. These apply to generalized Phrase-markers cyclically, in the following manner. First, the sequence of transformational rules applies to the most deeply embedded base Phrase-marker. ... Having applied to all such base Phrase-markers, the sequence of rules reapplies to a configuration dominated by S in which these base Phrase-markers are embedded ... , and so on, until finally the sequence of rules applies to the configuration dominated by the initial symbol S of the entire generalized Phrase-marker. ... That is, singular transformations are applied to constituent sentences before they are embedded, and to matrix sentences after embedding has taken place. The embedding itself is now provided by the branching rules of the base rather than by generalized transformations. We have, in effect, converted the specific properties of the Transformation-marker ... into general properties of any possible transformational derivation.
> The grammar now consists of a base and a linear sequence of singular transformations. These apply in the manner just described. ... The notion of Transformation-marker disappears, as does the notion of generalized transformation. ... Consequently, we may take a generalized Phrase-marker, in the sense just defined, to be the deep structure generated by the syntactic component.
> Thus the syntactic component consists of a base that generates deep structures and a transformational part that maps them into surface structures. The deep structure of a sentence is submitted to the semantic component for semantic interpretation, and its surface structure enters the phonological component and undergoes phonetic interpretation. The final effect of a grammar, then, is to relate a semantic interpretation to a phonetic representation – that is, to state how a sentence is interpreted. This relation is mediated by the syntactic component of the grammar, which constitutes its sole "creative" part.   Chomsky (1965:134-136)

- *Recursivity restricted to S-embeddings*

This proposal thus entails, first, that generalized T-rules are superfluous since the formation or rewrite rules of the base simply allow a re-entering into the rule system whenever a new constituent is to be embedded. This implementation of recursivity will result in one single deep structure tree (phrase marker) for each whole sentence. Secondly, only S-structures are to be embedded, so that any form of recursion in the base rules is restricted to S-structures. This much was already contained, though only half-explicitly, in Katz & Postal (1964). What Chomsky does in *Aspects* is make these ideas more explicit.

- *Restriction to S-embeddings leads to the Principle of Cyclicity*

It is above all the second restriction, which says that only S-recursion is allowed in the grammar, that has proved fruitful and influential. It also led Chomsky to postulate that the transformational component should be organized in such a way that at least some T-rules, the cyclic rules, apply first to the most deeply embedded S, which is the first cycle, to 'climb up' to the next most deeply embedded S, and so on till all cycles have been gone through, including the highest S-cycle dominating the whole sentence structure.

- *McCawley's argument for the Cyclicity Principle*

This idea is not supported by actual arguments in *Aspects*. It is simply put forward as a formal hypothesis. Soon after, however, a variety of linguists came forward with actual arguments showing the value of the cyclic principle. Among the clearest and most convincing of these arguments is the one proposed by McCawley in his article on English as a VSO-language (1970a). This argument centres on the two sentences:

(19)a.   Boris wants to seem to understand physics
    b.   Boris seems to want to understand physics

Both sentences involve the rules of Subject Deletion (often called 'Equi-NP Deletion' at the time) and Subject Raising. Subject Deletion occurs in an embedded argument clause S_1 when the verb of the higher clause S_0 is marked for this rule and when the subject term of S_1 is referentially identical to (or a pronominal pick-up of) one of the argument terms (most often the subject term) of the verb of S_0. For example, *Boris wants to understand physics* is derived from an underlying 'Boris wants $_S$[Boris/he understand physics]'. Since the English verb *want* is marked for Subject Deletion (controlled by its subject term), and since the subject of the embedded S_1, i.e. *Boris* (or *he*) is referentially identical with the subject term of the higher clause S_0, the lower subject is deleted, leaving only the verb phrase '(to) understand physics'. The rule is sketchily illustrated in the tree structures of (20). One notes that the verb *want* in the deep structure (20a) is marked for the rule SD (Subject Deletion), and that the higher subject *Boris* is resumed by the x-term in the direct object clause S_1. The rule SD is a cyclic rule and applies on the S_0-cycle, resulting in (20b), which has the particle *to* added as a routine procedure.

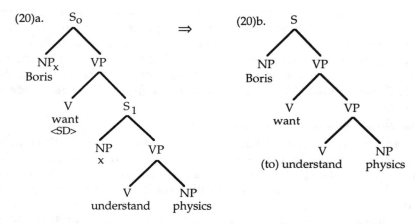

Subject Raising is another major cyclic rule in the rule system of English grammar. It also applies to the subject term of an embedded S_1, but instead of deleting it, this rule raises it to the position occupied by S_1 in the overall tree structure. The remaining VP of S_1 is then either left in place or, if it stands between the new subject term and the VP in S_o, extraposed to the far right. There are two possible positions for Subject Raising to take place: from a subject clause or from an object clause. In the former case one speaks of Subject-to-Subject Raising, in the latter case of Subject-to-Object Raising.[7] This rule is illustrated as follows for the sentence *Boris seems to understand physics*, with Subject-to-Subject Raising:

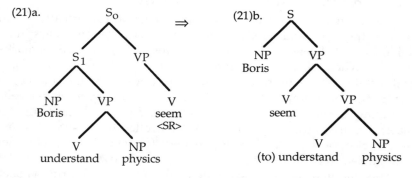

Here the main verb of S_o is *seem*, which induces Subject Raising (SR). The subject $_{NP}$[Boris] of S_1 is thus promoted to the position of its own S_1, while the remaining $_{VP}$[understand physics] is removed from its position between the new subject term and the VP of S_o, to end up as quasi direct object to *seem*, as shown in (21b). Again, the rule is cyclic, and it does not apply till the S_o-cycle. One

---

[7] Note that in Latin grammar, Subject-to-Object Raising has traditionally been known as 'Accusativus cum Infinitivo', while Subject-to-Subject Raising has been known as 'Nominativus cum Infinitivo'.

notices that (20b) and (21b), despite their surface similarity, are the products of two entirely different generation processes.

McCawley's argument is now that the sentences (19a) and (19b) cannot be generated unless it is assumed that the two rules concerned apply cyclically. The deep structure of (19a), according to the principles adhered to, should be (22a), while the deep structure of (19b) should be (22b). If the grammar is organized in such a way that the rules SD and SR are simply ordered linearly, (19a) and (19b) cannot come about. For if the order is taken to be SD-SR, SD can never apply to (22a) since the structural condition is not fulfilled ($_{NP}[x]$ is the subject of S_2, not of S_1). SR does apply there, giving 'x seems to understand physics' as S_1, but SD will then have no chance to do its work any more as its turn has passed. But if the order is taken to be SR-SD there is a similar problem with (22b). For then SR will give 'Boris seems to $_{VP}[$want $_{S2}[x$ understand physics]]', and the structural condition for application of SD will be destroyed. So neither order will do. One may propose to leave the rules unordered and stipulate simply that the derivation must be such that both rules are applied, both being obligatory. Any wrong application order will then result in an abortive generation process. This proposal does work, generally, but it then appears that the actual order followed is always the cyclic one, bottom up from the most deeply embedded S. This is also what appears from (22a) and (22b). Cyclic ordering does the trick: SR first for (22a) and SD first for (22b).

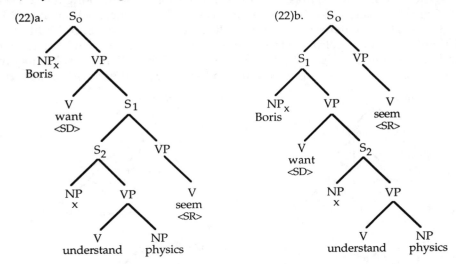

- *The Cyclicity Principle leads to the VSO-hypothesis*

McCawley then proceeds to argue that the rules in question, and other rules as well, are greatly simplified if it is assumed that the underlying word order for a language like English is not NP-VP but Verb-Subject-Object. SR, for example, then allows for a uniform formulation for Subject-to-Subject and for Subject-to-Object Raising. One can then say that in both cases the lower subject is promoted to the position of its own S, which becomes a VP and is moved one position to the right. This is illustrated in (24) and (25) for the sentences:

(23)a.   John is likely to win the race
    b.   I expect John to win the race

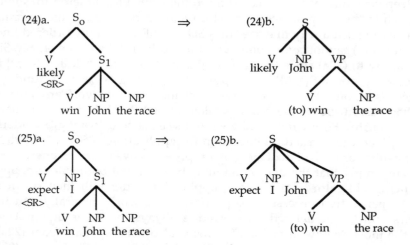

This VSO-hypothesis requires, of course, a provision for promoting the subject-NP from its position to the immediate right of V to the position it has in English surface sentences, i.e. as the NP in an NP-VP structure. Although McCawley does not yet make this proposal in his (1970), this can be done naturally by assuming a higher tense operator that induces SR and is subsequently lowered onto the verbal complex of the embedded S, as illustrated in (26a-d):

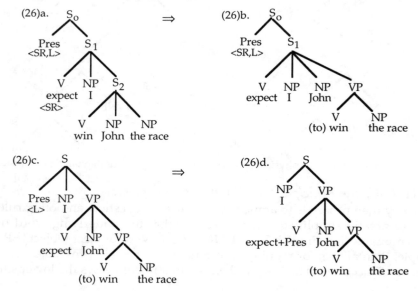

All this, however, is pure syntax, and we are running ahead too fast. Still, this example of syntactic theorizing well after Chomsky's *Aspects* shows how the *Aspects* model naturally led to these developments. Meanwhile, the principle of cyclicity rapidly became one of the most solid and central elements of transformational grammar. It is now widely agreed that the T-rules of a grammar fall into two classes, the cyclic and the postcyclic rules. The cyclic rules form the main body of the grammar and have a high degree of universality, whereas the postcyclic rules appear to be more language-specific and affect less central elements of sentence structure.

7.3.2 Generative semantics

7.3.2.1 The untenability of the *Aspects* model

• *The* Aspects *model proved self-destructive*
The *Aspects* model did not hold out long. It and its immediate predecessor, the 1964 Katz & Postal model, proved self-destructive for two reasons. The first reason was that it was soon realized that semantic representations, if anything, should be considered linguistic expressions themselves, which made the entire semantic component superfluous. The second reason was that certain semantic differences in surface sentences, especially differences to do with scope of quantifiers and other sentential operators, if expressed in deep structures, require deep structures of much greater abstractness than those proposed in *Aspects*. In fact, what is required to render those differences is nothing less than the language of predicate calculus.

• *First: semantic representations are identical with syntactic deep structures*
Soon after the appearance of *Aspects* some linguists (McCawley 1967; Seuren 1969) realized that there is no other generally practical way of specifying the meaning of a sentence than by rephrasing it, either in the same language or in a different one. No matter how hard one tries to escape from this *synonymous circle*, one stays caught in it. Model-theorists have proposed that meanings should be specified as sets of possible worlds, but we have seen (6.1.3) that there is no practical way of doing so. The alternative is to specify sentence meanings as sets of truth conditions, but apart from the fact that a truth-conditional specification is *per se* incomplete and inadequate, this method again amounts to the use of a paraphrase, circumstantial though it may be, of the sentence in question. Semantic representations of sentences, therefore, are best considered to be paraphrases of the sentences in question, but paraphrases with a special status, formulated in some semantically favourite language. If so, semantic representations are themselves representable as tree structures. Therefore, the mysterious oval in fig. 3 and fig. 4 can now be replaced by a proper triangle: SRs are tree structures.

But this implies that the projection rules postulated in the Katz & Postal model are in fact, if anything, transformations, since they transform linguistic structures into linguistic structures. This then raises the question of what such transformations are supposed to do. If syntactic deep structures are conceived as structures that carry all semantic information in an unambiguous and explicit form, then what reason is there to think that the transformational projection rules can add anything not already present in the syntactic deep structures? It would seem, therefore, that the semantic representations postulated in Katz & Postal (1964) can be dispensed with, as the syntactic deep structures themselves can act perfectly well as semantic representations. This answers, at a stroke, the two main questions hanging over the Katz & Postal model: what should semantic representations be thought to look like, and what is the form and function of the projection rules?

- *Secondly: semantic representations must be made much more abstract*
The second reason why the *Aspects* model was doomed lay in its inadequacy as a means for representing certain classes of semantic distinctions. As we have seen (7.3.1.2), some sentences are ambiguous as to the scope of certain scope-bearing elements, while other sentences are not but have close counterparts that express the other scope. The example sentences (4a,b) and (5a,b) are illustrative of this kind of semantic distinction. Further examples are provided by McCawley (1973:283), who quotes the following non-ambiguous sentences:

(27)a.   I often don't answer my mail
    b.   I don't often answer my mail

(28)a.   Have you never kissed a girl?
    b.   Have you ever not kissed a girl?

In (27a) the speaker asserts that it often occurs that (s)he does not answer his or her mail, while in (27b) it is asserted that it is not the case that the speaker often answers his or her mail. In (28a) it is asked whether it is indeed not the case that there ever was an occasion on which the addressee kissed a girl, while (28b) asks if there ever was an occasion on which the addressee did not kiss a girl. The members of each pair of sentences are clearly semantically distinct, and if deep structures are to express all semantic content they must be formulated in a language that allows them in any case to express these scope differences systematically and unambiguously.

The problem now with the *Aspects* model was that it did not allow for the expression of semantic differences such as those shown in (27) and (28) in the deep structures generated by the base rules proposed there. *Aspects* contains an 'illustrative fragment of the base component' (p. 107) which is deplorably poor in that it leaves out most of the interesting and difficult elements of deep structure generation. It concentrates heavily on selection restrictions, which McCawley (1968a) subsequently showed to be semantic and not syntactic in character.[8] There is nothing on complementation, nothing on negation, nothing

---

[8] This conclusion was later endorsed in Jackendoff (1972:17-21), where it was confusingly presented in a context meant to argue against generative semantics (cp. Huck & Goldsmith 1995:63).

on adverbial or quantificational scope, etc. In light of the principle expressed on pp. 132-3 of *Aspects* (see the quote given above) that deep structures should be deemed to contain all semantic information expressed by a sentence, the actual rules proposed in *Aspects* are without any interest at all.

7.3.2.2 Predicate calculus as the language of deep structure

• *The language of predicate calculus must be enriched and adapted*
After 1965 some transformational grammarians, mainly James McCawley, George Lakoff, Paul Postal, and John Robert Ross, thus began to discuss the question of what language and what kind of structures would be adequate for the expression of scope differences and related semantic phenomena. They soon agreed that the answer to this question is straightforward: there exists a language that comes very close to doing exactly what is required of semantic representations, namely the language of predicate calculus as devised in modern logic by, mainly, Bertrand Russell. That being so, why not use that language as the language of deep structure semantic representations? However, the language of standard predicate calculus had to be enriched and adapted in several respects, as was pointed out by McCawley (1970b), but it would remain that language.

• *Predicate calculus formulae should be represented as tree structures*
McCawley (1970b) argued, first, that in some respects the way in which logicians normally look at predicate calculus formulae should be made more linguistically relevant. Thus, instead of using brackets to indicate structure one should use constituent tree diagrams of the kind normally used in linguistics (see 4.4.5). There is nothing wrong with brackets *per se*, but bracketing is awkward when the formulae are subjected to (transformational) rules that change constituent structure. Tree diagrams are a much better notation.

• *Quantifiers as deep structure predicates*
Then, McCawley argued, it seems counter-productive to treat quantifiers as elements without categorial status, as is normally done in logic, where they are introduced syncategorematically, i.e. by stipulation, with separate definitions for the attainment of truth in a model (see Dowty et al. 1981:57-61). It is much more productive to treat quantifiers as predicates over (pairs of) sets.

The predicate status of quantifiers is incontrovertible. As was shown in section 5.5 on quantification theory, quantifiers, whether in restricted or unrestricted quantification theory, or as generalized quantifiers, are in fact higher order predicates assigning mathematical properties to (pairs of) sets. The standard Russellian unrestricted existential operator says of the set denoted by its subject term that it is non-empty, while its counterpart, the universal quantifier, says that the set equals the total domain of individuals in the universe of discourse. Both the restricted and the newer generalized quantifiers are binary higher order predicates over pairs of sets. Apart from refinements, the restricted or generalized existential quantifier says that the two sets have a nonempty intersection, while the restricted or generalized universal quantifier says that one set is a subset of the other. Restricted or generalized quantification theory allows for a similar treatment of other quantifiers as well (Barwise & Cooper 1981). This makes it difficult not to treat quantifiers as predicates in the language of predicate calculus, expressing properties of (pairs of) sets, since, simply, that is what they are in that language.[9]

However, owing to the fact that logicians had never emphasized the predicate quality of quantifiers and had treated them as syncategorematic elements in their own right (see above), the simple and incontrovertible statement that they are predicates came as a shock not only to some logicians (who should have known better) but above all to some linguists. Chomsky, for example, wrote in a letter to McCawley dated 20 December 1967 (Huck & Goldsmith 1995:65):

> Evidently it won't do to have quantifiers as "higher verbs", if one wants to preserve the structure of quantification theory. In fact, I have to say that I really don't know at all what you are talking about when you make these remarks about "logic" in the framework of phrase-markers and transformations.

thereby showing that he had an insufficient grasp of the issues concerned.

• *Predicate status for negation, connectives, and the tenses unifies grammar*
Analogous arguments were developed by McCawley for negation and for conjunction (*and*) and disjunction (*or*). These should not be described simply as truth functions taking truth values as input and delivering a truth value as output, but should also be given predicate status. In fact, all functions yielding a truth value, including the truth functions, should be treated as predicates.

As for negation, treatment as a unary predicate over propositions will do it no harm in predicate calculus, while in grammar such treatment has distinct advantages. McCawley observed (1970c [1973:282]):

> There are many languages (e.g. Finnish) in which the negative element is morphologically a verb: it is inflected for tense and for agreement with its surface subject. English differs from Finnish in having rules which insert a semantically empty verb (the *do* of *I don't have any money*) or puts *not* after a verb which at earlier stages of the derivation it precedes (*I haven't bombed the White House yet*), thus avoiding structures in which *not* would have to be inflected. The analysis proposed here identifies the difference between Finnish and English as a difference in morphology plus the transformations needed to avoid combinations which the morphology of the language does not allow.

This may seem ad hoc, since why should the grammatical treatment of negation in Finnish have any special significance? But on closer inspection, and in a wider perspective, it appears not to be ad hoc at all.

---

[9] The fact that they bind variables is merely a consequence of the notation used to specify sets, i.e. as S-structures with an empty term position, and of the necessity of distinguishing what (pairs of) sets are assigned what property when quantifiers are stacked.

Consider the tenses. It was proposed (McCawley 1971) that the tenses, too, should be treated as deep structure predicates.[10] In fact, McCawley proposed to adopt and adapt the analysis of tenses provided in Reichenbach (1947).[11] In this analysis there are two tenses (disregarding futuricity). The highest tense t_1 locates the argument proposition either at 'now' or at some contextually or pragmatically defined time in the past. The second tense t_2 is relational and places its proposition at a time that is either simultaneous with or precedes the time defined by t_1. The four possible combinations of present/past and simultaneous/preceding yield the four tenses of the English tense system:

present	+	simultaneous	→	simple present	(I run)
past	+	simultaneous	→	simple past	(I ran)
present	+	preceding	→	present perfect	(I have run)
past	+	preceding	→	pluperfect	(I had run)

The position of these tenses in deep structure trees would be as in (29a) (we adopt McCawley's 1970 VSO-hypothesis discussed above in 7.3.1.3). The cyclic Lowering of the tense operators on the lexical main verb *eat* plus Subject Raising on V_{t1} results in the V-cluster of (29b):[12]

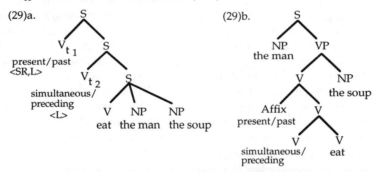

A postcyclic rule affecting nodes labelled 'Affix' will then have any such node right-attached to the non-zero Verb just below it. Together with one or two further rules (one of which must take care of *do*-insertion), and together with obvious provisions for morphophonological alternations, this simple system produces all the correct verbal forms.

One immediate advantage, then, of treating the tenses as predicates is that, like with ordinary lexical predicates, they can be made to induce certain cyclic transformations, as demonstrated in (26) and (29).

Moreover, and perhaps more importantly, it appears that the assignment of predicate status to sentential operators opens the way towards the realization

---

[10] Model-theoretically, they are interpretable as functions that take pairs of situations and moments or time spans as input and deliver a truth value as output.

[11] See the end of section 2.3.3 above on the tense system developed by the 18th century French grammarian Beauzée.

[12] This is exactly as in (26a-d) above, except that V_{t2} has been added, inducing Lowering, and the internal structure of the V-cluster has been made explicit.

of a long-standing ideal of linguistic theory, the unification of grammars of different languages. Ideally, one single grammar **G** will generate the sentences of a large number of different languages, perhaps even of all languages. **G** will contain an ordered set of parameters whose values are filled in by the individual languages concerned, which then turn out to differ only as regards the values assigned to the parameters of the common grammar **G**.

This can be demonstrated neatly for the tenses. In English surface structures only 'preceding' occurs as a morphological verb (*have*, followed by the past participle of the main lexical verb), whereas the other three tenses are expressed either by means of morphological elements (present/past) or as zero (simultaneous). This means that, at some stage in the derivation, the elements 'present' and 'past' have to be relabelled, presumably as 'Affix', while 'simultaneous' has to be deleted. The obvious place for carrying out these operations is the cycle: as the tenses are processed cyclically they undergo whatever category change is in store for them.

Since the four tense system occurs in many other languages as well, this allows for a uniform analysis of the tenses for the languages in question, but for the categorial relabellings. One may thus say that these languages have one single grammar for the tenses, with a small number of inbuilt parameters that can take on a small variety of values. The individual languages then turn out to be identical up to the values assigned to the parameters and, of course, the phonological make-up of the morphemes. The realization of such a system will bring linguistic theory significantly closer to the old idea of universal grammar, which may now begin to find a well-motivated implementation.[13]

In Latin, for example, the perfect tenses are not composed with an auxiliary verb but morphologically. All Latin grammar has to do to get the perfective tenses right is relabel 'preceding' as 'Affix' and specify the phonological form of the affixes concerned. Another example is Berbice Dutch, a Dutch-based Creole language once spoken in Guyana but now moribund (Kouwenberg 1994). This language does the opposite of what most modern European languages do. Whereas most European languages use morphological elements to express 'present' and 'past', and an auxiliary verb ('have' or 'be') for the perfective tenses, Berbice Dutch expresses 'present' and 'past' by means of auxiliary verbs but 'preceding' through a morphological affix:

(30)   o   wa   kriki-tɛ   o   hiri
        he   past get-preceding it here
        'he had got it here'

---

[13] One has to be extremely cautious in this respect. It may be objected, for example, that the tenses do not have the same meanings in all the languages concerned. Thus, the English simple past is used under different conditions from its German counterpart. Such complications are easily multiplied. The point is, however, that identity of grammar (or membership of the same class of grammars) does not at all imply translation equivalence. To achieve that, a great deal more is required, and it is doubtful that it will ever be realized.

Most other Creole languages use preverbal particles (most of which are verbs etymologically) for the expression of all four tenses (with the occasional zero form). In French-based Mauritian Creole, for example (see 2.5), one finds:

(31) a. Mo pe   mãz   diri
      I present eat   rice
      'I eat/ am eating rice'

    b. Mo ti   mãz   diri
       I past   eat   rice
       'I ate rice'

    c. Mo fin   mãz   diri
       I preceding eat   rice
       'I have eaten rice'

    d. Mo ti fin   mãz   diri
       I past preceding eat   rice
       'I had eaten rice'

In these languages, the tenses are not relabelled as 'Affix' but may be taken to remain 'V' or, if one prefers, to be relabelled 'Particle'.

This way of treating tenses can be extended to futurity. In the Germanic languages, futurity is mostly expressed by means of a modal verb whose original meaning implies volition or obligation, such as English *will* and *shall*, respectively. In the course of time, these verbs tend to be amalgamated into the tense system, which results in their being placed between the tense operators V_{t1} and V_{t2}. This has happened in English for a variety of modal verbs besides *will* and *shall* (i.e. *may, can, must, ought to*), which explains their well-known defective paradigm, and in German for the futurity verb *werden*.[14] The deep structure configuration of 'future' is shown in (32):

(32)

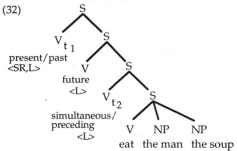

---

[14] In Dutch the modal verb *zullen* expresses futuricity. This verb must be taken to be a full main verb; it has not become an auxiliary verb placed between the two tenses. In this respect Dutch differs from German, where the futuricity verb *werden* is best taken to be a modal auxiliary, just like English *will*. This explains why German does not allow for a sentence like (i), with the infinitive *werden*, whereas Dutch fully accepts the analogous sentence (ii):

(i) *Ich hoffe, das Auto verkaufen zu werden
    I   hope the car   sell   to will
    'I hope that I will sell the car'

(ii) Ik hoop de auto te zullen verkopen
    I hope the car to will   sell
    'I hope that I will sell the car'

In languages like German and English, the operator 'future' need not be re-labelled and remains 'V'. In many other languages, however, such as Latin and the Romance languages, futuricity is expressed morphologically, for which reason they are often said to have a 'real' future tense.[15] Here, too, the futuricity operator is to be positioned between the two tenses. The only difference with English and German is then that in the languages with a morphological future tense, v[future] is relabelled as Affix[future], whereas the languages with a modal future tense do not apply such relabelling.

This little excursion into semantically based syntax shows that McCawley's proposal to treat higher sentential operators as deep structure predicates is far from trivial and has clear advantages for the unification of the grammars of different languages. These advantages were not immediately obvious at the time, but the method of describing and analyzing languages according to the principles of generative semantics was apparently sufficiently inspiring to attract a great deal of attention and win over large numbers of linguists all over the world.

• *Conjunction, disjunction, adverbs and prepositions likewise as predicates*
McCawley's proposal implied the assignment of predicate status also to the conjunctive and disjunctive connectives *and* and *or*, as well as to sentential adverbials and to prepositions. It would take us too far, in the present context, to elaborate any details of this part of his proposal. It may suffice to show how, for example, prepositions can be given predicate status. Consider the sentence

(33)   John sleeps on the floor

This can be given a deep structure in generative semantics terms as in (34). There, on the first S-cycle up from s[sleep + John], the prepositional predicate *on* is found, which takes a subject term and an object term. Its object term is NP[the floor]; its subject term is s[sleep + John]. The predicate *on* induces two cyclic rules, Object Incorporation and Lowering, in that order. Object Incorporation takes the object term and unites it with *on* into a composite predicate v[on the floor], which is subsequently lowered into s[sleep + John], and placed at the far right. Further tense treatment then gives (33).

(34)

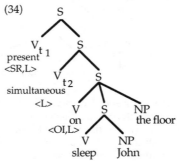

Semantically, the treatment of prepositions as predicates is easy to understand. Often one finds verbs as equivalents for prepositions, as in (35b):

(35) a.   The moat ran around the castle
    b.   The moat surrounded the castle

This, however, can hardly be used as a syntactic argument, unless it is found that the phenomenon of systematically using verbs for prepositions, as in (35b), is widespread enough to be a factor in the theory of universal grammar.

The treatment as exemplified in (34) has the advantage that prepositional phrases are given scope. In (34) the scope of *on the floor* is simply $_S$[sleep + John], but it is easy to find cases where the scope relation of a prepositional phrase has to be defined with respect to other scope-bearing elements, such as the negation. This is shown in, for example:

(36) a.   He did not leave the house because of the noise
    b.   Because of the noise he did not leave the house

If (36a) is read without an intonational break after *house* the prepositional phrase *because of the noise* is in the scope of *not*. In (36b), read in a normal non-contrastive intonation, the relation between the two operators is inverted: there *not* is in the scope of *because of the noise*. Such semantic facts impose restrictions on deep structures if these are to fulfil the function of semantic representations. In a deep structure like (34) such scope differences are naturally expressed, as the prepositional predicate occupies the position of a sentential operator and can thus stand above as well as below other sentential operators. This, then, is a clear advantage of the treatment as illustrated above.

- *Other extensions of standard predicate calculus*

So far, no real modifications or extensions of standard predicate calculus were involved. All that was at issue was ways of handling predicate calculus structures. McCawley did, however, also propose some real enrichments of the language of predicate calculus. He first made the obviously correct proposal:

> The repertoire of quantifiers will have to be much broader than that generally found in symbolic logic. For example, not only *all* and *some* but also *most, almost all, hardly any*, and *many* must be available.   McCawley (1970b:231)

Apart from the extension of the class of quantifiers McCawley also proposed that the sentential connectives *and* and *or* should not be considered binary operators but 'must be allowed to take an arbitrary number of operands' (ib.). His argument, in this respect, is based on certain funny properties of 'exclusive' *or* (i.e. 'A or B' is true just in case either A or B is true, but not both) if it is restricted to binary argument structures. It is, however, open to serious doubt that natural language has an exclusive *or* distinct from the standard inclusive *or*. If language does not have an exclusive *or* the argument must be dropped.

A further point is that the quantifiers should be considered to be the restricted quantifiers of section 5.5.3 above, not the standard Russellian unrestricted quantifiers. This is now generally accepted, as the generalized quantifiers are nothing but a variety of the restricted quantifiers (see 5.5.5).

Then, the language of predicate logic will have to contain provisions for deictic elements (*I, you, here, now, then*), as well as for referential indices. As regards the latter, McCawley stressed (1970b:233) the necessity of accepting intensional entities (see 6.1.3.4 and 6.2.6.1), so as to account for the semantic phenomena, in particular the anaphora relation, in sentences like:

(37)   The Trobriand Islanders believe in Santa Claus, but they call him Ubu Ubu

Finally, he proposed that speech act qualities should be expressed as operators at the top of deep structure trees, as in Ross (1970). However, given Fraser's (1974) critique of Ross (1970) and given the total silence that has hung over this issue ever since, one would be wise to reserve judgment on this issue.

In conclusion we say that in general terms McCawley was no doubt right in arguing that the language of standard predicate calculus, if used for the purpose of semantic representation, must be extended in several directions, even though one may have reservations about some of his precise proposals.

7.3.2.3 The generative semantics movement

Considerations such as those expressed 7.3.2.1 and 7.3.2.2 above led to a radical overhaul of existing transformational grammar. As has been said, the main leaders in this renewal were James McCawley, George Lakoff, Paul Postal, and John Robert Ross, though it was McCawley who contributed most of the seminal ideas. The renewal took on the characteristics of a movement, which went under the name of *Generative Semantics*. This movement is comparable in important respects to that of the Young Grammarians in 19th century Germany, except that its history has been a great deal less fortunate.

●   *The history of the term 'Generative Semantics'*
According to McCawley (1976:43), the term 'Generative Semantics' was used first in an informal, internally circulated paper by George Lakoff of 1963, not published until McCawley (1976). In this paper Lakoff proposed that the base component of a transformational grammar should generate structures that represent the meanings of the corresponding sentences. Lakoff (1963) thus antedates Katz & Postal (1964), but the many references to it suggest that the book was known to Lakoff before it was published. In this 1963 paper, Lakoff defends the term 'Generative Semantics' in the following way:

> There are several motivations for proposing a generative semantic theory. One is the intuition that we know what we want to say and find a way of saying it. A theory that maps meaning onto syntactic structures might account for this intuition. Then there is the purely practical motivation (theorists should shut their eyes at this point) that researchers in machine translation will sooner or later be forced to develop such a theory. Ideal machine translation programs will have to include both interpretive and generative semantic devices, just as they must include interpretive and generative syntactic devices. And last, there is the formal motivation. A generative semantic theory may well be simpler and more economical than an interpretive theory.

One notices that the term 'Generative Semantics' is used here in a much more psycholinguistic sense than is customary in theoretical linguistics. The idea that the generative character of rules in a generative-transformational grammar should reflect the actual process of formulating a sentence is generally rejected. In theoretical linguistics, a generative grammar is nothing but a formal, algorithmic specification of precisely the set of all sentences in a given language, not an account of how they are actually produced. In his (1963) paper, Lakoff blithely ignores this point, and speaks of 'generative' grammar and semantics in the sense of meaning-and-sentence production. Later, in Lakoff (1971), he corrects this position:

> As in the case of generative grammar, the term 'generative' should be taken to mean 'complete and precise'.   Lakoff (1971:232)

When, about 1966, the term 'Generative Semantics' came to be used to refer to the movement now known under that name, Lakoff's original meaning was forgotten and the term was used to express the fact that the machinery of projection rules postulated in Katz & Postal (1964) had been incorporated into the machinery of generative grammar, thus giving something like 'generative semantics'.[16]

- *How the Generative Semantics movement quickly gained ground*

During the academic year of 1966-67 the new ideas about semantically-based syntax were keenly absorbed by the sizeable classes of students taught by Ross at MIT and by Lakoff at neighbouring Harvard. After that, there was a series of landmarks, each increasing the status of generative semantics and the numbers of its followers.

In April 1967 a conference was held at the University of Texas at Austin on Universals in Linguistic Theory. Four of the papers presented, i.e. those by Fillmore, Bach, McCawley and Kiparsky, were subsequently published in Bach & Harms (1968). Both the quality of these papers and the status and positions held by the largely sympathetic participants made for widespread recognition. This was followed by a Linguistic Intitute held in the summer of 1968 at the University of Illinois under the auspices of the Linguistic Society of America. Here Lakoff, McCawley and Ross taught courses that were attended by large numbers of students. Then, 'the fifth annual conference of the Chicago Linguistic Society (CLS), in April 1969, attracted a large proportion of those who were engaged in G[enerative] S[emantics] research and dwarfed all previous CLS conferences in attendance, number of submissions, and number of papers presented' (McCawley 1994:1401). By 1969 virtually the whole world of theoretical linguistics was agreed that generative semantics was the word.

But then cracks began to appear. The first public sign of profound disagreement came with a second Texas conference, held in October 1969, again at the University of Texas at Austin, this time on the Goals of Linguistic Theory (see

---

[16] Seuren (1974) considered 'Generative Semantics' a misnomer, as it is not semantics but syntax, albeit semantically based syntax. He therefore uses the term 'Semantic Syntax'.

Peters 1972). Here a severe clash developed between Chomsky on the one hand and Ross and Postal on the other. We shall revert to this episode in 7.3.3.

• *Ross's 1967 thesis and the anecdote of William James and the old lady*
During this period Ross wrote his 1967 dissertation under Chomsky's direction at MIT. Its immense popularity and great influence was not in the least diminished by the fact that it remained unpublished till 1986. In it, he proposed a number of universal constraints on rules of syntax, two of which have held out remarkably well through the years: the Complex-NP Constraint and the Co-ordinate-Structure Constraint. The former forbids movement into or out of complex NPs (i.e. NPs with a head noun and an embedded S, such as *the fact that ...*, or relative clauses), the latter does the same for co-ordinated structures.[17]

Ross, who had a reputation for anecdotes and jokes, opens his dissertation with a half-jocular 'Fragestellung', which is an anecdote about William James and a little old lady. After a lecture that James had given on the structure of the solar system the lady came up to him, saying:

> "Your theory that the sun is the center of the solar system, and that the earth rotates around it, has a very convincing ring to it, Mr. James, but it's wrong. I've got a better theory," said the little old lady.
> "And what is that, madam?" inquired James politely.
> "That we live on a crust of earth which is on the back of a giant turtle."
> Not wishing to demolish this absurd little theory by bringing to bear the masses of scientific evidence he had at his command, James decided to gently dissuade his opponent by making her see some of the inadequacies of her position.
> "If your theory is correct, madam," he asked, "what does this turtle stand on?"
> "You're a very clever man, Mr. James, and that's a very good question," replied the little old lady, "but I have an answer to it. And it's this: the first turtle stands on the back of a second, far larger, turtle, who stands directly under him."
> "But what does this second turtle stand on?" persisted James patiently.
> To this, the little old lady crowed triumphantly, "it's no use, Mr. James — it's turtles all the way down!"   Ross (1967[1986]:xii)

The point of this anecdote has puzzled many of Ross's readers. One possible answer may lie in the fact that the linguists of those days were dazzled by the degree of abstraction they were having to deal with in the new deep-structures-cum-semantic-representations, which were beginning to look more and more like structures of predicate calculus, a subject unknown to linguists at the time. In this interpretation, the little lady personifies the young linguists

---

[17] Interestingly, these two constraints appear to hold for quantifier scope phenomena as well, as was noted in Seuren (1972b:259-60). Sentences like (i), with a complex NP, or (ii), with an embedded co-ordinate structure, only allow for a small scope reading for *many*. The large scope readings are excluded because they involve movement of the quantifier into a complex NP and a co-ordinate structure, respectively:

(i)   Tom believes the rumour that Fred knows many girls
(ii)   Tom believes that Fred is charming and knows many girls

This supports the theory that the rules of syntax and the rules of semantic interpretation are one and the same.

of the new school, who made a daring intellectual leap into the realm of the infinite. In a different reading, the lady personifies Chomsky, who stubbornly refused to accept the force of the arguments and of the evidence presented and persisted in relegating facts of meaning to the realm of mysteries.

- *Lakoff's 1970 dissertation and other contributions to generative semantics*
In October 1965 Lakoff finished his PhD-thesis, presented at Indiana University and published as Lakoff (1970). He had meanwhile moved to the Computation Laboratory at Harvard University, having failed to get access to MIT. In the dissertation he discusses the question of how to deal with exceptions in syntax. He does so in terms of the principles and rules proposed in Chomsky's *Aspects* of 1965, i.e. on the presumption that deep structures contain all relevant semantic information. While working with the *Aspects* rule system he quickly discovered its basic inadequacy and began to develop ideas that were to become essential to Generative Semantics.

As Lakoff was investigating exceptions in syntax he inevitably strayed into the lexicon which, as Bloomfield put it, is 'really an appendix of the grammar, a list of basic irregularities' (Bloomfield 1933:274). In order to reduce irregularity and find a reason for the apparently irregular syntactic behaviour of lexical items he started to dissect lexical predicates into more primitive, general semantic elements such as 'inchoative', 'causative' and the like, and link these up with rules of syntax. This, together with important work being done by Jeffrey Gruber around the same period,[18] laid the foundations for a large amount of interesting, albeit controversial, work in 'prelexical syntax' between 1965 and 1975.

In this context he also devoted a great deal of attention to nominalizations, already discussed extensively in Lees (1960) and in Katz & Postal (1964), and to other forms of lexical derivation. He found (as many others had found before him) that there are incidental 'gaps' in the lexicon. For example, while the lexicon of English contains *transgressor, transgression* and *transgress*, it also has *aggressor* and *aggression* but not **aggress*. His proposal was

> that the proper way to restrict the occurrence of lexical items such as *aggress* is by the use of structural description features. *Aggress* can be looked upon as absolute exception. ... <W>e can look upon *aggress* as an item which can never occur in a grammatical sentence of English without undergoing nominalization. This is, *aggress* can occur in a grammatical sentence of English only if it has met the structural description of the nominalization transformation and undergone that rule.
>
> Lakoff (1970:59)

This proposal is interesting in the light of Chomsky's 1967 paper 'Remarks on Nominalization', as we shall see in 7.3.3 below.

---

[18] See Gruber (1976), which contains his 1965 MIT doctoral dissertation 'Studies in Lexical Relations' and his influential 1967 report 'Functions of the Lexicon in Formal Descriptive Grammars', written for the System Development Corporation, Santa Monica, California.

Another idea, presented in chapter 6 of Lakoff (1970), was that the number of (apparent) exceptions or idiosyncrasies in syntax can be substantially reduced if it is assumed for a large number of rules in syntax that they are induced by individual lexical predicates (precisely as in McCawley's arguments for cyclicity and underlying VSO-structure discussed in 7.3.1.3 above). This idea is now widely accepted in a number of different theories of syntax.

Apart from his dissertation, Lakoff became an active contributor to the generative semantics movement, not least through his paper 'On Generative Semantics', first read at the fifth CLS meeting in Chicago in 1969, then published in revised form in Steinberg & Jakobovits (1971). In this paper Lakoff makes a valiant attempt at defining the general tenets of the generative semantics position and at providing all sorts of arguments in favour of that position. He raises a large number of extremely interesting questions, ranging from quantifier scope to prelexical syntax, proposing a large number of perhaps not always entirely coherent solutions. The breakthrough to predicate calculus is now complete, and no fear is left of abstract structures in syntax.

- *Postal's arguments on Psych-Movement, Cross-over and Raising*

Paul Postal does not count among Chomsky's students. He was Chomsky's colleague at MIT from 1961 until 1965, when he moved to the City University of New York. In 1967 he accepted a research post at the IBM Research Center at Yorktown Heights, just outside New York. There he gradually took distance from Chomsky's ideas to become one of his main opponents.

Postal, too, became embroiled in matters of lexical decomposition, seeking syntactic regularities as a correlate of semantic elements in lexical meanings.

Postal (1970, 1971) concentrated heavily on verbs and adjectives that 'designate psychological states, processes, or attributes' (1971:39). With these predicates he noticed a systematic correlation between sentence forms where the role of experiencer is expressed as a grammatical subject and those where it is expressed as a direct or indirect object, as in (38a) and (38b), respectively:

(38)a. I am excited about that
     b. That is exciting to me

On the basis of observations on the possibility of reflexive and non-reflexive pronouns in the argument positions of such sentences he postulated a rule of Psych-Movement, informally described as follows:

> This rule is formally rather similar to passive in that it moves an NP from grammatical subject position into the predicate and causes it to be supplied with a preposition, usually *to* but occasionally *for* and maybe once in a while *from*. At the same time, the rule moves an NP from the predicate into grammatical subject position.
>
> Postal (1971:39)

This rule would transform an underlying predicate-argument structure as in (39a) into (39b):

(39)a. I $_{VP}$[$_V$[excite about] that]
     b. That $_{VP}$[$_V$[excite] to me]

The rule would interact with other rules to achieve more complex results. Thus, a sentence like *John reminds me of a gorilla* would be the result of the derivation sketched in (40a-e), involving the rules indicated:

(40)a. I $_{VP}$[$_V$[perceive] $_S$[John similar to a gorilla]]   Subject Raising $\Rightarrow$
   b. I $_{VP}$[$_V$[perceive John] $_S$[similar to a gorilla]]   Psych-Movement $\Rightarrow$
   c. John $_{VP}$[$_V$[perceive me] $_S$[similar to a gorilla]] Predicate Raising $\Rightarrow$
   d. John $_{VP}$[$_V$[perceive similar] me to a gorilla]   Lexical insertion $\Rightarrow$
   e. John reminds me of a gorilla

Unfortunately, the notions about reflexivization and pronominalization that were entertained in those days were of a primitive kind. During the 1960s it was commonly believed that the riddles of reflexivization and pronominalization were, if not solved already, about to be solved soon. Nowadays we realize that these problems are much deeper than was thought previously, and that, for the time being, they exceed our powers of analysis. Moreover, the operations performed on the lexical items in question were badly underdetermined by facts as well as arguments, and the actual analyses proposed remained vague and sketchy. Consequently, Postal's arguments in this respect failed to make much of an impression.

Yet it is clear that there are certain processes at work in language that are responsible for regular correspondences like that between the English sentence (41a) and its French equivalent (41b):

(41)a. I miss my children
   b. Mes enfants me manquent   (lit.: my children fail me)

But whatever correspondence there is must be internal to the lexicon and is therefore not to be described in the syntax of the languages concerned.

Dutch allows for such pairs as (42a,b) within the same language, both meaning 'nothing is wrong with me':[19]

(42)a. Ik mankeer niks   (lit.: I fail nothing)
   b. Mij mankeert niks   (lit.: me fails nothing)

Historically, it seems, the forms with the experiencer as (in)direct object precede those where the experiencer stands in subject position, so that the rule of Psych-Movement would run in a direction opposite to the historical process.

The same fate that struck Postal's analysis of lexical predicates beset his description of cross-over phenomena. On the basis of his observations regarding predicates presumably undergoing Psych-Movement he believed he saw the outlines of a constraint that would forbid, under certain conditions, transformational movement of a referring expression E_1 across another such expression E_2 when E_1 and E_2 are co-referential. Here, too, both the observations

---

[19] These processes are sometimes productive in cases of imperfect language acquisition. A Moroccan immigrant labourer in the Netherlands was recorded as saying, in reply to a question whether he preferred an apartment on a corner or one flanked by other apartments, 'I make no difference', obviously intending to say 'It makes no difference to me' (the Dutch equivalents are: 'Ik maak niks uit' and 'Het maakt mij niks uit', respectively).

and the analyses relied on were too weak to support the conclusions. Consequently, these attempts by Postal, though understandable and probably legitimate in their context, made little impression.

His work on Subject Raising is a different story, which started at the 1969 Texas conference mentioned earlier. At this conference Chomsky attacked Postal's analysis of the verb *remind* as sketched in (40) above. He did so not by pointing out the weaknesses of the argument, which were real, but by casting doubt on the rules involved:

> The first question to be asked is whether these transformations are syntactically motivated. Predicate-raising surely is not; it is simply a device to convert phrases that are to be replaced by a lexical item into a single constituent. Though the matter is not relevant here, I might mention that the permutation rule that gives [(40c)] as well as subject-raising into object position seem to me to be at best dubious rules. However, I will not pursue the issue here, because even if these rules are assumed, the case for lexical insertion after they apply seems to me extremely weak.
>
> Chomsky (1972b:86)

This raised Postal's ire, understandably.

We now know that to call into question the syntactic motivation for Predicate Raising was a blunder. The rule had been proposed in McCawley (1968c) to account for the prelexical analysis of *kill* as 'cause to become dead', indeed without independent syntactic motivation. Subsequently, however, it was shown (Seuren 1972c; Evers 1975) that Predicate Raising is a central rule in the complementation system of French, Dutch, German, Japanese, and many other languages. The evidence was so overwhelming that even the adherents of the Chomsky school, who insist on calling it 'Verb Raising', had to accept the rule (though one still sees occasional feeble attempts to get rid of it). In fact, if McCawley's analysis of *kill* as 'cause to become dead' is to survive it will be because the rule of Predicate Raising has turned out to be so well-motivated.

The status of Psych-Movement (Chomsky apparently shuddered at the term, calling it a 'permutation rule') was indeed shaky. But to deny reality to Subject-to-Object Raising, on the other hand, was to defy reason. If any rule in the syntax of English is well-entrenched it is Subject Raising, whether from subject to subject or from subject to object. At the conference, Postal was so enraged that he instantly produced and circulated a paper with a large number of arguments showing the reality of Subject-to-Object Raising. This he later elaborated into his book *On Raising* of 1974.

Chomsky defended the position that what is normally considered a raised subject, such as *him* in (43a), is not a raised subject at all but is still, in surface structure, the subject of *win the race*, as the bracketing indicates. He accepted, in other words, an analysis in which an infinitival construction, *to win the race*, takes an actual subject term, a situation otherwise unheard of in English and other languages. The fact that *him* appears in an oblique (accusative) case is attributed to 'Exceptional Case Marking' or ECM.[20]

---

[20] Given the status assigned to this ECM in Chomskyan circles, its motivation as found in the literature is astoundingly weak. Cp. Van Riemsdijk & Williams (1986:235):

(43)a. I expect [him to win the race]
    b. Bill believes [John to have left]

Against this, Postal marshalled an impressive array of observations, a small selection of which follows here:

(44)a. I believed (that) we were right
    b. *I believed us to be right   (p. 77)

(45)a. Harry believes that not many pilots like Racine
    b. *Harry believes not many pilots to like Racine   (p. 98)

(46)a. They proved that he, who was Turkish, was innocent
    b. *They proved him, who was Turkish, to be innocent   (p. 226)

(47)a. I figured out that he was a swindler
    b. *I figured out him to be a swindler
    c. I figured him out to be a swindler   (p. 413)

(44) exemplifies the Inclusion Constraint, which forbids referential overlap between arguments of the same predicate, but not between the subject of a matrix verb and that of an embedded verb. (45) exemplifies a restriction on negative quantifier phrases like *not many* or *not all*, which can occur as the subject term of a clause but not as (in)direct object. (46) is an instance of the rule that non-restrictive relative clauses with a pronominal antecedent can occur only if the antecedent is in subject position, which rules out (46b). (47), finally, shows that Particle Movement, which is obligatory in English across a pronominal object term (*I pulled out him* versus *I pulled him out*) functions in precisely that way in cases of Subject-to-Object Raising.

Compared with the feeble motivation produced by Chomsky and his followers for their treatment of the cases at hand, Postal's defence of Subject-to-Object Raising must be considered a monument of solid syntactic argumentation. The fact that Chomsky neither replied nor changed his position is a measure of his unwillingness to be persuaded by argument.

After this, Postal lost interest in transformational grammar and concentrated entirely, together with David Perlmutter, on the development of a new theory of syntax, Relational Grammar, which is based on functional argument positions such as subject, direct and indirect object. This theory will not be discussed here, as it is too recent to be counted as part of the history of linguistics.

We now pass on to a discussion of the central tenets of the generative semantics movement, and of the model of grammar that stood at its centre.

Since [(43b)] is very much the exception, rather than the rule, especially in the context of the world's languages generally, we should not expect the correct solution to have the flavor of a natural phenomenon in language. It should have the flavor of the unusual.

The weakness of this 'motivation' shows the degree to which an academic community can be indoctrinated. One wonders which is more shocking, the statement that Subject-to-Object Raising is an isolated quirk of English, the fact that a totally ad hoc measure is made to look as a natural consequence of the theory, or the gullibility of those linguists who allow themselves to be taken in by this kind of 'argument'.

7.3.2.4 The generative semantics model of syntax

What, then are the central tenets of generative semantics? The question is important because, as we shall argue in 7.3.3, the downfall of generative semantics that occurred in the early 1970s was due in large part to the fact that its defenders were unable to separate essential from peripheral issues.

- *The overall model*

In general terms, the model of syntax that was proposed in generative semantics was like the Katz-Postal-*Aspects* model of fig. 4, but for the semantic component, which was dropped altogether, given the postulated identity of semantic representations and syntactic deep structures. These were defined formally by generative base or formation rules, and semantically in terms of whatever semantics one wishes to let loose on predicate calculus structures. Fig. 5 shows the structure of the generative semantics model of grammar:

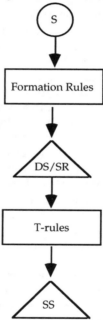

Figure 5   *Overall architecture of a syntax according to generative semantics*

The syntax (grammar) is now seen as a two-tiered system of rules, the base or formation rules that generate the deep-structures-cum-semantic-representations, and the transformational rules which form a mapping system from the semantic representations to the corresponding surface structures.

- *What this model actually claims*

A few important claims are inherent in this model. First, it requires that a deep-structure-cum-semantic-representation (DS/SR), apart from any elements expressing a speech act quality, be able, given proper contextual anchoring, to express a proposition which has a truth value. Since DS/SRs are formal structures they must be open to a formal procedure of semantic interpretation, model-theoretic or otherwise, showing them to be propositional.

Then, the language of the DS/SRs is that of predicate calculus (with extensions such as those described above), so that anyone with a sufficient training should be able to read them and grasp their meaning. DS/SR structures are adequately representable as tree diagrams, just like their surface structure (SS) counterparts.

Thirdly, the rules that transform DS/SR structures into surface structures must not change in any way the meaning that has been fixed for the corresponding DS/SRs. That is, any T-rule that would result in a structure intuitively understood by native speakers to mean something else than the underlying DS/SR is inadmissible. This principle of semantic invariance places a strong empirical restriction on the machinery that transforms SD/SRs into SSs, not a restriction on the form of the rules but on their empirical effect.

General and non-specific as this model is, it has relatively few direct consequences for the system of T-rules. One such consequence is that the theory must contain a well-motivated mechanism for the movement of predicate calculus sentential operators, including the quantifiers, to their surface positions. This mechanism must consist of so-called 'lowering rules', as they lower the operators in question from their high position in the DS/SR tree to their position in the matrix sentence.

This is just about all, which makes this model of grammar extremely general. Yet specific enough not to be without interest. The central issue is the constraining role of the semantic invariance principle on the transformational machinery. The semantic aspect had remained unaccounted for until the appearance of Katz & Fodor (1963) and Katz & Postal (1964), and the account given in the generative semantics model of grammar differed in essential respects from that given in either of these other two alternatives.

7.3.2.5 The counterpart: autonomous syntax

If we rule out the Katz & Postal 1964 model (prematurely called the 'Standard Theory' by Chomsky) as an alternative, on the grounds that it makes little sense to distinguish a separate semantic component if SRs are structures of the same kind as syntactic deep structures and both are to contain all semantic information in an unambiguous form, we still have the Katz & Fodor 1963 theory as an alternative. This was defended by Chomsky and soon became known as 'autonomous syntax' or as 'interpretive semantics', and also, for a while, as the 'extended standard theory' or EST.

Autonomous syntax postulates semantic freedom for transformation rules. It is neutral on the question of whether semantic representations are linguistic structures in the formal language of predicate calculus (though, given the absence of a reasonable alternative, most adherents of autonomous syntax take it that they are). And it does not require that the syntactic deep structures express full propositions with or without speech act qualities. As a theory of grammar or syntax it is, therefore, less constrained than its generative semantics rival. If semantic properties are to be taken into account, autonomous syntax does require rules of semantic interpretation and thus a separate semantic component, since the structures defined by the syntax may well be meaningless by themselves. The semantic interpretation rules will then turn the potentially meaningless structures produced by the syntax into meaningful structures that are open to formal semantic processing.

The positions taken by generative semantics on the one hand and by autonomous syntax or EST on the other, general though they may be, thus embody clear but contrary claims as to the optimal overall structure of an adequate grammatical and semantic description of a language. It is generally known that the opposition between the two schools of thought quickly developed into what has been described as a war of ideologies and personalities (Newmeyer 1980; Harris 1993; Huck & Goldsmith 1995). This war, which was won by the autonomous syntax party, was of a particularly nasty and, one may say, unworthy character, and there can be no doubt that it has left the field of linguistics in an unhealthy state.

7.3.3   An analysis of the episode

Various authors, in particular Newmeyer (1980; 1986), McCawley (1980; 1994) Harris (1993), Huck & Goldsmith (1995), have presented analyses of the events that occurred between, say, 1965 and 1975.

- *Newmeyer's analysis*

Newmeyer (1980) attributes the rapid downfall of generative semantics in the early 1970s, apart from its 'whimsical style of presentation' and its urge 'to be funny' (1980:171-2), largely to itself:

> It is tempting to think that it was the weight of the interpretivist counterattack that led to the demise of generative semantics. While it played an important role, it was not the deciding factor. ...
>
> No, the fact is that generative semantics DESTROYED ITSELF. Its internal dynamic led to a state of affairs in which it could no longer be taken seriously by anyone interested in the scientific study of human language. Generative semantics simply gave up on attempting to EXPLAIN grammatical phenomena, leaving the field open to its competitors.
>
> The dynamic that led to the abandonment of explanation for pure description flowed irrevocably from the decision to abandon scientific idealizations and therefore consider ANY speaker judgment and ANY fact about morpheme distribution as a matter of grammatical analysis. ...
>
> Attributing the same theoretical weight to each and every fact about language had disastrous consequences. Since the number of facts is, of course, absolutely overwhelming, simply DESCRIBING the incredible complexities of language became the all-consuming task, with formal explanation postponed to some future date. ...
>
> The data fetishism reached its apogee in fuzzy grammar. Many staunch generative semanticists who had followed every step of Lakoff's and Ross's up to that point, turned away from fuzzy theoretical constructs.   Newmeyer (1980:167-8)

McCawley (1980), however, showed, on the basis of facts and quotations, that the picture of generative semantics painted by Newmeyer bears little relation to reality. It is, in fact, a gross misrepresentation, inspired by the false rhetoric that Chomsky had been applying for years to generative semantics. We shall, therefore, dismiss this part of Newmeyer's analysis as irrelevant.

Newmeyer (1986), the second edition of 1980, is more moderate in this respect, ceding some ground to McCawley. Yet in this edition he still cites (1986:136-7) the whimsical, flippant, and at times vulgar style of presentation common among the generative semanticists as an important factor in the rapid downfall of the generative semantics movement in the early 1970s. While Newmeyer is right in mentioning this particular aspect of in particular the American adherents of generative semantics, it is doubtful that it was a factor of any significance. One should realize that those were the days of the hippies and flower power, of liberation movements of all sorts, and of experimenting with existing norms and traditions. In hindsight, the attempts at being funny or trendy, or outright shocking, appear a little forced and at times embarrassing. But at the time there was no strong adverse reaction of any kind. On the contrary, the world was obviously amused. The only objections came long afterwards, and they came from the very Chomskyan quarters that were keen on attacking generative semantics for totally independent reasons.[21]

A further factor mentioned by Newmeyer, and by others as well, was the sociological structure of the group of leading generative semanticists. Unlike the circles around Chomsky, where strict discipline and obedience ('loyalty') is exacted, the generative semanticists cultivated an atmosphere of personal freedom and even anarchy. No authority or 'leadership' was recognized. The movement was expected to live by the strength of the ideas that were generated. This idealistic attitude inspired many but it had disastrous organizational consequences for the movement, which lacked the machinery required for a systematic spreading of the word. The leading generative semanticists were unable systematically to organize the acquisition of funds for graduate students, and to ensure that the graduates were appointed in strategic posts. This undoubtedly made them vulnerable against a rival movement that had

---

[21] One is reminded, in this connection, of an episode that occurred in the Roman empire at the beginning of the third century AD. The boy emperor Heliogabalus, who reigned from 218 till 222, had turned the whole of Rome into one continuous licentious feast, thereby trampling on age-old traditions and values and, of course, shocking the ordinary citizens' normal sense of decency. After a few years he was overthrown and succeeded by his cousin, Severus Alexander, who had received a stern military education, and who introduced the grim period of the military emperors, which lasted till the end of that century. In this case, one may indeed say that the downfall of Heliogabalus was due mainly to the debauchery he brought about and to the total administrative disorder that resulted. In comparison, the downfall of generative semantics may have been due in part to 'administrative disorder', but not to the perhaps somewhat licentious counterculture attitudes of its adherents. The quirks were mainly stylistic, and certainly innocent and without guile.

its organization under tight control. One can do little else but list the anarchistic tendencies among the leading generative semanticists as one of the factors that led to the collapse of the movement. Yet how important this factor actually was remains a matter of debate.

- *The conflict was fuelled by clashes of personalities, not of issues*

It is to be noted, meanwhile, that neither the style of presentation nor the sociological structure of the group concerned are factors that have a bearing on the actual content and the academic merits of the issues concerned. They are external factors to do with personalities, not with issues. In this respect we fully agree with Huck and Goldsmith, who write in their Preface (1995:ix):

> But while the Generative Semanticists unquestionably faced theoretical obstacles of various sorts, there are also good reasons to believe that the demise of their program was not a consequence of theoretical weakness. Indeed we will argue in what follows that it is not possible to find, internal to the idea of Generative Semantics as it was evidently originally understood by Lakoff, McCawley, Postal and Ross, adequate grounds to explain its widespread abandonment in the 1970s. We will be concerned to evaluate the linguistic evidence on its own terms, paying particular attention to the theoretical assumptions that underlay the various critiques, and will conclude that one must turn to external explanations to account adequately for what transpired. But although external factors undoubtedly affected the way that the various proposals in the dispute were understood and received, we would also suggest that a focus on the relatively dramatic personal and social aspects of the interactions in which the participants were involved has tended to obscure the conceptual significance of the positions they took. In fact, those positions were considerably more compatible theoretically than one might suppose, given the animosities that developed as the issues were debated.

- *No arguments were produced, just rhetoric*

Despite twenty-odd years of disparagement from the side of Chomsky and his followers, one has to face the astonishing fact that not a single actual argument was produced during that period to support the attitude of dismissal and even contempt that one finds expressed, as a matter of routine, in the relevant Chomsky-inspired literature. Quasi-arguments, on the contrary, abounded.

- *Jackendoff (1983) as an example of a quasi-argument*

A typical example of the kind of quasi-argument produced during the period at hand is found in Jackendoff (1983). This 'argument' is aimed less at generative semantics than at the very notion that the language of predicate calculus should be taken to be the best language available for the representation of meanings, even though it is presented as an argument against generative semantics and in favour of the Chomskyan brand of grammatical theory, so-called interpretive semantics:

> Naturally, there are good reasons for adopting the formalism of quantificational logic, having to do with solving certain aspects of the inference problem. Yet one could hardly expect a language learner to learn the complex correspondence rules required to relate quantificational formalism to surface syntax. The logician might respond by claiming that this aspect of the correspondence rules is universal and thus need not be learned. But then we could ask on a deeper level why language is

the way it is: Why does it display the constituent structure and embedding relations it does, if it expresses something formally so different? In short, the Grammatical Constraint does not permit us to take for granted the use of quantificational logic to model natural language semantics. A competing model that accounts for the same inferences but preserves a simpler correspondence of syntactic and semantic structure is to be preferred.   Jackendoff (1983:15)

We notice, first, that Jackendoff does not even make the beginning of an attempt at actually formulating a rule system that would relate predicate argument structures to surface structures. He does make several attempts, however, to show that any rendering of meanings in terms of predicate calculus must be enormously baroque, which would make predicate calculus structures unrealistic as input structures to a grammatical rule system. He writes:

Consider a simple sentence like (4.1).

(4.1)   Floyd broke a glass violently

This sentence includes five referring expressions, picking out two #things#, an #event#, an #action#, and a #manner#. A possible logical form for (4.1), as closely parallel to standard logical practice as I can make it (though hardly first order), is (4.2). "Floyd" corresponds to a constant, but all the other referential phrases are translated as variables bound by existential quantifiers.

(4.2) $\exists x(Event(x)\ \&\ x = \exists z(Action(z)\ \&\ z(Floyd)\ \&\ z = (\exists w(glass(w)\ \&$
         $break(w)\ \&\ \exists u(violently(u)\ \&\ u(z))))))$

Though one could certainly quibble over details, the point is that (4.2) represents the general degree of complexity that any standard logical translation must contain: four existential quantifiers, each of which binds a variable of the appropriate ontological category. All vestiges of resemblance to natural language have vanished.   Jackendoff (1983:58-59)

One could indeed 'quibble over details', though the details are pretty momentous. There is, for example, the curious use of the identity predicate '=', (one probably has to read (4.2) as saying, among other things, that there is an action z, and z consists in there being a glass that breaks). More importantly, Jackendoff gives no justification at all for the proliferation of quantifiers over abstract elements like 'Action' or 'Event', or over the predicate 'violent'. Then, (4.2) does not even render the element 'past', clearly present in (4.1).

In fact, as a predicate calculus translation of (4.1), (4.2) is a travesty. A more constrained and more serious attempt at giving an adequate predicate calculus translation of his (4.1) is (48), where the verbal tense is treated according to the Reichenbach system outlined above in 7.3.2.2. The element 'past' is a context-bound deictic and hence a constant. 'Simultaneous' is there for systematic reasons but is semantically vacuous. The predicate 'violent' is taken to be subcategorized, inter alia, for a lexically specified S-structure as subject, in which case its semantics is fixed by meaning postulate as that of a manner adverb. Any causativity inherent in the predicate 'break' is again specified lexically by meaning postulate. Elements like 'event' or 'action' are likewise assumed to be lexically inherent in both the abstract elements and the lexical predicates used.

(48)

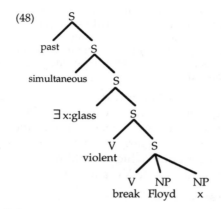

In general, Jackendoff fails to take into account the many proposals put forward by generative semanticists to render meanings in the (extended) language of predicate calculus, without having to resort to baroque and often inadequate paraphrases. He ignores, in particular, the possibility of storing a great deal of unruly semantic information in the semantic description of lexical predicates, by way of meaning postulates. Had he been more sympathetic towards predicate calculus and had he tried his hand at actual rule writing, he might have found what was found in Seuren (1996), namely that the rule system required to convert well-constrained predicate calculus structures like (48) into surface structures is, in fact, compact and straightforward.[22]

Given his failure to produce or refer to any actual rule system that relates well-motivated predicate calculus structures to surface structures, his contention that such systems must be complex beyond the learning capacity of the natural language learner must be deemed gratuitous.

Moreover, standard Chomsky-inspired models of grammar fully accept the language of predicate calculus as the optimal means of representing meanings, their so-called 'logical form'. One wonders, therefore, why Jackendoff's criticism does not extend to these grammatical models, since they all imply a rule system relating surface structures to predicate calculus structures, which, according to Jackendoff, 'one could hardly expect a language learner to learn'. Whatever validity there might be, therefore, to Jackendoff's position, will affect Chomsky grammar as much as generative semantics. But one must fear that there is very little validity to the argument. For if there were, Jackendoff would have produced a superior alternative to predicate calculus as a means of computing entailments and rendering meanings, a highly improbable accomplishment that would have shaken the world if it had any substance.

What remains is the question of why humans do not use the language of predicate calculus for their needs of linguistic communication but use the surface structures of their respective languages instead. This is a valid question

---

[22] It is ironical to note that Jackendoff adopts a 'transformationalist' position to attack generative semantics, where a 'lexicalist' position would immediately help it out. Cp. the comments made below on the issue of 'transformationalists' versus 'lexicalists'.

and it applies to all theories that posit a level of semantic representation different from surface structure, including generative semantics and autonomous syntax. If one implies, as Jackendoff does, that this question has no adequate answer, all one can do is embrace the position of surface semantics (see 7.2.3), but that is not what Jackendoff does, which suggests inconsistency.[23] On the whole, therefore, Jackendoff's argument seems to be more inspired by personal preferences than by a careful analysis of the issues concerned.

- *Generative Semantics is blamed for lack of constraints*

Another quasi-argument, often encountered in the literature, is that generative semantics suffered from a fatal lack of constraints on the rules of grammar required or adopted. What is meant is that generative semantics did not take part in the frantic rush for formal constraints on transformational rules that was started by Chomsky in 1970. The fact that generative semantics is practically defined by the constraint of semantic invariance of T-rules is usually left unmentioned. Moreover, no generative semanticist has or had any principled objection to the search for universal formal constraints. They just felt that the Chomskyans had, and have, a tendency to jump to premature formulations and hypotheses, a feeling that has been confirmed by the fact that over the past twenty-five or so years the Chomsky school has issued a confounding proliferation of such proposals, all of which have meanwhile proved untenable given the facts. On the whole, the generative semanticists preferred to stay more relaxed in this respect, and to adopt a more inductive attitude, concentrating on the production of analyses and descriptions that did justice to the facts in optimally insightful ways. From there on one could begin to try to formulate hypotheses of possible universal constraints. The difference was thus one of method, not of principle. After all, Ross's 1967 thesis contained a number of proposals for precisely such constraints. And these proposals, as has been said, have held out extremely well, much better than any proposal put forward after 1970 by the Chomsky school.

- *Most of the issues discussed were not essential*

During the early years of generative semantics, between 1965 and 1970, the main difficulty was the inability to identify and formulate precisely the essential generalities of the theory. What one did was come forward with a number of descriptive and analytical proposals that seemed to support the general outlook but were in no way indispensable or essential.

This is understandable given the emphasis that was placed, in those days, on the criterion of immediate falsifiability of scientific proposals and the

---

[23] What the answer should be is an interesting question that affects a good many theories of grammar. It is probably to be sought in the functional requirements of human language. One factor may be the primary use of the predominantly sequential acoustic medium for the transmission of linguistic messages. Other factors may be to do with the structure of the cognitive processing units that are involved in the use of language. In general, however, one must admit that no satisfactory answer has so far been provided to this question.

lack of appreciation for the status of a theory as a whole compared with other possible theories. Presenting a theoretical framework without specifying the grounds of immediate falsification was considered unscientific and disreputable. In fact, many in those days, including Chomsky, would say that such a framework was devoid of content and vacuous. It was for that reason that refuge was sought in analytical and descriptive proposals that were actually subject to direct falsification but were in no way defining features of the generative semantics research programme.

The most important issues that were thus discussed as if they were essential to generative semantics were:

(a) Ross's analysis of auxiliaries as main verbs
(b) the status of nominalizations: lexical or grammatical transforms
(c) the mechanism of lexical insertion and the status of 'deep structure'
(d) the internal analysis of lexical predicates (prelexical syntax)
(e) the status of derivational constraints
(f) Postal's analysis of the verb *remind*
(g) the status of thematic roles or functions

In the wake of Chomsky (1972b), where they are all discussed, these issues occur in virtually all of the literature dealing with the history of that period as the issues around which the debate between the 'generativists' and the 'interpretivists' revolved. Chomsky (1972b) shows a tendency to dismiss most of these issues as merely notational or terminological. Even so, however, he consistently rejects the positions taken by the generative semanticists and defends those of himself and his followers. He summarizes his position vis-à-vis generative semantics as follows, strangely omitting any mention of the semantic invariance principle:

> Summarizing so far, we have specified a general framework and three specific variants: the standard theory, the extended standard theory, and generative semantics. In my opinion, the standard theory is inadequate and must be modified. The evidence now available seems to me to indicate that it must be modified to the extended standard theory (EST). Furthermore, when some vagueness and faulty formulations are eliminated, I think we can show that generative semantics converges with EST in most respects. There are a few differences, which I will try to identify and discuss, but in most cases I think that the differences are either terminological, or lie in an area where both theories are comparably inexplicit, so that no empirical issue can, at the moment, be formulated. The clearest and probably most important difference between EST and generative semantics has to do with the ordering of lexical and nonlexical transformations. This, in fact, seems to me perhaps the only fairly clear issue with empirical import that distinguishes these theories. My feeling is that present evidence supports the narrower and more restrictive assumption of the (extended) standard theory that nonlexical transformations follow all lexical transformations, so that "deep structure" is a well-defined notion, and that the conditions on deep structure given by base rules narrowly constrain K (the class of derivations Σ). This, however, is an empirical issue, as distinct from a number of others that seem to me to be terminological, or in an area of indeterminacy and vagueness.   Chomsky (1972b:74-5)

• *Ross's analysis of auxiliaries as main verbs*

The thesis that English auxiliaries are best treated syntactically as main verbs was first proposed in Ross (1969). Chomsky (1972b:65-6, 120) dismisses this as being in part merely notational and for the rest unconvincing. Whether this is or is not so, however, is immaterial in the context of generative versus interpretive semantics. Both generative semantics and EST can live with or without this thesis. The only difference is that if there are good empirical arguments for labelling auxiliaries as 'Verb' this supports the methodological preference of generative semantics to reduce the number of categories in semantic representations to 'S', 'V', and 'NP'. But if this preference has to be given up that will not be the end of generative semantics.

• *Lexicalism and transformationalism*

Chomsky does recognize the question of how grammatical and lexical rules relate to each other as a truly empirical issue which, moreover, he sees as essential for the distinction between EST and generative semantics. This question underlies the topics (b), (c), (d), and (f) just mentioned. It was destined to become a major bone of contention in the war between Chomsky and the generative semanticists.

It all began with George Lakoff's dissertation of 1965, mentioned in 7.3.2.3 above, where Lakoff proposed to fit out lexical predicates with rule features defining which transformational rules are and which are not induced by them. Among these rules were nominalization rules, which would produce, for example, *transgressor* from *transgress*, and also *aggressor* from a postulated underlying verb *aggress* whose rule features would forbid it to occur as a verb.

For some reason Chomsky felt he had to get up in arms against this, and against the whole trend of linking up meaning with syntax, of which Lakoff was one of the main champions. In 1966-67 Chomsky spent a sabbatical at Berkeley, during which he apparently took the decision that the new movement of generative semantics had to be stopped:

> So it was, in Ray Jackendoff's phrase, "a dreadful surprise" when Chomsky returned to MIT from his Berkeley sabbatical in 1967, and launched a series of lectures that completely reversed the abstract syntax trend of deepening deep structure. His students, after some initial shock and puzzlement, found these lectures invigorating; Jackendoff, a second-year doctoral student, was particularly thrilled that his own recent research, research which had no home at all in generative semantics and compromised the *Aspects* model considerably, was resonating with Chomsky.
>
> There was no puzzlement about where these lectures – the "Remarks" lectures, named after the famous paper that came out of them, "Remarks on Nominalization" (1972a[1967]) – were aimed. Everyone immediately perceived them as an attack on generative semantics, a reactionary attempt to cut the abstract legs out from underneath the upstart model. The best term for the lectures is Newmeyer's. He calls them a "counteroffensive" (1980:114; 1986:107), which captures the air of reaction, assault, and upping-the-ante in which they were received. Chomsky, though – here the story gets particularly bizarre – says he wasn't much interested in generative semantics or in abstract syntax at the time, that he "knew virtually nothing about" [it] either, that he barely noticed the work Postal, Lakoff, Ross, and McCawley were up to. His 1967 MIT lectures, he says, were just a delayed reaction to Lees's

Grammar of English Nominalizations (written in the very late fifties with considerable input from Chomsky).   Harris (1993:139)

What followed was a bitter and personal conflict between the so-called 'lexicalists', who sided with Chomsky, and the generative semanticists' school of
'transformationalists'.

Chomsky's volte-face was indeed surprising to anyone still believing that
academic issues ought to be settled on the strength of the arguments involved,
and not on grounds of personal ambition or resentment. Chomsky's rhetoric also
puzzled many:

> ["Remarks"] dresses up surprising new proposals as natural extensions of the
> *Aspects* model, and characterizes the natural extensions pursued by the "transfor-
> mationalists" as a misguided detour. ...
>   Chomsky repudiated successful earlier work, proposed radical changes to the
> *Aspects* model, and opened ad hoc escape channels for those changes – all on the
> basis of quite meager evidence – with no more motivation, as far as anyone could
> see, than to cripple the work of his most productive colleague and of some of the
> most promising former students they shared.   Harris (1993:141-2)

The actual issue, however, of how nominalizations are best derived is, as
Chomsky said, of an empirical nature. It remains to be seen whether an internal lexical system of derivations for nominalizations is preferable to a system
where nominalizations are generated as part of transformational syntax. It
even seems plausible that Chomsky's lexicalist position is, in principle, to be
preferred. Yet, contrary to what Chomsky said and his followers took to be
the case, the issue is entirely indifferent as to the question of the superiority
of either generative semantics or EST (or whatever later incarnation of EST
emerged). There is nothing in either theory that favours or disfavours 'lexicalism' or 'transformationalism'. Both theories are fully compatible with
either position.

● *'Deep structure'?*

The same goes for the question of whether there is a level of 'deep structure'
defined as a watershed between lexical and transformational rules: the former
apply before, the latter after the coming about of this alleged 'deep structure'
level in the generative procedure. The generative semanticists rejected this
notion of 'deep structure' (cp. McCawley 1968c). Their deep structure was the
level of representation of a sentence produced by the base or formation rules
containing also primitive or 'prelexical' lexical forms.

Again, whether the lexical insertions carried out in the base rules necessarily have to involve only actual surface items or whether they should be
allowed to involve more abstract lexical items that will then combine and be
replaced by appropriate surface items during the transformational treatment,
is an empirical question whose answer is neutral between generative semantics
and EST.

In practice, the generative semanticists tended to favour the view called
'prelexical syntax', which implies that the base rules allow for the introduction of abstract items that are to be combined and replaced by surface items

during the transformational process, hoping that this would enhance the explanatory force of the description. And, again in practice, the Chomskyans were against prelexical syntax and in favour of unitary lexical insertion by the base rules of surface items only. But if one looks at the issue dispassionately, from the proper distance of purely academic significance, one has to admit that this issue, too, is neutral between the two theories. In fact, it has to be, since the very same ideas of prelexical syntax that were rejected with abhorrence by Chomsky, Fodor (1970) and others are now accepted and treated with respect by the same protagonists. The difference is, apparently, that this time they have been proposed by people with the right credentials.

- *What is the real issue?*

If the issues that were debated during the period at hand were on the whole not germane to the actual conflict, one will wonder what the real issue was. The answer to this is fairly simple. The real issue was, and is, whether the transformational rules should take semantic representations as input. It is a question of the overall superiority of one theory over another. The question is not who was right on this or that point of grammar, but which theory, as a whole, provides the better descriptions in terms of coverage of data and degree of generalization. As regards the latter, one strives for maximal generalizations first over the data of the language at hand, then over the languages of the world, and, finally, over the totality of scientific knowledge.

- *The issue is not decidable on grounds of simple falsification*

Isolated issues of directly falsifiable grammatical description are germane to this general question only in so far as they are compatible with one but not the other theory, and such issues are few in number. Other than that, if generative semantics succeeds in producing factually adequate and insightful grammars of languages with a minimum of fuss and a maximum of unity, while the other party systematically fails to produce such descriptions, it wins. And, of course, vice versa. But this has not been the way the comparison has been conducted. On the contrary, as has been noted by a number of authors, strategies consisting of false rhetoric, obfuscation and personality cult took the place of an orderly academic contest.

- *What were the real causes of the collapse of generative semantics?*

It would seem, in hindsight, that the sudden collapse of generative semantics during the first half of the 1970s was due not to the hippy style of presentation, nor to the exuberance of some of the structures presented, nor to any lack of constraints on rules of grammar, but mostly to the generative semanticists' inability to find an answer to the obfuscations, equivocations, false rhetoric and other unprofessional forms of sophistry employed by Chomsky in his war against them. In addition, they suffered from a lack of organization and the resulting inability to acquire funds for large numbers of students and have them appointed to university posts. The generative semanticists were obviously nonplussed at Chomsky's ruthless machiavellism. That being so, we shall now have a closer look at Chomsky's role in the conflict.

- *Chomsky's role*

Ironically, it was Chomsky himself who, in his younger years, defended precisely the view we put forward here. In *Syntactic Structures* (1957:51-3), as we pointed out in section 4.5.1, Chomsky proposed the view that the proper way of deciding between two competing grammars is to compare them and see 'which is the better grammar of the language from which the corpus is drawn' (1957:51). Analogously, the general theory in terms of which the better grammars are produced is to be preferred over a competing general theory whose grammars are inferior. This evaluation criterion 'is still strong enough to guarantee significance for a theory that meets it', and 'the correctness of this judgment can only be determined by the actual development and comparison of theories of these various sorts' (1957:53).

How different is the Chomsky of barely ten years later, when it became clear that no 'actual development' was coming about of a theory that would produce actual grammars (cp. note 27 on p. 252 above). Here we see him try all sorts of contortions in order to impress upon his readers the notion that the two competing theories are, for the most part, just notational or terminological variants. We see him present so-called points of logic or of philosophy of language which are not only not germane but also insufficiently understood.

It was shown above, in 7.3.2.2, how, in correspondence with McCawley, he proved unable to grasp the idea that quantifiers are higher order predicates. In itself this is forgivable and not serious. The point is, however, that this was a symptom of a general attitude of resistance and unwillingness to accept the role of the language of predicate calculus in the theory of grammar, an unwillingness which remained totally unsupported by argument. Any loose thought that suggested to him that generative semantics was not viable was immediately embraced as a fatal argument.

The same keenness to declare generative semantics dead is manifest in his 'argument' of opaque reference in intensional contexts, a problem of philosophy of language, with which the linguists of those days were hardly familiar. Huck & Goldsmith quote him, again from correspondence with McCawley in December 1967, as follows:[24]

> Consider the context: (1) "everyone realizes that $4 = —$." If we substitute "four", (1) becomes true. If we substitute "the only natural number between three and the square root of twenty-five", (1) becomes false. Therefore, [the two alternatives] are not mutually deducible; they must have different meanings. ... The fact is that referentially opaque contexts have the property that truth or falsity (hence, obviously, meaning) depends not only on the intrinsic semantic content, but also on the form in which a belief or a concept is expressed, hence ultimately on surface structure. This observation seems to me to destroy the possibility of Generative Semantics.   Huck & Goldsmith (1995:31)

---

[24] The same view is expressed, as is pointed out by Huck & Goldsmith (ib.), in Chomsky (1971:197), though there the phrasing is less explicit, vaguer and less committal, and therefore less suitable for critical comment.

Again, as in the case of quantifiers as predicates, Chomsky shows an inadequate grasp of the topic at hand. As we had ample occasion to point out in the sections 6.1.2.2, 6.1.4, 6.1.5.1, and 6.2.6.2 above, intensional contexts do, of course, allow for different meanings of two embedded propositions P_1 and P_2, where P_1 and P_2 are identical but for two co-referential terms. We also saw there why this is a problem and that it was to solve that problem that Frege introduced his distinction between meaning ('Sinn') and reference ('Bedeutung'). But Chomsky twists the issue round in order to fabricate an argument against generative semantics, messing up things in the process.

As regards the sentences *Everyone realizes that 4 = four* and *Everyone realizes that 4 = the only natural number between three and the square root of twenty-five*, nobody doubts that 'the two alternatives ... must have different meanings'. But what does it mean to say that 'referentially opaque contexts have the property that truth or falsity (hence, obviously, meaning) depends not only on the intrinsic semantic content, but also on the form in which a belief or a concept is expressed, hence ultimately on surface structure'? One would think that 'intrinsic semantic content' is the same as 'meaning', in which case Chomsky says that 'truth or falsity (hence, obviously, meaning) depends not only on the *meaning*, but also on the form in which a belief or a concept is expressed', which is an odd platitude. Obviously, different forms can have different meanings. And different forms in intensional contexts may produce different meanings, even though in fact they refer to the same entity. In terms of the Aristotelian notion of truth the latter should not be possible, yet it is possible, which causes a problem. But this problem is of a purely semantic nature and has no bearing on the theory of grammar. No matter what solution one proposes to it, there is nothing here that would 'destroy the possibility of Generative Semantics'. All that is required is that semantic representations, whether in generative semantics or in EST, should contain a principled way of distinguishing the different meanings concerned.

In his discussion of Quantifier Lowering, just about the only kind of rule that does make a difference between generative semantics and EST, a similar attitude is displayed (Chomsky 1972b:106-114). The example sentences are:

(49) a. Many men read few books
     b. Few books are read by many men

They are taken to differ in meaning, according to quantifier scope. Chomsky criticizes Lakoff, who proposed to take the (then) normal predicate calculus analysis of the sentences at hand as their underlying structure, to be converted into surface structures by means of transformational rules. As is well-known, in order to get the scope readings right it is necessary to assume a derivational constraint that ensures (with certain exceptions) that no higher quantifier or other scope-sensitive operator is lowered over a previously lowered scope-sensitive operator, so that, in principle, the left-to-right order of the scope-sensitive operators in the surface sentence reflects the scope hierarchy in the underlying semantic representation. This is rejected by Chomsky, because:

Given this apparatus, we can say that deep structure ... relates directly to "logical form". Thus we could convert [the tree structure representing the semantic representation of (49a)] directly to a pseudo-quantificational form such as [(50)]:

[(50)]   for many x∈ Men, for few y∈ Books, x read y

Exactly the same is true if we drop the rule of quantifier lowering from the grammar, eliminate the derivational constraint, and take the deep structure of [(49a)] and [(49b)] to be (approximately):

[(51)]

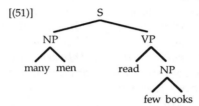

with [(49b)] formed by the ordinary passive transformation. There is a trivial algorithm which, applied to the surface structures, gives the pseudo-quantificational forms such as [(50)].   Chomsky (1972b:107)

Apart from the curious distinction made between what is called a 'pseudo-quantificational form' such as (50) and a tree structure of the kind commonly used by generative semanticists (which is indeed only a notational distinction), Chomsky says in effect that a rule system converting (50) (or its tree structure equivalent) to a corresponding surface structure is bad because it requires a derivational constraint, while a rule system that converts (51) (or its passive counterpart) to the corresponding predicate calculus structure is good because it is 'a trivial algorithm'.[25] He does not mention the fact that this 'trivial algorithm' will then also have to contain a derivational constraint, which will be entirely analogous, but formulated in terms of opposite directionality, not top-down but bottom-up. That algorithm will then have to contain a rule of Quantifier Raising, which can only be the counterpart of Quantifier Lowering, again bottom-up instead of top-down.[26] The only difference is that in generative semantics this rule system is part of the grammar, while for Chomsky it is not. Yet even if it is not it has to be acquired and must be considered part of any native speaker's linguistic competence. We have here another example of Chomsky's by now familiar technique of equivocation.

In addition, as is amply documented in chapter 3 of Huck & Goldsmith (1995), one notices Chomsky's tendency to resort to empty rhetoric, even in

[25] One notes the curious difference with Jackendoff, quoted above, who feels that such rule systems are so complex and ad hoc that a child would never be able to acquire them.

[26] May (1977) is in fact an attempt at formulating this 'trivial algorithm'. Much to the amusement of the linguistic world, this work does indeed have the rule of Quantifier Raising, complete with the derivational constraint so despised by Chomsky. However, much to the bewilderment of the linguistic world, May made only one passing reference to Lakoff and none to McCawley and other authors who had proposed the converse rule of Quantifier Lowering before May even began his studies.

private correspondence.[27] For example, in a letter to John Searle of 19 June 1972, he describes generative semantics as follows, calling its central claim 'exalted':

> [I]f they are saying anything at all, it is that these "readings" [i.e. logical form, P.S.] are so fundamental that in fact they are in some sense the "basis" of all syntax: i.e. they constitute S[emantic] R[epresentation] = P1,...., where P1 is the initial phrase-marker of all derivations. I make no such exalted claim, ...
>
> Huck & Goldsmith (1995:34)

Frequently one finds him use the term 'exotic' when referring to proposals or theories that he wishes to reject, whereas anything proposed by himself or his followers is 'natural' or 'standard'. Many more examples of Chomsky's peculiar choice of evaluative predicates can be adduced, but we shall leave it at this.

One further, particularly striking feature of the Chomsky school must be mentioned in this context, the curious habit of referring to and quoting only members of the same school, ignoring all other linguists except when they have long been dead. The fact that the Chomsky school forms a close and entirely inward looking citation community has made some authors compare it to a religious sect or, less damningly, to a village parish. No doubt there is a point to this kind of comparison, but one should realize that political considerations probably play a larger part in Chomskyan linguistics than is customary in either sects or village parishes.

In general, the whole episode was characterized by emotions rather than by matter-of-fact argument. A famous example of this is the unpleasant clash that occurred between Chomsky and his one-time student, then colleague, Ross at the Texas Conference of October 1969, mentioned earlier in section 7.3.2.3. Postal, in Huck & Goldsmith (1995), gives a vivid account of this event:

> After his [i.e. Chomsky's] verbal presentation, there was an opportunity for the audience to use a microphone, up toward the front. Those who wanted to ask a question or comment had to raise their hand and be called on by whomever was in charge. Haj Ross did that, took the microphone, started to talk, hadn't finished and Chomsky interrupted him. Quite brutally, Haj just turned around and walked away while Chomsky went on with his interruption. Ross's gesture signaled that this was a breakdown of communication, that he felt Chomsky had broken the rules. Which I believe he had.
>
> Huck & Goldsmith (1995:134)

What had happened was that Chomsky had simply applied one of his well-known strategies during question time: interrupt your opponent and finish his sentence for him. In a footnote to the quote given above, Postal comments:

> That Chomsky was willing to publicly exploit his academic/professional dominance and temporary control of the forum to treat someone standing in such a close relation to him with contempt before a large and important linguistic meeting had to communicate several important lessons to anyone who was aware of what was going on. One clear implication was that disagreeing with Chomsky, even then the most

---

[27] This suggests that he actually, in his private mind, mulled over the issues at hand in such terms, which in turn suggests a fundamental uncertainty and lack of confidence.

renowned and influential person in the field, would have a high price. A second
was that the controversies which had arisen were not being treated by Chomsky as
(only) technical matters to be resolved in normal scientific ways but as somehow
sufficiently threatening to induce strongly emotional responses and even clear
violations of normal standards.   Huck & Goldsmith (1995:161-162)

It will be clear by now that Chomsky's role in this whole course of events is
hardly an example of proper academic conduct. In fact, one would not be too far
off the mark if one felt that this behaviour should be qualified as petty, cyni-
cal and above all unprofessional. It certainly is also unwise, as chickens like
these tend to come home to roost. Some have admired him for it, praising his
versatility, his capacity to present his sudden theoretical changes as natural
extensions of his theory, even his talent for dividing the field and creating
violent animosities.[28] These would do well to realize that this very behaviour on Chomsky's part has caused great harm to linguistics. Largely as a result
of Chomsky's actions, linguistics is now sociologically in a very unhealthy
state. It has, moreover, lost most of the prestige and appeal it commanded forty years ago. And, finally, the overall quality not only of linguistic theorizing
but also of linguistic analyses and descriptions in terms of generative grammar
has declined dramatically, to the point even of threatening to make that
whole school of linguistics intellectually irrelevant.[29] A far cry indeed from
Frege, to whom Russell paid the warm and moving tribute quoted on p. 335
above for his 'almost superhuman ... dedication to creative work and knowledge instead of cruder efforts to dominate and be known'!

---

[28] Cp., for example, Harris (1993:240-260), where, to one's surprise after all the damning
evidence presented in the preceding pages, Harris depicts Chomsky as a hero of science,
calling him, among other things, 'a tremendously skilled rhetor' and 'an especially impressive prose stylist' (1993:244), and comparing him to Aristotle, Ptolemy and Coper-
nicus (1993:260). Pinker (1994) is another admirer:

> Chomsky is currently among the ten most-cited writers in all of the humanities ... and
> the only living member of the top ten. ... Chomsky gets people exercised. Reactions
> range from the awe-struck deference ordinarily reserved for gurus of weird reli-
> gious cults to the withering invective that academics have developed into a high art.
> In part this is because Chomsky attacks what is still one of the foundations of twen-
> tieth-century intellectual life – the "Standard Social Science Model", according to
> which the human psyche is molded by the surrounding culture. But it is also because
> no thinker can afford to ignore him.   Pinker (1994:23)

This is a curious passage. If Pinker wants to say that Chomsky is both idolized and despised because he attacked innatism and because 'no thinker can afford to ignore him', the
present author, who would not be reckoned to be one of the awe-struck idolizers, must be
an exception, since he has no problem with innatism, and he certainly bears no general
grudge against academics, living or dead, whom nobody can afford to ignore. It seems that
Pinker forgot to take into account the possibility that there may also be valid professional
reasons for uttering severe criticisms vis-à-vis Chomsky.

A different kind of admiration altogether is found in Barsky (1997), which is a typical
instance of the totally uncritical, artificially sweetened hagiographies one normally finds
produced in musty sects to boost the image of their leaders.

[29] It is ironical to think that this same man has frequently stressed the responsibility of
intellectuals, but this aspect of his activities has to be left out of account in this context.

There is an inevitable further and equally sobering aspect to this episode in the very recent history of linguistics. The fact that Chomsky's behaviour was accepted, even admired, by large sections of the linguistic community, which clearly took the side of the man with the strongest rhetoric, shows that neither the discipline of linguistics nor the community of linguists have achieved the degree of maturity one expects to find in a real science.

7.4 Epilogue

On this sad note we have come to the end of this book. Yet there is also some reason for optimism. Since 1975, a variety of theories and approaches to grammar have sprung up, besides Chomskyan linguistics. Without aiming at completeness we can mention Relational Grammar (Paul Postal and David Perlmutter), Lexical Functional Grammar (Joan Bresnan), Generalized Phrase Structure Grammar (Gerald Gazdar), Head-Driven Phrase Structure Grammar (Ivan Sag), Cognitive Grammar (Ronald Langacker and George Lakoff), Autolexical Syntax (Jerry Sadock), categorial and other logic-inspired forms of grammar in a variety of guises, etc.

We have to leave these newer developments undiscussed here. An adequate discussion would not only exceed this author's competence but also the admissible length of this book. Moreover, all these theories are of such recent date that a proper historical perspective is out of the question. Later historians will no doubt find it possible to assign to these developments a just place in the history of the subject. All we can hope for, in this respect, is that this book will contribute to a better understanding of the roots and backgrounds of, and the motivations for, the theories concerned.

However, from the point of view of academic sociology and politics, one cannot fail to notice that, whatever the intrinsic merits and the potential of these (and other, older) developments, which are likely to be considerable, they tend not to show the divisive characteristics that we have observed in the Chomsky-led school of linguistic theory. On the contrary, there appears to be a clear, though implicit, wish to avoid the attitudes and behaviour that have placed the Chomsky movement, powerful though it has become, under a cloud, and to revert to less innovative standards of academic conduct. It is to be hoped that a return to normal standards of academic quality, regardless of allegiances, prejudices, animosities, ambitions or whatever other improper factors have played a role in the recent developments, will restore to theoretical linguistics some of the status and prestige it had in the eyes of neighbouring disciplines in happier times, when parochial group arrogance and the brazen-faced presentation of nonsense as the latest wisdom had not yet become part of the linguist's repertoire. That may then be, after all, the most important lesson to be drawn from the Chomsky epiphany.

Bibliography[1]

Aarsleff, Hans

    1970   The history of linguistics and professor Chomsky. *Language* 46.3:570-85.

    1982   *From Locke to Saussure. Essays on the Study of Language and Intellectual History.* Athlone, London.

Allen, W. Sidney

    1948   Ancient ideas on the origin and development of language. *Transactions of the Philological Society of Great Britain* 1948. Pp. 35-60.

Ameka, Felix,

    1990   The grammatical packaging of experiencers in Ewe: a study in the semantics of syntax. *Australian Journal of Linguistics* 10:139-81.

Amsterdamska, Olga

    1987   *Schools of Thought. The Development of Linguistics from Bopp to Saussure.* Reidel, Dordrecht.

Andresen, Julie T.

    1990   *Linguistics in America 1769-1924.* Routledge, London-New York.

Arens, Hans

    1955   *Sprachwissenschaft: der Gang ihrer Entwicklung von der Antike bis zur Gegenwart.* Karl Alber, Freiburg-Munich.

Aristotle

    1946   De Poetica. In: W.D. Ross (ed.), *The Works of Aristotle.* Vol. xi. Clarendon Press, Oxford.

    1956   *Metaphysics.* Edited and translated by John Warrington. Dent & Sons, London.

Arnauld, Antoine and Pierre Nicole

    1662   *La logique, ou l'art de penser contenant, outre les règles communes, plusieurs observations nouvelles, propres à former le jugement.* Pierre le Petit, Paris.

Asher, R.E. and J.M.Y. Simpson (eds)

    1994   *The Encyclopedia of Language and Linguistics.* 10 vols. Pergamon Press, Oxford.

Atlas, Jay D.

    1989   *Philosophy Without Ambiguity. A Logico-Linguistic Essay.* Clarendon Press, Oxford.

---

[1] For names beginning with *De*, *Van* and *Von*, see *De*, *Van* and *Von*, respectively.

Austin, John L.

1961 *Philosophical Papers.* Edited by J.O. Urmson & G.J. Warnock. Clarendon Press, Oxford.

1962 *How to Do Things with Words.* The William James Lectures delivered in Harvard University in 1955. Edited by J.O. Urmson. Clarendon Press, Oxford.

Bach, Emmon

1964 *An Introduction to Transformational Grammars.* Holt, Rinehart & Winston, New York-Chicago-San Francisco.

1968 Nouns and noun phrases. In: Bach & Harms: 91-122.

Bach, Emmon and Robert T. Harms (eds.)

1968 *Universals in Linguistic Theory.* Holt, Rinehart & Winston, New York.

Bar-Hillel, Yehoshua

1953 A quasi-arithmetical notation for syntactic description. *Language* 29:47-58.

1959 Decision procedures for structure in natural languages. *Logique et Analyse* 2:19-29.

Baratin, Marc and Françoise Desbordes

1981 *L'analyse linguistique dans l'Antiquité classique.* Klincksieck, Paris.

Barsky, Robert F.

1997 *Noam Chomsky: A Life of Dissent.* MIT Press, Cambridge, Mass.

Bartlett, Barrie E.

1975 *Beauzée's* Grammaire Générale. *Theory and Methodology.* Ianua Linguarum, Series Maior, 82. Mouton, The Hague.

Bartley, III, William Warren

1977 *Lewis Carroll's Symbolic Logic. Part I, Elementary, 1896. Fifth Edition. Part II, Advanced, never previously published.* Harvester Press, Hassocks, England.

Barwick, Karl

1957 *Probleme der stoischen Sprachlehre und Rhetorik.* Abhandlungen der sächsischen Akademie der Wissenschaften zu Leipzig. Philologisch-historische Klasse, Band 49, Heft 3. Akademie-Verlag, Berlin.

Barwise, Jon and Robin Cooper

1981 Generalized quantifiers and natural language. *Linguistics and Philosophy* 4.2:159-219.

Barwise, Jon and John Perry

1983 *Situations and Attitudes.* MIT Press, Cambridge, Mass.

Beauzée, Nicolas

1767 *Grammaire générale, ou exposition raisonnée des éléments nécessaires du langage, pour servir de fondement à l'étude de toutes les langues.* (2 vols.) J. Barbou, Paris (Modern edition: B.E. Bartlett (ed.), Frommann-Holzboog, Stuttgart-Bad Cannstatt, 1974, 2 vols.)

Bickerton, Derek

1981 *Roots of Language.* Karoma, Ann Arbor.

1989 Seselwa serialization and its significance. *Journal of Pidgin and Creole Languages* 4:155-183.

1990 If it quacks like a duck ... *Journal of Pidgin and Creole Languages* 5:293-303.

Bierwisch, Manfred

1967 Some semantic universals of German adjectivals. *Foundations of Language* 3:1-36.

Black, J.A.

1989 The Babylonian grammatical tradition: the first grammars of Sumerian. *Transactions of the Philological Society* 1989:75-99.

Bloch, Bernard

1948 A set of postulates for phonemic analysis. *Language* 24.1:3-46.

Bloch, Bernard and George L. Trager

1942 *Outline of Linguistic Analysis.* Special Publications of the Linguistic Society of America. Waverly Press, Baltimore Md. 82 pp.

Bloomfield, Leonard

1914 *An Introduction to the Study of Language.* Henry Holt, New York. (Photostatic reprint 1983 by Benjamins, Amsterdam/Philadelphia, with Foreword by Konrad Koerner and Introduction by Joseph Kess.)

1917 *Tagalog Texts with Grammatical Analysis.* 3 vols. University of Illinois Press, Urbana Illinois.

1924 Review of *Cours de linguistique générale* by Ferdinand de Saussure. *Modern Language Journal* 8:317-19.

1926 A set of postulates for the science of language. *Language* 2.1: 153-64. (Also in Joos 1957:26-31)

1933 *Language.* Henry Holt, New York.

1939a Linguistic Aspects of Science. *International Encyclopedia of Unified Science* 1.4. 59 pp. The University of Chicago Press, Chicago.

1939b Menomini morphophonemics. *Etudes phonologiques dédiées à la mémoire de N.S. Troubetzkoy* (= Travaux du Cercle Linguistique de Prague 8). Pp. 105-15.

1942   *Outline Guide for the Practical Study of Foreign Languages.* Special Publications of the Linguistic Society of America. Waverly Press, Baltimore Md. 16 pp.

1944   *Colloquial Dutch.* Henry Holt, New York.

1944-1945   *Spoken Dutch: Basic Course.* 2 Vols. Henry Holt, New York.

Boas, Franz

1911   Introduction. In: *Handbook of American Indian Languages, Part I.* Bureau of American Ethnology, Bulletin 40. Pp. 5-83. Government Printing Office, Washington.

Boër, Steven E. and William G. Lycan

1976   *The myth of semantic presupposition.* Indiana University Linguistics Club.

Boole, George

1847   *The Mathematical Analysis of Logic.* Cambridge University Press, Cambridge.

1854   *An Investigation of the Laws of Thought on which are Founded the Mathematical Theories of Logic and Probabilities.* Macmillan, London.

Borbé, Tasso

1974   *Kritik der marxistischen Sprachtheorie N.Ja. Marrs.* Scriptor Verlag, Kronberg.

Borst, Arno

1957-1963   *Der Turmbau von Babel. Geschichte der Meinungen über Ursprung und Vielfalt der Sprachen und Völker.* 6 vols. Hiersemann, Stuttgart.

Botha, Rudolf P.

1989   *Challenging Chomsky. The Generative Garden Game.* Blackwell, Oxford.

Bréal, Michel

1893   On the canons of the etymological investigation. *Transactions of the American Philological Association* 24:17-28.

Bresnan, Joan

1978   A realistic transformational grammar. In: M. Halle, J. Bresnan, G.A. Miller (eds), *Linguistic Theory and Psychological Reality.* MIT Press, Cambridge, Mass. Pp. 1-59.

Breva-Claramonte, Manuel

1983   *Sanctius' Theory of Language. A Contribution to the History of Renaissance Linguistics.* Benjamins, Amsterdam.

Brugmann, Karl

1900   Zu dem 'Vorwort' zu Band 1 der *Morphologischen Untersuchungen* von Osthoff und Brugmann. Indogermanische Forschungen 11. *Anzeiger für indogermanische Sprach- und Altertumskunde. Beiblatt zu den indogermanischen Forschungen* 11. Pp. 131-2.

Buffier, Claude

1704   *Examen des préjugés vulgaires, pour disposer l'esprit à juger sainement & précisément de tout.* J. Mariette, Paris.

1714[2] (1709[1])   *Grammaire françoise sur un plan nouveau, pour en rendre les principes plus clairs et la pratique plus aisée, contenant divers traités sur la grammaire en général, sur l'usage, sur la beauté des langues et sur la manière de les apprendre, sur le style, sur l'orthographe.* Pierre Witte, Paris.

Bühler, Karl

1934   *Sprachtheorie. Die Darstellungsfunktion der Sprache.* Fischer, Jena.

Bursill-Hall, Geoffrey L.

1972   *Thomas of Erfurt Grammatica Speculativa. An Edition with Translation and Commentary.* Longman, London.

Busse, Adolf (ed.)

1897   *Ammonius in Aristotelis* De Interpretatione *Commentarius.* Royal Prussian Academy of Sciences, Georg Reimer, Berlin.

Cantrall, William R.

1969   *On the Nature of the Reflexive in English.* PhD-diss. University of Illinois.

1974   *Viewpoint, Reflexives, and the Nature of Noun Phrases.* Mouton, The Hague.

Carlson-Radvansky, Laura and David E. Irwin

1993   Frames of reference in vision and language: Where is above? *Cognition* 46:223-44.

Cary, M., J.D. Denniston, J. Wight Duff, A.D. Nock, W.D. Ross, H.H. Scullard (eds.)

1953   *The Oxford Classical Dictionary.* Clarendon Press, Oxford.

Chafe, Wallace

1976   Givenness, contrastiveness, definiteness, subjects, topics, and point of view. In: Charles N. Li (ed.), *Subject and Topic.* Academic Press, New York-San Francisco-London. Pp. 25-55.

Chomsky, Noam

1951   *Morphophonemics of Modern Hebrew.* MA-dissertation, University of Pennsylvania.

1953   Systems of syntactic analysis. *Journal of Symbolic Logic* 18:242-56.

1955a   *Transformational Analysis.* PhD-dissertation, University of Pennsylvania.

1955b Logical syntax and semantics: their linguistic relevance. *Language* 31.1:36-45.

1956 Three models for the description of language. *Institute of Radio Engineering Transactions on Information Theory* IT-2:113-24.

1957 *Syntactic Structures* (=Ianua Linguarum 4). Mouton, The Hague.

1959a Review of Skinner (1957). *Language* 35.1:26-58.

1959b Review of Greenberg (1957). *Word* 15:202-18.

1959c On certain formal properties of grammars. *Information and Control* 2:137-67.

1959d A note on Phrase Structure Grammars. *Information and Control* 2:393-5.

1961 Some methodological remarks on Generative Grammar. *Word* 17:219-39.

1964 *Current Issues in Linguistic Theory* (=Ianua Linguarum, series minor 38). Mouton, The Hague.

1965 *Aspects of the Theory of Syntax.* MIT Press, Cambridge, Mass.

1966a *Cartesian Linguistics. A Chapter in the history of Rationalist Thought.* Harper & Row, New York - London.

1966b *Topics in the Theory of Generative Grammar* (=Ianua Linguarum, series minor 56). Mouton, The Hague.

1967 Remarks on Nominalization. Published in Chomsky (1972a:11-61).

1969 Linguistics and politics. *New Left Review* 57:21-34.

1971 Deep structure, surface structure, and semantic interpretation. In: Steinberg & Jakobovits:183-216. (Also in Chomsky 1972a:62-119.)

1972a *Studies on Semantics in Generative Grammar* (=Ianua Linguarum 107). Mouton, The Hague.

1972b Some empirical issues in the theory of transformational grammar. In: Peters: 63-130. (Also in: Chomsky 1972a:120-202)

1975 [1956] *The Logical Structure of Linguistic Theory.* Plenum Press, New York & London.

1980 Rules and representations. *The Behavioral and Brain Sciences* 3:1-15; 42-61.

1982a *The Generative Enterprise.* Foris, Dordrecht.

1982b *Lectures on Government and Binding. The Pisa Lectures.* Foris, Dordrecht.

1986 *Knowledge of Language: Its Nature, Origin and Use.* Praeger, New York.

1995 *The Minimalist Program.* MIT Press, Cambridge, Mass.

Chomsky, Noam and Morris Halle

1968 *The Sound Pattern of English.* Harper & Row, New York, Evanston, and London.

Chomsky, Noam and Howard Lasnik

   1977   Filters and control. *Linguistic Inquiry* 8.3:425-504.

   1993   The theory of Principles and Parameters. In: J. Jacobs, A. von Stechow, W. Sternefeld & Th. Vennemann (eds.), *Syntax. Ein internationales Handbuch zeitgenössischer Forschung = An International Handbook of Contemporary Research*. De Gruyter, Berlin. Pp. 506-69. (also in Chomsky 1995:13-128.)

Chomsky, Noam and George A. Miller

   1958   Finite State languages. *Information and Control* 1:91-112.

Chomsky, Noam and M.P. Schützenberger

   1963   The algebraic theory of Context-Free languages. In: P. Braffort & D. Hirschberg (eds.), *Computer Programming and Formal Systems*, North-Holland, Amsterdam. Pp. 118-161.

Christmann, Hans H.

   1966   *Beiträge zur Geschichte der These vom Weltbild der Sprache.* Akademie der Wissenschaften und der Literatur. Abhandlungen der Geistes- und Sozialwissenschaftlichen Klasse Nr. 7. Pp. 441-69.

Clark, Ronald W.

   1975   *The Life of Bertrand Russell.* Jonathan Cape and Weidenfeld & Nicolson, London.

Collinge, N.E.

   1985   *The Laws of Indo-European.* Benjamins, Amsterdam/Philadelphia.

Copi, Irving M.

   1961   *Introduction to Logic.* Macmillan, New York.

Coseriu, Eugenio

   1975   *Die Geschichte der Sprachphilosophie von der Antike bis zur Gegenwart. Eine Übersicht. Vol. 1: Von der Antike bis Leibniz.* Narr, Tübingen.

Cotter, A.C.

   1931   *Logic and Epistemology.* Stratford Cy, Boston.

Covington, Michael A.

   1982   *Syntactic Theory in the High Middle Ages. Modistic Models of Sentence Strcuture.* PhD-thesis, Yale University.

   1994   *Natural Language Processing for Prolog Programmers.* Prentice Hall, Englewood Cliffs, N.J.

Cresswell, Max

   1985   *Structured Meanings. The Semantics of Propositional Attitudes.* MIT Press, Cambridge, Mass.

Darnell, R.

1994a   American linguistics: anthropological origins. In: Asher & Simpson: 93-7.

1994b   Sapir, Edward (1884-1939). In: Asher & Simpson:3655-6.

De Beaugrande, Robert

1991   *Linguistic Theory. The Discourse of Fundamental Works.* Longman, London.

De Clercq, Jean and Pierre Swiggers

1996   La linguistique française aux XVIIe et XVIIIe siècles: mutations théoriques, réception et contexte global. In: R. Lorenzo (ed.), *Actas do XIX Congreso Internacional de la Lingüística e Filoloxía Románicas. Universidade de Santiago de Compostela, 1989. Vol. VIII.* Fundación "Pedro Barrié de la Maza, Conde de Fenosa". A Coruña. Pp. 751-69.

De Mauro, Tullio

1971   *Senso e significato. Studi di semantica teorica e storica.* Adriatica Editrice, Bari.

De Morgan, Augustus,

1847   *Formal Logic: or, The Calculus of Inference, Necessary and Probable.* Taylor & Walton, London.

De Rijk, Lambertus M.

1967   *Logica Modernorum. A Contribution to the History of Early Terminist Logic. Vol. II.1: The Origin and Early Development of the Theory of Supposition.* Van Gorcum, Assen.

1986   *Plato's Sophist. A Philosophical Commentary.* Koninklijke Nederlandse Akademie van Wetenschappen, Verhandelingen Afdeling Letterkunde, Nieuwe Reeks, Deel 133. North Holland Publishing Company, Amsterdam.

De Rijk, Rudolf P.G.

1974   A note on prelexical Predicate Raising. In: Seuren:43-74.

De Saussure, Ferdinand

1916   *Cours de linguistique générale.* Edited by Charles Bally and Albert Sechehaye, with the collaboration of Albert Riedlinger. Payot, Paris-Lausanne.

De Vaugelas, Claude Favre

1647   *Remarques sur la langue françoise utiles à ceux qui veulent bien parler et bien escrire.* La Veuue Iean Camusat & Pierre le Petit, Paris.

Delbrück, Berthold

1901   *Grundfragen der Sprachforschung.* Trübner, Strasbourg.

1904[4] *Einleitung in das Studium der indogermanischen Sprachen. Ein Bei-*
trag zur Geschichte und Methodik der vergleichenden Sprachfor-
schung. Breitkopf & Härtel, Leipzig.

Diels, Hermann A. and Walther Kranz

1951 *Die Fragmente der Vorsokratiker: griechisch und deutsch. Vol. 1.*
Weidemann, Berlin.

Dittmar, Norbert

1976 *Sociolinguistics. A Critical Survey of Theory and Application.* Edward Arnold, London.

Dowty, David, Robert E. Wall, Stanley R. Peters

1981 *Introduction to Montague Semantics.* Reidel, Dordrecht.

Du Marsais, César Chesnau

1977 (1730[1]) *Traité des tropes ou des différents sens dans lesquels on peut*
prendre un mëme mot dans une mëme langue. [Postface de Claude
Mouchard, suivi de Jean Paulhan, Traité des figures ou la rhétorique
décryptée.] Le Nouveau Commerce, Paris.

1987 *Les Véritables principes de la grammaire et autres textes 1729-1756.*
Corpus des œuvres de philosophie en langue française. Fayard, Paris.

Dummett, Michael

1973 *Frege. Philosophy of Language.* Duckworth, London.

Egli, Urs

1983 The Stoic theory of arguments. In: R. Bäuerle, Chr. Schwarze, A. von
Stechow (eds.), *Meaning, Use, and Interpretation of Language.* De
Gruyter, Berlin-New York. Pp. 79-96.

Elffers-van Ketel, Els

1991 *The Historiography of Grammatical Concepts. 19th and 20th*
Century Changes in the Subject-Predicate Conception and the
Problem of their Historical Reconstruction. Rodopi, Amsterdam.

Evers, Arnold

1975 *The Transformational Cycle in Dutch and German.* PhD-thesis,
Utrecht University.

Fauconnier, Gilles

1985 *Mental Spaces. Aspects of Meaning Construction in Natural Langu-*
age. MIT Press, Cambridge, Mass.

Fernàndez Garcìa, Fr. Mariani

1902 *B. Joannis Duns Scoti Doct. Subtilis O.F.M. Grammaticae Specula-*
tivae nova editio. Ex Typographia Collegii S. Bonaventurae, Ad
Claras Aquas (Quaracchi) prope Florentiam.

Fillmore, Charles J.

   1968   The case for case. In: Bach & Harms: 1-90.

   1971   Types of lexical information. In: Steinberg & Jakobovits:370-92.

Firth, John R.

   1957   *Papers in Linguistics 1934-1951.* Oxford University Press, Oxford.

Fodor, Jerry A.

   1970   Three reasons for not deriving "kill" from "cause to die". *Linguistic Inquiry* 1.4:429-38.

Fowler, Thomas

   1895   *Logic, Deductive and Inductive.* Clarendon Press, Oxford.

Fraser, Bruce

   1974   An examination of the performative analysis. *Papers in Linguistics* 7:1-40.

Frege, Gottlob

   1879   *Begriffsschrift. Eine der arithmetischen nachgebildete Formelsprache des reinen Denkens.* Louis Nebert, Halle.

   1884   *Die Grundlagen der Arithmetik: eine logisch mathematische Untersuchung über den Begriff der Zahl.* Köbner, Breslau.

   1892   Ueber Sinn und Bedeutung. *Zeitschrift für Philosophie und philosophische Kritik* 100:25-50. (Also in: Patzig 1969:40-65.)

   1906   Ueber die Grundlagen der Geometrie. *Jahresberichte der deutschen Mathematiker-Vereinigung* 15:293-309, 377-403, 423-30.

Gamut, L.

   1991   *Logic, Language and Meaning.* 2 vols. University of Chicago Press, Chicago-London.

Gardiner, Sir Alan H.

   1951[2] (1932) *The Theory of Speech and Language.* Clarendon Press, Oxford.

Garza Cuarón, Beatriz

   1996   Main trends in the history of linguistics in Mexico. Paper read at the Seventh International Conference on the History of Linguistics, Oxford, 12-17 Sept. 1996.

Gazdar, Gerald

   1979   *Pragmatics. Implicature, Presupposition, and Logical Form.* Academic Press, New York-San Francisco-London.

Gazdar, Gerald, Ewan Klein, Geoffrey Pullum & Ivan Sag

   1985   *Generalized Phrase Structure Grammar.* Blackwell, Oxford.

Gazdar, Gerald and Chris Mellish

   1989   *Natural Language Processing in Lisp. An Introduction to Computational Linguistics.* Addison-Wesley, Wokingham, England.

Geach, Peter Th.

   1950   Russell's Theory of Descriptions. *Analysis* 10:84-8.

   1962   *Reference and Generality. An Examination of Some Medieval and Modern Theories.* Cornell University Press, Ithaca, New York.

   1969   Quine's syntactical insights. In: D. Davidson & J. Hintikka (eds.), *Words and Objections. Essays on the Work of W.V. Quine.* Reidel, Dordrecht.

   1972   *Logic Matters.* Blackwell, Oxford.

Geach, Peter and Max Black (eds.)

   1952   *Translations from the Philosophical Writings of Gottlob Frege.* Blackwell, Oxford.

Geeraerts, Dirk, Stefan Grondelaers and Peter Bakema

   1994   *The Structure of Lexical Variation. Meaning, Naming and Context* (=Cognitive Linguistics Research 5). Mouton de Gruyter, Berlin-New York.

Gerhardt, C.I.

   1890   *Die philosophischen Schriften von Gottfried Wilhelm Leibniz. Vol.VII.* Olms Verlagsbuchhandlung, Hildesheim.

Giannakidou, Anastasia

   1997   *The Landscape of Polarity Items.* PhD-thesis. Groningen University.

Gilbert, Glenn

   1994   Hugo Schuchardt (1847-1927). In: Asher & Simpson:3684-5.

Girard, Gabriel

   1747   *Les vrais principes de la langue françoise: ou la parole réduite en méthode, conformément aux lois de l'usage.* Prault, Paris. (Modern edition: Pierre Swiggers (ed.), Droz, Genève-Paris, 1982.)

Godel, Robert

   1957   *Les sources manuscrites du cours de linguistique générale de F. de Saussure.* Droz, Geneva-Paris.

   1966   F. de Saussure's theory of language. In: Th. A. Sebeok (ed.), *Current Trends in Linguistics. Vol. III, Theoretical Foundations.* Mouton, The Hague-Paris. Pp. 479-93.

Graffi, Giorgio

   1991   *La sintassi tra ottocento e novecento.* Il Mulino, Bologna.

Greenberg, Joseph H.

   1957   *Essays in Linguistics.* The University of Chicago Press, Chicago.

   1963a   *The Languages of Africa.* Publication 25 of the Indiana University Research Center in Anthropology, Folklore, and Linguistics. *International Journal of American Linguistics* 29.1, part II.

1963b Some universals of grammar with particular reference to the order of meaningful elements. In: J.H. Greenberg (ed.), *Universals of Language*. MIT Press, Cambridge, Mass. Pp. 73-113.

1974 *Language Typology: A Historical and Analytic Overview* (=Ianua Linguarum, series minor, 184). Mouton, The Hague.

1987 *Language in the Americas*. Stanford University Press, Stanford, CA.

1993 *Indo-European and its Closest Relatives: the Eurasiatic Language Family*. Stanford University Press, Stanford, CA.

Grice, H. Paul

1989 *Studies in the Way of Words*. Harvard University Press, Cambridge, Mass (= William James Lectures, Harvard 1967).

Groenendijk, Jeroen and Martin Stokhof

1991 Dynamic Predicate Logic. *Linguistics and Philosophy* 14:39-100.

Gruber, Jeffrey S.

1976 *Lexical Structures in Syntax and Semantics*. North-Holland, Amsterdam.

Haiman, John (ed.)

1985 *Iconicity in Syntax*. Proceedings of a Symposium on Iconicity in Syntax, Stanford, June 24-26 1983. Benjamins, Amsterdam.

Hajičová, Eva (ed.)

1993 *Functional Description of Language*. Proceedings of the Conference (Prague, November 24-27 1992). Faculty of Mathematics and Physics, Charles University, Prague.

Hall, Robert A. (ed.)

1987 *Leonard Bloomfield. Essays on his Life and Work*. Benjamins, Amsterdam/Philadelphia.

1990 *A Life for Language. A Biographical Memoir of Leonard Bloomfield*. Benjamins, Amsterdam/Philadelphia.

Harman, Gilbert

1980 Two quibbles about analyticity and psychological reality. *The Behavioral and Brain Sciences* 3:21-2.

Harris, Randy A.

1993 *The Linguistics Wars*. Oxford University Press, New York-Oxford.

Harris, Zellig S.

1946 From morpheme to utterance. *Language* 22.1:161-83. (Also in Joos 1957:142-53.)

1951 *Methods in Structural Linguistics*. The University of Chicago Press, Chicago.

1952 Discourse analysis. *Language* 28.1:1-30 (also in 1981:107-42).

1957   Co-occurrence and transformation in linguistic structure. *Language* 33.3:283-340 (=Presidential Address LSA 1955; also in 1981:143-210).

1965   Transformational theory. *Language* 41.3:363-401 (also in 1981:236-80).

1970   *Papers in Structural and Transformational Linguistics.* Reidel, Dordrecht.

1981   *Papers on Syntax.* Edited by Henry Hiż. Reidel, Dordrecht.

't Hart, August C.

1979   *Recht en staat in het denken van Giambattista Vico.* Tjeenk Willink, Alphen a/d Rijn.

Hawkins, John A.

1983   *Word Order Universals.* Academic Press, New York.

Heath, Peter

1988   *On Language. The Diversity of Human Language-Structure and its Influence on the Mental Development of Mankind.* With an introduction by Hans Aarsleff. Cambridge University Press, Cambridge.

Heeschen, Volker

1972   *Die Sprachphilosophie Wilhelm von Humboldts.* PhD-thesis Ruhr University Bochum.

1977   Weltansicht-Reflexionen über einen Begriff Wilhelm von Humboldt's. *Historiographia Linguistica* IV.2:159-90.

Heim, Irene

1982   *The Semantics of Definite and Indefinite Noun Phrases.* PhD-diss., University of Massachusetts at Amherst.

1983   File change semantics and the familiarity theory of definiteness. In: R. Bäuerle, C. Schwarze & A. von Stechow (eds.), *Meaning, Use and Interpretation of Language.* De Gruyter, Berlin. Pp. 164-89.

Heinekamp, Albert

1975   Natürliche Sprache und Allgemeine Charakteristik bei Leibniz. *Akten des II. Internationalen Leibniz-Kongresses, Hannover, 17.-22.Juli 1972.* Vol. IV. (=*Studia Leibnitiana*, Suppl. 15). Steiner Verlag, Wiesbaden. Pp. 257-86.

Herder, Johann Gottfried

1772   *Abhandlung über den Ursprung der Sprache.* Voss, Berlin.

Hjelmslev, Louis

1953   *Prolegomena to a Theory of Language.* (Translated from the Danish *Omkring sprogteoriens grundlaeggelse*, 1943, by Francis J. Whitfield) Indiana University Publications in Anthropology and Linguistics. Memoir 7 of the International Journal of American Linguistics. Waverly Press, Baltimore Md.

Hockett, Charles F.

1942 A system of descriptive phonology. *Language* 18.1:3-21. (Also in Joos 1957:97-108.)

1948 A note on 'structure'. *International Journal of American Linguistics* 14:269-71. (Also in Joos 1957:279-80.)

1954 Two models of grammatical description. *Word* 10: 210-31. (Also in Joos 1957:386-99.)

1955 *A Manual of Phonology.* Indiana University Publications in Anthropology and Linguistics. Memoir 11 of the International Journal of American Linguistics. Waverly Press, Baltimore Md.

1958 *A Course in Modern Linguistics.* Macmillan, New York.

Hoijer, Harry

1951 Cultural implications of some Navaho linguistic categories. *Language* 27:111-20.

Holm, John

1988 *Pidgins and Creoles.* 2 vols. Cambridge University Press, Cambridge.

Horn, Laurence R.,

1969 A presuppositional analysis of "only" and "even". *Chicago Linguistic Society* 5:98-107.

1985 Metalinguistic negation and pragmatic ambiguity. *Language* 61:121-74.

1989 *A Natural History of Negation.* The University of Chicago Press, Chicago-London.

Householder, Fred W.

1981 *The Syntax of Apollonius Dyscolus.* Translated, and with commentary by — (=Studies in the History of Linguistics 23). Benjamins, Amsterdam.

1994a Aristotle and the Stoics on language. In: Asher & Simpson:212-19.

1994b Dionysius Thrax, The Technai, and Sextus Empiricus. In: Asher & Simpson:931-5.

Hovdhaugen, Even

1982 *Foundations of Western Linguistics. From the Beginning to the End of the First Millennium AD.* Universitetsforlaget, Oslo.

Huck, Geoffrey J. and John A. Goldsmith

1995 *Ideology and Linguistic Theory. Noam Chomsky and the Deep Structure Debate.* Routledge, London & New York.

Husserl, Edmund

1900 *Logische Untersuchungen. Vol 2: Untersuchungen zur Phänomenologie und Theorie der Erkenntnis. Teil 1.* Niemeyer, Halle.

Hymes, Dell, and John G. Fought

1975   American Structuralism. In: Th. A. Sebeok (ed.), *Current Trends in Linguistics. Vol.13: Historiography of Linguistics.* Mouton, The Hague. Pp. 903-1176. (Reprinted as *American Structuralism*, Mouton, The Hague, 1981.)

Ildefonse, Frédérique, Jean Lallot, Marc Baratin and Irène Rosier

1994   *Sujet-prédicat de l'Antiquité grecque au Moyen Age latin.* Archives et Documents de la Société d'Histoire et d'Épistémologie des Sciences du Language (SHESL), 2nd series No. 10, Dec. 1994.

Israel, David

1987   Review of Cresswell (1985) in: *Computational Linguistics* 13.3-4:358-63.

Jackendoff, Ray S.

1972   *Semantic Interpretation in Generative Grammar.* MIT Press, Cambridge, Mass.

1983   *Semantics and Cognition.* MIT Press, Cambridge, Mass.

Jakobson, Roman

1941   *Kindersprache, Aphasie und allgemeine Lautgesetze.* Uppsala Universitets Årsskrift 9, Uppsala. [English translation: *Child Language, Aphasia and Phonological Universals.* Mouton, The Hague, 1968.]

1958   Typological studies and their contribution to historical comparative linguistics. In: E. Sivertsen et al. (eds.), *Proceedings of the Eighth International Congress of Linguists.* Oslo University Press, Oslo. Pp. 17-25.

Jakobson, Roman, Gunnar M. Fant and Morris Halle

1952   *Preliminaries to Speech Analysis. The Distinctive Features and their Correlates.* MIT Press, Cambridge, Mass.

Jespersen, Otto

1894   *Progress in Language; with special reference to English.* Swan Sonnenschein/Macmillan, London.

1909-1949   *A Modern English Grammar on Historical Principles.* Vols. I-VII. Allen & Unwin, London / Ejnar Munksgaard, Copenhagen.

1922   *Language. Its Nature, Development and Origin.* Allen & Unwin, London.

1924   *The Philosophy of Grammar.* Allen & Unwin, London.

1937   *Analytic Syntax.* Munksgaard, Copenhagen. (Reprint: Holt, Rinehart & Winston, New York, 1969.)

Johnson-Laird, Philip N.

1983   *Mental Models. Towards a Cognitive Science of Language, Inference, and Consciousness.* Cambridge University Press, Cambridge-London.

Jones, Daniel

    1957   *The History and Meaning of the Term "Phoneme"*. International Phonetic Association, London.

Joos, Martin (ed.)

    1957   *Readings in Linguistics. The Development of Descriptive Linguistics in America since 1925*. American Council of Learned Societies, Washington.

Joseph, Brian D.

    1983   *The Synchrony and Diachrony of the Balkan Infinitive. A Study in Areal, General, and Historical Linguistics*. Cambridge Studies in Linguistics, supplementary volume. Cambridge University Press, Cambridge.

Joshi, Aravind K., L. Levy and M. Takahashi

    1975   Tree Adjunct Grammars. *Journal of the Computer and System Sciences* 10:136-63.

Kalepky, Theodor

    1928   *Neuaufbau der Grammatik als Grundlegung zu einem wissenschaftlichen System der Sprachbeschreibung*. Teubner, Leipzig.

Kamp, Hans

    1981   A theory of truth and semantic representation. In: J.A.G. Groenendijk, T.M.V. Janssen, M.B.J. Stokhof (eds.), *Formal Methods in the Study of Language 1*. Mathematisch Centrum, Amsterdam. Pp. 277-322.

Kamp, Hans, and Uwe Reyle

    1993   *From Discourse to Logic. Introduction to Model-Theoretic Semantics of Natural Language, Formal Logic and Discourse Representation Theory*. Kluwer, Dordrecht.

Karttunen, Lauri

    1973   Presuppositions of compound sentences. *Linguistic Inquiry* 4.2:169-93.

    1974   Presupposition and linguistic context. *Theoretical Linguistics* 1.1/2: 181-94.

Katz, Jerrold J. and Jerry A. Fodor

    1963   The structure of a semantic theory. *Language* 39.2:170-210.

Katz, Jerrold J. and Paul M. Postal

    1964   *An Integrated Theory of Linguistic Descriptions*. MIT Press, Cambridge, Mass.

Kayne, Richard S.

    1975   *French Syntax. The Transformational Cycle*. MIT Press, Cambridge, Mass.

Kiparsky, Paul

    1968   Linguistic universals and linguistic change. In: Bach & Harms: 171-
           202.

Kiparsky, Paul and Carol Kiparsky

    1971   Fact. In: Steinberg & Jakobovits:345-69.

Klima, Ed

    1964   Negation in English. In: J.A. Fodor & J.J. Katz (eds.), *The Structure of
           Language: Readings in the Philosophy of Language*. Prentice Hall,
           Englewood Cliffs. Pp. 246-323.

Kneale, William

    1962   Modality, *de dicto* and *de re*. In: E. Nagel, P. Suppes & A. Tarski
           (eds), *Logic, Methodology and the Philosophy of Science: Proceed-
           ings of the 1960 International Congress*. Stanford University Press,
           Stanford. Pp. 622-33.

Kneale, William and Martha Kneale

    1962   *The Development of Logic*. Clarendon Press, Oxford.

Kneepkens, C.H.

    1995   The Priscianic tradition. In: S. Ebbesen (ed.), *Sprachtheorien in
           Spätantike und Mittelalter*. Narr, Tübingen. Pp. 239-64.

Koerner, E.F. Konrad

    1994a Saussure, Ferdinand(-Mongin) de (1857-1913). In: Asher & Simpson:
           3662-4.

    1994b Kruszewski, M.H. (1851-87). In Asher & Simpson:1878.

    1994c Typology and language classification: history. In Asher & Simpson:
           4813-17.

Kolakowski, Leszek

    1972   *Positivist Philosophy. From Hume to the Vienna Circle*. Pelican,
           Penguin Books.

Koster, Jan

    1975   Dutch as an SOV-language. *Linguistic Analysis* 1:111-36.

Kouwenberg, Silvia

    1994   *A Grammar of Berbice Dutch Creole*. De Gruyter, Berlin-New York.

Kripke, Saul A.

    1972   Naming and necessity. In: D. Davidson & G. Harman (eds.), *Seman-
           tics of Natural Language*, Reidel, Dordrecht. Pp. 253-355.
           (Also 1980, *Naming and necessity*. Blackwell, Oxford.)

Kučera, Henry

    1983   Roman Jakobson. Obituary. *Language* 59.4:871-83.

Kuhn, Thomas S.

1962   *The Structure of Scientific Revolutions*. Chicago University Press, Chicago.

Kühner, Raphael and Carl Stegmann

1955[3]   *Ausführliche Grammatik der lateinischen Sprache. Satzlehre*. 2 Vols. Gottschalk, Leverkusen.

Kuno, Susumo

1987   *Functional Syntax. Anaphora, Discourse and Empathy*. The University of Chicago Press, Chicago.

Labov, William

1972   *Sociolinguistic Patterns*. University of Pennsylvania Press, Philadelphia.

Ladusaw, William A.,

1979   *Polarity Sensitivity as Inherent Scope Relations*. PhD-thesis. University of Texas at Austin.

Lakoff, George

1963   Toward generative semantics. Internal memorandum of the Mechanical Translation Group, Research Laboratory of Electronics, MIT. (Published in McCawley 1976: 44-61.)

1970   *Irregularity in Syntax*. Holt, Rinehart & Winston, New York.

1971   On generative semantics. In: Steinberg & Jakobovits: 232-96.

Lakoff, Robin

1969a   Review of Herbert H. Brekle (ed.), *Grammaire générale et raisonnée, ou La grammaire du Port Royal*. Fromann, Stuttgart-Bad Cannstatt, 1966. *Language* 45.2:343-64.

1969b   Some reasons why there can't be any *some-any* rule. *Language* 45.3:608-15.

Lancelot, Claude

1653[3] (1644[1]) *Nouvelle méthode pour facilement et en peu de temps comprendre la langue latine*. Pierre le Petit, Paris.

Lancelot, Claude and Antoine Arnauld

1660   *Grammaire générale et raisonnée contenant Les fondemens de l'art de parler; expliquez d'une manière claire & naturelle; Les raisons de ce qui est commun à toutes les langues, & des principales differences qui s'y rencontrent; Et plusieurs remarques nouvelles sur la Langue Françoise*. Pierre le Petit, Paris. (Facsimile reprint by The Scolar Press Ltd., Menston, England, 1967.)

Law, Vivien

   1996   Memory and visual representation in early modern Latin grammars. Paper read at the Seventh International Conference on the History of Linguistics, Oxford, 12-17 Sept. 1996.

Leech, Geoffrey N.

   1969   *Towards a Semantic Description of English.* Longman, London.

Lees, Robert B.

   1957   Review of Chomsky (1957). *Language* 33.3:375-408.

   1960   *The Grammar of English Nominalizations.* Mouton, The Hague.

Leitzmann, Albert (ed.)

   1907   *Wilhelm von Humboldts Werke.* 15 vols. Behr, Berlin.

Leskien, August

   1876   *Die declination im Slavisch-Litauischen und Germanischen.* Hirzel, Leipzig.

Levelt, Willem J.M.

   1974   *Formal Grammars in Linguistics and Psycholinguistics.* 3 Vols. (=Ianua Linguarum, series minor 192). Mouton, The Hague.

   1989   *Speaking. From Intention to Articulation.* MIT Press, Cambridge, Mass.

Levinson, Stephen C.

   1983   *Pragmatics.* Cambridge University Press, Cambridge.

   1996   Frames of reference and Molyneux's question: cross-linguistic evidence. In: Paul Bloom, Mary A. Peterson, Lynn Nadel & Merrill F. Garrett (eds.), *Language and Space.* MIT-Press, Cambridge, Mass. Pp. 109-69.

Lewis, Clarence I.

   1946   *An Analysis of Knowledge and Valuation.* Open Court, La Salle, Illinois.

Lewis, Clarence I. and Cooper H. Langford

   1959[2]   *Symbolic Logic.* Dover, New York.

Lewis, David K.

   1970   General semantics. *Synthese* 22:18-67.

   1973   *Counterfactuals.* Blackwell, Oxford.

Linebarger, Marcia

   1980   *The Grammar of Negative Polarity.* PhD-thesis. MIT.

Lipps, Theodor

   1893   *Grundzüge der Logik.* Dürr, Leipzig.

Luhrman, Gerard J.

1984 *C.L. Pasius, T. Linacer, J.C. Scaliger. Een kritisch-vergelijkende studie omtrent xvi^{de} eeuwse taalkundige theorievorming.* PhD-thesis. Groningen University. Niemeyer, Groningen.

Luhtala, A.

1994 Grammar, Early Medieval. In: Asher & Simpson:1461-8.

Lyons, John

1966 Firth's theory of meaning. In: C.E. Bazell, J.C. Catford, M.A.K. Halliday, R.H. Robins (eds.), *In Memory of J.R. Firth.* Longman, London. Pp. 288-302.

1968 *Introduction to Theoretical Linguistics.* Cambridge University Press, Cambridge.

1977 *Semantics.* (2 vols.) Cambridge University Press, Cambridge.

MacCorquodale, Kenneth

1970 On Chomsky's review of Skinner's Verbal Behavior. *Journal of the Experimental Analysis of Behavior* 13:83-99.

Mandelbaum, David G. (ed.)

1961 *Edward Sapir. Culture, Language and Personality. Selected Essays.* University of California Press, Berkeley and Los Angeles.

Marty, Anton

1897 Ueber die Scheidung von grammatischem, logischem und psychologischem Subject resp. Prädicat. *Archiv für Systematische Philosophie* 3:175-190; 294-333.

1950 *Ueber Wert und Methode einer allgemeinen beschreibenden Bedeutungslehre.* New edition by Otto Funke. Francke, Bern.

Mathesius, Vilém

1928 On linguistic characterology with illustrations from modern English. In: *Actes du Premier Congrès International de Linguistes à La Haye.* Reprinted in: J. Vachek (ed.), *A Prague School Reader in Linguistics.* Indiana University Press, Bloomington, Indiana, 1964. Pp. 59-67.

May, Robert

1977 *The Grammar of Quantification.* PhD-thesis MIT.

McCawley, James D.

1967 Meaning and the description of languages. *Kotoba no Uchu* 2.9:10-18; 10:38-48; 11:51-7. (Also in McCawley 1973:99-120)

1968a Concerning the base component of a transformational grammar. *Foundations of Language* 4.3:243-269. (Also in McCawley 1973:35-58.)

1968b The role of semantics in a grammar. In: Bach & Harms:125-69. (Also in McCawley 1973:59-98.)

1968c Lexical insertion in a transformational grammar without deep structure. In: *Papers from the Fourth Regional Meeting, Chicago Linguistic Society*. Linguistics Department, University of Chicago. Pp. 71-80. (Also in McCawley 1973:155-66.).

1970a English as a VSO-language. *Language* 46.2:286-299. (Also in McCawley 1973:211-28, and in Seuren 1974:75-95.)

1970b Semantic representation. In: Paul M. Garvin (ed.), *Cognition: a Multiple View*. Spartan Books, New York. Pp. 227-47. (Also in McCawley 1973:240-56.)

1970c On the deep structure of negative clauses. *Eigo Kyoiku* 19.6:72-75. (Also in McCawley 1973:277-84.)

1971 Tense and time reference in English. In: Charles J. Fillmore & D. Terence Langendoen (eds.), *Studies in Linguistic Semantics*. Holt, Rinehart & Winston, New York. Pp. 96-113.

1972 A program for logic. In: Donald Davidson & Gilbert Harman (eds), *Semantics of Natural Language*. Reidel, Dordrecht. Pp. 498-544. (Also in McCawley 1973:285-319.)

1973 *Grammar and Meaning. Papers on Syntactic and Semantic Topics*. Taishukan Publishing Company, Tokyo.

1980 Review of Newmeyer (1980). *Linguistics* 18.9/10:911-30.

1994 Generative Semantics. In: Asher & Simpson:1398-1403.

McCawley, James D. (ed.)

1976 *Notes from the Linguistic Underground* (=Syntax and Semantics 7). Academic Press, New York-San Francisco-London.

Meillet, Antoine and Marcel Cohen

1924, 1952² *Les langues du monde*. Par un groupe de linguistes sous la direction de A. Meillet et Marcel Cohen. Société linguistique de Paris. Centre national de la recherche scientifique. Champion, Paris.

Mel'čuk, Igor A. and Nikolaj V. Pertsov

1987 *Surface Syntax of English. A Formal Model within the Meaning-Text Framework*. Benjamins, Amsterdam-Philadelphia.

Meyer-Lübke, Wilhelm

1899 *Romanische Syntax* (=Grammatik der romanischen Sprachen III). Reisland, Leipzig.

Miller, George A.

1991 *The Science of Words*. Scientific American Library, New York.

Miller, George A. and Noam Chomsky

1963 Finitary models of language users. In: R.D. Luce, R.R. Bush & E. Galanter (eds), *Handbook of Mathematical Psychology*. Vol. 2. Wiley, New York. Pp. 419-91.

Miller, George A. and Philip N. Johnson-Laird

    1976 *Language and Perception*. Harvard University Press, Cambridge, Mass.

Mitchell, John

    1986 *The Formal Semantics of Point of View*. PhD-diss. University of Massachusetts.

Monk, Ray

    1990 *Ludwig Wittgenstein. The Duty of Genius*. Jonathan Cape, London.

Montague, Richard

    1973 The proper treatment of quantification in ordinary English. In: K.J.J. Hintikka, J.M.E. Moravcsik & P. Suppes (eds.), *Approaches to Natural Language. Proceedings of the 1970 Stanford Workshop on Grammar and Semantics*. Reidel, Dordrecht. Pp. 221-42.

Morpurgo-Davies, Anna

    1978 Analogy, segmentation and the early Neogrammarians. *Transactions of the Philological Society, Commemorative volume: The Neogrammarians*. Pp. 36-60.

Morris, Charles W.

    1938 Foundations of the theory of signs. In: O. Neurath, R. Carnap & Ch. W. Morris (eds.), *International Encyclopedia of Unified Science*. The University of Chicago Press, Chicago.

Mostovski, Andrzej

    1957 On a generalization of quantifiers. *Fundamenta Mathematica* 44:12-36.

Moxey, Linda M. and Anthony J. Sanford

    1986/7 Quantifiers and focus. *Journal of Semantics* 5:189-206.

Mullally, Joseph P.

    1945 *The* Summulae Logicales *of Peter of Spain* (=Publications in Medieval Studies VIII). The University of Notre Dame Press, Indiana.

Müller, F. Max

    1861 *Lectures on the Science of Language*. Lectures delivered at the Royal Institution of Great Britain in April, May and June 1861. Longman, London.

Murray, Stephen O.

    1994 *Theory Groups and the Study of Language in North America. A Social History*. Benjamins, Amsterdam/Philadelphia.

Myers-Scotton, Carol

    1993 *Duelling Languages. Grammatical Structure in Codeswitching*. Clarendon Press, Oxford.

Newmeyer, Frederick J.

　1980　*Linguistic Theory in America. The First Quarter-Century of Transformational Generative Grammar.* Academic Press, New York-London-Toronto-Sydney-San Francisco. (2nd revised edition 1986)

Nida Eugene A.

　1949 [1946[1]] *Morphology. The Descriptive Analysis of Words.* The University of Michigan Press, Ann Arbor.

Norden, Eduard

　1898　*Die antike Kunstprosa vom VI. Jahrhundert v. Chr. bis in die Zeit der Renaissance.* 2 vols. Teubner, Leipzig.

Nuchelmans, Gabriel

　1973　*Theories of the Proposition. Ancient and Medieval Conceptions of the Bearers of Truth and Falsity.* North-Holland, Amsterdam.

Ogden, Charles K. and Ivor A. Richards

　1923　*The Meaning of Meaning. A Study of the Influence of Language upon Thought and of the Science of Symbolism.* Routledge & Kegan Paul, London.

Osgood, Charles E. and Thomas A. Sebeok (eds.)

　1954　*Psycholinguistics. A Survey of Theory and Research Problems.* Report of the 1953 Summer Seminar Sponsored by the Committee on Linguistics and Psychology of the Social Science Research Council. (=Indiana University Publications in Anthropology and Linguistics, Memoir 10.) Waverly Press, Baltimore.

Osthoff, Hermann and Karl Brugmann

　1878　*Morphologische Untersuchungen auf dem Gebiete der indogermanischen Sprachen.* Vol. I. Hirzel, Leipzig.

Parsons, Terence

　1995　Thematic relations and arguments. *Linguistic Inquiry* 26.4:635-62

Patzig, Günther (ed.)

　1969　*Gottlob Frege. Funktion, Begriff, Bedeutung. Fünf logische Studien.* Vandenhoeck & Ruprecht, Göttingen.

Paul, Hermann

　1920[5] (1880[1]) *Prinzipien der Sprachgeschichte.* Niemeyer, Halle.

　1888　*Principles of the History of Language.* Transl. by H.A. Strong. Sonnenschein London. (Macmillan, New York, 1889; revised edition Longman, London, 1890.)

Percival, W. Keith

　1976　On the historical source of immediate constituent analysis. In: James D. McCawley (ed.), *Notes from the Linguistic Underground.* (=Syntax and Semantics, Vol. 7). Academic Press, New York-San Francisco-London. Pp. 229-42.

1981   The Saussurean paradigm: fact or fancy? *Semiotica* 36:33-49

Peters, P. Stanley (ed.)

1972   *Goals of Linguistic Theory.* Prentice Hall, Englewood Cliffs.

Peters, P. Stanley and Richard W. Ritchie

1973   On the generative power of transformational grammars. *Information Sciences* 6:49-83.

Pike, Kenneth L .

1967 [1954]   *Language in Relation to a Unified Theory of the Structure of Human Behavior.* Mouton, The Hague. (First published by Summer Institute of Linguistics, Glendale, California, 1954.)

Pike, Kenneth L . and Eunice V. Pike

1955   *Live Issues in Descriptive Linguistic Analysis.* Summer Institute of Linguistics, Glendale, California. 23 pp.

Pinborg, Jan

1967   *Die Entwicklung der Sprachtheorie im Mittelalter. Beiträge zur Geschichte der Philosophie und Theologie des Mittelalters.* Band XLII, Heft 2. Aschendorff, Münster.

1975   Classical Antiquity: Greece. In: Thomas A. Sebeok (ed.), *Historiography of Linguistics.* 2 vols. Mouton, The Hague. Pp. 69-126.

Pinker, Steven

1994   *The Language Instinct. How the Mind Creates Language.* Morrow & Co., New York.

Pittman, Richard S.

1948   Nuclear structures in linguistics. *Language* 24:117-31. (Also in Joos 1957:275-78.)

Postal, Paul M.

1964:   *Constituent Structure: A Study of Contemporary Models of Syntactic Description.* International Journal of American Linguistics 30.1, Part III. (=Publication Thirty of the Indiana University Research Center in Anthropology, Folklore, and Linguistics.) Indiana University, Bloomington.

1970   On the surface verb 'remind'. *Linguistic Inquiry* 1.1:37-120.

1971   *Cross-over Phenomena.* Holt, Rinehart & Winston, New York.

1972   The best theory. In: Peters:131-70.

1974   *On Raising. One Rule of English Grammar and Its Theoretical Implications.* MIT Press, Cambridge, Mass.

Pullum, Geoffrey K.

1991   *The Great Eskimo Vocabulary Hoax and Other Irreverent Essays on the Study of Language.* The Universiy of Chicago Press, Chicago-London.

1996   Nostalgic views from Building 20. *Journal of Linguistics* 32.1: 137-47.

Quine, Willard Van Orman

1953   *From a Logical Point of View.* Harvard University Press, Cambridge, Mass.

1960   *Word and Object.* MIT Press, Cambridge, Mass.

Reichenbach, Hans

1947   *Elements of Symbolic Logic.* Macmillan, New York.

Rescher, Nicholas

1973   *The Coherence Theory of Truth.* Clarendon Press, Oxford.

Robins, Robert H.

1961   John Rupert Firth. Obituary article. *Language* 37.2:191-200.

1967   *A Short History of Linguistics.* Longman, London.

1980   Functional syntax in medieval Europe. In: K. Koerner, H.-J. Niederehe and R.H. Robins (eds.), *Studies in Medieval Linguistic Thought. Dedicated to Geoffrey L. Bursill-Hall on the occasion of his sixtieth birthday on 15 May 1980.* Benjamins, Amsterdam. Pp. 231-40.

1994   Traditional grammar. In: Asher & Simpson:4644-9.

Rocher, R.J.

1994   Sanskrit: Discovery by Europeans. In: Asher & Simpson:3651-4.

Ross, John Robert

1967   *Constraints on Variables in Syntax.* PhD-thesis MIT. (Published as *Infinite Syntax!* Ablex, Norwood, NJ, 1986.)

1969   Auxiliaries as main verbs. In: W. Todd (ed.), *Studies in Philosophical Linguistics I.* Pp. 77-102.

1970   On declarative sentences. In: R. Jacobs & P. Rosenbaum (eds.), *Readings in English Transformational Grammar,* Ginn & Co, Boston. Pp. 222-72.

Rousseau, Jean-Jacques

1755   *Discours sur l'origine et les fondemens de l'inégalité parmi les hommes.* (Modern edition: J. Starobinski (ed.), Gallimard, Paris, 1989.)

1781   *Essai sur l'origine des langues où il est parlé de la mélodie et de l'imitation musicale.* (Modern editions: C. Porset (ed.), Ducros, Bordeaux, 1968; A. Belin (ed.), reprod. of 1817 edition, Copedith, Paris, 1970.)

Russell, Bertrand

1896   *German Social Democracy.* Longman, Green & Co, London.

1900   *A Critical Exposition of the Philosophy of Leibniz.* Cambridge University Press, Cambridge.

1903a   *The Principles of Mathematics.* Allen & Unwin, London.

1903b   A free man's worship. *The Independent Review.*

1905   On denoting. *Mind* 14:479-93.

1908   Mathematical logic as based on the theory of types. *American Journal of Mathematics* 30:222-62.

1919   *Introduction to Mathematical Philosophy.* Allen & Unwin, London.

1956   *Portraits from Memory and Other Essays.* Allen & Unwin, London.

1957   Mr Strawson on referring. *Mind* 66:385-89.

1967   *The Autobiography of Bertrand Russell. 1872-1914.* Allen & Unwin, London.

1969[5] (1946[1]) *History of Western Philosophy and its Connection with Political and Social Circumstances from the Earliest Times to the Present Day.* Allen & Unwin, London.

Russell, Bertrand and Alfred N. Whitehead

1910-1913   *Principia Mathematica.* 3 vols. Cambridge University Press, Cambridge.

Ryle, Gilbert

1931-2   Systematically misleading expressions. *Proceedings of the Aristotelian Society* 32:139-70.

1949   *The Concept of Mind.* Hutchinson, London.

Sandmann, Manfred

1954   *Subject and Predicate. A Contribution to the Theory of Syntax.* University Press, Edinburgh.

Sapir, Edward

1921   *Language. An Introduction to the Study of Speech.* Harcourt, Brace & Cy, New York.

1925   Sound patterns in language. *Language* 1.1:37-51. (Also in Joos 1957:19-25.)

1929   The status of linguistics as a science. *Language* 5.2:207-14.

1933   Language. In: *Encyclopedia of the Social Sciences, vol.9.* Macmillan, New York. Pp. 155-69.

Sasse, Hans-Jürgen

1987   The thetic/categorical distinction revisited. *Linguistics* 25:511-80.

Schaars, Frans A.M.

1988   *De Nederduitsche Spraekkunst (1706) van Arnold Moonen (1644-1711). Een bijdrage tot de geschiedenis van de Nederlandstalige spraakkunst.* PhD-thesis. Nijmegen University. Quarto, Wijhe.

Schachter, Paul

1974   A non-transformational account of serial verbs. *Studies in African Linguistics,* Supplement 5:253-70.

Scharten, Rose

1997   *Exhaustive Interpretation. A Discourse-Semantic Account.* PhD-thesis. Nijmegen University.

Schiller, F.C.S.

1912   *Formal Logic. A Scientific and Social Problem.* Macmillan, London.

Schleicher, August

1863   *Die Darwinsche Theorie und die Sprachwissenschaft: Offenes Sendschreiben an Herrn Dr. Ernst Häckel.* Böhlau, Weimar. (Reprinted in *Linguistics and Evolutionary Theory,* Benjamins, Amsterdam, 1983.)

1868   Eine fabel in indogermanischer ursprache. *Beiträge zur vergleichenden Sprachforschung* 5:206-8.

Schmidt, Johannes

1872   *Die Verwandtschaftsverhältnisse der indogermanischen Sprachen.* Böhlau, Weimar.

Schuchardt, Hugo

1885   *Ueber die Lautgesetze. Gegen die Junggrammatiker.* Oppenheim, Berlin.

1914   *Die Sprache der Saramakkaneger in Surinam.* Verhandelingen der Koninklijke Akademie van Wetenschappen te Amsterdam, Afdeeling Letterkunde. Nieuwe Reeks, XIV.6. Johannes Müller, Amsterdam.

Seuren, Pieter A.M.

1967   Negation in Dutch. *Neophilologus* 51.4:327-63.

1969   *Operators and Nucleus. A contribution to the theory of grammar.* Cambridge University Press, Cambridge.

1972a   Taaluniversalia in de transformationele grammatika. *Leuvense Bijdragen* 61:311-70.

1972b   Autonomous versus semantic syntax. *Foundations of Language* 8.2:237-65. (Also in Seuren 1974:96-122.)

1972c   Predicate Raising and dative in French and sundry languages. Magdalen College, Oxford. Unpublished.

1975   *Tussen Taal en Denken. Een bijdrage tot de empirische funderingen van de semantiek.* Oosthoek, Scheltema & Holkema, Utrecht.

1977   Forme logique et forme sémantique: un argument contre M. Geach. *Logique et Analyse* 79, vol. 20:338-47.

1982   Internal variability in competence. *Linguistische Berichte* 77:1-31.

1985   *Discourse Semantics*. Blackwell, Oxford.

1988   Presupposition and negation. *Journal of Semantics* 6.3/4:175-226.

1990   Still no serials in Seselwa. *Journal of Pidgin and Creole Languages* 5:271-92.

1993   Why does 2 mean "2"? Grist to the anti-Grice mill. In: Hajičová:225-35.

1994   Presupposition. In: Asher & Simpson:3311-20.

1996   *Semantic Syntax*. Blackwell, Oxford.

in prep. *The Study of Meaning*.

Seuren, Pieter A.M. (ed.)

1974   *Semantic Syntax*. Oxford Readings in Philosophy. Oxford University Press.

Shannon, C.E. and W. Weaver

1949   *The Mathematical Theory of Communication.* University of Illinois Press, Urbana, Ill.

Sidgwick, Alfred

1895   Context and meaning. *Mind* 4:281-306.

Siertsema, Bertha

1954   *A Study of Glossematics. Critical Survey of its Fundamental Concepts*. Nijhoff, The Hague.

Sigwart, Christoph

1895   *Logic*. Translated by Helen Dendy. Swan Sonnenschein & Co, London; Macmillan, New York. (Original German edition 1873.)

Skinner, Burrhus F.

1957   *Verbal Behavior*. Appleton-Century-Crofts, New York.

Sobel, Dava

1996   *Longitude. The true story of a lone genius who solved the greatest scientific problem of his time.* Fourth Estate, London.

Staal, J. Frits (ed.)

1972   *A Reader on the Sanskrit Grammarians*. MIT Press, Cambridge, Mass.

Stankiewicz, Edward (ed.)

1972   *A Baudouin de Courtenay Anthology. The Beginnings of Structural Linguistics*. Indiana University Press, Bloomington.

Starobinski, Jean

1979   *Words upon Words. The Anagrams of Ferdinand de Saussure*. Transl. by Olivia Emmet. Yale University Press, New Haven & London.

Stegmüller, Wolfgang

1957   *Das Wahrheitsproblem und die Idee der Semantik. Eine Einleitung in die Theorien von A. Tarski und R. Carnap.* Springer, Vienna.

Steinberg, Danny D. and Leon A. Jakobovits (eds.)

1971   *Semantics. An Interdisciplinary Reader in Philosophy, Linguistics and Psychology.* Cambridge University Press, Cambridge.

Steinthal, Heymann

1848   *Die Sprachwissenschaft Wilh. von Humboldt's und die Hegel'sche Philosophie.* Dümmler, Berlin. (Reprint: Olms, Hildesheim-New York, 1971.)

1855   *Grammatik, Logik und Psychologie, ihre Prinzipien und ihre Verhältnisse zueinander.* Dümmler, Berlin.

1860a   *Charakteristik der hauptsächlichsten Typen des Sprachbaues.* (Neubearbeitung von Dr. Franz Misteli). Dümmler, Berlin.

1860b   Assimilation und Attraktion, psychologisch beleuchtet. *Zeitschrift für Völkerpsychologie und Sprachwissenschaft* 1:73-89.

1890-1   *Geschichte der Sprachwissenschaft bei den Griechen und Römern mit besonderer Rücksicht auf die Logik.* 2 vols. Dümmler, Berlin.

Stern, Gustaf

1931   *Meaning and Change of Meaning. With Special Reference to the English Language.* Göteborgs Högskolas Årsskrift XXXVIII, Gothenburg. (Reprint: Greenwood Press, Westport, Conn., 1975.)

Stout, George F.

1909[3] (1896[1]) *Analytical Psychology.* 2 vols. Sonnenschein, London / Macmillan, New York.

Strawson, Peter F.

1950   On referring. *Mind* 59:320-44.

1952   *Introduction to Logical Theory.* Methuen, London.

1954   A reply to Mr Sellars. *Philosophical Review* 63.2:216-31.

1964   Identifying reference and truth-values. *Theoria* 30.2:96-118.

Stuart, Tineke

1986   *Burley's vroege opvattingen over de Exclusivae.* MA-thesis, Nijmegen University.

Svedelius, Carl

1897   *L'analyse du langage appliquée à la langue française.* Almqvist & Wiksell, Uppsala.

Swadesh, Morris

1934   The phonemic principle. *Language* 10.1: 117-29.

Sweet, Henry

  1877   *A Handbook of Phonetics.* Clarendon Press, Oxford.

Swiggers, Pierre

  1983   Grammaire et théorie du langage chez Buffier. *Dix-huitième siècle* 15:285-93.

Taine, Hippolyte

  1911 (1870[1]) *De l'intelligence.* 2 vols. Hachette, Paris.

Taylor, D.J.

  1994: Classical Antiquity: Language Study. In: Asher & Simpson:559-65.

Thomsen, Vilhelm

  1902   *Sprogvidenskabens historie. En kortfattet fremstilling.* G.E.C. Gad, Copenhagen.

Toman, Jindrich

  1995   *The magic of a common language : Jakobson, Mathesius, Trubetzkoy, and the Prague Linguistic Circle.* MIT Press, Cambridge, Mass.

Trabant, Jürgen

  1990   *Traditionen Humboldts.* Suhrkamp, Frankfurt.

Travis, Charles

  1981   *The True and the False: the Domain of the Pragmatic.* Benjamins, Amsterdam.

Trubetzkoy, Nikolai S.

  1939   *Grundzüge der Phonologie.* Travaux du Cercle Linguistique de Prague 7. [2nd edition: Vandenhoeck & Ruprecht, Göttingen, 1958.]

Uldall, Hans Jørgen

  1957   *Outline of Glossematics. Part One* (=Travaux du Cercle Linguistique de Copenhague 10). Nordisk Sprog- og Kulturforlag, Copenhagen.

Van Fraassen, Bas

  1971   *Formal Semantics and Logic.* Macmillan, New York-London.

Van Heijenoort, Jan (ed.)

  1967   *From Frege to Gödel. A Source Book in Mathematical Logic, 1879-1931.* Harvard University Press, Cambridge, Mass.

Van Riemsdijk, Henk and Edwin Williams

  1986   *Introduction to the Theory of Grammar.* MIT Press, Cambridge, Mass.

Verner, Karl A.

  1875   Eine Ausnahme der ersten Lautverschiebung. *Zeitschrift für vergleichende Sprachforschung* 23.2:97-130.

Von der Gabelentz, H. Georg C.

1869   Ideen zu einer vergleichenden Syntax. Wort- und Satzstellung. *Zeitschrift für Völkerpsychologie und Sprachwissenschaft* 6:376-84.

1901² (1891¹) *Die Sprachwissenschaft. Ihre Aufgaben, Methoden und bisherigen Ergebnisse.* Tauchnitz, Leipzig.

Von Humboldt, Wilhelm

1836   *Ueber die Verschiedenheit des menschlichen Sprachbaues und ihren Einfluß auf die geistige Entwickelung des Menschengeschlechts.* Königliche Akademie der Wissenschaften. Dümmler, Berlin.

Von Schlegel, August Wilhelm

1818   *Observations sur la langue et la littérature provençales.* Librairie grecque-latine-allemande, Paris.

Von Schlegel, Friedrich

1808   *Ueber die Sprache und Weisheit der Indier.* Mohr & Zimmer, Heidelberg.

Von Wright, Georg H. (ed.)

1974   *Letters to Russell, Keynes and Moore by Ludwig Wittgenstein.* Blackwell, Oxford.

Warnock, Geoffrey J.

1963   John Langshaw Austin 1911-1960. *Proceedings of the British Academy* 49:345-63.

Wegener, Philipp

1885   *Untersuchungen über die Grundfragen des Sprachlebens.* Niemeyer, Halle.

Wells, Rulon S.

1947   Immediate constituents. *Language* 23.1:81-117. (Also in Joos 1957:186-207.)

Wheeler, G.

1994   Port Royal tradition of Grammar. In: Asher & Simpson:3229-33.

Whitney, William D.

1867   *Language and the Study of Language. Twelve Lectures on the Principles of Linguistic Science.* Scribner, New York.

1875   *The Life and Growth of Language. An Outline of Linguistic Science.* Appleton, New York.

Wilson, Deirdre

1975   *Presuppositions and Non-Truth-Conditional Semantics.* Academic Press, London-New York-San Francisco.

Wittgenstein, Ludwig

    1922   *Tractatus Logico-Philosophicus.* Transl. by C.K. Ogden. Routledge & Kegan Paul, London.

    1953   *Philosophical Investigations.* Transl. by G.E.M. Anscombe. Blackwell, Oxford.

Woodhouse, J.R.

    1994   Dictionaries, Italian Monolingual. In: Asher & Simpson:919-22.

Wooldridge, T.R.

    1994   French Dictionaries: Estienne to the Late Twentieth Century. In: Asher & Simpson:1301-3.

Wundt, Wilhelm

    1880   *Logik. Eine Untersuchung der Prinzipien der Erkenntnis und der Methoden Wissenschaftlicher Forschung.* Enke, Stuttgart.

    1901   *Sprachgeschichte und Sprachpsychologie. Mit Rücksicht auf B. Delbrücks "Grundfragen der Sprachforschung".* Engelmann, Leipzig.

    1922[4] *Völkerpsychologie. Eine Untersuchung der Entwicklungsgesetze von Sprache, Mythus und Sitte. Volume 2, Die Sprache, Part 2.* Kröner, Leipzig. (1st impression: Engelmann, Leipzig, 1900.)

Zholkovsky, Aleksandr K. and Igor A. Mel'čuk

    1965   O vozmožnom metode i instrumentax semantičeskogo sinteza [On a Possible Method and Some Tools for Semantic Synthesis]. *Naučnotexničeskaja Informacija* 6:23-8.

Index

(For names beginning with *De*, *Van* and *Von*, see *De*, *Van* and *Von*, respectively.)